MELVILLE
"AMONG THE NATIONS"

PROCEEDINGS OF AN INTERNATIONAL CONFERENCE;

VOLOS, GREECE, JULY 2–6, 1997

EDITED BY

SANFORD E. MAROVITZ

AND

A.C. CHRISTODOULOU

KENT STATE UNIVERSITY PRESS

Library of Congress Card Catalog Number 00-046486

ISBN 0-87338-696-5

Designed & composed by A. C. Christodoulou

Manufactured in the United States of America

06 05 04 03 02 01   5 4 3 2 1

Library of Congress Cataloging-in-Publication Data

Melville "Among the nations" : proceedings of an international conference,
Volos, Greece, July 2–6, 1997 / edited by Sanford E. Marovitz
and A. C. Christodoulou

p.   cm.

Includes bibliographical references and index.

ISBN 0-87338-696-5 (alk. paper) ∞

1. Melville, Herman, 1819–1891—Criticism and interpretation—Congresses.
2. Melville, Herman, 1819–1891—Appreciation—Foreign Foreign countries—
Congresses.

I. Marovitz, Sanford E. II Christodoulou, A. C. (Athanasios C.), 1943–

PS2387.M37 2001

813'.3—dc21

00-046486

British Library Cataloging-in-Publication data are available.

To Melville Scholars Everywhere:
Past, Present & Future

Sanford E. Marovitz
A. C. Christodoulou

TABLE OF CONTENTS

7

List of Illustrations

COLOR PLATES FOLLOWING PAGE 450

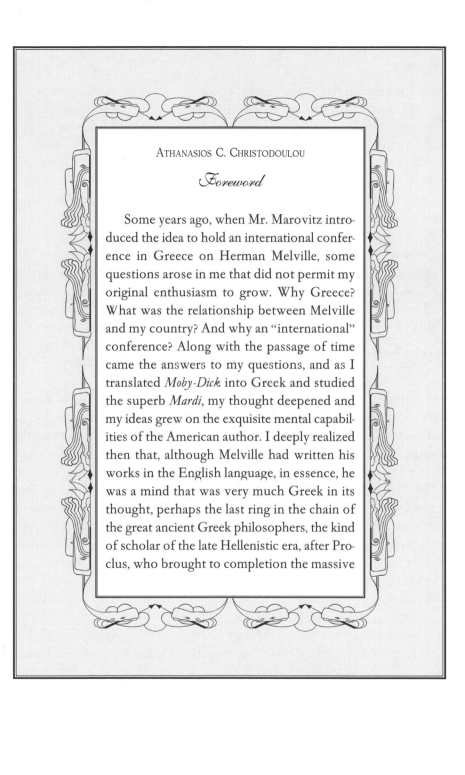

ATHANASIOS C. CHRISTODOULOU

Foreword

Some years ago, when Mr. Marovitz introduced the idea to hold an international conference in Greece on Herman Melville, some
questions arose in me that did not permit my
original enthusiasm to grow. Why Greece?
What was the relationship between Melville
and my country? And why an "international"
conference? Along with the passage of time
came the answers to my questions, and as I
translated *Moby-Dick* into Greek and studied
the superb *Mardi*, my thought deepened and
my ideas grew on the exquisite mental capabil-
ities of the American author. I deeply realized
then that, although Melville had written his
works in the English language, in essence, he
was a mind that was very much Greek in its
thought, perhaps the last ring in the chain of
the great ancient Greek philosophers, the kind
of scholar of the late Hellenistic era, after Pro-
clus, who brought to completion the massive

volume of ancient Greek philosophy. This may sound a bit exaggerated, but as my studies expanded, this idea became so deeply fixed in me that I finally pushed aside my original doubts, and thought of Dr. Sanford E. Marovitz's beautiful idea to be a very attractive one. There was, however, another issue to be resolved. Holding a conference in Greece was indeed a very attractive idea. Still, though, why did this conference have to be "international"? Why, in short, should there be Melville scholars from all over the world? My answer was related to my belief that Melville is the most important authority on ancient Greek philosophy and thus the most important philosopher of later Western thought, considering the fact that Western philosophy from the Middle Ages to Melville's time was nothing more than an "unfurling" of ancient Greek ideas. Inside that great tradition, Melville was that restless and authentic, even *primitive*, spirit that had spoken the boldest, most sincere and profound words about "man," irrespective of color, race, nationality, class, or religion. This was another belief that took deep root in me and completely pushed aside the final doubts about Dr. Marovitz's invitation. With this bizarre faith that an international conference in Greece on Melville would contribute in the "repatriation" of a filial and close person—in the Melvillian sense—and would be an incentive for the gathering of my unknown and scattered "brothers"—in the Melvillian sense again—I embraced the enthusiasm of my very good friend and decided to recruit all my strength for the realization of this bold project. No matter my lack of experience, I was so confident in the experience, organizational skills, dedication, diligence, and good heart of Dr. Marovitz that not only did I believe in the success of the conference, but I also started having the ambition for our conference to acquire a memorable dimension. I wanted another kind of conference, one that would not be just an exchange of scholarly views, but also a complete intellectual interaction based on the "humanitarian" spirit of Melville. I requested the assistance of my town and the Ministry of Culture for the realization of this project. And I succeeded. The conference took place in Volos according to our schedule, and I believe that it was very successful. I will not comment on the participants' impressions, which, by the way, found voice in a most elegant issue of the *Melville Society Extracts*, but only on mine. The most impressive element of the conference was the exceptional organization of the various events, the work of Dr. Marovitz, and the wholehearted participation of all members in all the events. The president of the Melville Society, Dr. Elizabeth Schultz, during our first evening told me that she felt Melville's presence among us. That was my sensation during those unforgettable days. Under Melville's watchful eye, therefore, people who were strangers among each other, speaking different languages but sharing the same mind, united their thoughts and hearts in a common effort to hear as clearly as possible his distant voice. Proof of this kind of unanimity were the characteristic cases of some members who, no matter their health problems, were among the first to participate in the activities that indeed required vigorous and robust physical abilities. Another proof of the success of the conference was the fact that several important decisions were made that I now witness being realized. To me, however, this conference was a very special one because I had the opportunity to work closely with my good friend Sanford E. Marovitz, to learn from him, and to benefit from his wisdom, kindness, and magnanimity. From where I stand now I thank him once more.

MELVILLE "AMONG THE NATIONS"

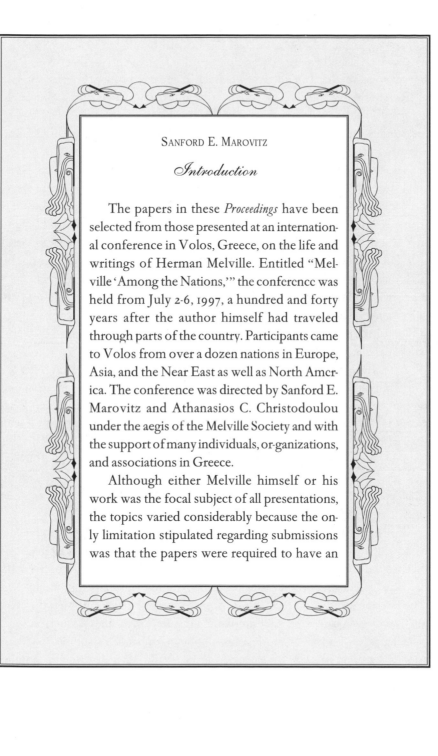

SANFORD E. MAROVITZ

Introduction

The papers in these *Proceedings* have been selected from those presented at an international conference in Volos, Greece, on the life and writings of Herman Melville. Entitled "Melville 'Among the Nations,'" the conference was held from July 2-6, 1997, a hundred and forty years after the author himself had traveled through parts of the country. Participants came to Volos from over a dozen nations in Europe, Asia, and the Near East as well as North America. The conference was directed by Sanford E. Marovitz and Athanasios C. Christodoulou under the aegis of the Melville Society and with the support of many individuals, or-ganizations, and associations in Greece.

Although either Melville himself or his work was the focal subject of all presentations, the topics varied considerably because the only limitation stipulated regarding submissions was that the papers were required to have an international theme. The range of possibilities included source studies; the visual arts; critical, theoretical, and comparative approaches; literary and philosophical parallels; Melville's travels abroad; influences of the world around him on his writings and his own impact on the works of others—all of these and more were considered suitable topics for "Melville 'Among the Nations.'"

The possibility of arranging an international Melville conference in Greece originated with informal conversations in years past among several members of the Melville Society. What was only a vague idea in those early days began to materialize into tentative plans when I first met A. C. Christodoulou at his home in Volos during the mid-1980s. He had begun bringing out his splendid Greek translation of *Moby-Dick* in segments, but he soon decided against continuing with this lengthy procedure in favor of completing the translation and publishing it in a single volume. It was published in Athens by Gutenberg in 1991, the cover embellished with an early nineteenth-century illustration of the sperm-whale fishery by the French maritime painter Ambroise-Louis Garneray, whose work Melville greatly admired.

After learning of his developing translation, I had been eager to meet Mr. Christodoulou because I was then writing an essay on Melville's international reputation for John Bryant's compendious *A Companion to Melville Studies* (Greenwood 1986). His translation is only one of several projects related to Melville that are either completed or in progress. The most ambitious of these is his five-volume bilingual edition and study of *Moby-Dick*, the first volume of which appeared in mid-1997, only days before the conference opened. Translated, the English title of this project is Moby-Dick; or, The Whale: *Introduction, Text, Translation, Commentary, and Notes.*

Shortly after Mr. Christodoulou and I began seriously considering the idea of organizing a Melville conference in Greece, I formally introduced the possibility to the Melville Society and eventually put the matter to a vote of the membership. The idea was enthusiastically received, and from that point on the planning became more definite. Calls for papers were publicized through the Modern Language Association, the International American Studies Association, and other agencies. Surprised over the large number of outstanding submissions from countries around the world, we decided against artificially restricting the number of participants and expanded our plans to include as many sound presentations on suitable topics as the conference facilities in Volos could reasonably accommodate. The result was illuminating and exciting to a degree far beyond our expectations. In addition to, and complementing, a program filled with remarkably strong presentations were the congenial discussions and camaraderie that Melville himself would have relished—a gam entirely devoted to him and his writings.

Not surprisingly, because the conference was held in Greece, as many as twenty-five percent of the papers incorporate a Hellenic theme. This was not a matter of the authors' forcing the theme to suit the circumstances but of their perceiving the extent to which Greek literature, thought, and art affected Melville's own life and writing. What he absorbed and assimilated from the Greek Classics and culture often manifested itself in his prose and poetry during the course of his long auctorial career.

Whereas some of the papers remain virtually unchanged from the time of their presentation, others have been extensively revised to clarify points as needed and provide additional support where advisable for publication in an altogether different venue. Many of the slides used by presenters to illustrate their papers in Volos have been reproduced as photographs in this volume, so the visual advantage of textual references to individual works of art will not be lost.

Certainly, Herman Melville was among the most widely traveled of American authors. Not yet twenty when he made his first voyage abroad, he sailed as a green hand to England and back in the summer of 1839. Less than eighteen months later he shipped out again, a-whaling in two oceans and island-hopping in the Pacific until mid-summer 1843, when he signed onto the frigate *United States* that brought him back to Boston late the following year. After drawing from these travels for much of the substance of his first five long narratives, Melville sailed again on a voyage to England and the Continent that would keep him away from home for nearly four months late in 1849 and early in 1850.

By the time he left the country again in October 1856, he had brought out three more full-length novels (a fourth, *The Confidence-Man*, was ready for his publisher before he left) and a volume of stories that included only a few of those he had published over the past three years in the monthly magazines. During his seven months abroad, Melville examined historical sites and monuments of Egypt, Palestine, Turkey, Greece, and several countries of western Europe, while carefully observing the life around him as he traveled.

He had long wished to visit Greece before the opportunity to do so finally came. In fact, he had expected to continue heading eastward from Vienna to Constantinople and Athens as part of his European voyage of 1849-50. "Think of it!," he had entered in his journal on October 15, 1849, while sailing to England; "Jerusalem and the Pyramids—Constantinople, the Egean, & old Athens!"[1] But the funds he had anticipated from book sales did not materialize, so he had to forgo the Middle-Eastern leg of his journey that he had been so eager to make. When at last he did tour parts of Greece, from Syra through Athens and Thessaloniki, in December 1856 on his way to the Near East and in February 1857 on the way back to Europe, Melville was struck by the chaotic diversity of peoples and the tangled narrow streets amidst what remained of a culture glorified by centuries of literary representation, painting, and illustration. Despite the thread of disillusionment occasionally exposed in his journal entries for Greece, he was clearly fascinated by much of what he observed and described there, often in sharp detail with accompanying impressions of the moment jotted down as well.

On leaving Greece, Melville spent two months touring Italy before stopping over briefly in several more countries on his way back to England, then home again to Arrowhead early in May. In 1860 he sailed around the Horn for the last time, aboard the clipper ship *Meteor*, captained by his brother Thomas, but instead of continuing with the vessel from San Francisco, the weary seafarer returned home by way of Panama late the same year. That voyage ended his international travels.

But as a glance through *Melville's Reading* (by Merton M. Sealts, Jr.) unquestionably confirms, Melville's hunger to read enabled him to traverse all bounds of time and place throughout his adult life. Although Melville had not been to Greece before his major fiction (excepting *Billy Budd*) was already published (or

---

1   Herman Melville, *Journals*, vol. 15 of *The Writings of Herman Melville*, ed. Harrison Hayford, Hershel Parker, and G. Thomas Tanselle (Evanston and Chicago, IL: Northwestern University and the Newberry Library, 1989), p. 7.

soon to be so), his familiarity with Classical authors had seeped into his consciousness to the extent that their pronounced influence on him is immediately apparent to serious readers of his work. If his reading was limited to works in English, he was not at all reluctant to take in translations, particularly of Classical, French, and German literatures but also of history and philosophy originally published in those languages. From this array of resources, he acquired a cosmopolitan familiarity with the art, thought, and cultures of his own day in addition to what he learned of the past. Then with the aid of his eclectic imagination, he incorporated in his own writing allusions to specific images and phrases from a veritable library contained in part on his bookshelves but as well in his extraordinarily retentive memory.

If he drew abundantly from the work of others, Melville also became no less influential on countless authors and artists who followed him, many of whom infused their productions with implicit and explicit references to specific features from his writings, most notably, of course, from *Moby-Dick*. Who can deny the wonderful universality of Ahab and the White Whale, whose images are likely to appear without warning almost anywhere in the world that one might travel? Without having sought them out, I offhandedly recall spotting Moby Dick signs over store or restaurant windows in Belgium, the Netherlands, and Israel, and I feel confident that most readers of this volume can identify other locations outside the United States where such signs may be seen. From the beginning Melville has indeed been a writer for the world.

———

The forty-five papers selected for this volume are organized in six occasionally overlapping sections, each arranged with the chronology of Melville's publications as the principal guideline and vaguely with an expansion from the specific to the general as the secondary one.

The collection begins with "Among the Nations," papers that represent Melville as an acute and critical observer of the world around him, from both social and aesthetic vantage points. The next three sections focus on his works, specifically on themes, sources, and parallels: the papers in section two, "Truth's Ragged Edges," consider Melville's writings from a philosophical and religious perspective; those in the third section, "Thematic Patterns," identify and trace prominent motifs in the narratives and poetry; and section four, "Theoretical Insights," which opens with a paper on Melville's memory, introduces a gamut of critical approaches that explore Melville's works from manifold cultural perspectives. Section five, "Melville and the Visual Arts," places his literary achievements in the context of his keen appreciation for paintings, graphics, sculpture, and architecture. He alluded profusely to such works of art in his writing, and artists in turn after him based compositions of their own on his fiction and poetry. The concluding section, "Projection and Reflection," is pedagogical and comparative. It opens with "Projection," a paper on the pleasures and problems of teaching Melville in China. "Reflection" begins with an explanation of Charles Olson's controversial reaction to the Melville Society and continues with papers on interconnections between Melville and France over time, the expanding attraction of Melville's writing in Japan along with the concomitant critical response to it there, and insights into translating one of Melville's late poems into Italian. The two papers that close the volume trace thematic correspondences with twentieth-century authors from Poland and St. Lucia (in the Caribbean Sea). The global range and diversity of the concluding section thus anchors the international theme of the conference.

The editors of these *Proceedings* and the Melville Society are profoundly grateful to the following individuals and organizations for their generous support: the Municipality of Volos and especially the Mayor of Volos, Mr. Dimitris Pitsioris; the Prefecture of Magnissia and its Governor, Mr. Panos Scotiniotis; the Greek Ministry of Culture; the National Book Center of Greece; the University of Thessaly; Kent State University and especially Prof. Fredric Schwarzbach, Chair of the English Department; the Hellenic Association of American Studies; the Association of Foreign Language Schools' Owners of Magnissia; and Gutenberg Publications, the publisher of these *Proceedings*, who also contributed all necessary printed matter for the conference itself. We wish, also, to acknowledge again our profound gratitude to the Program and Organizational Committees of the conference and to all participants on the conference program.

The editors of Melville *"Among the Nations"* acknowledge with gratitude the generous support of the Kent State University Libraries and the Melville Society for the publication of these conference proceedings.

Finally, we are immensely indebted to Eleonora D. Marovitz, whose capacity for superb impromptu translation between Greek and English greatly facilitated all activities related to the conference from initial explorations to interpersonal relations while the gathering was in progress and afterwards throughout the editing of this volume. Similarly, Tasoula Christodoulou, and the Christodoulous' magnificent crew of three—Kostas, Filitsa, and Nikos—all contributed significantly to the success of our first international Melville gam in more ways than we, the directors and editors, can count. Thank you all many times over! *Efharistó! Merci! Grazia! Dankje wel! Dzienkuje! Mange tak! Arigato! Xie xie ni! Shukran! Dank u! Tesekkur ederim!*

———

We regret deeply to announce that during the course of preparing our conference program and this subsequent volume of *Proceedings*, cancer took the lives of two contributors, Professor Hennig Cohen and Mr. Charles Watts. Professor Cohen's paper on Melville and Diogenes the Cynic had been accepted when his death occurred late in 1996, and Professor Marovitz had the honor of reading it in his place at the conference. Mr. Watts presented his paper in Volos and finished revising it for publication early in 1998, when it was accepted for publication. His untimely death occurred later the same year. We feel their loss profoundly and consider ourselves privileged that we could include their papers in this collection.

I
AMONG THE NATIONS

MARY K. BERCAW EDWARDS

MELVILLE'S WHALING YEARS

erman Melville reworked his own experiences at sea into his fiction, especially in his early books. Therefore, any information about his time at sea can throw light on how he wrote—how like a magician of words he transformed his experiences into great art. One of the early investigators of Melville's time at sea—and among the greatest of them—was Wilson L. Heflin. His "Herman Melville's Whaling Years" was, like so many early Melville dissertations, a tremendous piece of scholarship. Heflin combed through hundreds of logs, searching for any mention of the whaleship *Acushnet*. He also studied the documents that Ida Leeson found in the Mitchell Library in Sydney, Australia, concerning the mutiny on board the *Lucy Ann*. But he didn't stop there: he continued his researches into the mutiny especially through documents now in France which he sought out, studied, and quoted. Heflin identified Melville's third whaler, the *Charles and Henry*, and first published his find in 1949. When the dissertation is published, it will prove immensely valuable to future scholars.

But "Herman Melville's Whaling Years" has never been published. It was approved by the faculty of Vanderbilt University as a dissertation in 1952. At present, however, it only exists as a scratchy Xerox from University Microfilms, which is how I first read it in the early 1980s at the Newberry Library in Chicago.

The dissertation was supposed to be published by New York University Press. The report to the editorial committee of the New York University Press "strongly" urged the publication of "Herman Melville's Whaling Years" (p. 1), although "the study must be drastically cut and completely rewritten" (p. 4). The report glowingly praised Heflin's work: "With energy which seems inexhaustible Heflin has consulted letters, logs of ships, newspaper reports, consular records and other official documents, and the rewarding consequence of all this is plain here—the account of Melville's actual whaling experiences told with unsurpassed accuracy" (p. 1).

Throughout his life, Heflin continued to work on "Herman Melville's Whaling Years." Some of the excellent scholars he found to read over the manuscript include Jay Leyda, Charles F. Batchelder, Jr., Wilson Follett, Leon Howard, and Harrison Hayford. All of them, including an unknown writer who "humbly tendered" his suggestions on sheets of examination paper, made extensive suggestions. Jay Leyda, author of *The Melville Log*, wrote: "Dear Wilson, here is a first—or preliminary report, just on the major changes I'm suggesting. I'll save all the pettier things for later, after I see how these suggestions strike you. First, though, I believe its value, + I believe that it's a book." Leyda wrote later, with another set of suggestions, "Bravo Wilson! . . . This is a *really* definitive work." Leyda continued to make suggestions up through 1986.

Charles Batchelder was one of the premiere collectors of printed whaling material. His suggestions are the most valuable: twenty pages of closely typed comments keyed to the pages of the dissertation. Batchelder, with his thorough knowledge of whaling, whaling gear, whaleships, and the officers and men aboard them, pays close attention to Heflin's details to be certain that he is consistently accurate. For example, Batchelder says of Heflin's ch. 8, p. 5: "Wrong. He would have had the iron in his hands in order for the mate to give the order to strike" (p. 3) and of his ch. 13, p. 18: "Nix Hix [spell out]; his name was William B. Hicks [spell out]" (p. 8). Later, in reference to Heflin's ch. 14, p. 2—evidently a page with which Batchelder was none too happy—"irons draw, whales don't. / please, oh please: *fathoms* of whale *line*. / My two pet hates, leviathans and blubber-hunters, side-by-side!" (p. 11).

The suggestions of Wilson Follett, Heflin's editor at the New York University Press, were even more extensive than those of Batchelder: 37 typed pages. His comments are blunt and sharp but good. He writes of Heflin's phrase "had such not been the case": "Jargon. Why not 'otherwise'? or, 'if he had not been'? And 'literary geneticists' and 'complementary investigations of the experiential background' are pretty heavy and learned-sounding about a very simple matter" (p. 3). What would Follett have thought of some of the articles published today? But Follett can also be very encouraging: he writes of Heflin's p. vi, "A grand point well stated" (p. 3).

Wilson Heflin died on November 11, 1985, leaving his dissertation unpublished. He had continued researching and published his finds in short articles. But at the time of his death, his dissertation still needed major work.

In the summer of 1987, Thomas Farel Heffernan catalogued Helfin's correspondence, manuscripts, and other papers for the Wilson Heflin archive in the Newberry Library Special Collections: 17 boxes of papers and three cartons of additional material. Kitty Heflin, Heflin's daughter, asked Heffernan if he would be willing to edit her father's manuscript, and he agreed. Heffernan got the University of Texas Press to agree to publish the book, and he asked me, in 1990, to co-edit it with him.

So, what makes Heflin's manuscript so valuable? Why has so much work been willingly expended in editing it? Most of all it is the extent of his research. Look at Heflin's chapter on the crew of the *Acushnet*, for example. Charles Roberts Anderson, in *Melville in the South Seas* (1939), discusses the crew and quotes Melville's manuscript memoranda, "What became of the ship's company of the whale-ship 'Acushnet,' according to Hubbard [Henry F. Hubbard] who came home in her . . . and who visited me in Pittsfield in 1850" (Anderson, p. 33; WH, p. 68, n. 18). Anderson identifies 18 of the 25 men in Hubbard's list. Leon Howard, in his *Herman Melville: A Biography* (1951), describes the crew in general terms. But Heflin identifies the original 26 crew members and the three who joined while Melville was aboard. He mentions 26 others shipped by Captain Pease after Melville's desertion, making a total of 55 men who served aboard the *Acushnet* on her maiden voyage.

Anderson and Heflin both report that Henry F. Hubbard told Melville that Frederick Raymond, the first mate, "had a fight with the Captain & went ashore at Payta" (WH, p. 69). Heflin, however, additionally confirms this with a consular certificate signed on December 14, 1842, by the United States Consul at Payta.

Heflin identifies the *Acushnet*'s deserters and those discharged from her, citing consular certificates and sworn affidavits ferreted out from archives around the world. The amount of work Heflin did in digging out information is astounding. The prose in his dissertation may not have the beauty of Anderson's, who ended his chapter on the *Acushnet*: "With this crew, normal in all respects save that in addition to mortal harpoons it carried an immortal pen, the *Acushnet* set sail on its maiden voyage, January 3, 1841" (Anderson, p. 35), but Heflin's facts are irrefutable and invaluable.

Heflin's greatest interest, however, was not the crew but the ships. The searching out of logbooks, journals, and newspaper reports enthralled him.

So far as is known, the original log of the *Acushnet*, Melville's first whaler, has not survived. No personal journals of the voyage have yet been found. The log of the *Acushnet* was abstracted, however, by Captain Daniel McKenzie in 1848 for Lieutenant Matthew Fontaine Maury. This abstract log still exists, and it contains much information, including latitude and longitude, weather, when whales were raised, the bearings and distances of islands sighted, etc. But much is missing, too. First of all, the abstract log does not begin until March 22, 1841, 77 days after the *Acushnet* left port on January 3, 1841. And, although it records every time whales were sighted, it does not tell whether the boats were lowered or whether any whales were captured. Filling in the information left out of the abstract log occupied much of Heflin's time, and it is in this that his true genius shows.

Heflin combed through all the logs he could find of vessels which were at sea when the *Acushnet* was. For instance, the *Acushnet* was fighting her way around Cape Horn in mid-April 1841, and Heflin notes: "It is quite possible that the *Acushnet* passed in these waters the homeward-bound whaler *Huntress* on either April 16 or April 17. A comparative plot of the tracks of the two ships (based on their abstract logs. . .) shows that between noons of April 16-17 their tracks were almost parallel and no more than five miles apart. Their possible meeting is of significance because Melville mentions the *Huntress* in *Redburn* as the vessel in which Harry Bolton perished" (pp. 142-43, n. 7).

The *Acushnet* cruised through the In-Shore and Off-Shore Grounds. When another vessel was sighted, the two vessels "spoke": exchanged names, home-ports, months out to sea, and barrels of whale oil stowed. Heflin writes, for example: "Just before she reached the Line the *Acushnet* hailed on Saturday, October 23, the barque *United States* of Westport, Massachusetts, twelve months, 300 barrels... Captain Pease reported 720 barrels of sperm oil for his ship's ten months of whaling" (p. 187)—a fact that was duly recorded in the *United States*'s logbook and later found by Heflin. Often the logbooks themselves do not survive, but their information does, recorded in newspapers. The Boston *Courier* on February 10, 1842, stated: "Our Edgartown correspondent reports the *Acushnet*... 7 mos out, 610 brls" (p. 179, n. 18). Gathering all these facts—150 barrels of oil stowed down aboard the *Acushnet* by March 13 (p. 137, n. 9), 160 by May 8 (p. 153, n. 10), 350 by July 4 (p. 158, n. 18), 600 by September 25 (p. 179, n. 18), 720 by October 23 (p. 187), etc.—Heflin figured out the details of the voyage. He knew from the abstract log that a lone "Sperm Whale" was sighted on July 25, but the day was "rugged with rain" (p. 174) and evidently the whale was not taken. Heflin deduced the latter from the newspaper account of the whaleship *Midas*, which spoke the *Acushnet* on August 9 and reported the same number of barrels as the whaleship *William Wirt* had on July 4. Thus, like a detective, Heflin sorts through all the evidence and sets his conclusions before us for week after week and month after month of Melville's years at sea.

Even a scene seemingly as unrealistic as it is wanton, the scene of the whaleship *Dolly* surrounded by a shoal of Nukahivan girls in *Typee*, Heflin has confirmed. Chapter 2 of *Typee* ends with the arrival of the Polynesian girls: "As they drew nearer, and I watched the rising and sinking of their forms, and beheld the uplifted right arm bearing above the water the girdle of tappa, and their long dark hair trailing beside them as they swam, I almost fancied they could be nothing else than so many mermaids:—and very like mermaids they behaved too."

We were still some distance from the beach, and under slow headway, when we sailed right into the midst of these swimming nymphs" (*Typee*, ch. 2; NN p. 14). Amongst various primary documents, Heflin cites the logbook of the *Potomac* of Nantucket which came to anchor only eleven days after the *Acushnet*. "[I]n a few minutes the decks [of the *Potomac*] were crowded with Kanackas mostly girls swimming off like schools of porpoises" (p. 286). Mary Malloy rediscovered the Potomac's logbook/journal, kept by William H. Macy during the 1841-1845 voyage, and wrote up her discovery in 1990. Malloy's rediscovery of a work closely studied by Heflin highlights yet again that "Herman Melville's Whaling Years" needs to be saved from the fuzzy life-in-death of University Microfilms.

Another find which illustrates the need for the publication of Heflin's work is the acquisition of the log of the whaleship *Charles* of New Bedford, 1841-1844, Gardner, Master, by the Kendall Whaling Museum just a few years ago. The entry for Wednesday, July 13, 1842, includes the following: "PM The Acushnet appears of[f] the harbour sends in a boat gets 2 out of the 4 men that deserted from him 5 days prev[ious]" (KWM Log # 920-1, p. 76). Guess which two men the *Acushnet* did *not* get! Comfort Whiting, Jr., was the keeper of the log. Heflin does not mention this entry, but he does cite the log of the *Charles*, noting that the *Charles* came to anchor while Melville and Richard Tobias Greene were still in the hills (Log of the whaleship *Charles*, p. 312, n. 63).

Despite John Bryant's January 31, 1997, comment on Ishmail: "Just to keep professional respectability, a 'professional Melvillean' needs to have a Melville text s/he really hates in order to be able to claim some sort of objectivity and/or link to reality. But Mardi as Bad Text? It's too much over the top to be bad. Now Omoo really . . . [is] a desultory bore," I was intrigued with Heflin's research in connection with Melville's second book, *Omoo*. *Omoo* has been called perhaps Meville's most autobiographical book. Yet, as with *Typee*, Melville did not simply tell his story, but changed, extended, and borrowed to create the book as it now reads. Through Heflin's reseach, I set out to discover how Melville the man who shipped on board the *Lucy Ann* had reacted to foreign authority—Australian, British, French, and Polynesian—in comparison with the character known as "Typee" who shipped on the *Julia*.

When Charles Roberts Anderson published *Melville in the South Seas* in 1939, the documents concerning the revolt on board the Australian whaleship *Lucy Ann* had not yet been found. The incident on the *Lucy Ann* might have seemed an episode of "pure fiction" (p. 205), Anderson wrote, but both he and R. S. Forsythe independently discovered a brief entry in the logbook of the French flagship *La Reine Blanche* mentioning the mutineers. Anderson wrote: "What a treasure to the biographer would be these documents which are said to tell the whole story of the Lucy Ann! But all search for them has proved unavailing"

(p. 214). What a surprise, then, in 1940, must have been the publication of just those documents by Ida Leeson in the *Philological Quarterly*. Harrsion Hayford reprinted the documents in the Hendricks House edition of *Omoo* (1969). The documents in question are the papers of Acting Consul Charles B. Wilson, which were transferred from the British Consulate at Papeete, Tahiti, to Sydney, Australia, in 1935—for reasons having nothing to do with Melville, but fortuitous nonetheless! Heflin studied the British documents as well as any French documents he could find.

The story begins before Melville joined the crew in Nukahiva. The *Lucy Ann* was towed into the bay at Santa Christina in the Marquesas in July of 1842 by boats of the French warship *L'Embuscade*. Despite the impertinence of Captain Henry Ventom towards the French commandant, all went well for the first ten days of provisioning. Then the second mate, the carpenter, and seven of the men, including two boatsteeres, ran away, leaving the vessel with only two-thirds of its crew. As Heflin notes, "Officers of whale ships who were dissatisfied with their lot usually chose to be honorably discharged; Gabriel King, second mate of the *Lucy Ann*, deserted" (p. 356). Conditions aboard the *Lucy Ann* steadily worsened. At the captain's request, eight mutinous seamen were seized from the *Lucy Ann* and imprisoned aboard a French transport. Each night an armed party of Frenchmen stayed aboard the whaleship to protect the captain and remaining officers. Finally, his provisioning completed, Captain Ventom left port, towed out to sea by French sailors. Six of the eight imprisoned whalemen returned to duty, but Captain Ventom sent a written request to the commandant, asking that George Lefevre and John Peter continue to be held in irons. As Heflin writes, "When the *Lucy Ann* sailed the next day, it was not without pleasure that Captain Halley [the French commandant] watched her go hull down on the distant horizon" (p. 358).

Captain Ventom went to Nukahiva to replace his depleted crew. Instead, three more men deserted, including John B. Troy, Melville's "Doctor Long Ghost." The three men were recovered and the captain signed on three additional men, a carpenter and two foremast hands. He then signed on Melville as an able seaman—no longer a greenhand—at a 1/120th lay.

The *Lucy Ann* was a contentious ship on which "the refractory members outnumbered those who remained loyal" (p. 361). One of the biggest difficulties was that the *Lucy Ann* had sailed from home without enough officers—and then lost more. The vessel carried thirty men and lowered four whaleboats. Most whale-ships with that complement would have carried four officers in addition to the captain, one to command each whaleboat. Yet the *Lucy Ann* left Sydney with on-ly two officers. After the desertion at Santa Christina of the second mate and two of the four boatsteerers (or harpooneers), the vessel was left with only one officer, the "evidently capable" (p. 363) first mate, James German, and two petty officers, the two loyal boatsteerers. Captain Ventom signed an additional boat-steerer, John Garritson, at La Dominica, but he later joined with the mutinous crew against the captain. Captain Ventom's incompetence is most apparent in his continuing to cruise for sperm whales with a vessel so inadequately officered. Within two days of leaving port, Captain Ventom became severly ill and was confined to his cabin. As Heflin writes, "If Mate James German had felt during the first six months of the voyage that his broad shoulders had been uncom-monly burdened, the new demands of his situation were of a sort calculated to drive him to the habits of intemperance with which he was later charged" (pp. 364-65). He had to navigate the ship, care for the sick captain, and solely officer a disharmonious crew.

In *Omoo*, the drunken mate Jermin, despite the illness of much of the crew and without revealing his daily position, heads for an undiscovered cruising ground full of tame whales. When the captain becomes increasingly ill, he pro-poses to Melville (known as "Typee"), Doctor Long Ghost, and a few others, that should the captain die, they continue to head to the cruising ground and become rich on sperm oil. Doctor Long Ghost, backed by Typee, is the respon-sible one, who says that they must head "to the nearest civilized port, and de-liver [the ship] . . . into an English consul's hand" (ch. 13; NN p. 51). In actuality, German, seeing the captain's debilitated condition, had steered the *Lucy Ann* to-wards Tahiti even before the captain had made the decision to head to port. Thus emerges a pattern which continues throughout the first part of *Omoo*. Typee and Long Ghost are portrayed as responsible crewmembers, trying to get the other men to act reasonably. When the crew discovers that Captain Guy is to be put ashore while the *Julia* continues at sea, they threaten mutiny. "It was

34

with much difficulty," Melville writes, "that we could bring these rash spirits to a calm consideration of the case" (ch. 19; NN p. 70) and later, "Long Ghost and I labored hard to diffuse the right spirit among the crew; impressing upon them that a little patience and management would, in the end, accomplish all that their violence could; and that, too, without making a serious matter of it" (ch. 20; NN p. 73). Typee suggests the "round robin" statement of their grievances for the British consul. It is Typee who steers the *Julia* to safety after Bembo foully tries to wreck the vessel. When the British consul determines to send the mutineers to the French frigate, the mate "—who had always been friendly—stated the service rendered by myself two nights previous, as well as my conduct when he announced his intention to enter the harbor... But Wilson would hear nothing" (ch. 27; NN p. 103). So, despite his responsibility and reasonableness, Typee is counted a mutineer and held in irons aboard the *Reine Blanche*.

From the documents, Melville emerges as neither a leader nor a renegade. He prudently waited to see what would happen before joining those protesting against the captain and mate. He was never imprisoned on board the French frigate, only joining the revolters when they were sent to the Tahitian jail. In his deposition, the mate James German testified that when the men were re-examined by Acting Consul Wilson and Dr. Myrick, "'Herman Melville' also said that he would do no more duty and would share the same as the others who refused to do their duty" (HH, p. 324).

During his time on the *Lucy Ann*, Melville encountered Australian, British, French, and Polynesian authority. The ship was Australian, the Acting Consul British, the rulers of Tahiti French, and both the boatsteerer Benbow Byrne, who rose to power as acting third mate of the *Lucy Ann*, and the man in charge of the Tahitian jail Polynesian. The French supported the British acting consul, Charles B. Wilson, but not completely: they declined to be part of the examination of the mutineers. The rough-note translation of their reply reads: "We announce to you with regret that our position permits us not of forming part of a council to judge the conduct of mariners on board of Foreign Vessels" (HH, p. 317). Heflin attests that the "cordial treatment [of the mutineers in the Tahitian jail] was attributable in part to their compliance with the orders of their keepers, but was primarily due to the fact that the native authorities disliked the acting English consul"; he cites a letter from Wilson in confirmation (pp. 373-74 and n. 85). Benbow Byrne was appointed acting third mate of the *Lucy Ann*, but demoted to boatsteerer after the shipping of additional crew. So the forms of authority encountered by Melville were overlapping and shifting. In the face of such authority, he prudently bided his time. In *Omoo*, he writes: "I must explain myself here. All we wanted was to have the ship snugly anchored in Papeete Bay; entertaining no doubt that, could this be done, it would in some way or other peaceably lead to our emancipation. Without a downright mutiny, there was but one way to accomplish this: to induce the men to refuse all further duty, unless it were to work the vessel in... Nor was it without certain misgivings, that I found myself so situated, that I must necessarily link myself, however guardedly, with such a desperate company... But any thing like neutrality was out of the question; and unconditional submission was equally so" (ch. 22; NN pp. 83-84).

<h2 style="text-align:center">REFERENCES</h2>

Anderson, Charles Roberts. *Melville in the South Seas*. New York: Columbia University Press, 1939.

Batchelder, Charles. Undated manuscript comments on "Herman Melville's Whaling Years," by Wilson L. Heflin; see below.

Bryant, John. Message over "Ishmail" listserv, 31 January, 1997.

Follett, Wilson. Undated manuscript comments on "Herman Melville's WhalingYears," by Wilson L. Heflin; see below.

Hayford, Harrison, ed. "Documents on the *Lucy Ann* Revolt," appendix to *Omoo*, by Herman Melville. New York: Hendricks House, 1969.

Heflin, Wilson L. "Herman Melville's Whaling Years," PhD diss., Vanderbilt University, 1952.

Howard, Leon. *Herman Melville: A Biography*. Berkeley: University of California Press, 1951.

Leeson, Ida. "The Mutiny on the *Lucy Ann*," *Philological Quarterly*, 19 (October 1940): 370-79.

Leyda, Jay. Undated manuscript comments on "Herman Melville's Whaling

Years," by Wilson L. Heflin; see above.

Malloy, Mary. "'Bound to the Marquesas': Tommo Runs Away," *Melville Society Extracts*, no. 82 (September 1990): 1, 3-6.

Melville, Herman. *Omoo*, ed. Harrison Hayford, Hershel Parker, and G. Thomas Tanselle; vol. 2 of *The Writings of Herman Melville*. Evanston and Chicago, IL: Northwestern University Press and the Newberry Library, 1968.

——. *Typee*, ed. Harrison Hayford, Hershel Parker, and G. Thomas Tanselle; vol. 1 of *Writings*, 1968.

"Report to the Editorial Committee, New York University Press," undated manuscript.

Whiting, Comfort, Jr. Log of the whaleship *Charles* of New Bedford, 1841-44, Gardner, Master. Kendall Whaling Museum Log # 920-21.

CHRISTOPHER STEN

MELVILLE'S COSMOPOLITANISM:

A MAP FOR LIVING IN A (POST-) COLONIALIST WORLD

t was perhaps inevitable that Herman Melville would become America's most cosmopolitan writer of his time—the most widely traveled, with the broadest cultural experience and the most carefully considered views on the colonialism and cultural imperialism that defined his century in the South Seas, Latin America, Africa, and North America. The son of a Dutch patroon mother and a Scottish father and importer of French dry goods, Melville as a boy identified especially with his father, as seen in *Redburn*, where he reports listening eagerly to the older man's tales of travel to Havre and Liverpool; devouring the old books and colored prints of distant places his father would bring home; and falling into "long reveries about distant voyages and travels" to Africa or New Zealand.[1] Growing up in such an atmosphere, it's clear Melville came by his fascination with other cultures quite naturally. Given his parents' class standing, or aspirations for such, and his father's line of work, it is perhaps surprising he would become such an ardent critic of colonialism. But when we factor in his father's financial collapse and sudden death, even that aspect of his cosmopolitanism has a certain inevitability about it.

Melville's first works, *Typee* and *Omoo*, provide early evidence of the cosmopolitanism that marks his whole career. After jumping ship in the Marquesas and living with the Typees for several weeks, he went on to Tahiti where he claimed (falsely) to have witnessed the French take-over of the island and observed clear evidence of the decline of Tahitian life as a consequence of half a century of foreign rule and the meddling of missionaries. He then came back home and turned these episodes into two popular travel narratives. But he also turned them into two unusual anthropological studies, in that they attempt to treat the Otherness of these cultures with understanding and respect, despite a certain lingering condescension. For Melville, the crucial discovery of this period was the discovery of other cultures, not as resources to be exploited by Western nations, but as worlds unto themselves, and worthy of preserving. To borrow a phrase from Raymond Williams, Melville had the kind of experience that "pluralized the concept of culture." After observing the Typees and the Tahitians, it was no longer possible for him to think there was just one "correct" pattern of human development.[2]

One important consequence of his discovery was this: rather than support the imperialist take-over of the islands by the British and the French that had been occurring throughout the South Seas in earlier decades, Melville chose to critique the Western institutions that had been making inroads there, and he did so in such a way as to defend the native cultures. There were a few good things, in his view, that came from the European presence in Polynesia—improved roads, new plants and animals, and the spiritual *opportunity* the missionaries offered by translating the Bible into the natives' own tongue.[3] But to his eyes, just about every other foreign influence was bringing the natives harm—in work and dress; politics and religion; and manners and morals. Speaking of the Sandwich Islands in *Typee*, Melville says, "as in every case where Civilization has in any way been introduced among those whom we call savages, she has scattered her vices, and withheld her blessings" (198). At the same time, while he portrayed himself initially as superior to Typee culture—its simplicity, its cannibalism, its lack of industry—he soon became so enamored of it as to be tempted to join it himself—to give up his American past and assume an identity as one of them. But of course eventually he pulls back, unable to give up his old self, unable to forget about Mother and Home. In both respects, however, what he shows is something of the process of becoming cosmopolitan: he acquires a new respect for another culture *as a culture*, in all its material forms; and a new sense of himself as different from, but in no way superior to, his hosts.[4]

39

Melville provides an early model of the cosmopolitan in *Typee* itself, in the character of Marnoo, the taboo figure who moves at will from valley to valley, tribe to tribe, throughout the Marquesan Islands. Though the source of his capacity to cross borders with impunity remains something of a mystery to Melville,[5] it is tied to the fact that his face is free of tattoos, and to his natural eloquence—the most extraordinary eloquence Melville had ever witnessed, he says (137). This is an important feature of Melville's notion of cosmopolitanism, I think, and I will come back to it in my remarks about *The Confidence-Man*.

When Melville/Tommo asks how it is that he could travel so freely from Nukuheva, Marnoo explains blandly, "'Ah! me taboo,—me go Nukuheva,—me go Tior,—me go Typee,—me go everywhere,—nobody harm me,—me taboo.'" Melville then adds that he recalls hearing of "a singular custom among these islanders" whereby a native of one tribe, at war with another, may venture into enemy territory if he "has ratified friendly relations with some individual belonging to" that other tribe (139). Such "personal friendships" are so honored among the natives that "the individual so protected is said to be 'taboo,' and his person ... is held as sacred" (140).[6] (Queequeg and, through him, Ishmael are important later examples of taboo figures.)

Let me interject a bit of theory before going any further and say that I take my definition of cosmopolitanism from Arnold Krupat, author of *The Voice in the Margin: Native American Literature and the Canon* (1989) and, more recently, *Ethnocriticism: Ethnography, History, Literature* (1992). Krupat's conception is based on Bakhtinian notions of polyphony and dialogism, which he appropriates as techniques for including otherness and difference in the ongoing conversation among nations. The call to polyphony or many-voicedness, he says, understands cosmopolitanism as "urging the refusal of imperial domination, and so of the West's claim legitimately to speak for all the Rest." At its simplest and most direct, "this call is ... an exhortation to proceed humbly and with care; it asks that we Westerners stop shouting, as it were, and that we speak with our ears open."[7] On several levels, Melville practices such polyphony in *Typee* and *Omoo*, particularly where he makes an effort to let the natives speak through his text—the natives *and* certain representatives of Western culture as well, himself of course most of all in all his heterodoxy, but also some of the orthodox representatives, such as the missionaries and government authorities, whom he quotes or echoes and otherwise engages in the controversies over colonialism in the South Seas.

For Krupat, cosmopolitanism involves speaking and listening; it is a form of discourse. However, there is also a larger social dimension to it, and for this he turns to Paul Rabinow, who offers his own definition of this complex and fascinating term. For Rabinow, cosmopolitanism is "an ethos of macro-interdependencies, with an acute consciousness (often forced upon people) of the inescapabilities and particularities of place, characters, historical trajectories, and fates."[8] What is needed here, though, adds Krupat, is "to avoid 'reif[ying] local identities or construct[ing] universal ones'"; and this, both Krupat and Rabinow agree, "requires a rather delicate 'balancing act,'" one so difficult as to be practically utopian.

While Melville can hardly be said to promote such "macro-interdependency" among nations in *Typee* and *Omoo*—for the most part he clearly says to the West, "hands off" these island cultures—he doesn't simply attempt to "reify" their local identities either, and of course neither does he advocate the construction of universal identities or of a single, monolithic world culture defined as white, Christian, and European. He is sensible of the fact that the Tahitians have something to gain from Western culture—a Bible presented in their own language, a new road around the island, and so on. Though he writes in defense of native cultures, he is not a purist or a sentimentalist about them. He recognized it was, and is, an interdependent world.

As he makes clear in his next book, *Mardi*, however, Melville had seen enough of colonialism to recognize that the power imbalance between major and minor cultures was such that the strong European nations would continue to dominate and enslave the rest of the world, to the point where the peoples of the weaker, or less aggressive, cultures would be destroyed—destroyed or trapped in slavery. He also recognized that throughout the world colonialism depended on monarchical rule or on the tyranny that stems from such rule (and as he goes on to show in the Vivenza section, there is a tyranny of the majority that can be as ruthless as the tyranny of any king).[9] Melville's third book is a satire of kings; indeed, on a map of the spheres, King Media tells his cohorts, Mardi is marked "the world of kings" (542). Of the fifteen islands visited by Taji and company (not counting the utopian Serenia) the misrule of the reigning monarch is a major point of focus in Melville's treatment of twelve of them. On island after island—Odo, Valapee, and so on—Melville condemns the reigning king's senseless treatment of his own people, and the bizarre forms of suffering they are forced to experience because of his rule. Near the end, when the travelers move out of the imaginary portion of the archipelago and into an allegorical realm (where Dominora stands for England, Porpheero for Europe, and Vivenza for the United States) Melville's target becomes more specifically the colonialism of these Western cultures, and most importantly of the American South, where the tribe of "Hamo" is enslaved in spite of the country's professed republicanism.

Melville's next three books—*Redburn*, *White-Jacket*, and *Moby-Dick*—leave the realm of satire and social theory and return the author to his earlier experience at sea. In these narratives, his critique of colonialism continues, but the focus shifts from the exploited colonies to the exploited working classes, particularly the sailing classes—merchantmen, fighting men, whalers—who undergird the imperialist nations' economies. Clearly not satisfied with what he had been arguing in *Mardi*, where the happiness found on Serenia was more a spiritual state of mind than a place on any map, Melville continued to gnaw at the bone of the exploited working man in the Western world's colonialist enterprise, complaining in *Redburn*, in particular, that the upper classes in the world's economy rode in their coach on the wheels of the lower classes.[10] Only in *Moby-Dick* do we see anything like a dramatic representation of the cosmopolitanism that marked Melville's first three books—in the form of the Presbyterian Ishmael turned ecumenicalist (sharing a bed with the cannibal Queequeg, practicing idolatry [or pretending to] by worshiping Queequeg's little Yojo, etc.). The *Pequod* itself, with its Anacharsis Clootz deputation of sailors, is something of a paradigm of international cosmopolitanism—but only fitfully, in the crew's milder, sperm-squeezing moods or when flanked together performing their duties, hunting the whale. In its darker moods, at night and under the influence of grog, as in Chapter 40, "Midnight, Forecastle," the crew is seen to harbor racial hatreds and national animosities—the product of a competitiveness that is defined by their position at the bottom of the class hierarchy and that not even Ahab's autocratic rule can completely contain. (Given the talk of mutiny against Ahab, it was a natural step for Melville to go on to explore the slave mutiny on the *San Dominick*, in *Benito Cereno*, as a means of castigating the slave trade that provided yet another cornerstone of colonialist Europe and white America.) Finally, in *The Confidence-Man* Melville turned his attention to a full-scale examination of cosmopolitanism, not in international terms exactly (though a case could be made that the U.S. conflict with Native Americans, which features so centrally in this narrative, was an international one) but in a multicultural context.

In fact, Melville examines a good many dimensions of cosmopolitanism in this novel, to the point where one begins to wonder whether it is not as important a subject as confidence. Indeed, America itself is envisioned as an extraordinarily cosmopolitan, if deeply suspicious culture, bringing together a multiplicity of people of diverse ethnic, racial, and national origins, a fact Melville emphasizes from the beginning when he characterizes the passengers on the *Fidèle* as "a piebald parliament, an Anacharsis Cloots congress of all kinds of that multiform pilgrim species, man," and speaks of the "all-fusing spirit of the West" as being symbolically captured (or "typed") in the novel's Mississippi River setting, "which, uniting the streams of the most distant and opposite zones, pours them along, helter-skelter, in one *cosmopolitan and confident tide*."[11] What this group of people does, of course, while the boat makes its way down the river is to engage one another in business transactions or confidence schemes, most of which have a cosmopolitan angle, involving as they do people of disparate cultures. It's a mixed and fluid, multicultural, polyglot world, Melville seems to say, with special tensions and distinctive social difficulties, requiring unusual wariness and at the same time unusual faith, and we Americans must learn to live in it. There is, for example, a black cripple from Guinea (or so he claims) who begs for coins from the white passengers. There is a man with gray coat and white tie, a Caucasian, who tries to raise funds for a Widow and Orphan Asylum recently founded among Seminoles. There is a fellow who schemes to *methodize* all the world's benevolence in a single World's Charity, along the lines of the recent World Fair in London. And there is the man with an international scheme for contracting out the missionary work of converting all the world's pagans to Christianity, offering "so much for converting India, so much for Borneo," and so on (35). There is even talk of some reverse colonialism, whereby Jesuits from Europe disseminate so-called "popery" in the United States. More matter-of-factly, there is a leathery old Missouri bachelor, a reluctant sort of cosmopolitan to be sure, who has tried 35 boys from 35 cultures—Irish, African, Chinese; white and black—in a fruitless search for a reliable personal factotum; but all he finds are "rascals" (102).

Of course there is no character so "cosmopolitan" as the one who goes by that name, a figure who enters the narrative midway through as a curious latter-day savior or Christ-figure (the segment before his entrance being analogous to the Old Testament, the segment coming after it being equivalent to the New) and dominating the story from then on. An outlandishly dressed figure ("no bigot but a liberalist in dress") who speaks extravagantly yet with candor, too, and spends his money and himself with equal liberality, he is in every respect a "man of the world"—a "king of traveled good fellows" (114); a "catholic man who ties himself to no narrow tailor or teacher," as he says, and to whom no man is a stranger; a "true citizen of the world," who professes to follow the Christly principle of "return[ing] good for ill" (and seems to do so, repeatedly), and—as we learn in his exchanges with the misanthropic Missouri bachelor and the cautious barber—a man who goes around the boat spreading the gospel of trust in the face of doubt (203). He is, in other words, an instance of the confidence man, the book's last and major example.

Even so, he is an unusual version of the title character, not simply because he spreads a philosophy of cosmopolitanism, or faith in humanity, in a world of provincials and strangers, but because, unlike his predecessors, he never seems to try to dupe anyone in the process—unless we take the (cynic's) position that trying to win people's faith is a form of duping, the ultimate con game. To be sure, I have to admit to some uncertainty as to whether the cosmopolitan might be operating in *bad faith*, like the devil himself, though I have to add that I can never quite bring myself to believe with firmness that he does. He never seems to slip up, though like the other putative con artists on the *Fidèle*, he remains an enigma. Even when he asks for money (something he does just once, when he surprises the hypocritical Charlie Noble with a request for a $100 loan), that seems to me, rather patently, to be intended as a "test case," to expose the depths of Charlie's mistrust and try to pull Charlie back from the brink of cold faithlessness about his fellow man.[12]

Enigmatic though the cosmopolitan may be, from a functionalist point of view, it seems clear his job in the narrative is to test the faith of the other characters he meets (and indirectly to test our faith as readers), and in that way keep alive what I call the "dialogue of crisis"—the internal dialogue between faith and doubt, confidence and skepticism, that is our lives as moral agents. The characters he meets—whether Pitch or Charlie, or even the Emerson look-alike, Mark Winsome—are all doubters, even cynics; they may waiver on occasion (as Pitch does, to his credit, when he finally agrees to purchase one more boy from the PIO man), but basically they mistrust humanity implicitly. And insofar as they do so, they lack humanity themselves. They are machines.

By contrast, the cosmopolitan represents an attitude of *faith in humanity*, and as such he keeps alive the dialectical, dialogical process—the mental, moral, social process—the book explores, the process of human interaction, of trying to preserve one's "humanity" in an age, and a nation, defined by self-aggrandizement, chicanery, and cynicism. As the cosmopolitan tells Pitch, after the latter accuses him of being in reality a doubter like himself, a "Diogenes masquerading as a cosmopolitan," he comes to the Missouri bachelor as an "ambassador *from* the human race, charged with the assurance that for your mislike [misanthropy] they bore no answering grudge, but sought to conciliate accord between you and them. Yet you take me not for the honest envoy, but I know not what sort of unheard-of spy" (120). Despite the note of mischievous irony, I take this to be a serious defense of cosmopolitanism, one with almost religious overtones, for the character of the cosmopolitan, and for Melville as well.

The most serious threat to cosmopolitanism, however, is not cynicism or misanthropy, but solitariness, the opposite of cosmopolitanism—the kind of solitariness Melville himself must have experienced for the better part of a decade, when he went "up garret" to do his job as a writer, and then suddenly stopped. In the book's central exchange between the cosmopolitan and the Missouri bachelor, the cosmopolitan warns the latter that it's the solitary man who has the sorriest misconceptions about humanity, because to him all humanity are strangers. Without real, continuous interaction, he is likely to have an extreme or misguided conception. The Missouri bachelor is himself a case in point, believing as he does that the only reason a man like the cosmopolitan would want to have his fellow-creatures around him or venture into a crowd is to pick their pockets (119).

Such seems to be the point of the story of John Moredock, the book's most extreme example of the solitary man, whose Indian-hating makes him not simply a misanthrope but a cold-blooded killer. For a long time now, critics have been urging us to view the Indians as devils incarnate, the most evil and duplicitous avatars of the confidence man in Melville's narrative, and hence deserving of the genocidal fury John Moredock visits on them. According to this theory, confidence schemes constitute a powerful disease, and a strong disease calls for a strong purge.[13] But I think there are a few hints to the contrary, within the story of John Moredock itself, that should lead us to question the idea that the extermination of the Indians was, in Melville's own view, a matter of America's "manifest destiny."

Unfortunately, I don't have time to look closely at Melville's rendering of this complex story of the Indian hater. A few choice details will have to suffice to suggest how it fits within Melville's career of anti-colonialism. First of all, Melville makes the imperialist connection explicit, when he says that the backwoodsman, like John Moredock, "would seem to America what Alexander was to Asia—captain in the vanguard of conquering civilization." Also, it is not too coyly suggested that the backwoodsman *trespasses* when he goes into the woods: his "lonely path," we are told, "lies a long way through their [the Native Americans'] lands" (126). Third, Moredock, in seeking revenge against the Indians who killed his family, leaps from the example of this small group of killers to stereotype all Indians as evil even though "the actual transgressors," those who killed his mother and siblings, were "outlaws even among Indians" (133).

I said earlier I would come back to the idea of the cosmopolitan as a figure of eloquence, an artist figure. More than anything, the cosmopolitan in *The Confidence-Man* reminds me of Mark Twain's "Mysterious Stranger," another slippery, savior figure who happens also to be a big talker. A character with similarly mysterious origins, he enters the world to test Melville's other characters (and his readers), and reveal themselves to themselves, as Twain would say. Their "poor servant," he comes to set them free; yet like Twain's mysterious stranger, he is mistrusted and misunderstood.

This capacity to reveal us to ourselves makes the cosmopolitan an image of the artist. Indeed, I would say that the cosmopolitan in this book is as close to a portrait of the artist as Melville ever sketched of himself. A figure of faith and of doubt, one might even say cosmic faith and cosmic doubt, he nonetheless insists on promulgating a philosophy of *charity* toward his fellow man: "Charity, charity," the cosmopolitan exclaims to Charlie Noble, when the latter accuses Pitch of being a "comprehensive Colonel Moredock"; "never a sound judgment without charity. When man judges man, charity is less a bounty from our mercy than just allowance for the insensible lee-way of human fallibility," and then he goes on to show that he himself combines such charity with a good deal of mental work—looking, observing, even prying to uncover the truth—as he does at the end of his encounter with Pitch when, seizing an opportunity to inspect the Missouri bachelor's heart, he is "undeceived" and finds it "an inviting oyster in a forbidding shell" (136). To be sure, this last admission has an ominous ring to it, but only if we think of the cosmopolitan as a nefarious figure. If instead we think of him as the artist who, infinitely curious, escapes the self, escapes the local, in an effort to understand the many-sidedness of humankind; who makes an imaginative, empathic leap into the minds and hearts of his fellows, one can begin to understand the reasons behind the shapeshifting of what Melville avowed to be the most "original" character he ever created, the one who "like a revolving drummond light," lights up everything as never before (204-5). By the end of his career as a publishing fiction writer, cosmopolitanism had become a defining activity of the imagination for Melville, in politics and in art, one requiring the capacity to see and feel other people, other worlds, as though they were one's own, and to treat them with the same kind of charity or caring as if they were, even though they were indeed Other.

Notes

1   *Redburn, His First Voyage*, ed. Harrison Hayford, Hershel Parker, and G. Thomas Tanselle (Evanston and Chicago, IL: Northwestern UP and the Newberry Library, 1969), pp. 7 and 5. Subsequent references are to this edition and appear in the text.

2   As quoted in John Tomlinson, *Cultural Imperialism: A Critical Introduction* (Baltimore, MD: Johns Hopkins UP, 1991), p. 5.

3   See *Typee: A Peep at Polynesian Life*, ed. Harrison Hayford, Hershel Parker, and G. Thomas Tanselle (Evanston and Chicago, IL: Northwestern UP and the Newberry Library, 1969), pp. 178, 182-83, 198. Subsequent references are to this edition and appear in the text. Note that otherwise, in Melville's view, the missionaries had pretty much botched the job of Christianizing the islanders.

4   This state of affairs is intriguingly similar to the one described in Pascal's parable of a man shipwrecked on an unknown island. The natives treat him as their lost king but he cannot forget his real condition. He thus "had a double thought: the one by which he acted as king, the other by which he recognised his true state," and had "nothing naturally superior to" the natives. (Quoted in Tomlinson, 29.)

5   Melville says, "if a native to that region, I could not account for his friendly reception at the hands of the Typees," who were notoriously hostile to members of neighboring tribes (137).

6   That cosmopolitanism isn't necessarily the same as diplomacy is revealed when Marnoo tries to help Melville/Tommo escape from Typee Valley and almost starts a fight, but that the two are at least connected is suggested in the end of the narrative when Melville learns it was Marnoo, after all, who had made possible his rescue (252).

7   Arnold Krupat, *The Voice in the Margin: Native American Literature and the Canon* (Berkeley: U of California P, 1989), pp. 16-17.

8   Quoted in *Voice*, 197-98.

9   See, for example, pp. 468 and 471-72 in *Mardi: And A Voyage Thither*, ed. Harrison Hayford, Hershel Parker, and G. Thomas Tanselle (Evanston and Chicago, IL: Northwestern UP and the Newberry Library, 1970). Subsequent references are to this edition and appear in the text.

10   Cf. *Redburn*, 139: "Now, sailors form one of these wheels: they go and come round the globe; they are the true importers, and exporters of spices and silks, of fruits and wines and marbles; they carry missionaries, embassadors, opera-singers, armies, merchants, tourists, scholars to their destination: they are a bridge of boats across the Atlantic; they are the *primum mobile* of all commerce. . . ."

11   *The Confidence-Man: His Masquerade*, ed. Hershel Parker (New York: Norton, 1971), p. 6. Subsequent references are to this edition and appear in the text.

12   It finally comes out in this episode that Charlie's position gets whittled down to that of the simple-minded Polonius, "neither a borrower nor a lender be."

13   See esp. John W. Shroeder, "Sources and Symbols for Melville's *Confidence-Man*," *PMLA*, 66 (June 1951): 364-80; and Hershel Parker, "The Metaphysics of Indian-Hating," *Nineteenth-Century Fiction*, 18 (September 1963): 165-73.

MARVIN FISHER

THE AMERICAN CHARACTER, THE AMERICAN IMAGINATION,

AND THE TEST OF INTERNATIONAL TRAVEL IN *REDBURN*

hen Melville seemingly dismissed his fourth novel as that "beggarly Redburn," he invited the critical underestimation of the past century and a half. That critical consensus describes a book shaped by economic despair and the dispiriting unpopularity of *Mardi*. Because *Redburn* incorporates so many autobiographical elements, the narrator is too readily identified with Melville and the novel too often read as a boy's initiation into manhood and mature knowledge. For these reasons *Redburn* seems to mark Melville's abandonment of *Mardi*'s wide-ranging philosophical satire, ridiculing religion, politics, occupations, and the literary marketplace.

My view, however, is that Melville here explores the territory, tries out the themes, and first practices the techniques we associate with Henry James. We have a quintessential young American now grown older who, as a narrator, is almost as unreliable as his callow adolescent self. Sheltered by a well connected family and untested moral assumptions, he is as unprepared for the world of work and shipboard indignities as he is for the cultural, intellectual, aesthetic, and moral challenges of a foreign society. Having argued elsewhere that Melville's short fiction embodies art as subversion, I now propose that Melville was already a subversive writer in *Redburn* and that his subversion targeted not only the religious establishment and the cruel disparities between the socially privileged and the socially impoverished, it was directed also at those qualities in the

American character that abetted moral hypocrisy and an impoverished imagination, qualities that also demonized the decorative and expressive arts because they threatened American purity and innocence. In our time these attitudes underlie the recurring attacks on the National Endowment for the Arts and the limitations imposed on individual artists and group grant recipients. Young Redburn bore the impress of these culturally imposed limitations; they are the hallmark of what Melville called his "young inland imagination." The cultural exponents of these hostile and suspicious attitudes include Cotton Mather in the seventeenth century, Benjamin Franklin in the eighteenth century, and the Connecticut Wits in the nineteenth century. They shaped American literary history through a combination of moralism, didacticism, and patriotic concern for the failure of fiction and poetry to bolster the gross national product.

Redburn, the naïve heir to this historical legacy, might himself be his country's grossest national product, and, *Redburn*, the book, a stronger indictment of the American embarking on a voyage of international experience than Henry James would produce and a more ironic and embittered portrait of the young protagonist's incapacity for art than James Joyce would produce. If I may create a category for it, I would call it Melville's counter-*künstlerroman*.

Redburn longs for excitement, adventure, and the cosmopolitan experience of travel but is woefully unequipped to understand what he sees and to benefit from his experience. Like the brittle fragility of the glass ship in his family parlor, his assumptions and preconceptions leave him vulnerable to frustration, disappointment, self-pity, and ultimate alienation. His voyage begins well before he boards the *Highlander*, and it shatters his precarious idealism and provincial security. The variable price structure of a free market economy and the exploitative initial interview with Captain Riga, who manages to convert all of Redburn's genteel pretensions into economic disadvantages, place Redburn in the company of cannibals before he is even 20 miles from home. Just as the early signs of his material poverty foreshadow the later exposure of his impoverished imagination, Redburn's failure to catch on to Riga's game foreshadows the irony of initiation without development, a bildungsroman that doesn't build, and travel that doesn't broaden or inform.

Redburn's "young inland imagination" has its counterpart in his young inland education. Placing Bremen in France and Hamburg in Holland stamps his exuberant ignorance and unreliability. Melville exposes his protagonist's naïve, nativist anti-Semitism in his visits to pawnbrokers—another form of social impoverishment. He is oblivious even to stereotypes; his only association with stereotyped Jewish features is Judas Iscariot. Ostensibly free of racist prejudice, he nevertheless imagines that a public drinking glass from which a Negro had previously drunk retained an unpleasant taste.

Less than a year after the publication of *Redburn*, there appeared Melville's review of "Hawthorne and His Mosses" with its overt attention to the accomplishment of his Berkshire neighbor and its covert concern for public recognition of the genuine artist in America. It is an indisputable compendium of Melville's own values, beliefs, and hopes—all of them in marked contrast to Redburn's. From the moment that the dramatically conceived "Virginian" and his charming cousin Cherry discard Dwight's *Travels in New-England* and take up Hawthorne's *Mosses*, the American literary canon comes under attack and an alternative literary history emerges. Ranked with Shiloh and Shakespeare, the messianic Hawthorne nevertheless offers a New World literary testament built upon but clearly distinguishable from its Old World precursor. "Who reads a book by an Englishman that is a modern?" our Virginian asks rhetorically. What he means, of course, is that the literary history of the future lies with those potential rivals to Shakespeare who "are this day being born on the banks of the Ohio" and who are "bound to carry republican progressiveness into Literature, as well as into Life." Viewed by many today as blatant literary nationalism, these assertions by a young, white, American male also constitute an early self-interested affirmative action challenging the dominance of English writers and the popularity of their American imitators.

The first to suffer by this critical revaluation is Washington Irving, unnamed though recognizable as "that very popular and amiable writer . . . [who] owes his chief reputation to the self-acknowledged imitation of a foreign model, and to the studied avoidance of all topics but smooth ones." Further candidates for decanonization are those also unnamed but recognizable poets whose efforts "but furnish an appendix to Goldsmith and other English authors. And we want no American Goldsmiths; nay we want no American Miltons." The earlier toss of Dwight's

New England guidebook and elevation of Hawthorne's *Mosses* was an act of literary iconoclasm, for Timothy Dwight was foremost among those once-revered poets known as the Connecticut Wits. He had celebrated pastoral America and the industry and thrift of its simple citizenry in *Greenfield Hill*, much in the manner of Goldsmith's *Deserted Village*, and allegorized the American Revolution in a Miltonic poem that does Milton no credit—*The Conquest of Canaan*. His better known colleagues included John Trumbull, Joel Barlow, and David Humphreys.

Just as Dwight's guidebook to New England and New York, posthumously published in 1821-22, failed the test of Melville's Virginian, the guidebook to Liverpool left by Redburn's late father fails to meet Redburn's needs; but unlike the Virginian, whose standards are synonymous with Melville's ambitions. Redburn will not discard or abandon his revered guidebook. His confidence in the infallibility of the guidebook foreshadows Amasa Delano's naïve faith in appearance and preconception or the callow vulnerability of the confidence man's victims aboard the *Fidèle*. Refusing to acknowledge the failure of an outdated guidebook, Redburn fails the test that might declare his own intellectual independence. Even apart from his naivete, Redburn's inclinations and attitudes run counter to the central ideas of Melville's review, and his limitations coincide with those whose moral, aesthetic, and intellectual servility blocks American artistic expression.

Redburn's sentimental excesses as he follows his sainted father's footsteps on the very street his father trod half a century before reflect the same maudlin rhapsodizing and emotional self-manipulation that Mark Twain satirized in his description of a young American overcome at encountering his ancestral past at Adam's tomb in *The Innocents Abroad*.

Redburn's moral constraints and awkward innocence are comically rendered in his juvenile membership in anti-smoking and alcoholic abstinence societies, his views of religion, and his embarrassment at the mysteries and décor of Aladdin's Palace. In these matters he is heir to the advice Cotton Mather in his late years directed at young ministers who might be too much attracted to the literary beauties of Homer and Virgil. In depicting gods acting in roguish fashion, Homer became, in Mather's eyes, the "universal corrupter" who "set open the floodgates for a prodigious inundation of wickedness." Because of the effectiveness of his art, this pagan poet "was one of the greatest apostles the Devil ever had in the world," and such poetic mischief can poison the soul:

I cannot but advise you, withhold thy throat from thirst. Be not so set upon poetry, as to be always poring on the passionate and measured pages. Let not what should be a sauce rather than food for you, engross all your application. Beware of a boundless and sickly appetite for the reading of poems ... and let not the Circaean cup intoxicate you. But especially preserve the chastity of your soul from the dangers you may incur, by a conversation with Muses that are no better than harlots: among which are... Ovid's epistles, which for their tendency to excite and foment impure flames ... deserve rather to be thrown into the fire, than to be laid before the eye... Indeed, ... the powers of darkness have a library among us, where of the poets have been the most numerous as well as the most venomous authors. Most of the modern plays, as well as the romances and novels and fictions, ... belong to ... this cursed library... As for those wretched scribbles of madmen, ... touch them not, taste them not; thou wilt perish in the using of them. They are the dragons whose contagious breath peoples the dark retreats of death. (*Manductio ad Ministorium*, 1726)

Old guardians of morality such as Sen. Jesse Helms or Newt Gingrich's phalanx of economic puritans may not quote Cotton Mather directly, but manage to evoke his spirit and make political hay by attacking immorality and alleging rampant sacrilege in an arts community they view as "elitist."

In less violent language and from a more enlightened perspective Benjamin Franklin, in his *Autobiography*, approvingly recalls how a wise friend discouraged a would-be-poet: "and advised him to think of nothing beyond the business he was bred to: that, in the mercantile way, tho' he had no stock, he might, by his diligence and punctuality, recommend himself to employment as a factor, and in time acquire wherewith to trade on his own account." Redburn would do no less for his friend (or artistic-alter-ego) Harry Bolton. Franklin, summing up his anecdote, seems to glance back to Cotton Mather: "I approv'd the amusing one's self with poetry now and then, so far as to improve one's language, but no farther." Practical as ever, Franklin realizes that using the skill sharpened by his poetry exercises for productive purposes, he would never have to write a "Dollars damn me" letter complaining about the deficiencies of public taste or the economics of the publishing market.

Redburn, taken to the opulent and sinister Aladdin's Palace by Harry Bolton, feels himself in a graphic counterpart to Mather's library of literary seductiveness. Artifice, mimicry, and deception are intermingled with splendor and indulgence in strange liquors and frequent cigars. Pornographic paintings (wholly unlike the landscapes and seascapes in his father's library) line the walls. They are described with no reference to their content, but with reference to their similarity to what might have been seen in the private recesses of the orient, ancient Greece, decadent Rome, or the Aztec kingdom—all pagan and foreign places. Discomforted by his esoteric surroundings and by Harry's feverish behavior. Redburn seems to experience the dangers Mather predicted: "The whole place seemed infected; and a strange thought came over me, that in the very damasks around, some eastern plague had been imported. And was that pale yellow wine, that I drank below, drugged?. . . This must be some house whose foundations take hold on the pit. But these fearful reveries only enchanted me fast to my chair; so that, though I then wished to rush forth from the house, my limbs seemed manacled" (*Redburn*, ch. 46). The spirit of Cotton Mather lives in these words and in Redburn's moralistic judgment "that though gilded and golden, the serpent of vice is a serpent still." The manacles encase his mind as well as his limbs and leave him immobilized and vulnerable to plagues of foreign origin that lead to decadence and damnation.

The spirit of Benjamin Franklin, however, would regard the costliness of this indulgence, the unprofitableness of the escapade, and the implicit dangers as effective deterrents, a compendium of what he called in the *Autobiography* his *errata*, instances of immoral behavior that served a didactic purpose. That didactic purpose can also produce poetry of a sort, not great poetry but poetry that Redburn could admire and that Melville knew from the tribe of Dwight, whose leader was not alone in praising Puritan virtue and industry. David Humphreys's *Poem on the Industry of the United States of America* patriotically traced the emergence of a thriving commercial society from the "hideous and desolate wilderness" that Bradford recorded:

> The immense of forest! Where no tree was fell'd,
> Where savage-men at midnight orgies yell'd,
> Where howling round burning pyres each ravening beast,

As fiend-like forms devour'd their bloody feast,
And hoarse resounded o'er the horrid heath,
The doleful war-whoop, or the song of death,
. . . the dun forest's thickest foliage frown'd,
And night and horror brooded o'er the ground;
Where the swart savage fix'd his short abode,
Or wound through tangled wilds his thorny road;
Where the gaunt wolves from crag-roof'd caverns prowl'd,
And mountains echoed as the monsters howl'd;
Where putrid marshes felt no solar beams,
And mantling mire exhal'd mephictic steams.

But the warm sun of colonial enterprise purges the gothic landscape of the primitive pestilence and produces an image that any subsequent chamber of commerce would love:

See, mid the rocks a Paradise arise,
That feels the fostering warmth of genial skies!
While gurgling currents lull the enchanted soil,
The hill-tops brighten and the dingles smile.

Of course Redburn did not read Humphreys's poem but he encountered its English equivalent in the pages of the guidebook that proves so futile and false when he puts it to use. It is *The Picture of Liverpool* found in his father's library amid the romantic paintings, sentimental and stylized prints, and pristine artificiality of the carefully crafted glass ship. All of these artifacts serve, like the neoclassical doggerel in the guidebook, as objective correlatives for the debased beauty, false ideality, and pretentious gentility of American aesthetic taste. The fact that the first lines quoted from the guidebook and dated 1772 seem so similar to Humphreys's poem fifty years later further stresses the servility and imitativeness of some of the most admired American poetry during the early decades of the nineteenth century. The lines of poetry that grace the more prosaic passages of the guidebook include a borrowed prologue and a more contemporary account of Liverpool's commercial importance cast in epic form. The prologue exalts the virtue and industry of those who first settled where the Mersey ran to the sea:

> Where Mersey's stream, long winding o'er the plain,
> Pours his full tribute to the circling main,
> A band of fishers chose their humble seat;
> Contented labor blessed the fair retreat,
> Inured to hardship, patient, bold, and rude,
> They braved the billows for precarious food:
> Their straggling huts were ranged along the shore,
> Their nets and little boats their only store.

The lines are remotely democratic in subject but condescendingly aristocratic in tone. They tell as little about the struggle and impoverishment of these fishermen and their families as the paintings and prints which Redburn so avidly admires tell about life at sea.

More than fifty years ago, Willard Thorp compared the poetry quoted in *Redburn* with that included in *The Picture of Liverpool* and concluded that most of it was quoted verbatim, some rearranged, and some made up by Melville. Melville's purpose, it now appears, was to stress the anomaly of presenting proletarian and bourgeois themes in a neoclassical and aristocratic style, resulting in an inadvertent burlesque that was nevertheless accepted as art. Thus the less-than-mellifluous sound of "Liverpool" evokes these lines from the guidebook:

> Now o'er the wondering world her name resounds,
> From northern climes to India's distant bounds
> Where'er his shores the broad Atlantic waves;
> Where'er the Baltic rolls his wintry waves;
> Where'er the honored flood extends his tide,
> That clasps Sicilia like a favored bride.
> Greenland for her its bulky whale resigns,
> And temperate Gallia rears her generous vines:
> Midst warm Iberia citron orchards blow,
> And the ripe fruitage bends the laboring bough:
> In every clime her prosperous fleets are known,
> She makes the wealth of every clime her own.

Though these lines attest to the commercial and geographical centrality of Liverpool, the style cannot account for such a phenomenon of commercial capitalism as Captain Riga, the wily Irish fisherman who cons them out of the rope thrown to him, or the assortment of land-sharks, land-rats, landlords, barkeepers, clothiers, crimps, and consorts, who prey upon the sailors. Nor can it deal with the casualties of Launcelot's Hey or the conditions of the Highlander's immigrant cargo. Redburn's uncritical acceptance of such poetry allies him with the tribe of Dwight and their successors, whom Melville in his *Mosses* review described as "these smooth, pleasing writers that know their powers . . . but furnish an appendix to Goldsmith, and other English authors." Redburn, however, would rather "sell his Shakespeare, and even sacrifice his Hogarth" than part with his misguided guidebook and its praiseful poetry. He clearly affirms his preference for the kind of literature that Melville detested.

When he tried to speak Addisonian English to his hosts in the English countryside, Redburn became more than a curiosity. Here he was a representative of a brash New World democracy trying to sound like a ridiculous relic of Augustan England. He inhabits an intellectual time warp; he constitutes the embodiment of a lingering cultural dependence on Europe in general, England in particular. The courtly muses that Emerson warned of are still singing their siren song to Redburn. To the extent that young Redburn is representative of young America, Melville would seem to imply, we live in cultural and aesthetic thralldom. Although he finds a handful of American writers worthy of praise, Haw-thorne and Emerson in the forefront, Melville the critic saw the literary artist penned in by deficiencies in present taste—the various immaturities of Redburn—and burdened by the constraints of literary history which imposed the form, vocabulary, and syntax of a distant culture in a past century.

Redburn's Christian piety and American patriotism reveal further instances of timidity, hypocrisy, and self-deception. He depicts himself as an unabashed admirer of monumental church architecture and of the church's role in extending hospitality and democratic community across national borders. However, the empirical reality of his visits to the more prosperous and imposing Liverpool churches clearly contradicts but does not cancel his benign preconceptions. Invariably the sexton seeing his less than fine garb places him in the least convenient seat where the most prominent architectural feature is an immense pillar blocking his view of the pulpit and the congregation's view of him. But the experience of segregation and social stratification seems not to challenge his belief in Christian hospitality and open-handed democracy. His capacity for muting contradiction and embracing Orwellian doublethink affirms his intellectual subordination while assuring his survival.

Doublethink underlies Redburn's apparent support for liberal immigration policies and his celebration of ethnic diversity. Beginning with praise for the piety and industry of German emigrants en route to New York from Liverpool, he proceeds to praise American tolerance, which, despite the nativist sentiment so prominent by mid-century, will successfully "extinguish the prejudices of national dislikes":

Settled by the people of all nations, all nations may claim her for their own. You can not spill a drop of American blood without spilling the blood of the whole world. . . . We are not a narrow tribe of men with a bigoted Hebrew nationality—whose blood has been debased in the attempt to ennoble it, by maintaining an exclusive succession among ourselves. No: our blood is as the flood of the Amazon, made up of a thousand noble currents all pouring into one. We are not a nation, so much as a world; for unless we may claim all the world for our sire, . . . we are without a father or mother. [¶] For who was our father and our mother? . . . Our ancestry is lost in the universal paternity; and Cæsar and Alfred, St. Paul and Luther, and Homer and Shakespeare are as much ours as Washington, who is as much the world's as our own. We are the heirs of all time, and with all nations we divide our inheritance. On this Western Hemisphere all tribes and people are forming into one federated whole; and there is a future which shall see the estranged children of Adam restored as to the old hearthstone in Eden.

But such political correctness, then as now, does not mean what it seems to mean, and Redburn's affirmation of multiculturalism stems more from the lip than from the heart.

Even as he echoes the American liberal vision of a new chance for mankind, a new beginning in an American Eden, he immediately dispells that benign belief with a harsher apocalyptic exclusiveness hostile to religious and linguistic difference. Alluding to European discovery of the New World and to the anonymous sailor whose deep-sea-lead "brought up the soil of Earth's Paradise," he injects a fundamentalist evangelical note that not only rejects but destroys the liberal vision: "Not a Paradise then, or now; but to be made so, at God's good pleasure, and in the fullness and mellowness of time. The seed is sown, and the harvest must come; and our children's children, on the world's jubilee morning, shall go with their sickles to the reaping. Then shall the curse of Babel be revoked, a new Pentecost come, and the language they shall speak shall be the language of Britain. Frenchmen, and Danes, and Scots; and the dwellers on the shores of the Mediterranean, and in the regions round about; Italians, and Indians, and Moors; there shall appear unto them cloven tongues as of fire" (*Redburn*, ch. 33).

Partial or selective references to these two incompatible visions of American destiny have resulted in undue praise for Redburn's democratic sentiments, ignoring how quickly these sentiments succumb to the dire language of Christian Apocalyptic thought. From the liberal perspective, the language of the book of Revelation is like the serpent whose efforts dispel the hope of the New Eden; from the evangelical perspective, the optimism of a New Eden for unfallen mankind is the message of a deceiver whose cohorts must be defeated in an inevitable Armageddon. In Redburn's choplogic the effort to shun "a bigoted Hebrew nationality" produces an American chosen people and a new strain of bigotry. Similarly, the effort to assimilate people of all nations, races, and languages leads to the divine decree: English only! Melville's criticism targets the capacity for doublethink in his protagonist, who is of course the product of his country, his culture, and their inherent contradictions.

Eighty years ago, George Santayana, in a sort of farewell address to America, used the phrase "the genteel tradition" in a highly descriptive and keenly analytical way. Having characterized America as "a young country with an old mentality," he went on to refine his diagnosis: "it is a country with two mentalities, one a survival of the beliefs and standards of the fathers, the other an expression of the instincts, practice and discoveries of the younger generations. In all the higher things of the mind—in religion, in literature, in the moral emotions—it is the hereditary spirit that still prevails, so much so that Mr. Bernard Shaw finds that America is a hundred years behind the times." Neither Mr. Santayana nor Mr. Shaw is likely to have read Redburn, but Melville seems to have preempted their argument, and, on the subject of literary history and the canon, or the limitations of the American character and imagination, some others as well.

Melville's young American cannot esteem what is honest, original or true in

American experience and expression nor comprehend the subtleties and ambiguities of his first adventure among the nations. Tested by the novelty of foreign travel, he denies the lessons of his own experience and maintains the fixed ideas or ideological preconceptions of his puritan forebears, his provincial upbringing, and his patriotic clichés. Fearful of being enticed into "notorious Corinthian haunts" whose depravities rival those of the bottomless pit, he remains a young insular moralist whose mind is closed to what his travel might teach. Instead his lesson seems to be that travel corrupts and international travel corrupts absolutely. For these reasons, "beggarly Redburn" disparages the character of the protagonist rather than the quality of the book.

WYN KELLEY

THE STYLE OF LIMA:

COLONIALISM, URBAN FORM, AND "THE TOWN-HO'S STORY"

I n *Moby-Dick* Melville's references to Lima seem to substantiate Hershel Parker's claim that, "no other city in the Americas, not crooked old Boston, not Manhattan belted with wharves, not heavy-walled Quebec bristling with cannon, ever caught and haunted his imagination the way Lima did" (281). Melville certainly gives a haunting description of Lima in his chapter, "The Whiteness of the Whale": "Nor is it, altogether, the remembrance of her cathedral-top-pling earthquakes;...—it is not these things alone which make tearless Lima, the strangest, saddest city thou can'st see. For Lima has taken the white veil; and there is a higher horror in this whiteness of her woe. Old as Pizarro, this whiteness keeps her ruins for ever new; admits not the cheerful greenness of complete decay; spreads over her broken ramparts the rigid pallor of an apoplexy that fixes its own distortions" (193). This passage makes several of the allusions commonly found in nineteenth-century accounts of Lima: to Pizarro and the Spanish Conquest; to Lima as a veiled woman, with suggestions of both feminine allure and spiritual renunciation; and to the earthquakes that figured regularly in contemporary travel accounts.[1] But Melville also creates a mysterious and conflicting set of meanings around this central image. And he goes on, in his chapter "The Town-Ho's Story," to foreground Lima in even more problematic ways. Here Ishmael promises to tell a story of Moby Dick, in "the style in which I once narrated it at Lima, to a lounging circle of my Spanish friends, one saint's eve, smoking upon the thick-gilt tiled piazza of the Golden Inn" (243). I want to determine what Ishmael means by "the style in which I once narrated it at Lima" by looking at three dimensions of the figure of Lima: first as an urban form containing a plaza capable of openly enacting cultural conflict, second as a site from which to engage romantic American historiography, particularly as represented by William Hickling Prescott in his histories of Spanish colonialism, and third as a model for a distinctive "style" of narrative which stages conflict as a monumental national drama while at the same time revealing the more sordid operations of colonial power. Although Melville surely shared the distaste of some Americans for Spanish Catholicism, conquest, and colonialism, he also saw in the plaza a ground for resistance to that hegemony. Ironically, democratic New York had no such plaza, no place where the victims of North American colonialism might meet and stare down their rulers as Babo does the Spanish at the end of "Benito Cereno" (1853).

New York in the early 1800s was surveyed and laid out on a grid plan suitable for commercial expansion and real estate speculation. Designed with little open public space, the city was frequently portrayed and imagined as a dense, constricted urban landscape that paved over evidence of its earlier history as colonial settlement, as Indian land. New York was a post-colonial and post-revolutionary city that constantly tore itself down and reinvented itself, leaving scattered signs of its history. Its cultural meaning was displayed, not in a central, monumental plaza but in its many streets which obliterated the past.[2]

Lima in 1844, however, when Melville's ship, the *United States*, visited it, still loudly proclaimed its colonial history. Though recently liberated in 1821, its structure, architecture, and urban life showed the influence of centuries of European dominance. The central plaza prominently displayed Pizarro's statue, cathedral, and government palace. Subject to numerous earthquakes, Lima had been rebuilt many times but never in ways that effaced its colonial past. For Melville, it provided a vivid symbol of European might.[3]

But the plaza also allowed cultural conflict between colonizers and oppressed to be staged in a more generous public space than in North American cities. Unlike in North America, plazas already existed in several South American cities before the Europeans arrived, built, of course, by Aztec and Mayan imperial rulers. The history of urban planning in Central and South America shows evidence of architectural compromise between colonizers and native culture. Aztec and Inca cities had enormous central squares where religious ceremonies, military exercises, and popular festivals and markets took place. The cross-fertilization between Spanish and South American urban planning produced cities that, ironically, proclaimed European political and religious authority while at the same time yielding to Native American topography and urban form.[4]

Furthermore in the way that South American plazas were used as public space, they forcefully demonstrated an interactive relationship between conquerors and conquered. In Peru, as the nineteenth-century accounts repeatedly emphasized, the subject culture held its own through racial mixture and was a visible presence in the plaza. The *mestizo* class combined not only European whites and Mayan Indians but also a large number of Africans, who moved rapidly into the racial mixture, as they did not do until much later in North America. Melville, then, would have seen a forceful European presence and at the same time a convergence of multiple races and powerful cultures on the same urban site: a phenomenon he would later be drawn to in ancient cities like Jerusalem, Thessaloniki, and Constantinople.

For his use of Lima in *Moby-Dick*, Melville drew, as he did in most of his works, not only on his memories of visiting the place but also on a range of texts. Charles Wilkes's *Narrative of the United States Exploring Expedition* and other nautical accounts have been extensively studied as a source for Melville's South American passages. I would like to look at two less noticed texts, William Hickling Prescott's histories of Spanish conquest and an essay, "Lima and the Limanians," that appeared in the Oct. 1851 issue of *Harper's New Monthly Magazine*, the same issue that published Melville's "The Town-Ho's Story" from *Moby-Dick* as a separate story.[5] (Although the *Harper's* essay appeared too late for *Moby-Dick*, it may well have influenced "Benito Cereno.") I want to suggest that Melville chose Lima in part because of its emerging significance in American cultural dialogue.

A logical place for Melville to turn to in this dialogue would have been Prescott's popular *History of the Conquest of Peru*, published in 1847. We can be certain that he knew of Prescott's work, particularly the 1843 *History of the Conquest of Mexico*. Melville was at sea when the book came out, but he would have come across Prescott's first book, *Ferdinand and Isabella*, in the library of the *United States*. On his return home in 1844, he found his brother Gansevoort and others fervently excited over Mexico; among the many people who were reading Prescott's *Conquest of Mexico* during the Mexican War was Melville's future·sister-in-law Sophia Thurston (Parker, 464). Through his Boston relatives, Melville even had an opportunity to meet Prescott at a dinner in December 1846, but Melville apparently skipped the dinner and missed the rendezvous (Parker, 467). In any case, there can be no question that he knew of Prescott's writings and of his reputation as the eminent historian of the Spanish colonial enterprise in South America.

But Prescott's *Mexico* might well have dismayed Melville with its romantic view of European civilization and its racist treatment of the Aztecs. As Jenny Franchot has argued, Prescott displaced American anxieties over the immigration of Catholics from Europe onto the Aztec subject. In Prescott's cultural drama, the Aztecs shared many of the faults perceived in European Catholics: idolatry and superstition, religious violence and fanaticism, and a love of gaudy display. On the other hand, Cortes, though himself Catholic, seemed to show North American discipline and effectiveness, permitting American readers to identify with the conqueror rather than the victims.

Prescott's history of Peru, however, acknowledged the difficulties of its subject in ways that Melville might have endorsed. As Prescott admitted in his "Preface," "here, the subject...does not afford so obvious advantages to the historian, as the Conquest of Mexico" (727). That earlier conquest, he asserts, followed closely the plot structure of a national epic: "The natural development of the story, there, is precisely what would be prescribed by the severest rules of art...It is a magnificent epic, in which the unity of interest is complete" (727). The story of Peru, however, does not offer so tidy a plot nor so stirring an epic: "The action, so far as it is founded on the subversion of the Incas, terminates long before the close of the narrative. The remaining portion is taken up with the fierce feuds of the Conquerors" (727). The main conflict, then, is not between one superior and another inferior culture, but between rival groups in a single culture. And Pizarro, as an elderly leader, an illegitimate son, a diplomatic failure, has little of the heroic aura surrounding the energetic, inspired Cortes. As Prescott is also forced to emphasize, the Incas do not deserve what they get, the way he was able to argue that the Aztecs did. In the *History of the Conquest of Peru*, the cultural values of the history of Mexico seem almost reversed, with the conquerors appearing like barbarians and the Incas like rational, civilized people. To Melville, who satirized European civilization in *Typee*, who asked "what has he [the Indian] to desire at the hands of Civilization?" (124), the conquest of Peru would have seemed a great abomination, as Prescott often, though covertly, implies.

Even if Melville might have agreed with Prescott's view of Spanish conquest, however, he would have balked at its celebration of Pizarro's city-building. For Prescott's greatest enthusiasm for Pizarro comes when he founded Lima in 1535. Prescott admires the "regular plan," the orderly streets "much wider than usual in Spanish towns, and perfectly straight, crossing one another at right angles, and so far asunder as to afford ample space for gardens to the dwellings, and for public squares" (1007). He also makes special note of: "The *plaza*, which was extensive, [and] was to be surrounded by the cathedral, the palace of the viceroy, that of the municipality, and other public buildings." Pizarro apparently threw himself into the work with sober zeal: "the sword was exchanged for the tool of the artisan" (1007). And although he went on to found other cities, "nothing claimed so much of Pizarro's care as the rising metropolis of Lima" (1014). Prescott's conclusion suggests without irony that Pizarro's city was his greatest monument: "This peaceful occupation formed a contrast to the life of incessant turmoil in which he had hitherto engaged. It seemed, too, better suited to his own advancing age, which naturally invited to repose. . . [A]midst the woe and desolation which Pizarro and his followers brought on the devoted land of the Incas, Lima, the beautiful City of the Kings, still survives as the most glorious work of his creation, the fairest gem on the shores of the Pacific" (1914).

If we return now to Melville's description from "The Whiteness of the Whale," we can see it as a direct challenge to this assertion. Whereas Prescott downplays the woe, Melville emphasizes it. Whereas Prescott points to Lima's beauty, glory, and fairness, Melville takes pains to underscore its ruin, desolation, and decay. What Prescott oxymoronically calls a "peaceful occupation," the creation of a city out of enslaved native labor, Melville calls the "rigid pallor of an apoplexy that fixes its own distortions" (193). Thus although Melville might have felt sympathy with Prescott's criticism of Pizarro's civilization, he could not have accepted this characterization of the conqueror as peaceful city-builder.

This ambivalence about Spanish urbanism deeply informs "The Town-Ho's Story" in *Moby-Dick* and is revealed in the way Ishmael tells his story, in the "style in which I once narrated it at Lima" (243). I see the "style of Lima" as having two implications here. On the one hand, Ishmael uses a narrative structure that imitates the form of the plaza in admitting into his story a rich cultural mixture of influences. On the other hand, his narrative uses the plaza as a point from which to enact cultural tensions that the colonizers cannot either suppress or understand. Ishmael, then, speaks to two audiences, his Spanish listeners, who see without fully comprehending the cultural diversity displayed in the plaza of his story, and his New York readers, who understand the colonial history that lends sinister violence to the narrative.[6]

The plaza creates a richly ironic setting for Ishmael's narration, subtly reminding the reader of Lima's complex class divisions. Ishmael, an American sailor, is unaccountably entertaining a group of Spanish "cavaliers," who are drinking their *chicha* and drunkenly spilling it on their "silvery ruffles" (250). As Ishmael unfolds his mysterious tale of Steelkilt's revolt, the cavaliers interrupt with uncomprehending questions about baffling details in the story, particularly those related to American class distinctions. Ishmael patiently explains the meaning of Nantucketers, Lakemen, and Canallers, each a particular subculture of American boatmen. Periodically the sounds of the festival interrupt the story as well, reminding the reader that while the city-dwellers are observing a religious holiday, the cavaliers are profaning it with their drinking. Similarly, as Ishmael proceeds with his story of Moby Dick, whom he calls "a certain wondrous, inverted visitation of one of those so called judgments of God" (242), his listeners profane his narrative with their obtuse questions and observations. Ishmael's story, however, makes room for these interventions and skillfully works them into his account. Thus his flexible, inclusive narration imitates the structure of the plaza itself, with its multicultural characters, its permeable boundaries between classes, and its fluid movements in space and time that permit tremendous variety and cultural interchange within a generous public space.

At the same time, Ishmael's genial narrative reveals a deadly, submerged conflict between oppressors and victims. In the telling of his story, Ishmael seems to accommodate his rambunctious listeners, yet at the same time he inserts comments that, if they were listening carefully or were less drunk, would strike terror into their hearts. For example, in describing the Erie Canal boatmen, Ishmael talks about their barbaric existence: "For three hundred and sixty miles, gentlemen, through the entire breadth of the state of New York, . . . through all the wide contrasting scenery of those noble Mohawk counties, . . . flows one continual stream of Venetianly corrupt and often lawless life. There's your true Ashantee, gentlemen; there howl your pagans; where you ever find them, next door to you; under the long-flung shadow and the snug patronizing lee of churches. For by some curious fatality, as it is often noted of your metropolitan freebooters that they ever encamp around the halls of justice, so sinners, gentlemen, most abound in holiest vicinities" (248-49). Ishmael's threatening address to his South American listeners, and by extension Melville's to his North American ones, overturns the whole Eurocentric tradition of the urban metropolis, opposed to the barbaric wilderness outside. In this passage he makes it clear that the "true" barbarians inhabit the populous cities and seek shelter under the lee of churches. Pagans sit "next door to you," and "sinners, gentlemen, most abound in holiest vicinities."

Ishmael's listeners *seem* to understand his meaning, as they humorously thank him for referring to Venice as the epitome of corruption rather than Lima itself: "we have by no means overlooked your delicacy in not substituting present Lima for distant Venice in your corrupt comparison. Oh! do not bow and look surprised: you know the proverb all along this coast—'Corrupt as Lima'" (249). Later Don Pedro nervously, or drunkenly, spills his drink as he recognizes the universality of human depravity: "No need to travel! The world's one Lima" (250). To the Spanish, then, the "style of Lima" would seem to be an urbane style that recognizes its own corruption, that in its tolerance of cultural diversity signals that it accepts the presence, even the necessity, of violence in the empire. But Ishmael's pointed references to the barbarism at the heart of urban civilization stab at the Spanish cavaliers' confidence in their own city, their own culture. He reveals that in the "holiest vicinities," revolutionary violence threatens the conquerors and displays itself openly at the center of the plaza.

Lima appears in this story as containing many of the cultural meanings Prescott ascribes to it: as a Catholic stronghold, as a colonial power, as a place of corruption and class division. But Melville goes beyond Prescott in using a narrative form that like the plaza itself displays colonial splendor and arrogance in uneasy and unacknowledged juxtaposition with "barbarian" energies of revolt. Unlike Prescott, whose narrative tries to give a rational structure for imperial violence, Melville uses a structure that admits challenges to imperial power from below.

If the plaza serves "The Town-Ho Story" as an open stage for cultural conflict, it works in "Benito Cereno" even more directly to display and heighten racial violence. Although the "mutiny" in this story of a slave revolt takes place at sea, it ends in Lima, where Babo is tried and decapitated. "The body was burned to ashes; but for many days, the head, that hive of subtlety, fixed on a pole in the Plaza, met, unabashed, the gaze of the whites; and across the Plaza looked towards St. Bartholomew's church, in whose vaults slept then, as now, the recovered bones of Aranda: and across the Rimac bridge looked towards the monastery, on Mount Agonia without; where, three months after being dismissed by the court, Benito Cereno, borne on the bier, did, indeed, follow his leader" (315). Babo's sightless gaze at his white owners, at the churches and monasteries of the European enslavers, forcefully challenges their supremacy. Melville capitalizes "Plaza" here, as he did not in *Moby-Dick*, and emphasizes the word by saying it twice in a way that makes a mockery of Pizarro's delusions of urban grandeur.

This subtle reference takes issue, then, with the moral certainty of the *Harper's* article, "Lima and the Limanians." That essay ends with a lengthy description of Pizarro's monuments, which it points out fell to the ravages of nature, the disastrous earthquakes, rather than to human agency. The article ends with a pious reflection on Lima's modest housing design: "The very architecture of Lima—its houses of a singly [*sic*] story—its plastered upper walls, its cane roofs, its towers and steeples of stuccoed wicker work—is a perpetual prayer against an evil which no human foresight can avoid, and no mortal power avert, and in respect to which the utmost that man can do, is in some degree to mitigate its circumstances" (609). The anonymous author of the article is referring to the "evil" of nature, the earthquakes. Melville in "Benito Cereno," however, makes it obvious that the "evil which no human foresight can avoid" is the evil of colonial power, of court-sanctioned slavery, of mutilating violence against the oppressed. In 1853, Melville did not feel that it was enough to "mitigate . . . [the] circumstances" of such evils. In the plaza, one sees them only too clearly, and in "Benito Cereno" Melville uses the plaza as the stage from which Babo can make them visible.

NOTES

1   Besides the descriptions of Lima in Prescott's *History of the Conquest of Peru* and the *Harper's* "Lima and the Limanians" discussed below, see also Samuel R. Franklin's *Memoirs of a Rear-Admiral* (New York and London: Harper and Brothers, 1898); and Charles Wilkes's *Narrative of the United States Exploring Expedition* (Philadelphia: C. Sherman, 1844).

2   For a fuller discussion of New York and Melville's experience of it, see my *Melville's City: Literary and Urban Form in Nineteenth-Century New York* (New York: Cambridge University Press, 1996).

3   For the architectural history of Lima and its urban planning, see Dora P. Crouch, *Spanish City Planning in South America* (Cambridge, MA: Massachusetts Institute of Technology Press, 1982); Valerie Fraser, *The Architecture of Conquest* (New York: Cambridge University Press, 1990); and Ralph Gakenheimer, "Determinants of Physical Structure in the Peruvian Town of the Sixteenth Century" (diss., University of Pennsylvania, 1964).

4   See Setha M. Low, "Cultural Meanings of the Plaza: The History of the Spanish-American Gridplan-Plaza Urban Design," in Robert Rotenberg and Gary McDonogh, eds., *The Cultural Meanings of Urban Space* (Westport, CT: Bergin & Garvey, 1993).

5   I am indebted for this reference to Kathleen E. Kier, *A Melville Encyclopedia: The Novels* (Troy, NY: Whitson Publishing Company, 1960), 1:588.

6   For a fuller discussion of this subject, see my chapter, "Town Ho," in *Melville's City*.

REFERENCES

Franchot, Jenny. *Roads to Rome: The Antebellum Protestant Encounter with Catholicism*. Berkeley: University of California Press, 1994.

"Lima and the Limanians." *Harper's New Monthly Magazine* 17 (Oct. 1851), 598-609.

Melville, Herman. *Moby-Dick, or The Whale*. Ed. Harrison Hayford, Hershel Parker, and G. Thomas Tanselle. Vol. 6 of *The Writings of Herman Melville*. Evanston and Chicago, IL: Northwestern University Press and the Newberry Library, 1988.

——. *The Piazza Tales and Other Prose Pieces 1839-1860*. Ed. Harrison Hayford, Hershel Parker, and G. Thomas Tanselle. Vol. 9 of *Writings*, 1987.

——. *Typee: A Peep at Polynesian Life*. Ed. Harrison Hayford, Hershel Parker, and G. Thomas Tanselle. Vol. 1 of *Writings*, 1968.

Parker, Hershel. *Herman Melville: A Biography. Volume 1: 1819-1851.* Baltimore: Johns Hopkins University Press, 1996.

Prescott, William Hickling. *A History of the Conquest of Mexico* and *A History of the Conquest of Peru*. New York: Modern Library/Random House, n.d.

James Emmett Ryan

Melville in the Brotherhood:

Freemasonry, Fraternalism, and the Artisanal Ideal

The Problem of the Universe is like the Freemason's mighty secret, so terrible to all children. It turns out, at last, to consist in a triangle, a mallet, and an apron,—nothing more!
Herman Melville: letter to Hawthorne, 16 April 1851

"You do not comprehend?" he said.
"Not I," I replied.
"Then you are not of the brotherhood."
Edgar Allan Poe, "The Cask of Amontillado"

lthough generally speaking they have been a contentious lot, cultural historians of the nineteenth century have come to broad agreement that Americans in the antebellum period were a nation of "joiners"— enthusiastic participants in a wide variety of voluntary organizations and clubs ranging from literary salons (most famously the Transcendentalist Club) to temperance societies, religious benevolent groups, budding labor organizations like the Knights of Labor, and fraternal groups based on freemasonry. As Gordon Wood has noted for the Revolutionary period, increasing personal mobility in the young republic, fueled by the dismantling of monarchical traditions and values and brought to a feverish pitch by the huge influx of immigrants, made America ripe for new forms of community behavior and meaningful group activities.[1]

However, literary historians of the nineteenth century have been less suc-

cessful than religious historians at charting the broad continuum of spirituali-
ties available on the American scene. We know, for example, a tremendous
amount about Emerson's Unitarian roots and about Emily Dickinson's and Herman Melville's Calvinist background, but we know considerably less when it
comes to understanding our canonical writers in relation to the broader nineteenth-century cultures of sociability and volunteerism. With the eventual aim of
unfolding the significance of antebellum social-group behavior, then, and using
Melville's work as both context and illumination, what I will try to do first is to
provide a general sketch of the historical phenomenon that was, and still is,
freemasonry in the United States. Within that discussion, I will try to outline
both the historical basis and ethos of freemasonry and the specific practice of
freemasonry as it proliferated in nineteenth-century America after beginnings
during the Revolutionary period.[2] Lastly, I will begin to mark the parameters of
a study intended to show how the writings of Herman Melville at numerous
points confront the same general issues to which popular masonic fraternalism
was responding during the period that Melville wrote. A study of this kind seeks
to answer, in part, Andrew Delbanco's recent formulation of the main question
presented to modern Melville scholars: "[H]ow imprisoning is culture, and how
far did Melville break out?" (Delbanco 710). Above all, my thesis is that within
Melville's writings can be found both an implicit critique and an extensive elaboration of certain views of social and convivial life that were constructed in part
for American society by the saturation of culture with fraternalism in the nineteenth century.[3] At the most elementary level, the axis to be explored in this
historicization of Melville has as its poles the contradictory, but absolutely essential, twin concepts embodied in fraternalism and articulated by a welter of
antebellum masonic organizations and popular texts: egalitarianism and hierarchy, both of which are bound in service to a secularized force with divine powers, a force linked to the figure of the "Supreme Architect."

By the end of the nineteenth century, a century marked in the United States
by, among other things, the rise of industrialism and representative democracy,
the cult of domesticity and a concomitant feminization of labor, a dramatic increase in the number of literate women (providing a market for popular novels

and stories), and the Civil War, the United States male population had reached approximately 22 million. Of these men, who had just ended a century marked by profound shifts within society in the definitions of labor, hierarchy, gender, and race, approximately 3-5 million (and possibly more, although exact figures are not available; see Clawson 7) were members in an array of fraternal organizations deriving generally from the ancient practice known as freemasonry. Even into the twentieth century, and probably beyond, these organizations continue under such names as the International Order of Oddfellows, the Loyal Order of the Moose, and the Benevolent and Protective Order of the Elk, among numerous others that have attained the status of marginal and eccentric clubs. But in the eighteenth and nineteenth centuries, and during Herman Melville's lifetime in particular, these fictive kinship organizations, based on historical forms, rituals, and values dating back at least as far as the Crusades, enjoyed an enormous popularity and comprised an all-male social movement of remarkable proportions, eventually exerting significant political influence that reached into the formation of labor unions (some of which began as masonic groups) and political parties.

One twentieth-century historian of freemasonry has observed that "Fraternalism is above all about boundaries, in both their institutional and symbolic aspects—their construction, their bridging, and occasionally their dismantling" (Clawson 248). Within Melville's predominantly all-male narratives, boundaries of this kind are also undergoing a process of being constructed, bridged, and dismantled. For example, in the *Moby-Dick* "Cetology" chapter, whales, like freemasons in the thirty-three degrees of Scottish Rite Masonry, are divided into categories; knowledge about the whales stems directly from knowledge about the boundaries between species. As in freemasonry, whose histories and commentaries tend to categorize and create boundaries but which do not take the position of being comprehensive (for them, like the white whale, freemasonry is too large and multifarious to be grasped in its entirety), Melville's narrator in *Moby-Dick* is willing to leave his task of boundary-drawing incomplete. Melville (in his narrator's voice) conceives of himself as a builder—a gothic stone-mason of the kind his contemporary, the English cultural critic John Ruskin, would have approved:[4] "I now leave my cetological system standing thus unfinished, even as the great Cathedral of Cologne was left, with the crane still standing up-

73

on the top of the uncompleted tower. For small erections may be finished by their first architects; grand ones, true ones, ever leave the cope-stone to posterity" (*Moby-Dick* 145).

Setting aside for the moment the rich ancient history of freemasonry, which many masonic historians have traced as far back as the Sumerian architects (dating to 3100 BC), a group whose traditions lie behind many Biblical narratives including that of the Tower of Babel, the modern version of masonry, called "Accepted Masonry" began in England in the first part of the seventeenth century. About that time, masonic lodges that had previously been organizations only for craftsmen became a variant on that tremendously popular institution of Enlightenment England and America, the gentleman's club. In Scotland around 1600, for example, John Boswell, Laird of Auchinleck and ancestor of the avid club attendee and toastmaster, James Boswell, became the first known "accepted mason" (non-craftsman) in the Edinburgh masonic lodge, thereby initiating the transformation of the lodges into meeting-places for the aristocratic classes. But masonic lodges differed from other exclusively male clubs in important ways. Beyond the centrality of conviviality and witty and cultivated conversation (cf. the clubbing of Johnson and Boswell and their circle in London and the "Tuesday Club" of Alexander Hamilton in America; see Micklus), Masons "involved themselves in the remnants of a tradition-laden medieval institution whose elaborate rituals and mythical accounts of ancient origin remained centrally important to Accepted Masonry's definition of itself" (Clawson 55). In particular, secrecy, inter-lodge brotherhood, ritual and initiation, and a deep artisanal ethos remained vital to these organizations even as fraternal memberships bore less and less resemblance to the guild craftsmen for whom the organizations were first intended. For disillusioned Christian intellectuals of the Enlightenment in Europe, rocked by the scientific discoveries of Newton and the rise of empiricism, freemasonry had become a utopian impulse that "had within it the potential of becoming nothing less than a new religion" (Jacob 109).

Freemasonry in America can be dated to 1730, with the first masonic lodge being constructed, appropriately enough, in Philadelphia (the city of brotherly love), where Benjamin Franklin was an avid life-long Mason (as were George Washington and Thomas Jefferson). Although gentleman's freemasonry made an early appearance in the colonies, it was not until the nineteenth century that it began to accumulate a large number of members. The millions of men who would be members of fraternal organizations in America by century's end numbered only 3,000 in the year 1800. However, by the 1820s, membership in masonic organizations had been increased dramatically (Clawson 115), even to the extent that there was a great anti-masonic backlash, which accused the masons of being both "unchristian and uncharitable" and ridiculed masonic claims of an ancient history (Vest 294-98). Much of the Melville family's own involvement in the politics of anti-masonry has been amply documented in Hennig Cohen's recent article on Melville and freemasonry, in which Cohen shows that numerous members of Melville's family were themselves freemasons and also details many allusions to masonic lore in Melville's fiction.[5] Cohen's research into the archives of American masonic organizations led him to conclude that, although it seems unlikely that Meville himself belonged officially to a fraternal lodge, several generations of his Gansevoort-Melville relatives did belong to masonic organizations.

Apart from Melville's allusions to freemasonry in his novels and stories, references which are unsurprising given that so many persons in Melville's family were members of fraternal orders (Cohen 3-5), it is also necessary to begin to chart the relationship between the antebellum cultural phenomenon of freemasonry and Herman Melville's writings, and in particular to show how a quasifamilial domain in which idealized forms of kinship could be construed was a part of Melville's thinking that was mirrored in society at large. Along with his biographical research into the connections between Melville's extended family and masonic traditions—connections that he traces primarily to the family's Jacksonian political sympathies—Hennig Cohen has carefully documented Melville's repeated references to the lexicon of freemasonry within the novels *Typee*, *Mardi*, *Redburn*, *White-Jacket*, *Moby-Dick*, *Pierre*, *The Confidence-Man*, and in Melville's poetry and stories as well. These many references Cohen attributes to Melville's usual practice of responding to various strands of popular culture discourse. Cohen also notes that the "quest structure of so much of Melville's writing" corresponds closely to the rhetoric of masonic initiation; likewise, Cohen found that the paradoxical rational/mystical elements of freemasonry fit naturally with Melville's investigations of religion and epistemology. Stylistically, of course, it has been a commonplace observation that Melville's works are loaded with symbolism; nearly all of his writings can, like the values at the heart of freemasonry, be understood as a system of morality veiled in elaborate allegory and illustrated by symbols and mythic language. But there is more to the Melville-freemasonry connection than shared language and an interest in symbolism. The following pages propose extending Cohen's discoveries of masonic language in Melville's fiction and his findings about the Melville family and freemasonry to suggest that Melville's themes of fraternalism and craft were dovetailed with the fraternal concerns held by large numbers of nineteenth-century American men and expressed through the literature of freemasonry. I will argue that despite the marginalization and unpopularity of Melville's writings dating at least from *Moby-Dick*,[6] he—like his contemporary, John Ruskin—was nonetheless aligned quite precisely with the preoccupations of popular freemasonry in those very writings by his charting of the limits of kinship and fraternalism, as well as by his exhaustive critique of the artisanal ideal.

Fraternalism—broadly conceived—figures as an important motif in much of Melville's fiction. The unctuous fraternalism present in Melville's story "The Paradise of Bachelors," for example, in fact turns out to be a perversion of the original intent and values of freemasonry, as Melville's knowing references to the Crusades indicate. Likewise, when the "thing called pain [and] the bugbear styled trouble" (*Piazza Tales* 322) are invoked by the narrator, they are dismissed as "fables" or "Catholic miracles"; in other words, the core values and beliefs of the fraternal ethic have been replaced by a superficial conviviality and good cheer that Melville's Bartleby would reject so steadfastly. Fraternalism for the good-natured nine bachelors[7] of this story is reduced to ornament, while the actual impoverishment of their fellowship is lost behind a haze of alcohol. A similar conviviality is seen in "Benito Cereno," with the perpetually sanguine Amaso Delano serving as the figure of the bachelor, to whom conflict, violence, and hardship are invisible, and thus nonexistent. Like the nine bachelors of "The Paradise of Bachelors," Delano knows that he is in the presence of a besieged fraternalism; for example, he notes at one point that "The young sailor's eye was again fixed on the whisperers, and [he] thought he observed a lurking significance in it, as if silent signs, of some Freemason sort, had at that instant been interchanged" (*Piazza Tales* 66). Delano also appears to be well-versed in the early modern history of freemasonry. Like the narrator of "The Paradise of Bachelors," who describes the bachelors' club as a "cloister" (literally, "bar") and waxes lyrical in his narrated history of the fabled "monk-knights," Delano invokes the metaphor of monastic fraternalism and particularly when he first sees the ship *San Dominick:* "Peering over the bulwarks were what really seemed, in the hazy distance, throngs of dark cowls; while fitfully revealed through the open port-holes, other dark moving figures were dimly descried, as of Black Friars pacing the cloisters" (*Piazza Tales* 48).

Fraternal pride in craft and labor gives way to aristocratic ease even as Melville's fictional bachelors congratulate themselves on their "remarkable decorum" (*Piazza Tales* 323). "The Paradise of Bachelors," with its bourgeois-class appropriation and commodification of a proud legacy of freemasonry, is one example of the erosion to which fraternal ideals had been subject. On the other hand, however, it features prominently a component of eighteenth-century American men's clubs that had come under strong attack by the first half of the nineteenth century. Although it is fair to say that fraternalism had been radically altered by 1855, lodges did, in the face of the powerful temperance movements of the nineteenth century, continue to supply a form of "fraternalism that provided a ritual to create the togetherness formerly engendered by alcohol" (Clawson 146). Melville's story, from this perspective, can be seen simultaneously as nostalgic for a fraternalism and bonding engendered by heavy drinking in the company of other men, while at the same time identifying the lodge itself, as social vehicle, as an eviscerated parody of itself.

While "The Paradise of Bachelors" primarily provides a framework for a critique of nineteenth-century masonic concerns, Melville's story "The Bell-Tower" more explicitly, because of its direct concern with the ethics of architect and stone-mason, can be understood as a variant history of freemasonry. The hubris of Bannadonna, the great architect of "The Bell-Tower," is analogous to the degeneration of architecture that John Ruskin saw as having occurred in Venice. Bannadonna is an example of the self-serving builders who caused the original purity of Venetian architecture to become corrupted, a corruption described in methodical and comprehensive detail in Ruskin's *Stones of Venice,* with which

Melville, as an avid reader of Ruskin, would doubtless have been familiar.

Apart from contemporary political ideology, however, freemasonry of the sort practiced in the eighteenth and nineteenth centuries was marked by a unique set of often contradictory values and practices that updated the ancient masonic values of Beauty, Strength, and Wisdom. First, the boundary-crossing gentlemen who joined masonic organizations in the early eighteenth century and turned masonry into a practice of bourgeois sociability also transformed freemasonry into a set of organizations with egalitarianism at their core. Members were encouraged to put aside differences of class and belief, and toleration for difference was the official watchword so that the lodge could become a social space built around instinctive and spontaneous fellowship and sympathy. At the same time, ranks (called "degrees") and hierarchy were crucially important for freemasonry, as evidenced by the dozens of official ranks that were assigned to members within the lodges, not to mention the preoccupation with elaborate ritual initiations complete with secret incantations and prescriptive arrays of garish costumes. In theory, all ranks within masonic organizations are open to all members, so that it exists as a gender-exclusive paradigm of a society founded on social mobility, a kind of idealized model of the American dream, or as Clawson suggests, "a defense of capitalist relations as encapsulated within the heroic figure of the craftsman" (82).

The other value system that remained central to nineteenth-century freemasonry in particular was that of the artisanal ideal. In this respect, Melville's writings, and those of the freemasons and trade unionists, can be understood in relation to John Ruskin's ongoing romantic obsession with craft and the ideals of labor, as in Ruskinian remarks such as "When men are rightly occupied, their amusement grows out of their work, as the colour of petals out of a fruitful flower" (Ruskin 88). For Ruskin (like Melville and Whitman, born in 1819), the anonymous builders of the great Gothic churches were the true heroes and prototypes for modern artistic and social reform. Uncannily aligning himself with the freemasons, he saw in these workers a level of conscientiousness, dignity, and genuine religious fervor that fostered the perfected naturalism of their handicrafts. The stones themselves, in these Gothic churches, thus comprise a literal written record of the accumulated wisdom of the medieval artisan. Melville had owned (Sealts 89) and read Ruskin's *Modern Painters* enthusiastically because of his great interest in the paintings of J. M. W. Turner (see Wallace), but it is the Ruskin of *The Stones of Venice* who matches Melville's artisanal preoccupations with his own highly elaborated theory of architecture and craftsmanship—a theoretical framework for the fraternal ethos that may have complemented the more mundane popular masonic literature with which Hennig Cohen has shown Melville to be so familiar. The seeds of Ruskin's eventual turn toward writings focused on social reform had already begun to germinate by the time of the publication of his *Stones of Venice* (1851-53). Ruskin had embarked on a reformist crusade against the age of machinery and the process of industrialism by which workers were made into tools, into cogs in a huge and impersonal machine. Resonating with a number of Melville's own concerns, Ruskin denounced the rising tide of individualism as a cultural ideology, an individualism that led, he felt, to extreme heartlessness, which formerly had been restrained by sincere religion and strong family life.

In "The Bell-Tower," the twin concerns of craft and brotherhood as articulated through the lexicons of architecture and freemasonic myth appear once again. Melville makes it clear in his description that the constructions that his architect Bannadonna is capable of are attributable neither to science nor alchemy. He is a "practical materialist" who, like Owen Warland in "The Artist of the Beautiful," is first and foremost a craftsman; he creates "not by logic, not by altars; but by plain vice-bench and hammer" (184).[8] Because he desires his craft to transcend nature, however, he is doomed to failure. In terms of Bannadonna's specific design, Melville's narrator likens Bannadonna's bell-tower not only to the Tower of Babel, but also to the Campanile of St. Mark's cathedral, which features prominently in *The Stones of Venice* as an example of proper Gothic architecture. Bannadonna will not build a tower in accord with "correct" Gothic principles, and instead he combines bell-tower with clock-tower and violates Ruskin's (and masonic) dictates concerning proportion in a properly crafted tower by making the bell too heavy for the supporting structure.[9] In addition, Bannadonna's murder of the helpless laborer for the sake of his tower eventually provides a fatal flaw in the bell: "where man's blood had flawed it, that will prove to destroy it. It is well known that the literature of freemasonry subscribes to an understanding of God as the Supreme Architect, but also prominent in the writings of nineteenth-century masonic historians is the prototype of the gifted human architect, a person who is able to unite the two branches of freemasonry: speculative (morality) and operative (actual building). According to legend, when Solomon decided to build a temple in Jerusalem, he contracted the services of Hiram Abiff, master architect of Tyre: "He was the most accomplished designer and operator on earth, whose abilities were not confined to building only, but extended to all kinds of work, whether in gold, silver, brass, or iron; whether in linen, tapestry, or embroidery; whether considered as an architect, statuary, founder, or designer, he equally excelled" (Macoy 536). The unnamed southern European city of "The Bell-Tower," like Solomon's Jerusalem, has grown prosperous through "commerce with the Levant" (*Piazza Tales* 174), but the Italians are building a tower in honor of their own wealth rather than as a tribute to God, and "the unblest foundling, Bannadonna" (174), is likewise driven by personal motivations instead of conscience. The homicide of the laborer by Bannadonna is forgiven by the magistrates as merely one of his "transports of esthetic passion" (176), thus revealing the imbalance between craft and morality in his practice of architecture. As with pure freemasonry, "Gothic art is an art based on the proper working of conscience. When an artist receives an inspiration, he has the choice of interpreting it in a personal and limited way or of surrendering his personal will and of making the inspiration serve the universal purpose of its origins" (Anderson 22).

Once again, Melville includes the figure of a monk, this time shrouded and mysterious under a "domino" and smuggled to the belfry in service of Bannadonna's creation. As in "The Paradise of Bachelors" and "Benito Cereno," the monk represents a religious manifestation of masonic ideals: a figure embodying religious devotion and artisanry and conscience wedded to labor. The chain-mail armor described in "The Paradise of Bachelors" as authentic garb for the original Knights Templar of the Crusades (before they succumbed to immorality) can be glimpsed again after the architect is dead and the figure of Haman is discovered by the magistrates beneath the monkish cloak: his limbs "seemed clad in scaly mail, lustrous as a dragon beetle" (*Piazza Tales* 182). In keeping with Bannadonna's materialism, Haman (half-man?), the modern monk, is pure technology, with conscience removed. Echoing the evil disposition of the villainous character "Haman" from the Hebrew Bible's book of Esther, Melville's Haman is also an extension and product of Bannadonna's commitment to a debased ethic of building—debased because no longer an ethic developing out of fraternalism and piety.

Apart from the literature of freemasonry itself, which seems not to have been assessed in a thorough manner by modern literary and religious historians, there are consistent indications that Melville was writing with an acute awareness of the phenomenon of lodge-joining that marked the nineteenth century. Melville's writings broach the social issues that drove the development and reconfiguration of freemasonry in the antebellum period in America. Like the freemasons, his "constructions," that is to say his fictions, respond to a perceived decline in religion (and the ceremonial space that religion comprises), they respond to the various temperance movements (movements that created a need for "men's space for conviviality"), they respond to a cult of domesticity which valorized family life and the centrality of women as mediators of morality, and above all they respond to a form of "men's reading" or literary habitus and convivial epistemology divorced from a rising tide of sentimentalist texts attuned primarily to the growing numbers of women readers. Finally, far from being a comprehensive account of the interwoven histories of masonic texts and Melvillian texts, the foregoing is intended to suggest additional points of contact as well. For example, how can Melville's concerns with racial power (as in *Moby-Dick*, "Benito Cereno," and *The Confidence-Man*) be understood within a culture that gave rise not only to *Uncle Tom's Cabin*, but also to the Ku Klux Klan as a variant on the masonic lodge? How are the problematic gender crises found in the novels *Pierre* and *Moby-Dick* related to the fetishization of the mother (versus the wife) within the popular literature of freemasonry? And perhaps most challenging, what is the relationship between the masonic fascination with symbols and terrain of the Holy Land (as the site of the overlapping origins of freemasonry and Christianity) and *Clarel*—the preoccupation of Melville's later writing years—which begins with a student: "In chamber low and scored by time, / Masonry old, late washed with lime—/ Much like a tomb new-cut in stone" (3). The "stone pine" fabricated by the master mason in "The Bell-Tower" is only one of the early signs of

Melville's trajectory toward an extended meditation in *Clarel* concerning the raw materials and the holy origins of freemasonry, craft, and art.

NOTES

1   Gordon Wood, *The Radicalism of the American Revolution*. New York: Vintage Books, 1991. The best extended treatment of freemasonry in the early American republic is Steven C. Bullock's recent *Revolutionary Brotherhood: Freemasonry and the Transformation of the American Social Order, 1730-1840*.

2   The literature devoted to freemasonry is extensive, but for general overviews of the many ideas associated with lodge fraternalism in America and Europe, see Robert Macoy, *General History, Cyclopedia and Dictionary of Freemasonry* (1872); Albert G. Mackey, *A Lexicon of Freemasonry* (1852); and Deed Vest, *Pursuit of a Thread* (1983). For modern critical accounts of freemasonic practices, see Margaret Jacob, *The Radical Enlightenment: Pantheists, Freemasons, and Republicans* (1981); and Mary Ann Clawson, *Constructing Brotherhood: Class, Gender, Fraternalism* (1989).

3   For a more extensive discussion of Melville's preoccupation with male friendship and homoeroticism, see especially Robert Martin, *Hero, Captain, and Stranger*.

4   For a broader discussion of the significance of Gothic architecture for Euro-American intellectuals of the nineteenth century, see William Anderson, *The Rise of the Gothic* (1988), and John Ruskin's seminal discussion of Gothic architecture as the historically preeminent building style in *The Stones of Venice* (1853) and, more briefly, in *Sesame and Lilies* (1871).

5   Allusions to freemasonry in Melville's works are also discussed in Michael Stanton, "Masonic Symbolism in Melville's *Pierre*" (1982).

6   The remarkable jacket in Melville's *White-Jacket* may indeed be a variant on the apron of the artisan as described by freemasons: "The pure white lambskin apron is to the operative Mason an ancient and spotless emblem. The investiture of this symbol of the purity of the order, [is] the first gift bestowed upon the candidate.... The investiture of the candidate with the apron, among the primitive Masons, formed an esential part of the ceremony of initiation, and was attended with rites equally significant and impressive" (Macoy 87).

7   Numerology, for practical and mystical reasons, is central to masonic teachings; thus Viola Sachs's surprising admonition to center attention on apparently trivial aspects of Melville's writing such as "numbers, cardinal directions, elements, metals, celestial bodies, zodiacal signs" (239) is not as unreasonable as it first appears. The number nine has specific significance in freemasonry, for example, in relation to the nine muses.

8   "The blow of the Master's hammer commands industry, silence, or the close of labor, and every brother respects or honours its sound; ... the hammer is a symbol of the power of the master" (Mackey 530).

9   There is great irony associated with Melville's choice of the St. Mark's Campanile for his

example of gothic tower-building. In the year 1900 (the year of Ruskin's death), after having stood for over 1,000 years, the Campanile collapsed to the ground, requiring reconstruction that was not completed until 1912.

References

Anderson, William. *The Rise of the Gothic*. New York: Dorset Press, 1988.

Bullock, Steven C. *Revolutionary Brotherhood: Freemasonry and the Transformation of the American Social Order, 1730-1840*. Chapel Hill and London: Institute of Early American History and Culture and the University of North Carolina Press, 1996.

Clawson, Mary Ann. *Constructing Brotherhood: Class, Gender, Fraternalism*. Princeton: Princeton University Press, 1989.

Cohen, Hennig. "Melville's Masonic Secrets." *Melville Society Extracts* 108 (March 1997): 2-17.

Delbanco, Andrew. "Melville in the 1980's." *American Literary History* 4 (Winter 1992): 709-725.

Hawthorne, Nathaniel. "The Artist of the Beautiful." *Selected Tales and Sketches*. New York: Penguin, 1987.

Jacob, Margaret J. *The Radical Enlightenment: Pantheists, Freemasons, and Republicans*. London: George Allen, 1981.

Mackey, Albert G. *A Lexicon of Freemasonry*. Charleston, SC: Walker and James, 1852.

Macoy, Robert. *General History, Cyclopedia and Dictionary of Freemasonry*. New York: Masonic Publishing Company, 1872.

Martin, Robert K. *Hero, Captain, and Stranger: Male Friendship, Social Critique, and Literary Form in the Sea Novels of Herman Melville*. Chapel Hill: University of North Carolina Press, 1986.

Melville, Herman. *Clarel: A Poem and Pilgrimage in the Holy Land*. Edited by Harrison Hayford, Alma A. MacDougall, Hershel Parker, and G. Thomas Tanselle. Vol. 12 of *The Writings of Herman Melville*. Evanston and Chicago, IL: Northwestern University Press and the Newberry Library, 1991.

——. *Correspondence*. Edited by Lynn Horth. Vol. 14 of *The Writings*. 1993.

——. *Moby-Dick, or, The Whale*. Edited by Harrison Hayford, Hershel Parker, and

G. Thomas Tanselle. Vol. 6 of *The Writings*. 1988.

——. *The Piazza Tales and Other Prose Pieces, 1839-1860*. Edited by Harrison Hayford, Hershel Parker, and G. Thomas Tanselle. Vol. 9 of *The Writings*. 1987.

——. *Pierre, or, the Ambiguities*. Edited by Harrison Hayford, Hershel Parker, and G. Thomas Tanselle. Vol. 7 of *The Writings*. 1971.

——. *White-Jacket, or the World in a Man-of-War*. Edited by Harrison Hayford, Hershel Parker, and G. Thomas Tanselle. Vol. 5 of *The Writings*. 1970.

Micklus, Robert. "The Secret Fall of Freemasonry in Dr. Alexander Hamilton's *The History of the Tuesday Club*." *Deism, Masonry, and the Enlightenment*. Edited by J. A. Leo Lemay. Newark, DE: University of Delaware Press, 1987. 127-36.

Poe, Edgar Allan. *Complete Tales and Poems*. New York: Vintage Books, 1975.

Ruskin, John. "Of Kings' Treasuries." In *Sesame and Lilies*. New York: Thomas Y. Crowell, 1871.

——. *The Stones of Venice*. Edited and abridged by J. G. Links. New York: Hill and Wang, 1966.

Sachs, Viola. *The Game of Creation: The Primeval Unlettered Language of* Moby-Dick; or, The Whale. Paris: Editions de la Maison des Sciences de l'Homme, 1982.

Sealts, Merton M., Jr. *Melville's Reading: A Check-List of Books Owned and Borrowed*. Madison: University of Wisconsin Press, 1966.

Stanton, Michael N. "Masonic Symbolism in Melville's *Pierre*." *Melville Society Extracts* 49 (1982): 11-13.

Vest, Deed Lafayette. *Pursuit of a Thread*. Waco, TX: Watercress Press, 1983.

Wallace, Robert K. *Melville and Turner: Spheres of Love and Fright*. Athens, GA: University of Georgia Press, 1992.

Wood, Gordon S. *The Radicalism of the American Revolution*. New York: Vintage Books, 1991.

Ekaterini Georgoudaki

Herman Melville in Thessaloniki:

Following the Steps of European Travelers[1]

I. Introduction

n the eighteenth century, there was a revival of Western interest in the classical Greek world and a tendency to idealize it. "In the nostalgia for the Greek Ideal [was] that nostalgia for a Golden Age, an Eden, an ideal time and place and condition of humanity" which the eighteenth century hoped that might be achieved again in the future.[2] Therefore, Westerners who visited Greece were attracted to its antique monuments rather than to modern Greece, which was under Ottoman rule (Tsigakou 28-29).[3] This cult continued through the nineteenth century Romantic Movement. When the Greek Independence War against the Turks broke out in 1821, attention shifted to modern Greece but the tendency to idealize the country and its people continued. As a result, the Greeks were often seen "as being more or less the heirs of the antique Grecian world, classical figures in a classical landscape" (Runciman 8). In early nineteenth-century republican America, admiration of the ancient Greek language, literature, philosophy, and the arts produced a passionate anticipation of the regeneration of modern Greece through its Independence War (Larrabee 3, 24, 54).[4]

Americans in Greece during the first half of the nineteenth century were mainly missionaries, tourists, volunteers in the Independence War, relief agents, artists, scholars, diplomats, naval officers and crews, merchants, scientists, and pilgrims on their way to the Holy Land (Larrabee 56, 245, 247). Several Americans and Europeans systematically observed and discussed the geography and landscape, as well as the socioeconomic and political condition of their contemporary Greece.[5] Since the search for survivals of the ancient Greek spirit and civilization in modern Greece continued (*British Travellers* 18-19, 24, 80-81), "comparisons and correspondences, as well as contrasts, between ancient Greek civilisation and the contemporary Greeks became increasingly specific and concrete, influencing and to some extent determining opinions about the Greeks" (Koumarianou xix).[6]

Most travelers after 1830 visited Athens and some other parts of the free Greek nation. Few went north through Macedonia, whose uprisings had been violently suppressed by the Turks, and which became liberated only during the Balkan Wars (1912-13). Melville seems to be the first American tourist who visited Thessaloniki, the major city in Macedonia.[7] In the following discussion of his journal entries about Thessaloniki I will compare his view of the city and its people, in December 1856, with the views of some Europeans who lived in or visited Thessaloniki from the end of the eighteenth century to 1860.[8] I will also explore to what extent the writer's remarks were objective and historically accurate and to what extent they were shaped by the prevailing Western attitudes about Greece mentioned before, or about countries in the Near Orient, Greece included.

II. Approaching Thessaloniki

Melville came to Thessaloniki at a time when the activity in its port and its transactions with European cities had increased considerably. Already in 1843, Raul de Malherbe (386) considered it a major commercial center. B. Nicolaidy in 1859 (33) and Mary Adelaide Walker soon after (37) called it the most important city after Constantinople.[9] Melville's ship departed from Liverpool on 18 November 1856 with a destination to Constantinople and, through Algiers, Malta, and Syra, it reached Thessaloniki on Saturday, 6 December. His first journal comments recreated certain landscape features. It seems that the author was particularly impressed by the mountains he saw while the ship was approaching Thermaikos Gulf where Thessaloniki is situated: "At day break roused by the Captain to come on deck. Did so. Saw Mount Olympus, covered with snow at the summit, & looking most magestic in the dawn. Ossa & Pelion to the South. Olympus 10,000 feet high, according to the Captain's chart. O & P about 4 or 5000. Long ranges of hills along the Thessalain shore. Mount Athos (rather conical) on the opposite shore" (54-55). The above and other journal passages illustrate Melville's special attraction to Mt. Olympus, the mythical abode of Zeus and other gods worshiped by the ancient Greeks. It was probably its association with the Greek gods that made Olympus look more majestic and beautiful in Melville's eyes than Ossa, Pelion, and Athos. Moreover, the weather conditions enhanced Melville's idealized image of Olympus. During his departure, on 9 December, for example, he remarked: "A moonlight night followed. Passed Olympus glittering at top with ice. When it was far astern, its snow line showed in the moonlight like a strip of white cloud. Looked unreal—but still was there. Passed Ossa & Pelion. Rounded Athos" (57). The winter view of the high Greek mountains gave Melville aesthetic pleasure. Two other British visitors, Colonel William Martin Leake, MD, in November 1835, and the landscape painter Edward Lear, in September 1848 (15-16), were similarly impressed. The former referred to "the grand outlines of Olympus, Ossa, and Pelium" (240), and the latter to the "lines of noble mountain grandeur."[10]

Yet, Melville's moments of pleasure were spoiled by his obsession with metaphysical speculation. On 8 December, for instance, he interpreted the remoteness and coldness of the snow-covered Mt. Olympus as proof of divine indifference to human affairs: "Upon the uproar at the landing Olympus looked from afar cold & snowy. Surprising the Gods took no interest in the thing. Might at least moved their sympathy" (56). Quite different from his was the reaction of Mary Adelaide Walker whose religious faith made her see Olympus as "the giant monarch of Thessaly" that had the power to "elevate the mind of the christian spectator to the world beyond the grave" (66).

The first things Melville noticed and described as the ship anchored in Thermaikos Gulf were the city's fortifications, the Turkish military presence, and some of its Islamic characteristics, such as minarets and cypress trees: "About nine o'clock came to anchor before Salonica. A walled town on a hill side. Wall built by Genoese. Minarets & cyprus trees the most conspicuous objects. The Turkish men of war in harbor" (55). Melville's brief reference contains a historical inaccuracy: The walls had not been built by the Genoese, as he claimed.[11] The city became fortified by the Venetians who fought against the Turks. This, however, happened in the fifteenth century. The first walls had been built just after the city was founded in 316 BC by the Macedonian king Cassander, brother-in-law of Alexander the Great, and were later repaired and strengthened by the Romans and Byzantines. Their largest part was constructed at the end of the fourth century AD by the Emperor Theodosius I. After the Turks conquered the city in 1430, they repaired the walls and added towers to them.[12] After Melville's visit, about 1869, the Turks demolished the sea wall first and then parts of the eastern and western walls. Thus the people living behind them were able to breathe more fresh air and make a wharf, and Thessaloniki expanded eastward and westward. Luxurious homes were built in the new eastern suburbs by wealthy Turks, Greeks, Jews, and western Europeans. In an effort to modernize, i.e., to Westernize the Ottoman Empire, the Turkish authorities repaired the city streets and constructed a railroad to connect Thessaloniki with Balkan and central European cities.

As regards the minarets that Melville mentioned, they had a variety of shapes and colors, and they ranked among "the most important minarets of the sixteenth-eighteenth century" (Moutsopoulos 29). In 1812, Henry Holland, MD, stated that they contributed to "the exterior magnificence of the city" (316). The cypress trees that Melville also noticed were the Turks' favorite trees (Moutsopoulos 27), which explained their large number in the city.

As we can see from Melville's telegraphic comments quoted before, he noticed, at first glance, those characteristics of the amphitheatrically built city, which always made it attractive to foreign visitors. However, the remarks of some visitors appearing below are more enthusiastic than his. For example, in November 1821, John Madox, Esq. found the distant view of the city "very striking" (80). Leake (1835) stressed "the most imposing appearance" of the "lofty whitened walls" and the city, seen from the sea (238). In October 1849, George Ferguson Bowen underlined its "imposing look from the sea" and its "old whitewashed, painted, and battlemented walls" (27); and, in 1860, Walker was particularly impressed by the walls and an old fortress high on the hill, a round tower at the water's edge, the "rounded domes and tapering snowy minarets" which contrasted well with the straight lines of the houses, and the little Greek sail boats enlivening the whole scene (31).

III. The City and Its Monuments

At a closer view, however, Thessaloniki lost much of its attraction. Melville's journal comments reflect his disappointment with the condition of its monuments and people. On 6 December, for instance, he wrote: "Several of the mosques formerly Greek churches, but upon the conquest of the Turks turned into their present character. One of them circular & of immense strength. The ceiling mosaic. Glass. Peices continually falling upon the floor. Brought away several.—Saw Roman remains of a triumphal arch across a street. Fine sculpture at the base representing battle scenes. Roman eagle conspicuous. About the arch, miserable buildings of wood" (55).

The two monuments he mentions above are the Rotonda and the triumphal arch of Galerius. They were parts of the palace complex constructed by the Roman Emperor Galerius next to the Hippodrome, in the eastern part of the city, when Galerius made Thessaloniki his capital at the beginning of the fourth century AD. The Rotonda probably served the needs of the official cult. Among the foreigners who knew more about the history of the monument than Melville and who connected it with the worship of the Cabeiri were Cousinéry (35-42), French consul in Thessaloniki, and Walker (44).[13] The ceiling mosaics that Melville saw belonged to the end of the fourth century, when the Rotonda was turned into a church, and they represented saints of the early Eastern Christian church. About 1590, the Rotonda was converted into a mosque.[14] Melville was not the only one who took with him glass pieces. In her detailed description of the interior of the mosque Walker also mentioned "the gaily-coloured little cubes" that were "constantly falling from the dome" and afforded "a small income to the guardian of the mosque" (45) and to some little boys who collected them from the floor and sold them. She also mentioned that an entire pattern had been lately removed (45).

The Triumphal Arch, commonly called Kamara, was part of a four-arched gateway that linked the Rotonda with the palace complex. It was built to celebrate the emperor's victory over the Persians, about 306 AD.[15] Its reliefs depicted battle scenes, as Melville correctly remarked, and also Galerius's triumphant return to Thessaloniki and the religious ceremonies he performed. The "miserable buildings of wood" about the arch that Melville noticed were little shops and homes which probably belonged to the Greeks living in the area. For, when Melville visited Thessaloniki, non-Muslims were forbidden to build stone houses or houses higher than 5.76 meters. Only after the Ottoman law changed around 1864 were they allowed to do so.[16]

Previous visitors made comments about the arch and the attached buildings. For instance, in August 1828, von Osten, Austrian spy and later the first Austrian consul in Athens, pointed out the state of neglect and filth of the monument and the horrible huts suppressing it (qtd. in Enepekides *Thessaloniki-Makedonia* 23). Captain J. J. Best also mentioned on 8 May 1839: "a very fine triumphal arch . . . almost entirely obscured by a number of small houses that have been built about it" (208). A few years after Melville, Walker referred to the small shops and homes attached to the lower part of the arch, and to the many sculptured figures that were seen inside a coffeeshop. Walker also mentioned that they were painted blue to honor the Sultan or Prince Alfred (51).

In addition to the Arch of Galerius and the Rotonda, Melville saw the remains of another important ancient monument as he walked through the town center: "A Turkish cafe near one pier. Also saw remains of a noble Greek edifice. 3 columns &c. used as gateway & support to outhouse of a Jew's abode. Went into the Bazaar" (55). The author most probably meant the five Corinthian-style marble pillars which were the remains of a two-story colonnade that had a double facade and was in the lower section of the Roman forum (Papazoglou 5).[17] The Roman forum, capitolium, theater, and baths were situated at the site of the ancient Greek agora and near a Cabeirian temple in the city center, northwest of Galerius' palace and the Hippodrome (about a mile). One of the important Jewish quarters, "Rogoz," was formed in the lower section of the forum (Papazoglou 21).

The Jews called the mythological figures sculptured on the upper story of the colonnade "Las Incantadas," the Greeks called them "The Idols," and the Turks "Suret-Maleh," i.e., figures of angels (Papazoglou 7)—the Jewish name prevailed. The British architects and painters Nicholas Revett and James Stuart made sketches of the monument and the Jewish home attached to it in 1753 (Moutsopoulos 10). Stuart also made an engraving. L. F. Sebastien Fauvel, painter and French consul in Athens, made another engraving in 1790 (Papazoglou 11, 37). The monument attracted the admiration of several travellers. Its most detailed description was made by von Osten on 24 August 1828, who considered the colonnade and the figures the most beautiful ancient monument of Thessaloniki.[18] It is rather surprising, therefore, that Melville mentioned only the columns and not the sculptured figures. In 1865, Emmanuel Miller took the sculptures to the Louvre. Miller's action was not unique. Plundering the archaeological treasures of Greece and selling them abroad was a common practice among foreigners, diplomats like Fauvel included. A frequent excuse of plunderers was that they rescued the treasures from the "ignorant" Greeks and the "barbarous" Turks, who "were not fit keepers of a great heritage."[19]

In addition to Roman, Melville saw two of the major early Christian monuments of the city: "Went into the mosques Tomb of an old Greek saint shown in a cellar"(55). This monument was the church and tomb of St. Demetrius, a high official in the Roman army who was arrested because of his Christian zeal. Demetrius was imprisoned and executed (26 October 306 AD), after the order of the Emperor Galerius, in the basement of the oldest Roman public baths in the city, situated north of the forum. Some Christians secretly buried his remains there and, when the Christian religion was officially accepted, they erected a chapel over his tomb. Demetrius was named the city's patron saint and his underground burial place (crypt) that Melville saw was turned into a place of worship. When Walker visited it, after Melville, she remarked that the shrine of the saint was well preserved and that it was venerated by both Christians and Muslims (44). A large church was built on that spot in the fifth century.[20]

The second monument which Melville mentioned, rather vaguely, on 8 December, was "the pulpit of St. Paul in the court of a mosque. Beautiful sculpture—all one stone. Steps &c. The chief lion of Salonica, is this" (56). Melville did not give the name of the mosque. The later visitor Walker remarked that the local people pointed out to her "no fewer than six places" where St. Paul had preached in 50 AD: a pulpit within St. Sophia, another one beneath it, one outside St. Demetrius, etc. (51). I think that Melville's description fits better the sculptured pulpit outside the Rotonda. Other places where St. Paul preached were the synagogue in Ets-ha-Haim, the oldest Jewish quarter (first century BC) near the sea wall and a Greek man's (Jason's) house.[21]

Melville's omission of the names of the Roman and Byzantine monuments he saw and his brief comments about them, as well as his wrong reference to the Genoese as the constructors of the first city walls, show his ignorance of Thessaloniki's long history, in contrast to his knowledge of Greek mythology and the Athens-centered classical civilization. Yet, through his telegraphic journal comments about the Roman and Byzantine monuments, he conveyed the multicultural character of Thessaloniki and the changes the city had undergone, especially after its conquest by the Turks.

As the passages quoted before illustrate, Melville followed the Western trend, and thus he kept comparing his contemporary with the past Thessaloniki, and idealizing the past. Since he was not aware of the economic, educational, and other institutions that its inhabitants had established by the mid-nineteenth century, institutions which contributed to its progress, he saw Turkish Thessaloniki as a city in a state of cultural decadence.[22] He conveyed this decadence through visual contrasts: the fine quality and strength of the buildings, sculptures, and mosaics connected with its Greco-Roman and Byzantine past, versus the poor construction, plain aspect, and cheap material of nineteenth-century buildings.

A previous visitor, Warington Smyth, also referred to the decline of its antique monuments in 1854: "though much mutilated, they contrast strongly with the mean but often picturesque character of the modern architecture" (188). Yet, Smyth was more positive than Melville, when he stated that "the relics" survived "the ravages of time and the barbarians" (188). On the contrary, Melville's images of neglect, destruction, poverty, and filth, his references to bad smell, and his comparison of Thessaloniki's streets to New York City's Five Points slum, on 6 December, enhanced the feeling of decline: "Went into the Bazaar. Quite large, but filthy. Streets all narrow, like cow lanes, & smelling like barn-yards. Very silent. Women muffled about the face. All old. No young. Great numbers of Jews walking in long robes & pelisses. Also Greeks mixed with the Turks. Aspect of streets like those of Five Points Rotten houses. Smell of rotten wood. Three months ago a great fire, overrunning several acres. Not yet rebuilt" (55).

Melville's description of the streets is historically accurate. There existed no city plan in Thessaloniki in his time. Some of the main streets were comparatively broad but the majority were very narrow. Although there was mobility of population within the city, after the fifteenth century the Greeks concentrated in the Kamara and the Hippodrome districts, whereas the Jews lived mainly near the harbor, behind the sea wall, and in the downtown market area, close to the remains of the ancient forum. Most of them were the descendants of Spanish Jews who had fled to and settled in Thessaloniki towards the end of the 15th and the beginning of the sixteenth century, because they had been persecuted in Spain.[23] Their wooden homes were overcrowded—more than one family often lived in them. Only the Jews who had been converted to Islam had the right to make permanent homes in the Muslim areas on the upper hill which Melville saw from the sea—the only Muslim areas he walked through were those near the Rotonda and St. Sophia.

The Jewish quarters were the poorest and the dirtiest—the scavengers did not enter them. The bad smell that annoyed Melville came from decaying corpses of animals, garbage, and sewage that accumulated in the streets (Moutsopoulos 17, 33; Vakalopoulos 313-14). In contrast, the upper hill, predominantly Muslim, was thinly populated, cleaner, and less noisy than the downtown area which the author saw (Moutsopoulos 27). Melville's bad impressions of the city center resembled those of other foreign visitors. According to Leake, for example, Thessaloniki bore "the usual characteristics of a Turkish town; no attention [was] paid to cleanliness or convenience in the streets" (239). Lear pointed out the "labyrinth of lanes in the lower town" (23). Von Osten expressed his disgust for the filth of the Jewish quarter and wondered how it was possible for human beings to choose to live in such a sewer (qtd. in Enepekides, *Thessaloniki-Makedonia* 22). Madox underlined the "horrible" misery one witnessed in passing through the streets, and he called the local Jews "the most degenerate of any in the Turkish dominions" (80). The British vice-consul at Mytilene, Charles Thom-as Newton, who visited Thessaloniki in February 1853, called it "a dirty town, full of Jews" from Spain (121). In 1859, B. Nicolaidy contrasted the neglected homes and pestilential exhalations infecting the air in the Jewish quarters with the nice homes, gardens, and fountains on the upper hill (32); and Walker contrasted the "miserably paved, tortuous streets" (31), "the dirt and unpleasant odours of the low quarter of Salonica" with the "pleasant airy spot, about two miles distant along the shore" (32), where the English consul lived.

The only visitor who did not express disapproval was Holland who remarked that "as respects cleanliness and internal comfort, Salonica may contrast favorably with most other places in Turkey of large size and population" (314). He praised its business and abundance of goods and saw them as criteria of its superiority to other Turkish cities (315). Leake (239) and Walker also knew something that Melville apparently ignored, i.e., that the poor appearance of Jewish people and their homes was often a disguise. According to Walker, several wealthy Jews chose to: "keep up a sordid outward appearance, in their persons and dwellings, hoping thus to escape, in some measure, the cupidity of their grasping Turkish rulers. Many an old Hebrew, hobbling over the rough pavement in a ragged chintz robe, like a dressing gown made from bed curtains, patched and grimy, might probably buy up half Salonica" (56-57).

Melville became aware, however, of a frequent problem Thessaloniki faced, that of epidemics.[24] He mentioned going "with Captain with papers to the quarantine. All right & shook hands. (Usual ceremony of welcome)" (55). They finished with the formalities quickly because there was probably no epidemic at that time. Previous visitors like Adolphus Slade, however, mentioned their own unpleasant experiences with fever and the lack of adequate medical care. In 1830, Slade presented Thessaloniki as "the headquarters of the tertian fever, which ravages more or less, every part of Turkey in the summer and autumn" and saw it as the natural consequence of uncultivated lands around the town (469) and as the cause of the depopulation of Turkey (470). Similarly, Holland (332) and Capt. Best (229) blamed the great marshes in the vicinity of the city for the epidemics of fever. Moreover, Lear (14, 17-19) described the gloomy atmosphere in Thessaloniki during an epidemic of cholera in September 1848 and the consequences of the epidemic on the economic life (unemployment of poor people, desertion of the city, closing down of bazaars, etc.). Like Holland, Slade, and Best, Walker blamed the "pestilential marshes on the opposite side of the bay" and the breeze which blew from their direction and brought "the terrible fever and ague from which the inhabitants suffer frightfully" (34). According to her, Salonica fever was much dreaded in Turkey, and most of its victims came from the poorer class-es, due to their "unwholesome food, and habits of intemperance" (34-35).

IV. The People

As both the preceding and the following passages illustrate, Melville's first good impressions of the amphitheatrically located city changed after he walked through parts of its historical and commercial center and saw the bad condition of its streets, monuments and homes, and the poor clothes of its inhabitants. It is true that certain other travellers were attracted to the multicultural and poly-glot population of Thessaloniki and the liveliness of its port.[25] Smyth, for in-stance, remarked that the town offered novelty in regard to the language and costumes of its people, i.e., Greeks, Bulgarians, Albanians and others who spoke their own languages or used Turkish when they mingled together (189). Melville, however, saw these characteristics of Thessaloniki as further proof of its back-wardness. For example, he referred to the deck passengers of an arriving ves-sel, coming from different ethnic and religious backgrounds, as a struggling "mob" sunk in poverty and "wrangling in all tongues."

Although he appeared detached and objective, his language ("plague," "mob," "rags," "struggling," "wrangling," etc.) betrayed a rather critical and superior at-titude towards the deck passengers who came from a lower social class and a cultural background different from his own.[26] His description of them not as distinct individuals but as a "dense mob" gesturing wildly and unable to speak properly reinforced some of the negative Western stereotypes about the inhabi-tants of the eastern Mediterranean, such as irrational (Said 38, 40), racially infe-rior (209), and backward (205-6) people.[27] He also presented the Thessaloniki port as a new Tower of Babel: "At the landing watched for an hour or two a vast crowd & tumult. An Austrian steamer from Constantinople just in, with a great host of poor deck passengers, Turks, Greeks, Jews &c. Came ashore in boats, piled up with old dusty traps which the Plaige seemed shaken. Great up-roar of the porters & contention for luggage.—Imagine an immense accumula-tion of the rags of all nations, & all colors rained down on a dense mob, all strug-gling for huge bales & bundles of rags, gesturing with all gestures & wrangling in all tongues. Splashing into the water from the grounded boats" (56).

95

Negative descriptions of the polyglot crowd of passengers and the porters were also made by some British visitors. For instance, Best compared the crowded deck-passengers of different nationalities to "pigs in an Irish steam-vessel," and referred to their "Babel-like confusion of tongues" (231). Lear, on the other hand, travelled on a ship that carried a double load of passengers from Constantinople, because the second steamer available had a problem (13). Lear called the lower deck, which was "crammed" with people from different nationalities, a "herring-barrel" (12). He also called its passengers a "motley cargo" and "the throng below" (13). He further described very vividly "the wildest confusion" that "scizcd all the passive human freight" (16), when the ship reached Thessaloniki. His description focused on how "crowds of black-turbaned" Hebrew porters rushed into the water, seized his arms and legs, tore him out of the boat, almost tore his clothes, fell upon his enraged dragoman, and started fighting with each other over his luggage (17), and how severely the Turkish police beat them with sticks and whips in order to stop their fight (18). Lear attributed the porters' large numbers and aggressive behavior to the existing epidemic of cholera which "had rendered employment scarce" (17).

More negative comments about the porters were made by Smyth and Walker. Smyth described how he and other passengers were "hustled by clamorous porters in turbans and red shoes, all Jews!" and how they managed to extricate themselves from the porters' "clutches" and reach the custom-house (186). Smyth further referred to the Jewish petty officers and searchers as a "mob," with a "continual gabble," searching his luggage "to extract a backshish" (186). Several years later Walker described the porters as "a crowd of miserable-looking Jews ... pushing and vociferating in their attempts to pounce upon their customary prey, the traveller" (31). She also mentioned how helpless she and her companion felt "amidst the clamour of Turkish, Spanish, Greek, Bulgarian, Albanian, and various other tongues" in their futile search for the British consulate, until a "cool," "clean," "brisk young Armenian man" offered to help them "through the struggling crowd" (32).

It is obvious from the above that neither Melville nor the European visitors liked to mix with the local crowds. Their attitude and comments remind us of Said's portrait of the Western orientalist: a man who appeared as a supposedly detached, objective, and neutral informer (103, 205) but who actually believed in the Western superiority over oriental backwardness (7, 227) and therefore acted as a superior judge or interpreter (109, 208), and assumed the right to generalize about race (227), or to (re)define the domain he surveyed (228).

Melville felt more comfortable when he moved away from the overcrowded city center. On 7 December, he rode to the country estate of the wealthy English-Greek ship-agent Abbot at Urendjik, together with the ship captain, a guide and a guard.[28] In his journal, he telegraphically mentioned the camels, the Muslim cemetery, the barren hills, a water fountain with an inscription from the Koran, and the grape vines he saw (55). He also mentioned the high thick stone wall that enclosed and the armed men that guarded Abbot's estate, as well as the polite secretary who read Abbot's letter and let them in (55-56). Melville praised the "oriental style" and beauty of Abbot's place, its "hot houses & fountains & trellises & arbors innumerable," as well as the hospitality with which he was received (56). But, through his description of the landscape and Abbot's luxurious villa, so different from the city houses, Melville reproduced another stereotypical image of the Orient: a place of romance and sharp contrasts (wealth versus poverty, beauty versus ugliness, pleasure versus pain), exotic, mysterious, and often dangerous (Said 1, 51-52).[29]

V. Conclusion

Abbot's rich estate did not erase from Melville's mind the scenes of decay, poverty, and filth that he had witnessed in the city center on 6 and 8 December 1856. These scenes gave him the impression that nineteenth-century Turkish Thessaloniki, with its predominantly Jewish population, was cut off from its past and lacked the potential to create a civilization comparable to the classical or the Byzantine.[30] Even when he visited Syra and saw from his ship Delos, Patmos, Tinos, and other Aegean islands, which were parts of the new Greek nation, Melville felt that they had lost their connection with their glorious past. Only the Parthenon in Athens enabled him to temporarily bridge the gap between the actual and the ideal Greece, and to revive the dead classical world through his imagination.[31] In the other places Melville saw, the Hellenic ideal remained "unrealizable, lost" for him, as for most travellers: "Visiting the land itself, recovering the sites and the works of art, enhance[d] the sense of loss" (Constantine, *Early Greek Travellers* 4) in his mind. Moreover, like other visitors, he idealized the classical Orient to such an extent that he saw modern orientals, Greeks included, as the degraded remnants of a former greatness (Said 233).[32]

NOTES

1   A short version of this paper, written (in Greek) at the initial stage of my research, appeared in *Makedoniko Imerologio.*

2   I am quoting from Constantine, "Poets and Travellers and the Ideal of Greece" (253), abbreviated as "Poets" in subsequent references. Also, according to Constantine, "Hellas, as an ideal, ... was the state before the Fall, or after the Revolution.... Hellas was the natural sunny condition of man before the shadow of Christianity came over it" for eighteenth-century Westerners (*Early Greek Travellers and the Hellenic Ideal* 3, abbreviated as *Early Greek Travellers* in subsequent references). We find a similar concept of Hellas in Melville's poems "Syra" and "The Apparition," *Timoleon*, 62-65 and 66 respectively.

3   Constantine (*Early Greek Travellers* 5-7) provides information about the kind of people who travelled to Greece in the eighteenth century and the dangers they faced. Among the mid-eighteenth-century British travellers he mentions are James Stuart and Nicholas Revett (4) who were sent by the London Society of Dilettanti to Athens in 1751 to make drawings of the classical remains—they stayed for two and a half years. Information about the two young architects is also provided in Constantine ("Poets" 256) and in *British Travellers in Greece 1750-1820*, 3, 6-8, and 10-12—the title appears abbreviated as *British Travellers* in subsequent references.

4   According to Larrabee, one prominent strand of the philhellenism in American thinking was the belief that "the existence of a Platonic Hesperia in America should possess the power of an ideal made real, which would prove capable of regenerating the East, where the ideal had been conceived" (261). Said also refers to the Romantic sense of the mission to revive a dead world by discerning its potential underneath a degenerate surface (172).

5   Larrabee mentions James O. Noyes, MD, American surgeon in the Ottoman army, as a man who gave a truthful description of the everyday life of Greeks and other people whom he visited in the mid-1850s (272) in his book about Roumania (1857). See also Weber's reference work about nineteenth-century travel literature concerning Greece and other countries in the Near Orient.

6   Many Europeans saw the real Greece of their time as "a land of poverty and squalor, full of thieves and superstitious clergy, dominated by corrupt if courteous Turks" (Runciman 8). A characteristic example of negative criticism at the end of the eighteenth century was the portrayal of modern Greeks by the French consul in Thessaloniki (1794-96), baron Félix de Beaujour. In his report of 15 March 1798 from Thessaloniki, qtd. in Enepekides *Thessaloniki ke Makedonia, 1798-1912* (15-

20), he stated that modern Greeks were unworthy of their ancestors. For, enslaved for a long time, they became ignorant, superstitious, vain, egocentric, corrupted, cowardly, etc. (20). Beaujour wrote several reports about the economic, political, and military affairs of the Ottoman Empire (1798-99 and 1816-18). See his relevant books. Vakalopoulos attributes Beaujour's hatred for the Greeks, reflected in his reports, to the latters' commercial success which resulted in the marginalization of the French, after 1792 (289). Some nineteenth-century Americans who expressed negative views of modern Greeks were: Nicholas Biddle of Philadelphia who lamented (1806) the "degeneracy" of Greeks under the Turkish rule (qtd. in Larrabee 17); the Philo-Turk James Ellsworth Dekay, New York doctor and naturalist, who pointed out (1830) the inner depravity and gross moral defects of Greeks (qtd. in Larrabee 218-19), and who made sarcastic comments against the philhellinists that idealized Greeks (qtd. in Larrabee 219-20); and the merchant George Francis Train who thought of modern Greece (1850s) as mainly the "home of renegade Greeks" and "robber hordes" (qtd. in Larrabee 262).

7   The first American consul, W. B. Llewellyn, was appointed in January 1835 (Vakalopoulos 320).

8   Horsford and Horth, editors of Melville's *Journals* (1989), provide information (247, and 448, item 98.38) about Sir George F. Bowen, president of the University on Corfu (1847-51), and his publications about Greece, including his *Handbook for Travellers in Greece* (1854) which was probably one of Melville's sources. However, none of the comments from the *Handbook* and Melville's journal, which the editors compare (391, 450), refers to Thessaloniki. In my essay and notes I am citing Bowen's *Mount Athos, Thessaly, and Epirus.* I am also quoting passages from the above edition of the journal, keeping Melville's spelling and punctuation.

9   The data of present day historians validate the views of nineteenth-century visitors. For example, according to Hasiotis, steamships revived the commercial links of Thessaloniki to other Western and Mediterranean ports. Between 1836 and 1869, the number and size of the ships entering Thessaloniki increased from 25,000 to 243,000 tons (167). Also in his relevant book, Vakalopoulos discusses the history of Thessaloniki and its important position as an ancient Greek, Roman, Byzantine, and Ottoman city.

10   Runciman considers Edward Lear "as the most delightful of all" the landscape artists who arrived, especially from Britain, after "the sheer beauty of Greece was discovered" by the Romantics (8).

11   The journal editors also underline Melville's error about the Genoese and contrast the "strikingly beautiful appearance" of the white walls from a distance with "the squalor and filth within" the town (391, item 55.2).

12   In 1835, Colonel Leake noticed that the lower part of the town walls was partly composed of ancient marbles (235). He particularly referred to the mile-long sea wall, flanked with three great towers and constituting the maritime defences of the town (239). In 1859, Nicolaidy mentioned two rows of canons by the walls (27) in addition to describing the walls and towers (27-29). For information about the latter see also (our) contemporary scholars: Moutsopoulos (8, 14-16, 38),

99

Aspioti (7-9, 11-15, 27, 38, 52-53, 69, 73-74), and Papagiannopoulos (21-29).

13   Consul Cousinéry's *Voyage dans la Macédoine* and his reports about: life in Thessaloniki, the effects of the French Revolution and other sociopolitical events, as well as his archaeological research provide us with valuable historical information. He served as consul during the years 1773-79, 1783-85, and 1815-18.

14   See Aspioti (25) and Moutsopoulos (31, 34) about the various names given to the Rotonda, and Papagiannopoulos (34-37) about the history of the monument. Among nineteenth-century foreigners describing the Rotonda were: Cousinéry 34-38, Leake 240-41, and Bowen 38. Bowen (38) repeated Leake's 1835 description (241) of the representations of buildings and saints on the dome mosaic and his comment about the ornaments being little injured by the Turks. Walker compared the Rotonda to the Pantheon (44). She mentioned seeing mosaics of the ancient temple (aerial structures, like fantastic aviaries) which reminded her of frescoes at Pompei (45). Melville's journal editors similarly compare the Rotonda to the Roman Pantheon (392, item 55.9). Moreover, they quote Charles Dudley Warner's information (330) that the ceiling mosaics represented fourteen saints and that the architectural designs included peacocks and bright blue birds which showed the monument's ancient beauty, in contrast to the walls which were "white and barn-like."

15   For more details about the Arch of Galerius see Moutsopoulos (9 and 227, notes 27 and 28), Papagiannopoulos (38-40), and H. I. Makaronas (8-10, 13-15, 27-28, and 32-50). Makaronas compares Galerius to Pericles and the architectural-artistic significance of the palace complex in Thessaloniki to those of the Acropolis in Athens (18). At the beginning of the nineteenth century, Cousinéry gave information about the arch (29-32, 34) and adopted Zosimus's view that the arch had been made by the Emperor Constantine the Great (30). His book (28a) also included a late eighteenth-century lithograph of the arch by L. F. S. Fauvel, which showed poor homes attached to it (see Velenis 19, *British Travellers* 22, 58, and Simopoulos 572-82 about Fauvel's activities and his engravings). Other foreigners who connected the arch with Constantine were Holland 317; Madox 77; Slade 451; Bowen 35; Newton 122; and Walker 39, 49-50—the same wrong view was adopted by Horsford and Horth (392, item 55.14). A different but also wrong view was expressed by Leake who attributed the construction of the arch to Emperor Theodosius for the celebration of his victory over the Goths (245). Melville does not refer to any emperor.

16   Velenis provides information about Ottoman laws concerning house construction by Muslims and non-Muslims (17-19). According to Velenis, when foreign visitors mentioned poorly built homes in Thessaloniki, they meant Greek and Jewish. For, only the ruling Turks had the legal right to construct two-story (or higher) homes of stone (18). Velenis quotes A. Pisani, a late eighteenth-century visitor who described wooden Turkish homes, with their facades painted red (upper part) and black (lower part) and bearing inscriptions from the Koran, and with cypress trees in their yards (18, and 28, note 14).

17   The colonnade was not the propylaeum of the Hippodrome, i.e., southward to the Arch of Galerius, as Horsford and Horth wrongly suggest (392, item 55.14).

18 Von Osten's description was included in his memoirs from the Orient published in 1836, which Enepekides considers very important for the study of Greeks from August 1824 to November 1828. Von Osten's description of the Incantadas and his comments about Thessaloniki are translated by Enepekides (*Thessaloniki-Makedonia* 21-29) whom I am quoting. Foreigners who mentioned the house of a Jew attached to the Corinthian-style pillars were: Cousinéry, Madox (77), Leake, and Malherbe (381). According to Cousinéry, the pillars were located on the street of triumph, on the same line with the triumphal arch (32-33). He included (32a) an engraving by Fauvel. Like Cousinéry, Leake placed the pillars westward to the arch, i.e., near the forum, but he mentioned only four columns whose shafts were half buried in the ground (245). He explained that the figures acquired the name Incantadas because the Jews considered them to be human beings petrified through magic (246). He also supported the view that their central position and nature of construction showed that they were connected with the ancient agora (246). About fourteen years later, Bowen's description of the Incantadas and other monuments (36-37) was similar to Leake's. Besides, Newton called the Incantadas the most interesting relic of classical antiquity (121). Holland and Lear saw four columns. Holland, however, believed that they formed the entrance to a Greek and not to a Jewish house (318). Today, the eight figures have been identified as Maenad, Dionysus, Ariadne, Leda, Ganymede, Dioscurus, Aura, and Nike (Papazoglou 13).

19 I am quoting Constantine *Early Greek Travellers*, 8. In the same book, Constantine also remarks that from the seventeenth century onwards it was "established that western Europe needed classical Greece as a main ingredient of her culture" (8), and therefore it was thought proper that travellers should take all they could with them to rescue them from the Turks and from the Christians who detested the representations of the body and maltreated the pagan carvings. Moreover, Constantine refers to the vandalism committed by crude Europeans motivated by acquisitiveness (9). Constantine (214) and Tsigakou (23) refer to the plunder of ancient monuments by European and Larrabee (92, 213) by American travellers in the nineteenth century. Simopoulos criticizes European plunderers, and especially Fauvel who took advantage of his position as a diplomat to conduct a thriving business of selling Greek antiquities to museums and private collectors (572-77). Moutsopoulos (10), Papazoglou (10, 12, 18, 23), and Vakalopoulos (334) discuss the removal of Las Incantadas by Miller.

20 Xygopoulos (5-6, 9), Maitos (7, 15-17, 65-67, 80, 92, 95), and Moutsopoulos (9-10, 31, and 228, note 48) give information about the saint and the church. See also Horsford and Horth 392, item 55. 9, in which the editors quote Warner's comments about St. Demetrius being the most perfectly preserved of the city's thirty-seven former churches, with "fine mosaics of marble, beautiful in design and color" (331).

21 Stamboulis (174) and Vakalopoulos (52) mention Jason's house. Vakalopoulos (46) and Nehama (I, 39) also refer to Ets-ha-Haim synagogue as the place where Paul preached. Horsford and Horth (394, item 56.31) quote Warner's comments (329-30) about the mosque of St. Sophia—he referred to the "magnificent" stone pulpit, but he questioned the validity of the information that St. Paul preached there. Instead, he considered a synagogue the most probable place. Below is a

variety of opinions about the location of the pulpit: Slade found it in the street near the church of the S. S. Apostles from which it was later removed to the St. Sophia mosque (451)—Madox gave similar information (78); Holland located the pulpit in a subterranean church, underneath St. Demetrius's church built on the site of a Jewish synagogue (317), Bowen in St. Demetrius church (40), von Osten (qtd. in Enepekides *Thessaloniki-Makedonia* 23-24), and Smyth saw it outside the Rotonda (188). The Rotonda pulpit was taken to the museum of Constantinople at the end of the nineteenth century (Vakalopoulos 52).

22   Hasiotis (170-71), Papastathis (224, 226), and Vakalopoulos (329, 331) mention the educational and other institutions that the Greeks created in Thessaloniki, which enabled them to retain their cultural heritage and their ideological-political links with the free Greek nation and thus prepare the way for their own liberation from the Turks. One of the foreign visitors who stressed the Greeks' progress in population, commerce, education, literature, and their independent consciousness of power necessary to their future liberation was Holland (530).

23   Slade called Thessaloniki the headquarters of the Turkish Jews (448). Other foreign travellers who discussed them were Holland (320-21) and Walker (56-63). For further information about the origin, settlement, and development of Thessaloniki Jews see Hasiotis (166-69), Papastathis (227-30), Moutsopoulos (14, 20-22), Vakalopoulos (25-26, 46, 215-18), Veinstein (45-106), Nehama (vols. I-IV), and Hamoudopoulos's book. According to Vakalopoulos, the Jews called Thessaloniki "Mother of Israel" (218).

24   Moutsopoulos (33) and Vakalopoulos (313-15) refer to the frequent malarial fever and to epidemics caused by the filth in public places or brought by ships. Enepekides also discusses the poor medical and hygienic conditions, the epidemics, and quarantine houses in the Ottoman Empire, Thessaloniki included (*I Thessaloniki sta hronia 1875-1912* 237-47).

25   Moutsopoulos discusses the cosmopolitan character of Thessaloniki and its polyglot, noisy, multicultural population from the Roman period to the early twentieth century (19-20).

26   Melville's attitude shows that as a traveller, he did not "surely" acquire "a broader appreciation of the liberal, transcultural perspective of a citizen of the world," as Bryant claims (36).

27   Other such stereotypes about Orientals were: sensuous, primitive, queer, eccentric, mysterious, devious, capricious, passionate, lazy, and childish. Moreover, the inhabitants of the Near Orient were seen as the degenerate remnants of great ancient civilizations. For greater details, see Said, 1, 7, 14, 23, 51, 97, 103, 119-20, 171, 178, 203, 233, and 247. Also see Larrabee about some American travellers' comparison of nineteenth-century Greeks to American Indians and of the Greek scenery to the American Far West (264-65). In the context of such comparisons, Melville's association of the Greek islands/islanders with the "primitive" Polynesia/Polynesians is not surprising.

28   Holland mentioned the Abbott family as the most striking example of a Frank family which lost its national characteristics through its long stay in the Levant—the first Abbott, Bartholomew Edward, spoke better Turkish than English and married a Greek woman (313). Holland further pointed out that many Greek merchants acquired considerable property and that he saw large collections of books in some of their houses (320). Leake also referred to some "opu-

lent Greek merchants" who increased their wealth, thanks to their protection by European missions, but he believed that these protections would be abolished and their situation would be precarious (251). Leake (250) and Bowen (29) considered the Jews in Thessaloniki generally rich.

29 According to Dorothee Finkelstein, "the picturesqueness of the Near East with its 'challenge of contrasts' was a significant attribute in [Melville's] Orientalism" (8). He often tended to contrast the economic and social backwardness of the Muslim world with the material progress and worldliness of the West (278).

30 In contrast to Melville, Walker, who spent several weeks in Thessaloniki and got to know the city and its people, expressed her faith in the city's regenerative powers. She wrote that the town was "equally remarkable for the frightful tragedies formerly enacted there, and for the apparent ease with which... it has always risen again from its misfortunes" (37). Much earlier Holland had stated that the ancient Greeks could not be revived in nineteenth-century Greeks, because the race had undergone many changes, but he expressed his faith that a Greek nation might be created (530-31).

31 As Said points out, throughout the nineteenth century, the Orient was a place of pilgrimage and all pilgrimages passed through the Biblical lands. Most pilgrims attempted to relive some portion of Judeo-Christian or Greco-Roman actuality (168). Melville tried to do the same. In his effort he experienced the same feelings of disappointment, disenchantment, and demystification as Flaubert, Neval, and other Western pilgrims to the east did (Said 103, 180-81).

32 Melville's only journal comment about Athenian Greeks—"Greeks in cafes smoking" (98)—and his descriptions of Syra's low-class inhabitants (Georgoudaki "Melville's Trip to Syra" 5-6) reproduced the stereotypical image of the lazy, backward Orientals (Said 38, 178). Moreover, the wealthy Abbot served as his model for the character of the rich middle-aged wealthy English-Greek banker from Thessaloniki, in *Clarel* (1876). Melville made the banker "a bitter caricature of MAMMONISM" (Clarel 532) and hedonism which the writer blamed for the loss of the higher (moral/spiritual/aesthetic) values inherited from the glorious past civilizations in the Near Orient. For a more thorough discussion of Melville's prototype and the banker's function in *Clarel* see also Georgoudaki "Melville's Artistic Use" 90-91, and "Djékis Abbot."

REFERENCES

Aspioti, Lila. *Ta kastra tes Thessalonikes [The Walls of Thessaloniki]*. Thessaloniki: n.p., 1985.

Beaujour, Le baron Louis Auguste Félix de. *Tableau du commerce de la Gréce, formé d' aprés une année moyenne, depuis 1787 jusqu'en 1797.* 2 vols. Paris: Renouard, 1800.

——. *Voyage militaire dans l' Empire ottoman, ou, Description de ses frontiéres et de ses principales défenses, soit naturelles; soit artificielles, avec cinq cartes géographiques.* 2 vols. Paris: Firmin Didot, 1829.

Best, Capt. J. J. *Excursions in Albania: Comprising a Description of the Wild Boar, Deer, and Woodcock Shooting in That Country; and a Journey from thence to Thessalonica & Constantinople, and up the Danube to Pest.* London: Allen, 1842.

Bowen, Sir George Ferguson. *Mount Athos, Thessaly, and Epirus: A Diary of a Journey from Constantinople to Corfu.* London: Rivington, 1852.

——. *Handbook for Travellers in Greece.* London: Murray, 1854.

Bryant, John. "Citizens of a World to Come: Melville and the Millenial Cosmopolite," *American Literature* 59.1 (March 1987): 20-36.

Constantine, David J. "Poets and Travellers and the Ideal of Greece." *Journal of European Studies* 7 (1977): 253-65.

——. *Early Greek Travellers and the Hellenic Ideal.* Cambridge: Cambridge UP, 1984.

Cousinéry, Esprit-Marie. *Voyage dans la Macédoine, contenant des recherches sur l' histoire, la géographie et les antiquités de ce pays.* 2 vols. Paris: Imprimerie Royale, 1831.

Enepekides, Polychronis K. *I Thessaloniki sta hronia 1875-1912* [*Thessaloniki during the Years 1875-1912*]. Thessaloniki: Kyriakides, 1981.

——. *Thessaloniki ke Makedonia, 1798-1912* [*Thessaloniki and Macedonia, 1798-1912*]. Athens: Hestia, 1982.

Finkelstein, Dorothee. *Melville's Orienda.* New Haven: Yale UP, 1961.

Georgoudaki, Ekaterini. "Melville's Artistic Use of His Journeys to Europe and the Near East." Diss. Arizona State U, 1980.

——. "Djékis Abbot of Thessaloniki and the Greek Merchant in Herman Melville's *Clarel.*" *Melville Society Extracts* 64 (Nov. 1985): 1-6.

——. "Herman Melville's Trip to Syra in 1856-57." *Melville Society Extracts* 74 (September 1988): 1-8.

——. "I Thessaloniki tou 1856, opos tin ide o Herman Melville." *Makedoniko Imerologio* ["Thessaloniki in 1856, as Herman Melville Saw It." *Macedonian Journal*] 1996: 21-28.

Hamoudopoulos, A. H. *I Israelitai tis Thessalonikis* [*The Israelites of Thessaloniki*]. Athens: Kyklos, 1935.

Hasiotis, I. K. "I Thessaloniki tis Tourkokratias" ["Thessaloniki under Turkish Rule"]. *Nea Hestia* 118. 1403 (Christmas 1985): 161-71.

Holland, Henry, M.D. *Travels in the Ionian Isles, Albania, Thessaly, Macedonia, etc. during the Years 1812 and 1813.* London: Longman, 1815.

Koumarianou, Catherine. Introduction. *British Travellers in Greece 1750-1820.* Exhibition Catalogue. Ed. Georgios Tolias. London: Foundation for Hellenic Culture, 1995. x-xxi.

Larrabee, Stephen A. *Hellas Observed: The American Experience of Greece, 1775-1865*. New York: New York UP, 1957.

Leake, William Martin. *Travels in Northern Greece*. 4 vols. London: Rodwell, 1835.

Lear, Edward. *Journals of a Landscape Painter in Albania, Illyria, etc*. 2nd ed. London: Bentley, 1852.

Madox, John, Esq. *Excursions in the Holy Land, Egypt, Nubia, Syria, etc., Including a Visit to the Unfrequented District of the Haouran*. London: Bentley, 1834.

Maitos, Ioannis. *O naos tou Agiou Demetriou Thessalonikes* [*St.Demetrius's Church in Thessaloniki*]. 2nd ed. Thessaloniki: n.p., 1982.

Makaronas, H. I. *I Kamara: To thriamviko toxo tou Galeriou sti Thessaloniki* [*Kamara: Galerius's Triumphal Arch in Thessaloniki*]. Thessaloniki: Society of Macedonian Studies, 1969.

Malherbe, M. Raul de. *L' Orient 1718-1845: Histoire, Politique, Religion, Moeurs, etc.* Paris: Gide, 1846.

Melville, Herman. *Clarel*. Ed. Walter E. Bezanson. 1960. New York: Hendricks House, 1973.

——. *Timoleon*. Norwood, PA: Norwood, 1976.

——. *Journals*. Ed. Howard C. Horsford and Lynn Horth. Vol. 15 of *The Writings of Herman Melville*. Evanston and Chicago, IL: Northwestern UP and the Newberry Library, 1989.

Moutsopoulos, Nikos. *Thessaloniki 1900-1917*. Thessaloniki: Molho, 1980.

Nehama, Joseph. *Histoire des Israélites de Salonique*. Vol. 1-4. Salonique: Librairie Molho, 1935-36. 7 Vols. 1935-1978.

Newton, Charles Thomas. *Travels and Discoveries in the Levant*. 2 vols. London: Day & Son, 1865.

Nicolaidy, B. *Les Turcs et la Turquie Contemporaine: Itinéraire et Compte-rendu des voyages dans les provinces ottomanes, avec cartes détaillées*. Paris: Sartorius, 1859.

Noyes, James O., MD. *Roumania: The Border Land of the Christian and Turk, Comprising Adventures of Travel in Eastern Europe and Western Asia*. New York: n.p., 1857.

Osten, Ritter Prokesch von. *Denkwürdigkeiten und Erinnerungen aus dem Orient*. 3 vols. Stuttgart: Hallberger, 1836.

Papagiannopoulos, Apostolos. *Monuments of Thessaloniki.* Thessaloniki: Rekos, 1983.

Papastathis, Haralambos. "I kalliergia ton grammaton sti Thessaloniki kata tin Tourkokratia" ["The Cultivation of Letters in Thessaloniki during the Turkish Rule"]. *Nea Hestia* 118. 1403 (Christmas 1985): 221-35.

Papazoglou, Aris. *Las Incantadas: I akrivis thesi tou mnemiou sto syngrotima tes archaias agoras tes Thessalonikis* [*Las Incantadas: The Precise Location of the Monument in the Ancient Forum Complex in Thessaloniki*]. Thessaloniki: Pimenides, 1997.

Pisani, A. *Letters from Different Parts of Europe, Asia and Africa Visited in 1788 and 1789.* London: n.p., 1791.

Runciman, Sir Steven. Introduction. Tsigakou 7-8.

Said, Edward. *Orientalism.* London: Routledge, 1978.

Simopoulos, Kyriakos. *Xeni Taxidiotes stin Ellada* [*Foreign Travelers in Greece*]. vol. 4. Athens: Ekdotiki, 1975. 4 vols. 1970-1975.

Slade, Adolphus, Esq. *Records of Travels in Turkey, Greece, etc. and of a Cruise in the Black Sea with the Capitan Pasha, in the Years 1829, 1830, and 1831.* 2 vols. London: Saunders and Otley, 1832.

Smyth, Warington W. *A Year with the Turks, or, Sketches of Travel in the European and Asiatic Dominions of the Sultan.* London: Parker, 1854.

Stamboulis, Yorgos N. *I zoe ton Thessalonikeon prin ke meta to 1912: Laografika-ithi-ethima* [*The Life of Thessalonicans before and after 1912: Folklore-Mores-Customs*]. Thessaloniki: Dioskouri, 1984.

Tsigakou, Fani-Maria. *The Rediscovery of Greece: Travellers and Painters of the Romantic Era.* London: Thames, 1981.

Vakalopoulos, Apostolos. *Istoria tes Thessalonikes, 316 p.c.-1983* [*History of Thessaloniki, 316 BC-1983*]. Thessaloniki: n.p., 1983.

Veinstein, Gilles. Introduction-Afterword. *Salonique, 1850-1918: La "ville des Juifs" et le réveil des Balkans.* Greek trans. Yorgos Kalamantis. Athens: Hecate, 1994.

Velenis, Yorgos. "Istorikes tomes sti metabyzantini architectoniki tes Thessalonikes" ["Historical Cross-sections in the Meta-byzantine Architecture of Thessaloniki"]. *Thessaloniki 2.300 chronia* [*Thessaloniki 2.300 Years*]. Magdalini Goula et al., eds. Thessaloniki: Sfakianakis, 1985. 17-32.

Walker, Mary Adelaide. *Through Macedonia to the Albanian Lakes.* London: Chapman, 1864.

Warner, Charles Dudley. *In the Levant.* Boston: Osgood, 1877.

Weber, Shirley Howard. *Voyages and Travels in the Near East Made during the Nineteenth Century.* Princeton, NJ: Princeton UP, 1952.

Xygopoulos, Andreas. *Ta psifidota tou naou tou Agiou Demetriou Thessalonikes* [*The Mosaics of St. Demetrius's Church in Thessaloniki*]. Thessaloniki: Society of Macedonian Studies, 1969.

MARYHELEN C. HARMON

IDEALITY, REALITY, AND INSPIRATION:

MELVILLE AND WORDSWORTH IN ROME

"Can art, not life, make the ideal?"

ach of us is a traveler, "wandering to-and-fro over the deserts"; were it not so, many of us would not have gathered in July 1997 in Volos, Greece, celebrating the life of Herman Melville. Where each of us had already visited, of course, is unique. What one does in such places, what one is confronted with and is forced to cope with, and how one responds to challenges is critical. Such a situation, Melville in Rome, and how experiences there were remarkably analogous to those of an earlier traveler in Italy, the British poet William Wordsworth, in ideality, reality, and inspiration is the topic of this study.

After returning to his home and family in 1857 after his visit to the Eternal City, Melville felt he must make use of the storehouse of material in his voluminous journals of his travels. How could he yield a profit on this accumulated capital, that which Wordsworth earlier described in his sonnet beginning "I Wandered Lonely as a Cloud" as "What wealth the show to me had brought"? Melville wrote that he had "been trying to scratch my brains for a Lecture. What is a good, earnest subject?" Thus "Statues in Rome" began to take shape, a public lecture for the Lyceum circuit, in which he would be speaking "of the impressions produced upon my mind as one who looks upon a work of art as he would upon a violet or a cloud." Wordsworth had earlier observed in his collection titled "Memorials of a Tour in Italy" that "Who that travels far / To feed his mind with watchful eyes could share / Or wish to share it." Wordsworth cautioned those who could cull and reflect on images of beauty, in "Plea for the Historian," to honor the Muse who "taught her faithful servants how the lyre / Should animate, but not mislead, the pen." Melville's program was first to describe objectively the particulars of the selected statues that he had viewed in "the bliss of solitude," then to "speculate upon the emotions and pleasures that appearance is apt to excite in the human breast." In *The Prelude* (Book 14) Wordsworth expressed such an effort as keeping "in wholesome separation the two natures, / The one that feels, the other that observes."

There is no doubt that at this time in his career Melville was quite familiar with much of Wordsworth's thought and poetry; in 1853 he had parodied a passage from "Resolution and Independence" in "Cock-A-Doodle-Doo!" In "Statues in Rome" he would specifically cite Wordsworth as "that best of all pastoral poets," having earlier journalized about sculptured animals in the Vatican museum showing "a Wordsworthian appreciation of the gentle in Nature." What has received scant critical attention is the surprising extent that specific Wordsworthian images (the violet and the cloud, for example), Wordsworth's central poetic theme of the correspondence of stimulation and deferred sensation ("emotion recollected in tranquility"), his word choice ("the language really used by men," "a man speaking to men"), as well as the British poet's concept of artistic creation ("the spontaneous overflow of powerful feelings"), all articulated in the "Preface" to the second edition of the *Lyrical Ballads*—are embedded in Melville's Italian journal and, in this same air of "tranquility," are presented in his subsequent anunciatory public recollections of his experiences in Rome.

By comparing such literary relationships between Melville and Wordsworth, I intend to focus on the many ways in which the American wandering "lonely as a cloud," despite his personal suffering, apparently assuaged his loneliness realistically among the "mute marbles" of Rome as well as elsewhere in Italy. Notwithstanding the passage of time since their creation, he would contend they "live on, and speak with a voice that echoes through the ages," and Wordsworth-like, he will share his emotional reaction to the "impressions produced" in Rome, "recollected in tranquility" in his Lyceum lectures presented under difficult circumstances for little profit in America.

Few have noted the curiously similar biographical correspondences between the two writers. Each lost his father when in early adolescence, both lived as adults in overcrowded conditions which made sustained artistic endeavors difficult, and each loved to travel. Both served long in government jobs. Each was immeasurably affected by a relatively brief, difficult, and painful relationship with another now-celebrated writer; and the masterpiece of each was dedicated to that other writer, Wordsworth's *Prelude* to Coleridge and *Moby-Dick* to Hawthorne. Each writer would experience neglect and critical censure in his attempts to communicate directly with readers. Each lived beyond seventy years.

But my main concern is with the two literary men who shared similar circumstances of their visits to Rome: each was there in an effort to restore health and depressed spirits, and each was realizing a long-held aspiration. Wordsworth wrote retrospectively, "During my whole life I had felt a strong desire to visit Rome, but did not think myself justified in incurring the necessary expense." Melville was greatly disappointed in 1849 in London when his negotiations with English publishers did not yield sufficient funds to travel to Italy. He wrote in his journal, "bad news enough—I shall not see Rome—I'm Floored." It is ironic that two of the greatest Romantic writers—exalting emotion, intuition, imagination, and individualism, opposing the ideals of restraint and harmony characteristic of Classicism—would yearn to visit classical Rome. It is therefore not surprising that the reality of the actual experience did not fulfill either writer's expectations, and that their immediate response was not overwhelmingly enthusiastic. As Melville observed, such decay and ruins ("everywhere are fallen columns and sculptured fragments" in "the great pile of confused architecture") cannot sustain inspiration, the artistic vision, in face of the reality of physical and mental demands of travel, especially for those whose health is not robust.

Melville obviously wanted to be moved significantly by the sites and artifacts, "the ideal statuary," of a center of Western civilization, his expectation as an artist. In his lecture he asserts that "Rome contains more objects of interest than perhaps any other place in the world." Yet in his search for ideality he was forced pragmatically by his choice of topic to comment on the realities of Rome; nevertheless he felt constrained to wax philosophic by allusions to Plato, among others, or expatiated about sculptured horses being "idealized by the ancient artists as majestic next to man." An equestrian group he described exemplified "this ideal and magnificent conception of the horse," thereby raising "that animal into a sort of divinity." In his lecture's conclusion, an overview of the collection of statues in Rome, he will claim they are "the works of the dreamers and idealists of old." He then would question his audience rhetorically: "Can art, not life, make the ideal?" As early as 1814 in the long didactic poem *The Excursion* Wordsworth too had grappled with the dilemma of an overly optimistic idealist in the world of reality, the Solitary who is despondent about the hopes for mankind.

The manuscript of Melville's lecture does not exist, for it is presumed he destroyed it following the termination of his Lyceum circuit. In response to Newton Arvin's 1942 call for "the whole evidence on Melville as lecturer," Merton M. Sealts, Jr., responded, painstakingly reconstructing the lecture from contemporary newspaper reviews of Melville's presentations of "Statues of Rome," twenty-eight articles in all. Sealts's 1957 *Melville as Lecturer* provides both details and critical analyses, as well as the composite text of the Roman lecture in addition to the other two Lyceum topics: "The South Seas" and "Traveling: Its Pleasures, Pains, and Profits." Without Professor Sealts's labors I could not have attempted this study. Also extremely helpful was the article "Melville the Traveler" in *A Companion to Melville Studies* (1986, ed. John Bryant) by Thomas Farel Heffernan, who emphasized that Melville was "a mental traveler as well as a physical one."

Wordsworth the physical traveler asserted, "I traveled among unknown men, / In lands beyond the sea"; in a poem beginning with those lines, describing himself as a "lonely traveler," he was also a mental traveler when musing in *The Excursion* (Book 1) about "the things which he had seen; and often touched, / Abstrusest matter, reasonings of the mind / Turned inward." Melville the traveler both mental and physical began his Lyceum presentation by defending his position as lecturer, being "Neither critic nor connoisseur ... [but one who] admires or condemns as he finds an answering sentiment awakened in his soul." He draws an analogy between the poet Robert Burns and the botanist Linneaus as each in his own way having an understanding of flowers, and that in art too "the rude and uncultivated feels its influence as well as the polite and polished." One is reminded of Wordsworth's rude leech gatherer in "Resolution and Independence" whose "Choice word and measured phrase [are] above the reach of ordinary men." Melville's mention of Linneaus also recalls the British poet's indictment in "The Poet's Epitaph" of the scientist: "a fingering slave, / One that would peep and botanize upon his mother's grave." Elsewhere, in "The Tables Turned," he excoriates "our meddling intellect / [that] Mis-shapes the beauteous forms of things:—/ We murder to dissect./ Enough of Science . . . bring with you a heart / that watches and receives." Melville watched, received, and argued persuasively his right "to paint . . . the appearance of Roman Statuary objectively and afterward to speculate upon the emotions and pleasure that appearance is apt to excite in the human breast."

My scheme now is to review Melville's Italian journal and its transcription into the lecture "Statues in Rome," citing what I see as specific and particularly strong Wordsworthian resonances. Melville complained that his chosen Lyceum lecture topic was so vast and challenging that much had to be omitted so that he might "keep within the limits of an hour," and I too must be succinct.

It is surprising that Melville had the strength after his demanding twenty-six hour stagecoach journey from Naples to Rome to begin his Roman sightseeing so soon, but he records that on the day he arrived he "Walked to Capitol." Wordsworth too was anxious to begin: as his party neared the city he exulted in "Musings at Aquapendente": "Let us now / Rise, and to-morrow greet magnificent Rome." Melville's hotel was less than half a mile from the Capitoline Hill, and he noted that he took a view from a tower there, which would have been part of the Palace of the Senators. He had been advised by his friend John Murray to visit the site early for help in orientating himself to Rome. Having visited this spot many times, I was shocked to read that the view did not impress Melville; "Rome fell flat on me. Oppressively flat." Surprisingly Wordsworth too was at this site disappointed, as he expressed in his "Musings": though "free to rove . . . yet Art's noblest relics, history's rich bequests, / Failed to reanimate and but feebly cheered." Melville rationalized pragmatically that he hadn't had any sleep the previous night, and that perhaps the glories of the sights he had seen in the Near East might have jaded him. But the anticipation that had been building up over a long time was for the moment crushed. A Wordsworth poem, "At Rome," begins in a similar negative response to the site: "Is this, ye Gods, the Capitolian Hill?"

From this advantageous vantage point Melville describes the Tiber River as a "ditch, yellow as saffron. The whole landscape nothing independent of associations." As he looks toward the Vatican he thinks that St. Peter's looks small, but nevertheless he walks toward it, about one and a half miles by the most direct route. He notes regretfully that the view of the façade was disappointing, despite its grand approach; the interior, however, would come up to his expectations, even if the dome was "not so wonderful as St. Sophia's in Constantinople." It comes as no surprise to any traveler that he records that by 3 P.M. on his first day in Rome he was exhausted, so he had an early supper and went to bed. Another day Melville would revisit the Capitoline Hill, mentioning again the Tarpeian Rock with its trashy "dirty yard at base," covered by shabby buildings. Twenty years earlier the sight had moved Wordsworth to exclaim in "At Rome": "Yon petty steep in truth the fearful Rock? / Tarpeian named of yore, and keeping still / That name, a local Phantom proud to mock the Traveler's expectation."

On Melville's second day in Rome he walked to the Pincian Hill overlooking the Piazza del Popolo, where he had a "Fine view of St. Peter's." Yet on this day he complained bitterly and poignantly that there is "No place where a lonely man will feel more lonely than in Rome." Similarly, Wordsworth's first view of "the whole majesty of Rome" was first apparent from "the Pincian Height / Crowned with St. Peter's everlasting dome" as he expressed it in "The Pines of Monte Mario at Rome."

Melville would stay in Rome three and a half weeks, longer than anywhere else in his arduous seven-month foreign journey. The classical sights would remind him of those at home—the Colosseum prompts the image of the "Hopper of Greylock," his favorite mountain; the banks of the Tiber River are as "primeval as Ohio's in the midst of all these monuments of the centuries." When Wordsworth visited Italy in 1837, his traveling companion, Henry Crabb Robinson, wrote: "It often happened that objects of universal attraction served chiefly to bring back to his mind absent objects dear to him." In a sonnet the traveling poet would write of being "rich in thoughts of home,"—for him, always Grasmere and the Lake District.

Samuel Johnson once observed, "The use of travelling is to regulate imagination by reality." Heffernan speculated that Melville's compilation of the Lyceum lecture "Statues in Rome" was "an articulation of the way Melville did his looking when he traveled...the regulation of reality popularly explained." Melville began his presentation of how he "did his looking" by narrating his itinerary of Rome and its statues, thereby escorting his listeners by circuiting the city, first to provide factual data about the antiquities, and then to share his estimations and reactions to them. In *The Prelude* (Book 6) Wordsworth observed: "I looked upon these things / As from a distance; heard, and saw, and felt. / Was touched." In stressing the importance of honest response, elsewhere, in *The Excursion* (Book 1), he counseled: "Why then should we read / The forms of things with an unworldly eye?"

Melville does not limit himself to only those statues that are in Rome. The Vatican Apollo reminds him of the Venus de Medici in Florence, a fair woman in whom "the ideal and actual are blended." Wordsworth's poem "She Was a Phantom of Delight" describes "A lovely apparition, sent / To be a moment's ornament;... I saw her upon nearest view, / A Spirit yet a Woman too!... A perfect Woman, nobly planned, / To warn, to comfort, and command; / And yet a Spirit still, and bright / With something of angelic light." Not surprisingly, Mel-ville is reminded by this Venus of a native maiden of Typee, the legendary Fayaway. One newspaper account of a Melville lecture observed that he would venture a bet that Mr. Melville, with all his admiration for the Medicean Venus, thinks Fayaway worth a score of cold inhabited marbles.

Next Melville cited the Laocoon, an example of the "ideal statuary of Rome expressing the doubt and the dark groping of speculation in that age when the old mythology was passing away and men's minds had not yet reposed in the new faith." Wordsworth also in his sonnet "The World Is Too Much With Us" had noted humanity being out of tune: "Great God! I'd rather be / A pagan suckled in a creed outworn: / So might I, standing on this pleasant lea, / Have glimpses that would make me less forlorn: / Have sight of Proteus rising from the sea:/ Or hear old Triton blow his wreathed horn." The Vatican Hall of Animals then is cited, and it is here that Melville specifically mentions Wordsworth: "The quiet, gentle, and peaceful scenes of pastoral life are represented in some of the later of Roman statuary, just as we find them described by the best of all pastoral poets, Wordsworth." The opening lines of *The Prelude* are typical of this pastoralism: "O there is blessing in this gentle breeze. / A visitant that while it fans my cheek / Doth seem half-conscious of the joy it brings / From the green fields and from yon azure sky."

As Melville draws to his conclusion, he suggests bringing all the extant statues of Rome together "and speak[ing] of them as a whole." Wordsworth-like, he observes that statues "are rather of a tranquil, subdued air such as men have under the influence of no passion." He argues that what makes Roman museums so impressive is this "same air of tranquility," asserting "Here, in statuary, was the Utopia of the ancients expressed." Yet, in truth, both Melville and Wordsworth were suspicious of the utopian: Melville wrote of an "almost entire impracticality" of the notion; Wordsworth observed in *The Prelude* (Book 11) that both "the meek and lofty" are "called upon to exercise their skill, / Not in Utopia.../ But in the very world, which is the world / Of all of us,—the place where, in the end, / We find our happiness, or not at all!" Melville saw the Vatican itself as "the index of the ancient world." In Wordsworth's best-known reference to a statue in *The Prelude* (Book 3), that of Sir Isaac Newton in Cambridge, he cites "his prism and silent face, / The marble index of a mind for ever / Voyaging through strange seas of Thought, alone"—a fitting estimation of Melville himself.

Rising to a conclusionary hortatory pitch, Melville the lecturer sharply contrasts the role of "visionaries and dreamers" among the ancients who embodied their conceptions of perfection in idealized statuary with the diminishing significance, as he saw it, of the modern artist in his own time, overvaluing practical science and technology at the expense of art. Here it must be recognized, with regret, that the aging Wordsworth in 1833 wrote a paean to "Steamboats, Viaducts, and Railways," in which he felt that although these technological marvels are "at war / With old poetic feeling... Poets should not judge them amiss" even if their presence and "harsh features... Mar the loveliness of nature." Melville's final comments bring into focus this tension between ideality and reality: "The ancients of the ideal description, instead of trying to turn their impractical chimeras, as does the modern dreamer, into social and political prodigies, deposited them in great works of art... [which] seem to breathe inspiration through the world."

In Sealts's opinion Melville's lectures were "the bridge between his fiction and his poetry." I have tried here to identify the bridge between the thought and the reaction of the earlier visitor Wordsworth to Melville's intense response to his visit to Rome as he articulated it in his Journal and Lyceum lecture. Leon Howard found the lecture "a significant revelation" of Melville's attempt, at this turning point of his career, "to order his thoughts on art." A poem of Meville's last years, aptly titled "Art," attempts to articulate his idea of the nature of artistic creation, happening when "unlike things must meet and mate." When composing the lecture "Statues in Rome," however, he had not arrived at this resolution, when he told his audience that "things . . . so totally unlike cannot be brought together." Wordsworth in his 1800 "Preface" to the *Lyrical Ballads* anticipated Melville's matured vision when he recognized "a principle which must be well known to those who have made any of the arts the object of accurate reflection; namely, the pleasure which the mind derives from the perception of similitude and dissimilitude. This principle is the great spring of the activity of our minds, and their chief feeder."

Wordsworth would experience in his long life the tragedy of the loss of artistic inspiration, his "chief feeder." In Book 12 of *The Prelude* he appears to have a presentiment of his dilemma, his poetic anticlimax from about 1815 until his death in 1850. For a writer whose most characteristic posture was that of the rememberer of things past—one who would trace the growth of a poet's mind—a calculus points out that one's earlier emotional experience is not an inexhaustible resource. Wordsworth lived dangerously upon his capital and he knew it; from *The Prelude* (Book 12): "The days gone by / Return upon me almost from the dawn / Of life; the hiding-places for man's power / Open, I would approach them, but they close. / I see by glimpses now: when age comes on, / May scarcely see at all."

It was observed journalistically about Melville at the time of his lectures: "He had so completely exhausted his personal experiences that his attempts to please the public led him into commonplace generalities and verbal repetitions of himself" (Howard, quoted in Sealts 257-58). Yet in concluding his comments about Melville as lecturer, Sealts pointed to this critical way-station in his life as anticipating that "the writing which lay ahead, the persistence of memories, and the value of the past" would be his major themes, quieter echoes of his earlier life and writing—the prevailing mood of reminiscence—quintessential Wordsworthian characteristics all. Whereas Wordsworth's emotional capital would be found sadly wanting, as evidenced by his over three closing decades of mostly pedestrian verse, Melville's last years produced poetry of a high quality, only lately coming toward a recognition long overdue, not to mention the incomparable *Billy Budd*.

In this triumphant final work Melville recounts the fate of Billy, the Handsome Sailor, a "superior figure," one whose "masculine beauty" marked him as "a fine specimen of the genus homo who in the nude might have posed for a statue," "Apollo with his portmanteau." Billy's noble descent was as evident in him as in a blood horse." His body hanging from the yardarm is statue-like, "no motion was apparent." After the execution the "air in the clearness of its serenity was like smooth white marble in the polished block." In life "he showed in face that human look of reposeful good nature which the sculptor gave to his heroic strong man, Hercules." These references offer only an echoing sampling of Melville's earlier commentary about the statuary of Rome. In his lecture he had proclaimed that "The statue which most of all in the Vatican excites the admiration of all visitors is the Apollo, the crowning glory, which stands alone . . . Its very presence is overawing." He stated assertively, "How well in the Apollo is expressed the idea of the perfect man!" He spoke of the statue as having "a kind of divinity in it that lifts the imagination of the beholder above." The allusion to Hercules in describing Billy too was heard earlier at the Lyceums: "a noble statue, . . . which in its simplicity and bovine good nature reminds us of cheerful and humane things and makes our hearts incline towards him." Captain Vere observes, "With mankind forms, measured forms, are everything"; in speaking of the statues Melville asserted, "They were formed by those who had yearnings for something better." The plethora of reference in *Billy Budd* to notions expressed in the lecture delivered almost three decades earlier challenges the widely held opinion that what Melville said publicly about his Roman experience was nothing more that a scheme for monetary gain.

Wordsworth and Melville each suffered failing physical eyesight as they aged. As to the British poet's visionary gleam, "the light that never was on sea or land," by his later years it had almost departed: "A power is gone, which nothing can restore," as he ruefully acknowledged in "Elegiac Stanzas." At this point a marked difference between the two writers becomes apparent. Melville's visionary gleam persisted, burning like a Fresnel light, inspiring him to write both powerful poetry and moving fiction. In "Statues in Rome" Melville proclaimed that "The ancients live while these statues endure, giving purpose, shape, and impetus to what was created." What Melville created, even to the end of his life, I argue was inspired to a degree, not often noted, by the tension between the ideality and the reality of his 1857 visit to Rome.

REFERENCES

Heffernan, Thomas Farel. "Melville the Traveler," *A Companion to Melville Studies,* ed. John Bryant. New York: Greenwood Press, 1986. 35-61.

Melville, Herman. *The Piazza Tales and Other Prose Pieces 1839-1860.* Evanston and Chicago, IL: Northwestern University Press and Newberry Library, 1987.

——. *Journals.* Evanston and Chicago, IL: Northwestern University Press and the Newberry Library, 1987.

Sealts, Merton M., Jr. *Melville as Lecturer.* Cambridge, MA: Harvard University Press, 1957.

Wordsworth, William. *The Poetical Works of William Wordsworth,* ed. Ernest de Selincourt. 2nd ed. Revised by Helen Darbishire, 5 vols. Oxford: Oxford University Press, 1952-59.

Lyon Evans, Jr.

The Significance of Melville's Greece Poems

in His Late World-View

I

n 1837, Ralph Waldo Emerson observed, "Authors we have, in numbers, who have written out their vein, and who, moved by a commendable prudence, sail for Greece or Palestine . . . to replenish their merchantable stock" (71). Two decades later, Herman Melville followed the path of those earlier writers himself. Having "written out his vein" of bleak and bitter satire in *The Confidence-Man,* Melville sailed to England in the autumn of 1856 to arrange for British publication of the novel. After a notable reunion with Hawthorne in Liverpool, Melville boarded a ship, *The Egyptian,* bound for the Mediterranean. Before returning to America six months later, Melville visited Malta, Constantinople, Egypt, Palestine, Greece, and Italy, recording his impressions in a travel journal (Howard 237-53; Melville, *Journals*).

That Melville in his travels succeeded in replenishing his merchantable stock—creatively, if not financially—is confirmed by what he later produced. *Clarel: A Poem and Pilgrimage in the Holy Land* (1876) draws on Melville's observations and experiences in Palestine; "Fruit of Travel Long Ago," an eighteen-poem sequence in *Timoleon and Other Poems* (1891), records his impressions of Italy, Greece, and Egypt. Although many of these poems may have been written shortly after Melville's return to America, it is possible that some, at least, were revised for publication in *Timoleon* (Howard 265, 333). Furthermore, that Melville, a few months before his death, chose to self-publish these poems (the printing was limited to 25 copies) is itself noteworthy. With *John Marr and Other Sailors* (1888), *Timoleon*, the last of his works to be published in Melville's lifetime, makes clear that to the end of his days, Herman Melville continued to transmute his merchantable stock of experiences into art.

Compared to the ambitious scope and sheer size of *Clarel*, the "Fruit of Travel" poems appear to be something of an afterthought. Few in number, brief in length, modest in their evident themes and aspirations, most of the poems stay close to their source material in Melville's travels, offering impressionistic reflections on the locale or edifice being described. Seven poems, however, which address classical Greek architecture in its natural setting, are of more far-reaching significance than may be evident at first glance. Melville's arrangement of the poems (Italy/Greece/Egypt), which reverses the order of his 1856-57 travels, also is significant. In my paper, part of a longer work in progress, I will unpack the ambiguities and ironies in the Greece poems, making clear their central importance in Melville's late world-view; explain why the recollected travels end in Egypt; and briefly assess these poems' thematic relationship to Melville's posthumously published *Weeds and Wildings, with a Rose or Two* (1924). In his last years, I will show, Melville, still searching for something that might win his "soul's allegiance," was also increasingly preoccupied with intimations of mortality, with the inexorable, the inescapable encroachment of "that terminating season": death.

II

The first poem in the Greece series, "The Attic Landscape," sets the tone for those that follow. The traveler, newly arrived from Italy, with its "Picturesque," its "Old Romance," is enthused, even dazzled, by the contrasting ambience of Greece. Warmly praising the "pure outline" and "linear charm" of a classical temple set against the "clear-cut," "sculptural" hills, Melville adds, buoyantly, "'Tis Art and Nature lodged together, / Sister by Sister, cheek to cheek; / Such Art, such Nature, and such weather / The All-in-All seems here a Greek" (245-46).

In the next poem, aptly titled "The Same," Melville observes, "A circumambient spell it is, / Pellucid on these scenes that waits [*sic*], / Repose that does of

Plato tell—/ Charm that his style authenticates" (246).

Although these poems may appear to evoke what Catherine Georgoudaki terms "the idea of unity between art and Nature" (qtd. in Robillard 255), the language of "The Attic Landscape" and "The Same" is equivocal. As William Bysshe Stein has noted, the use of the verb "seems" in the line, "Such Art, such Nature. . . / The All-in-All *seems* here a Greek" (emphasis added), as well as the use of "spell" and "charm" in "The Same," "bespeaks unconscious depreciation . . . the presence of optical illusion" (121).

That the Greek landscape indeed casts a spell on the traveler, clouding his judgment and leading him to mistake appearances for reality, is confirmed, with dry humor, in the third poem in the Greece series, "The Parthenon." After warmly apostrophizing the Parthenon, "Seen Aloft from Afar"—"You look a sun-cloud motionless / In noon of day divine"—Melville adds, "Like Lais, fairest of her kind, / In subtlety your form's defined—/ The cornice curved, each shaft inclined, / While yet, to eyes that do but revel / And take the sweeping view, / Erect this seems, and that a level, / To line and plummet true" (246-47). The point of the comparison appears straightforward enough: as Lais was the fairest of women, so is the Parthenon the fairest of temples. But why does Melville honor Lais, a prostitute and priestess of Venus in notoriously corrupt Corinth, herself one of "the most notorious women of ancient times" (Stein 122), as "fairest of her kind"? In the ancient world, Helen of Troy, not Lais, was held to be the most beautiful of women.

The next stanza is more curious still: "Spinoza gazes; and in mind / Dreams that one architect designed / Lais—and you!" (247). It is one thing to say that the Parthenon and Lais are the apex of two different kinds of beauty, something else to say they share a common essence, which is here implied. The Parthenon is inert and made of stone; Lais was a sexually active woman, made of flesh and blood. As Bryan C. Short has aptly said, "'One architect' did not design both girl and temple" (111). To Short, Melville's point in asserting the contrary is to show that "the human artist produces a unique form of beauty" (111). This reading, however, overlooks the irony of the qualifying phrase, "Spinoza gazes; and in mind / Dreams," which implies that the unity of the Parthenon and Lais is not an indisputable fact, but rather is a mere dream of Spinoza, a metaphysical monist who would have assumed, *a priori*, that a single creator—"one architect"—made both the marble temple and the living woman.

That "one architect" did not "design" both the Parthenon and Lais becomes clear when Lais's notoriety as a priestess of Venus is considered. Venus was the Roman goddess of love (her Greek counterpart was Aphrodite): sister, but also antithesis, of Minerva, virgin goddess of reason. As the Parthenon was dedicated to Athena (prototype of Roman Minerva), the comparison of Lais to the Parthenon thus really involves an implied *contrast* of *eros* and *logos*, passion and reason, sexuality and virginity, much as Nietzsche, in *The Birth of Tragedy*, contrasts Apollonian *stasis* and repose with Dionysian dynamism and frenzy. "One architect," then, could not have designed both the Parthenon and Lais, because their ruling deities, Athena/Minerva and Aphrodite/Venus, although sisters, are mutually incompatible, irreconcilably opposed to one another.

Awareness of this antithesis casts an ironic light on Melville's claim, in "The Attic Landscape," that the classical temple and its surrounding "sculptural" hills are "Art and Nature lodged together, / Sister by sister, cheek to cheek" (246). Although the temple and the surrounding hills may resemble one another, sisterhood, as the example of Athena/Minerva and Aphrodite/Venus reminds us, is no guarantee that the respective natures will be similar or complementary.

Spinoza's dream that "one architect designed" both the Parthenon and Lais is, then, an illusion: another "charm" or "spell." The concluding section of "The Parthenon," "The Last Tile," confirms this with dry humor. "When the last marble tile was laid / The winds died down on all the seas; / Hushed were the birds and swooned the glade; / Ictinus sat; Aspasia said / "Hist—Art's meridian, Pericles!" (247). Ictinus was the architect of the Parthenon; he was not, however, the architect of Lais—or of Aspasia, either. Although educated and cultured, Aspasia was also a *hetaera*, or courtesan, who became Pericles' mistress after he divorced his wife. Denounced as a "child of debauchery," Aspasia was eventually tried for immorality (Ehrenberg 231, 238; Stein 122). In the symbolism of the poem, then, Aspasia and Lais have similar functions. Both serve *eros*; both are signifiers of sexuality, passion, Dionysian release; both oppose Athenian virginity, rationality, self-control. Unlike Aphrodite and Athena, Aspasia and Lais are sisters whose natures really *are* similar.

As the Parthenon is being dedicated, Ictinus is respectfully silent; the birds, too, cease chirping; the glade "swoon[s]"; the wind dies down "on *all* the seas" (emphasis added). So seductive is the classical temple's "charm," the poem implies, so potent its "circumambient spell," that living Nature itself appears to be on the verge of metamorphosing into the marble Parthenon's counterpart or double: reposeful, inert, still. But then the irrepressible Aspasia speaks up: "Hist!— Art's meridian, Pericles!" Her words, I suggest, are a revenge, however whimsical, of Aphrodite against Athena: *eros* vanquishing *logos*, a Dionysian return of the repressed. Thanks to Aspasia's intervention, the poem implies, the birds will not give up chirping, the winds on the seas will not cease blowing, after all.

The antithesis of living Nature and classical Art, passion and repose, dynamism and *stasis*, is elaborated obliquely, and with dry humor, in "The Parthenon." A grimmer, more explicit version of the same dichotomy is offered in "Off Cape Colonna." This brief poem begins with an arresting description of the temple of Poseidon, which stands majestically at the summit of Cape Colonna (today called Cape Sounion), much as the Parthenon overlooks Athens from the high ground of the Acropolis: "Aloof they crown the foreland lone, / From aloft they loftier rise—/ Fair columns, in the aureola rolled / From sunned Greek seas and skies. / They wax, sublimed to fancy's view, / A god-like group against the blue" (248). The columns of Poseidon's temple—"aloft," "fair," "god-like"—resemble the Parthenon, "Seen Aloft from Afar": "[a]erial gleaming, warmly white . . . / a suncloud motionless / In noon of day divine" (246).

The next stanza, however, shifts abruptly from the godlike temple, elevated and remote, to the "fallen" world of Nature below: "Over much like gods! Serene they [the columns] saw / The wolf-waves board the deck, / And headlong hull of Falconer, / And many a deadlier wreck" (248).

As in poems in *John Marr and Other Sailors*, Nature in "Off Cape Colonna" is signified by a shipwreck. The characterization of the classical temple's columns as "aloft," "god-like," and serenely indifferent to the human tragedy below thus reiterates in a darker tone the underlying theme of "The Parthenon." The classical temple may be "Art's meridian"—an embodiment in stone of Platonic metaphysical idealism, exposing what Melville calls in "Greek Architecture" a "reverence for the Archetype" (248)—but in its very inert perfection it has little in common with living Nature, represented by devouring "wolf waves" in one poem and by chirping birds and undying winds, as well as by Lais and Aspasia, in the other.

Melville's Greece poems, then, are less an encomium to the classical ideal than a telling critique of it. This realization helps to clarify the meaning of another poem in *Timoleon*, the much-discussed "After the Pleasure Party." In this dramatic monologue, the protagonist, Urania, is an astronomer who "hailed for sister / Starred Cassiopea in Golden Chair" (217). That is, Urania (whose namesake was the goddess of astronomy) allied herself with rationalty and science. Urania's worship of the stars—she terms it a "dream" (217), a "spell" (219)—and of her sisterhood with Cassiopea, a mortal woman transformed (ironically, as punishment) into an immortal constellation, links astronomical science, itself an expression of Hellenic rationalism, to the classical temples in Melville's Greece poems. Like the "god-like" columns in "Off Cape Colonna," like the Parthenon, "aloft" and "motionless," Cassiopea and the stars are also elevated in the heavens, remote and aloof from "fallen" Nature, below.

Attending a pleasure party in Rome, Urania finds herself, for the first time in her life, passionately aroused. Unfortunately, the man who attracts her is drawn not to Urania but to another, younger, woman. Torn between her devotion to science and her desire to "plunge / Deeper than Sappho, in a lunge / Piercing Pan's paramount mystery" (219), Urania at last enters an ancient temple, and kneels prayerfully before "an antique pagan stone," a "[c]olossal" statue of the "helmeted . . . armed Virgin." "Transcender!" Urania cries out to Minerva, "raise me up to thee, / Raise me and arm me!" (221). Urania has resolved to arm herself with Minerva's strength and banish passion once and for all. Her prayer, however, is answered not by Minerva, but by Amor (Cupid), son of Venus. "[I]ncensed" that Urania has prayed not to him, but to his adversary, Amor, in "vengeance," inflicts on Urania a fresh wave of painful passion. Forced to acknowledge her dual nature—her sisterhood with Venus as well as with Cassiopea—Urania sadly concludes: "[N]ever passion peace shall bring, / Nor Art inanimate for long / Inspire" (221).

The phrase "Art inanimate" refers both to the mute, stone statue of Minerva and to the classical ideal the statue represents. It is also applicable to the Parthenon. In its reasoned perfection, its marble inertness, the Parthenon, like the statue of Minerva, cannot "long inspire": it denies and excludes "Pan's paramount mystery," living Nature itself.

This realization helps clarify the meaning of "The Apparition," the final Greece poem in "Fruit of Travel Long Ago." Saving his most exalted praise of classical architecture for last, Melville favorably compares the Parthenon to the "supernatural Cross" that "[s]mote the Emperor Constantine / And turned his soul's allegiance there" (253). That this comparison is deeply equivocal becomes clear when one realizes that elsewhere in *Timoleon*, Melville is an outspoken *opponent* of Christian supernaturalism. In "The Age of the Antonines," for example, Melville contrasts the "Halcyon Age" of the pagan Antonine emperors (the most famous of whom was the Stoic Marcus Aurelius, author of *The Meditations*), with its this worldy tolerance and pluralism, and the benighted Christian supernaturalism that supplanted it: "The sting was not dreamed to be taken from death, / No Paradise pledged or sought, / But they reasoned of fate at the flowing feast, / Nor stifled the flowing thought" (235).

It was Constantine himself who ended the pagan "Halcyon Age" by imposing Christianity as the official religion of the Roman Empire. The consequences of this action for Western civilization are suggested in "The New Zealot to the Sun." Reflecting the biblical scholarship of the day, the poem traces Christian supernaturalism to its origin in Persia, "arch type of sway," and its subsequent sweep westward from "orient climes," "Mid terrors dinned," "Transmitted, spread in myths and creeds, / Houris and hells, delirious screeds / And Calvin's last extreme" (226).

In view of this Arnoldian antithesis of tolerant, this-worldly Hellenism and Hebraic, other-worldly fanaticism and dogmatism, which is emphasized as well in *Clarel* (Detlaff 214-18), the favorable comparison of the Parthenon to the "supernatural Cross" cannot be taken at face value. A clue to the underlying irony is suggested in the poem's title and subtitle. The Parthenon, "uplifted on its rock, first challenging the view on the approach to Athens" (253), is an "apparition," an appearance—much as the "supernatural Cross" that appeared to Constantine in the heavens was an apparition, an illusion. While the Cross "smote" Constantine and "turned his soul's allegiance" to Christianity, however, the classical temple's power is more limited. "If cynic minds you [the Parthenon] scarce

125

convert," Melville observes, "You try them, shake them, or molest" (253). Although not without appeal—the classical Antonine Age is itself appealing—the Parthenon, and the classical ideal it represents, has no power to "turn," or win, the "soul's allegiance." "Art inanimate" cannot "long inspire."

No wonder "Fruit of Travel Long Ago" ends not in Greece or in "Picturesque" Italy—where Melville's Mediterranean journey concluded in 1857—but elsewhere. Having rejected supernatural Christianity decades earlier, in *Clarel*, and classical "Art inanimate" in *Timoleon*, Melville turns, at the end of "Fruit of Travel," to another edifice that might conceivably win his "soul's allegiance": the Great Pyramid of Egypt, an object of fascination for Melville since *Moby-Dick*. Pondering the Great Pyramid's unimaginable antiquity, Melville observes, "Craftsmen, in dateless quarries dim, / Stones formless into forms did trim, / Usurped on Nature's self with Art, / And bade this dumb I AM to start, / Imposing him" (255).

The Great Pyramid, then, is "Art and Nature lodged together"; but who were its "craftsmen"? Resembling an Alp or a Grampian, the Great Pyramid appears "[m]ore like some Cosmic artisan's" handiwork than something fashioned by man. Indeed, in its mysterious antiquity, its incomprehensible vastness, its "dumb I AM," the Great Pyramid, rather than winning the soul's allegiance, threatens to engulf and annihilate it: "Slant from your inmost lead the caves / And labyrinths rumored. [He] who braves / And penetrates (old palmers said) / Comes out afar on deserts dead / And, dying, rave[s] (255).

Melville in his last years has not lost sight of the labyrinth that led Ahab and Pierre to madness, and eventually destroyed them; but he has no wish to re-enter the labyrinth himself. The poem that follows "The Great Pyramid," "L'Envoi," is also the last in *Timoleon*. "The yearning infinite recoils, / For terrible is earth!" Melville asserts (256). Having rejected the "supernatural Cross" and turned away from the Parthenon, Melville at the conclusion of *Timoleon* "recoils" from the Grampian-like Great Pyramid and all it represents.

Melville will continue searching for something in which he might believe, something capable of winning his "soul's allegiance," in his posthumously published Rose poems (in *Weeds and Wildings, with a Rose or Two*). In *Melville and His Circle: The Last Years*, William B. Dillingham explains how Melville came to write his Rose poems. Recently retired after 19 years in the New York Customs House, Melville began to cultivate roses in his backyard in New York City; he also read, and marked, two books in which the cultivation of roses is likened to a religious experience, a form of worship (140-44). The appeal of the Rose for Melville is not hard to fathom. Resonant with centuries of amatory, religious, and aesthetic symbolism, the archetypal Rose of Art is also iconically identical to the living rose of Nature, the queen of the flowers, cultivated and valued for its fragrance and beauty. In the Rose, then, Art and Nature are lodged together harmoniously at last, on a human scale, in a concrete universal that appeals in equal measure to the intellect and the emotions alike.

With their tone of gentle amorousness, of whimsical devotion, the Rose poems are among Melville's most charming productions. An undercurrent of chilliness is present in these poems, however: the cherished roses are subtly but unmistakably associated with death. In "The Vial of Attar," for example, Melville praises attar, a fragrant oil distilled from rose petals, but then laments, "There *is* nothing like the bloom; / And the Attar poignant minds me / Of the bloom that's passed away" (298). The attar and the bloom, then, replicate the Art/Nature dichotomy of Melville's Greece poems. As a work of Art, the attar may remind Melville of the bloom of Nature, but it is no substitute for the living rose itself: like the "inanimate" marble of the Parthenon, the inert rose of Art is, also, in a sense, dead. But, then, the living bloom from which the attar is distilled is itself transitory and mortal; like every natural organism, the living rose will "pass away," will die. Wherever one turns, then, whether to the living but mortal rose of Nature, or to the immortal but "inanimate" rose of Art, one cannot escape or evade death. Death is everywhere.

Melville explores this impasse not only in his Rose poems, but elsewhere in *Weeds and Wildings*. In "Rip Van Winkle's Lilac," the "laughing," eternally youthful Lilac planted by Rip (a symbol of Art) is juxtaposed with the decay and dissolution that carries away the lilac of Nature, the willow tree, Rip's house, Rip's wife, and eventually Rip himself (283-87). In "The Year," the wildflowers, birds, and woodland creatures that Melville recalls from his years at Arrowhead, his farm near Pittsfield, Massachusetts, are innocent and benign. In Melville's ironic rendering of them, however, they are also frozen by memory, archetypally unchanging and inert. The flora and fauna of "The Year," like the Rose, like the inert, marble columns in Melville's Greece poems, are frosted with the chill of death: "that terminating season," Melville dryly calls it (482).

In another venue I will offer a fuller explication of the relationship between artistic representation, Platonic archetypes, memory, and death, in *Weeds and Wildings*, the Rose poems, the Greece poems, and *Billy Budd*. Eventually I hope to show that in his final years, when Herman Melville was elderly, infirm, and near death himself, the secret motto of his late world-view and final works was neither "testament of acceptance" nor "unabated quarrel with God," but, rather: *memento mori*.

REFERENCES

Detlaff, Shirley. "Ionian Form and Esau's Waste: Melville's View of Art in *Clarel*." *American Literature* 54 (1982): 212-28.

Dillingham, William. *Melville and His Circle: The Last Years*. Athens: Georgia UP, 1996.

Ehrenberg, Victor. *From Solon to Socrates*. London: Methuen, 1968.

Emerson, Ralph Waldo. "The American Scholar." *Selections*. Ed. Stephen E. Whichler. Boston: Houghton Mifflin, 1957. 69-80.

Howard, Leon. *Herman Melville: A Biography*. Berkeley: U of California P, 1967.

Melville, Herman. *John Marr and Other Sailors*. Vincent 159-206.

——. *Journals*. Ed. Howard Horsford and Lynn Horth. Chicago: Northwestern UP, 1989.

——. *Timoleon and Other Poems*. Vincent 209-56.

——. *Weeds and Wildings, with a Rose or Two*. Vincent 259-310, 481-82.

Robillard, Douglas. "Wrestling With the Angel: Melville's Use of the Visual Arts in *Timoleon*." Sten 246-56.

Short, Bryan C. "'Like Bed of Asparagus: Melville and Architecture." Sten 104-16.

Stein, William Bysshe. *The Poetry of Melville's Late Years*. Albany: State U of New York P, 1970.

Sten, Christopher, ed. *Savage Eye: Melville and the Visual Arts*. Kent, OH: Kent State UP, 1991.

Vincent, Howard P., ed. *Collected Poems of Herman Melville*. Chicago: Hendricks House, 1947.

II

TRUTH'S RAGGED EDGES

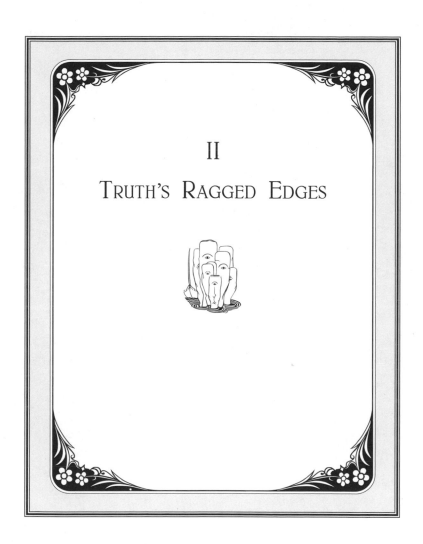

Hennig Cohen

Melville and Diogenes the Cynic

iterate Americans in the nineteenth century, Herman Melville among them, were familiar with the apocryphal doings and sayings of Diogenes the Cynic (ca. 412-332 BC). Accounts of his domicile in the tub, his persistent search for an honest man, his impudence, and his raillery were known to schoolboys even though neither Diogenes himself nor any contemporary provides us with the firm evidence to substantiate them. In fact, their ultimate source is Diogenes Laërtius' *The Lives and Opinions of Eminent Philosophers* (London, 1853; Sealts 183a) that appears to date from the early part of the third century. Melville surely imbibed such hand-me-down information, further diluted, as a pupil of "Latin Language" and "Classical Biography" enrolled in "a standard course leading to classical studies" (Titus 4-8) and as a sailor aboard the frigate *United States* casually browsing the ship's library that probably included another source, the "superexcellent biographies" in Plutarch's *Lives* (M, *W-J* 167-69). Melville's most originative source of information on Diogenes was Pierre Bayle's *Historical and Critical Dictionary* (Sealts 51), purchased in 1849.

The earliest example of Melville's exploitation of the Diogenes apocrypha occurs in the "romance," *Mardi* (1849), in Babbalanja's recitation of Bardianna's genially cynical "last Will and Testament" (M 3:582). It echoes the search for an honest man. Bardianna bequeaths his friend "Minta the Cynic" (Apemantus, Timon's cynical friend?—of whom more later) a considerable estate "to have and to hold, in trust [NB] for the first through-and-through honest man" who is "issue" of a succession of designated neighbors, but "in default of such issue, to any through-and-through honest man, issue of any body, to be found through the length and breadth of Mardi" (584). In a turn that looks forward to *The Confidence-Man* (1857), Bardianna further prescribes "Minta the Cynic to be the sole judge of all claims to the above-mentioned devise" and the residual trustee "until the aforesaid person be found" (584).

Melville used the tub motif in *Redburn* (1849) in a lame attempt at comic relief to offset the account of the starving Irish passengers during the return voyage of the *Highlander*. When Pat, a comic Irish stereotype, steals food, Captain Riga has him "coopered up" in a portable, makeshift pillory, half of "one of the large deck-tubs," with openings for his head and hands. His appearance is "so ridiculous" that he "laughed with the rest at the figure he cut," genially used his situation to con food and sympathy, "and would fain have continued playing Diogenes in the tub for the rest of this starving voyage" (M 4:284).

As Melville matured, Diogenes reference became one way of voicing the conflict between acceptance and skepticism, trust and no trust, heart and head, evidenced in a memorable letter to Hawthorne written during the composition of *Moby-Dick* (1851): "I stand for the heart. To the dogs with the head" (M 12:192)— the dogs of Diogenes, presumably, for the cynical philosopher was linked with dogs from the time of Aristotle, who explained that the Cynics, like dogs, "attack and bite" fools and knaves (Chambers's *Cyclopaedia*; in Sealts 128). They make a subtle appearance in "The Try-Works" chapter, where the progression is from the factual and straightforward to the rhapsodic, significant, and complex. Thus the chapter begins with a prosaic description of the works and their maintenance. The try-works are as capacious as a large tub and "polished . . . till they shine within like silver punch-bowls. During the night-watches some cynical old sailors will crawl into them and coil themselves away there for a nap" (M 6:421). Once more, although at a lower layer, we have Diogenes' tub, its presence confirmed by association with "cynical" and the comparison of old sailors curled up in it like sleeping dogs. The word *cynic* is linked etymologically to the Greek word for *dog*, the kind of linkage of special interest to Melville, given his play on the derivation of *whale* in the "Etymology" preamble to *Moby-Dick* (M 6:xv-xvi).

Diogenes Laërtius reports that the burial place of Diogenes the Cynic was marked with a shaft surmounted by a marble dog. The association of canines with cynics in general, and Diogenes in particular, trickled down through the centuries. In Melville's day it appeared in reference works such as *Anthon's Classical Dictionary* (Sealts 70; Bercaw 16) and schoolbooks. For example, Anthon, whose main source is Diogenes Laërtius, explains that *cynic* derives "from the Greek term for a 'dog,' an allusion to the *snarling* humour" of the Cynic philosophers. In similar language, a footnote to an extract from a sermon by Henry Ward Beecher, titled "The Cynic," anthologized in a typical textbook of the period, explains: "The name is derived from a Greek word for 'dog' because they lived more like dogs than men" (*National Fourth Reader* 124).

Melville could expect an educated reader to know the connection between cynics and dogs. Precisely when *he* came to know it cannot be determined, but the article on Diogenes in Bayle's *Dictionary* was a storehouse of information and incitement. He bought his set of the *Dictionary*, in the Tonson translation of 1710, soon after *Mardi* but prior to *Redburn*, and entranced by it, wrote Evert Duyckinck from Boston on 5 April 1849, that he intended "to lay the great old folios side by side & go to sleep on them thro' the summer" (M 11:128). Indeed, he does seem to have absorbed Bayle through the pores of his skin.

Bayle makes much of the tub and much more of Diogenes and dogs, justifying the etymological connection: "As for *Diogenes* the Cynick, his Name shews what he was; for 'tis as one should say, *Diogenes* who lived like a Dog." Dogs, like Diogenes, were physically dirty, immodest in their behavior, and "continually barking or biting People." When Alexander the Great came to pay his respects (Plutarch's "Antony" is Bayle's source), Diogenes is said to have inquired, "Art thou not afraid that I should bite thee, for I am a mad Dog?" The extent of Diogenes' "honesty" and his con-man logic, according to one of Bayle's anecdotes, may have exceeded the limits of Melville's Rabelaisian humor. Bayle reports that Diogenes "*brutishly* performed several lewd Actions"; for instance, "believing that it was a lawful thing to lie with a Woman, he concluded that there was no harm in laying with her in public." Bayle cites as a possible cause of Diogenes' death "the biting of a Dog," and he mentions the funerary monument topped with a marble dog (1101-3). He credits the bulk of his information to Diogenes Laërtius.

Melville marked his copy of Diogenes Laërtius heavily, including references to the tub, and he lined a number of Diogenes' acerbic apothegms and his comparisons of himself to a hunting dog, "a sort which most of those who praise do not like to take out hunting with them, because of the labor of keeping up with them; and in a like manner, you cannot associate with me, from fear of the pain I give you" (Cowen 491-92). Could Melville have been thinking of reader response, himself the dog who ran too far ahead? And what is the date of his purchase and his marginal marking? The publication date is 1853, but the book was rebound uniformly with a volume of Aristotle, dated 1889-90 (Sealts 14a and 14b).

Melville's most notable serving up of cynics and dogs (cf. "that good dish, man," 10:133), nicely seasoned with Timon and a dash of Diogenes, is to be found in *The Confidence-Man* (1857). The flavor is often sharp, although sometimes subtly blended. The word "'cynic' reaches a peak of frequency" in this novel (Coffler xi). Elizabeth Foster, commenting on one of the many references in canine terms to Black Guinea, an early manifestation of the Confidence-Man, notes that "Connotations of 'cynic,' 'misanthrope,' and 'fawning insincerity' cluster about Melville's use of *dog*" (Foster 296).

The Missouri bachelor, Pitch, at heart a philanthropist, assumes the role of misanthropic cynic to protect himself. It is a role that anticipates the old Dansker in *Billy Budd, Sailor* who observes the ship world "with a somewhat cynical regard" and whose "leading characteristic" is a "pithy guarded cynicism" (M *BB* 71), Pitch is quick to identify another, the agent of a Philosophical Intelligence Office, who slinks about "with a sort of canine deprecation" and wears a kind of dog collar engraved with what might be called the initials of his master, "P.I.O." Pitch denounces him as "a fair specimen" of a "Swindling" concern "kept by low-born cynics, under a fawning exterior wreaking their cynical malice on mankind" (10:114-15). In the "Tusculan disputations" that follow, Pitch is beguiled into dropping his cynical guard for a sort of "conditional degree of confidence" (10:127) and is victimized.

Pitch's confidence is rightly conditional, and he has second thoughts as he contemplates the riverside, a "swampy and squalid domain; and over it audibly mumbles his cynical mind to himself, as Apemantus' dog may have mumbled his bone" (10:129). Apemantus, epitomized in the folio cast list of Shakespeare's

Timon of Athens as a "churlish philosopher," is called a dog by others and is quick
to return the compliment. He feeds and feeds on Timon's misanthropy. When
he visits Timon in his cave, he accuses Timon of imitating his own churlish "manner," to which Timon replies, "'Tis, then, because thou does not keep a dog,
Whom I would imitate" (IV iii 199-200). Later in the same scene, when Timon
cynically asks who could possibly love anyone without "means," i.e., without a
fortune, and Apemantus replies, "Myself," Timon bites back: "I understand thee;
thou hadst some means to keep a dog" (IV iii 313-16), that is, to keep himself.
Melville placed a check mark at this point in his copy of *Timon* (Cowen 289).

Pairing Diogenes and Timon was not unusual. Montaigne in his *Essays* (Sealts
366), like Melville, considered "Diogenes . . . a juster judge than Timon, surnamed
the Man-hater" (197). Timon and Apemantus inhabit the narrowly defined world
of dog-eat-dog. They are like the whale, "a self-consuming misanthrope" (M
6:422) that fuels the try-works with its own bulk. The world of Diogenes and
Pitch is more flexible, contingent, shifty. In such domain a philanthrope may
appear, may in fact *be*, a misanthrope—and the reverse may also obtain. Pitch,
pondering the margins of swampy terrain and mumbling his bone, is accosted
by a self-titled "cosmopolitan" (10:132) in full fig and fully primed to win his
confidence. Having escaped the herb-doctor's scam when misanthropic but been
taken in by an employment agent when philanthropy swayed him, and with Timon the categorical man-hater, freshly in mind, Pitch stands his ground.

In a last attempt to garner Pitch's confidence, the Cosmopolitan poses a question: "was not that humor, of Diogenes . . . better than that of the less wise Athenian, which made him a skulking scare-crow in pine-barrens? An injudicious gentleman, Lord Timon" (10:137). Pitch extends his hand, which the Cosmopolitan
takes as a token of brotherhood until Pitch, albeit his sincerity in question, embraces him as a fellow misanthrope, but at the same time reminds him that "a
brace of misanthropes" can hardly "be brothers." The Cosmopolitan stares "in
blank amaze," and Pitch, as if Timon and Diogenes are one and the same, wa-
vers: "Won't do. You are Diogenes, Diogenes in disguise. I say—Diogenes masquerading as a cosmopolitan" (10:137-38). The Cosmopolitan can distinguish between a "man-hooter" like Diogenes and "a man-hater" like Timon, but at this
point the befuddled Pitch conflates them. Momentarily for Pitch, all cynics

merge—Diogenes, Timon, Apemantus, dogs, and cynics humane and philanthropic or whatever. Nor does the Cosmopolitan make too fine a point of it. He is not looking for an honest man but for confidence and trust, and he advises, for reasons, benign or otherwise: "[G]et you confidence. See how distrust has duped you. I Diogenes?" Pitch, not the Cosmopolitan, if anyone is Diogenes, "Diogenes, that honest heart," Melville, in a late poem, would call him. In fact, in the final sentence of a chapter headed "A philanthropist undertakes to convert a misanthrope," a "philanthropist . . . less lightsome" takes leave of a "discomfited misanthrope," and our misanthrope vacillates in his misanthropy.

The cynical dogs of Diogenes make their appearance in Melville's verse explicitly in "The Apparition" but are submerged among the elements of a complex imagery cluster in "The House-top." "The House-top" in *Battle-Pieces* (1866) is about the New York draft riots of July 1863. The city is burning. Above, the red star, Sirius, in the constellation Canis Major, the star of dog days, "Balefully glares red Arson." Below "civil charms / And priestly spells . . . dissolve" into anarchy. Then: "Wise Draco comes. . . / In code corroborating Calvin's creed / And cynic tyrannies of honest kings; . . . / . . . and the Town, redeemed, / Gives thanks" (*SP* 24).

The imagery of jungle, parching flame, riot, and military power are appropriate to Melville's subject, which he underpins with a hint of the Diogenes material. The dog Sirius relates to Diogenes' dog, and both are paired with Draco, who like Diogenes, seeks through extreme behavior to restore moral and civic order.

On 16 June 1891, a copy of *Timoleon* was deposited at the Library of Congress. Melville died the following September. The content of *Timoleon* is predominately Hellenic. A concluding group of eighteen poems is captioned "Fruit of travel long ago." The first six have Italian settings, the next ten are Greek, the last two Egyptian. Their tone is one of "Repose that does of Plato tell—," as a quatrain following "The Attic Landscape" (and entitled simply "The Same") has it (*CP* 246). The last of the Greek poems, "The Apparition," begs questions and provokes conjectures. Its subject, Melville states in a headnote, is "The Parthenon uplifted on its rock first challenging the view on the approach to Athens" (*SP* 156). Melville's source is revealed in a laconic entry in his travel journal of 8 February 1857: "Parthenon elevated like cross of Constantine" (15:99). In another poem titled "The Parthenon," he describes the temple "Aerial gleaming . . . / In noon of day divine" (*SP* 153). An apparition is a divine manifestation, so the word is appropriate to both the temple of Athene Parthenope, the virgin Athene herself, and the cross of Constantine. They are equated in the poem.

The first stanza of "The Apparition" describes the vision of the "supernatural Cross" and the conversion of the emperor. The second notes the effect of the Parthenon on the Athenians: "If cynic minds you scarce convert, / You try them," lines clarified with reference to those in an earlier draft that reads, "Miraculous human Fane! / You strike with awe the cynic heart, / Convert it from disdain" (*SP* 156 and 248).

The final stanza is a speculation on the effect an apparition of the Parthenon could have had on Diogenes the Cynic: "Diogenes, that honest heart, / Lived ere your date began; / Thee had he seen, he might have swerved / In mood nor barked so much at Man" (*SP* 156). Diogenes transformed? Converted to a mild and genial cynicism? The idea was good but anachronistic. Melville erred in his dates. Diogenes was alive in 438 BC when the Parthenon was built.[1]

Melville began with commonplace lore associated with Diogenes. In *Mardi* the search for an honest man is an occasion for a brash young writer to show off his wit. In *Redburn* the tale of the tub is ineptly used to touch up a picture of human misery. Reference to cynics and dogs in the try-works tub in *Moby-Dick* is a deft and delicate touch. The baroque elaboration in *The Confidence-Man* is stunning in every sense.

"The Apparition" is a winding down, visionary, envisioning the possibility of conversions. Melville asks: had Diogenes not lived before the Parthenon was built, might he have behaved in a different manner? "The Apparition" is positioned toward the end of Melville's last published work. Although his hypothesis is undermined by his evidently mistaken chronology, it nevertheless leads one to ponder how much, if at all, is "The Apparition" a last new testament? Acceptance? Irony? Conversion?

NOTES

1 Cf. Bryant, 238-39 and 249. Please note that I have slightly revised this paragraph with respect to the apparent anachronism after discussing it briefly with Professor Cohen. Had he been

able to do so, he would have clarified the passage himself, but time did not allow it; if the reading is erroneous, the error is mine (S.E.M.).

REFERENCES

Anthon, Charles. *A Classical Dictionary*. New York: Harper, 1855.

Bayle, Pierre. *Historical and Critical Dictionary*. Trans. Jacob Tonson. London: C. Harper et al., 1710.

Beecher, Henry Ward. *Seven Lectures to Young Men*. Indianapolis, IN: Cutler, 1844 (quoted in *National Fourth Reader*, listed below).

Bercaw, Mary K. *Melville's Sources*. Evanston, IL: Northwestern University Press, 1987.

Bryant, John. *Melville and Repose*. New York: Oxford University Press, 1993.

Chambers, Ephraim. *Cyclopaedia; or, Universal Dictionary of Arts and Sciences*. London: D. Midwinter [etc.], 1738.

Coffler, Gail H. *Melville's Classical Allusions*. Westport, CT: Greenwood Press, 1985.

Cowen, Walker. *Melville's Marginalia*. New York: Garland, 1987.

Diogenes Laërtius. *Lives and Opinions of Eminent Philosophers*. Trans. C. D. Yonge. London: G. Bell, 1915.

Duban, James. "The Translation of Pierre Bayle's *An Historical and Critical Dictionary* Owned by Melville," *Papers of the Bibliographical Society of America* 71 (1977): 347-51.

Foster, Elizabeth S., ed. *The Confidence-Man*, by Herman Melville. New York: Hendricks House, 1954.

Melville, Herman. *Billy Budd, Sailor*. Ed. Harrison Hayford and Merton M. Sealts, Jr. Chicago: University of Chicago Press, 1962.

——. *The Collected Poems*. Edited by Howard P. Vincent. New York: Hendricks House, 1947.

——. *Selected Poems*. Ed. Hennig Cohen. New York: Fordham University Press, 1991.

——. *The Writings*. Ed. Harrison Hayford, Hershel Parker, and G. Thomas Tanselle. Evanston and Chicago: Northwestern University Press and the Newberry Library, 1968-.

Montaigne, Michel Eyquem. *Essays*. Trans. Charles Cotton. London: Navarre Society, 1923.

National Fourth Reader. Ed. Richard G. Parker and J. Madison Watson. New York: A. S. Barnes, 1862.

Sealts, Merton M., Jr. *Melville's Reading*, 2nd ed., Columbia, SC: University of South Carolina Press, 1988.

Titus, David K. "Herman Melville at the Albany Academy," *Extracts* 42 (1980): 4-8.

RACHELA PERMENTER

PYTHAGORAS AND NONDUALITY:

MELVILLE AMONG THE PRE-SOCRATICS

In the "Stowing Down and Clearing Up" chapter of *Moby-Dick*, Melville writes about how "man-killing" life is. After oil, blood, blubber, and bone drench the decks in "The Try-Works," Ishmael describes the men having "tea by the moonlight" on the pristine "piazza of the forecastle" as though nothing horrendous occurred at all. (What messy murder? "Away, and bring us the napkins.") In one of the hundreds of necessary and "unnecessary duplicates," doubles, and dichotomies in the novel, Melville gives us the striking contrary of blood-washed fiery hell in "The Try-Works" and "spotless dairy room" in "Stowing Down." After the Sisyphean task of cleaning up, then another whale, then cleaning up, then "there she blows," and "the whole weary thing again," Ishmael repeats, "Yet this is life." He refers to Pythagoras's theory of reincarnation as he invokes the ancient demi-god: "Oh! The metempsychosis! Oh! Pythagoras, that in bright Greece, two thousand years ago, did die, so good, so wise, so mild; I sailed with thee along the Peruvian coast last voyage and, foolish as I am, taught thee, a green simple boy, how to splice a rope!" (429).

In this most recent incarnation, so Ishmael's joke goes, he taught Pythagoras how to be a seaman and philosophically how to make the severed unified with the central Pythagorean concept that the world as perfect whole is also the many. When woven as a rope, fragments at the same time exist separately and are lost to the whole.

Since Harrison Hayford's "Unnecessary Duplicates,"[1] scholars have been talking about the "twoness" of *Moby-Dick:* two narratives, two titles, two whaling ports, two inns, two beds, two Queequegs (one as Bulkington), two Ahabs (one as Peleg), the "double value of terminology,"[2] and "double talk speaking,"[3] as well as the narrative splits in *Pierre* and *The Confidence-Man*, and most recently the coexistence of Melville's sexism and his feminism, his blending of masculine and feminine,[4] and his anti-colonialism in tandem with his colonialism.[5] Are these mistakes? Inevitabilities? Warring opposites? Statements about Narcissism?[6] Deconstructions of binary oppositions?[7] A lament against our post-lapsarian condition? A complaint against Descartes' gift to us—splitting our souls from our bodies? I argue that they are all of the above, although not likely "mistakes," and as such indicate only one "side" of the novel's larger counterpoise of double vision and single vision as well as of the many and the one.

Ishmael's invocation of Pythagoras is one of the many golden keys to the "great floodgates" of the novel's "wonder-world." That key offers a glimpse of what reminds us of Emerson's bridge "where Being passes into Appearance and Unity into Variety" (*CW* III: 9) and Thoreau's fishing line which flies up to the sphere then down to the elements, catching "two fishes as it were with one hook" (*Walden* 118). It is Walden Pond itself, "earth's eye" and "God's drop," which "lying between the earth and the heavens ... partakes of the color of both" (*Walden* 119), and Melville's "equal eye" in "doubts of all things earthly, and intuitions of some things heavenly" (*Moby-Dick* 374). Perhaps it is his attempt to "strike the uneven balance." As Wenke describes it, the sperm whale embodies "the living nexus between phenomenal and noumenal realms" (111), and he argues that Ishmael places "the interpreting self at some precarious boundary, a point at which 'visible' surfaces give way to intimations regarding the nature of 'invisible spheres'" (116). Ishmael describes those two realms as seemingly incompatible, but nevertheless the only life we have: "For hardly have we mortals by long toilings, extracted from this world's vast bulk its small but valuable sperm; and then, with weary patience, cleansed ourselves from its defilements, and learned to live here in clean tabernacles of the soul; hardly is this done, when—There she blows!" (429).

It is that point of perception; in fact, it is this (non)dual perception itself, particularly that which deals with the spirit/flesh dichotomy, for which Melville uses Pythagoras in *Moby-Dick*.[8] Moreover, it is nonduality in its postmodern form which I believe will keep Melville studies alive and well for quite awhile.

First, let me define the term *(non)duality*. The "non" of the term is best understood if imagined as placed in parentheses, since without them "nonduality" may easily, but mistakenly, suggest *not duality* or perhaps *oneness*. With the parentheses, the prefix *(non)* does not annul the duality, but *adds* oneness to the twoness. This is a crucial addition. Although there is no difference in the meaning of the term with or without parentheses, I use them intermittently for the purpose of emphasis and to jog the reader's memory of the term's meaning.[9] The concept of nonduality is part of a perennial thread some would label Romantic, which ties East to West and pre-Socratics and primitive to postmodern.[10] The most substantial occasions of nonduality as a mode of perception with varying degrees of ontological, epistemological, and metaphysical implications have been made with the pre-Socratic Greeks, traditional Eastern thought, the literature and philosophy of the Romantics, Native American literature, recent continental philosophy, and contemporary physics.[11]

I use the term *(non)duality* to indicate "the two-and-the-one," as it is presented in many philosophical constructs. It is the *coexistence* of "two" and "one." It indicates a concept and a mode of perception which embrace both duality and oneness in one thought. When referring to Chaucer and Shakespeare, Peter Elbow affirms that the Boethian counterpoise of "saying opposite things at the same time" (16) is valuable and "one of the patterns of thought that makes wise people wise" (161). As Mircea Eliade stresses in much of his work as a religious historian,[12] "the *summum bonum* is situated beyond polarities" (*Quest* 169). Hélène Cixous links her belief in "truth as tension, as movement" to Archimedes, Montaigne, Shakespeare, Dostoyevsky, and Derrida (*Root-prints* 85). She calls it "thinking of/on both sides" (*Root-prints* 25).[13] Irigaray explains, "We are luminous. Beyond 'one' or 'two'" (71).

In a detailed and complex study of nonduality, David Loy argues that of the three Eastern traditions which have been the most influential in Asia—Mahayana Buddhism, the Vedanta branch of Hinduism, and Taoism—each asserts a condition or perception of (non)duality which eases the struggle with human dualisms and which reveals truth but only in small, nonlethal doses which must remain both inside and outside us.[14] Loy also uncovers the nondual in an impressive gathering of Western thinkers, which begins with the pre-Socratics and ends with Gadamer and Derrida.

It is no coincidence that D. H. Lawrence begins his essay "The Two Principles" with reference to Melville's use of the sea "as the great protagonist" (Lawrence 227). In looking for "some terms to express such elemental connections as between the ocean and the human soul" (227), Lawrence turns to the pagan world of the Pythagoreans and the Orphists, and to Heraclitus. He looks past the dualities of Plato and Aristotle to describe the "apparently perfect" ancient cosmic theories. I am convinced that Lawrence refers to Melville before he unravels his own theories of nonduality because he has experienced a sound reading of *Moby-Dick*.[15] Such a reading of Melville's work emphasizes the importance of ancient Greek worldviews as they blend with Eastern influences in Melville's thought. His familiarity with the pre-Socratics, particularly through his reading of Pierre Bayle and Goethe, helped create his grasping for the "pagan" nondual realms in *Moby-Dick*.

Pythagoras, an Ionian Greek born about 570 BC on the island of Samos, was the first to call the universe "kosmos" and according to Bayle was "the first of the ancient sages who took the name of Philosopher" (665). Plato wrote about him, as did Aristotle, and Xenophanes satirized his belief in the transmigration of souls.[16] He was later rather canonized by Christians and neo-Platonists and obscured by legend although he remains to be considered a father of contemporary mathematics. Melville also would have been familiar with Pythagoras through Edmund Burke, Thomas Browne, and several of his philosophical reference books.[17]

Those familiar with the pre-Socratics refer to The Pythagorean Table of Opposites usually in this manner: limited/unlimited, odd/even, one/many, right/left, male/female, rest/motion, straight/curved, light/darkness, good/evil, square/oblong. As associated with their number theory, odd numbers are "limiting," and even numbers are "unlimited"; the number one, however, is both even and odd, and represents the total universe. One can see how Plato's forms and idealism were related to the Pythagoreans, but we should keep in mind that the table itself, as a dualistic view of the universe, was neither original with the Pythagorean school nor accepted by all its members. In fact, many scholars believe that the Pythagoreans instead used the table to emphasize (non)duality rather than duality.

According to G. E. R. Lloyd, for example, the early Greeks were as divided about binaries as their schematic table itself was about the cosmos.[18] Melville most likely read Bayle's analysis: Pythagoras "said that unity was the principle of all things, and that out of it came the subject it made use of as it's [*sic*] matter, and that out of it's [*sic*] action upon that matter came out numbers, figure, elements, the visible world... for, according to Plutarch, he admitted of *two independent principles, Unity and Binary*, and ascribed to the first the Divine Essence... and to the second... matter" (674, my emphasis). Along the lines of Heraclitus, who saw the unity of opposites, Pythagoreans saw the world as a *mixture* or commingling of principles, cosmological forces, or "moving causes"; yet from the binary classifications of the table, some of the early Greeks and Aristotle drew logical and specious divisions which were concretized in social and philosophical thought. Although not the dominant Pythagorean intention, many of these static splits and their columnar associations have endured as implacable contradictories, the most pernicious of which is the forced homologizing from the powerful and sustaining tropes *male* and *female*. Despite Pythagorean intentions about fiery water as God-stuff (much like "The Candles" chapter of *Moby-Dick*), the ensuing logic found the (non)duality aspect less rational and emphasized the duality part so strongly as distinct "parts" of a whole that Aristotle's hierarchal way of looking at these pairs remains preferred today despite being challenged by a postmodern Zeitgeist.[19]

The Pythagoreans, then, stressed the dependence of the dynamics of world structure on the interaction of contraries or pairs of opposites, believing that the cosmos is an organism. This (non)duality is evident in the "two independent principles, Unity and Binary," and the *oneness* and *oddness* of the number one in its number theory. Thom points out the "Pythagorean belief in a basic and pervasive constitutive principle, whether it be 'breath' or 'number';... by breathing in the void, the undivided universe (the one) becomes divided, which division is the origin of numbers" (187). Although the mortal/immortal, spirit/flesh dichotomy is used by the Pythagoreans, for the most part, they deny the basis of ancient Greek religion, namely, the fundamental opposition between the divine and mortal spheres (Thom 108). Pythagoras, for example, was believed to be semi-divine, a representation of the nonduality of spirit and flesh, related to Apollo, able to fly among the spheres, and is said to have a golden thigh (Thom 173). In the "Doubloon" chapter of *Moby-Dick*, Flask notes that Queequeg seems to think the sun is in his thigh, as he looks at his hieroglyphic tattoos. The sun in Libra (the scales, of course) shines above on the gold coin.

A commonly repeated belief of scholars who try to capsulize Pythagorean thought is that Phythagoreanism interweaves rationalism and irrationalism "more inseparably than does any other movement in ancient Greek thought" (Guthrie, "Pythagoras" 37). As well, *Moby-Dick* forms such a nonduality with the apparent dichotomies of idealism/empiricism, spirit/flesh, and subject/object. Lightheartedly one could see that Moby Dick himself followed the Pythagorean dictum "Wear white clothes" and, more seriously, he certainly followed their rule "Refrain from speaking about the Holy." Bayle relates legends which suggest that some Pythagoreans "chose to die rather than to reveal so great a secret. A Pythagorean woman cut out her tongue, lest the severity of the torments should force her to speak" (671). In "The Prairie" chapter, we are told that the sperm whale's great genius comes from his Sphinx-like repose. Ishmael is reminded by this "pyramidical silence" that "had the great Sperm Whale been known to the young Orient World, he would have been deified" as was "the crocodile of the Nile, because the crocodile is tongueless; and the Sperm Whale has no tongue, or at least it is so exceedingly small, as to be incapable of protrusion" (347).

Melville also mentions Pythagoras in the first chapter of the novel, "Loomings." As a joke about gastric wind and a statement about mortal struggle, Ishmael tells us, "For as in this world, head winds are far more prevalent than winds from astern (that is, if you never violate the Pythagorean maxim)" (6). That maxim being of course, "Don't eat beans," part of the dietary restrictions of the Pythagoreans' spiritual discipline (Bayle 670-72). This mention of Pythagoras in chapter one is significant because it is all right there in "Loomings" really. Not a small feat. It appears Melville had taken all of *Moby-Dick* and condensed it into its opening chapter, challenging the reader to add water to it as one would to a packet of dried soup—seas of water, of course, "that unsounded ocean" of water we "gasp in" which Ishmael calls Life (321) and which Melville attempts with grandeur and self-mockery to put into one novel. "Loomings" balances profundity with what the "Hyena" chapter describes as the humor necessary to see both the magnitude and the "general joke" that is the universe. The universe of *Moby-Dick*, and perhaps for Melville, plays incessant sleight-of-hand with the eternal white truth which is and is not there, which is both many and one, as is Ishmael's spliced rope in his lesson to Pythagoras.

Ishmael introduces the sea as having both material and mystical powers, with both its hard-knock, salty, and sensual actuality and its metaphorical role as the unknown, the unconscious which bids us all to dive. Getting "just as nigh the water as they possibly can without falling in" is the human response to some "magnetic virtue" of the sea that makes most of us at some time or another want to be divers and philosophers, to try to learn what Truth and human *being* are. Yet with chiding self-mockery, Ishmael makes it clear that actually going to sea is as suicidal as a "pistol and ball" or "Cato's sword." And why is that suicidal? Because in *Moby-Dick* the human condition (or the normal human perspective) is divided, but Truth is the (non)duality of divided and whole. We can have moments when we see that, but we cannot *be* whole. This is our tragedy. This is why we hang ourselves when we say "God" and separate ourselves from whatever *is* "God." Using language keeps us in duality or divided perception, and we lose that moment of (non)duality. It is akin to being thrown out of Eden and forced to name things. Melville writes, "as soon as you say *Me*, a *God*, a *Nature*, so soon you jump off from your stool and hang from the beam" (that is, affirm one side of the duality, which is mortal).[20]

It seems that Melville's central concerns had not changed much since he had Babbalanja in *Mardi* speak about the Truth of human *being* and the mysterious link/separation of body and soul: "Oh, Man, Man, Man! thou are harder to solve, than the Integral Calculus—yet plain as a primer; harder to find than the philosopher's-stone—yet ever at hand; a more cunning compound than an alchemist's—yet a hundred weight of flesh, to a penny weight of spirit; soul and body glued together, firm as atom to atom, seamless as the vestment without joint, warp or woof—yet divided, as by a river, spirit from flesh" (433). Seamless *and* divided.

This nondual concept can help with the conundrum of why Ahab is both monomaniacal and split from crown to sole, split like a river, yet his soul bleeds into his body. Ahab's problem is that he thinks he could be whole. As if Truth were only singular and can be lived as such, he wishes the blacksmith could smooth out the seam between his eyes with anvil and hammer. This is madness, of course; one cannot live there, as Pip clearly shows. For Babbalanja, babbler of the Truth for which Ishmael searches, the Truth is at the boundary line which reveals no boundary; the seamless seam is in each of us: "We are twain—yet indivisible; all things—yet a poor unit at best" (433). Similar in spirit to Pip or to one of Shakespeare's babbling fools and precursor in some ways to Queequeg, Babbalanja speaks "heaven's sense" as "man's insanity." In Persian, *baab* means "gate" or "gateway," at the border between truth and ignorance, spirit and separation.[21] Finally, "Loomings" introduces the "appalling" color-inclusive and color-exclusive whiteness of nonduality, the two and the one. Ishmael's "wild conceits" of whales are processing "two by two" before him, but in the center is the multifarious "one"—"one grand hooded phantom" (7).

Carolyn Porter maintains that Ishmael, speaking largely from a boundary, "both subverts authority and clings to it" (106). I would further clarify, however, that there is no *autonomous* authority to which Ishmael clings; rather, with the idea "Who ain't a slave?" he forwards the proposal that we all have to be subservient to some "code" or another at different times for different purposes; in that sense the authority is both Necessity and our own creation, our "practical presence." As Melville presents it, the (non)dual may allow an appearance of Truth which we can occasionally glimpse as if, like a frightened doe, it runs through the forest (and which afterward we can remain aware of), but it is not a place where we can live. Part of human *being* is living only in partial truth since we cannot live in the elusive interstice where "all" can be perceived.

According to *Moby-Dick*'s narrative pattern, we cannot deny those rare appearances nor can we rely on them. Ishmael's narrative can lead the reader to glimpses of nonduality by (1) presenting dualities, (2) blurring the distinctions between those dualities, (3) forcing the reader to choose a "side" as a temporary configuration of truth, and (4) shaking a buffalo robe of some kind to lead the reader to question that choice. For as soon as we decide that Queequeg is more

"Christian" than Christians, we are reminded of his savageness; as soon as we decide that he has the wisdom of a holy man, we are reminded that he prefers to eat human flesh. It is Queequeg the flesh-eater who is life-giver as he performs the "delivery of Tashtego" from the life-oozing, spermaceti-filled head of the dead sperm whale (344). Queequeg is overtly (non)dual: in one being, a civilized savage, a rational nonrational creature with dark and light checkerboard skin who designs a coffin life-buoy. Lined with carved symbols which he embodies as tattoos of all his unspeakable holy/savage truths of the two and the one, Queequeg's box of death is life, and in the end saves Ishmael. With golden thigh, Queequeg the cannibal is a kind of incarnation of Pythagoras the vegetarian.

Moby-Dick offers blueprints for balance and openings to (non)duality as it foregrounds, accepts, and refuses dualities. As well, it offers balance as it denies hope for maintaining it. For example, Ishmael uses a philosophical metaphor in describing the hoisting of a right whale's head as it balances the weight of the sperm whale's head on the opposite side of the ship. He declares that "When on one side you hoist in Locke's head, you go over that way; but now, on the other side, hoist in Kant's and you come back again; but in very poor plight." Ishmael, although aware that he cannot resist his own philosophical dives, recommends throwing "all these thunderheads overboard, and then you will float light and right" (327). According to Ishmael, we cannot take on board, that is, fully embrace any ideology without being somehow wrong or only partially right. If we try to balance it by taking on another, we can only be counterpoised for a moment before we lose sight of the larger (non)dual truth and we become confused in apparent contradictions in the search for right mindedness. Such a truth may bring a moment of insight, but no one will be designing any bridges or getting through the comfortable demands of a normal day with (non)dual vision.[22]

The nonduality of the whales' heads also shows us the nondualities of Stoicism and Platonism, empiricism and idealism. We see this (non)duality only for a fleeting moment, however, before, as Ishmael reminds us, first one head, then the other will be returned to the sea. His presentation and denial of first one-sidedness and then duality do not preclude all apprehensions of nonduality; despite centuries of poetic efforts, no one has yet learned to live in and write from an interstice, even when praising it. Nonetheless, much of *Moby-Dick* can be found in those interstices, floating "light and right," and many of Melville's "truths" lie hidden between gross dualities, "forced to fly like a scared white doe in the woodlands."[23]

A helpful metaphor for nonduality is that of a knife blade. As Thoreau explains, "If you stand right fronting and face to face with a fact, you will see the sun glimmer on both its surfaces, as if it were a cimeter" (66). If the blade were held before you, it would appear to have two sides, but it is not two, nor is it a fusion of two of anything. It is one, but its oneness is perceived as two. If the blade could be held at the bridge of your nose, and if your eyes could focus in such a position, you could see the dissolution of dualism by the change of perceptual viewpoint. If we wish to extend the metaphor to conceptualize much Eastern and Romantic thought, we can tack binary concepts to alternate sides of the blade: form ↔ formlessness, subject ↔ object, good ↔ evil, unity ↔ plurality, spiritual ↔ material, eternal ↔ temporal, duality ↔ (non)duality. With our limited perceptual abilities, normally only one side of the blade can be dominant in our vision at one time. We can only turn the blade over in our hands and take it on faith or from some suggestive glimpses that the other side exists as we look at its "opposite." Subject thus appears distinct from object, spiritual is separate from material, and separateness is the "opposite" of wholeness. Yet in some rare "good moments," we can see at the same time that there are binaries and there are no binaries; we can see the "two and the one."

It is suggested then that the *apprehension* of the nondual, or such *experiences* of the oneness in multiplicity or in spirit/flesh are only available in moments of epiphany. As Thoreau continues his metaphor of the scimitar, he suggests, "you will . . . feel its sweet edge dividing you through the heart and marrow, and so you will happily conclude your mortal career" (66). Beholding the nondual for too long of course ends in the truth or reality of giving up our mortal existence. Nonetheless, many Romantic and Eastern thinkers, as well as many other Westerners, have written volumes in attempts to use words and images to help even the "nonspiritual" among us form concepts of nonduality. Despite the claims that the *experience* or the *true* understanding can only be apprehended non-rationally, it is also claimed that an intellectual acceptance of the condition of nonduality is possible, desirable, and *close* to understanding—at least somehow more "true" than a rational denial of it. We can list Eastern and literary descriptions of transcendental moments: Hindu and Buddhist nirvana, Buddhist satori, Emerson's moment of "perfect exhilaration," Whitman's moments of "peace and knowledge that pass all the argument of the earth"; and Bloom lists, "Stevens's 'irrational moment,' Wordsworth's 'spot of time,' Pater's 'privileged moment,' Joyce's 'epiphany,' Yeats's moments when he is blessed and can bless, Browning's 'good moment,' Blake's 'moments in each day that Satan's Watch Fiends cannot find,' Lawrence's moments of breakthrough, Hart Crane's 'sudden revelations'" (Bloom 327). Implications and "uses" of such moments are distinct for each writer, and certainly not all of them are helpful to an understanding of Melville or of the Romantic element in postmodernism. One thing is clear, however: all these moments are attempted descriptions of some kind of nondual experience. Our usual experience is dualistic, and so is the language that expresses the nondual, yet at some points in some minds these metaphors work to help conceptualize (non)duality. In Melville's famous "Dollars damn me" letter to Hawthorne, he describes the "all feeling" when he recognizes an uncomfortable affinity with Goethe: "In reading some of Goethe's sayings . . . I came across this, '*Live in the all.*'. . . As with all great genius, there is an immense deal of flummery in Goethe, and in proportion to my own contact with him, a monstrous deal of it in me. . . . This 'all' feeling, tho', there is some truth in. You must often have felt it, lying in the grass on a warm summer's day. Your legs seem to send out shoots into the earth. Your hair feels like leaves upon your head. This is the *all* feeling" (Leyda 413). Melville then immediately warns that too long in such revery will cause one to plummet from the masthead. He writes, "But what plays the mischief with the truth is that men will insist upon the universal application of a temporary feeling or opinion" (413). If *universal* is read in the sense of *general, common, widespread, or ubiquitous*, rather than *cosmic* or *absolute*, then Melville is perhaps not dismissing the feeling or perspective as silly flummery, but is struck by the requisite elusiveness of flummery that is clearly impractical as it gives a glimpse of the all and the many.[24]

As Melville represents some kind of (non)dual truth as Moby Dick, Ishmael describes the eyes of a sperm whale and presents "a curious and most puzzling question" but hesitates to articulate it; instead, he tells us, "I must be content with a hint" (330). He then presents Melville's strongest trope for nonduality by continuing our examination of the whales' heads and comparing a human's eyes with those of a whale. First, the human eye: "So long as a man's eyes are open in the light, the act of seeing is involuntary... Nevertheless... it is quite impossible for him, attentively, and completely, to examine any two things—however large or however small—at one and the same instant of time... But if you now come to separate these two objects, and surround each by a circle of profound darkness; then, in order to see one of them, in such a manner as to bring your mind to bear on it, the other will be utterly excluded from your contemporary consciousness" (330-31). Whereas the human eye sees objects as unified, Ishmael's description of the whale's vision, on the other hand, suggests something different: a coalescence of double vision and single vision. For the eyes of a whale are situated on its head approximately where our ears are and the animal cannot see anything directly in front of it: "True, both his eyes, in themselves, must simultaneously act; but is his brain so much more comprehensive, combining, and subtle than man's, that he can at the same moment of time attentively examine two distinct prospects, one on one side of him, and the other in an exactly opposite direction? If he can, then is it as marvellous a thing in him, as if a man were able simultaneously to go through the demonstrations of two distinct problems in Euclid" (331). Thus when Ishmael describes perceptions of the whiteness of the whale, he does so to give his reader the eyes of a whale that "can at the same moment of time attentively examine two distinct prospects" (331). In this respect, Melville holds a knife blade between our eyes to allow us Pythagorean visions of (non)duality which subtly combine "twoness" into one without loss of the two, but then quickly drops both heads separately back into the depths of the sea. He reminds us that we cannot live here—it is a dangerous place. Just when we learn to live "in the clean tabernacles of the soul," there she blows. In addition to the *Pequod* crew as victims of Ahab's unwillingness to see this truth, Melville arranges the deaths in *Pierre* of those who are too heavenly for earth, and of Pierre who strove to be. The narrator insists that "the gods love the soul of a man... but they abominate his body" and no "Pythagorean... dietings on apple-parings... ever fit thy body for heaven" (299).[25]

This, ultimately, is the tragedy of *Moby-Dick*. The truth is in forms of (non)duality, but a sustained perception of it by ordinary mortals is fatal. Diving into one or the other side of the Cartesian split will kill us.[26] Cixous very succinctly explains with a Christian metaphor what can be specifically applied to the fatal error of Pierre and more generally to that of Ahab: "whoever imitates Jesus Christ on this planet kills. The plane of the absolute lurks, divides, cuts, kills on this earth" (*Rootprints* 75). As Pip demonstrates, we cannot look for long at the form of God. As far as Moby Dick is Melville's trope for such a look, the white whale's nondual vision blinds him from the front and causes him to crash that prairie-like brow into sure death for the humans who follow Ahab's drive to be seamless. Ishmael's "insular Tahiti" saves him in the form of Queequeg's coffin of hieroglyphs that represent the nondual. A belief in it as some kind of needed truth can calm and center us, but it is only beheld in brief glimpses from the boundary.

Nonduality helps us see Melville's skeptical Romanticism. Where most Romantics focus more on idealism and the possibilities of those unifying moments and a little less on the dangers of reaching for them, Melville consistently reminds us that there are sharks out there whenever he balances idealism with nascent existentialism and the "all feeling" with "this *Being* of the matter" in Pythagorean nondualities.

NOTES

1   Others, such as Sheila Post-Lauria, have argued that duplicates were indeed necessary in Melville's use of a "heterogeneous form" using "metaphysical discussions, genre shifts, use of Shakespearean conventions and mixtures of facts and romance" which also appear in "mixed form" narratives, "a popular yet subversive trend within antebellum literary culture" (303).

2   According to Sanford E. Marovitz in "More Chartless Voyaging," Melville's interest in the "double value of terminology" was roused by discussions with George J. Adler.

3   Carolyn Porter is convincing in her argument that Ishmael's voice resides "at the boundary" where his stance "not only enables him to blur it but to defend it against the total dissolution that would render him, like Pip, a mad mimic rather than a sane one." His survival and "outrageous" narrative behavior "reflect the 'cunning spring' and 'buoyancy' of his double-voiced discourse" (106).

4   Leland Person's overview of the Melville gender debate is helpful (1-3). Arguing that Melville reverses gender polarities, Neal L. Tolchin reveals that Ahab is a female mourner, and David Leverenz insists that Ahab is a female hysteric. Robert K. Martin maintains that Melville contests the power of the patriarchy with homosexuality. In separate works, Robyn Wiegman and Joseph Allen Boone expose Melville's critique of the cultural power of male bonding and argue that Melville "ex-

poses the bond's reiteration of a privileged masculine perspective" (Wiegman 188). Wiegman points out, however, that Boone and Martin tend to forget that Melville's critique is still within the male privileged space. Person, perhaps too simplistically, sees Wiegman as "unable to conceive of manhood except as anti-female," but insists that "the sea represents not so much an exclusively male sphere that reinforces partriarchal authority as a fluid realm in which all constructs dissolve" (3-4). Eric J. Sundquist claims that Moby Dick is "both mother and father, womb and phallus" (148). Julian Rice sees Ishmael as born of the union of male Ahab and female Moby Dick, while Sanford E. Marovitz maintains that Melville "apparently developed his heroines with a strong if not wholly conscious sense of his own intersexual tendencies" ("Queenly" 8).

5   Lawrence Buell, for example, argues that *Omoo* treats American nationalism ironically in a demonstration of the country's nineteenth-century "postcolonial anxiety" about creating a separate culture from Britain. Juniper Ellis points out the appropriation of the South Pacific exotic for artistic purposes as a continuation of colonialism and argues: "the cartographies that U.S. writers have provided should not be taken for mimetic reproductions of the South Pacific" (25).

6   Sweeney, Wenke, and Mancini build on Melville's introduction of Narcissus in "Loomings" as a metaphor central to his philosophical questioning.

7   See especially William Spanos for his poststructural readings of Melville's works.

8   Melville also refers to Pythagoras in *Pierre* and *Israel Potter*. For helpful reference, Gail Coffler in *Melville's Classical Allusions* lists these and other references to the pre-Socratics.

9   For that purpose, it is worth the risk of appearing to float in the wake of 1980s' poststructural trendiness, especially since Ishmael's ability to float in the poststructural wake signals the timeliness and timelessness of Melville's philosophical concerns.

10   Defining the postmodern as accommodation to fragmentation, and by extension, to ambiguity and the deferral of definite meaning tells only half the stories of both post-Newtonian science and postmodernism. In much of the new science, although humanity comes up short of a God's-eye view, the belief in a protean and incomprehensible common reality is strong. When Lyotard compares science to postmodernism, he suggests that the new sciences "wage war on totality" (82), referring to some of the findings of quantum physics. But in his comments on the implications of science to postmodernism, Lyotard ignores quantum field theory, which suggests the interconnectedness of all phenomena, and the recent chaos and complexity studies that look for universality in unpredictability and randomness.

11   Consequently, I use the work of David Loy and Mircea Eliade (religious scholars), G. E. R. Lloyd (analytical philosopher), Hélène Cixous and Luce Irigaray (French feminists and Derridean poststructuralists).

12   See especially his *The Two and the One* and chapter one in Rennie for Eliade's explication of the *coincidentia oppositorum*.

13   In "The Laugh of the Medusa," Cixous calls it "the other bisexuality" (155). Melville is hardly the "bisexual writer" Cixous is calling for, but aspects of his work (particularly in *Pierre* and *Clarel*) support the concept of the "other bisexuality." The concept does not purport a fantastic disap-

pearing act of sexual difference, but a "non-exclusion either of the difference or the one of sex," a perception which "doesn't annul differences, but stirs them up" ("Medusa" 155).

14   Kulkarni's work refers to many scholars who have shown, as he has, that "Melville's references to Hindu myth and thought, however peripheral to his works some have thought them to be, are so numerous that there can be no doubt about his extensive knowledge of Hinduism" (1).

15   Harry T. Moore praises Lawrence's readings of Melville, noting that Lawrence was "one of the first voices in the great Melville revival" (288).

16   These and the following details about Pythagoras are taken from Bennett Ramsey, Pierre Bayle, Johan Thom, and W. K. C. Guthrie.

17   Pierre Bayle's *Dictionary* agrees, surprisingly, with a 1995 study of the *Pythagorean Golden Verses* that makes a stronger connection to the neo-Platonists than thought for the 120+ years since 1875. See Sealts's *Melville's Reading*, items 51, 97, 128, 147, 228. Also see his "Melville and the Platonic Tradition."

18   For studies of the history of binary thinking in the Western tradition, I highly recommend Genevieve Lloyd's *The Man of Reason: "Male" and "Female" in Western Philosophy*. Lloyd's work is thorough in analyzing the informal logic of pre-Socratic thought and its influence on Aristotle. She traces the ideals of Reason from the Greeks through de Beauvoir. Her work is evidence that "philosophers can take seriously feminist dissatisfaction with the maleness of Reason without repudiating either Reason or philosophy" (109).

19   As Irigaray, Cixous, Derrida, and others convincingly argue, this use of *logos* has persisted with an unshakable male bias. See Scott for a well-written overview.

20   See Marovitz, "Melville's Problematic *Being*," on Melville's comments in this "April[?] 16[?], 1851" letter to Hawthorne (*Letters* 124-25).

21   It was a title given to the men who transmitted the messages of the last of the hidden messengers of Mohammed (A. Bausani in Eliade, *Encyclopedia* 2:32-33).

22   As does much postmodern thought, *Moby-Dick* takes (non)duality seriously and at the same time leaves us with a sensible pragmatism that warns against it, but which is not exactly in conflict with it.

23   In "Hawthorne and His Mosses," Melville writes, "In Shakespeare's tomb lies infinitely more than Shakespeare ever wrote. And if I magnify Shakespeare, it is not so much for what he did do, as for what he did not do, or refrained from doing. For in this world of lies, Truth is forced to fly like a scared white doe in the woodlands, and only by cunning glimpses will she reveal herself" (*Piazza* 244).

24   On this I disagree with the finality with which Wenke, for example, falls on the "thundering No" side of Melville's philosophical wrestling. Wenke reads the "all feeling" as a "rhapsodic thrill fictionalized as one's passage into the empyrean" (163). Certainly Melville warns against the fatal "blending of the self with the Absolute," but *Moby-Dick* is not final about Melville's "belief in the nontranscendent capacity of human consciousness" (Wenke 163). See Djelal's argument that "Melville's 'all' recuperates the many and the one of Plato and Plotinus, filtered through a refocused Coleridgean lens" (219).

25 In *Pierre*, Millthorpe tries to explain to Pierre (as Melville alludes to *Macbeth*'s equivocal Porter), "the trick!—the whole world's a trick. Know the trick of it, all's right, don't know, all's wrong. Ha! ha!" (319). Pierre never sees humor in this cosmic joke (the "general joke" introduced in "Loomings") and fails as clearly as Ahab because of his obsession for absolutes. For attempting, as Romeo and Juliet do, to bring the heavens to earth or the corporeal to the stars, Pierre leaves corpses all over the stage.

26 Matthew Mancini studies the scientific and philosophical roots of Melville's "Descartian Vortices" and points out that *Moby-Dick*'s "philosophical agenda is signalled by the ironic rejection of Descartian vortices. Not in the pure, airy realm of self-sufficient consciousness (the Descartian vortex), nor yet in the crude, impenetrable world of material objects,... but in a synthesis of both, lies the real relation of subject and object. In this respect the key tropes are those of warp and woof . . . in the weaving of the sword-mat" (325).

REFERENCES

Bayle, Pierre. *A General Dictionary, Historical and Critical.* 10 vols. London. J. Bettenham, 1734-1741.

Bloom, Harold. *The Ringers in the Tower.* Chicago: U of Chicago P, 1971.

Boone, Joseph Allen. *Tradition Counter Tradition: Love and the Form of Fiction.* Chicago: U of Chicago P, 1987.

Buell, Lawrence. "Melville and the Question of American Decolonization," *American Literature* 64.2 (1992): 215-37.

Cixous, Hélène. "The Laugh of the Medusa." Trans. Keith Cohen and Paula Cohen. *Signs* 1 (1976): 875-99. Rpt. Eds. Elaine Marks and Isabelle de Courtivron. *New French Feminisms.* Brighton: Harvester, 1980: 245-64.

Cixous, Hélène, and Mireille Calle-Gruber. *Hélène Cixous Root-prints: Memory and Life Writing.* Trans. Eric Prenowitz. New York: Routledge, 1997.

Coffler, Gail. *Melville's Classical Allusions.* New York: Greenwood, 1985.

Djelal, Juana Celia. "All in All: Melville's Poetics of Unity." *ESQ: A Journal of the American Renaissance* 41 (1995): 219-37.

Elbow, Peter. *Oppositions in Chaucer.* Middletown: Wesleyan UP, 1975.

Eliade, Mircea. *Encyclopedia of Religion.* 16 vols. New York: Macmillan, 1987.

——. *The Quest: History and Meaning in Religions.* Chicago: U of Chicago P, 1969.

——. *The Two and the One.* Trans. J. M. Cohen. 1965. Chicago: U of Chicago P, 1979.

Ellis, Juniper. "Melville's Literary Cartographies of the South Seas." *Massachu-setts Review* (Spring 1997): 9-29.

Emerson, Ralph Waldo. *The Collected Works of Ralph Waldo Emerson.* Ed. Robert E. Spiller, Alfred R. Ferguson, et al. 5 vols. Cambridge, MA: Harvard UP, 1971-94.

Guthrie, W. K. C. *In the Beginning: Some Greek Views on the Origin of Life and the Early State of Man.* Ithaca, NY: Cornell UP, 1957.

——. "Pythagoras and Pythagoreans." 9 vols. Vol. 7 of *The Encyclopedia of Philosophy.* New York: Macmillan, 1967.

Hayford, Harrison. "Unnecessary Duplicates." *New Perspectives on Melville,* ed. Faith Pullin. Kent, OH: Kent State UP, 1978. 128-61.

Irigaray, Luce. "When Our Lips Speak Together." Trans. Carolyn Burke. *Signs* 6 (1980): 69-79.

Kulkarni, H. B. Moby-Dick: *A Hindi Avatar. A Study of Hindu Myth and Thought in Moby-Dick.* Logan: Utah State UP, 1970.

Lawrence, D. H. "The Two Principles." *Phoenix II: Uncollected, Unpublished, and Other Prose Works by D. H. Lawrence,* ed. Warren Roberts and Harry T. Moore. 1959. New York: Viking, 1968. 227-237.

Leverenz, David. *Manhood and the American Renaissance.* Ithaca, NY: Cornell UP, 1989.

Leyda, Jay. *The Melville Log.* 2 vols. New York: Gordian, 1969.

Lloyd, G. E. R. *Polarity and Analogy: Two Types of Argumentation in Early Greek Thought.* Cambridge: Cambridge UP, 1966.

Lloyd, Genevieve. *The Man of Reason: "Male" and "Female" in Western Philosophy.* London: Methuen, 1984.

Loy, David. *Nonduality: A Study in Comparative Philosophy.* New Haven, CT: Yale UP, 1988.

Lyotard, Jean-Francois. *The Postmodern Condition: A Report on Knowledge.* Trans. Geoff Bennington and Brian Massumi. Minneapolis: U of Minnesota P, 1984.

Mancini, Matthew. "Melville's 'Descartian Vortices.'" *ESQ: A Journal of the American Renaissance* 36 (1990): 315-27.

Marovitz, Sanford E. "Ahab's 'Queenly Personality' and Melville's Art." *Melville Society Extracts* 65 (Feb. 1986): 6-9.

——. "Melville's Problematic Being." *ESQ: A Journal of the American Renaissance* 28 (1982): 11-23.

——. "More Chartless Voyaging: Melville and Adler at Sea." *Studies in the American Renaissance*, ed. Joel Myerson. Charlottesville: U of Virginia P, 1986. 373-84.

Martin, Robert K. *Hero, Captain, and Stranger: Male Friendship, Social Critique, and Literary Form in the Sea Novels of Herman Melville*. Chapel Hill: U of North Carolina P, 1986.

Melville, Herman. *The Letters of Herman Melville*. Eds. Merrell R. Davis and William H. Gilman. New Haven: Yale UP, 1960.

——. *Mardi, and A Voyage Thither*. Ed. Harrison Hayford, Hershel Parker, and G. Thomas Tanselle. Vol. 3 of *The Writings of Herman Melville*. Evanston and Chicago, IL: Northwestern UP and the Newberry Library, 1970.

——. *Moby-Dick*. Ed. Harrison Hayford, Hershel Parker, and G. Thomas Tanselle. Vol. 6 of *Writings*. 1989.

——. *The Piazza Tales and Other Prose Pieces 1839-1860*. Ed. Hayford Harrison, Alma A. MacDougall, and G. Thomas Tanselle. Vol. 9 of *Writings*. 1987.

Moore, Harry T. *The Priest of Love: A Life of D. H. Lawrence*. 1954. New York: Farrar, Straus and Giroux, 1974.

Person, Leland. "Melville's Cassock: Putting on Masculinity in *Moby-Dick*." *ESQ: A Journal of the American Renaissance* 40 (1994): 1-26.

Porter, Carolyn. "Call Me Ishmael, or How to Make Double-Talk Speak." *New Essays on* Moby-Dick, ed. Richard H. Brodhead. Cambridge: Cambridge UP, 1986. 73-108.

Post-Lauria, Sheila. "Philosophy in Whales . . . Poetry in Blubber: Mixed Form in *Moby-Dick*." *Nineteenth-Century Literature* 45.3 (1990): 300-316.

Ramsey, Bennett. "Pythagoras." 16 vols. Vol. 12 of *Encyclopedia of Religion*. Ed. Mircea Eliade. New York: Macmillan, 1987.

Rennie, Bryan S. *Reconstructing Eliade: Making Sense of Religion*. Albany: SUNY, 1996.

Rice, Julian. "Male Sexuality in *Moby-Dick*." *American Transcendental Quarterly* 39 (1978): 239-40.

Scott, Joan W. "Deconstructing Equality-versus-Difference: Or, the Uses of Post-structuralist Theory for Feminism." *Feminist Studies* 14 (1988): 33-50.

Sealts, Merton M., Jr. "Melville and the Platonic Tradition." *Critical Essays in Herman Melville's* Moby-Dick. Ed. Brian Higgins and Hershel Parker. New York: G. K. Hall, 1992. 355-76.

——. *Melville's Reading*, revised ed. Columbia: U of South Carolina P, 1988.

Spanos, William. *The Errant Art of* Moby-Dick: *The Canon, the Cold War, and the Struggle for American Studies.* Durham, NC: Duke UP, 1995.

Sundquist, Eric J. *Home as Found: Authority and Genealogy in Nineteenth-Century American Literature.* Baltimore: Johns Hopkins UP, 1979.

Sweeney, Gerard M. *Melville's Use of Classical Mythology.* Amsterdam: Rodopi, 1975.

Thom, Johan C. *The Pythagorean Golden Verses.* Religions in the Graeco-Roman World Series. Vol. 125. New York: E. J. Brill, 1995.

Thoreau, Henry David. Walden *and* Resistance to Civil Government. 2nd ed. Ed. William Rossi. New York: W. W. Norton, 1992.

Tolchin, Neal L. *Mourning, Gender, and Creativity in the Art of Herman Melville.* New Haven, CT: Yale UP, 1988.

Wenke, John. *Melville's Muse: Literary Creation and the Forms of Philosophical Fiction.* Kent, OH: Kent State UP, 1995.

Wiegman, Robyn. "Melville's Geography of Gender." *American Literary History* 4 (1989): 735-53.

ATHANASIOS C. CHRISTODOULOU

THE "TRAGICALNESS OF HUMAN THOUGHT"

AN INTRODUCTION TO MELVILLE'S THEORY OF KNOWLEDGE

translated from the Greek by

CONSTANTINE A. CHRISTODOULOU

Preliminary Remarks

O n the 11th of April 1851 Herman Melville visited Hawthorne carrying a clock and a bedstead for his friend. During that visit Hawthorne gave him the newly published *The House of the Seven Gables*.[1] Five days later, on the 16th of April 1851, Melville wrote a unique letter to Hawthorne about that book. It is a small but profound essay, where Melville uses a language "full of implications, windings and curves" to talk not only about the essentials of Hawthorne's art, but also about the central theme that he himself was trying to "materialize" in *Moby-Dick*. Inside this letter there is a crucial phrase which, had it been studied more closely, would have become the key to deciphering the "abysmal" ideas both of Melville and of Hawthorne. I quote: "And here we would say that, did circumstances permit, we should like nothing better than to devote an elaborate and careful paper to the full consideration and analysis of the purport and significance of what so strongly characterizes all of this author's writings. There is a certain tragic phase of humanity which, in our opinion, was never more powerfully embodied than by Hawthorne. We mean the tragicalness of human thought in its own unbiassed, native, and profounder workings."[2]

Even the most unsophisticated reader can perceive almost immediately Melville's implication: that he had a thorough knowledge of the ideas that constitut-

159

ed the secret core of Hawthorne's philosophy, as well as the artistic methods that the great writer used in order to realize, to express, that is, the various "iridescences" of this philosophy; furthermore, that this philosophy was related to an element hidden inside all of Hawthorne's works which was none other than the *tragicalness of human thought*, "in its unbiassed, native, and profounder workings." Melville's comment, however, would be of no particular value without the term "unbiassed."[3] Because even the most uninformed reader cannot but be surprised by this adjectival complement. *Human thought in its unbiassed workings;* please, notice here that he refers to "human thought," and not the "human mind"; not the *functions* of the brain—imagination, memory, sense, perception—but only *thought*, the *intellectual process*. He refers, that is, to the intellectual function and not the human mind itself, as a *separate* thing. What exactly does Melville mean with this strange intimation? Hasn't Aristotle spoken clearly about the intellect? Doesn't *thinking* mean the actual production of concepts, judgments and syllogisms? And the strangest of all: why is "human thought" considered tragic? why is human nature ("humanity") tragic? why does Melville, with this equation, secretly associate and equate human thought with human nature? Both Aristotle and later philosophy never discerned any "tragicalness" in our intellectual faculties whatsoever. On the contrary, they considered our intellect "a gift from God," a unique tool for self-knowledge and generally the discovery of truth, and man as the most favored and gifted creature in all the universe.

What does Melville imply, therefore, when talking about the "unbiassed, natural" workings of human thought? It is not difficult to understand that both Melville and Hawthorne *do not accept* the theories of Aristotle and later philosophy on the function of our intellect but consider all the principles[4] summarized in the *Formal Logic* to be "prejudices," ideas that are misleading and false. Based upon these observations, I will attempt to describe the functions of human thought the way they were perceived by Melville and Hawthorne. This small paper, therefore, substitutes for the paper that Melville had dreamt of writing but never did, due to the circumstances of his time, because it would have caused an uproar, as it refuted the whole of Aristotelian logic and destroyed thus the foundations of life itself. Hence, my paper, being a substitute of that unwritten and nightmarish paper, is already condemned and rejected. For who could accept the dreadful and outrageous truth that "man" or whatever we call "intellect" or "mind" is a *double-natured being*, a being with two faces, with two hypostases? Who could accept that this being is the only one in the universe that *destroys itself* thousands of times each minute, so that whatever we call "life" is essentially nothing else but an eternal and indestructible self-destruction, so that "life" of life is merely an undying death? Who could accept that whatever we call "man" is just a bodiless, *non-existent* being which constantly self-destructs on the verge of life and death, without ever being able to be born[5] or to die? Neither Shakespeare, nor Hawthorne, nor Melville, who constituted a *secret brotherhood*, could openly speak about such terrible things, i.e., the "annulling reason's laws."[6] The only solution for them was to express those terrible truths, by concealing them under the "skin" of the very same words they used to "fictionalize" and to simply suggest, to illuminate from the side, that is, the eternal tragedy of man.

The Profound "Thought" of Melville

Both Hawthorne and Melville were among the few *practical* people[7] who had their feet firmly on the ground and knew with mathematical precision the physiology of their own self—their other appalling self.[8] In the limited space I have, I will try to communicate to you their strange ideas, as well as the artistic or practical ways which they used to express them. I will ask you to be very careful and pay the utmost attention to the following phrases because each one constitutes a secret pattern for both writers' art. This brief philosophical submersion can only be fulfilled with the "ropes" and "respirator" of Aristotle's *Formal Logic*,[9] that is with the standard rules of *categorical* (reasoning) *syllogism* we use in every step of our lives, which is based upon the four fundamental principles that govern rational thought: the principles of *identity*, of *contradiction*, of the *excluded middle* or *third* and of *sufficient reasoning* or *determination*.

At some point in their lives, both Hawthorne and Melville realized that in a "tree," for example, are hidden *two* things; the *concept* "tree" and the *real, genuine thing* that we call tree; in other words they realized that one thing is the term "tree" and another the *unknown and unnamed object* hidden beneath the term "tree."[10]

Their next discovery was that the object we call "tree" acquires its own individuality, its own *body* and *essence*, that is, when it is "clothed" with the concept or term "tree."[11] By removing this cloth, whatever we call "tree" is no different and cannot be distinguished from the object that lies, for example, behind the concept or term "mountain," "sea," "man," "Melville," "Hawthorne."[12]

In other words, they discovered that the universe is an infinite sum of concepts,[13] a universal conceptual *brotherhood*,[14] and that the creator of this conceptual universe is exclusively the human mind,[15] that obscure force that man calls "mind," "intellect," "spirit," "soul," "imagination,"[16] "memory," "sense," "perception," etc.[17] They also realized that the actual and anonymous universe remains shielded and impervious to man exactly because this opaque net of concepts or masks, like an impenetrable wall, intervenes;[18] they realized, furthermore, that our mind not only cannot dispense with this net in order to come into direct contact with that unknown world, but on the contrary, in its anguished effort to perceive the world, it constantly creates more and more names, weaving thus more and more "eyelets" into that net, and making, thus, its prison even more stifling.

If, therefore, all of the universe is nothing but a net of concepts, an enormous and inexhaustible dictionary, then the essence of man is concealed beneath only one word, what we call "concept." *What is a concept?*—was Hawthorne's and Melville's fatal question. Although Aristotle had given a clear answer to that question many centuries ago, which, however, was never questioned (nor proven), the two inquisitive Americans, by doubting Aristotle's definition and eventually the whole Aristotelian logic, began a feverish search which would inevitably end in an harrowing tragedy. According to Aristotle, *"concept* is a representation that includes the basic traits of a being or the characteristics that form its essence."[19] These two Americans were the only ones to realize that that definition was false. Because the *object of study* itself can never be used as a definition of its own essence. In other words, one cannot define what a "concept" is by using one or more concepts because even these concepts need previously a definition of their own essence. In other words, Aristotle, in order to provide a definition of the *concept*, used other concepts, without having previously determined the *essence* of those concepts. Neither Aristotle nor later philosophy realized this tragic and "grand error."[20]

Melville and Hawthorne rightly rejected this definition and, being very practical, intuitively perceived that "concept" is nothing but a "transubstantiation" of the mind itself, a disguise, a reincarnation or a transformation or even a bizarre "body" of the intellectual faculty itself.[21]

At the same time they also realized that whatever we call "mind," "intellect," or "human mind" is not something absolute, self-existent, and independent that simply "floats" in mid-air, but something that *constantly moves*,[22] that *constantly thinks*,[23] something that is constantly transformed into a "concept."[24] Whenever, therefore, we say "mind" or "intellect," *mind* or *intellect* is exactly these terms, the *fleeting* concepts "mind" or "intellect."[25]

A "tree," therefore, is simply a disguise, a mask of the mind itself,[26] which, however, has the innate ability, at that particular moment of its transformation into concept, to be fully aware of this transformation. Based on this last conclusion, Melville and Hawthorne discovered that whatever we call "mind" or "intellect" is a *double-natured being* [27] because only a being with two hypostases can "suffer" and *simultaneously* "know or witness itself suffering." The double nature of the mind becomes ever more apparent when the mind creates the concept "I." It is at that infinitesimal moment, when the mind creates the concept "I," that it also fulfills a monstrous delivery: it *extracts*, that is, from within its own self the whole of itself, giving to that extract an *other*, separate life; the mind is both womb and fetus, watching at the same time like an outsider this bizarre delivery. Even the most naive man understands that only *one* being with *two* hypostases or with two selves can have one "I" or one (other) "self," can simultaneously be both the subject and the object of this self-knowledge, both "creator" (ποιοῦν) and "created" (πάσχον) according to Aristotelian terminology. The one self, the ποιοῦν is the creator, the one that forms the concept "I"; the other self, the πάσχον is the created, "the concept I itself." Grasping *intuitively* this truth,[28] humanity and all of civilization change or rather lose their historical course.[29]

When the two astounded Americans perceived their double nature and understood that all the inanimate or living things, all the so-called real or imaginary ideas, all the memories and various feelings were nothing more than simple concepts,[30] that is, infinite double-faced masks,[31] disguises or transubstantiations or duplicates of our intellect,[32] then they wondered in awe, *who am I?* With this question, Melville and Hawthorne initiated the most ruthless and *monomaniacal hunt* the human mind could ever conceive. In order for the mind to exist, it must provide an answer to the agonizing question "Who am I." In order to answer, however, it must invent another concept, which concept is actually another disguise of the mind itself. In order to define this second concept, it must invent a third concept and so on. For example: I ask: "Who am I?" I answer: "I am a man." I ask: "What is man?" I answer: "Man is a two-legged being with soul." I ask: "What is two-legged, what is being, what is soul?" and so on.[33] Every new concept the mind invents in order to create itself or to define its identity is also a new disguise of itself, a replacement or substitution of its own self,[34] a new mask. In order for the mind to transform into a new concept, however, it must *destroy* its previous concept, its *own* concept.[35] Every disguise, therefore, is equal to a self-destruction of the mind or "I"—if we consider the infinite *disguises* that the mind assumes with inconceivable speed throughout life, then it is easy to understand the infinite self-destructions, the endless death that man lives every single moment.[36] The tragedy in this desperate pursuit is that the unsatisfied <m>*I*<nd> *denies* and constantly *rejects* like a sovereign king whichever concept it invents,[37] pursuing like a captive slave some other concept which, however, can never be its true concept.[38] Hence, man or mind is a double-natured apparition, a *shadow* that desperately hunts in all the archipelagos and oceans its inconceivable concept.[39] During this hunt it eats its own "flesh" like a cannibal in order to exist. So *hunter* and *prey* in this ruthless hunt is always the double-natured mind,[40] which is and will forever be an *incomplete* or *maimed* or *crippled* being, because without the invisible, living *limb*[41] it is missing, without "its true concept," that is, it can never exist. Essentially, therefore, "man," whose "corporeal hypostasis" is not but a concept, is a *non-existent* being[42] which constantly is on the verge of life and death. The mind self-destructs and will continue to do so forever without ever being able to utter its true name.[43] Substance of self-consciousness is *emptiness*[44] or <s>*I*<lence>.

This relentless hunt is a cyclical voyage without meaning or ending. Starting from itself, the mind always ends up back to itself,[45] destroying (in the process) countless times its own false and delusory concept.

The tragedy, however, does not end here. Melville and Hawthorne, by refuting Aristotle's *Formal Logic* and thus arriving at the tragic conclusion that every thought is a delusion and every syllogism an illusion of the mind, they realized that even this truth was also another delusion, was based upon those same rules of *categorical syllogism* they had just refuted, that it was, in other words, one more "thesis," one more "language." They realized, that is, that they had reached the truth with the "crutches" of Aristotle's logic, and that since those "crutches" were worm-eaten and rotten, then the concept of self-destruction could never be true. Melville and Hawthorne were just one step away from the abyss that gaped in front of the them—the *sane madness*.[46] To escape from this chasm, the mind sealed its lips and never spoke again.[47] Grammars and dictionaries were all useless now.

The Great Art of Telling the Truth

Melville and Hawthorne are the only ones to have journeyed in the abyssal kingdom of the sane madness. They were saved by clinging to the "gunwale" of literature, by a *coffin*, that is, just like Ishmael. In realizing that all aspects of life, all the wealth and endless variety of the external world called "reality," and the whole of the spiritual and intellectual world of man, even God Himself, were nothing but the mind's own masks, *deceptive words* or *concepts*, that is, they found consolation in literature, in the art of writing.[48] In that great art which, although using the false and deceitful language of man, it can still suggest and constantly tell the truth, it can still imply the self-delusion and self-destruction of the mind in all its manifestations. Behold the *secret* of this *great art:* although both writers adhere to the rules of grammar and syntax for purely narrative purposes, *every* word, phrase, image, metaphor, chapter, or myth of these narratives is simply an incarnation of the double-natured, self-destructive mind. *All* the heroes of their novels, all the characters, things and animals, all thoughts, fantasies, dreams, feelings, myths and anecdotes included in their works, are all disguises and embodiments of that unknown being which is gifted with what we call "intellectual capability" and is destined to eternally self-destruct without any reason and without any logic—all these are delusory images of a being that will remain "unpainted to the last."[49] Especially "for Melville the mind and its means of expression, the language, that is, can never speak *precisely* or *literally*. On the other hand, conventional language, being a reflection of our Aristotelian logic, is the only one that can "illuminate," *always sideways*, this inconceivable tragedy, not by being precise or literal, but by using its material (words) and its forms (grammar and syntax) in one and only one way—always *metaphorically* and *allusively*. Melville's lan-

165

guage, therefore, never *literally* "states" but always "suggests," never *means* but always *implies*, leading constantly the inquisitive reader from literal commonplaces to ineffable implications that basically express, in a persistent and even monotonous way, the bizarre iridescences of the mind—its multi-faceted speechlessness or self-destruction. Melville was prudent to hide the "essence" of the mind, that is, to incorporate into as many words as he could, *another meaning, another secret word* that expresses one of the many peculiarities of this strange being. The reader must find, with the help either of a dictionary, or through etymological research, but mainly with the help of his imagination,[50] this *secret* and *second* meaning *under the obvious meaning* of Melville's word (or even his myth); the reader must break into pieces the Melvillean sentence and find this hidden and *second* word in its debris, in between the letters of his words, that is, either as an *extract*, or as an *anagram* of two or more letters, or as an *echo* hidden in the pronunciation of the word. Each historical, mythological, or imaginary name that Melville uses or invents is a symbol that reveals, expresses, and embodies, with its own *secret story*, its *secret etymological structure*, or with the *form of its letters*, one of the above peculiarities of the mind. For Melville the parts of speech are not ten, as traditional grammar teaches, but *one and only one:* the insubstantial (non-existent) and double-natured personal pronoun *"ego"* or "I." The *object* is nothing but a mask of the subject, of the *ego*, that is—a second self-destruction. The *verb* is simply the desultory and incomprehensible leap of this peculiar being from one concept to another—the leap of self-destruction. So, the phrases, the paragraphs, the chapters, and all the books of Melville constantly refute all human institutes, beliefs, opinions, sciences, and philosophies, sometimes in a tragic, sometimes in a comical or parodic way.[51] Indeed, Hawthorne's and Melville's true minds are hidden not in their magnificent language but in its ruins which constitute the foundations of their splendid but delusory "logo-technical" edifice.

Epilogue

Here I stop, apologizing for my distressing ideas. I can't expect you to perceive and adopt this peculiar theory of knowledge in all its aspects in the few minutes I have available. Should, however, these ideas ever arouse your curiosity, I would be the happiest of the lecturers, and I would be in the position to say that for the three writers I mentioned above a new day is dawning. Before ending my paper, and in order to stir even more your curiosity, I will bring forward some striking examples that, I am sure, will make you think seriously whether the peculiar things you heard in this distant corner of the earth are of some import or not. Read chapters CXXXIII (133)[52] and CXLIII (143)[53] from the extraordinary *Mardi*, where Babbalanja talks about his double-natured self. Remember the demon Azzageddi who constitutes the *alter ego* of this bizarre philosopher. Remember Babbalanja's strange philosophy and his incessant babbling which always ends in his own self-destruction. Remember the endless string of bizarre names that Melville constantly invents in *Mardi*, which is nothing else but an autobiography of the *mar<re>d I*.[54] Remember the ineffectual voyage of *Mardi*'s double-natured hero (Taji) who is and remains until the end a man without a *real name*, who, in order to be able to even pseudo-exist and to speak, he must settle for, just like Ishmael, with a simple *pseudonym*.[55] Compare Taji's voyage to Ahab's. Remember Bartleby's speechlessness. Remember "Monsieur du Miroir," "Egotism; or, the Bosom-Serpent," "The Minister's Black Veil," "The Great Carbuncle," and "Earth's Holocaust," Hawthorne's tales. Remember Hawthorne's and Melville's stigmatized heroes—they are nothing but personifications and embodiments of the mind, of a *mark*, of a *scar* that each man has had from his very birth. Remember that Hester's scarlet letter, the letter A, is the first letter of the alphabet, the first and fatal embodiment of the mind, a *scar letter*, the scarred mind itself. Remember the Unpardonable Sin of the "branded" Ethan Brand or Melville's "Original Sin"[56]—it is the "knowledge" that Adam and Eve acquired by eating from the forbidden fruit—God never forgave their disobedience. Notice that the word *Moby-Dick* is a compound word comprising two words joined with an odd hyphen; notice that under the skin of the word "Moby" lies the fake word "moby"[57] or "mo-by,"[58] which means "an enormous collection of similar things"; and that the word "Dick," which means "fellow, lad, man,"[59] "fine language, long words," is actually an abbreviation in the common language for the word "dictionary";[60] notice, that is, that the word "moby-dick" suggests that this book is an enormous dictionary, an enormous collection of concepts; notice how Melville with his phrase "or, the Whale" identifies this enormous dictionary with the whale, implying that all the words of this book are simply the conceptual

ATHANASIOS C. CHRISTODOULOU

characteristics, the embodiments, the personifications of his "own whale." Remember CETOLOGY, chapter 32 in *Moby-Dick*, where again Melville compares whales with books, with collections of concepts, that is. Remember Melville's own comment to Hawthorne that "the pervading *thought* that impelled the book"[61] constitutes the central theme of *The Whale*. Notice the two preliminary chapters, ETYMOLOGY and EXTRACTS, in the Harper & Brothers edition of 1851— Melville distributes the text of the first pages in two facing pages with two facing titles. Remember Queequeg's "broken heads."[62] Remember *Moby-Dick*'s ETYMOLOGY which is actually a clear implication to the reader that this book is nothing else than an *etymological research* for the revelation of the true meaning of the *one and only* concept. Notice that the awkward words that Melville chooses to build his sentences in *Moby-Dick* are often connected to each other in a strange way—they are either *synonymous* in a more profound analysis of their meaning or they form *pairs* and *groups* with common initial letters. Investigate the biography of the characters that Melville introduces in *The Whale*, and you will discover that their tragic countenance always enlivens some aspect of the secret "tragicalness of human thought." Discern among the phonemes of the introductory sentence in *Moby-Dick*, when you pronounce the famous words "Call me Ishmael," the phonemes ⟨c⟩*all me is*⟨h⟩*m*⟨a⟩*e*⟨l⟩, i.e., *all me is me*. And when you read Melville's and Hawthorne's books remember the answer that Hamlet gives to Polonius when the latter asks—"what do you read, my lord?"—"Words, words, words."[63]

NOTES

1   Herman Melville, *Correspondence*, edited by Lynn Horth, Evanston and Chicago, IL: Northwestern University Press and the Newberry Library, 1993, p. 184. Laurie Robertson-Lorant, *Melville, A Biography*, New York: Clarkson Potter, 1996, p. 270.

2   I copy out the text from the NN edition.

3   It is clear that by this term, which means (*fig.*) "not unduly or improperly influenced or inclined; unprejudiced, impartial" (OED, 2), Melville indirectly castigates all the scientific and philosophical views concerning the nature and functions of human thought, implying that they all are false and delusive.

4   As it will be proven later, Melville implies the four fundamental principles of the *Formal Logic*, those of *identity*, of *contradiction*, of *excluded middle* or *third*, and of *sufficient reasoning* or *determination*. The same idea also is repeated by Babbalanja in *Mardi* (NN) 574: "There is no supreme stan-

dard* yet revealed, whereby to judge of ourselves; 'Our very instincts are prejudices,' saith Alla Mallolla; 'Our very axioms,** and postulates*** are far from infallible.' 'In respect of the universe, mankind is but a sect,' saith Diloro; 'and first principles but dogmas.'"

5   Cf. *Mardi* 368: "My memory is a life beyond birth."

6   See *Mardi* 627. In the notes I often quote from *Mardi*, because there Melville expresses his theory of knowledge more clearly than in any other of his books. Most of the time these quotations have at least two meanings; the one *phenomenal* or *sensible* (mostly hard to explain) and the other *secret* or *imperceptible*. The phenomenal or sensible one is related to the narrative or the logical structure of the context; the secret or imperceptible is related to the deeper thinking of Melville and is hidden beneath the phenomenal that is used both as a *spur* and as a *transparent glass* through which we must discern the exact meaning of the hidden intimation in order to understand his true ideas. Therefore, Melville is one of those authors "who falter in the common tongue, because they think in another" (*Mardi* 395) and whose "words are exceedingly ambiguous" (*Mardi* 412). These second meanings would be used as proof to the *rightness* of my views, if the reader could make out the "bottom landscape" of each extract. Unfortunately, I have to restrict myself to a bare record of these extracts, otherwise I should be beyond the scope of this essay. However, I hope that the thoughtful reader will be able on his own to dive into them with the help of the ideas of this essay.

7   As well as Bishop Berkeley. Cf. *Mardi* 63: "my Right Reverend friend, Bishop Berkeley—truly, one of your lords spiritual—who, metaphysically speaking, holding all objects to be mere optical delusions, was notwithstanding, extremely matter-of-fact in all matters touching matter itself."

8   Cf. *Mardi* 593: "No mailed hand lifted up against a traveler in woods, can so appall, as we ourselves."

9   What I mean by the term *Formal Logic* is explained by Sir William Hamilton: "The doctrine which expounds the laws by which our scientific procedure should be governed, in so far as these lie in the forms of thought, or in the conditions of the mind itself . . . may be called Formal, or Subjective, or Abstract, or Pure, Logic" (*Lectures on Logic*, xxvii, 1860, 231 App. i. quoted from OED 1 b); and by J. D. Morell: "The purport of Logic then is to investigate these fixed laws of thought; to show us the principles by which our understanding is governed; and to guard us in this way against all possible fallacies in reasoning" (*Handbook of Logic*, Robert Theobald, London, 1855, p. 11).

10   Cf. *Mardi* 269: "Judge not things by their names." 283: "truth is in things, and not in words: truth is voiceless." 283: "things visible are but conceits (= *concepts*) of the eye (= I): things imagina-

---

* **standard**: criterion ⟨of truth⟩ (OED 10 b).   ** **axiom**: *Logic* and *Math*. 'A self-evident proposition, requiring no formal demonstration to prove its truth, but received and assented to as soon as mentioned'" (Hutton. OED, 3).   *** **postulate**: *Logic* and *gen*. "A proposition demanded or claimed to be granted; something claimed taken for granted, or assumed, as a basic of reasoning, discussion, or belief; hence, a fundamental condition or principle" (OED, 2).

tive, conceits of the fancy." 362: "The shadows of things [= thinks, *sb. dial.* or *colloq.* "an act of (continued) thinking; an idea; a thought." (OED)] are greater than themselves, and the more exaggerated the shadow, the more unlike to the substance."

11 Cf. *Mardi* 437: "nature is an immaculate virgin, forever standing unrobed before us. True
poets but paint the charms which all eyes (=*I*<s>) behold."

12 Cf. *Mardi* 638: "Nations are but names." 394: "We are only known by our names; as letters
sealed up, we but read each other's superscriptions." 528: "Names make not distinctions." 616: "Saturn, and Mercury, and Mardi, are brothers, one and all."375: "theology, or amber, or ambergris, it's all
the same." 383: "Philosophical Necessity and Predestination One Thing and The Same." 538: "In kings,
mollusca, and toad-stools, life is one thing and the same." 428: "orthodoxy and heresy are one."

13 Or "souls" that invigorate the mind/man (see also note 21). Cf. *Mardi* 594: "We are fuller
than a city." 367: "And like a frigate, I am full with a thousand souls." 367: "Ay: many, many souls
are in me." 593-94: "We are full of ghosts and spirits." 368: "my memory, my library of the Vatican." 367: "And my soul sinks down to the depths, and soars to the skies; and comet-like reels on
through such boundless expanses, that methinks all the worlds are my kin."

14 Cf. *Mardi* 367: "all the worlds are my kin." 615: "In me, in me, flit thoughts participated
by the beings peopling all the stars." 625: "is not Oro the father of all? Then, are we not brothers?" 12: "all generations are blended: and heaven and earth of one kin . . . one and all, brothers in
essence—oh, be we then brothers indeed! All things (= *thinks*, see note 10) form but one whole."
616: "Saturn, and Mercury, and Mardi, are brothers, one and all."

15 Cf. *Mardi* 489: "the imagination [or the *I ma*<gination> -> *I am*<gination>] is the Voli-Donzi-
ni; or, to speak plainer, the unical, rudimental, and all-comprehending abstracted essence of the
infinite remoteness of things [=*thinks*, see note 10]."

16 Cf. *Mardi* 577: "The universe can wax old without us." 577: "The firmament-arch has no key-
stone; least of all, is man its prop." 559: "The world revolves upon an I." 616: "Kill me, and generations die."489: "when I die, the universe will perish with me." 230: "for to Himself His own universe
is He." 488-89: "talk not to me of Ohonoo. To me it is not, except when I am there. If it be, prove it.
To prove it, you carry me thither; but you only prove, that to its substantive existence, as cognizant
to me, my presence is indispensable." 488: "It is this imagination of ours, my lord, that is at the bottom of these things." 594: "And all our dead sires, verily, are in us; that is their immortality."

17 Cf. *Mardi* 574: "In respect of the universe, mankind is but a sect." 210: "as old Bardianna
has it, if not against us, nature is not for us." 210: "All vanity, vanity, Yoomy, to seek in nature
for positive warranty to these aspirations of ours."

18 Cf. *Moby-Dick* (NN) 164: "All visible objects, man, are but as pasteboard masks. But in each
event—in the living act, the undoubted deed—there, some unknown but still reasoning thing puts
forth the mouldings of its feature from behind the unreasoning mask. If man will strike, strike
through the mask! How can the prisoner reach outside except by thrusting through the wall?"

19 "When an abstract or a generalised idea has been formed in the mind, we call it *a Concept;*
and when expressed by an outward sign, we call it *a Term*" (Morell, p. 12).

20 I borrow this expression from *Mardi* 525, where "a fiery youth" mentions the "grand error⟨s⟩" of his "boisterous days." Cf. *Mardi* 429: "it would hardly answer for Oro himself, were he to come down to Mardi to deny men's theories concerning him."

21 Cf. *Mardi* 385: "the thoughts of men are each a soul." 594: "Every thought's a soul of some past poet, hero, sage." (See also note 13).

22 Cf. *Mardi* 504: "'True to your nature, Babbalanja; you stay nowhere.' 'Ay, keep moving is my motto.'" 556: "by some mystic impulse am I moved, to this fleet progress."

23 Cf. *Mardi* 396: "whose whole existence is an unintermitting consciousness of self."

24 Cf. *Mardi* 459: "much of the wisdom here below lives in a state of transition."

25 Cf. *Mardi* 337: "'Oro is but a sound,' said the boy: 'They call the supreme god, Ati, in my native isle; it is the soundless thought of him, oh guide, that is in me.'"

26 Cf. *Mardi* 297: "I, the man (= *am* ⟨n⟩) in the iron (= *I*⟨ron⟩) mask [= *am*⟨sk⟩ or/and ⟨m⟩*ask*]." 339: "Peace, peace, my soul; on, mask, again." *Moby-Dick* 147: "behind those forms and usages, as it were, he sometimes masked himself."

27 Cf. *Mardi* 613-4: "I have found that the heart (⟨he⟩*art* ∿ "*are*") is not whole, but divided." 433: "I give thee up, oh Man! thou art twain—yet indivisible; all things [*"are twain—yet indivisible"* it is understood]—yet a poor unit at best." 456: "For aught I know, I may be somebody else. At any rate, I keep an eye (=*I*) on myself, as I would on a stranger. There is something going on in me, that is independent of me . . . for what they commend pertains not to me, Babbalanja; but to this unknown something that forces me to it." 457: "So present is he always, that I seem not so much to live of myself, as to be a mere apprehension of the unaccountable being that is in me. Yet all the time, this being is I, myself." 397: "The truest poets are but mouthpieces; and some men are duplicates of each other." 317: "devils, doubly bedeviled." 616: "I bear a soul in germ within me." 338: "I blindly follow, where I seem to lead." 368: "Yet not I, but another: God is my Lord." 368: "I and all mine revolve round the great central Truth." 559: "The world revolves upon an I; and we upon ourselves; for we are our own worlds." 457: "they do not govern themselves, but are governed by their very natures." 427: "all my acts, are Oro's." 596: "he was not his own master: a mere amanuensis writing by dictation." 615: "All are parts of One." 416: "Every unit is made up of parts." "In reading some of Goethe's sayings . . . I came across this, '*Live in the all.*' That is to say, *your separate identity* (emphasis added) is but a wretched one—good." (Melville's Letter to Hawthorne of June 1?, 1851; Herman Melville, *Correspondence*, NN, 193). *Moby-Dick* 312: "not the smallest atom stirs or lives in matter, but has its cunning duplicate in mind."

28 Cf. *Mardi* 338: "I but feel Oro* in me, yet can not declare the thought."

29 Cf. *Mardi* 580-1: "All Mardi's history—beginning, middle, and finis—was written out in capitals in the first page penned. The whole story is told in a title-page. An exclamation point is entire

---

* By the name of Oro Melville implies the "*speaking Ego*" or "*I*," because this Polynesian name (of the god Oro) morphologically identifies with the first person singular of the present tense of the Latin verb *orare* ("oro") which means "I speak" (cf. the English word "oral").

Mardi's autobiography." 389: "For the more we learn, the more we unlearn; we accumulate not, but substitute; and take away, more than we add. We dwindle while we grow; we sally out for wisdom, and retreat beyond the point whence we started." 578: "The first man's thoughts were as ours." 461: "In himself, he was the whole history of Mardi, amplified, not abridged, in one volume."

30   Cf. *Mardi* 428: "For in things abstract, men but differ in the sounds that come from their mouths, and not in the wordless thoughts lying at the bottom of their beings."

31   Cf. *Mardi* 597: "there are things infinite in the finite; and dualities in unities."

32   Cf. *Mardi* 229: "In all the universe is but one original." 428: "The universe is all of one mind." 426: "in all things Oro is immutable." 427: "Oro is not merely a universal on-looker, but occupies and fills all space; and no vacancy is left for any being, or any thing but Oro. Hence, Oro is *in* all things, and himself *is* all things."

33   Cf. *Mardi* 458: "To exist, is to be; to be, is to be somethig: to be something, is—" 412: "all subjects are inexhaustible, however trivial; as the mathematical point, put in motion, is capable of being produced into an infinite line." 597: "there are things infinite in the finite. . ." 339: "I doubt my doubt."

34   Cf. *Mardi* 389: "we accumulate not, but substitute. . ." 580: "new fashions but revivals of things previous." 594: "we go on multiplying corpses in ourselves; for all of which, are resurrections." 507: "Mere substitutions of sounds for inexplicable meanings, my lord. In some things science cajoles us."

35   Cf. *Mardi* 599: "For I am critic and creator; and as critic, in cruelty surpass all critics merely, as a tiger, jackals. For ere Mardi sees aught of mine, I scrutinize it myself, remorseless as a surgeon. I cut right and left; I probe, tear, and wrench; kill, burn, and destroy. . . It is I that stab false thoughts, ere hatched." 376: "All thought is a puff." 376: "But life itself is a puff and a wheeze."

36   Cf. *Mardi* 385: "death is but a mode of life." 587: "We die because we live." 238: "Living is dying." 237: "But dead, and yet alive; alive, yet dead." 616: "These myriad germ-dramas in me." 385: "How can the unhoused spirit hope to live when mildewed with the damps of death." 368: "my thoughts crush me down till I groan." 238: "Thy own skeleton, thou thyself dost carry with thee, through this mortal life." 593-94: "We are full of ghosts and spirits; we are as grave-yards full of buried dead, that start to life before us. . . From sire to son, we go multiplying corpses in ourselves." 593: "We die of too much life." 458: "I live while consciousness is not mine, while to all appearances I am a clod."

37   Cf. "There is the grand truth about Nathaniel Hawthorne. He says NO! in thunder; but the Devil himself cannot make him say *yes*. For all men who say *yes*, lie; and all men who say *no*,— why, they are in the happy condition of judicious, unincumbered travellers in Europe; they cross the frontiers into Eternity with nothing but a carpet-bag,—that is to say, the Ego." (See Melville's letter to Hawthorne of April, 16, 1851.)

38   Cf. *Mardi* 578: "Common sense is a sturdy despot." 630: "Reason no longer domineers; but still doth speak."

39   Cf. *Mardi* 337: "Nor he, nor thou, nor I, nor any; Oro, to all, is Oro the unknown."

40 Cf. *Mardi*, the tilte of chapter 100 (305): "THE PURSUER HIMSELF IS PURSUED." 576: "The soul needs no mentor, but Oro; and Oro, without proxy. Wanting Him, it is both the teacher and the taught." 654: "pursuers and pursued flew on, over an endless sea."

41 Cf. *Moby-Dick* 131: "The living *me*<m>*be*<r>—that makes the living insult, my little man."

42 Cf. *Mardi* 237: "Thou art not even a sightless sound; not the echo of an echo." 460: "we are air, wind, breath, bubbles; our being is told in a tick."

43 Cf. *Mardi* 456: "though I have now been upon terms of close companionship with my-self for nigh five hundred moons, I have not yet been able to decide who or what I am. To you, perhaps, I seem Babbalanja; but to myself, I seem not myself." 454: "Let me, oh Oro! be anony-mously known!"

44 Cf. *Mardi* 411: "Full to the brim of themselves, for that reason, the Tapparians are the emptiest of mortals." 413: "these Tapparians have no brains." 412: "It is from our very abundance that we want." 429-30: "'my talk is my overflowing, not my fullness.' 'And what may you be so full of?' 'Of myself.'" 459: "the vagueness of the notion I have of myself."

45 Cf. *Mardi* 460: "'You everlastingly travel in a circle.' 'And so does the sun in heaven, my lord; like me, it goes round, and gives light as it goes. Old Bardianna, too, revolved'. . .'All things revolve upon some center, to them, fixed.'" 368: "I and all mine revolve round the great central Truth, sun-like, fixed an luminous forever in the foundationless firmament." 339: "From dark to dark!—What is this subtle something that is in me, and eludes me? Will it have no end? When, then did it begin?" 559: "that man so highly prizes his sweet self, that he cares not to profane the shrine he worships, by throwing open its portals. He is locked up; and Ego is the key. Reserve alone is vanity. But all mankind are egotists. The world revolves upon an I; and we upon our-selves; for we are our own worlds." 575: "our mortal lives have an end; but that end is no goal: no place of repose. Whatever it may be, it will prove but as the beginning of another race." 238: "and all revolve:—systems and asteroids; the sun wheels through the zodiac, and the zodiac is a revolution." 458: "Mardi is alive to its axis."

46 See Melville's *Hawthorne and His Mosses* (Herman Melville, *The Piazza Tales and Other Prose Pieces, 1839-1860*, Evanston and Chicago: Northwestern University Press and the Newberry Li-brary, 1987, 244).

47 Cf. *Mardi* 630: "Beyond one obvious mark, all human lore is vain." 620: "The last wisdom is dumb."

48 Cf. *Mardi* 579-80: "Every man an author! books plenty of men!"

49 *Moby-Dick* 264. Cf. *Mardi* 339: "What is this subtle something that is in me, and eludes me?"

50 *Moby-Dick* 192: "without imagination no man can follow another into these halls."

51 I copy out this paragraph from my unpublished book "Melville's Secret Thought & Art."

52 Chapter CXXXIII (133): "They Still Remain upon the Rock" (*Mardi* 419-21).

53 Chapter CXLIII (143): "Wherein Babbalanja Discourses of Himself" (*Mardi* 455-60).

54 Cf. *Mardi* 581: "An exclamation point is entire Mardi's autobiography."

55 Melville reveals (in his letter of 29 June 1851 to Hawthorne) that the "secret motto" of

The Whale is the (secret) meaning of the phrase "Ego non baptizo te in nomine"—notice that he omits the words "Patris, et Filii et Spiritus Sancti—sed in nomine Diaboli." [See *Moby-Dick* 970 and 489]. In other words Melville implies that the main theme of the book is the "Ego," which rejects all the consecrated names of the common language (*non baptizo in nomine*). See note 37.

56 See Melville's *Hawthorne and His Mosses* (Herman Melville, *The Piazza Tales and Other Prose Pieces, 1839-1860*, Northwestern University Press and the Newberry Library, 1987, 243).

57 **mob**: *sb.*[1] *transf.* and *fig.* "a heterogeneous collection or crowd of things" (OED, 4 b); -y: an adjective-forming suffix meaning *full of* (*Webster's Dictionary of the English Language*, encyclopedic edition, J. G. Ferguson Publishing Company, Chicago, 1977. *Concise Oxford Dictionary*).

58 **mo**: *adj.* as the comparative of "much": "More or greater in amount or quantity." (OED, C 1); -by: suffix, forming descriptive personal appellations, playful or derisive (OED).

59 **dick**: A familiar pet-form of the common Christian name *Richard*. Hence generically (like *Jack*) = fellow, lad, man, especially with alliterating adjectives (OED, wd. "dick," *sb.*[1]).

60 See OED, wd. "dick," *sb.*[4], *slang*.

61 See Melville's letter to Hawthorne of 17 November 1851.

62 Cf. *Mardi* 442: "to those identical cracks, was he indebted for what little light he had in his brain."

63 William Shakespeare, *Hamlet*, II, ii, 193-94.

Basem L. Ra'ad

Uneasiness in "Bartleby":
Melville and Lockean Philosophy

Our occasion here in Volos is relevant to the meaning of my paper. I come from a land Melville visited 140 years ago and then devoted many years to writing his undervalued verse novel, *Clarel: A Poem and Pilgrimage in the Holy Land*. He had no difficulty in calling that land Palestine then. It is a land of many uneasinesses that Melville anticipated. He made it the setting for the issues of faith and doubt but also for the opposition of two modes of living that preoccupied his earlier writing as well: the simple and accepting vs. the obsessive and acquisitive.

Melville visited Greece too during the same trip. It is a beautiful land that shares with other parts of the eastern Mediterranean a deep history and the origin of much of what we call civilization today—together with the mythologies that developed into religions. It is the land where the tradition of "democracy" was born. At the same time there existed slavery and inequality. The American Revolution was based in part on that tradition as well as on a political philosophy derived largely from John Locke's writings. John Locke wrote about freedom, liberty, and the pursuit of happiness. But he also found ways to justify slavery and oppression. For Locke, for example, the forays of the Royal Africa Company into the African coast were a "just war," and the African people captured had forfeited their own lives by committing unjust acts that deserved death. But once he has them in his "power," the "lawful Conqueror" can delay taking their lives and put them to "his own Service" instead (*Treatises* 284-85).

Melville recognizes the contradictions between principle and practice in his culture. He deconstructs the assumptions underlying the duplicitous use of ideals to conceal power motives. The power exercised in this way exploits a type of knowledge based on a strategy of co-opting authorities of justification—religious, racial, philosophical, or other. Melville invokes a counter knowledge, one that is more difficult to attain in the normal exercise of human affairs. This knowledge means a deeper self-examination than human consciousness is usually capable of—since it requires uncovering self-deceptive, self-serving strategies. It is higher human knowledge that occupies Melville in "Bartleby," as it does in other works.

Every reading of "Bartleby" yields a different configuration and clustering of ideas. Sets of recurring words and concepts, or their combination, suggest new interpretations. I have never experienced such words in any way that made me feel uneasy, but they never fail to give me a "foreboding" and expectation. One single word, however, remained constantly puzzling, demanding to be solved if the story's total mood and its underlying psychology are to become more easily revealed.

One such word (we might think) could be "preference"—as in Bartleby's famous retort. Certainly this word is important, among other words and phrases: the "advent" of Bartleby, his silence, his blankness, his "passive resistance," the artificial "green" and "imprisoned turf" that is pointed up as consolation. Or there is, on the other hand, the narrator's first self-ironic premise about himself as "an eminently *safe* man," or his injunctions about the practices of reason-justice-charity-common sense, or his responses to Bartleby that range from "fear" to empathy, from "pity" to the "Adam of resentment." Many of these and other notions are capable of being pursued (as some have been) in their associations in the text, in Melville's writings, in the literary traditions, and in the history of thought.

But it is "uneasiness" that has intrigued me most, a word used three times in unusual circumstances (21, 27, 32). Its variants, antonyms, and synonyms, once explored, form a pervasive pattern in the story. Antonyms of "uneasiness" and "unease" are conspicuous: "easiest," "safe," "cozy," "snug," "idle," "content"; "peace," "pleasure," "happiness," "joy" (the last nouns are also philosophical concepts). Such words, linked to the lawyer or the public, have an opposing set of antonyms of "unease" associated with Bartleby's "passivity," his "stillness" and self-possession, often formed curiously as adverbs ("silently"; "tranquilly"; "dimly calm"; "cadaverously gentlemanly *nonchalance*"). The range of synonyms and variants is even more striking. I list some of them:

Nouns	Adjectives	Verbs
melancholy, repulsion, ambition, perplexity, impulse, motive, resentment, doubts, curiosity, apprehension, pain, passions, excitement, incentives, fear, tribulation, discontent, desire	restless, energetic, indignant, disturbed, displeased, inflamed, exasperated, flurried, nervous, reckless, uncomfortable, flighty	pained, (is) haunting, disconcerted, (being) incensed, burned, aggravates

Coincidentally, the same emotion is expressed in word forms of "unease" eight times in "Benito Cereno," another of Melville's works from the same period that fictionalizes complex psychological and power relationships. "Uneasiness" and "uneasy" occur eight times in Conrad's *Heart of Darkness* (1899) in most significant contexts that I believe are central to the novel. With Conrad, the condition of being uneasy is psychological and existential, cultural and aesthetic, and it defines the observer/actor relationship between Marlow and Kurtz as well as the responses, in a variety of uneasinesses, to the system of colonization, to the manager, to the city, to the wilderness, to the narrative itself.

In Defoe's *Robinson Crusoe* (1719), "uneasiness" is a key motivational concept, associated with "distempers, of body or mind" and with motives for economic improvement that drive Crusoe to his adventures. The influence of Locke's philosophy (especially *An Essay Concerning Human Understanding* and *Treatises on Government*) on Defoe's works has been discussed in a number of studies (e.g., Watt, Bell). Perhaps paradoxically, puritan thinking in Defoe runs in tandem with the adaptation of Locke's theories to economic matters.

The response to uneasiness in Conrad and Defoe are worlds apart, with Defoe's novel expressing the workings of the economic man and the justifications of the colonizing mind and Conrad's novel exploring the problematic of colonization and the destructiveness to the mind (in Kurtz) of its duplicitous aspects.

More than economic motive is involved in the concept of uneasiness elaborated in Locke's *Essay*. In fact, the economic motive is only one of the "irregular" or "adopted" desires included under "the fantastical uneasiness (as itch after honour, power, or riches, &c.)" (II.xxi.46, p. 343). Uneasiness is, as Locke puts it, "the chief, if not only[,] spur to human industry and action. . . . [It] alone determines the will" (II.xx.6, p. 304; II.xxi.37, p.336). The uneasiness can be either of body or of mind, and the "desire" that arises from it has, as its object, avoidance of pain and attainment of pleasure. This is a process to which we are continually subjected. The bodily or "natural" uneasinesses are those of "hunger, thirst, heat, cold, weariness. . . &c." (II.xxi.46, p. 343), while mental uneasinesses include fear, sorrow, shame, aversion, anger, and envy (II.xx.6, pp. 305-6; II.xxi.40, p. 338). Uneasiness generates a desire to remove pain or discomfort in order to reach "happiness," "joy," or "ease" again. "Joy" is "a delight of the mind, from the . . . approaching possession of a good," whereas despair is "the thought of the unattainableness" of any good (II.xx.6-11, p. 305).

What is crucial is that Locke included the concept of uneasiness only in the second edition of the *Essay* (1694), using it to replace the "established and settled . . . maxim . . . *the greater good*" in the first edition (1690) as the primary mover of the will (II.xxi.35, p. 335). Locke's change of mind is a significant point in his thought and in popular Western philosophy, and it both rises out of and influences religious, cultural, social, economic, and aesthetic developments.

Initially, Locke's new model of the mind and his empirical psychology of human motives generated a good deal of praise but also attack. The Scriblerus Club, founded shortly after publication of the *Essay*, including members like Swift and Pope, parodied some of Locke's theories and examples (see Fox). The religious attacks were even more vehement. The *Essay* was attacked in "pulpit and pamphlet" because it contained a "philosophy that denied innate ideas of God and morality and dared to suggest man's mind may be a material rather than a spiritual substance, a philosophy that proved human knowledge limited and demonstrated the inferiority of the intellect of a being supposedly formed in the image of the Creator" (MacLean 5-6).

In fact, this replacement of "greater good" with "uneasiness" was specifically rejected, decades later, by Jonathan Edwards, the American philosopher of religion, who admired and was strongly influenced by Locke. Edwards preferred the text of Locke's first edition because he thought that Locke's change negated the pervasiveness of God's will in the conduct of human affairs—in effect placing natural necessity above moral necessity and making human will independent of divine providence (*Philosophy* 67; *Freedom* 433).

But the influence of Locke's ideas grew in the eighteenth century. His works, of course, influenced later philosophical discussion in Europe and America, and they were commented on by major English literary figures. His thinking directly affected literary works (Defoe, Fielding, Richardson, Sterne, Johnson, Goldsmith, Addison, and others; see MacLean). I do not need to remind you of the influence Locke's political thought had on the philosophical foundation of the American Revolution and its writers (MacLean 44; Caws). Also, Locke's empirical assumptions about the workings of the mind helped to create, according to one view, an evolution in literary sensibility and the concept of the imagination: "the transference of the 'locus of reality' to the perceiving mind made necessary eventually a radically new conception of art as effect . . . it was necessary to reconstruct 'conscience' and 'the means of grace' in terms of a theory of the mind that denied the possibility of occult and supernatural influences on the personality. By a natural process . . . imagination came to be a means of grace within the world of actual, physical sense impressions" (Tuveson 2).

Locke's philosophy influenced Melville, directly and indirectly. Locke's model of the mind raised ontological and epistemological issues that we know Melville responded to in his writing. The opposition between Kant and Locke is played out in the whale-head metaphor in *Moby-Dick* (as in chapter 73), and Melville demonstrates awareness of the polemic against innateness. He cites Locke's comparison of "the human mind at birth to a sheet of blank paper; something destined to be scribbled on, but what sort of characters no soul might tell" ("Tartarus of Maids" 333). (Note the change from Locke's "white paper" to "blank paper," and the use of "scribbled.")

Locke's "uneasiness" thus contains possibilities for both traditional and deconstructive applications—in that it can be a model for practical motives, for capitalistic impulse (for power, riches, and so forth) as well as, implicitly, for ideal motives and the absence of "the greater good." Such double possibilities also exist in a strange way in Locke's political thinking. Locke's model for political organization (consent, liberty, equality, property) contains an acceptance of inequality and provides justification for slavery and colonial power. This same problematic is available in the political environment of the American Declaration of Independence.

In "Bartleby," there are what might be considered echoes of Locke's title. The narrator says that a description of his office and surroundings is "indispensable to an adequate understanding of the chief character about to be presented," and this character, we find out later, has nothing "ordinarily human about him" in that he is not subjected to usual desires. In fact, he is not "like other men" and does not seem to share the state of "a human creature with the common infirmities of our nature" (13, 21, 28, 26). We get the story from the perspective of a person who is trying to understand the Bartleby phenomenon but is really incapable of doing so because of normal and popular motives. In this way, the story deconstructs Locke's concepts.

Uneasiness

The change by Locke from "greater good" to "uneasiness" is fundamental to the conflict dramatized in "Bartleby." While Locke replaces a classical and idealistic principle with a pragmatic one based largely on a causal chain of motives and impulses, his text preserves the possibilities of ambiguity and still suggests that the "greater good" may be desirable but impractical to attain: "Let a man be ever so well persuaded of the advantages of virtue, that it is as necessary to a man who has any great aims in this world, or hopes in the next, as food to life: yet, till he hungers or thirsts after righteousness, till he *feels an uneasiness* in the want of it, his *will* will not be determined to any action in pursuit of this confessed greater good; but any other uneasiness he feels in himself shall take [its] place, and carry his will to other actions" (II.xxi.35, p. 335).

This kind of problematic (impulses vs. obligations, wants vs. duties) is explored in Kant's philosophy. It allows Melville to construct a critical response to the duplicitous application of principles in a materialistic American context.

What is particularly portentous about uneasiness is that it represents a set of emotions and priorities to which only the lawyer and other characters become subjected—whereas Bartleby does not feel uneasiness at all. The "advent of Bartleby" begins to generate a process of psychological uneasiness, an invasion of the lawyer's "peace." The lawyer is in effect being challenged in his "assumptions" and eventually asked, as the reader is asked, to question the "easiest way of life" (he concedes, though, that his profession is "energetic and nervous"— that is, motivated and uneasy; 14-15). The narrator, in other words, is now only marginally subjected to the primary motives of the capitalistic enterprise. He has become a parasite at the service end of already established American capital—a "safe" man who is self-congratulatory about the rich he services and resentful of any threat to his established self-interest. This self-ironic premise by the narrator is carefully sketched at the beginning of the story (especially in the ironic parallels to landscape painting). So, we can say that the narrator is controlled by popular Lockean psychology, being a slave to acquired or fantastical desires—which for him become "necessities" (32). He has grown at ease about them.

But Lockean philosophy is capable of enlightening Bartleby's position as well, in ways that Locke would not have intended. Bartleby is a figure that transcends normal necessities. He eats little (and finally nothing), he is propertyless, all his worldly belongings fit into a handkerchief. If he is uneasy about anything, his uneasiness takes the form of moral resignation at the absence of the greater good—as his fixed glance upon the bust of Cicero suggests (30). Locke explains that "the will being the power of directing our operative faculties to some action, for some end, cannot at any time be moved towards what is judged at that time unattainable: that would be to suppose an intelligent being designedly to act for an end, only to lose its labour; for so it is to act for what is judged not attainable; and therefore very great uneasinesses move not the will, when they are judged not capable of a cure" (II.xxi.41, p. 339). The "uneasiness is cured or allayed by that consideration [unattainableness]" (II.xx.6, p. 305).

Melville provides an ironic echo of Locke's explanation when he has the narrator explain the limits of his pity by saying that such limits come about from "a certain hopelessness of remedying excessive and organic ill. To a sensitive being, pity is not seldom pain. And when at last it is perceived that such pity cannot lead to eventual succor, common sense bids the soul be rid of it" (29). Pity, charity, love, the greater good are all in the same category—now truly impossible, unattainable. When they are cited their application is limited by practicalities and necessities. Here Blake's lines from "The Human Abstract" come to mind: "Pity would be no more / If we did not make someone poor."

Bartleby's inaction is the action that leads the narrator to greater and greater existential uneasiness. Locke may be useful to explain inaction in this context: "I would crave leave here, under the word *action*, to comprehend the forbearance too of any action proposed" (II.xxi.28, p. 330).

Preference

Locke's "forbearance" is connected to "preference"—a concept that is crucial in the dramatic confrontation on the issue of labor between the lawyer and Bartleby. Bartleby prefers rather than wills, whereas the narrator insists on necessity:

> "You *will* not?"...
> "I *prefer* not"....
> "You *must*" (25, 33).

For Locke the ideas of liberty and necessity are connected to the power in human beings "to begin or forbear, continue or put an end to several actions." Uneasiness determines the will: "the will, or power of setting us upon one action in preference to all others, is determined in us by uneasiness" (II.xxi.7, p. 315; II.xxi.39, p. 338). Locke distinguishes the will from preference (whereas, coincidentally, Edwards rejects such a distinction completely): "So far as a man has power to think or not to think, to move or not to move, according to the preference or direction of his mind, so far is a man *free*" (II.xxi.8, p. 315; compare Edwards's *Freedom* 138).

Bartleby's primary objection is to labor. This objection allows him to transcend the limits of a work contract in order to preserve his sense of freedom. In "preference" Bartleby is, in effect, asserting his freedom by suspending the necessity determined in action and therefore insisting on higher and greater good as a value.

"Innate and incurable disorder"

This concept in Melville's story is actually an ironic assertion of good that is perceived as disorder. Lockean philosophy may be an operative one in the story, but the character of Bartleby can be seen as an insistence on some innate values, to which lip service is given in the conduct of human society and its merciless practicalities. This might explain the narrator's assumption that Bartleby suffers from an "innate and incurable disorder," an "aberration"—that he does not adhere to requests made "according to common usage and common sense" (29, 31, 22). The context of the story forces us to think of "disorder" or "aberration" as a challenge to the established rules of vulgar common sense. For the narrator tries to ease his uneasiness by construing Bartleby's position as "disorder" (sure enough, it would lead to disruption of prescribed order). How else can we make consistent the narrator's admission of having "evil impulse" or committing an "inadvertence" by making demands on Bartleby to do certain tasks, in the face of Bartleby's "paramount consideration"? And what else will reconcile the contradictions in his exclamation after another refusal by Bartleby: "How could a human creature with the common infirmities of our nature, refrain from bitterly exclaiming upon such perverseness—such unreasonableness?" (22, 24, 26). In ironic typological mode, the Christ parallel points to the tragic incompatibilities, religious and political, between principles and practices (a dominant theme in *Pierre*, *The Confidence-Man*, and *Clarel*). The practice of charity, particularly as developed in America from Winthrop on (where self-interest is accepted into the philanthropic motive), is a source of the assumption of perverseness in the holder of the ideal.

To clarify the issue in other philosophical terms, we can cite the Kantian tension between two types of common sense (vulgar and higher), between the world of phenomena or experience (controlled by causal relationships and sensuous impulses) and the world of rationality (where moral duties, reason, and true freedom reside). In Kant, "the will is considered to be the source of obligation which directs moral attention away from heteronomous, unworthy maxims of actions, to those consistent with the moral law" (Caygill 414). Kant also makes a distinction between common will and transcendent will.

I hope to pursue further the significance of the concept of "uneasiness" in "Bartleby" and in the other works I mentioned. This has been only a brief overview of possible applications. An inward look at the work through a concept such as "uneasiness" might help to establish a sort of landmark against which possible interpretations, past and future, could be gauged. Let me give four fairly random examples of what I consider to be serious fallacies in critical interpretation:

1. The story's reference to Edwards on the will and Priestly on necessity (33; see summary in Newman 33-34): In the anxiety of discovering sources, the context in the work is not examined fully. Necessity is rejected in Bartleby's posture. The narrator uses Edwards and Priestly as a source of consolation—as a way to "ease" his confusion—because they maintain that the will is not free, that all is predestined.

2. Religious and theological explanations for "the doctrine of assumptions" (35; see summary in Newman 58): Such explanations do not seem to follow the context either, where "assumptions" are clearly opposed to "preferences"—assumptions being the premises of the system that require "compliance," whereas "preferences" can be equated with freedom of choice. Kuebrich's economic reading is to the point here, although it would need to be modified by adding the philosophical elements.

3. The significance of the color green (e.g., 35; Newman 38, 63): "Bartleby rejects the green of the grass pointed out to him by the lawyer. . . . The lawyer's awareness of the green grass is a measure of hope of his eventual salvation. The color symbolism reinforces the 'sympathy and hope for the average man' expressed in the story as well as 'the severity of its treatment of the artist'"(Marx; in Inge 102-5). Such a conclusion seems to contradict the suggestions of the artificiality of the greens used in the story: the screen in the office, the "soft imprisoned turf" in the prison compound (44). Bartleby's response to the narrator's attempt to console him with "Look. There's the sky, and here's the grass" (43; "Benito" 116) is a measure of the unavailability of "hope" and of the narrator's duplicitous position.

4. The defense of the lawyer (e.g., Newman 65-66; McCall 153): A recognition of ambivalent self-irony by the narrator is crucial to the story. Melville's purpose can be transmitted to us without necessarily implying an eventual development or understanding in the narrator's sensibilities. The narrator's attitude of playfulness, pity, vindictiveness, attraction, and doubleness toward Bartleby (similar to that between Marlow and Kurtz) is an indication of complexity in the relationship. The narrator (and we, as we remain affiliated with the system)

may grow wiser or more aware while experiencing the story but not change or become necessarily purer.

The connections I have outlined may also help in understanding how Melville often applies and inverts sources:

1. "Some of the compassionate and curious bystanders joined the party; and headed by one of the constables arm in arm with Bartleby, the silent procession filed its way through all the noise, and heat, and joy of the roaring thoroughfares at noon" (42). The "joy" of pedestrians on Wall Street, so incongruous here, is given pointed meaning in light of Locke's definition of joy as "a delight of the mind, from the consideration of the present or assured approaching possession of a good" (II.xx.7, p. 305).

2. "What earthly right have you to stay here? Do you pay any rent? Do you pay any taxes? Or is this property yours?" (35). These questions by the narrator can be placed consistently within the story by seeing them in the context of Locke's *Second Treatise on Government*. In the state of nature, property is common and labor then gives title to property: "Though the Earth, and all inferior Creatures be common to all Men, yet every Man has a *Property* in his own *Person*. This no Body has any Right to but himself. The *Labour* of his Body, and the *Work* of his Hands . . . are properly his. . . . Thus the Grass my Horse bit; the Turfs my Servant has cut; and the Ore I have digg'd . . . become my *Property*, without the assignation or consent of any body" (287-89). America, which is now controlled by money, was once according to Locke "wild woods and uncultivated wast [*sic*]": "Thus in the beginning all the World was *America*, and more so than that is now; for no such thing as *Money* was any where known" (294, 301). In his posture, Bartleby therefore repudiates the narrator's servility to the system and also his role as a "conveyanser and title hunter" (19). Bartleby affirms original principles of property and an original hope of America in a pure moneyless condition. America is repeating Old World cycles: its promise, as Ungar says to the pilgrims in *Clarel*, has become that "squandered last inheritance" (IV.xxi.166).

Bartleby violates the expectations implicit in a popular application of Lockean psychology: he, in effect, refuses to be "scribbled on" and keeps himself outside the cycle of daily uneasinesses. Bartleby is not subjected to the uneasiness of hunger (his food is minimal and he starves himself at the end) or of thirst for power or property or riches (he does not touch the lawyer's payment). One could argue that his only uneasiness is one about the absent "greater good." This may be akin to Pascal's anxiety and ennui (as Hildebrand describes it), but it strikes me as more directed—for Bartleby is not as much miserable as he is watchful and determined. That uneasiness being totally in the realm of "impossibility or unattainableness . . . is cured or allayed by that consideration" (II.xx.6, p. 305; II.xxi.41, p. 339).

"Uneasiness," in short, provides an over-arching concept that subsumes many other concepts in the work. Bartleby assumes the position of one who holds to the greater good and who reminds us of its absence. His gesture is therefore cognizant of the system and its requirements for compliance. His act of preferring not to act is itself an action that, while it may be fatal, succeeds in challenging and testing the system. When Bartleby says to the narrator, "I know you" (43), therefore, he is making an epistemologically meaningful statement that has far-reaching implications.

References

Bell, Ian A. "King Crusoe: Locke's Political Theory in *Robinson Crusoe.*" *English Studies* 1 (1988): 27-36.

Blake, William. "The Human Abstract." In *Songs of Experience* (1794).

Caws, Peter. *Two Centuries of Philosophy in America.* Totowa, NJ: Rowman and Littlefield, 1982.

Caygill, Howard. *A Kant Dictionary.* Cambridge, MS: Blackwell, 1995.

Conrad, Joseph. *Heart of Darkness* (1899).

Defoe, Daniel. *Robinson Crusoe* (1719).

Edwards, Jonathan. *Freedom of the Will.* Ed. Paul Ramsey. New Haven: Yale UP, 1957.

——. *The Philosophy of Jonathan Edwards From His Private Notebooks.* Ed. Harvey G. Townsend. Eugene, OR: U of Oregon P, 1955.

Fox, Christopher. *Locke and the Scriblerians.* Berkeley: U of California P, 1988.

Hildebrand, William H. "'Bartleby' and the Black Conceit." *Studies in Romanticism* 27 (1988): 289-313.

Inge, M. Thomas, ed. *Bartleby the Inscrutable: A Collection of Commentary on Herman*

Melville's Tales. Hamden, CT: Archon Books, 1979.

Kuebrich, David. "Melville's Doctrine of Assumptions: The Hidden Ideology of Capitalist Production in 'Bartleby.'" *New England Quarterly* 69 (1996):381-405.

Locke, John. *An Essay Concerning Human Understanding*. 2 vols. New York: Dover, 1959.

——. *Two Treatises of Government*. Cambridge: Cambridge UP, 1988.

MacLean, Kenneth. *John Locke and English Literature of the Eighteenth Century*. New York: Russell & Russell, 1962.

Marx, Leo. "Melville's Parables of the Walls." *Sewanee Review* 61 (1953): 602-27. Rpt. in Inge, 84-106.

McCall, Dan. *The Silence of Bartleby*. Ithaca, NY: Cornell UP, 1989.

Melville, Herman. "Bartleby, the Scrivener." In *The Piazza Tales and Other Prose Pieces, 1839-1860*. Vol. 9 of *The Writings of Herman Melville*. Evanston and Chicago: Northwestern UP and the Newberry Library, 1987.

——. "Benito Cereno." In *Piazza Tales*.

——. *Clarel: A Poem and Pilgrimage in the Holy Land*. Ed Walter E. Bezanson. New York: Hendricks House, 1960.

——. "The Tartarus of Maids." In *Piazza Tales*.

Newman, Lea Bertani Vozar. *A Reader's Guide to the Short Stories of Herman Melville*. Boston: G. K. Hall, 1986.

Tuveson, Ernest Lee. *The Imagination as a Means of Grace: Locke and the Aesthetics of Romanticism*. Berkeley: U of California P, 1960.

Watt, Ian. *The Rise of the Novel: Studies in Defoe, Richardson and Fielding*. Harmondsworth, U.K.: Penguin, 1957.

Weiner, Susan. *Law in Art: Melville's Major Fiction and Nineteenth-Century American Law*. New York: Peter Lang, 1992.

Hendrika Klijn Neuburger

Currents in Common:

Christianity in Selected Writings of Melville and Kierkegaard

oncern with the interpretation of Christianity is a topic of importance for both Melville and Kierkegaard as they share a desire for purity, or truth in Christian thought and practice. In selected works the authors treat certain concepts and themes related to the perceived meaning of Christianity in a similar fashion. At times, the parallels are striking, giving an impression of double exposures. This paper deals with a number of these parallel ideas and, to an extent, considers their literary application in the works of Melville.

First, it will be useful to distinguish briefly between the individual perceptions of the authors with regard to Christianity.

Kierkegaard's concern is of an existential nature. He devotes his work to the question of what it means "to be or, rather, to become Christian," applying the relevant psychology primarily to himself. Later, somewhat reluctantly, he intends to reach those who, in his view, are equally in need of spiritual edification.

The initial reluctance to publish stems from a scruple of knowing himself not yet to be fully Christian, having borne Christ's Cross only "externally," and from his doubt if one then has the right to let others know one's thoughts on the subject. Kierkegaard circumvented his self-imposed moral obstacle by writing and publishing most of his early work under various pseudonyms which gave him a measure of freedom in expressing his ideas. The pseudonyms also served as identifications, or potentialities of characteristics in his own nature, as well as allowed him to communicate indirectly, which he thought to be more effective than to convey his thoughts directly under his own name. In this we see a kinship with Melville's frequent use of irony in thoughts expressed or, interpreted through his various literary characters.

Melville's concern, as we know, is to expose through satire or irony the spiritual and emotional poverty that is evident in the social application of traditional Christian beliefs and thus to contrast the deficiency with that which appears to him to be the essential meaning of Christianity.

I have selected passages from *White-Jacket, Redburn, Moby-Dick,* and *Pierre* by Melville and from a number of works by Kierkegaard as acknowledged in the Notes. In these particular works the authors have employed kindred ideas with a view to, in Kierkegaard's words, "a condemnation of Christendom, as an attempt to introduce Christianity into Christendom."[1]

Not only does this assessment of intent inform us of Kierkegaard's aim, it reverberates through Melville's work as well. For example, it occurs in *White-Jacket* when, at the end of a satirical meditation on Indian exploits, the protagonist, questioning the cruelty of so-called civilized "fellow Christians," asks rhetorically: "Are there no Moravians in the moon, that not a missionary has yet visited this poor pagan planet of ours to *civilize civilization* and *christianize christendom?*" (*WJ* 273; emphasis added).

Apart from the similarity in the concept expressed by the different authors, it is worth noting that Moravians were reformers, *against* the power of the Church, but *for* Moral Reformation of the Christian faith. The movement, known as the Bohemian Brethren, originated in Czechoslovakia and spread through Europe and North America where it was established in 1734. Søren Kierkegaard's brother, Peter, did at one time belong to the Brethren; their father did attend some meetings. Interesting, in this context, is Søren Kierkegaard's allegation that the State Church (of Denmark) rests "only on a phantom of Christian faith . . . which by pretending to be Christian commits the most serious of impostures."[2]

As if consolidating the observation of a fellow participant in an "unconscious community of artists," Melville deftly paints the tragedy resulting from applying socially the mere "phantom of Christian faith," rather than ministering Christianity in its gospelized fullness of brotherhood and compassion. In *Red-*

burn, as the protagonist hears a wail "which seemed to come out of the earth, [an] endless wail of someone forever lost," the plight of the starving woman and children tragically personifies this "phantom of Christian faith." Redburn asks himself, "who were these ghosts that I saw? Were they not human beings? A woman and two girls? With eyes and lips, and ears like any queen? With hearts which, though they did not bound with blood, yet beat with a dull, dead ache that was their life?" (*RB* 253).

Later, he exclaims: "Tell me, oh Bible, that story of Lazarus again, that I may find comfort in my heart for the poor and forlorn" (*RB* 257). And, wandering through Liverpool, he muses how it is "a most Christian thing, and a matter most sweet to dwell upon and simmer over in solitude, that any poor sinner may go to church wherever he pleases" (*RB* 279). Strengthening the impact of the message still further, young Redburn notes: "It speaks whole volumes of folios, and Vatican libraries, for Christianity."

Albeit from different perspectives and in dissimilar contexts, both authors expose the spiritual poverty and dearth of compassion in the general avowal of traditional Christian faith. Where Kierkegaard highlights poverty of spirit as adhering to the foundation of the Church, Melville employs satire and/or irony to poke holes in the imposture of a socially accepted veneer, thus exposing the un-Christian practice underneath.

Since *Redburn* appears to be the spawning ground for many of Melville's literary themes, it will be interesting to take a further look at a concept developed by Kierkegaard which has its parallel in *Redburn*.

Kierkegaard gives voice to his conception of the archetypal castaway as he reminds himself "that at *birth* a man is cast out into the world and from that moment lies with a depth beneath him of a thousand fathoms, and the future before him every instant, yea, every instant, *which is as the darkest night*" (emphasis added).[3]

Redburn ushers in the outcast and wanderer when narrating the ship's passage into the open sea. He feels cast out as he meditates on how the ship "is steering right out among those waves, and leaving the bright land behind, *and the dark night coming*" (emphasis added; *RB* 81).

The still innocent Redburn paints a vivid picture of his rite of passage, describing how the vessel is going through the Narrows, the doorway to and from

New York Harbor, and how at sunset they were "fairly 'outside,' and well may it so be called, for I felt thrust out of the world" (*RB* 83). The emotional description, with its overtones of a physical birth, strongly resembles the already cited Kierkegaardean *birth*.

Redburn who, to an extent, is modeled on Esau (kin of Ishmael), confirms his role of friendless outlaw as he finds himself to be a "sort of Ishmael in the ship" (*RB* 114), thereby foreshadowing the emergence of the full-fledged Ishmael in *Moby-Dick*.

In *Moby-Dick*, the mature Ishmael appears at center stage, taking on biblical dimensions while dramatically addressing the audience and establishing a lasting relationship with the invitation: *Call me Ishmael.*

Due to the nature of the tales, Kierkegaard's "depth ... of a thousand fathoms," is in Melville's *Redburn* and *Moby-Dick* mirrored in the protagonists' circumstantial abodes. In *Pierre*, however, this type of imagery also occurs. Albeit a land-tale, the work is in the context of what Professor Sedgwick has termed "Melville's most wonderful of symbols," veined with references to the sea. Pierre's discovery of a particular mass of rock, for example, which he christens the "Memnon Stone" and describes as with "its crown being full eight fathoms under high-foliage mark during the great spring-tide of foliage" (*P* 160), places the work, metaphorically, in the same league.

In a similar context, Kierkegaard seems to have foreseen the mirage of Ishmael's near-drowning and miraculous survival at the end of *Moby-Dick*, through the fine mist thrown up by ocean waves. His existential chant begins with the emphasis on "I am again myself," moving on to the expression of a deeply felt elation with his own rescue to, in his terms, "the idea ... the high flight of thought." I quote the pertinent part. "Hail to the solemn exultation of victory! Hail to the dance in the vortex of the infinite! Hail to the breaking wave which covers me in the abyss! Hail to the breaking wave which hurls me up above the stars!"[4]

Ishmael's testimony of being "but slowly drawn to the closing vortex" (*MD* 687), and his description of reaching the center of the whirlpool and seeing the buoyant coffin "rising with great force" out of the vacuum, echoes the essence of Kierkegaard's chant of thanksgiving, if not its level of exultation. Although I include two other, prior instances of kinship between a Melville passage and

Kierkegaard's poetic exclamation, I have noted Ishmael's example first, since his rescue is not only most dramatic in nature but, occurring at the very end of *Moby-Dick*, the language with its anti-climactic last words, "only found another orphan," beautifully matches the equally soulful, "Call me Ishmael," at the beginning of the tale. These words, at beginning and end, frame the story.

In the context of the author's attempt to "Civilize Civilization and Christianize Christendom," Melville brings together two disparate perspectives—the pagan and the biblical (O.T.)—and intertwines them into One Truth. With the doubly coiled vision generated in Ishmael through his friendship with the pagan shipmate, Queequeg, and through the latter with the indecipherable mystery of life, sealed within the life-buoy coffin, Melville highlights a glimpse of the Truth of Reality, that is, the Act of Being.

Also in *Moby-Dick*, one of the earlier examples of what sounds like Kierkegaard's "Exsultate, Jubilate," may be found in the apotheosis, projected by Ishmael, of the mysteriously invisible Bulkington. In spiritually charged words, Ishmael urges the aloof sailor to "Take heart, take heart, O Bulkington! Bear thee grimly, demigod! Up from the spray of thy ocean-perishing—straight up, leaps thy apotheosis!" (*MD* 203).

Another allusion occurs in *White-Jacket*, when the protagonist, at the point of drowning, will shed his confining jacket. Finding himself sinking, a "wild and heartlessly jubilant sound" rang in his ear, and in an appropriate analogy (for this conference) with Greek geography, White-Jacket chants: "Oh soul! thou then heardest life and death: as he who stands upon the Corinthian shore hears both the Ionian and the Aegean waves." He goes on: "Quicker and quicker I mounted; till at last I bounded up like a buoy, and my whole head was bathed in the blessed air" (*WJ* 403). A further theme, advanced by Kierkegaard and reflected in Melville's work as well, could have been written by the Danish author with the spiritually challenged, or despairing Pierre in mind.

In putting forward a particular theme, the Kierkegaardean voice easily "fits" the characteristic voice of the authorial narrator in *Pierre*, if not in substance, certainly in style, as in: "The heathen . . . has this anxiety; for heathenism is precisely self-torment. Instead of casting all his care upon God, the heathen has all the worries; he is without God [without spiritual paternity], and hence he is the worried man, the self-tormenter. For since he is without God it cannot in any sense be God that imposes worry upon him. The situation is not this: without God—no worry, with God—with worry; but it is this: with God—no worry, without God—with worry."[5]

Pierre becomes a heathen, he has cast out his paternity—his past—since he defiantly wishes to be "untrammeledly his ever-present self! free to do his own self-will and present fancy to whatever end!" (*P* 232). Kierkegaard sees defiance as leading to "the despair of willing despairingly to be oneself."[6] His work *The Sickness unto Death* deals with sickness, or despair in the spirit which in his Christian philosophy is to be remedied with religion, that is, through faith (the opposite of despair), that consciously worships Christ. Pierre's despair is, in Kierkegaardean terms, a self-consuming despair. It is impotent, for it is "not able to do what it wills."[7]

Interesting are the various literary applications of the self-consuming aspect of despair in works of Melville. In *Redburn* there is Jackson who, plagued "by an incurable malady, full of hatred and gall against every thing and every body . . . is but the foul lees and dregs of a man, thin as a shadow" (*RB* 112).

There is Ahab who, in his monomaniacal obsession with the White Whale by whom he was dismembered, attempts to wreak vengeance "on a dumb brute" and thus becomes a blasphemer. He confirms what he has become when venting his feelings of megalomania, yet knowing himself to be "damned in the midst of Paradise" (*MD* 266).

Pierre, too, is part of the procession of self-consumers. Gradually losing his spiritual hold on reality and on himself, he calls out to Lucy and Isabel when they enter the prison-dungeon to go away: "For Pierre is neuter now!" (*P* 403).

Another concept dealt with by both Melville and Kierkegaard in similar metaphors occurs at the end of *Pierre*. Pierre's friend, Charlie Millthorpe, on finding Pierre lifeless, exclaims: "The dark vein's burst, and here's the deluge-wreck all stranded here!" (*P* 405), showing an understanding of the defiance that drove Pierre. Charlie's utterance is akin to the conscious characterization of Kierkegaard's autobiographical despair (which he regards as the natural consequence of defiance) in the form of "the shipwreck of freedom."[8]

Among further similarities between Kierkegaard and Melville, there is

Kierkegaard's personal decision to renounce his engagement to *Regina* and the decision of Melville's character, Pierre, to renounce his engagement to *Lucy*. Albeit for different reasons, both felt honor-bound to break the respective relationships, as they believed themselves called to fulfill a divine mission. Moreover, both Kierkegaard and Pierre adopt the same method in achieving a complete break. They make themselves seem unworthy in the eyes of their fiancées, in order to enable them to more or less accept the situation. As well, Kierkegaard's moral dilemma, *Regina* or *God*, is echoed in *Pierre* as the "infatuated young enthusiast" (*P* 213) is confronted with his own "all-including query—*Lucy* or *God?*" (*P* 213).

The last example in this paper of apparent simultaneous vision in works of Melville and Kierkegaard appears most striking in its similarity. I refer to a Kierkegaardean *Discourse*, published in 1847-48, titled "Of the Difference between a Genius and an Apostle" and a chapter in *Pierre*, titled "Church of the Apostles." *Pierre* was published in 1852.

Kierkegaard describes an Apostle as someone receiving or having received a mission; to "become an Apostle is not preceded by any potential possibility; essentially every man is equally near to becoming one."[9]

As the title of the *Discourse* indicates, Kierkegaard also addresses the concept of Genius, analyzing its meaning. From his perspective, Genius is born, "Genius is what it is of itself," but an Apostle is called, "an Apostle is what he is by his divine authority."[10]

Dr. Lowrie, who has translated many Kierkegaard works and has written an extensive biography of the author, writes that "S. K. was aware that he was a genius, and sadly aware also how much he had to suffer for it."[11]

With an appreciable dose of irony, Pierre, who thinks of himself as an Apostle, and who in a zealous burst of righteousness cries out that he will "gospelize the world anew" (*P* 310), appears to intertwine the concepts of Genius and Apostle. Initially he comes forward as an Apostle, believing himself to have been called by divine authority to be his sister's keeper. He begins, however, to think of himself as a Genius in the writing of his gospel which, in reality, is autobiographical; to wit, "Pierre seems to have directly plagiarized from his own experience to fill out the mood of his apparent author-hero" (*P* 342).

Thus, in Kierkegaard's terms which parallel, albeit from a different perspective, those of Melville, Pierre becomes a blasphemer: "a man is called by a revelation to go out in the world, to proclaim the Word, to act and to suffer . . . as the Lord's messenger. But that a man should be called by a revelation to sit back . . . momentarily clever, and afterwards as publisher and editor of the uncertainties of his cleverness: that is something approaching blasphemy."[12]

Although Pierre never manages to have his work published, it is what he strives for while residing in New York.

A footnote to Kierkegaard's thoughts explains that his observations refer to Adler, one-time follower of Hegel. As discussed by Kierkegaard, he saw in the Reverend A. P. Adler "not only an example of misguided enthusiasm . . . confused by a complete misunderstanding of the present age, but a caricature of his own position."[13]

The above view, expressed by Kierkegaard, could have served as a blueprint for the character of Pierre. Taking into account the authorial intrusions in *Pierre*, one could substitute the voice of Melville for Kierkegaard's voice, and Pierre, Melville's "infatuated young enthusiast" for Adler, without in any way altering the strength of the assertion. Taking this further, Melville may have seen in Pierre, as one of his literary personae, a caricature of himself.

In addition, there is the phenomenon that Melville, the author and the Genius of Pierre's writing, becomes the Apostle, called upon to write the in principle not-to-be-written gospel.

In conclusion, the various parallel ideas and, at times, similar ways of expressing them in the discussed works of Melville and Kierkegaard, point first to *Currents* [of thought] *in Common*, flowing through a particular era as the spirit of its time (Zeitgeist) or, in T. S. Eliot's view, spring from an "unconscious community of artists."

Second, the similarities show that both Melville and Kierkegaard saw as their mission (in Melville's case, as part of a mission), the task of being literarily instrumental in demolishing the edifice of nineteenth-century Christian thought, in order to "Christianize Christendom" and thus to help instigate a Moral Rebirth.

NOTES

1 Walter Lowrie, transl., *The Sickness unto Death* by Søren Kierkegaard (Princeton, NJ: Princeton University Press, 1968), 136.

2 Jacques Collette, ed., *The Difficulty of Being Christian* by Søren Kierkegaard (Notre Dame, IN: University of Notre Dame, 1968), 17.

3 Søren Kierkegaard, *Christian Discourses* (London: Oxford University Press, 1952), 263.

4 Søren Kierkegaard, "Repetition: An Essay in Experimental Psychology," *A Kierkegaard Anthology*, ed. Robert Bretall (Princeton, NJ: Princeton University Press, 1946), 136.

5 Kierkegaard, *Discourses*, 79.

6 Kierkegaard, *Sickness*, 200.

7 Kierkegaard, *Sickness*, 151.

8 Walter Lowrie, *A Short Life of Kierkegaard* (Princeton, NJ: Princeton University Press, 1965), 92.

9 Søren Kierkegaard, *Of the Difference Between a Genius and an Apostle* (London: Oxford University Press, 1962), 107.

10 Kierkegaard, *Difference*, 105.

11 Walter Lowrie, *Kierkegaard*, 2 vols. (Gloucester, MA: Peter Smith, 1970), 102.

12 Kierkegaard, *Difference*, 125.

13 Søren Kierkegaard, *The Present Age* (London: Oxford University Press, 1962), 11.

REFERENCES

Auden, W.H. *The Living Thoughts of Kierkegaard.* Bloomington & London: Indiana University Press, 1963.

Brodtkorb, Jr., Paul. *Ishmael's White World. A Phenomenological Reading of* Moby-Dick. New Haven and London: Yale University Press, 1965.

Hamilton, Kenneth. *The Promise of Kierkegaard.* Philadelphia and New York, J. B. Lippincott Company, 1969.

Kierkegaard, Søren. "Christian Discourses." Trans. W. Lowrie. London: Oxford University Press, 1952.

——. *The Concept of Dread.* Trans. W. Lowrie. Princeton: Princeton University Press, 1967.

——. *Fear and Trembling* and *The Sickness Unto Death.* Trans. Walter Lowrie. Princeton, NJ: Princeton University Press, 1968.

——. *Kierkegaard: The Difficulty of Being Christian.* Ed. Jacques Collette and trans.

Ralph M. McInnery and Leo Turcotte. Notre Dame, IN: University of Notre Dame Press, 1968.

——. *Kierkegaard: Either/Or.* Trans. Walter Lowrie. Princeton, NJ: Princeton University Press, 1949.

——. *The Present Age* and *Of the Difference Between a Genius and an Apostle.* Trans. Alexander Dru. London: Oxford University Press, 1962.

——. "Repetition: An Essay in Experimental Psychology." Pseudonymn Constantine Constantius (1843). *A Kierkegaard Anthology.* Ed. Robert Bretall. Princeton, NJ: Princeton U P, 1946.

Lowrie, Walter. *Kierkegaard's Attack upon "Christendom." 1854-1855.* Princeton, NJ: Princeton U P, 1968.

——. *Kierkegaard.* Gloucester, MA: Peter Smith, 1970. Vol. 1. 2 vols.

——. *A Short Life of Kierkegaard.* Princeton, NJ: Princeton University Press, 1965.

Melville, Herman. *Moby-Dick.* Ed. Harold Beaver, Harmondsworth, Middlesex M: Penguin Classics, 1986.

——. *Pierre: or, The Ambiguities.* New York: New American Library, 1964.

——. *Redburn.* Ed. Harold Beaver. Harmondsworth, Middlesex: Penguin Classics, 1987.

——. *White-Jacket: or The World in a Man-of-War.* Scarborough, Ontario: New American Library of Canada, 1988.

Murray, Henry A. Introduction to *Pierre,* by Herman Melville. New York: Hendricks House, 1962.

III

THEMATIC PATTERNS

Milton Reigelman

Looking at Melville's First Hero
Through a Homeric Lens:
Tommo and Odysseus

uring several months in the middle of the 1840s, 27-year-old Herman Melville wrote his first book, *Typee*, which more or less recounts his earlier adventures in the Marquesas Islands. In the process he created the first Melville narrator/protagonist, the largely autobiographical Tommo. Twenty-eight centuries earlier Homer, over long years of oral performances, gave shape to *The Odyssey*. In the process he created the most enduring archetypal hero of western literature, Odysseus.

Certainly there are vast differences between these two literary characters, the one in an ancient epic and the other in a nineteenth-century autobiographical novel. The similarities between the two are more unexpected. Both leave home on ships as young men, sail around the charted and imagined world for some time, and then return home. The variable narrative styles, the landscapes, and even the incidents of Melville's work many times remind us of Homer's. In both works there are islands and mountains and wild forests in the midst of the endless sea. Odysseus hangs in space suspended by an olive tree to escape Kharybdis' whirlpool (Book XII); Tommo hangs onto branches "suspended over [a] yawning chasm" swinging "to and fro in the air" (61). In *The Odyssey* we learn of the seductiveness of the Lotos plant; in *Typee* of the "arva" plant that exerts "a narcotic influence produc[ing] a luxurious sleep" (165). Both heroes suffer heroically from sleeplessness, hunger, and thirst. Both encounter taboos,

201

cannibals who would eat them, and beautiful women who bathe them with sweet oils. And as Christopher Sten has observed, both gain their freedom only after doing violence to a menacing, one-eyed, cannibal giant.

What I wish to do here is use Odysseus as a lens through which to observe Tommo, bringing into sharper focus certain features of Melville's first protagonist that might otherwise pass unnoticed. These features will give us a slightly different view not only of Tommo, but by extension of Tommo's creator, the author himself.

The aspect of Odysseus that has most captured our imagination is not his strength, his resoluteness, or his cunning, but his eternal wanderlust. Like Dante, we moderns have taken the hint from Teirêsias's prophecy in Book XI of a strange, further journey; we like to imagine an Odysseus well after the action of the epic has ended. The most well-known Odysseus avatar in recent times is probably the title character of Tennyson's dramatic monologue, "Ulysses." The old warrior tells us that he is "always roaming with a hungry heart," that he "cannot rest from travel." He can *never* reach a resting place because "all experience is an arch wherethro' / Gleams that untravell'd world whose margin fades / For ever and for ever when I move." The twentieth-century Greek poet Constantine Cavafy continues this reading of the hero. In his poem "Ithaca," Cavafy suggests that the importance of Odysseus's homeland kingdom is simply that it keeps him wandering and prolongs his journey. "Pray that the road is long," Cavafy's Odysseus advises.

We moderns favor an Odysseus so complex, divided, and self-deceived that he might slip unnoticed into a Hawthorne short story. We latch on to the passage in Book X after the woodland goddess Kirkê counsels the hero to remain with her long enough to "restore behind your ribs those gallant hearts." Homer's character then responds: "As we were men we could not help consenting. / So day by day we lingered, feasting long / on roasts and wine, *until a year grew fat*" (emphasis mine).

It is Odysseus's oft-distracted men who now have to pull their captain out of his year-long dalliance: "'Captain, shake off this trance, and think of home,'" they plead. This particular passage is especially appealing to us because Odysseus as incorrigible adventurer/wanderer resonates to a deeply felt need in our less heroic times. But this reading also distorts the ethos of Homer's poem taken as a whole. Both the action of *The Odyssey* and its hero's essential character argue against our modern predilections and can serve us here as a baseline with which to measure Melville's much later character.

In the opening lines of the epic, Homer announces the two goals that will drive the action and determine the plot of the adventure parts of the poem: Odysseus wishes "to save his life, to bring his shipmates home." Now bereft of his men, he "still hunger[s] for home and wife." He is famously distracted a time or two—we have already noted the most flagrant instance—yet neither he nor the reader is ever allowed to forget Ithaca. Athena carries us there for most of the opening two books, in Book X Odysseus approaches close enough to see his countrymen "building fires along the shore," and the action is firmly anchored on that rocky isle for the entire last half of the poem. In the most famous episode of the poem, Odysseus identifies himself to the Kyklops as "'homeward bound, but taking routes and ways / uncommon'" (Book IX). We remember the hero's lapses in focus only because they *are* lapses and stand out so sharply against the inexorable drift of the poem. Ithaca is both engine that powers the episodic plot and magnet that draws Odysseus back to where he began.

In stark contrast, the action of *Typee* begins on one aimless ship wandering the Pacific, *The Dolly*, and ends on a captainless ship with even less of a destination, *The Julia*. We assume, of course, that eventually Tommo does reach home and is composing the narrative from that place. Yet we get information about "home" only once, in an introductory phrase near the end of the novel. The narrator tells us that "Even now, amidst all the bustle and stir of the proud and busy city in which I am dwelling, the image of those trees seems to come as vividly before my eyes as if they were actually present" (244). What is surprising and significant is that these scant words—which might refer to any city on the globe—are the extent of our knowledge about "home" and its significance to Melville's first narrator/protagonist. In short, the very concept of "home" seems alien to the young writer's imagination.

While the word "home" (and variants such as "homeland") occurs continually in *The Odyssey*, the actual word itself used in reference to the author's place of origin occurs only once in *Typee*. At the very end of the book in a well-known passage as Tommo limps toward the sea hoping to meet Toby and make his escape, old Marheyo, the "father" of Tommo's family group, comes to his side "and emphatically pronounced the only two English words I had taught him 'Home' and 'Mother.' I at once understood what he meant, and eagerly expressed my thanks to him" (248). Because Marheyo then commands Kory-Kory to carry Tommo, most readers have assumed that the old man uses these two words— "Mother" was cut from the second American edition—to evoke the nurturing and maternal influence which Tommo is seeking: Mrs. Maria Gansevoort Melvill(e) snug in her Lansingburgh home. However, it is at least possible that Marheyo uses the two English words to call up for his friend the only environment Marheyo has ever known: the happy valley which has served as both home and mother to Tommo for the past twelve weeks. If the narrator has not shared with his intimate readers a single personal detail from his past in 248 pages, it seems a little improbable that he would have painted a nostalgic picture of his past for the Typeean chief who does not speak English. Tommo tells us that he "at once understood" what Marheyo meant by these words. It is significant that we cannot "at once" be sure. In *Typee*, there is no Ithaca.

Odysseus, like other epic heroes, defines himself largely through daring physical action. When he awakens to shouts on Phaiákia, he hesitates only momentarily before asking himself if he is among savages "or gentle folk, who know and fear the gods" (Book VI). After a quick reckoning he speaks what could well serve as his personal motto: "'Up again, man; and let me see for myself.'" Because Tommo's anthropological, analytical interest in the Typees occasionally seems pedestrian and repetitive to us, we tend to forget that Melville's hero has something of the same "let me see for myself" quality as his epic forebear. When he and Toby first come upon an "indistinctly traced footpath," for example, "curiosity to see where this path might lead" takes the two to the edge of a ravine. His athletic companion will go no further. Tommo insists on continuing because "there's something to be seen here, that's plain . . . and I am resolved to find out what it is" (45).

Having said this, we must say something else. The *sense* of adventure we have in *Typee* is very different from what we experience in *The Odyssey*. And the difference is even larger than what might be explained by the considerable distance between the epic and the autobiographical novel. The difference has mostly to do with motivation. While Odysseus is always moving toward something (Itha-ka), Tommo is always moving away from something, or escaping: *The Dolly*, Captain Pease, the Nukehevans trying to bring him back to the ship, the Happars, Karky-Karky, and finally the whole Typee tribe. Odysseus moves toward a place; Tommo moves away from places. Odysseus has a final destination toward which all of his activities are aimed; Tommo's only destinations are temporary way-stations from which he must soon escape.

Bryan C. Short has argued that Melville discovered in *Typee* a congenial nar-rative voice that he would continue to use and develop throughout his career. What interests us here about the persona of Tommo is his radical unconnect-edness. Like the drifting ships that bookend the novel, Tommo is tetherless, un-attached to place or family, invented ex nihilo without a past. In *The Odyssey* we are never allowed to forget Odysseus's "place" vis-à-vis others from his past. We continually see him in roles that are defined by his relationship to others: captain, husband, king, father, and son. Perhaps the most poignant description of Odysseus comes at the beginning of Book I when Athena tells us that "'such desire is in him / merely to see the hearthsmoke leaping upward / from his own island, that he longs to die'" (3).

Such a human desire flits through Tommo's mind only once, in the penulti-mate chapter of the book. Embedded within a dependent clause in the middle of a very long sentence, we find the only reference to those who have peopled his past: "For hours and hours during the warmest part of the day I lay upon my mat, and while those around me were nearly all dozing away in careless ease, I re-mained awake, gloomily pondering over the fate which it appeared now idle for me to resist. When I thought of the loved friends who were thousands and thou-sands of miles from the savage island in which I was held a captive, when I re-flected that my dreadful fate . . .—I could not repress a shudder of anguish" (243).

It is particularly telling that in this, perhaps the most nostalgic passage of the entire novel, Tommo refers neither to an exact place nor a named person, but merely to the generalized abstraction, "loved friends." Are these friends from the New York City of his youth? Albany? Are they male? Female? Siblings? Not only are there no individualized and therefore believable friends at "home," there is no Queequeg with Tommo as he journeys. To be sure, he does enlist Toby as a fellow deserter, but he describes him as "one of that class of rovers you sometimes meet at sea, who never reveal their origin, never allude to home, and go rambling over the world as if pursued by some mysterious fate they cannot possibly elude" (32). There is, Tommo tells us, "a certain congeniality of sentiment" between this person without home or past and himself.

Unlike history, which is prey to the randomness and looseness of time, myth signifies those recurring patterns that have a wholeness and a completeness within themselves. Even if the myth recounts a process of change, it characteristically moves toward some well-defined end. If Odysseus is always in movement, this movement is toward a goal, which comes at the conclusion of the poem with the suitors slain and peace in Ithaca. Movement becomes stasis, and the pattern is complete.

Rather than moving toward some kind of stasis, *Typee* ends where it begins, on a directionless ship. What Tommo fears more than anything else is becoming rooted, settling into one existence, and finishing a life of continual process. Tommo is granted a remarkable opportunity to return to what he calls a "Paradise" with lush vegetation, ample Poee-Poee, a clubhouse, swimming pool, body servant, dark-eyed nymphs, and sexual license. Odysseus lingers with Kirkê "until a year grew fat"; Tommo seems incapable of relaxing for a fourth (in Melville's actual experience, a twelfth) of that time.

In chapter 30 Tommo comes to the frightening realization that Karky-Karky wants to tattoo his face. After this, his life, he later tells us, is "one of absolute wretchedness" (231) because he fears being fixed in any one way—as seen by others and imagined by himself—forever. He would no longer have the possibility of moving among different cultures, as does the wandering Marnoo, whose face has escaped the tattooer's shark's tooth.

Facial tattooing in this work is closely related to Tommo's mysterious leg wound that swells up and subsides for no apparent reason. Tommo feels he needs to flee the happy valley both to prevent his face from being disfigured and to get modern medical treatment for the wound. Edgar A. Dryden has discussed the wound in relation to Tommo's desire "both to possess and to escape from the past, to have the advantages of both the primitive and civilized worlds" (42).

Dryden then draws a comparison from Greek drama: "Like the swollen foot of Oedipus, [the leg wound] is a symbol of his inability to possess the past entirely or escape it completely" (42). Supporting this interpretation, Faith Pullen sees the wound as a symbol of Tommo's acceptance or rejection of life in the happy valley. That is, when Tommo is comfortable about his existence in the valley, the swelling suddenly subsides, as it does in the exact middle of the narrative (chapter 17) when Tommo loses "all knowledge of the regular recurrence of the days of the week." He then "rambles around the valley" and experiences an "elasticity of mind which placed me beyond the reach of those dismal forebodings." At last he seems to be able to relax in his new environment: "I thought that for a sojourn among the cannibals, no man could have well made a more agreeable one" (123). Immediately, however, he reminds us that there are "limits to my wanderings" since the natives bar him from going toward the sea and "the green and precipitous elevations" bar his progress in the other direction. He is an anxious outsider still, even in this idyllic spot.

In double contrast to Melville's hero, Odysseus both moves toward the stability of home and at the same time participates fully in the worlds he discovers along the way. At Phaiákia, after telling of his lineage and past journey, he is treated as heir apparent to the kingdom and given a royal send-off. Tommo is incapable of entering any place fully, even this Typeean Eden. To the extent Tommo is interested in people, his interest is more intellectual than personal.

The book Melville writes immediately following the success of *Typee* takes up where his first book left off. The narrator of *Omoo* moves from place to place, revealing little about his home, family, friends, or past. Like Tommo, Melville's second narrator locates himself neither in some stable Ithakan existence nor in his present way-station. He is the eternal outsider, exploring ideas more than emotions, thoughts more than people. Ishmael continues the pattern. Except for one boyhood memory in "The Counterpane," we know very little about him, including his actual name. Ishmael cannot stay long in or be satisfied with any position, whether geographical or intellectual. His encounters are with floating ships, and his rich and dark observations signal a continual *process* of thought rather than any final product.

What is it about Melville, who wrote in the middle of the nineteenth century, that so fascinates us as we approach the twenty-first? Allow me to close by suggesting that the travel writer/anthropologist/philosopher Bruce Chatwin can provide us with at least one answer. In *The Songlines*, published in 1989, Chatwin ranges with Melvillean finesse over topics as various as the Australian Aboriginals, classical mythology, the Nemadi tribe of the western Sahara, dreams, and Konrad Lorenz. He concludes that the human race carries within it an instinctive urge to travel, akin to that of birds in autumn. To settle down is to begin the inevitable process of ownership of the land, jealousy, and human corruption. Among hundreds of sources, Chatwin uses stories from the Judaeo-Christian heritage: the settler Cain killing his free-ranging brother Abel, the wanderings of the ancient Israelites, and the peripatetic preachings of Jesus who was born on the road and who asked his disciples to sell all their possessions and come along.

The plot, the hero, and the ethos of *Typee*, as well as of Melville's later works and of Melville himself—but that's another and much more daunting topic—reflect what Chatwin believes is this ineradicable, instinctual, migratory urge in the species of which Odysseus, Tommo, and we, too, fortunately, are a part.

WORKS CITED

Chatwin, Bruce. *The Songlines.* New York: Penguin Books, 1987.

Dryden, Edgar A. *Melville's Thematics of Form: The Great Art of Telling the Truth.* Baltimore: Johns Hopkins University Press, 1968.

Homer. *The Odyssey.* Trans. Robert Fitzgerald. Garden City, NJ: Anchor Books, 1963.

Melville, Herman. *Typee: A Peep at Polynesian Life.* Ed. John Bryant. New York: Penguin Books, 1996.

Pullin, Faith. "The Failure of Eden." *New Perspecives on Melville.* Ed. Faith Pullin. Kent, OH: Kent State University Press, 1978.

Short, Bryan C. "'The Author at the Time': Tommo and Melville's Self-Discovery in *Typee.*" *Texas Studies in Literature and Language,* 31, no. 3 (Fall 1989): 386-405.

Sten, Christopher. *The Weaver-God, He Weaves: Melville and the Poetics of the Novel.* Kent, OH: Kent State University Press, 1996.

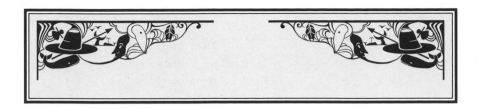

GAIL H. COFFLER

GREEKS AND ROMANS IN *WHITE-JACKET:*

THE POLITICS OF MELVILLE'S CLASSICISM

ver the course of his long writing life, Melville's idea of what it means to be "Greek" underwent some surprising transformations. At the end, after his trips abroad and his study of art and philosophy, his understanding of Greece was learned and complex, as we see in *Billy Budd.* But in the beginning—in *Typee* and *Omoo*—Melville's allusions to Greece show only the conventional concepts of Hellenism: the Greeks' love of democracy and independence, their reverence for beauty, respect for humanity, and interest in philosophical and metaphysical matters. With *Mardi* and *Redburn*, Melville's allusions to Greeks and Romans take on a political coloration that becomes stronger and more complex with each succeeding book. In 1849, when he wrote *White Jacket*, the terms "Greek" and "Roman" had an idiosyncratic meaning to Melville, with a particular political significance.

In 1849, Melville was embroiled more than he wanted to be in New York literary politics, partly because of his unorthodox positions on some sacred matters, partly because he had inherited some enemies through his political brother Gansevoort, and partly because of his friendship with Evert Duyckinck and Cornelius Mathews, who were beating the drum for a national literature, or "Home Literature" as they often called it.[1]

From Duyckinck's diary we know about Melville's involvement with Young America, a group of leftist-democrat writers headed by Cornelius Mathews, the novelist and editor-publisher who was the bosom friend of Melville's mentor,

Evert Duyckinck. From that diary and from letters that Duyckinck saved, we know that Melville wrote the "Old Zack" sketches for Mathews's magazine, *Yankee Doodle*. We have also identified several articles and reviews Melville wrote for Duyckinck's literary magazine, *The New York Literary World*, or simply "The World," as Melville alluded to it in a letter he wrote to Duyckinck from London, where he had taken the manuscript of *White-Jacket* to be published in December 1849.[2]

All through the 1840s, a battle had raged in the literary magazines where the critical attacks could be vicious enough to destroy an author's professional as well as personal reputation. In his biography, Hershel Parker prints several examples of attacks on Melville as well as on Duyckinck and Mathews. In *The Raven and the Whale*, Perry Miller gives a more detailed account of the battle between Duyckinck's circle and the Knickerbocker group, which was led by Lewis Gaylord Clark. In the late 1840s, the battle heated up and reached a climax for Melville in October 1849 when he boarded the ship to England, carrying the finished manuscript of *White-Jacket*.

As part of their artillery in this literary war, writers used allusions to Greece and Rome for propaganda—a custom going back all the way to Augustus Caesar: the point was to praise or condemn the persons in power by comparing them to figures from Greek and Roman history. In *Augustus Caesar in Augustan England*, Howard Weinbrot shows how eighteenth-century English writers portrayed the English king as Augustus, especially George II (whose actual name was George Augustus). A writer friendly to King George would write an essay showing Augustus in a favorable light, demonstrating how Rome flourished under Caesar Augustus, who was portrayed as a patron of the arts and a beneficent monarch. But other writers such as Pope and Swift (who believed the arts could flourish only in freedom) satirized George through *negative* allusions to the Emperor Augustus. Using "Augustus" as a code-word for "tyrant," they portrayed Augustus (i.e., King George) as a despot under whose reign the arts were controlled and manipulated. To put it simply, then, classical allusions indicated a writer's political stance: left or right.

With the romantic movement, Hellenism took the forefront. According to James Johnson in *The Formation of English Neo-Classical Thought*, the English Romantic was a Phil-Hellene. Just as the humanists took Greek nationalism and Greek ideals of personal heroism for their own, the romantics fostered the idea of the

Greeks' joyfully spontaneous individualism, their passion for physical sensation and emotional expression, their pleasure in the visual arts, their primitive simplicity and innocence. These were characteristics typically associated with the Hellenic spirit.

The stylized opposition between the "Greek" character and the "Roman" character seems simplistic now, but it was a fashionable topic in nineteenth-century America, for whom Greece represented art, philosophy, democracy, and freedom of thought, while Rome represented law, order, tradition, and military might. Americans aspired, literally, to attain the best of both worlds: the art of Greece, the order of Rome. Yet, as Melville came to know, the flourishing of the arts is not exactly possible in a society where law, order, and tradition are the strongest concerns.

In the politics of Melville's own time and place, "Roman" meant conservative, that is "Whig," while "Greek" signified liberal or "Democrat." This formula was already in use when Melville was growing up. In *The Jefferson Image in the American Mind*, Merrell Peterson cites the funeral oration for John Adams and Thomas Jefferson who died on the same day, July 4, 1826: "Adams was Roman, Jefferson was Grecian. . . / Adams was practical, Jefferson was theoretical; / Adams was a Whig, of the old school; Jefferson belonged to the modern liberal school; / Adams wished to restrain the popular will; Jefferson to ensure the supremacy of the popular will; / Adams believed in institutions, Jefferson believed in man" (11).

In 1849, this Graeco/Roman code had an even more particular meaning among Melville's literary contemporaries. America had just elected Zachary Taylor president and the Whigs were in power. Thus, in the New York publishing world, the power was in the hands of the Romans: Horace Greeley and the *New York Daily Tribune*, Hiram Fuller and the *Evening Mirror*, Lewis Gaylord Clark and the *Knickerbocker Magazine*, and Clark's friend and ally, Rufus Griswold, who, as author of best-selling anthologies, was both a recognized authority and the arch-arbiter of popular literary taste. To a man, the Knickerbockers were Whigs; these were the "Romans," who preserved order and tradition by promoting socially conservative literature.

Opposing them were the "Greeks," Duyckinck's circle and democratic allies, including the group called "Young America." They were liberal Democrats and literary nationalists—ardent workers for a "Home Literature," i.e., an *American* literature, fresh, original and democratic and "not an echo of effete English schools." At the center was Melville's friend and mentor Evert Duyckinck, editor of Wiley and Putnam's "Home Library of America," which included *Typee* among its first publications. Duyckinck and his brother recruited Melville to write several reviews for their magazine, the *Literary World*, an elite literary journal that quickly became the main rival of Clark's *Knickerbocker*. Also at the center was the writer Cornelius Mathews, who had edited *Yankee Doodle Magazine*, in which Melville published the satirical sketches of Zachary Taylor during the recent presidential campaign.

Duyckinck and Mathews had formed their group ten years earlier under the Greek name *Tetractys*, and together they had edited *Arcturus*, a short-lived but critically admired literary journal. The motto of *Arcturus* was printed on its cover—in Greek. All the members took on Greek names: Duyckinck's for example, was "Attic," and legend had it that they conducted their secret meetings in Greek.[3]

Young America's allies included the *Southern Literary Messenger* edited by John Thompson (whose code name was "Sigma"), William Gilmore Simms, an author in Duyckinck's "Home Library," and John O'Sullivan of the *Democratic Review*, which had published Hawthorne's *Mosses* and which was running the series "Flogging in the Navy" in 1849, when Melville began *White-Jacket*.

These writers subscribed to the democratic ideals of Jefferson and of 5th-century B.C. Greece, and they were fighting to establish an original national literature, freed from the tyranny of past tradition and from the militant, imperialistic stance of the "Roman" Whigs. Punning on the phrase "home literature," they called for America's "Homer" to arise, a "Homer of the Masses," who would write the national epic. On the other side, the "Romans" viewed the upstart nationalists as barbarians, whose "home literature" threatened to tear down the high standard of established English models.

The literary war escalated in late 1848. When the Duyckinck brothers bought the *Literary World* outright in order to promote the literature they believed in, the *Knickerbocker*, the *Tribune* and the *Whig Review* declared themselves under the standard of Rome: that is, on the side of the Republican-Whigs, territorial expansion, and a literature that reflected conservative values. Meanwhile, under the banner of Greece, Duyckinck and his allies pushed for a free, innovative, and "democratic" literature that would throw off the formal and artificial restrictions imposed upon contemporary American art by a tyrannical and reactionary tradition.

In January 1849, for example, a *Southern Literary Messenger* review of *Evangeline* accused Longfellow of "garbing his poetry in grotesque costume of hexameter verse, as to disguise all the natural loveliness" and included a parodic "tribute" to America's supreme author: "Longfellow might as well as strut about in an old *toga virilis*, / Or put a helmet on his little head, take a spear in his right hand / And play the part of Cicero, Pompey, or Coriolanus."[4]

All during 1849, in the allied magazines of both factions and under every pretext, essay after essay proclaimed the superiority of either the Romans or the Greeks. For instance, in September 1849, in the honored left-hand corner of page one, Greeley's *New York Tribune* printed H.T. Tuckerman's poem "The Siege of Rome," which condemned the "barbarians" bent on destroying Rome in the name of "freedom." Should they succeed, the poet prophesies, the Art of the glorious Empire shall be destroyed. That same month, September 1849, Duyckinck's ally, the *Messenger* started a series called "Rome: Papal and Republican," which attacked Roman authoritarianism, and in the same issue it began a series signed "the New Pythagorean," which outlined the strengths of the Greek civilization. Soon, Duyckinck's *Literary World* featured a lengthy review of a new translation of Winckelmann's "History of Ancient Art," which had definitively established Greece's superiority over Rome in the arts. The reviewer, most likely Evert Duyckinck, invited readers to learn about Greek art and Greek values: "The humane disposition of the Greeks, as compared with the Romans, was also favorable to Art. So also their free institutions.... The freedom of the Greeks, and the high thoughts and noble deeds it inspired, had also its effect, and with these were combined the social position of the artist, his intercourse with philosophers and statesmen."[5]

This was the action surrounding Melville as he wrote his fifth novel, and with *White-Jacket: The World in a Man-of-War*, he took a leading role in the fight. The New York war between "Greeks and Romans" over Home Literature is alluded to in a chapter entitled "Homeward Bound." In the ship's library White-Jacket picks up Plutarch's *Lives:* "superexcellent biographies ... which pit Greek against Roman in beautiful style" (168). On a subversive level, this passage was a clue to insiders that Melville was participating in the game: he would use allusions to Greece and Rome to support the cause of artistic freedom against authoritarian control in the war of literary politics.

In *White-Jacket*, as in all Melville's works, ship captains are portrayed as Romans, along with military officers, authoritarians, and those who uphold the aristocratic tradition. Democrats and idealists on the other hand are Greeks. The Roman officers include "the commodore—inaccessible in his cabin, silent and stately as the statue of Jupiter in Dodona" (6). Next is Captain Claret, who has "a small speck ... upon his imperial cheek—like the beard of [Roman Emperor] Hadrian." Then we have "The Professor, [who] quotes from the classics, generally Ovid" (24), and Mad Jack, the lieutenant, who has an "aquiline" (Roman) nose. "Look at the Barons of the gun-room—Lieutenants, Purser, Marine officers, Sailing-master—all of them gentlemen with stiff upper lips, and aristocratic-cut noses ... [From] living so long in high military life, served by a crowd of menial stewards and cot-boys, and always accustomed to command ... their very noses had become thin, peaked, aquiline and aristocratically cartilaginous [.] Even old Cuticle the surgeon had a Roman nose" (48).

While the officers are upper-class and Roman, Jack Chase and the enlisted men are portrayed as Greeks. Ushant, Captain of the Forecastle, is called "the Nestor of our crew," "our sea-Socrates," and "our bearded master" (one of Socrates' names). Captain Claret's order for the men to cut their beards corresponds to the Roman hair style, for Greeks of the classical period (until Alexander) wore full beards, while Romans were beardless. Ushant is the only seaman not to yield to the Captain's order. As Socrates took the hemlock, so Ushant submits to the lash rather than give up his prized "homeward-bounder." The term "homeward-bounder" refers to the seamen's contest to grow the fullest beard on the in-bound trip, but it also alludes to Young America's cause of Home Literature and to Mathews's being prohibited by the former publishers of the *Literary World* from writing about his pet cause in their journal. When his article was published, Evert Duyckinck was fired as editor, a brouhaha which led to the Duyckincks' buying the *World* outright in late 1848. As Mathews was dear to Duyckinck, so Ushant's fierce devotion to the cause makes him "of all the men ... most beloved by Jack Chase."

Jack Chase, the sailors' charismatic leader, is an "oracle of Delphi," advising his followers from his main-mast office (13). Jack's idol is of course Homer, whom he quotes to Captain Claret, alluding to the heroes who died at Troy for the Greek cause (the house of Atreus): "Happy, thrice happy [they] who in battle slain, / Press'd in Atrides' cause the Trojan plain" (214).

With a wink at Captain Claret, Jack adds, that's "*Pope's* version, sir, not the *original* Greek!" (214), with Melville here alluding to the English poet who used classical allusions to satirize King George and the "Roman" establishment.[6]

Only insiders among Melville's readers would catch the puns and allusions to Young America's cause of Home Literature—and to the American "Homer," who they believed would soon rise from the ranks to write the national epic. Jack tells White-Jacket, "They say Homer himself was once a tar. . . . I've that here, WhiteJacket [touching his forehead] that . . . might have made a Homer of me. But we Homers who happen to be captains of the tops must write our odes in our hearts, and publish them in our heads" (271). Later, White-Jacket says, "Were mine the style of stout old Chapman's Homer, even then I would scarce venture to give noble Jack's own version of the fight" (318).

With his irrepressible spirit, Jack Chase is a model of Greek-like independence. The maintop captain and his men, dressed in simple "duck," are the bravest, most tireless fighters on this otherwise-Roman warship. With mock heroics, White-Jacket pities the ship's officers who, even in battle, are constrained in regimental uniforms: "It must be a disagreeable thing to die in a stiff, tight-breasted coat. . . . At such times, a man should feel, free, unencumbered. . . . Seneca understood this, when he chose to die naked in a bath" (69).

Melville's literary-political point here is that even Seneca, the stoic Roman philosopher, felt the philosophical constraints of living in Rome; at last he killed himself rather than serve Nero and the Roman court. White-Jacket compares his own situation to being an outsider in a Rome of later times, a heretic in a society dominated by the Catholic Church: "I was a Roman Jew of the Middle Ages, confined to the Jews' quarter of the town, and forbidden to stray beyond my limits. Or I was as a modern traveler in the same famous city forced to quit it at last without gaining ingress to the most mysterious haunts—the innermost shrine of the Pope, and the dungeons and cells of the Inquisition" (128).

On its visible and literal level, *White-Jacket* states serious criticism of the navy and its practices. At the same time, on a little lower layer, Melville's book is a satire of literary politics and publishing. The *Neversink* is stuffed with Greeks and Romans, like the special Mediterranean pie the ship's cook makes from a "secret" recipe. Because the book succeeds so well as serious literature, some of its under layers have largely escaped detection. In this sense, it is a literary *tour de force*—topping "A Fable for Critics" by Lowell, "The Trippings of Tom Pepper" by Briggs or "Hop Frog" by Poe, all of which were produced during the same literary war in New York in the 1840s.

When the book was finished, Melville had developed considerably—as a stylist and as a satirist with double vision, a man who saw with two eyes, not just one. By 1850, Melville knew he had outgrown his New York companions and their limited viewpoints on many issues, including literary politics.

And having tweaked the noses of the "Romans," and of some of his "Greek" friends as well, he left New York and turned his sights on a "broad-browed" (in Greek, *platonic*) sperm whale. The meaning of Melville's allusions to Greeks took on different dimensions with *Moby-Dick* and again with each succeeding book. But it is in *White-Jacket* that Melville's allusions to Greeks and Romans are the most good-natured and playful in their satirical exposure of the world of literary politics.

NOTES

1 Melville's brother Gansevoort had won a reputation as a "fiery Tammany Hall orator and solid party man" in the Democrats' campaign to elect Polk president. Leon Howard, *Herman Melville*. (Berkeley and Los Angeles: UC Press, 1967), 89.

2 In December, Melville wrote to Duyckinck from London, "I shall write such things as the Great Publisher of Mankind ordained ages before he published 'The World'—this planet, I mean—not the Literary Globe" (*Correspondence*, Dec. 14, 1849).

3 See Miller and Stafford.

4 "Longfellow and Evangeline," *Southern Literary Messenger* 15 (Jan. 1849): 45-46.

5 Review of Winckelmann's *History of Art* in the *Literary World* 5 (Nov. 24, 1849): 439.

6 Pope's translations of Homer comprised volumes 32-34 in Harper's *Classical Library*, 37 v., purchased by Melville on 19 March 1849 (Sealts, No. 147).

REFERENCES

Greenspan, Ezra. "Evert Duyckinck and the History of Wiley and Putnam's Library of American Books, 1845-1847," *American Literature*, 64 (1992): 277-93.

Jenkyns, Richard. *The Victorians and Ancient Greece*. Oxford: Basil Blackwell, 1980.

Johnson, James. *The Formation of English Neo-Classical Thought*. Princeton, NJ: Princeton University Press, 1967.

Melville, Herman. *Correspondence*. Ed. Lynn Horth. Vol. 14 of *The Writings of Herman Melville*. Evanston and Chicago: Northwestern University Press and the Newberry Library, 1991.

——. *White-Jacket or The World in a Man-of-War*. Ed. Harrison Hayford, Hershel Parker, and G. Thomas Tanselle. Vol. 5 of *Writings*, 1970.

Miller, Perry. *The Raven and the Whale: The War of Words and Wits in the Era of Poe and Melville*. New York: Harcourt, Brace & World, 1956.

Parker, Hershel. *Herman Melville: A Biography, 1819-1851*. Baltimore: Johns Hopkins University Press, 1996.

Peterson, Merrill. *The Jefferson Image in the American Mind*. New York: Oxford University Press, 1960.

Robertson-Lorant, Laurie. *Melville: A Biography*. New York: Clarkson Potter, 1996.

Sealts, Merton M., Jr. *Melville's Reading*, revised ed. Columbia: University of South Carolina Press, 1988.

Stafford, John. *The Literary Criticism of "Young America": A Study in the Relationship of Politics and Literature, 1837-1850*. Berkeley and Los Angeles: University of California Press, 1952.

Weinbrot, Howard. *Augustus Caesar in Augustan England*. Princeton, NJ: Princeton University Press, 1978.

Yannella, Donald, and Kathleen Malone Yannella, eds. "Duyckinck's 'Diary: May 29-Nov. 8, 1847,'" *Studies in the American Renaissance*, 2 (1978): 207-58.

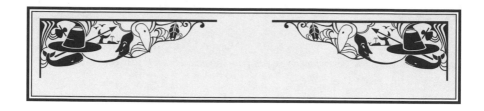

RICHARD HARDACK

"PAN AND THE PAGAN ORACLES":

GREEK NATURE AND AMERICAN IDENTITY IN THE WRITINGS OF HERMAN MELVILLE

ear Eastern Orientalism suffuses the work of many American Renaissance writers, especially that of Herman Melville: in the guise of the "pre-Western" pantheism Emerson develops and Melville critiques—but to which he also succumbs—American transcendentalism owes much of its force and fervor to the Old World.[1] This partly Greek pantheism provides the context for Melville's noted "paganism"—his reluctance to believe fully in Western Christianity—as well as his fascination with, and fears concerning, Emersonian transcendentalism. In this essay, I provide a cross section of background material on, and an informal overview of, the significance of Pan and pantheism in the mid-nineteenth century; I move toward addressing how Melville's obsession with Old World pantheism specifically helps structure his notions of geography and gender. (Pan as a figure and pantheism as a discourse reflect two disparate etymological traditions, but are almost uniformly conflated in the American Renaissance; Pan the Bacchic shepherd, the seductive god, is intercalated with the "pan" or All of an impersonal, universal nature, a natural law that unexpectedly turns out to be even more dangerously alluring.)[2] In America, the pantheist deification of the natural world foremost allows a merger of the otherwise autonomous, self-reliant Jacksonian white male self with a collective, non-Christian or "pre-Western" nature; the pantheist experiences a reverie in merging with other men in nature rather than society and thereby transcending his individual body and identity.

When Emerson first appears on the public stage, he masks his socially unacceptable, almost "foreign," belief in Pan the Greek deity as a symbol of a divine nature. Even in the first anonymously published version of "Nature" (1836), the word "nature" has been substituted for most of the original references to "Pan" found in the manuscript and journal versions, including the previous title of the essay. (In Emerson's case, this revision marks a self-imposed extension of the censoring of a pre-modern or pre-Western religious sensibility that Andrews Norton describes as having been impressed upon Spinoza: that is, at publication, both Spinoza and Emerson replace some of their initial draft references to "nature" with socially acceptable references to "God.") Emerson's self-censoring establishes the pattern for how Near Eastern sources are incorporated into, but also left largely hidden within, transcendental American writing. Perhaps appropriately, such elisions veil the literal figure of Pan, but Pan remains deeply embedded as natural law, and present under a variety of other subterfuges, throughout Emerson's essays. Through much of mid-nineteenth-century American culture, pantheism operates as a Masonic discourse; as Emerson conceived it in his journals, transcendentalism was available to the general public, but pantheism only to the initiated acolyte. If Emerson's peers would never worship Pan directly, or accept even in literary terms a pagan god configured as unadulterated nature, they could at least witness his effects all around them. For the most part, Emerson sees "in the woods perpetual youth. Within these plantations of God ... we return to reason and faith," elements that for Emerson are surprisingly contiguous in Pan and nature ("Nature," *W*, I, 9-10). Through much of his writing, Emerson's Pan, the god of the natural world, remains abstemious and benign on the surface: "I wondered at the continence of Nature under the sky, and truly Pan ought to be represented in the Mythology as the most continent of gods" (*W*, III, 177: or *JMN*, VII, 545). Pantheism begins as an enlightenment "religion" that overlooks the Bacchic elements or demonology of its own Romanticism. Even Emerson sometimes realizes, however, that the seemingly reasonable nature he loves will also betray him: "very seductive are the first steps from the town to the woods, but the End is want & madness" (*JMN*, X, 344).

Throughout the American Renaissance, Pan the Greek wood-god represents a variety of elements "foreign" to yet definitive of American Protestantism.[3] In

Democracy in America, for example, Tocqueville had predicted that pantheism and Catholicism would equally hold the greatest charm for representative men living in the new republic. Theologians worried about the way transcendentalism was leading Americans "backward" from Protestantism—first to Catholicism, and finally to pagan, pre-Christian Greece and Rome. For example, Theodore Parker wrote: "At the present day Pantheism seems to be the bugbear of some excellent persons. They see it everywhere except on the dark walls of their own churches. . . . M. Maret . . . finds it the natural result of Protestantism, and places before us the pleasant alternatives, either the Catholic Church or Pantheism! The rationalism of the nineteenth-century must end in skepticism, or leap over to Pantheism!"[4]

It is against this specific backdrop—a raging debate about pantheism largely lost to subsequent critics—that Melville writes to Hawthorne in November 1851 of his own transcendental impulses; here, he effectively mentions the Italian setting for his friend's final novel about the seductive religions of the ancient world, *The Marble Faun:* "So now I can't write what I felt. But I felt pantheistic then— your heart beat in my ribs and mine in yours, and both in God's. . . . Ineffable socialities are in me. I would sit down and dine with you and all the gods in old Rome's Pantheon. . . . Whence come you Hawthorne? By what right do you drink from my flagon of life? And when I put it to my lips—lo, they are yours and not mine. I feel that the Godhead is broken up like the bread at the Supper, and that we are the pieces. Hence this infinite fraternity of feeling."[5] (With reference to his lecture on Rome, *The Ohio Farmer* also describes Melville's disturbing "affection for heathenism [as] profound and sincere. He speaks of the heathenism of Rome as if the world were little indebted to Christianity."[6] Melville's frequent and sympathetic references to the heathenish pantheism of Rome and the ancient world reveal his nostalgia for pre-Christian religions of nature, a nostalgia strongly abetted by American transcendentalism.) Before Melville sends Clarel on a pilgrimage in search not just of a Judeo-Christian deity, but an Elysian Greece/Middle East, many of his characters also encounter the literal or veiled form of Pan. For Melville, Greece becomes the hybrid site bridging Western and pre-Western beliefs about nature, and a locus for contemporary reactions to the transformations of the American church.

Emerson invokes a pagan Pan throughout his writings, a fact critics have discussed primarily in formal and historical contexts, but insufficiently in terms of its ontological significance. In his day, however, many of Emerson's contemporaries situated his beliefs primarily in the context of his pantheism. The emergence of Emerson's controversial pagan persona takes place against the backdrop of a social and theological revolution, where the centralized church was being replaced by a universal natural law, and the doctrine of Christian transubstantiation was being challenged by early theories of development or evolution.[7] The absence of any anthropomorphic source of authority in Emerson's deontology also becomes one of the key targets of anti-pantheist polemicists: Mary Moody Emerson, a devout Calvinist, despairing of her nephew's insistence that nature is the voice of God, that the woods contain the creator, writes to Emerson, "[I]f this withering Lucifer doctrine of Pantheism be true what mortal truth can you preach or by what authority should you feel it?"[8] Despite the indisputably traditional tone of many of Emerson's early sermons, people closest to him and those who read him most carefully regarded a pagan pantheism, and not simply a Christian form of transcendentalism, as the essence of his theosophy.

In much of Emerson's writing, transcendental American nature is expressed as an incarnation of a pagan Greek cosmology: for Emerson, "mythology cleaves close to Nature; and what else was it they represented in Pan . . . ? Such homage did the Greek pay to the unscrutable force we call Instinct, or Nature . . . [Pan] could intoxicate by the strain of his shepherd's pipe . . . aboriginal, old as Nature, and saying, like poor Topsy, 'Never was born; growed'" ("Natural History of Intellect," *W*, XII, 35). The Greek figure of Pan and discourse of pantheism metamorphose to provide the basis for transcendental American attitudes regarding natural science and philosophy; American ideas about reproduction, race, and gender were derived from, validated by, and in turn themselves shaped that transcendental version of natural science. Through Emerson's invocation of a "primitive" Greece, we also encounter his notion of a black American nature and unconscious instinct: the black and female (and in Hawthorne a racialized, explicitly "pagan" Catholicism as well)—the elements "foreign" to white male Protestant identity—are often represented through the rhetoric of pantheism and imagined as the "not me" of Nature.

Emerson's invocations of the Greek deity serve as abstract and direct influences on many of Melville's personae, especially his young philosophers from Taji to Pierre. When Emerson and Pierre wander in the woods, the nature they encounter is half Native American and half Greek. To overcome their mortal, male nature, many of Melville's male protagonists seek the divine diffusion of Pan's animated flowers and trees. Divine nature is feminine and trans-individual, and seemingly allows men to transcend their super-individuated masculinity: when Pierre wants heaven "to confirm [him] in the Christ-like feelings" he first experiences, he swears he will "forsake the censuses of men, and seek the refuge of the god-like population of the trees.... Their high foliage shall drop heavenliness upon me; my feet in contact with their mighty roots, immortal vigor shall so steal into me. Guide me, gird me, guard me, this day, ye sovereign powers!... ye Invisibles" (*P*, 134). This Pan of nature represents "the surplus" of Christ—whatever cannot be contained by Christian views of divinity, or even the return of what Christianity represses: significantly, Pierre's "Christian" feelings can be validated only in that pagan nature.[9] As with Ishmael's repeated flirtations with pantheism at sea, however, Melville reveals how conscious he is of the price of such transcendence; immortal vigor is ours, identity is guaranteed, to the extent that we forsake the world of men and male individuality, and merge into a divine, impersonal, and inhuman nature.

At first, Pan offers Emerson's pilgrim a glimpse of the secret nature of the universe as well as the promise of a stable identity: "Gentle pilgrim, if thou know / The gamut old of Pan / And how the hills began / The frank blessings of the hill/Fall on thee.... / Enchantment fixed me here... / Can thy style-discerning eye / The hidden Builder spy?" ("Monadnoc," *W*, IX, 68). Pan, and what he represents, becomes the secret builder, organizer, and connective tissue of a world in flux. He is usually hidden, but almost always present, in the transcendental literature of the American Renaissance: like Moby Dick, he is ubiquitous, but cannot be fully represented. Emerson admits that Pan can only be seen beneath the surfaces of the American present—which extend even to his own work: "Pan, that is, All. His habit was to dwell in mountains ... [as in Hawthorne's "The Celestial Railroad"]. Yet he was in the secret of nature ... [but] he was only seen under disguises"; he is the "one hidden stuff" of Emerson's universe ("Natural History of Intellect," *W*, XII, 36). Though omnipresent, Pan always remains beneath a mask or veil.[10] Emerson and Melville, then, represent Pan mimetically, often hiding him in the very structures of their texts.

Edward Said's *Orientalism* provides a useful context for a discussion of the colonial representation of the East as site of a "pre-Western" nature. In the New World, nature is imagined through Eastern coordinates. In this regard, Said claims that the "American contribution to the history of Orientalism" can be dated to the period after World War II: for Said, "The American experience of the Orient prior to that exceptional moment was limited. Cultural isolatoes like Melville [*sic?*] were interested in it . . . the American Transcendentalists saw affinities between Indian thought and their own. . . . But there was no deeply invested tradition of Orientalism, and consequently in the United States knowledge of the Orient never passed through the refining and reticulating and reconstructing process . . . that it went through in Europe" (290). But Said fails to consider the ways in which the European fascination with Egypt and the Near East also characterizes the American Renaissance. As Mary Louise Pratt writes in *Imperial Eyes: Travel Writing and Transculturation*, taken against the "dehistoricized celebration of primal America and the primitivist view of the Amerinidians that went with it," a "powerful model for the archaeological rediscovery of America [came through] Egypt" (134). According to Emerson, for example, "As man's knowledge enlarges, that is, as his mind applies itself to a larger piece of the universe, he sees the unbroken prevalence of laws; the grass grows in Egypt by the same natural order as in Ohio."[11] In other words, Egypt becomes a linguistic and social model for interpreting America, as Emerson unself-consciously attests, and as other writers, such as Poe and Melville, more cannily propose. As John Irwin argues throughout *American Hieroglyphics: The Symbol of the Egyptian Hieroglyphics in the American Renaissance*, Egypt serves as a focal point for American self-representation of that period. A more generic cultural Orientalism differs from the specifically transcendental use of Greek pantheism, but the general fetishization of Egyptian culture is largely compatible with Emerson's transcendental equation of both Egypt and Greece with Ohio, or with Melville's obsessive use of specific Egyptian myths, hieroglyphics, and names.

In *Ishmael: A Study of the Symbolic Mode in Primitivism*, James Baird suggests that transcendental American Orientalism involved symbolic appropriation and an

atavistic referencing of Asian scriptures—"there can be no question [that] . . .
Emerson and Thoreau read every translation of Hindu scripture available to
Concord" (40). As Dorothee Finkelstein extensively writes in *Melville's Orienda*,
an unjustly overlooked reference for this subject, transcendentalists pursued
"an organic link between Christianity and the mystic creeds of the Orient to
confirm the[ir] concept of the unity of the world, man and God" (13). While
Emerson believed in the superiority of the West, he also "'used' the Orient to
demonstrate the truth of their conviction that there was [to quote Thoreau] 'a
kindred principle at the bottom of all affinities'" (14-15). Representing a somewhat imperial, early principle of multicultural commensurability, Pan (or natural law) transcends all particular geography and law to become transcendentally
universal, but remains especially representative of both Greece and America,
the centers of the old and new world.[12]

As Finkelstein notes, "pure physical sensuousness is associated with the
Bacchanalia of Greek Paganism," yet in much of Emerson's and Melville's writing this Greek pantheism also comes to reflect a metaphysics designed to transcend the male body. Luce Irigaray's comments on symmetry and universality
bear directly on the nature of heterosexual desire and self-representation in
American pantheism: "the Greek takes hold of himself as one who is separated
from infinite nature by his bodily being. . . . [But man] does not even remember
the fact that his body is the threshold, the portal for the construction of the universe, or universes. He exists in his nostalgia for a return to the ONE WHOLE;
his desire to get back toward and into the originary womb." Ironically, Irigaray
also echoes, but also implicitly corrects, D. H. Lawrence, who claims he wants
"in the Greek sense, an equilibrium between me and the rest of the universe,"
but also complains that "the Greeks began the cutting apart business."[13] Hence,
as Lawrence inchoately begins to suspect in *Studies in Classic American Literature*,
Pan presides over a dialectic of merger and amputation in the American Renaissance—the Ishmael who merges with Queequeg, and the Pierre who fuses with
nature and Isabel, are predicated on the amputations of characters like Samoa,
Cuticle, and Ahab. The oscillations of pantheism—between merger with the one
whole of a divine nature and amputation at the hand of a nature that represents
the market—chart a dialectic rather than an opposition. While "few thoughts of

Pan stirred Ahab's brain," Ahab also "merges" with other men by claiming to incorporate them—their arms and legs—into his own body (*MD*, 456). He represents a failed or forced merger, the demonology of pantheism that always disrupts Melville's transcendental reveries. The incessant fragmentations created by American society—what Tocqueville described as its tendency toward atomization—generate the need for a fantasy of transcendental unity, one locatable in pantheistic Greek conceptions of the All.

As Baird argues, once we look to Melville with this Near-Eastern pantheism in mind, we can see his use of Greece as one of his central referents for American transcendentalism: as Ishmael concludes in *Moby-Dick*, in a moment of transcendental reverie, "Lifted by those eternal swells, you needs must own the seductive god, bowing your head to Pan" (*MD*, 456). As D. H. Lawrence writes in "Pan in America"—his response to Tocqueville's *Democracy in America*—Pan was "an outlaw, even in the early days of the gods. A sort of Ishmael among the bushes. Yet always his lingering title: The Great God Pan."[14] The Near Eastern figures of Ishmael and Pan remain intimately connected in Melville's writing. Melville writes in *Clarel*, "Each germ of Pantheistic sway, / Whose influence, not always drear, / Tenants our maiden hemisphere. . . . Hither, to renew their old control—/ Pan and the pagan oracles."[15] In other words, Melville is centrally concerned with how these Pagan oracles are resituated in an "Ishmaelite" new world, how the old beliefs of pantheism infiltrate transcendentalism, and how and why the great god Pan is reborn in America.

Melville's pantheism is, then, a hybrid of these diverse sources: through Greek pantheism; through Emerson, and thus Goethe's European pantheism; Native American belief systems; and most of all through his own travels in Polynesia, Melville synthesizes an equally classical and aboriginal pantheism. We can perhaps find the best and most condensed example of this amalgamation in some of Melville's poems. In "The Parthenon," Melville links one of his many quintessential pantheists to a universal geography: "Spinoza gazes: and in mind / Dreams that one architect designed Lais—and you!"[16] (According to Hennig Cohen, "At one point in the draft, [Melville] considered substituting 'The Pantheist' for Spinoza."[17] Consistent with the way Emerson and Spinoza find euphemisms for Pan in "nature," Melville returns the trick and uses

Spinoza as a euphemism for *pantheist.*) Melville's attendant claim in "The Attic Landscape" that "The All-in-All seems here a Greek" in itself is not that surprising, but the importation of pantheism to the new world is.[18] As he writes in "To Ned," "Ned, for our Pantheistic ports:—/ Marquesas and glenned isles that be / Authentic Edens in a Pagan sea."[19] Melville here designates the Pacific Islands as sources of a valorized edenic pantheism—an association Melville's detractors accurately, if boorishly, used to censure him throughout his early career. In a startling juxtaposition, Melville also frequently links Greek pantheism with these Pacific Islands; island hopping, he brings Pan to Polynesia, finds him already there, and brings their island polytheism back to Greece. In "The Archipelago," Melville specifically identifies the Cyclades, Pan's first domain, through reference to his more familiar Marquesas: "They still retain in outline true / Their grace of form when earth was new / And primal. / But beauty clear, the frame's as yet, / Never shall make one quite forget / Thy picture, Pan, therein once set—/ Life's revel! / Tis Polynesia reft of palms."[20] In a turn that sets the stage for Derek Walcott's recent navigation of island cultures, "primal" Greece and "primitive" Polynesia are mirrored across space and time in a proto-postmodern, and finally Pan-American, zone. In the end, the "authentic" Edens of the Pacific become reflections of a space divine in representing a universal America. The more Melville sees of the world, the more he concludes he can arrive without traveling.

So the figure of Pan crosses over to the new world and finds his new manifestation not just in its nature, but its democracy. According to Lawrence, who traces the specific degeneration of Pan in the West from nature-god to cloven hooved devil, "Democracy in America is just the tool with which the old master of Europe, the European spirit, is undermined. Europe destroyed, potentially, American democracy will evaporate. America will begin. American consciousness has so far been a false dawn."[21] For Lawrence, democracy acts as a device for confronting fathers—an ironic claim given Melville's encounters with his democratic past. An old world pantheism in *Mardi*, *Moby-Dick*, and *Pierre* acts as a decisive determinant of these novels' estimations of new world democracy. *Pierre* chronicles the fall of a "soft-social pantheist" who tries to live in nature and forge a new democratic literature—but who, in committing incest, winds up sharing the fate of a variety of Greek figures, from blinded Oedipus to dismembered Enceladus (*P*, 286). Throughout the novel, Melville sardonically anticipates America as a machine of such Lawrentian transformations of the old world: "For indeed the democratic element operates as a subtle acid among us; forever producing new things by corroding the old. . . . Herein by apt analogy we behold the marked anomalousness of America; whose character abroad . . . is misconceived, when we consider how strangely she contradicts all prior notions of human things; and how wonderfully to her, Death itself becomes transmuted into life. So that political institutions, which in other lands seem above all things intensely artificial, with America seem to possess the divine virtue of a *natural law*; for the most mighty of nature's laws is still this, that out of Death she brings Life" (emphasis mine; 29). America resurrects by killing, creates life by transforming existing life; she institutionalizes a foreign, transcendental nature that allegedly brings good out of evil, out of death, life. Not Christ, but Pan's nature provides the "apt analogy" for American democracy: this is the "divine virtue of natural law." Though misconceived abroad, America is actually governed by a nature misappropriated from foreign pagan sources: through the guise of the representative proto-Western culture, Greece, this new pantheist democracy serves as the site for the eruption of the pre-Western. Through the cultural heritage of Pan and democracy, Greece returns to America so America can break away from Europe. Thought to kill paternal Europe, American democracy in fact resurrects and transforms its sources. If Pan/the father is killed, his ghost keeps returning.

The classical motif also reflects an obsession with what is imagined as the dangerous pagan unconscious—the Greek pantheism—beneath New England transcendentalism. What starts out with the promise of resurrection ends with the disintegration of the male self; to borrow the terminology of Richard Slotkin, pantheism regenerates the vitality of American religion, but at the price of American identity. The democratic "element," Melville puns, is a corrosive acid revealing the Greek layers beneath the facade of the new world.

Pan finally functions as a locus for instability and dismemberment rather than the unity of nature; he serves as the exemplary surrogate for Osiris in the American Renaissance, a ruler of nature dismembered by society. Emerson writes in "The Natural History of Intellect" that "Pan . . . wanting the extremities ... [is] a shapeless giant ... without hands or fingers or articulating lips or teeth or tongue..." (*W*, XII, 35). (Such a description again echoes the almost Catholicized Pan of Hawthorne's "The Celestial Railroad.") Similarly, Melville incessantly dismembers his larger than life characters, like Ahab, in the context of their relation to Nature or Pan, as in this instance from *Mardi:* "Ah! Sadly lacking was he in all the requisites of an efficient ruler. Deaf and dumb he was: and save arms, minus everything but an indispensable trunk and head"(470). In *Pierre*, the implicit connection between power, incest, and amputation in the American family is confirmed in the pivotal appearance of "the American Enceladus ... the Titan's armless trunk".(387-88). In dialectical fashion, figures of Pan/ Osiris come to connote not just merger with nature, but the Old World theme of incest (and hence amputation) in nature, reflected in Pierre's obsession with the Cenci and the dismembered Greek Titan. (In complex ways, Nature/Pan is then both dismemberer and dismembered.) "Wrought by the vigorous hand of nature's self," the Greek statue, like Greek nature, also represents Emerson's dismembered American Scholar and the American All—a giant male body amputated by nature (*P*, 388). (Much of this discourse also resuscitates Plato's myth of an original, undivided, and sexless being.) As Lawrence writes in "Pan in America," "Alas, poor Pan! Is this what you've come to? Legless, hornless, faceless, even smileless, you are less than everything or anything.... And yet here, in America ... old Pan is still alive" (24).[22]

The motif of Greek pantheism is also crucial for understanding other political manifestations of American transcendentalism: Pan's pagan oracles help determine America's own "tribal" unities. Melville makes this point regarding the political valence of pantheism more explicit in *Clarel:* "What if the kings in Forty-eight / Fled like the gods? even as the gods / Shall do, return they made: and sate / And fortified their strong abodes; / And, to confirm them there in state / Contrived new slogans, apt to please—/ Pan and the tribal unities. / Behind all this still works some power / Unknowable, thou'lt yet adore" (II, iv, 99-107). Pan is reborn in America in the discourse of Emersonian transcendentalism, a hybrid pantheism existing behind official surfaces: but behind that surface is great instability.

For Emerson, Pan had first represented a life of divine transformation:

"Tuned to the lay the wood-god sings . . ./ of chemic matters, force and form. . . The rushing metamorphosis / Dissolving all that fixture is, / Melts things that be to things that seem. / And solid nature to a dream" ("Woodnotes II," IX, 48-59). This Greek god through much of Emerson's writing represents not just a classical trope, but the governing discourse of natural science and human identity in American transcendentalism. But even for Emerson, man is cast adrift by divine mutability, Pan the nature-god's indeterminacy: "Gladly would we anchor, but the anchorage is quicksand. This onward trick of nature is too strong for us: *Pero si mouve*" ("Experience," *W*, III, 55). For Melville, who endlessly parodies but succumbs to Emersonian transcendentalism, Pan himself is finally overcome by his own laws of self-variation. As Patricia Merivale suggests in *Pan the Goat-God*, *Clarel* represents not the "fixed position but change itself."[23] In this hysteron proteron, even transcendental nature is overcome by its own system, by the transformation it purports to regulate; as Melville comes to lament, "Pan, Pan is dead! / Such fables old—/ From man's deep nature are they rolled, / Pained and perplexed awed, overawed / By sense of change?" (*Clarel*, IV, viii, 7-10).

In his letter to Hawthorne, Nov. 17, 1851, Melville—just after invoking his pantheistic feelings and the gods of Rome's pantheon—writes that like Pan he could not even know his own hand: "The very fingers that now guide the pen are not precisely the same that just took it up and put it on this paper. Lord, when shall we be done changing?"[24] Through most of *Moby-Dick*, this same aspect of pantheism—the inability to demarcate the borders of one's own body, and the mutability of the self in nature—overawes and destabilizes the male American self: Ishmael "takes the mystic ocean at his feet for the visible image of that deep, blue, bottomless soul, pervading mankind and nature. . . . In this enchanted mood, thy spirit ebbs away to whence it came: becomes diffused through time and space: like Cranmer's sprinkled Pantheistic ashes, forming at least a part of every shore the round globe over. . . . And perhaps, at mid-day, in the fairest weather, with one-half throttled shriek you drop through that transparent air into the summer sea, no more to rise for ever. Heed it well, ye Pantheists!" (*MD*, 162-63). Pan is far from dead in Melville's works; the transformative male nature he represents is resurrected in American transcendentalism, but his divine rebirth does not herald human redemption. Most dramatically, when Ishmael disappears from his own narrative, when he "witnesses" events aboard the *Pequod* and narrates solilo-quies to which he could not have been privy, and warns "ye pantheists" about dropping "through that transparent air," he has become Emerson's transcenden-tal, transparent eyeball, his observing machine of "Nature" (or "Pan"): at least for a time, he is nowhere, but sees All (*MD*, 162-63).

Pan's destabilizing effects often reach their apotheosis when Melville imag-ines transcending the individual male body through nature/pantheism. As he re-veals in his "pantheistic" letters to Hawthorne, Melville's profoundest sense of being involves a merger with a feminine nature that he continually dissimulates. In *Pierre*, which traces the failure of a young pantheist, Isabel takes up Melville's own sylvan, pagan prayer to Hawthorne in his letters: "I pray for peace—for mo-tionlessness—for the feeling of myself, as of some plant, reabsorbing life with-out seeking it, and existing without individual sensation. I feel that there can be no perfect peace in individualness. Therefore, I hope one day to feel myself drank up into the pervading spirit animating all things" (*P*, 146). Isabel meanwhile would "steal away into the beautiful grass, and worship the kind summer and the sun," which she refers to repeatedly as human. Able to merge without male hesi-tation into nature, Isabel would then serve as conductor for Pan to the superindi-viduated man still external to nature.[25] In "After the Pleasure Party," Melville suggests that the Greek Pan represents not just nature, but gender, the primal splitting from the All as sex itself: "Could I remake me! or set free / This sexless bound in sex, then plunge / Deeper than Sappho, in a lunge / Piercing Pan's para-mount mystery!"[26] These myriad elements of a usually Greek inflected panthe-ism play a crucial role in the representation of identity throughout Melville's writ-ings; and as this poem suggests, the central mystery of nature for Melville—in *Mardi*, *Moby-Dick*, and *Pierre*—is a pantheistic coding of gender that takes us back to the Greece of Sappho and Pan. For Melville, the All in All is a Greek, but the self divided by gender an American.

NOTES

1 Following Melville's, Emerson's, and Hawthorne's (problematic) lead, I situate ancient Greece as a partly pre-Western culture for the white American Renaissance writers I discuss in this essay: in the guise of a vairiety of Orientalisms, these writers imagine the West in terms of Christian-

ity, and any pre- or non-Chrsitian culture as animistic and hence at least partly "pre-Western." Greece then figures as kind of Near-Eastern, and thus putatively pre-Western, culture according to this historically rather dubious logic; for Melville especially, animism and pantheism mark Greece, Egypt, and the Roman Empire as both sources of and counterpoints to later Western European cultures.

2   The pantheism of the American Renaissance primarily does not serve as an invocation of wild sensuality, but a system of representation based on Neoplatonic idealism, the animation of a divine nature, and the systematic reification, or literalization and absolute generalization, of all particular metaphors. When it suits his purposes, however, Emerson seems deliberately to conflate Pan with pantheism. Throughout the American Renaissance, a Dionysian and emphatically somatic Pan comes to represent a presumably more ascetic pantheism/transcendentalism in sometimes stochastic and historically inaccurate ways. [¶ Though Emerson, "shy of names," and "Careful not to give his [creed] to his readers in any formulated shape," rarely defines his terms, other writers' equivalent use of an identified pantheism often reveals Emerson's implicit ideology. Invoked virtually in each of Emerson's essays, but under a hundred many-colored names, Pan appears as the woodgod, the Over-Soul, the laws of compensation, nature itself, "the inworking of the All"("Compensation," *W*, II, 106). In Emerson's protracted conflation, Pan becomes the symbol, but not the object of worship, of pantheism.

3   In oblique but consistent ways, for example, Pan is associated with the distant but looming "threat" of Catholicism, which is also equated with transcendental pantheism, most obviously in Hawthorne's *The Marble Faun*, but throughout the literature of the American Renaissance. Hawthorne's allegory of *The Marble Faun* is as much about New England as about Rome; Melville adumbrates this use of foreign sylvan settings to write allegories about American transcendentalism.

4   Theodore Parker, *A Discourse of Matters Pertaining to Religion* (Boston: American Unitarian Association, 1907), 77.

5   Merrell R. Davis and William H. Gilman, eds., *The Letters of Herman Melville* (New Haven, CT: Yale University Press, 1960), 142.

6   See Merton M. Sealts, Jr., "Statues in Rome," *Melville as Lecturer* (Cambridge: Harvard University Press, 1957), 34. David Mead, in *Yankee Eloquence in The Middle West: The Ohio Lyceum, 1850-1870* (East Lansing; Michigan State University Press, 1951), is credited with first highlighting the paper's reaction.

7   When "Nature" was first published anonymously in 1836, for example, many attributed the work to Robert Chambers, author of the proto-evolutionary tract *Vestiges of the Natural History of the Creation*.

8   David Williams, *Wilderness Lost: The Religious Origins of the American Mind* (Selinsgrove, PA: Susquehanna University Press, 1987), 164.

9   See *The Melville Log: A Documentary Life of Herman Melville, 1819-1891,* ed. Jay Leyda. (New York: Harcourt, Brace, and Co., 1951), 506. From *Omoo* on—where already "Oro, the great god of their mythology, was declared in the cocoa-nut log from which his image was rudely carved," and where "there stands a living tree, revered itself as a deity"—the great god Pan/Oro is associated with the living tree of nature, not the tree of the cross (*O*, 262-63). Most of Melville's characters follow Pierre

in imagining a divine presence in trees. Melville himself is said to have had an eccentric, sentimental attachment to Pan's totem: on a trip with Hawthorne and Oliver Wendell Holmes, Maunsell Field notes that Melville "took us to a particular spot on his place to show us some superb trees. He told me that he spent much time there *patting them upon the back*" (Leyda II:506).

10   Such a consideration should also change the way we read the metaphysical veils of *Moby-Dick*, as well as those found covering women in many Romantic American Renaissance novels.

11   See Edward Said, *Orientalism* (New York: Random House, 1979); Mary Louise Pratt, *Imperial Eyes: Travel Writing and Transculturation* (New York: Routledge, 1992); John Irwin, *American Hieroglyphics: The Symbol of the Egyptian Hieroglyphics in the American Renaissance* (New Haven, CT: Yale University Press, 1980); James Baird, *Ishmael: A Study of the Symbolic Mode in Primitivism* (New York: Harper, 1956); and Dorothee Finkelstein, *Melville's Orienda* (New York: Octagon, 1971).

12   Pan's all-representative nature also helps contextualize how various disparate cultures of the old world, from Egypt to China, could equally serve as sources for a transcendental Orientalism in which Nature became the universal law, transcending all local politics and transient laws.

13   See "Love of Same, Love of Other," in *An Ethics of Sexual Difference*, trans. Carolyn Burke and Gillian C. Gill (Ithaca, NY: Cornell University Press, 1984), 99-100; for Lawrence, see "Him With His Tail," *Phoenix* II, ed. Warren Roberts and Harry T. Moore (New York: Penguin, 1978), 433-34.

14   Lawrence, "Pan in America," *Phoenix* (New York: Viking, 1936, 1968), 22.

15   See *Clarel*, in *The Writings of Herman Melville*, XII, ed. Harrison Hayford, et al. (Evanston and Chicago, IL: Northwestern University Press and the Newberry Library, 1991, I, xvii, 159-65).

16   Melville, *Collected Poems of Herman Melville*, ed. Howard Vincent (Chicago: Packard and Co., 1947), 247.

17   See Hennig Cohen, "Comment on the Poems," in *Selected Poems of Herman Melville*, ed. Cohen (Carbondale: Southern Illinois University Press, 1964), 245.

18   *Collected Poems*, 246.

19   Ibid. 201.

20   Pantheism's version of manifest destiny indicates that today is equivalent to yet supplants the past, and that the American is equivalent to yet supplants the "primitive." *Collected Poems*, 249.

21   D. H. Lawrence, *Studies in Classic American Literature* (New York: Penguin Books, 1971), 12-14.

22   In Melville's version of America, tailed and cloven-hooved Pan is transformed not just into the devil, but the Confidence-Man.

23   See Merivale, *Pan the Goat-God: His Myth in Modern Times* (Cambridge, MA: Harvard University Press, 1969), 116.

24   See *The Letters of Herman Melville*, 142-44.

25   In a letter of early June 1851, Melville writes to Hawthorne of his longing for an edenic merger in nature: "If ever, my dear Hawthorne, in the eternal times that are to come, you and I shall sit down in Paradise, in some shady little corner by ourselves . . . we shall then cross our celestial legs in the celestial grass that is forever tropical." In the postscript to this letter, Melville shares with Hawthorne his feeling of splendor in this same grassy repose: "In reading some of Goethe's

sayings . . . I came across this, '*Live in the all.*' . . . what nonsense! . . . This 'all feeling,' though, there is some truth in. You must often have felt it, lying on the grass on a warm summer's day. Your legs seem to send out shoots into the earth. Your hair feels like leaves on your head. This is the all feeling." Melville simultaneously pursues and shies away from this merger in nature—depicted in terms clearly resonant for Isabel—and systematically represents that merger both as a mystical truth and as nonsensical Goethean "flummery" that leads to a dangerous form of self-delusion. See *Letters*, 126-33.

26   *Collected Poems*, 261.

All references to Emerson and Melville indicate the following editions :

Ralph Waldo Emerson: *The Journals and Miscellaneous Notebooks of Ralph Waldo Emerson*, vols. 1-16. Ed. William Gilman, et al. Cambridge: Harvard University Press, 1960-82. *Works* I-XII. Boston: Houghton, Mifflin and Co.: 1904.

Herman Melville: *The Confidence-Man.* New York: Signet, 1964.

——. *Mardi.* New York: Signet, 1964.

——. *Moby Dick.* New York: Signet, 1961.

——. *Omoo.* Eds. Harrison Hayford, Hershel Parker, and G. Thomas Tanselle. Vol. 2 of *The Writings of Herman Melville.* Evanston and Chicago, IL: Northwestern UP and the Newberry Library, 1968.

——. *Pierre.* New York: Signet, 1964.

233

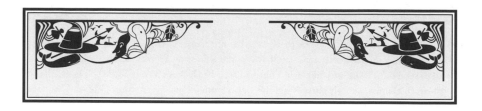

JOHN BRYANT

THE NATIVE GAZES:

SEXUALITY AND SELF-COLONIZATION IN MELVILLE'S *TYPEE*

n 1851, while finishing *Moby-Dick*, thirty-one-year-old Herman Melville wrote this stunning self-assessment in a letter to Hawthorne: "Until I was twenty-five, I had no development at all," he said. "From my twenty-fifth year I date my life. Three weeks have scarcely passed, at any time between then and now, that I have not unfolded within myself" (NN *Correspondence*, 193). Along with other early Melville scholars, Leon Howard used these lines to help explain the composition of *Moby-Dick*,[1] but in taking us back to Melville's twenty-fifth year, the passage also describes the moment when Melville first began to write. It was then, in 1845, that the author first experienced a phenomenon common enough to all writers. The act of writing became for him a kind of self-genesis. The "unfolding" Melville speaks of in his letter was a process of self-invention, and the product of that first year of unfolding was not *Moby-Dick* but *Typee*.

The working draft of *Typee*, dated 1845 but not discovered until 1983, records these very "unfoldings." They afford a "peep" at Melville's creativity and in particular how the young writer's emergent sexual and political awareness evolved through his writing process. To do this, I want to focus on Melville's manipulation of one word: Gaze. From Ishmael's "crowd of water-gazers" for whom "meditation and water are wedded" to Babo's "unabashed" head receiving "the gaze of the whites" at the end of "Benito Cereno," the word recurs in Melville's fiction not as an emblem of the ungraspable phantom of our subjective consciousness

234

or even as some elusive "doubloon" of objectivity, but as that condition of self-conscious wonder when subject acknowledges object. The word also appears dozens of times in *Typee*. And Melville uses it in three ways.

For him, the Gaze is not merely an act of seeing but a meditative state of mind bordering upon transcendence. In gazing, we contemplate the possibility of pushing our internal subjectivity out of ourselves and onto an objective Other. We are curious of this thing that is not us; we are caught in wonder over the existence of something so strange that it cannot possibly be just the usual projection of ourselves. This thing we gaze at is an awesome Not Me with which we anticipate an earnest integration, but in gazing we also maintain an anxious distance; the object of our gaze may stun us with its shifting reality; it may kill. This metaphysical Gaze of Wonder has obvious cultural and psychoanalytic implications. For Stephen Greenblatt the colonial gaze bespeaks the potential for assimilation. And Lacan asks us to consider the elemental beginnings of infant selfhood as one gazes into the mirror and recognizes an other which is one's self gazing back.

But there is also a more threatening sociological view. For Sartre, the gaze, or "*le regard*," is the Other's objectifying stare, which threatens to define our meaning. This second, more alienating Gaze of Control is one that Michel Foucault famously delineates in his study of the growth of prisons out of the monarchical practice of torture and execution. Foucault argues that modern discipline is based upon an awareness of institutional, panoptic surveillance rather than the king's abuse of a malefactor's actual body. Modern institutions, including factories, schools, hospitals, the military, a naval ship perhaps, as well as prisons, depend upon the individual's belief that a central, figurative "eye" is watching us, finding out incorrect behavior, and thereby inducing correction. In fact, the panopticon operates without an actual seer, for we internalize the seer; it becomes the "unseen seer" in our midst, an omniscient socializing gaze of control that commands us.[2]

We have, then, two kinds of Gaze: the metaphysical Gaze of Wonder that calls the very nature of Being into question and opens us to the possibility of self-awareness, growth, even cultural assimilation; and, the sociological Gaze of Control which more like the insistent stare of a bully bespeaks power, territory, and dominance. In *Typee*, Melville plays with both Gazes, attributing them generally but not exclusively to the natives he encounters. Tommo does not gaze at the Polynesian Other so much, as he is continually aware of that Other gazing at him. Tommo is their object of wonder and an object to control; and he is stunned by their objectification of him. But to these two Native Gazes, Melville incorporates a third, the sentimental Gaze of Sympathy.

But before inspecting these gazes, let us recall that up until the time he wrote *Typee*, Melville was always under the controlling scrutiny of some powerful authority—whaling captains, masters at arms, island police, the natives of Nuku Hiva, and, later at home, his mother. But in 1845, while residing in his brother's Manhattan rooms where he probably composed most of *Typee*, he found private space. Ironically, he was now more alone in the city than he had ever been at sea; and in this new, private place Melville began to unfold. He was inventing himself by gazing at himself. Essentially, the act of writing *Typee* was the enactment of a Gaze of Control over himself, his past, and emergent art. For once, he was not being gazed at; he was himself gazing.

Melville's shipboard life was a nightmare of Foucauldian surveillance. The day is divided into watches. Captains supervise mates who survey masters who oversee sailors from foretop to hold. White-Jacket, for instance, envies the "mob of incognitoes" and seeks their anonymity from the ship's "strict disciplinarians" (NN *White-Jacket*, 120-21). In cutting away his jacket, Melville's self-projected character liberates himself into this anonymity, but Melville, the writer, achieves his own more self-enabling liberation from the social Gaze when in Chapter 12 he discovers that his lofty maintop post "enable[s] him to give . . . a free, broad, off-hand, bird's-eye, . . . impartial account of our man-of-war world; withholding nothing; inventing nothing" (47). By turning his perch into a Panopticon and himself into an "unseen seer," Melville seizes artistic control over the naval institution that formerly controlled him with its oppressive gaze. *White-Jacket* marks a crucial aesthetic moment in Melville's narratorial development. But his masthead Panoptic vision, while it anticipates Ishmael's own mast-head reverie, is also a far cry from the "anxious" voice of *Typee*.

Melville had no certain plans when he set out to write *Typee*. He began simply by transcribing certain anecdotes of personal experience. Eventually, he began to dramatize those anecdotes, but he early on found that he had to go beyond personal experience. He had to do some research. These two writerly activities—dramatizing and researching—led Melville in essentially opposite directions. One route led him to a deeper self-awareness of sexuality; the other led him to a deeper political consciousness. On the one hand, Melville was essaying or, to use the whaling term, "trying out" his sexuality. He was giving voice to his homosocial, perhaps homosexual, bonding with jetty locked Toby (NN *Typee*, 32), and then his ferociously ugly island brother, Kory-Kory, whose fire-lighting scene (111) comically enacts male orgasm. But with Toby's departure, Tommo turns resolutely to blue-eyed Fayaway, with her masculine pipe (133), as if to dramatize and insist upon a heterosexual orientation. A sign of his success in this transition comes in the doubly erotic Chapter 18 when Fayaway joins Tommo in the taboo canoe, makes herself into a mast—a sight that in turn creates an erotic little mast in Tommo (134)—and sails off upon an imagined lake, to the distant transports of the watchful Kory-Kory. It's one boy (Tommo) watching another boy (Kory-Kory) watching him having sex. This kind of homosocial mirroring of heterosexual behavior is further confirmed in the chapter with the arrival of the physically striking Marnoo, whose "rich curling brown" hair recalls Toby. Marnoo's Roman beauty and cosmopolitan demeanor threaten Tommo who immediately takes the native to be a sexual rival.[3] This both affirms Tommo's heterosexuality as it threatens his performance in that orientation.

In dramatizing the sexualities of his Polynesian characters, Melville was seeking at his writing desk in New York to achieve control over the various sexual spheres he had inhabited in his former island life. He was exorcising adolescent homosexual tendencies and doubts in order to define himself in increasingly heterosexual terms. More precisely, he was achieving imperial dominion over his various sexualities. His first unfolding, then, was a self-colonization of his sexual being.

But running counter to this self-dramatization was his need to do some Polynesian researches. Although it was enough for him to work out in the writing process his sexual identity, that process did not yield enough pages to make a book. Research would allow him to augment his personal anecdotes and lend credibility to his travel narrative. However, the more Melville researched, the more his political consciousness grew. The works of naval warrior David Porter and missionary Charles Stewart supplied sufficient examples of colonial arrogance to trigger in the writer the kind of angry rebuttals which later on in print triggered the negative response from religionists that led to the expurgations of many of those passages in *Typee* that Melville had originally inserted to make his book into a book. Ironically, Melville's anti-colonialism ran counter to (although not in denial of) his own private colonization of his sexual being.

These twin developments are traceable in Melville's use of the Gaze. In jumping ship, Tommo by no means escapes the watchful eye of authority, for he must continually submit himself to chief Mehevi's "strange and steady glance," a male gaze of control that repeatedly unmans Melville's protagonist. Of his first encounter with this native gaze, Tommo says, "It revealed nothing of the mind of the savage, but it appeared be reading my own" (NN *Typee*, 71). This is a Melvillean expansion beyond the Foucauldian gaze of control. Mehevi is no "unseen seer": he is quite visible, but utterly incomprehensible. He is an "unknowable seer," and the dark bands of tattooing around his eyes heighten the strange otherness of this "regard." The native gaze unmans Tommo, for the native knows him better than he knows himself. The gaze has dominion over him; it has colonized him.

This native gaze of control is invariably male and suffuses Tommo's perceptions of nature. Take the early seaboard reverie in which Tommo awakens to a glittering ocean world which harbors the "evil eye" of the "prowling shark, that villainous footpad," and the "strange flashing" eye of the seahawk, "that piratical-looking fellow" (10). Pirates and footpads are watching Tommo, and King Mehevi is no different. The primal link between an ungraspable nature and an equally unknowable savage mind bears down upon Tommo, challenging his authority and manhood, like a never-blinking eye. At every turn, this masculinized native gaze belittles Tommo. Even when Tommo is the gazer, he experiences a form of speechless wonder that is equally unmanning, but often this alienation takes the form of his sudden awareness of silence, both in nature and among the natives, whose language he does not share. Recall Tommo standing stupefied before the silent cascades of the Typee valley (49, 65), or equally unmanned in contemplating his leap onto a tree-top growing up out of the abyss (63), or struck speechless at the "dumb stones" of ancient ruins (155). In each instance Melville's speechless wonder is expressed through his "gaze" at the scene before him, attesting more to his baffled seer status than to the scene itself.

To gain control in Nuku Hiva, Tommo must first overcome its silence. Despite his inability to speak Polynesian, he fancies by Chapter 18 with its interwoven tapestry of homo- and heterosexualities, that he can actually interpret "the nervous eloquence of [the natives'] looks and gestures" (142). In short, Tommo's mid-narrative sexual domination is accompanied by his sense that he can now read the native gaze. No longer a source of alienation, the gaze now becomes a vehicle of his gaining imperial control over his various sexual identities. To further effect this sexual self-colonization, Melville has Tommo feminize the alienating, male gaze. The Gazes of Wonder and Control, then, become a Gaze of Sympathy that is invariably united to Fayaway's female sensual eyes.

Melville's first description of Fayaway involves a curious solecism that in fact reveals as much about the young writer's sexual disorientation as it does his shaky sentence structure. Tommo writes: "Gazing into the depths of her strange blue eyes, when she was in a contemplative mood, they seemed most placid yet unfathomable" (86). The dangling modifier—"Gazing into the depths of her eyes"— requires a sentence in which Tommo performs the act of gazing, but as it is constructed, the actual sentence has its subject, "they," or Fayaway's eyes, do the gazing and in fact gaze impossibly into the depths of her own "strange blue eyes." Unintentionally, Melville has Fayaway gazing into herself, when he clearly intends Tommo to be gazing into her. The sentence error nevertheless speaks to Tommo's radically unstable identity. He intends to connect with the contemplative Fayaway, but trips over his grammar, and ends up making Fayaway oddly introspective—a fair reckoning of his own condition. Tommo cannot take visual control. All he can "see" is Fayaway seeing herself. She, like her male counterparts, still claims dominion over Tommo with her "unfathomable" eye.

But when Fayaway becomes aroused "by some lively emotion," Tommo fancies that her gaze becomes more readable. The *Typee* manuscript allows us to see this transformation from inscrutability to readability unfolding as Melville wrote. In Chapter 14, after Toby's departure throws Tommo into a depression and before Kory-Kory's erotic fire-lighting scene, Tommo finds himself comforted by Fayaway.

Initially in manuscript, Melville simply lists Fayaway's tenderness and sympathy, her sweet voice, and glance of pity, all of which assures Tommo that she "deeply compassionated *our* situation." Here is the clear reading text of the manuscript passage:

There was a tenderness *& sympathy in the tones of her sweet voice, and a glance of pity in her face* which it was impossible to misunderstand or resist. ◎ *It plainly assured me* that she deeply compassionated *our* situation, as being far removed from *our* countrymen & friends & seemingly placed beyond the reach of all hope of succer or releif. Indeed at times I was almost led to beleive that her *gentle bosom* was swayed by *thoughts & feelings* hardly to be anticipated from one in her condition—that she appeared to be conscious there were ties & connections rudely severed that had bound us to our homes, that there were sisters & brothers anxiously looking forward to our return who were *fated never* more to behold us.—¶ In this amiable light did *Faaua* appear in my eyes, & reposing full confidence in her *superior candor and intelligence*, it was no wonder that I now had recourse to her in the midst of *the apprehensions that afflicted me* with regard to my companion.[4]

Notice that the word "our" in Melville's original inscription includes both Tommo and Toby in the scene. But upon returning to revise the manuscript, Melville saw fit to eliminate this recollection of the physically absent but still mentally present Toby. Melville/Tommo wants Fayaway's "glance of pity" for himself only, and he therefore alters "our situation" to "my situation," thus removing the sexually ambivalent Toby altogether.

Quite possibly this small but meaningful shift—the elimination of Toby—also triggered the much larger revisions to come. Converting the sympathy, sweet voice, and glance of pity into the simple phrase "her sweet manner," Melville next proceeded to insert on a separate sheet now lost, a longer passage that effectively dramatizes Fayaway's "sweetness." In doing so, Fayaway's glance of pity is converted into a feminized gaze of sympathy. Here is the entire insertion:

Whenever she entered the house, the expression of her face indicated the liveliest sympathy for me; and moving towards the place where I lay, with one arm slightly elevated in a gesture of pity, and her large glistening eyes GAZING intently into mine, she would murmur plaintively, "Awha! awha! Tommo," and seat herself mournfully beside me.[5]

In contrast to Mehevi's "fixed and stern" regard, the emblem of male dominance in Tommo's first encounter with the Typees, Fayaway's glistening gaze of sympathy converts both alienating wonder and control into a vision that encourages a less-threatening, indeed redemptive integration of western and Polynesian sensibilities. Of course, this is merely Melville/Tommo's wishful interpretation of the "nervous eloquence of [Fayaway's] looks and gestures" (142). But at the same time it is also Melville's insistent reconstruction of his homosocial dependency upon Toby into a heterosexual relationship with one who understands and elevates him. It is an unfolding into artistic and psychological self-control.

But Melville's revising was not complete. The writer also modulates Fayaway's Polynesian sensibility. Initially, Melville has Fayaway's "gentle bosom" being "swayed by thoughts and feelings" not usually attributed to "savages." In this regard, Fayaway possesses a "superior candor and intelligence" in the original manuscript reading. But when Melville later added his description of Fayaway's glistening gaze, he also converted her "thoughts and feelings" to more emotional "impulses." That is, Fayaway's sympathy is revised from a mental state to something closer to a primal instinct. As such, the more elemental wording stresses the deepest links in Tommo and Fayaway's shared humanity.

And the revising was still not complete. Later, before going to press, Melville converted the phrase "gentle bosom" to "mind"; he also removed the word "superior" from the phrase "superior candor and intelligence." These modulations are counter-directional. The shift from bosom to mind restores a dimension of thought to Fayaway's sensibility, while it of course de-emphasizes an appealing part of her anatomy. But this intellectualizing of Fayaway is muted with the removal of "superior" from her candor and intelligence.

This building up of Fayaway's sympathetic sensibility—she is now more like us because her gaze reveals not a control over us but an understanding of us—and the toning down of her perhaps threatening superiority also coincides with Melville's anglicizing of Faaua to Fayaway. These revisions effectively familiarize the native gaze of control into a gaze of wonder that can understand him, and he it. Melville's strategy is to achieve, whether it is real or not, a sense of personal control. He can gain imperial dominion over himself sexually, and over primal Polynesia culturally, because he can now read the native gaze; and reading it as a mirror of himself he converts it from a controlling stare into a vehicle of imperial self dominance.

In converting the masculine gaze into a feminine gaze, Melville transformed the bisexual encounters of his island past into a willfully insistent heterosexual present. He was gazing upon himself, and unfolding as he wrote.

NOTES

1   *Herman Melville: A Biography* (Berkeley: University of California Press, 1951), 178.

2   *Discipline and Punish: The Birth of the Prison*, trans. Alan Sheridan (New York: Random House, 1977), 202. Jay Martin draws the parallel between Foucault's and Sartre's shared notion of the internalization of the social gaze (see "In the Empire of the Gaze: Foucault and the Denigration of Vision in Twentieth-century French Thought," in *Foucault: A Critical Reader*, ed. David Couzens Hoy (London: Blackwell, 1986), 190.

3   See my discussion of Marnoo as a cosmopolite in *Melville and Repose: The Rhetoric of Humor in the American Renaissance* (New York: Oxford University Press, 1993), p. 179, 184.

4   A full reading text of the three-chapter manuscript, presently located at the New York Public Library, appears as an appendix in Herman Melville, *Typee: A Peep at Polynesian Life*, ed. John Bryant (New York: Penguin American Classics, 1996). This passage appears on Leaf 14, page 27 of the manuscript and page 108 of the printed text. Italics indicate words and phrases Melville revised in subsequent versions. The enclosed circle after the word "resist" indicates the location of Melville's insertion mark in the manuscript.

5   Melville's insertion of Fayaway's gaze was composed on a separate sheet or sheets now lost. We can infer its existence as a late insertion in Melville's writing process because an insertion mark (an enclosed circle) appears mid-page on Leaf 14, page 27 at the point where the passage in question appears in the printed text. A tear at the top of manuscript Leaf 14 suggests that the sheet containing this insertion was straight-pinned to the leaf, the tear occurring when the now lost insertion leaf was pulled off.

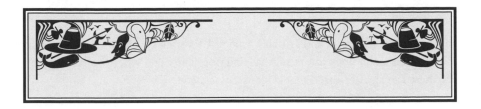

INGER HUNNERUP DALSGAARD

"THE LEYDEN JAR" AND "THE IRON WAY" CONJOINED:

MOBY-DICK, THE CLASSICAL AND THE MODERN SCHISM OF SCIENCE AND TECHNOLOGY

ithin a couple of pages in *Moby-Dick* Ahab's personality is likened to both a "Leyden Jar" and an "Iron Way." These two concepts or objects, electricity and the railway, are not only metaphors for certain of Ahab's personal qualities; *pars pro toto* they also stand for the larger systems to which they belong. The relationship between these "systems," science and technology, was a contemporary issue upon which Melville partly comments through the figure of Ahab in *Moby-Dick*. Technology and science as specific areas with certain parameters, procedures, and aims grew up together, from Plato to Diderot onwards, being defined conventionally in terms of contrast. We still understand them primarily in that way, as different realms which occasionally intersect. This was also the case in the United States in Melville's time, but there existed then a uniquely strong drive to make science seem directly useful to the growing industrial society. To carve out a place for themselves and gain funding, scientific communities in America had to make common cause with technology to serve manufactures and the transport industry. Melville's investigation of this relationship in mid-nineteenth-century industrializing America also reworks popular figures of science and technology from Greek mythology. The *Pequod* as America is inhabited as much by the fiery Prometheus as by the cunning, crafty, and skillful Daidalos and Hephaistos and the brave and the forceful heroes Herakles and Perseus. Melville uses these more or less popularly known figures, relating and redefining them prima-

rily via Ahab, to reflect and criticize aspects of a society where science was dependent on technology for its survival and popularity and where both in tandem
furthered an already unacceptable industrial society.

I

Melville grew up in a rapidly industrializing America. He spent his teens in
the 1830s, a period where railroad construction experienced a growth rate unprecedented in any other country. Aiming for a career in this prosperous area, he even
finished an engineering and surveying course during his late teens with an eye
on employment on the Erie Canal, which was considered the first, informal
"School of Engineering" in America. By this time, Jeffersonian suspicion towards
manufacturers had subsided and, along with improvements in transportation,
already well-established factories and mill-communities were continuing to grow
and prosper. In the 1830s, Lowell, the model industrial town of the New World,
was a show-piece for visitors. This form of large-scale manufacturing paved the
way for an expanding national economy and exemplified the enlightened route
to prosperity the United States celebrated. By the late 1830s and early 1840s, however, the happy image of a morally improving and financially rewarding life in
the mills was crumbling and in 1855 Melville's "The Tartarus of Maids" showed
the veritable hell which working women suffered in factories. They gave over
their own potential for reproduction to industrial production, letting the material supplant the maternal, so to speak. As for Melville's views on the boom in
transportation, we might look to his 1853 short story "Cock-A-Doodle-Doo!" It
was written in that *Annus Horribilis* of American Railroads when major accidents
totaled more than one hundred, killing 234 passengers and seriously injuring
another 496.[1] The narrator might well ask gloomily if life is a reasonable price to
pay for the (American System of) improvements as he describes the killing-spree
involving rutting trains animated by a strange mechanical attraction. Charon fer-
ries over the epitome of procreative promise, bride, groom, and baby, "baggage-
less, to some clinkered iron-foundry."[2] (Needless to say, contemporary railroad-
company advertisements prominently stated their strictly limited liability for
delayed and mislaid baggage.) Two years later in "The Bell-Tower" (1855), Melville
offers an allegorical critique of the type of mind-set, in both individual and socie-

ty, which fosters Frankenstein-like engineers who channel their libidos into out-sized constructions and try single-handedly to give birth to an alternative being—a "'Haman" rather than a human one in Bannadonna's case. In the 1850s machines were maiming both passengers and factory workers, and it could look as if toler-ant authorities were allowing this in the interest of the economy, industrial advance or—ultimately—in the name of "Progress."

Melville's criticism of the parts technology and society play in producing a dehumanizing type of industrialization is also recognizable in *Moby-Dick*. Ahab has an "iron soul" which turns his mates mechanical: "Like machines, they dumb-ly moved about the deck" ("The Hat"); and Starbuck comments that Ahab on the third day of the chase has a "heart of wrought steel" ("The Chase – Third Day"), that is, once malleable but now hardened in water.[3] The wrought iron rails of a railroad, which in "Cock-A-Doodle-Doo!" cut "straight as a die" through ob-stacles to reach the goal, are thus also present in Ahab:[4] "Swerve me? The path to my fixed purpose is laid with iron rails, whereon my soul is grooved to run. Over unsounded gorges, through the rifled hearts of mountains, under torrents' beds, unerringly I rush! Naught's an obstacle, naught's an angle to the iron way" ("Sunset," p. 266). Starbuck, whose soul was "overmanned" by this outburst, complains that Ahab has "drilled deep down, and blasted all my reason out of me!" ("Dusk," p. 267) just as a railroad-engineer drills a hole for gun-powder into an offending rock in the path of construction. When describing Ahab's purpose, Melville uses imagery and metaphors drawn from industrial society: in order to get his iron way, Ahab has had to blast through and level all obstacles so he can run the rails over the ground provided here by his crew. Ahab's project and rail-road engineering share an irony: a certain level of breaking down or destroying is necessary for the construction of something which itself, Melville fears, will ulti-mately bring total destruction.

If "iron way" functions as an extended industrial or technological metaphor, there is a related significance in its proximity to the "Leyden Jar" description of Ahab, which alludes to a distinctly scientific topic at the time. In "The Quarter-Deck" Ahab nails the golden doubloon to the mainmast and fires up his crew with demagogy and a drink from the pewter. He then has his mates (or "cup-bearers") cross their irons so he can touch the axis. In so doing Ahab creates his own voltaic pile or lightning rod, and it "seemed as though he would fain have shocked into them the same fiery emotion accumulated within the Leyden jar of his own magnetic life" ("The Quarter-Deck," p. 264). Ahab's mixture of mysticism, grail or tarot lore, and electrical charge is threatening and repulsive as well as magnetically attractive. In this scene the mates are under his sway, yet they also shy away from his power, much like magnetic poles. As they look away from his "strong, sustained, and mystic aspect," Ahab cries, "In vain!... but maybe, 'tis well. For did ye three but once take the full-force shock, then mine own electric thing, *that* had perhaps expired from out me. Perchance too, it would have dropped ye dead. Perchance ye need it not" ("The Quarter-Deck," p. 264). The exclusive hold Ahab has on this force also indicates science's esoteric and private nature. If he ever had delusions that his actions would have positive results for his fellow human beings, Ahab's doubts that others could handle the electric shock of his project obliterate the last vestiges of any attempt at shared understanding. Like scientist Victor Frankenstein before him, his project reveals itself to be solipsistic, arrogantly shutting out common sense to keep it "mine own electric thing," which in his mind no one else can handle nor needs a share in.

There is further significance to Melville's metaphoric choice of a somewhat old-fashioned electrical instrument, the Leyden jar. The device, a type of condenser for storing static electricity (or in Franklin's famous case "lightning"), was invented in 1745 and became somewhat outmoded in scientific circles after the first battery was invented by Volta 55 years later, when Galvanism was becoming all the rage. The Leyden jar outside the Galvani setting strongly hints at mesmerism and fittingly describes Ahab as an hypnotic, charismatic, Mesmer-like figure who has cast a spell over his congregation. His subsequent magic trick of remagnetizing the compass needle ("The Needle," p. 627) shows not only his utter control of technique and scientific principles but also his ability to put on a show for a superstitious audience. But the mention of magnetism in the Leyden-jar passage also hints forward in time from the heyday of Mesmer, animal magnetism, and electrostatics to a modern scientific hero like Michael Faraday. In *Mardi* Melville made reference to Faraday, whose discovery of the principles of electro-magnetism were well known at the time. In the decade between 1821 and 1831 Faraday had taken Ampère and Ørsted's ideas further and proven the relation between magnetic and electric forces. He used technology to test his theories by constructing a scientific apparatus (a primitive electro-motor and generator) and thereby also showed that mechanical energy could be turned into electrical force. This idea, though it was not to find industrial application for another four decades, could still be what informs the connection between the scientific and technological imagery surrounding Ahab: his physical drive, the iron way, is easily exchanged for his electrically charged personality, the Leyden jar, and vice versa.[5] One generates or drives the other. Ahab, though branded as if once struck by lightning ("Ahab," p. 219), no longer needs to draw it down to fire his purpose; he is self-supplying and generates enough energy also to drive the factory-ship in his command onto his own desired course.

II

Moby-Dick brings out an essential dilemma in the American approach to science. An individualistic project and search for fame, it also had to be a practical, material quest. Faraday could devote himself to discovering principles and could use technology merely to prove them. In contrast to this Englishman stood a now forgotten American, Thomas Davenport, who actually built and patented a functioning electric motor in 1837. In 1840 (on Independence Day) he started a weekly publication called *The Magnet*—the first American magazine on electricity printed on the first electrically driven printing press. Using rhetoric and the language of advertising, he recommends the publication because: "First—it is printed upon a new and improved conical rotary press. Secondly—this press is worked by our electro-magnetic engine. Thirdly—both are wholly American." Juggling these laudable qualities, Davenport also tried to incorporate the popular idea of progress, arguing "the great advantages this wonderful power has over steam, in regard to safety, cheapness and convenience." Much like Ahab in the "Needle" section, he also uses supernatural and sublime connotations to capture his audience: the slightly unscientific but very bold headline of the first number of *The Magnet* proclaimed "Lightning in Harness" and extolled electricity as a "POWERFUL and MYSTERIOUS agent." Finally, it also becomes clear in the pamphlet's last paragraph that this is not just Davenport's attempt to popularize and promote his own invention: behind the rhetorical barrage devoted to American Civil Religion, patriotism, and the practical application of electromagnetism to further his cause, he intends his publication to report "the experiments of others, more experienced in the science of Electricity, Galvanism, Magnetism, and Electro-magnetism . . . in order that the reader may get a general idea of the science, and the laws by which they are governed, and by which we are guided in controlling and working [it]." [6]

Davenport is a good example of how science in America had to sell itself with both hocus-pocus (as Ahab does to his crew) and material pragmatism (as Ahab does to the ship's owners) to seem both acceptable and loyal to a specific ideology. However, a close reading of the scientific journals of that time also reveals scientists tiring of discussing exploding steam-engines and devoting increasing amounts of time and space to the purer science of electricity! The growing scientific bias also saw correspondents in scientific journals depicting engineers as too uneducated and unscientific, too practical about their observations. Such representations were symptomatic of a growing gap in understanding between the learned scientists and the practical engineers, or those "sordid, ignorant" people to whom parts of the scientific community still felt they had to justify and popularize their activities.

In *Moby-Dick* shrewd Ahab sees that sort of inferior, practical version of himself in the Hephaistos figure of the emotionally and physically crippled blacksmith, Perth, and the carpenter whose "brain, if he had ever had one, must have oozed along into the muscles of his fingers" ("The Carpenter," p. 579). As craftsmen employed by industry, they may be ingenious like Daidalos, or creative like Hephaistos or Prometheus himself in some myths, but Ahab's ancillaries provide the "muscle part" only. The inferior positions given to the carpenter and blacksmith reflect not only the subjugation of craftsmanship by a mechanized, industrialized society, nor simply the disdain towards the malformed creator of beauty, Hephaistos, perceptibly displayed in ancient myths, but also the split in the Prometheus myth between the "Prometheus Plasticator" and the "Prometheus Pyrophoros." Melville was familiar with both strains of the myth: Prometheus as a molder of men, creating human kind from clay, and Prometheus as the stealer or carrier of fire, bringing enlightenment to mankind. From the classical era up to Francis Bacon's times, both functions were woven into the texture of one Prometheus figure. But in early industrial society the conjunctive logic had already ruptured. The growing split between the creative and the enlightening strains of human activity, between technology and science or body and mind, are also reflected in the way the Promethean epithet is divided between Ahab and his workers, whom he asks not to invent or create but to execute his design, turning his airy ideas into an artificial human being as tangible as the Thames Tunnel ("Ahab and the Carpenter," pp. 581-82). The scientific mind-set Ahab displays does not correspond to the old rhetorical promise that the primary goal of science was to assist the development of useful technology. Instead it seeks, via authority and financial rewards, to use technology for the less obviously rewarding objectives of experimental science, represented in Ahab's request for an artificial man as much as in his quest for Moby Dick himself. In this, Melville exposes the power-struggle between the two areas: it is clear that they are no longer part of the same texture, nor cooperating, but fighting for priority in a battle where the "Pyrophoros" (because it represents mind above matter) evidently wins out over the "Plasticator."

Ahab on board the *Pequod* represents a certain (misdirected) scientific mind-set on board a junket financed by industry, and he depends on ship and crew functioning like one well-oiled machine to pursue and conquer his object of desire (even Ishmael's style of science, whale-observation, needs the whaling ship which kills what he is trying to chart). To survive and secure financial backing, science in America had to pretend, like Ahab when amongst the crowd in Nantucket and financial backers like the Quaker owners, Peleg and Bildad, that its goal was to hunt and try out the oil of many whales, in a factory-like manner. But, like Ahab's, the hidden drive of science is for unproductive seeming abstract knowledge, of pursuing that one white whale. Ahab's hidden real project lacks obvious popular appeal, except to a captive audience steeped in the mechanized and magnetized atmosphere of the *Pequod*. Ahab's individualism and electrical charge transcend the quest for the Almighty Dollar which the sailors pursued through the "lays" system, where a share of the profits rewards the quantity of catch ("The Ship," p. 172) and turns the Dollar into the Doubloon. A "democratic" hierarchical distribution of wealth is replaced by the potential for one individual to strike it lucky. The shared performance bonus is forgotten for the higher ideal (gold or vengeance) of chasing the white whale. In the process, the ambition and freedom signified by the doubloon turn each sailor into a miniature Ahab rather than a "factory-worker" content with his daily drudgery for moderate pay. Overboard go the good republican values which preferred to have mass-production drive the American ship of state at a moderate human cost. The loyal factory ship instead commences a mono-maniacal scientific quest for one thing to satisfy one man. And, inevitably, Ahab ends up getting the doubloon himself ("The Chase—First Day," p. 655).

III

If a writer like Melville in some ways reflected a quite English-inspired, Carlylean, view of the dehumanizing effects of this wholesale pursuit of material gain by technology and industrial workers, or the reckless impetus of a scientific mindset, his forebodings did not fit well what Robert Bruce calls the "swelling current of American faith in the unalloyed benefice of technology." Americans in general did not spend much time worrying about the lessons to be learned from Eve, Pandora, Midas, Icarus, Faust, or Frankenstein: in fact, Greek myth was selectively rewritten when called upon to glorify America.[7] Hercules was often invoked as a metaphor for the unbending strength and determination of the industrial drive and, more curiously, the flawed Titan, the hubristic Prometheus of Homer, Hesiod, and Aeschylus also found a particularly positive American usage. Where in England Percy Shelley had resurrected this rebel against the power of Olympian gods and Mary Shelley had shown through *Frankenstein, or, the Modern Prometheus* (1818), the unacceptable face of scientific pursuits, Prometheus was welcomed into the American pantheon of cultural heroes as a beneficial bringer of enlightenment, skills, and civilization; as such he became a positive metaphor for progress in a quite different way. The Modern American Prometheus was a popular champion for integrated science and technology and had, like Hesiod's Prometheus, been allowed freedom by the interception of Heracles (Hercules): which can be seen as industry paving the way for scientific knowledge. The positive imagery attributed to this figure was typically illustrated in January 1846 when the benefits of physical sciences were lauded in the *United States Magazine and Democratic Review*. For "the Prometheus of the nineteenth century," the editor declared "no rewards are esteemed excessive, no dignities too exalted."[8]

Familiar with both classical and renaissance works on Prometheus from Aeschylus' *Prometheus Bound* and Francis Bacon's *The Wisdom of the Ancients* to Robert

Burton's *The Anatomy of Melancholy*, Melville, like Mary Shelley, could take off the "rose-tinted glasses of Romanticism," see through the rhetoric of progress, and recognize the dire connotations of the Promethean metaphor in their different societies.[9] His Prometheus is akin to Mary Shelley's, but he operates against a different background. Where Victor Frankenstein steals the spark of life secretly, American society officially sends Ahab to steal fire in the form of whale-oil. But Ahab becomes more Promethean and reprehensible in the classical, Aeschylean mold when his real project surfaces. By pursuing only Moby Dick (and not even for his oil), Ahab abandons the material objective of catching and trying inferior whales and thus in effect steals oil/fire from the coffers of Peleg and Bildad. He sins against a capitalist contract as much as against nature, god, or family life. Like the classical Prometheus, he convinces the lowly humans that what he is doing, though wrong, is really for their benefit, so that rather than eking out a minimum for existence they might be given something precious. Like that Prometheus, too, Ahab's pride and desire blind him to the worse consequences of his actions: the wrath of Moby Dick or Zeus. The American Prometheus Melville sends up through Ahab is a champion of industry who has lost sight of the humanitarian goal, the moral improvement possible through increased production, which politicians had originally promised and which technologists and scientists were still rehearsing in the prefaces to their books and pamphlets. Ahab's actions show that, on the flip-side, the rhetoric and the doubloon hold no guarantees for the majority of Americans of moral or even financial improvements.

IV

In conclusion, science's special relation to technology and industry in an American context describes the way in which Ahab's Prometheus is different from Milton's Satan, Byron's Manfred, and Goethe's Faust. He *is* darkly attractive to his crew, even to readers, perhaps, like those glorified Romantic sinners. But Melville does not seem to give in to the same personal sympathy or fascination with his lapsed creation to which the Romantics tended to succumb as Milton did in *Paradise Lost*. Moreover, Ahab is thoroughly modern, a master of practical engineering. A significant difference from Manfred and Faust is that Ahab's involvement with magic is not pre-industrial nostalgia on the part of his creator but his own conscious strategy for controlling his crew. Finally, Ahab is not a champion of freedom for the masses or the abstract individual but of his own liberty. A mad egotist, he seeks to use the world around him for his own purposes—which in Mary Shelley's view would have made him genuinely Romantic, like Byron or Percy Shelley (themselves supreme egotists in personal relationships whatever their outward ideals).

Ahab is truly modern because, like Shelley's Victor Frankenstein, it is possible to take him out of the religious equation and into the modern manufacturing one, where Ahab does not so much offend god and sin against natural order as primarily against other human beings and the protestant, productive ethos. In *Moby-Dick* Melville has produced an offensive, mad, raving Prometheus, who has hijacked his ship and men to pursue a metaphysical and unproductive goal, seen from Peleg and Bildad's point of view. He risks his men's lives, and the investment in the *Pequod* itself, which was unforgivable in contemporary American society, not because it did not happen frequently but because when it went wrong, as in Ahab's case, it would not pay off. American tolerance of risk-taking favored experimental technology above experimental science: as a ruthless representative of industrial capitalism Ahab was accepted, but his Frankensteinian side cannot easily be tolerated as part of the idealized Modern American Prometheus.

NOTES

1   John F. Stover, *American Railroads* (Chicago: University of Chicago Press, 1961), p. 50.

2   Herman Melville, Billy Budd, Sailor, *and Other Stories*, ed. Harold Beaver (Harmondsworth: Penguin, 1970), p. 104.

3   Herman Melville, *Moby-Dick*, ed. Harold Beaver (Harmondsworth: Penguin, 1972), pp. 644 and 677. References hereafter in parentheses in the body of the text.

4   Melville, *Billy Budd, Sailor,* p. 120.

5   H. J. Habakkuk, *American and British Technology in the Nineteenth Century: The Search for Labour-Saving Inventions* (Cambridge: Cambridge University Press, 1962), pp. 182-83.

6   *New York Herald*, April 27, 1837, n.p. *The Magnet: Devoted to Arts, Science, and Mechanism*, ed. S. J. Bauer vol. 1, no. 1, (New York; July 4, 1840), p. 1.

7   Robert V. Bruce, *The Launching of Modern American Science, 1846-1876* (Ithaca, NY: Cornell University Press, 1987), pp. 130-31.

8   Bruce, p. 131.

9   Gerard M. Sweeney, *Melville's Use of Classical Mythology* (Amsterdam: Rodopi, n. v., 1975), pp. 14 and 36.

REFERENCES

Aeschylus. *Prometheus Bound, The Suppliants, Seven Against Thebes, The Persians* (Harmondsworth: Penguin, 1961).

Bacon, Francis. *The Essays: The Wisdom of The Ancients and The New Atlantis* (London: Odhams Press Ltd., 1935).

Bruce, Robert V. *The Launching of Modern American Science, 1846-1876* (Ithaca, NY: Cornell University Press, 1987).

Democritus Junior [Robert Burton]. *The Anatomy of Melancholy: What Is It, With All The Kinds, Causes, Symptoms, Prognostics and Several Cures of It* (London: William Tegg and Co., 1849).

Habakkuk, H. J. *American and British Technology in the Nineteenth Century: The Search for Labour-Saving Inventions* (Cambridge: Cambridge University Press, 1962).

Katz, Barry M. *Technology and Culture: A Historic Romance* (Stanford: The Portable Stanford Book Series, 1990).

Kerényi, Carl. *The Gods of the Greeks* (Harmondsworth: Penguin, 1958).

The Magnet: Devoted to Arts, Science, and Mechanism. Ed. S. J. Bauer, 1, 1 [New York], July 4, 1840.

Melville, Herman. *Moby-Dick*, ed. Harold Beaver (Harmondsworth: Penguin, 1972).

Melville, Herman. Billy Budd, Sailor, *and Other Stories*. Ed. Harold Beaver (Harmondsworth: Penguin, 1970).

New York Herald. April 27, 1837.

Stover, John F. *American Railroads* (Chicago: University of Chicago Press, 1961).

Sweeney, Gerard M. *Melville's Use of Classical Mythology* (Amsterdam: Rodopi, n.v., 1975).

253

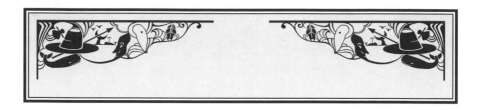

YUKIKO OSHIMA

THE RED FLAG OF THE *PEQUOD*/PEQUOT:

NATIVE AMERICAN PRESENCE IN *MOBY-DICK*

the Indian at the mainmast ... nailing the flag faster and yet faster to the subsiding spar.
Moby-Dick, 572

hy did Melville assign such an important role as hammering Ahab's flag on the mainmast of the sinking *Pequod* to such a minor character as the whaler's Third Harpooneer, Tashtego, whose roles have categorically eluded critics?[1] Prompted by the final scene and the fictional name of the *Pequod*, named after an indigenous tribe *officially* put into extinction by the Puritans in the seventeenth century, I suggest that the text contains a veiled homage to the tribe Pequot, and, in a broader sense, to the Native Americans in general as *one of its enormous multiple layers*.

Melville had a long-standing concern about the Native-white divide since *Typee* and a rare moral outlook sympathetic to the Native side. Only two years before the publication of *Moby-Dick* (1851), his unconventionally favorable view on the Amerindians appeared in a book review in *The Literary World* on Francis Parkman's *The Oregon Trail* (1849). Parkman despised the Natives he encountered on the plain as lazy and vulgar in the memorial summer of 1846 in the U.S. westward movement. Acknowledging the dangers of hostile Natives in the vast wilderness past the extreme frontier, and understanding Parkman's view as merely representative of the period, Melville nonetheless criticized this elite historian's sense of racial superiority: "But though it [i.e., this feeling] is almost natural, it is not defensible;

254

and it is wholly wrong. Why should we contemn them?—Because we are better than they? Assuredly not. . . . We are all of us—Anglo-Saxon, Dyaks and Indians—sprung from one head and made in one image" ("Mr Parkman's Tour" 291). He apologized to the editor Evert Duyckinck for writing such a "critical" review nine months later (Leyda I, 347), reconfirming the age's racism at that time. Through the hard-working Tashtego in this thriving national industry that the Native Americans started, as Ishmael narrates in "Nantucket," and to which a lot of them contributed, Melville covertly reversed Parkman's formulaic Native American representation.

Native Americans have often been invisible in textual analyses of American literature. In *Moby-Dick*, a prophecy about Ahab by a squaw Tistig (79), whose name is spelled like Tashtego's from the same island, has been neglected. By moving Tashtego to the forefront of the action as opposed to subordinating him to the background where Ishmael assigned him, it becomes clear Tashtego plays a crucial role in the main plot, Ahab's hunt for the White Whale. Tashtego is the first crew member who answers Ahab's quarter-deck speech:

"It's a white whale, I say . . . a *white* whale. *Skin* your eyes for him, men; look sharp for *white* water; if ye see but a bubble, sing out."

All this while *Tashtego, Daggoo, and Queequeg* had looked on with even more intense interest and surprise than the rest, and at the mention of the wrinkled brow and crooked jaw they had started as if each was separately touched by some specific recollection.

"Captain Ahab," said Tashtego, "that *white* whale must be the same that some call Moby Dick."

"Moby Dick?" shouted Ahab. "Do ye know the *white* whale then, Tash?" (162, emphasis mine)

On the surface, Ahab repeats "white whale," assuming his audience is unfamiliar with its proper name. By reiteration of its whiteness and the expression "skin" in "Skin your eyes for him," he appeals to the non-Caucasians' pent-up anger in free association. (Despite the title of the novel, "Moby Dick" is *far* less frequently used than "the White Whale.") "Some specific recollection" in the above can mean racial or other forms of discrimination taking place in this highly racialized text.[2]

Ahab's quarter-deck oratory, "To me, the white whale is that wall, shoved

near to me" (164), is multi-faceted. His hunt, made possible by the crew's agree-
ment, is a wish-fulfilling counterattack by a group of outcasts against a force
that keeps oppressing them and pushing them into lower social strata, into a
metaphorical ever-shrinking prison. Although of elite status, Captain Ahab
stands in front of them with a mutilated corporeal self as a visibly devastated
man, articulating a subaltern's pain. For the non-whites, the "white wall" in the
form of the White Whale can embody white supremacy experienced as racism.

The highlighted naming of "Tashtego, Daggoo, and Queequeg" confuses
their ranks: Tashtego, introduced as the Second Harpooneer in "Knights and
Squires" and as the Third in "The First Lowering," is here listed first while the
First one, Queequeg, is last. This shuffled ranking is carried forward to Ahab's
baptism of his harpoon with the harpooneer's blood as saying, "Ahoy, there!
Tashtego, Queequeg, Daggoo! What say ye, pagans! Will ye give me as much
blood as will cover this barb?" (489). To Queequeg and Daggoo, former princes
who came to the United States by their free will and thus can relish their luxurious pride, the White Whale vaguely embodies white men's power. For Tashtego,
the same white-wall analogy appears as a land confiscation and genocide that
characterize the Amerindian experience, in which the white wall overlaps the
ever-pressing frontier line that pushes them. The Natives had been shoved into
territories west of the Mississippi by the Indian Removal Act, advocated by
Andrew Jackson, passed by Congress in 1830, and virtually completed by 1850.
Tashtego—as "an unmixed Indian from Gay Head, the most westerly promontory of Martha's Vineyard, where there still exists the last remnant of a village of
red men" (120)—is a fit representative of his "vanishing race."

There is rapport between harpooneers and Ahab, who knows the racial Others in their Native settings; he has "been in colleges, as well as among the cannibals" (79). Shortly after the quarter-deck speech, reversing the ship's otherwise
rigid hierarchy as well as racial strata, Ahab makes the reluctant white mates
serve the harpooneers as "cup-bearers to my three pagan kinsmen there—yon
three most honorable gentlemen and noblemen, my valiant harpooneers" (166).
The harpooneers, in turn, have been faithful to Ahab; even when the others
come to fear the captain's growing madness, "a certain magnetism shot into
their [i.e., the harpooneers'] congenial hearts from inflexible Ahab's" (518), and

when Ahab later "seemed distrustful of his crew's fidelity; at least, of nearly all except the Pagan harpooneers" (538).

In spite of his less frequent appearances, Tashtego plays substantial roles. He sights the first sperm whale of the voyage. (Compare this with Daggoo's comical mistaking a giant white squid for Moby Dick in "Squid.") He is almost the first to sight Moby Dick, although to be precise, being spatially under Ahab, he is a split second later than the captain. True enough, it is an overstatement to posit that the two of them make concerted efforts throughout, growing maniacal on the third day of the chase and reducing the crewmen to his arms and legs, Ahab rejects Tashtego's claim of simultaneously sighting the whale. This split, however, proves to be momentary.

Tashtego's greatest role is in the closing scene, not just as the last crewman who goes down with the ship but the only one who responds to Ahab's desperate cry to protect the vessel. It is as if he textually emerged into existence only to sink again: "Meantime, for that one beholding instant, Tashtego's mast head hammer remained suspended in his hand; and *the red flag, half-wrapping him as with a plaid, then streamed itself straight out from him, as his own forward-flowing heart*; while Starbuck and Stubb, standing upon the bowsprit beneath, caught sight of the down-coming monster just as soon as he" (570, emphasis mine).

In conjunction with the name of the ship, the plaid cloth, red flag, and "red arm" of the red man, the Native American presence wins visibility here. Ahab's heart is embodied in the captain's flag which, unlike a company flag chosen by the ship owners, is his own choice. This flag enwraps Tashtego like a patterned blanket, which is often worn by Amerindians for their tribal identity, and "streamed itself straight out" from him. However futile his act might be, Tashtego's "forward-flowing heart" is set against the inactive renunciation of the rest of the crew, especially that of the mates, depicted at length right before this passage. As the whale staves in the ship, Ahab senses the fulfillment of one of Fedallah's prophecies, "the visible wood of the last one [i.e., hearse] must be grown in America" (541). The shipwreck of the *Pequod*, made of American wood, overlaps the disappearance of nature by America's ongoing industrialization and of sylvan Natives like the Pequot. The text's racial undertone reverberates in the way Tashtego's sense of victimization and motivation for vengeance overlaps those of Ahab. Receiving Ahab's very last words to a human, "What ho, Tashtego! let me hear thy hammer" (571), Tashtego nails the captain's flag while the whale charges the ship. Only the uppermost mainmast is out of the water: "[A] red arm and a hammer hovered backwardly uplifted in the open air, in the act of nailing the flag faster and yet faster to the subsiding spar. A sky-hawk that tauntingly had followed the main-truck downwards from *its natural home among the stars*, pecking at the flag, and incommoding Tashtego there; this bird now chanced to intercept its broad fluttering wing between the hammer and the wood; and simultaneously feeling *that etherial thrill*, the submerged savage beneath, in his death-grasp, kept his hammer frozen there; and so *the bird of heaven, with archangelic shrieks*, and *his imperial beak* thrust upwards, and his whole captive form folded in the flag of Ahab, went down with his ship, which, like Satan, would not sink to hell till she had dragged *a living part of heaven* along with her, and helmeted herself with it" (572, emphasis mine).

Tashtego does what Ahab would have done by himself had that been possible. In view of Manifest Destiny, in which religion and politics are conjoined, "*the* bird of heaven" (emphasis mine) can be the American national bird.[3] It is also the same kind of bird that took Ahab's hat ("The Hat"), which he had been wearing daily, as well as his flag away on the same day. Throughout the chase, actions simultaneously take place at such breathtaking speed that even Ahab's death appears anticlimactic. With a concentric force this tableau-like scene arrests the moment. Had this been on a hatchment at graveside or the church wall in the nineteenth century, its iconography with a hammer would suggest a quester, after someone desired had died (Reno 157).[4] The next paragraph, the very last one before the eiplogue, curiously omitted in the first English edition, either by mistake or on purpose, swoops away into the panoramic effect in time and space by sarcastically referring to Noah's ark that, unlike the damned *Pequod*, did not sink. Melville, however, paid tribute to the *Pequod* through this heraldic announcement of death.

With Tashtego's central role at the closure in mind, he becomes visible in other chapters as well. In "The Town-Ho's Story," the story-within-a-story told in threefold ways seems unnecessarily complicated. Also peculiar is that the white sailors on the *Town-Ho* chose Tashtego to tell the event in a gam, and that aloof Tashtego tells the story after revealing much of it in his sleep. The only possible way to account for his unusual excitement at this story would be that his pent-up anger as a subaltern bursts forth without inhibition in his sleep when his superego is weak, especially because the overbearing Radney is from his home island. Imagery clusters among Tashtego, rebellion, and hammer. Driven to "pull down and pulverize that subaltern's tower" (246) out of jealousy, the *Town-Ho*'s mate, Radney, begins to harass a common sailor, Steelkilt. When Radney grazes him with a hammer against warnings, Steelkilt smashes his oppressor's jaw. Melville made Ishmael the narrator of this story, which only iconographically prefigures Tashtego's later silent act as the *Pequod* sinks in order to avoid offending early readers by allowing an Amerindian to talk about his suppressed desire, an outright rebellion.

"Cistern and Buckets" discloses another opposition between "red" Tashtego and white supremacy. The professionally skilled Tashtego somehow falls headforemost into a whale's severed head. Had Queequeg not rescued him, he would have sunk to the ocean bottom. Though the chapter humorously concludes that this sort of possible death "in the very whitest and daintiest of fragrant spermaceti" (344) is the sweetest, once we overlap the Native plight trapped in the white man's intellect, his being nearly smothered in the whitest part of the head is potent. The controversial chapter, "The Whiteness of the Whale," can be read anew in this light. Imperialism is insinuated into the initial association with whiteness among the inflation of associations with the color white. Ishmael cites the remote Austrian Empire, a case seemingly irrelevant to the U.S. context, as "having for the imperial color the same imperial hue; and though this pre-eminence in it [i.e. whiteness] applies to the human race itself, giving the white man ideal mastery over every dusky tribe" (188-89). Amerindians had been defeated by the white man's technology, including both well-organized military strategies and the pervasive rhetoric championed by Andrew Jackson that fathers (the whites) can punish disobedient children (the Amerindians, "children of nature") (Rogin 115-24, 206-18). ·

Ishmael quickly chooses the *Pequod* with no specific reason. I suggest that the Pequots' tribal extinction is incorporated as *a* subtext in the ways the *Pequod* is destroyed—in a circle, in its eastward movement, in a gesture for fair play.[5]

No full-scale analysis of the Pequot War, which offers a thorough account of the Pequot response as well, appeared until recently (Cave 1-7). Thus, our argument in this paper is based on the information available to Melville. With rare foresight into white expansionism, the Pequot, one of the few tribes relatively less affected by smallpox, whose population was reduced only to one-fourth, tried to make allies with other tribes to push the Puritan settlers back into the sea. Neal Salisbury suggests that the spiritual crisis caused by the Antinomian controversy partly triggered the Pequot war to "redefine and adjust New England's proclaimed mission" (220). Had Roger Williams managed to hold the Narragansetts in check, the infant settler towns would in all probability have been wiped out of existence. Even a captain who attacked the village-fort admired the brevity and skill with which this tribe fought (Underhill 39). Its major village circle-fort on the Mystic River was surrounded by the British army and set afire in a pre-dawn surprise attack in 1637, while the vast majority of the villagers were asleep. Admitting this war has caused historical controversy, I regard it a massacre; two British out of eighty lost their lives while some four to eight hundred of the Pequots died within an hour. Losing a major tribal base and soon systematically hunted down, the formidable and, as Ishmael narrates, "celebrated" (69) tribe officially disappeared from historiography.[6] Although the Natives had never been desirable neighbors for the settlers, not until the Pequot War—when the settlers' demand for agricultural land into the Natives' areas became keener and the importance of trade disappeared as the beaver population neared extermination—did an all-out war set by the whites break out (Hauptman and Wherry 60-80; Steele 89-94).

The tribal fort and the ship are both destroyed in white circles, and that with unprecedented intent to massacre. Before this, as before the extinction policy by the whites, the White Whale has only taken one arm, leg, or life at a time from his enemies. The circle is used in the text twice as white whirlpools made by the whale; at their centers are Ahab on the first and his red flag on the last day of the chase. In "The Quadrant" Ahab crushes the ship's quadrant and maintains his persistent eastward voyage as the white corpusants, a rare phenomenon during a great storm, seem to force the ship back to the west in the next chapter: west is a direction fatal to the Amerindians. The massacre is further incorporated into Ahab's persistent demand for fair play as in "For could the sun do that, then could I do the other; since there is ever a sort of fair play herein" (164) in his quarter-deck speech or, stoically prohibiting the use of lightning rods in the middle of a great storm in a suicidal act in "The Candles," "let's have fair-play here, though we be the weaker side . . . out on privileges!" (505).

Further similarity exists between Ahab and Amerindians than some critics suggest,[7] as when Ahab's dedication of the voyage to his semi-personal vengeance collides with Starbuck's Puritan and capitalistic ethics of the Nantucket market economy.[8]

> "Starbuck; thou requirest a little lower layer . . . my vengeance will fetch a great premium *here!*"
>
> "He smites his chest," whispered Stubb. . .
>
> "Vengeance on a dumb brute!" cried Starbuck, "that simply smote thee from blindest instinct! Madness! . . ."
>
> "Hark ye yet again,—the little lower layer." (163-64)

Ahab is driven by his chest (the seat of emotion). As was seen in Tashtego trapped in the whitest part of a whale's head, the text manipulates the heart/head dichotomy. Ahab's way relates to the Natives' warpath, warring more for abstract ideas like honor and vengeance than for material gains. Nearing the sighted whale, the old captain of a rare old ship which started its voyage from an old harbor, acts more openly to this "little lower layer," bearing a stronger anachronistic air by dropping the lightning rods, quadrant, and industrial try-works.

Despite his strong ego—indeed the very thing on which the entire main plot seems drawn—Ahab is at the mercy of his anti-Christian signifiers, "Ahab of the *Pequod*"; The Old Testament Ahab was a wicked king and the Pequot was detested by the Puritans as devils. The fire-worshipping King Ahab provoked God more than any king before him and was described as savage. Once a good Christian, Captain Ahab turns into a fire-worshipper. He was hit by a white lightning and branded with a livid lash-like scar; then the White Whale deprived him of his leg and highly likely sexual potency. In "The Candles" as the white corpusants, whose color is redundantly repeated, Ahab bellows, "the white flame but lights the way to the White Whale!" (507). It is as if the storm pushes the ship to the west: as Starbuck says, "the gale comes from the eastward, the very course Ahab is to run for Moby Dick" (504). Although his hunt is similarly checked by thunder in "The Needles," the latter is placed *after* "The Candles" as if to confirm that Captain Ahab suffers the three visitations by whiteness in an unbroken succession. At rare moment of self-reflective derision on the second day of the chase, Ahab confesses that he has been controlled by Fate. Not his obsession, "God hunt us all, if we do not hunt Moby Dick to his death!" (166), nor his cry to the corpusants, "To neither love nor reverence wilt thou be kind; and even for hate thou canst but kill; and all are killed" (507), can translate that neither friendly approach ("love") nor race war ("hate") led to survival for the Natives who refused assimilation. Ahab continues, "Come in thy lowest form of love, and I will kneel and kiss thee; but at thy highest, come as mere supernal power; and though thou launchest navies of full-freighted worlds, there's that in thee that still remains indifferent" (507).

The passage below, written by a British major who attacked the Pequot fort, exemplifies how the Christian God's power is deployed to justify the massacre in history written by Puritan leaders and British military men: "And indeed such a dreadful Terror did the ALMIGHTY let fall upon their Spirit, that they would fly from us and run into the very Flames, where many of them perished. . . . But God was above them, who laughed his Enemies and the Enemies of his People to Scorn, making them as a fiery Oven" (Mason 8-9). Self-justification is nothing but the glaring sanctification of "history" that smoothes over the horrific agonies of the Natives in the exterminating fire.

Far from being filtered by the prevalent white desire of domesticating the Natives, it is as if Melville were to raise the ghost of the Pequot through Ahab of the *Pequod*, whose doubly anti-Christian signifiers as well as violent visitations by whiteness symbolically transformed him into a fit agent to enact the defensive-offense or wish-fulfilling counterattack that any tribe uneasy about the white expansion wished to make.

The Pequots' round fort about to be set afire, portrayed in Captain Underhill's well-known picture with the conspicuous shape of a circle, was with high probability seen by Melville in 1837 (Parker 109). Melville reencountered Pequot history during his composition of *Moby-Dick* at a literary meeting when there was a "cross examination on Hope Leslie and Magawisca" (Leyda I, 385) with Catherine Maria

Sedgwick about her best-selling novel, *Hope Leslie*. In spite of its rare account of the Pequot War by a Pequot survivor, Magawisca, a daughter of one of the sachems, and the description of her surviving father bent on revenge, *Hope Leslie*'s ideology as a whole endorses the Puritan ethics and the Natives' assimilation.

Of paramount importance is Melville's view on the Pequot in *Israel Potter* when the protagonist's emotions, which well up at his belated homecoming to the United States for whose independence he was to sacrifice his forty-five years without due reward, are compared to those of a fictitious "trespassing Pequod Indian" (164) on the former homeland now occupied by its rival Narragansett, who fought for the British in the Pequot War. Here, as in *Moby-Dick*, the Pequot seems to have figured prominently in the author's mind as an epitome of the race unfairly to be subjugated.

Nearing the completion of *Moby-Dick*, Melville wrote to Hawthorne mentioning the clear air through his open window in which Native Americans still seemed to be alive "in the boundless, trackless, but still glorious wild wilderness through which these outposts run, the Indians do sorely abound" (Leyda I, 415), and asks: "Shall I send you a fin of the Whale by way of a specimen mouthful? The tail is not yet cooked—tho' the hell-fire in which the whole book is broiled might not unreasonably have cooked it all ere this. This is the book's motto (The secret one),—*Ego non baptizo te in nomine*—but make out the rest yourself" (415). The "secret motto" is reminiscent of Melville's previous letter to Hawthorne, "What I feel most moved to write, that is banned,—it will not pay. Yet, altogether, write the *other* way I cannot" (412). The "secret motto" points to the text's key passage in Latin of Ahab's diabolical tempering of his newly forged harpoon for "the white fiend" (489) with the harpooneers' blood, as we have seen, addressing Tashtego first. It may well be that in teasing Hawthorne to "make out the rest," Melville provoked him to see not only blasphemy, which is after all overt, but the Native American presence in "a little lower layer" of his "wicked book." Moving to the Berkshires during the composition of *Moby-Dick*, he named the place Arrowhead after relics of the Natives found on the site. Besides a tabooed understanding of the Natives' desire and fantasy, a free-spirited layer of the text cherishes an impossible dream of racial intermarriage as an alternative. As Carolyn Karcher noted, its underlying racial theme is metaphorical intermarriage, presented in the Ishmael-Queequeg and Ahab-Pip bonds (70-72, 87, 89).

Young Melville encountered various races as a common sailor through whaling voyages which in those days were full of non-Caucasians. (On board, nonwhites could not be abstract racial Others but co-workers with their individualities.) Made aware of the commodity side of his work-in-progress, especially through his book review on *The Oregon Trail*, he navigated a difficult line and slipped racial themes into *Moby-Dick*, striving to be true to his inner conviction based on his experiences.

NOTES

1   Much has been made of Queequeg and the black characters. By suggesting another perspective, my essay counterbalances the criticism on the blacks in *Moby-Dick*, initiated by Carolyn L. Karcher's landmark study centered on slavery. As for the Native American in *Moby-Dick*, John Staud paid attention to the name *Pequod* in his typological reading identifying the ship "as a Babylonian tribe singled out for punishment" (342-43). Louise K. Barnett (180) and Elizabeth Lyons Ballard (138-72) also regarded Tashtego as a merely typical guide of white Ahab. Toni Morrison acknowledged D. H. Lawrence as a predecessor who had sensed what she terms a "white ideology" in *Moby-Dick*. For Lawrence, hunting down the whale, which embodies "the white mental consciousness" (160), serves the white men's expurgation.

2   A white sailor jeers at the Ishmael-Queequeg bond in "Wheelbarrow," sleepy Pip is made to play the tambourine, and Daggoo counterattacks a Spanish sailor in "Midnight, Forecastle." Hearing this revelry in his officers' cabin, Starbuck hastily blames the "pagan" crew without checking that a vast majority of the noise-makers are whites. Stubb reminds Pip of his sad existence as a commodity salable at a slave market. Tashtego is reticent toward the whites. Compare his aloofness in "Midnight, Forecastle," where he says to himself regarding the revelry, "That's a white man; he calls that fun: humph! I save my sweat" (175), with the lively Tashtego while he is with Queequeg in "The Cabin Table" or alone in "Midnight, Aloft."

3   Other critics also interpreted this bird as the national bird of the United States (Foster 33; Heimert 504, 507-8; Karcher 89).

4   Footnoted in Janet Reno's book were, John Morley, *Death, Heaven and the Victorians*. Pittsburgh: U of Pittsburgh P, 1971, figs. 41 and 42; and W. Cecil Wade, *The Symbolisms of Heraldry*. London: George Redway, 1898, 75, 98-99.

5   Unlike the *Pequod*, the *Essex*, to which Ishmael refers (206-7), presumably a model for the *Pequod*, was *stove*, not sucked into a whirlpool of an enraged whale's making, and that during its *westward* circumnavigation.

6   Timothy Dwight also praised the Pequots' statesmanship and bravery in his *Travels in New-England and New-York*. Roving solitary Pequots were characters in several works of Melville's time.

James Fenimore Cooper's *The Wept of Wish-ton-Wish* and Sedgwick's *Hope Leslie* had the same spelling of the tribe as Melville's.

7   Among other associations, Richard Chase suggested Ahab as a shaman-like primitive magician (43). Wai-chee Dimock related Ahab to the Amerindian in terms of their adamant will, which virtually undid them (136).

8   My reading of this passage is opposite to Donald Pease's; he regarded Ahab as "idealiz[ing] his profit motive into a version of manifest destiny on the quarter-deck" (242).

REFERENCES

Ballard, Elizabeth Lyons. "Red-Tinted Landscape: The Poetics of Indian Removal in Major American Texts of the Nineteenth Century." Ph.D. diss., U of Oklahoma, 1989.

Barnett, Louise K. *The Ignoble Savage: American Literary Racism, 1790-1890*. Westport, CT: Greenwood P, 1975.

Cave, Alfred A. *The Pequot War*. Amherst: U of Massachusetts P, 1996.

Chase, Richard. *Herman Melville: A Critical Study*. New York: Macmillan, 1949.

Dimock, Wai-chee. *Empire for Liberty: Melville and the Poetics of Individualism*. Princeton, NJ: Princeton UP, 1989.

Foster, Charles H. "Something in Emblems: A Reinterpretation of *Moby-Dick*," *New England Quarterly*, 34 (March, 1961): 3-35.

Hauptman, Laurence, and Wherry, James D. eds. *The Pequots in Southern New England: The Fall and Rise of an American Indian Nation*. Norman and London: U of Oklahoma P, 1990.

Heimert, Alan. "*Moby-Dick* and American Political Symbolism," *American Quarterly*, 15 (Winter, 1963): 498-534.

Karcher, Carolyn L. *Shadow over the Promised Land: Slavery, Race, and Violence in Melville's America*. Baton Rouge: Louisiana State UP, 1980.

Lawrence, D. H. *Studies in Classic American Literature*. New York: Penguin, 1986.

Leyda, Jay. *The Melville Log: A Documentary Life of Herman Melville 1819-1891*. 2 vols. New York: Gordian P, 1969.

Mason, John. *A Brief History of the Pequot War*. New York: Readex Microprint Co., 1966.

Melville, Herman. *Israel Potter*. Vol. 8 of *The Writings of Herman Melville*. Evanston and Chicago: Northwestern UP and the Newberry Library, 1982.

——. *Moby Dick*. Vol. 6 of *The Writings*, 1988.

——. "Mr. Parkman's Tour." *The Literary World*, 4 (March 31, 1849): 291-93.

Morrison, Toni. "Unspeakable Things Unspoken: The Afro-American Presence in American Literature." *Michigan Quarterly Review*, 28 (Winter 1989): 1-34.

Parker, Hershel. *Herman Melville: A Biography*, Vol. I, *1819-1851*. Baltimore: Johns Hopkins UP, 1996.

Pease, Donald. *Visionary Compacts: American Renaissance Writings in Cultural Context*. Madison: U of Wisconsin P, 1987.

Reno, Janet. *Ishmael Alone Survived*. London: Associated UP, 1990.

Rogin, Michael Paul. *Fathers and Children: Andrew Jackson and the Subjugation of the American Indian*. New York: Alfred A. Knopf, 1975.

Salisbury, Neal. *Manitou and Providence: Indians, Europeans, and the Making of New England, 1500-1643*. New York: Oxford UP, 1982.

Staud, John. "'What's in a Name?': The *Pequod* and Melville's Heretical Politics," *ESQ*, 38 (4th qtr. 1992): 338-59.

Steele, Ian K. *Warpaths: Invasions of North America*. New York: Oxford UP, 1994.

Underhill, John. *News From America*. Amsterdam & New York: DaCapo P, 1971.

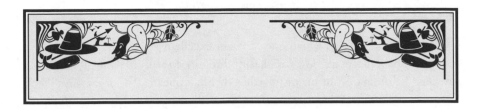

SANFORD E. MAROVITZ

SHAKESPEAREAN RESONANCE IN *MOBY-DICK* AND *PIERRE*

hen Melville first immersed himself in Shakespeare, his mind was acutely receptive and absorptive, and he responded to the Elizabethan as both a thinker and a writer. F. O. Matthiessen said that "Melville meditated more creatively on Shakespeare's meaning than any other American"; his meditation led to a catalytic experience that "released his work from limited reporting to the expression of profound natural forces" and thus transformed him from a popular travel-and-adventure writer of the day into the timeless, universal author he had yearned to become (Matthiessen, 424, 428). The magic of Shakespeare's genius in correlation with Melville's own energized *Moby-Dick* within a few months of its conception (Olson, 65-68). By the time it was published, Melville was planning, if not already drafting, *Pierre*. One of the strongest links between these two romances is the meditation theme in *Hamlet*. But in addition to retaining *Hamlet* as a principal source, Melville turned from *Macbeth* and *King Lear* to *Romeo and Juliet* and *Measure for Measure* as the other Shakespearean plays from which he drew most heavily when he shifted from a ship at sea to a social sphere on land and from a metaphysical quest to a moral enigma presented with a strong ironic twist.

In *Moby-Dick*, Shakespeare's voices are manifold. They operate on various levels, sound in different modes. One voice, the dramatist's own, appears indirectly as a compositional key to parts of Melville's romance. The other voices, those of his characters, represent emotional and moral conflicts that echo through Ishmael's narrative as he describes and ponders.

A recent book from which one can gain excellent insight into the resonant voice of Shakespeare in *Moby-Dick* has nothing to do with Melville. It is a study by David Young of four major tragedies by Shakespeare, *The Action to the Word: Structure and Style in Shakespearean Tragedy* (1990). Young emphasizes "the profound and productive tension [in the plays] between action and expressive language," that is, between structure and style, in Shakespeare's tragedies (Young, 106). He does not believe that the dramatist consciously introduced this tension into the plays but found it inherent in the situation he had created for each one.

To be sure, the situations differ vastly from play to play, and Shakespeare's strategy in employing the tension between style and structure differs accordingly. Having perceived Shakespeare's designs in the tragedies, Melville adapted them in *Moby-Dick*. Although language and action would not seem directly comparable because they are of different modes, Shakespeare's application of them appears contrastive, and the same is true of Melville's.

For instance, according to Young's analysis, *Hamlet* is a play at once "thrifty in . . . structure" but "lavish in language" with many soliloquies and extended dialogues that include much punning and other forms of word-play, and these occur mostly while the action is stopped (Young, 7, 9). Similarly, action occurs only intermittently in *Moby-Dick*, mostly in the three-day chase as Ishmael moves through the climax of his narrative. As in *Hamlet*, much of Melville's novel is speculative and philosophical, in conformity with a narrator who acknowledges at the outset that "meditation and water are wedded for ever" (*M-D*, 4).

Also in *Hamlet*, Shakespeare employs a device that Young calls "dramatic reflexivity," in which characters comment on the nature and techniques of the medium to illumine underlying themes and motives (Young, 31, 35). The most obvious example of this method occurs in Hamlet's acting instructions to the troupe of players who have come to perform at Elsinore. On many occasions Ishmael makes equally clear that in poeticizing the whaling trade he is also telling a story about writing a book. In "Cetology" he categorizes the whales by size, using books as his basis for classification. "This whole book is but a draught,— nay, but the draught of a draught," he says at the end of that remarkable chapter (*M-D*, 145).

Having read and heavily marked his Hilliard and Gray edition of Shakespeare, Melville knew the plays well, and of them all, as Charles Olson noted, "It was *Lear* that had the deepest creative impact" (Olson, 47; Markels, 64). In *Lear*, the expansive setting and scope take in all of England as well as a gamut of social classes from King to bastard to servant to Fool. Yet much of the dialogue, in contrast, is of "an intimate and inward style" in which "private thought" is exposed obliquely through such devices as songs and riddles while the language still seems natural. Shakespeare does this, Young says, by "stretching the limits of consistent and coherent characterization," though at the risk of sacrificing plausibility of character and action (Young, 87).

Melville portrayed Ahab similarly, as an heroic and tragic figure on the order of Lear, and the vast ocean setting is even more expansive than that of Shakespeare's play. Surely Ahab, Queequeg, and others aboard the *Pequod* are also stretched to "the limits of consistent and coherent characterization"; indeed, they, like Lear, are giants, however mortal, and it is largely through their singularly exaggerated features that they command attention and engage the reader. Nor are they always consistent, for even the crazed Ahab "has his humanities" (*M-D*, 79). Also, as in *King Lear* so in *Moby-Dick*, the *Pequod*'s crew descends from the colossal Captain to its "most insignificant member" (*M-D*, 411), as Ishmael identifies the ultimately deranged black "ship-keeper," Pip.

In addition, Young notes that *King Lear* exhibits various types of madness: "the Fool's professional version, Edgar's feigned version, and Lear's helplessly authentic version" (Young, 92). *Moby-Dick* does the same in presenting Ahab the monomaniac; Gabriel, the delirious fanatic aboard the *Jeroboam*; and again poor Pip, who lost his mind in the vast solitude of the ocean, where he saw "God's foot upon the treadle of the loom, and spoke it" (*M-D*, 414). Related to their madness, of course, is the most crucial likeness between Lear and Ahab: their stripping away of all the accouterments of social existence in attempting to apprehend Truth at the core of life. In Thoreau's words, they thrust away the trappings "to front only the essential facts of life . . . and reduce it to its lowest terms" (*Walden*, 143), but fanaticism and madness drive Lear and Ahab into an alien, existential state, whereas Thoreau's approach was through the discipline that he knew would lead him to a higher consciousness.

Finally of the three tragedies mentioned here, the influence of *Macbeth* on

Moby-Dick is most immediately apparent through Melville's use of the supernatural, particularly the ghostly Fedallah and his three fatally misinterpreted prophecies. The dramatic power in *Macbeth*, however, comes less through supernatural devices than from the tension that exists between such "primitive structural sources" as the prophecies, and the "sophisticated poetry" that seems so incongruous with them. Yet these contraries are ultimately united by magic, Young observes, thus making the play uncharacteristically "opaque and mysterious" (Young, 101). Similarly in *Moby-Dick* the spirit-spout, prophecies, and corposants reflect the magic in *Macbeth* as the lyricism of such chapters as "The Mast-Head," "The Grand Armada," and "The Symphony" conforms with the tragedy's "sophisticated poetry."

As for Macbeth himself, his consciousness is extraordinarily subtle; he is intensely alert, aware of all that occurs both inside his own mind and around him; preoccupied by his thoughts and imagination, he is compelled to act by their direction. But Macbeth's compulsion impresses the audience less than his "acute awareness of it," says Young, who might as well be describing Ahab's thoughts and behavior. "Even as he turns himself into a dry husk, an empty parody of a feeling human being . . . Macbeth continues to monitor his own descent, the success, as it were, of his failure" (Young, 113). So Ahab, as he drives madly toward his "topmost greatness [that] lies in [his] topmost grief" (*M-D*, 571), death in the wake of the white whale. Macbeth's mind, like that of Hamlet and many of Shakespeare's other major figures, is exhibited in astonishing detail. Of course, the same is true of Ahab and Ishmael.

Soon after his return from the Pacific late in 1844, Melville began to socialize with a number of influential actors, dramatists, critics, journalists, and other figures identified with the stage, whom he met through his friendship with Evert Duyckinck. Genial talk with Duyckinck along with such acquaintances as James Henry Hackett, best known in the role of Falstaff (Eddy, 35), and perhaps the Reverend Henry Norman Hudson, popular Shakespearean lecturer and idolater among Duyckinck's associates, probably helped Melville read and watch the plays from a more sophisticated and intense vantage point than might otherwise have been likely in a relatively short time. His concentrated reading of the plays and the way that Hawthorne's fiction apparently motivated him to ponder creatively over the evil and mystery in their depths—the "magic in the web" of them, to adapt an image from *Othello*—profoundly affected his own writing.

Of Shakespeare's grand themes, the most important for Melville emerged from the blackness he perceived in the plays, especially but not only the tragedies. It sets the tone for *Moby-Dick*, which is "shrouded" in blackness throughout. Suggestive of evil, sin, and mystery, including that of *being* itself, blackness hovers like the dark cloud over a stricken craft in the Spouter Inn painting. But no less important than its ominous foreboding is—as in Shakespeare's tragedies— its function as a backdrop to heighten the value of those "occasional flashings- forth of the intuitive Truth" that Melville had described in his review of Haw- thorne's *Mosses*. For "there is no quality in this world that is not what it is mere- ly by contrast. Nothing exists in itself," Ishmael says and illustrates it time and again (*M-D*, 53).

Comparing the relation of word to action in *Moby-Dick* with David Young's analysis of Shakespeare's ironic contrasts in the tragedies exposes the truth of Ishmael's observation on a broader scale. Most critics writing about the influ- ence of Shakespeare on *Moby-Dick* have begun with Melville's novel, then turned to the plays for parallels in form, theme, character, or language. By commenc- ing with Young's reading of four major Shakespearean tragedies, however, and considering *Moby-Dick* with reference to his perception of the tension in them between language and action, style and structure, I have attempted to examine the plays from a perspective closer to Melville's own in 1849 and 1850, shortly after he acquired his Hilliard and Gray edition.

According to George Adler, the novelist's traveling companion for a good part of his journey to England and the Continent late in 1849, Melville was eager to return home and work up "some beautiful chimaeras" (quoted in Metcalf, 139). Back in New York early the next year, he began drafting *Moby-Dick*, "a strange sort of work,...[in which] the poetry runs as hard as sap from a frozen maple tree," he wrote to Richard Henry Dana on May 1, adding that although it includes "a little fancy, I intend to give the truth of the thing, spite of this" (*Corresp*., 162). Near the end of June, the substance of his chimaeras became a lit- tle clearer when he wrote to his English publisher, Richard Bentley, "The Book is to be a romance of adventure, founded upon certain wild legends in the

Southern Sperm Whale Fisheries, and illustrated by the author's own personal experience" (*Corresp.*, 163). A poetic romance of adventure, then, based on legends and the truth of personal experience, *Moby-Dick* often exhibits dramatic tension with Shakespearean power, a tension similarly produced by a purposeful dissonance between language and action, style and structure. More than a matter of specific parallels, these integrated stylistic and structural correspondences between the tragedies and *Moby-Dick* add a new dimension to the influence of Shakespeare on Melville's grandest novel.

Ishmael's words on *contrast* are as applicable to *Pierre* as to his own narrative. Subtitled *The Ambiguities*, *Pierre* exposes an ever-darkening world of moral uncertainty and ambivalence. Driven by the dual aim of saving his dead father's reputation and protecting the young woman he accepts as his illegitimate sister, Pierre loses his patrimony as Lear does his kingdom, but the King is morally reborn before his death, whereas Pierre goes over the edge and dies a suicide in prison.

Although the narrator suggests that Pierre may seem "fond and foolish" (*P*, 13), as Lear sees himself "a very foolish and fond old man" (IV vii 60), Melville's seventh novel is closer akin to *Hamlet*, *Romeo and Juliet*, and particularly *Measure for Measure* than to *King Lear*. In fact, the novel is framed with reference to *Romeo and Juliet*. Soon after it opens, Pierre's mother addresses him as Romeo; in the dialogue she initiates, she reminds him that Shakespeare's Romeo meets a tragic end because he disobeys his parents and marries a Capulet against their wishes. Hence she foreshadows the pit into which Pierre likewise falls, thus bringing ruin and death upon his family and himself. The parallel with Shakespeare's early tragedy is sustained at the end, where the Capulet tomb becomes Pierre's dungeon, and a double suicide brings death to him and Isabel as it does to Romeo and Juliet.

The light/dark contrast so pronounced in *Romeo and Juliet* also appears in *Pierre*, though in the novel as Pierre more surely falls under Isabel's compelling influence, the darkness increases commensurately. Whereas the novel opens amid the summer brightness of his patrilineal estate at Saddle Meadows, shadowy visions of Isabel soon begin to cloud both Pierre's currently happy situation and thoughts of his future. Attempting to learn the truth of Isabel's claim to be his sister, he commits himself to a moral stand that calls for action once his questions are answered. As his speculations become more convincing, he no longer identifies with Romeo but with Hamlet. "His mind was wandering and vague;... he found the open Hamlet in his hand, and his eyes met the following lines: "'The time is out of joint,—Oh cursed spite, / That ever I was born to set it right!' [¶] He dropped the too true volume from his hand" (*P*, 168).

Still suffering over the early loss of his father, now exacerbated by the likelihood of paternal infidelity and deceit, Pierre readily identifies with Hamlet, whose father, too, dies before his time and whose mother seems faithless. As several scholars (Murray, Tolchin, Lehrman) have perceived, Melville himself may be closely identified with both Pierre and Hamlet through the theme of "guilt-ridden father-child relationships" (Lehrman, *DAI*, 6/87, 47:12).

From these few remarks, the thematic importance of *Romeo and Juliet* and *Hamlet* to *Pierre* should be clear, however undeveloped here, but the significance of *Measure for Measure* as a major source for that novel also warrants attention. Charles Olson implicitly dismissed it as inconsequential to Melville when he said: "Fortunately for *Moby Dick* the big truth was not sermons-on-the-mount. Melville found these in *Measure for Measure*" (Olson, 43). In fact, he found a great deal more than that in the play, one of Shakespeare's darkest comedies and one "closely bound to *Hamlet*" (Goddard, 1:50). Abusive power, hypocrisy, deception, betrayal, illicit sex, and dubious justice are themes developed ambiguously in *Measure for Measure* as in *Pierre*. Despite its ostensibly favorable resolution, *Measure for Measure* is justly considered a "problem play" laden with questionable values and unappealing characters, including Isabella, the vacillating heroine.

Coleridge called this play Shakespeare's "only painful" work, in which the "comic and tragic parts equally border" on lust and lewdness. For Henry Norman Hudson, whom Melville may have met (Rosen, 183) or at least heard in the lecture hall, it is among Shakespeare's "least attractive" works, too inherently sinful to dwell on; he said that although "the tone of sentiment and character is pure and lofty ... [the] events themselves are repulsive" (Hudson, 1:188). Hudson's lectures on Shakespeare, like much nineteenth-century commentary on the plays, emphasize theme and character assessment, an approach that Melville also took, though he read them holistically as well for their poetic, structural, and even theatrical qualities.

His thorough reading of *Measure for Measure* is evident from his abundant markings in his copy of the play, which, though undated, nevertheless document his empathic engagement with the work. Those marks call attention to thoughts on power, duality, deception, madness, and death—thoughts that become major themes in *Pierre*. Although these ideas appear also in much of Melville's other writing, *deception* is the principal term here because it is not central in his work prior to *Pierre*, though it is a basic motif from then on. Indeed, deception with all its variations is at the heart of that novel's ambiguities. So it is, also, in *Measure for Measure*, of which Walter Pater said: "the very intricacy and subtlety of the moral world itself, the difficulty of seizing the true relations of so complex a material, the difficulty of just judgement,... are the lessons conveyed" (in Rossiter, 169).

A. P. Rossiter observed that *Measure for Measure* is "full of equivocal speeches, of a kind there is no resolving the ambiguities.... Something like doubleness of vision or aim is present in words, situations,... and characters" (Rossiter, 163-64). Whereas *Hamlet* exposes "the psychological proximity of heaven and hell," Harold C. Goddard wrote, *Measure for Measure* "is saturated with antitheses"; it reveals that "everything breeds within itself the seed of its contrary," including passion. "Good and evil get inextricably mixed" throughout the play (Goddard 1:64-65). Similarly in *Pierre*, duality and deception—as Pierre sees them in his father, his mother, Isabel (whose name may be derived from Shakespeare's Isabella), the Rev. Falsgrave, Plotinus Plinlimmon, the harassing publishers, Glen Stanly, and others—increasingly disorder his mind, which in turn destroys the family and ends the Glendinning line.

Melville may also have been influenced in his narrative method by the character of the Duke, that is, by the Duke as a dramatis persona rather than as an actual person in a stage community. Hudson assessed the Duke as "mysterious," good but devious, more a politician than a statesman (Hudson 1:209). A century later, Goddard called the Duke "a curious character,... fond of experimenting on human beings and inquiring into their inner workings." His motive for leaving Vienna and returning as an observer seemed to Goddard "less political and social than psychological.... The Duke is as introspective as Hamlet" (Goddard, 1:52).

In *Pierre*, Melville transforms the Duke, no less "curious" and "mysterious," into the narrator, his first use of this omniscient third-person point of view. The narrator focuses on Pierre but treats him sardonically, hinting snidely at what will come of the youth's naivete and idealism, observing his disillusion as it increases from doubt to possibility, probability, and finally, certainty. He much resembles the Duke; both know what will come—the downfall of the protagonist—and they conspiratorially make the reader/audience privy to it.

In short, relating *Moby-Dick* and *Pierre* to their respective sources among Shakespeare's plays helps illuminate Melville's compositional method as well as thematic and structural matters in the fiction. Furthermore, critical insights into the plays indirectly provide not only greater understanding of the two novels but also an additional perspective from which to read them. Finally, although Shakespeare's major tragedies have long been recognized as a principal influence on *Moby-Dick* and *Pierre*, Melville's empathic engagement with *Measure for Measure* and its effect on the latter novel also warrant close critical attention.

By indirections, then, we, too, may find directions out.

REFERENCES

Coleridge, Samuel Taylor. *Coleridge's Shakespearean Criticism*. Ed. Thomas Middleton Raysor. 2 vols. London: Constable, 1930.

Eddy, Darlene Mathis. "Bloody Battles and High Tragedies: Melville and the Theatre of the 1840's," *Ball State University Forum*, 13 (Winter 1972), 34-45.

Goddard, Harold C. *The Meaning of Shakespeare*. 2 vols. 1951; Chicago: U of Chicago P, 1960.

Hudson, Henry Norman. *Lectures on Shakspeare*. 2 vols. New York: Baker and Scribner, 1848.

Lehrman, Adele Temin. "The Influence of Hawthorne and Shakespeare on Melville: Father Figures and Failure in *Moby-Dick* and *Pierre*." Ph.D. diss., George Washington U, 1987.

Markels, Julian. *Melville and the Politics of Identity: From* King Lear *to* Moby-Dick. Urbana: U of Illinois P, 1993.

Matthiessen, F. O. *American Renaissance: Art and Expression in the Age of Emerson and Whitman*. London and New York: Oxford UP, 1941.

Melville, Herman. *Correspondence*, ed. Lynn Horth. Vol. 14 of *The Writings of Her-*

man Melville. Evanston and Chicago: Northwestern UP and the Newberry Library, 1993.

——. *Moby-Dick; or, The Whale*, ed. Harrison Hayford, Hershel Parker, and G. Thomas Tanselle. Vol. 6 of *The Writings of Herman Melville*, 1988.

——. *Pierre; or, The Ambiguities*, ed. Harrison Hayford, Hershel Parker, and G. Thomas Tanselle. Vol. 7 of *The Writings of Herman Melville*, 1971.

Metcalf, Eleanor Melville, ed. *Journal of a Visit to London and the Continent by Herman Melville 1849-1850*. Cambridge, MA: Harvard University Press, 1948.

Murray, Henry A., ed. "Introduction," *Pierre; or, The Ambiguities*, by Herman Melville. New York: Hendricks House, 1949. Pp. xiii-ciii.

Olson, Charles. *Call Me Ishmael*. San Francisco: City Lights Books, 1947.

Rosen, Roma. "Melville's Use of Shakespeare's Plays." Ph.D. diss., Northwestern U, 1962.

Rossiter, A. P. *Angel with Horns: Fifteen Lectures on Shakespeare*. New York: Theatre Arts Books, 1961.

Shakespeare, William. *The Complete Works*, ed. G. B. Harrison. New York: Harcourt, Brace and Co., 1952.

Thoreau, Henry David. *Walden*. Vol. 2 of *The Writings of Henry David Thoreau*. Riverside Ed. Boston: Houghton Mifflin, 1883.

Tolchin, Neal L. *Mourning, Gender, and Creativity in the Art of Herman Melville*. New Haven, CT: Yale UP, 1988.

Young, David. *The Action to the Word: Structure and Style in Shakespearean Tragedy*. New Haven, CT: Yale UP, 1990.

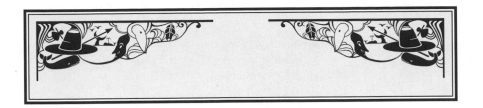

STANTON GARNER

AGING WITH THE ANTONINES

n the 1876 United States presidential election, Republican Rutherford B. Hayes ran against Democrat Samuel J. Tilden, a widely respected New York leader. Tilden led in the election, but in that unsettled time each of four states had submitted two competing panels of electors, one for Tilden and one for Hayes. Hayes could become president only by winning the electoral votes of all four states; otherwise, Tilden would win. An electoral commission, with a majority from the Republican party, was appointed to adjudicate the anomaly, and on March 2, 1877, it awarded all four states to Hayes, who took the oath of office on March 4. Three days later, amid the ensuing uproar, Herman Melville wrote a stoic message to a cousin: "what's the use? life is short, and Hayes' term is four years, each of 365 days."[1]

At the end of the same month, he sent a brother-in-law another commentary on the election, the poem "The Age of the Antonines," which, as it was published many years later, read,

> While faith forecasts millennial years
> Spite Europe's embattled lines,
> Back to the Past one glance be cast—
> The Age of the Antonines!
> O summit of fate, O zenith of time
> When a pagan gentleman reigned,

And the olive was nailed to the inn of the world
Nor the peace of the just was feigned.
A halcyon Age, afar it shines,
Solstice of Man and the Antonines.

Hymns to the nations' friendly gods
Went up from the fellowly shrines,
No demagogue beat the pulpit-drum
In the Age of the Antonines!
The sting was not dreamed to be taken from death,
No Paradise pledged or sought,
But they reasoned of fate at the flowing feast,
Nor stifled the fluent thought.
We sham, we shuffle while faith declines—
They were frank in the Age of the Antonines.

Orders and ranks they kept degree,
Few felt how the parvenu pines,
No law-maker took the lawless one's fee
In the Age of the Antonines!
Under law made will the world reposed
And the ruler's right confessed,
For the heavens elected the Emperor then,
The foremost of men the best.
Ah, might we read in America's signs
The Age restored of the Antonines.[2]

In the accompanying letter, he stated that the poem had been inspired by Edward Gibbon's *Decline and Fall of the Roman Empire* and added, in typically Melvillean fashion, "What the deuce the thing means I dont know." But that was the infirmity of jocularity to which he often treated his relatives; of course he knew what it meant, or else he would not have made a point of circulating it at all and of circulating it just after the stolen election. It is an important poem in that it is one of the few works in which, arguably, Melville presented his own ideas unmasked by literary devices. I say that the speaking voice is his, rather than that of

278

a created narrator with a different point of view, because the poem does not establish the criteria for a dramatic monologue. The clarity with which it can be read is a product of its contrapuntal design. It contrasts Melville's America unfavorably with the Roman era of the Antonine emperors, generally the second century of the Gregorian calendar, about which Gibbon wrote, "If a man were called to fix the period in the history of the world, during which the condition of the human race was most happy and prosperous, he would, without hesitation, name that which elapsed from the death of Domition to the accession of Commodus."[3] Since that era was represented as being uniquely felicitous, it provided Melville with a standard of comparison by which to criticize his own age.

The first stanza concerns war and peace. Although Melville overstates the peacefulness of the reigns of the Antonines, they did halt the military expansion of the Roman Empire, fighting battles and campaigns mainly to defend its borders. Thus, although their age was not wholly "halcyon," these "pagans" deserved credit for nailing the olive to the inn of the world as much as seemed to them possible. In contrast, Melville saw about him a population of optimistic meliorists who boasted that they were bringing about the biblical millennium in which the ideal state of civilization would be achieved, while at the same time Christian Europe was engaged in military maneuvers and conflicts arising from the rapaciousness of predatory emperors and nations.

Conventional though that complaint may have been, in the second stanza Melville gives us a remarkable insight into his religious views. Referring to the polytheism of the Romans, in which there was no single omnipotent deity to whose whims mortals were subject, and no expectation of salvation after death, the Romans were freed of anxiety about their eternal lives. Not only that, but, as Gibbon put it, religion was "not embittered by any mixture of theological rancour; nor was it confined by the chains of any speculative system."[4] Since in their religion the invisible deities were linked firmly to empirical reality, the relationship between gods and men was natural, personal, and comprehensible because self-evident. Melville admired their conception of death as a curtain beyond which they could not see but about which they could reason, in gala hours as well as sober. If they were to receive a pleasant surprise after death, as Clarel hints at the end of his Holy Land travels, so much the better. In Melville's words, the ancient Romans were "frank," rather than being shufflers.

In contrast, for the modern Christian, religion was not rooted in the things, conditions, and events of everyday life, but rather in abstract entities connected to mortals only through the agency of other abstractions. Thus the importance and the influence of the cleric in the pulpit, the "demagogue" who beat the "pulpit-drum" of exhortation, imprecation, and intimidation. His offices were essential to his congregation, who sought an eternal life in a heaven of which most could not conceive in terms other than self-gratification, ease, and luxury, perhaps as a well-lighted celestial shopping district. The result of this surrealistic "sham" was that true faith, the faith of stoic comprehension and acceptance, ebbed farther and farther away from his America.

In Melville's idiosyncratic vocabulary, the word "pagan" often implies a harmonious and comprehensible relationship between "heaven" and man, one deeply rooted in nature, as opposed to a theoretical religion in which a remote and often hostile and demanding Jehovah threatens men with eternal suffering. The gods of the Antonines were "friendly" and their shrines "fellowly," free of anger and terror.

In many ways, this is consistent with the religious ideas that emerge from *Battle-Pieces*, not in its polytheism, but in the idea that whatever god there may be is indifferent to human strife and unconcerned with redeeming souls. Rather, he is a supreme engineer of a fate which, regardless of the actions of men, directs the overall course of the universe. In this conception we may have an explanation of Melville's lifelong religious wanderings and of his constant disappointment in the preachers whose sermons never slaked his thirst for honest and liberating guidance.

Melville reserved his political, and therefore social, complaints for the third stanza, which sets the stage for his later fiction. It centers on the Antonines themselves, the half-dozen emperors whose reigns represented the "summit of fate," the "zenith of time," and the "Solstice of man." Taken altogether, their achievements would be impressive in any era. They improved the condition of their people by healing civil divisiveness—reintegrating exiles into society and discouraging informers—caring for the poor and orphans and encouraging charity as a public virtue, improving the lot of slaves, combating a decline in agriculture and population, and giving aid to needy cities and provinces. They repaired roads and aqueducts, and they sponsored great architecture and encouraged the arts and sciences and studied them—Marcus Aurelius both lectured in philosophy and wrote about it. They improved government by repeatedly reforming its laws to make them more humane and by making public administration lean and efficient and, above all, honest—that impressed Melville, who had been employed for over a decade in a government office where corruption was the unchanging password of the day. "No law-maker took the lawless one's fee," he wrote, reproachfully. In short, Gibbon claimed (confining himself to Antoninus Pius and Marcus Aurelius), "Their united reigns are possibly the only period of history in which the happiness of a great people was the sole object of government."[5]

In Melville's poetic celebration of the idea that "the heavens elected the Emperor then" and that the "foremost of men" were "the best" lies the principal key to the poem's meaning. As Gibbon put it, the "characters and authority" of the Antonines "commanded involuntary respect":[6] they were, in short, cynosures, natural leaders. It is significant that they became emperors not because of imperial birth but because of innate superiority. Beginning with Nerva, each emperor selected and adopted as his heir an able and qualified successor, even when he had children of his own, and there were no mistakes. That practice continued until Marcus Aurelius unaccountably allowed himself to be succeeded by his own son, Commodus, whose inferiority brought their noble period to an end. Thus Rome was ruled by what Melville later came to call "Handsome Sailors," those naturally virtuous, able persons who were peculiarly qualified for leadership.

This allows us to understand Melville's praise of the Antonine citizens for being content with their places in the order of things rather than being, as in nineteenth-century America, "parvenus" yearning to shoulder aside those above them in order to rise in status and influence. It was not that Melville objected to the class porousness that was the mother of the "American dream," but, rather, that he believed that a man should aspire to a status no more elevated than the order and rank for which nature, rather than influence and affluence, had fitted him. In other words, he saw Antonine Rome as a society in which the stations of men were dictated by nature, or "the heavens," which were essentially synonymous.

Melville had been developing the idea of the "Handsome Sailor" almost from the beginning of his career. There is an incomplete version of him in *Typee*, in the figure of Marnoo, but the concept is first embodied whole in the figure of Jack Chase in *White-Jacket*. Jack is not only a cynosure but also a literate one, a reader of Camões and Montaigne. He is first among the topmen, but he is also the first to step forward to defend the sailors under him. In this, he is the enlisted men's version of an Antonine emperor. And in *Moby-Dick*, the sailor Bulkington is a well enough developed example of a Handsome Sailor to be transplanted to *Billy Budd*, as, indeed, he may have been.

In comparison, the tainted election of Hayes was not ordained in heaven, but that was not Melville's only quarrel with the selection of American presidents. During his lifetime, he saw presidents and lesser office-holders whose characters and abilities fell far short of the level of excellence that an elective democracy should have been able to summon. This was particularly true in the post-Civil War era, in which, as Nathaniel Hawthorne had shrewdly predicted, "One bullet-headed general will succeed another in the Presidential chair."[7] Indeed, a procession of former warriors followed each other into office, each demonstrating that battlefield service alone did not qualify a man for civil leadership. Lieutenant-General Ulysses S. Grant, whom Melville had celebrated in *Battle-Pieces* as a sort of Handsome Sailor, was a disappointment as president. The presidency of Brevet Major-General Hayes was crippled by the divisiveness which its election had earned. Major-General James A. Garfield, whose assassination elevated to the presidency Quartermaster-General Chester A. Arthur, was no cynosure. Arthur, who had been Melville's employer in the custom house, became president just three years after having been fired in a corruption scandal, resulting in doubts about his qualifications for the presidency. None of these men sought the goal that Melville thought most important in the Reconstruction years, the reintegration of the defeated South into full partnership in the union of states.

In addition, Melville was employed in a key government office in which the criterion for selecting the principal officers was political expediency rather than suitability. These officers turned over the actual operation of the custom-house to more-or-less nameless subordinates while they filled their pockets and, under the spoils system, used their power of appointment to entrench their political parties. In sum, the men Melville saw occupying the highest ranks did so not because of their abilities but because the political system gave them offices that they did not necessarily merit. No wonder he yearned for a return to a time when native ability and character were avenues to power rather than the machinery of politics and influence.

He dramatized the idea of the Handsome Sailor in *Billy Budd*.[8] The very first paragraphs of the book are a sketch of the natural leader: a black sailor whose shipmates give him their "spontaneous homage" (p. 43). The sailor has not sought leadership: rather, because of his strength and beauty, his "natural regality," those about him have given it to him unasked (p. 43). The same is true of the title character, Billy Budd, on the *Rights-of-Man*. On this exemplary ship, exemplary in its model of society in its natural, "frank" state, the captain is in charge of the business of the ship, but he is not its disciplinarian. Consequently, the crewmen are badly behaved to the point that the ship is a "rat-pit of quarrels" (p. 46) until Billy establishes order by chastising an impudent sailor. Then the crew becomes a peaceful, Antonine-like community which takes its character from the virtue emanating from its "priestly" leader, and the ship sails serenely toward home. This is Melville's vision of man in his free state: he is ornery and fractious, but the natural peacekeeper infuses his world with harmony. That was the way of the Antonines.

The *Rights-of-Man* is one term of comparison, the ideal: the *Bellipotent* is the other, the artificial, outward-bound world which Melville found wanting. It is the urbane, landsman's community of structured cynicism. Here the peacemaker is Master-at-Arms John Claggart, an appointive functionary who is not only unqualified for the position but also the worst possible candidate. The arrival of nature's peacemaker, Billy, leads to Claggart's defeat, but a victory for the natural world of the *Rights-of-Man* is a capital crime in the hierarchical world of the *Bellipotent*, where the charlatan peacemaker is both a product of its structure of mandated authority and an officer in it.

In a further pairing of characters, Captain Vere suffers. His counterpart is another Handsome Sailor, the legendary Admiral Horatio Nelson. In the story, much of the character of Nelson is elided because, at the time of composition, it was common knowledge to schoolchildren. We are given only high points, such as the incident of H.M.S. *Theseus*, to which Nelson was transferred because

STANTON GARNER

its crew were suspected of mutinous tendencies. It "was thought that an officer like Nelson was the one, not indeed to terrorize the crew into base subjection, but to win them, by force of his mere presence and heroic personality" (p. 59) back to unquestioned allegiance. But a fuller biography of the great Handsome Sailor would have noted that, like the Antonine emperors, Nelson did not gain his rank through birth or influence, but, the son of a poor minister, he began his seagoing career as a common sailor and left it up to "heaven" to advance him to the highest level of command.

Nelson is a difficult example for Captain Vere, a decent enough person, to follow. A nobleman by birth, he had won his command through service as a staff officer rather than as a gallant shipboard warrior, and he exhibits few of the qualities of a Handsome Sailor. He is aloof and distant from his crew, and, unlike Nelson, prudent. He cannot inspire obedience through charisma, for one of the first things Billy encounters on the *Bellipotent* is a flogging meant to terrorize the crew into base subjection. Because of his remoteness, Vere misunderstands his crew, believing, incorrectly, that leniency toward Billy would have a dangerous effect upon them, when, in fact, they "instinctively felt that Billy was a sort of man as incapable of mutiny as of wilful murder" (p. 131). In the age of the Antonines, commanders would be Nelsons, not Veres.

Thus *Billy Budd Sailor* is a dramatization of the ideas enunciated in "The Age of the Antonines." But, it might be asked, are we justified in interpreting a work in terms of the author's earlier writings? Need an author think in his seventies as he thought decades earlier? In fact, for as long as most readers can remember, this question has been at the root of a radical critical disagreement about the meaning of *Billy Budd.* Those who maintain that Billy was victimized by Captain Vere can point back to a long tradition of Melville works in which sailors are oppressed by tyrannous captains—*Typee, Omoo, Redburn, White-Jacket,* and perhaps *Moby-Dick*—and to others containing notable objections to irresponsible privilege and expressions of sympathy for the underprivileged—works such as *Redburn,* "The Two Temples," "The Paradise of Bachelors and the Tartarus of Maids," and "Poor Man's Pudding and Rich Man's Crumbs." If these earlier attitudes infuse *Billy Budd,* then it follows that Melville must have meant Billy to be a sympathetic character at the expense of Vere—the stern condem-

284

nation of flogging in *White-Jacket* would alone be enough to establish that. But the counter-argument holds that *Billy Budd* is a product of new ideas, that very late in life Melville underwent a radical change of attitudes, to the point of valuing constituted authority over the common man, and that, therefore, Captain Vere, the defender of the adamantine *status quo*, is the hero of the story.

But the textual history of "The Age of the Antonines" suggest otherwise. When in 1877 Melville sent the poem to his relative, he stated that he had come across it "the other day . . . in a lot of papers,"[9] implying that it had been buried for some time in his files, and, in fact, Jay Leyda guessed that he had written it in 1862.[10] But whether or not the poem dates from 1862 or 1877, and whether or not the text Melville put in the mail was newly written or an earlier poem resurrected, the two extant versions, the one he mailed in 1877 and the one he published in 1891, are remarkably alike in both form and intention. Yet in Melville's last year or so, when he was finishing *Billy Budd*, he was also preparing "The Age of the Antonines" for publication. At that time, he could have revised the poem to reflect any change that had occurred in his thinking, or, alternatively, he could have omitted it entirely from *Timoleon*, but he did neither of those things: the published version presents his criticism of his society intact. The ideas of at least fourteen years earlier, and perhaps as much as three decades earlier, were still current as he completed *Billy Budd*.

When we read his last tale, then, we should do so remembering that "The Age of the Antonines" speaks unequivocally about precisely the same issues, valuing the individual over the codified ranks and regulations of hierarchical institutions. Melville did not demand a particular form of government; any usable arrangement would do. But up to the very end he asked that authority be confided in those who merit exercising it, the Handsome Sailors. He asked that we be governed by the Antonines and Nelsons and Billy Budds, not by the Claggarts and Veres.

NOTES

1   Ltr. to Catherine G. Lansing, 7 Mar. 1877, Herman Melville, *Correspondence*, ed. Lynn Horth, vol. 14 of *The Writings of Herman Melville* (Evanston and Chicago: Northwestern UP and the Newberry Library, 1993), 451.

2   *Collected Poems of Herman Melville*, ed. Howard P. Vincent (Chicago: Hendricks House, 1947), 235-36. The 1877 version may be found in ltr. Herman Melville to John C. Hoadley [31 March 1877], *Correspondence*, 453-54.

3   Edward Gibbon, *The History of the Decline and Fall of the Roman Empire*, intro. Hugh Trevor-Roper, 3 vols., vol. 1 (Everyman's Library) (New York: Knopf, 1993), 90.

4   Gibbon, I, 34.

5   Gibbon, I, 88.

6   Gibbon, I, 90.

7   "Chiefly About War Matters," vol. 12 of *The Complete Works of Nathaniel Hawthorne*, intro. George Parsons Lathrop, 12 vols. (Boston: Houghton Mifflin, 1883), 303.

8   *Billy Budd, Sailor (An Inside Narrative)*, ed. Harrison Hayford and Merton M. Sealts, Jr. (Chicago: U of Chicago P, 1962). Page numbers of quotations refer to this text.

9   Ltr. to Hoadley, 452.

10   *The Melville Log: A Documentary Life of Herman Melville, 1819-1891*, with suppl. (New York: Gordian Press, 1969), 760. However, there is a possibility that Melville was not being candid about the poem's origin. He could have written the poem in response to the presidential election, but, because he was sending it to a staunch Republican whose friendship he cherished, concealed the fact in order to mute its commentary on the Republican victory.

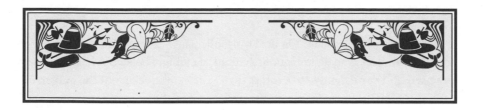

DENNIS BERTHOLD

MELVILLE'S MEDUSAS

e can all visualize some version of Medusa. In both appearance and associations, it is a public image already emplotted with the allusive weight of legend and centuries of pictorial representation. Melville, too, carried a portfolio of Medusan iconography in his mind. In fact, his many allusions to Medusa, as Gail Coffler's compendium *Melville's Classical Allusions* shows, make his works a register of the nineteenth-century's fascination with this figure from Greek mythology. And this fascination, as recent psychoanalytic and feminist studies have argued, has a specifically political dimension, embodying a conservative male reaction to revolution and female empowerment. When examined within this larger context, Melville's web of Medusa allusions helps explain his evolving politics and the contradictory tendencies they held in tension, a tension critics have repeatedly identified in *Billy Budd* that is also evident in his late poetry. Death and life, revolution and authority, male and female, beauty and horror, all combine in the complex ideology that underlies Medusa, a potent icon that reveals Melville's deep philosophical affinities with the myths of ancient Greece.

Although two critics have touched on Melville's appropriation of Medusan iconography, they conflate Medusa with Gorgon and thus miss the ambiguity inherent in the figure. In his analysis of "America," a poem from *Battle-Pieces*, Michael Paul Rogin links the explicit Gorgon allusion to violence, seeing America as "a gorgon who turns her children to stone" and linking her to the female fury of war that slays young men in "On the Slain Collegians" (276-77). William H. Shurr, too, sees Gorgon as an unambiguous symbol of evil, and believes Melville uses it precisely and consistently "to express [evil,] the central reality of the universe" (22). But Melville knew Greek myths well, as Gerard Sweeney has shown, and would have known that "Gorgon" is not synonymous with "Medusa." Although these terms were often used interchangeably, "Gorgon" is actually the collective name for Stheno and Euryale, two monstrous, immortal sisters who lived somewhere far west of ancient Greece. Charles Anthon's *Classical Dictionary*, Melville's personal reference work for mythological allusions, cites several other usages, including one from Homer that identifies Gorgon as a distinct monster unrelated to the two sisters. In this sense, then, "Gorgon" can be any hideous monster, as in the "Gorgonian head" of "The Maldive Shark," or the allusions Rogin and Shurr gloss. A far subtler symbol than Gorgon, Medusa represents the *mixture* of good and evil that defies any single moral interpretation. It functions more like the symbols of the Capitol's iron dome, or the Cincinnati eagle, or Vere's navy buttons which, as Rogin shows, encompass the uneasy dichotomies that political terms separate and submit *both* order and anarchy to moral scrutiny.

The Medusa myth, as Melville knew from Anthon, makes Medusa more than a simple allegorical representation of evil. Originally, she was a proud woman of great beauty. She had an affair with Poseidon in Athena's temple, and in retribution the goddess wound living snakes in her golden hair and exiled her to live with the two Gorgon sisters. When Perseus, the son of Zeus and the mortal Danäe, told his king he could slay Medusa, Athena armed him with a sword, shield, magic wallet, and winged sandals and sent him across the western ocean to the Gorgons' lair. By viewing Medusa in the reflection of his shield, Perseus avoided her stony gaze, and with Athena directing his blow he severed Medusa's head and placed it in his wallet. On his way back to Greece, he saw Andromeda chained to a rock and threatened by a huge sea-monster. Smitten by instant love, Perseus flew to Andromeda's rescue, using Medusa's head to petrify the sea-monster. He then gave the head to Athena who placed it on her shield to terrify her foes.[1]

Melville was drawn repeatedly to the story of Medusa and Perseus. His earliest references to Medusa stress her horror, associating her with a shark in *Mardi* (3:54), flogging in *White-Jacket* (5:386), and prostitution in *Redburn* (4:191). With

Pierre, whose subtitle indicates Melville's intention to pursue ambiguity more forcefully, Medusan allusions become more paradoxical. Pierre Glendinning, demonstrating his inability to entertain contradictory emotions, dissociates horror from beauty as he gazes at Isabel's portrait: "The terrors of the face were not those of Gorgon; not by repelling hideousness did it smite him so; but bewilderingly allured him, by its nameless beauty, and its long-suffering, hopeless anguish" (7:49). Pierre, of course, is not imagining Gorgon, but Medusa, a beautiful and alluring image like the Rondanini Medusa (fig. 1) whose mysterious, simultaneous appeal and repulsion Goethe analyzed in *Italian Journey*.[2] Although the Rondanini Medusa retains horns on her head, her hair and face appear natural, free of the obvious writhing serpents and protruding tusks characteristic of some Medusan iconography. In a move congenial to the romantic mind, the Rondanini mask ameliorates "repelling hideousness" with "nameless beauty" and effectively conflates the two. Jerome J. McGann has shown how Goethe influenced Shelley, Rossetti, and Morris, and Adrienne Munich further suggests how these writers infused the Medusa myth with male sexual anxieties over increasingly assertive female power. Melville read both Goethe and Shelley, and in the passage from *Pierre* clearly had in mind Shelley's poem "On the Medusa of Leonardo Da Vinci in the Florentine Gallery" (1819). Shelley praises Leonardo's painting for fusing opposites and rendering a horrid subject beautiful, even spiritual: "Its horror and its beauty are divine" (line 4), Shelley writes, and reveal "struggling underneath, / The agonies of anguish and of death" (7-8). "Yet it is less the horror than the grace / Which turns the gazer's spirit into stone" (9-10), the poem continues; our inability to look away reveals the appeal that terror has for us, "the tempestuous loveliness of terror" (33) mirrored in "all the beauty and the terror there" (38). Intellectually, Pierre resists the Shelleyean aesthetic of mixed beauty and terror, even though he is emotionally enveloped by its power. Etymologically "stone," Pierre is petrified by Isabel's Medusan blend of grace and horror, good and evil. This is the Medusa that Hawthorne wrestled with in his simplified retelling of the Perseus legend in *A Wonder-Book for Girls and Boys* (1852), a Medusa whose face is "the fiercest and most horrible face that ever was seen or imagined, and yet with a strange, fearful, and savage kind of beauty in it" (29).

What Pierre resists, Ishmael embraces. In chapter 55 of *Moby-Dick*, Ishmael cites Guido and Hogarth for their "Monstrous Pictures of Whales," both paintings of Perseus rescuing Andromeda from the sea-monster.[3] Ishmael correctly condemns the two artists' shared shortcomings as accurate painters of whales. But their depictions of Perseus are remarkably different and demonstrate the ambiguity of Medusa that was seeping into Victorian iconography. In later, Roman versions of the myth, for example Ovid's *Metamorphoses*, Perseus slays the sea monster with his sword instead of using Medusa's head to petrify the monster. Guido portrays the Ovidian Perseus astride Pegasus, sword in one hand and shield in the other, with Medusa hidden in his wallet. Hogarth shows the earlier Greek Perseus, flying through the air unaided, one hand holding a short sword and the other Medusa's head. Guido's Perseus replicates the iconography of conventional military valor, the man on a white horse rescuing the pale maiden; Hogarth's Perseus is a lonely wingless supernatural killer, as the gruesome head of Medusa reminds us.

Omitting Medusa sanitizes the myth's sexual violence, as Cellini recognized in his famous statue of *Perseus*, a statue Melville considered "an astonishing conception" (9:406; fig. 2).[4] What most astonishes, I think, is how Cellini emphasizes Medusa herself, both her head and body. Perseus thrusts the head forward, bringing the spectator under its awful gaze while the demigod looks down and away, one foot resting on his victim's writhing, naked body. Blood flows freely from head and torso, suggesting a frozen moment of life-in-death commonly associated with the *Laocoön* group in the Vatican. Yet amidst all this horror is great beauty, for Cellini follows the Rondanini Medusa and his own erotic bent to disturbingly convolute violence, eroticism, life, and death in one powerful image. There is nothing in the myth to suggest she was naked, and some depictions even give her a monster's body. Cellini emphasizes her female shape, particularly her breasts, and subordinates her body to Perseus's prominent genitalia and phallic sword. *Perseus* presents an image of male sexual predation, even rape, more than it does divinely ordained retribution. Though Medusa's gaze kills, so does the male gaze, both that of Perseus and Cellini, who petrifies her in statuary as an object of male lust, horror, ambition, and violence. As in Hogarth's engraving, the visible head complicates Perseus's heroism, for it reminds viewers that, before rescuing one woman, Perseus beheads another. These are, of course, the contradictory emotions and ethics Ishmael observes in Ahab, another heroic figure driven to violence by fate and chance, a woeful hero who, standing alone on the quarterdeck, reminds Ishmael of "Cellini's cast Perseus" (6:123).

Medusan iconography goes beyond aesthetics to incorporate issues of gender and politics peculiar to the nineteenth century. After the French Revolution of 1789, rebellion was frequently represented as feminine, as in Delacroix's famous painting of liberty scaling the barricades. At the same time, revolution became associated with decapitation, a result of the guillotinings in revolutionary Paris. This combination, according to Neil Hertz, created "a theory of representation—bound up with a still more explicit linking of what is politically dangerous to feelings of sexual horror and fascination" (168). Medusa—a beheaded female—thus represents a male fantasy of suppressing revolution by simultaneously disempowering both women and the lower classes. Adrienne Munich takes this logic one step further in her study of the Andromeda myth. Perseus plays the role of patriarchal oppressor, murdering and containing Medusa, the independent woman, while liberating Andromeda only to marry and domesticate her, keeping women safely within their separate sphere. This exchange, according to Munich, makes both women "cipher[s] for gender politics, useful for reinscribing traditional authority" (84). Although Munich does not distinguish the Greek from the Roman Perseus, most of the Victorian imagery she adduces portrays Perseus slaying the sea-monster with his sword rather than Medusa's head, reinforcing the semiotics of phallicism and virtually eliminating the powerful and rebellious woman who turns men to stone.

All of these connotations of Medusa figure in Melville's dense web of allusions to Medusa and Perseus in "At the Hostelry," the late unpublished poem celebrating Garibaldi's liberation of Italy and the merits of the picturesque aesthetic. In the debate on the picturesque, one of the key questions is whether disgusting subjects deserve a picturesque artistic treatment. Herman Swanevelt, a realistic Dutch painter, tries to mediate the debate with the example of Leonardo da Vinci's *Head of Medusa* (fig. 3), the painting that inspired Shelley's poem: "Like beauty strange with horror allied,—/ As shown in great Leonardo's head / Of snaky Medusa,—so as well / Grace and the Picturesque may dwell / With Terror. Vain here to divide—/ The Picturesque has many a side" (2: 65-69).[5] Art—

Leonardo's mastery of form and line, color and composition, or Cellini's "astonishing conception" of Perseus, or Shelley's recognition of Medusa's intermixed beauty and terror—conjoins opposites and offers spectators the *frisson* of Medusa's gaze, yet protects them from the consequences of actual experience. Hawthorne's friend George Stillman Hillard had been afraid to look at Leonardo's painting steadily and couldn't understand why Leonardo had painted it (78). Hillard was wiser than he knew, for the painting is no longer attributed to Leonardo. Yet Melville was ultimately wiser than Hillard, for he realized that great art should produce oppositional reactions, a mixed beauty and horror that destroys preconceived aesthetic categories—such as the picturesque—and forces viewers to divest themselves of the moral and aesthetic baggage they carry.

The shift away from judgmental aesthetics implicit in the painters' debate and imaged in Medusan iconography emblematizes the paradoxes at the heart of Melville's art and thought. Medusa is both a victim and a victimizer, one who suffers immeasurably but whose glance causes eternal suffering. She simultaneously displays the violence of Perseus and the beauty of Andromeda, and, because of her deathly gaze, becomes almost impossible to accept in her own terms. She is, as the surgeon would say in *Billy Budd*, "phenomenal," something that defies prescribed categories of moral and physical understanding. Like Billy, Medusa combines guilt and innocence, terror and beauty, anarchy and order. These are the paradoxes that Celio, the anguished seeker in *Clarel*, finds in Christ, a figure who, as the Prince of Peace bearing a sword, Celio views as a modern Medusa: "Yea, thou through ages to accrue, / Shalt the Medusa shield replace: / In beauty and in terror too / Shalt paralyze the nobler race—/ Smite or suspend, perplex, deter—/ Tortured, shalt prove a torturer" (12:42; 1.13.94-99). The Christ myth is but another version of the Medusa myth to Celio, who is as beguiled by the gaze of Christ as Shelley, Leonardo, and Cellini were by the gaze of Medusa.

The political connotations of Medusa arise when Melville compares Garibaldi to Perseus in the opening lines of "At the Hostelry." Garibaldi, as a "Redshirt Perseus," liberates Naples even as the Greek demigod liberated Andromeda. According to Anthon, Perseus, like Heracles, was one of classical myth's "just murderers" who "purify the stains of evil by force and by the shedding of blood," combining virtue and violence as "Mithraic" figures of intertwined goodness and evil (1007). In some myths, Heracles founded Naples, the city Garibaldi frees from foreign rule. Combining deeds of both Perseus and Heracles, Garibaldi partakes of the same contradictions as all revolutionaries who employ violent means to gain their ends. He too is a "just murderer," one who is chivalric, selfless, and virtuous, yet still wields his sword with brutal force wherever necessary. As Perseus, he shares in the violence and misogyny associated with Medusa, as well as the equivocal morality of all revolution.

The companion poem to "At the Hostelry," "Naples in the Time of Bomba," extends the political connotations of Medusa with the story of Masaniello, the Neapolitan rebel who led a nine-day revolt against Spanish authorities in 1647. Only twenty-five, Masaniello galvanized Neapolitans into action with charismatic speeches demanding economic justice. But when the authorities acceded to his demands, the mob turned against him and, in an act worthy of the Spanish authorities in "Benito Cereno," as the *Penny Cyclopedia* records it, "his head was cut off, fixed on a pole, and carried to the viceroy." For Jack Gentian, the conservative narrator of "Naples in the Time of Bomba," Masaniello is a specter of "incensed Revolt," a leader of "riff-raff," "Brigands and outlaws." Yet historically speaking, his rebellion seems justified, for he was goaded by an unjust and oppressive foreign authority into a revolt that presages Garibaldi's praiseworthy liberation of Naples. Masaniello, as a decapitated figure of revolt, shares in the intermixed "beauty and terror" of Medusa, an alternating victim and oppressor whose deeds testify to the situational ethics of history.[6] And as described in Melville's poem, he anticipates Billy Budd, an ambiguous figure of youthful innocence and murderous violence that complicates moral judgments: "And, see, dark eyes and sunny locks / Of Masaniello, bridegroom young, / Tanned marigold-cheek and tasseled cap; / The darling of the mob; nine days / Their great Apollo; then, in pomp / Of Pandemonium's red parade, / His curled head Gorgoned on the pike, / And jerked aloft for God to see. / A portent" (VII: 156-64).

The story of Masaniello combines Greek legend with Italian history to create a figure who, like Billy, is at once apotheosized and punished. As Gail Coffler has shown in her essay on classical iconography in *Billy Budd*, Billy's "significant beauty" derives from Melville's idealization of Apollo, a god who blends strength and beauty, the powers of life and death. To Melville, such figures are revolutionary, upsetting the normal order of things by combining traits usually considered opposites. This is what Jack Gentian fears in Masaniello, a beautiful young hero who portends the excesses of the French Revolution; and this is what Claggart and Vere fear in Billy, an Apollo-Hercules who signifies mutiny. Yet the beauty of both young men gives them, like Medusa, an unsettling (homo)erotic appeal: they are both "Handsome Sailors," "nautical Murats," "Apollos," symbols of transgressive sexual desires joined with the terrors of anarchy, unpredictable, volatile, and violent, gyrating from one extreme to another. Furthermore, as martyrs to "the Rights of Man," both represent political revolution as do Babo and John Brown. Masaniello's decapitated head is displayed on a pike like Babo's, and Billy is hanged like John Brown, just before the *Bellipotent* confronts the *Atheist*. All of these men are "portents" of war and revolution, and in their deaths extend the destructive and alluring power of Medusa's gaze into the present. They are male Medusas, figures who live on after death to inspire mixed admiration and revulsion.

The much-debated ambiguities of *Billy Budd* stem from the conflation of opposites Melville found in Medusa. They are evident as well in *Clarel*, *Timoleon*, and other late poems. The Medusa head symbolizes the ambiguities of revolt, instantiated in Ahab, Pierre, Babo, Billy, and, in Melville's time, Garibaldi. Such figures have noble aims and violent methods, and gaze at them as we will, we can never quite solve the riddle of unified contradictions they represent. Their actions, iconographically represented in the Medusa head, incorporate the contradictions of history, gender, art, and politics and, like so much of Melville's poetic, make a single vision impossible.

NOTES

1   This account follows the information in Anthon's various entries on Medusa, Perseus, and the Gorgons. Anthon's work is scholarly and thorough, and like modern mythographies offers variant stories and competing interpretations.

2   It was probably Goethe who ushered in the romantic phase of appreciation for Medusa's paradoxical qualities in 1788 when he expressed extravagant praise for the Rondanini mask in Rome: "the Medusa Rondanini—a marvelous, mysterious and fascinating work, which represents a state between death and life, pain and pleasure" (*Italian Journey*, 489). Melville owned a version of Goethe's book under the title *Letters from Italy*.

3   Ishmael mentions the Guido only briefly, but the specificity of the Hogarth description suggests that Melville had access to a copy of the engraving, either in a book or in his own art collection, although none is extant (see Wallace). Melville had access to numerous illustrations in books, periodicals, and even newspapers, and we know from his journals that he purchased numerous books and prints on his 1849 visit to London and Paris. Any of these could have provided a visual source for this passage. Reproductions of the painting and engraving are available in Stuart Frank and Dennis Berthold.

4   Although his journal entry is imprecise, Melville must have seen Cellini's statue when he visited the Uffizi in 1857. It stood in an arcade of the Piazza del Gran Duca, the same square that borders the Uffizi, and few visitors failed to comment on it (15:114, 491n; see also Hillard, 72). The allusion in *Moby-Dick* indicates Melville had seen engravings of the statue.

5   These verbal parallels strongly suggest that Shelley's poem, not Leonardo's painting, was the source for Swanevelt's meliorizing aesthetic formula. Although Melville could have seen the painting at the Uffizi in 1857, he makes no note of it; but he acquired a volume of Shelley in 1861 and obtained others in 1868 and 1873 (Leyda, 640, 694, 735, 950). My quotations are from Sandberg's edition.

6   Facts about Masaniello's life are taken from the article "Anniello, Tommaso" in *The Penny Cyclopedia*. Masaniello is a fixture in the travel literature on Italy, a well-known symbol of beauty and revolt. Melville's pastor Henry W. Bellows compared a picturesque beggar to Masaniello (2:61), while the popular historian Joel Tyler Headley quoted a peasant who said, "We want another Massaniello [sic] to lead us," and then made a beheading gesture (105). Headley considered him "the People's Washington" (105). Daniel Auber's opera *Masaniello* played frequently in New York during the 1840s.

REFERENCES

Anthon, Charles. *A Classical Dictionary...* New York: Harper and Brothers, 1841.

Bellows, Henry W. *The Old World in Its New Face: Impressions of Europe in 1867-1868.* 2 vols. New York: Harper & Brothers, 1869.

Berthold, Dennis. "Melville, Garibaldi, and the Medusa of Revolution." *American Literary History* 9 (Fall 1997), 425-59.

Coffler, Gail. "Classical Iconography in the Aesthetics of *Billy Budd, Sailor.*" In *Savage Eye: Melville and the Visual Arts*, ed. Christopher Sten. Kent, OH: Kent State UP, 1991, 257-76.

Coffler, Gail H. *Melville's Classical Allusions: A Comprehensive Index and Glossary.* Westport, CT: Greenwood P, 1985.

Frank, Stuart M. *Herman Melville's Picture Gallery: Sources and Types of the "Pictorial" Chapters of Moby-Dick.* Fairhaven, MA: Edward J. Lefkowicz, Inc., 1986.

Goethe, J. Wolfgang von. *Italian Journey.* Trans. W. H. Auden. New York: Pantheon, 1962.

Hawthorne, Nathaniel. "The Gorgon's Head," in *A Wonder Book. The Centenary Edition of the Works of Nathaniel Hawthorne*, Vol. 7, ed. William Charvat et al. Columbus: Ohio State UP, 1972, 10-34.

Headley, J[oel] T[yler]. *Letters from Italy*. Rev. ed. New York: Charles Scribner, 1851.

Hertz, Neil. "Medusa's Head: Male Hysteria under Political Pressure" in *The End of the Line: Essays on Psychoanalysis and the Sublime*. New York: Columbia UP, 1985.

Hillard, George Stillman. *Six Months in Italy*. Boston: Houghton, Mifflin and Company, 1853.

Leyda, Jay. *The Melville Log*. 2 vols. 1951; rpt. with a new supplement, New York: Gordian P, 1969.

McGann, Jerome J. "The Beauty of the Medusa: A Study in Romantic Literary Iconology." *Studies in Romanticism*, 11 (1972), 3-25.

Melville, Herman. *Billy Budd, Sailor (An Inside Narrative)*. Ed. Harrison Hayford and Merton M. Sealts, Jr. Chicago: U of Chicago P, 1962.

Melville, Herman. *The Writings of Herman Melville*. 15 vols. to date. Ed. Harrison Hayford et al., Chicago: Northwestern UP and Newberry Library, 1968—.

Munich, Adrienne Auslander. *Andromeda's Chains: Gender and Interpretation in Victorian Literature and Art*. New York: Columbia UP, 1989.

The Penny Cyclopedia of the Society for the Diffusion of Useful Knowledge. 14 vols. London: Charles Knight, 1833-43.

Rogin, Michael Paul. *Subversive Genealogy: The Politics and Art of Herman Melville*. New York: Knopf, 1983.

Sandberg, Robert Allen. Melville's Unfinished "Burgundy Club" Book: A Reading Edition Edited from the Manuscripts with Introduction and Notes. Dissertation, Northwestern, 1989.

Shelley, Percy Bysshe. "On the Medusa of Leonardo Da Vinci in the Florentine Gallery." *The Complete Poetical Works of Percy Bysshe Shelley*. Ed. Thomas Hutchison (1905). London: Oxford UP, 1948.

Shurr, William H. *The Mystery of Iniquity: Melville as Poet, 1857-1891*. Lexington, KY: UP of Kentucky, 1972.

Sweeney, Gerard. *Melville's Use of Classical Mythology*. Amsterdam: Rodopi, 1975.

Wallace, Robert K. "Melville's Prints and Engravings at the Berkshire Athenaeum." *Essays in Arts and Sciences* 15 (1986), 59-90.

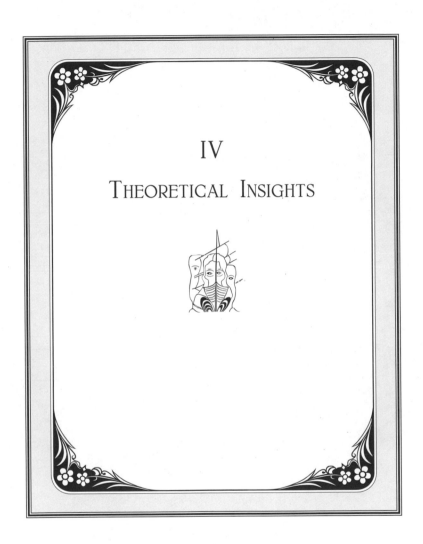

IV

THEORETICAL INSIGHTS

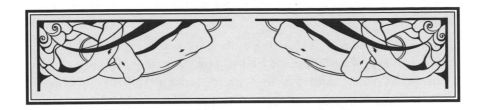

Bryan C. Short

Melville's Memory

N ear the end of "Benito Cereno," Amasa Delano implores Don Benito to forget the horrors of his recent ordeal: "See, yon bright sun has forgotten it all, and the blue sea, and the blue sky; these have turned over new leaves." The Spanish officer rejects the gesture: "Because they have no memory, because they are not human."[1] Toward the end of *Pierre*, Melville's hero justifies Lucy's return by crediting her with the power of "presentment"; Isabel responds, "Hath she that which they call the memory, Pierre; the memory?" (*P* 314).

Benito Cereno speaks for Melville in equating memory with humanness, and Isabel voices his understanding of memory as grounding the authenticity of the self. Benito's and Isabel's statements signal Melville's changing view of a theme prominent from the beginning: nowhere in his first six novels has a selfhood grounded in memory seemed so slippery.

Beginning with *Pierre* Melville's speculations, inspired by intense philosophical reading, become more specialized and technical.[2] Along with its sharper intellectual focus, Melville's thinking in the period from 1852 to 1857 is more sophisticated than it is earlier, more comfortable with international philosophical developments.

1. Memory in Melville's First Six Novels

Memory plays two straightforward roles in Melville's pre-*Pierre* works. First, it justifies the authority of first-person narrative. Remembrance of adventures undergone makes Tommo, Typee (the name given *Omoo*'s narrator by his ship-mates), Redburn, White-Jacket, and Ishmael worth attending. Melville's personae combine Tommo's claim to speak the "unvarnished truth" (*T* xiv) with Ishmael's ability to "see a little into the springs and motives" determining his fate (*MD* 7). The narrator of *Omoo* credits his tale to "simple recollection" (xiv).

At the same time memory grounds the authority of Melville's first-person narrators, it links his characters to a past preceding the events of the fictional testimony. The strength or weakness of such links signals the degree of personal integration or fragmentation underlying their motives. Ishmael feels his "splintered heart" to be "redeemed" (*MD* 51) after waking up in Queequeg's arms reconnects him to his childhood by way of the dreamlike memory recounted in "The Counterpane." Redburn, on the other hand, cannot put the glass sailor of his youth "on his legs" until he gets on his own (*R* 9). The struggle to redeem (or revenge) a painful or hidden past is by definition a struggle with memory. Melville's characters seek to establish ties to a pre-fictional past similar to those which link his narrators to the tales they recount. The function of memory in Melville's early novels shows a repeated pattern: a fictional character haunted by disturbing or thwarted recollections is "induced" to undergo adventures and gain new memories, which, when narrated, establish an authoritative, if not always happy, selfhood.

2. Philosophical Backgrounds of Melville's Memory

Plato presides over Melville's early philosophical speculations.[3] Plato's notion of *anamnesis*—the possibility of "recollecting" supersensible knowledge—turns fiction into "the great Art of Telling the Truth" by promising discovery within oneself of insights that transcend the pride and pleasure of "simple recollection."[4]

Emerson, to whom Melville's letters refer in 1849 (*C* 119-22), raises an issue crucial to Melville's grudging Platonism when he writes in *Representative Men*, "In man, the memory is a kind of lookingglass, which, having received the images of surrounding objects, is touched with life, and disposes them in a new order" (151). Melville criticizes Emerson for "the insinuation, that had he lived in those days when the world was made, he might have offered some valuable suggestions"

(C 121). The past is too clear to him. By giving memory a living, active power to "dispose" objects "in a new order," Emerson extends it too far. In terms made obvious to Melville by his reading, Emerson confuses memory with imagination and thus stumbles into a central philosophical pitfall of the day.

A key insight of enlightenment empiricism is that a memory is, after all, a present experience; its status as a representation of the past must somehow be indicated at the moment it is called to mind. Our relation to the past is tenuous in that it rests on qualitative markings of current mental experience. Locke explains that "our ideas are said to be in our memories, when indeed they are actually nowhere, but only there is an ability in the mind when it will to revive them again" (97). Hume asserts that "the ideas of the memory are much more lively and strong than those of the imagination" (317) and as a result induce our belief that they have occurred before. By linking memory to belief, Hume opens even wider the Pandora's box of memory's presentness: if the authenticity of a memory signals itself in the belief which it inspires, what is to stop belief from retroactively treating the stuff of fancy as remembered? Melville's understanding of Locke and Hume can be inferred from his references to them, their ubiquity, and discussions of their and related views in works acquired by Melville or in his possession before 1851: Coleridge's *Biographia Literaria*, bought in 1848 (S 168); Hartley's *Observations on Man*, borrowed in the same year (S 182); and Carlyle's *Sartor Resartus*, borrowed in 1850 (S 163), Akenside's *The Pleasures of Imagination*, residing in the family library (S 150), Rousseau's *Confessions*, bought in London in 1849 (S 209), and De Quincey's *Confessions of an English Opium Eater*, acquired at the same time (S 172).

Pierre hinges on the issue of whether Isabel remembers or imagines the experiences that justify his adopting her as his sister—whether or not their truth is retroactively imposed by his belief in her. The novel can be read as a primer on the pitfalls of associationism. How can special insight or authority be claimed, Melville asks, when, as Hume says, "the memory, senses, and understanding are, therefore, all of them founded on the imagination" (545)?

The associations cemented together by Pierre's wish-fulfillment decision come apart when he begins to doubt. Isabel's past remains ambiguous, "nowhere." The novel's ending demonstrates Coleridge's perception that "the objects of any two ideas need not have co-existed in the same sensation in order to become mutually associable" (62-63). Associationism, for Coleridge, confounds the distinction between memory and fancy, actual and imagined past.

The irony of empiricist epistemology as conveyed to American writers like Melville is that its inability to derive a clear theory of memory finally leaves the mind alienated from the sensations on which it supposedly depends. In contrast, romanticism worships imagination unfettered by "simple recollection." Carlyle in *Sartor Resartus* postulates a "Time-annihilating" hat that would enable one to roam the ages. He concludes: "Or thinkest thou it were impossible, unimaginable? Is the Past annihilated, then, or only past; is the Future non-existent, or only future? Those mystic faculties of thine, Memory and Hope, already answer. . . . Yesterday and Tomorrow both *are*" (261).

Wordsworth's formula of "emotion recollected in tranquillity" (886) relies on feelings to bridge the gap between belated present and shadowy past. Wordsworth mirrors Rousseau, who declares in *The Confessions*, that as a child he "had no idea of the facts, but I was already familiar with every feeling. I had grasped nothing; I had sensed everything" (20). "Emotion recollected in tranquillity" is an oxymoron in which one technology of memory (tranquil reflection) calls up its contrary (heightened emotion). The recollection of emotion says little about the event responsible for it. Yet one's emotions, for Wordsworth as for Rousseau, ground one's selfhood.

Wordsworth, in a formula close to Melville's, calls on his listeners to witness and share; if the feeling which authorizes a continuous self can be communicated, its authenticity is reinforced and given a moral dimension. When no reliable witness, like Dorothy in "Tintern Abbey," is present, the narrator must direct his appeal to the reader.

3. Memory in *The Confidence-Man*

The trickery in *The Confidence-Man* begins after the man in cream-colors has gone to sleep and "the last transient memory of the slumberer vanished" (8).[5] The world of the *Fidèle* is characterized by forgetting, by the disabling of memories which would connect one avatar of the hero to the next or his victims to a sense of identity that would permit resistance. In the spirit of Montaigne's essay "Of Liars," acquired in 1848, bad memory is a key to the truths the novel uncovers.[6]

When pressed for someone "who can speak a good word for you" Black Guinea answers "as if his memory, before suddenly frozen up by cold charity, as suddenly thawed back into fluidity" (13). He describes eight "ge'mmen," five of them subsequent guises of the confidence man. Guinea's list links his "thawed" memory to the novel's most important assertion of the continuity of the self. Without it, arguments for a single confidence man collapse.[7] Two circumstances give the list, as a recollection, theoretical significance. First, its truth depends on the witness of the reader. The confidence man as a continuous self exists only for himself and the reader. Second, Guinea's list is a memory of the future not the past. Melville understands the presentness of memory in empiricist thought. The notion that memory as a marker of mental representations points forward as much as backward in time counts as one of his important theoretical departures.

Almost immediately after Guinea stumps out of sight, Ringman, the man with the weed, accosts Roberts, the country merchant, with an appeal to "supply the void in your memory" (20). During their conversation, Ringman revises a traditional metaphor: "You see, sir, the mind is ductile, very much so: but images, ductilely received into it, need a certain time to harden and bake in their impressions, otherwise such a casualty as I speak of will in an instant obliterate them, as though they had never been. We are but clay, sir, potter's clay" (20). What determines remembrance is not merely the event in itself but the mind's subsequent action upon it—an assertion akin to Rousseau's claim that "objects generally make less impression on me than does the memory of them."[8]

The net effect of the confidence man's theory of mental ductility is to undercut memory as a source of belief. To the extent that Melville's hero can subvert confidence in the self by subverting confidence in recollection, he can assert the necessity of witness, of his victim's having confidence in him. The confidence man's modus operandi is to force the transition from memory to imagination. In the immemorial world of the *Fidèle*, event and story become indistinguishable in motive power; stories proliferate to "supply the void" left by the lack of helpful recollections.

Chapter 13, in which the story of Goneril and her unfortunate husband is discussed, starts with "an anticipative reminder to such readers" as may be surprised by the confidence man's "philosophic and humanitarian discourse" (64). Chap-

ter 14, the first of Melville's metafictional treatises, then commences with a reminder "glancing backward" at the "reminder looking forwards" (69) of the previous chapter. Proleptic memory, the "anticipative reminder" that introduces the
discussion of the "touching" story, has the purpose of preserving the readers'
"own good opinion of their previous penetration" (64). Now that the confidence
man has appeared in three of the guises introduced by Guinea, it is the continuity of the reader's responses to him which is at stake.

As the grounds of a pragmatic or ethical selfhood are undercut by Melville's
protagonist, the reader's responses and the novel's metafiction take center stage.
Chapter 14 introduces two important aspects of Melville's theory of memory.
First, "The grand points of human nature are the same to-day they were a thousand years ago" (71), even if variations in expression make them impossible to
remember. Second, "no man's experience can be coextensive with *what is*" (70).
English naturalists cannot accept the "duck-billed beaver of Australia" as real
because their system of classification prevents it. What we remember depends
on our training, on what Althusser would call the ideology of the surrounding
culture.

After Chapter 14, the outlandish capers and guises of the confidence man
increasingly justify the narrator's judgment of the work to be "comedy" (71).
Among the most memorable is Charlie Noble's retelling of Judge Hall's story
of John Moredock, Indian-hater. After recounting "The Metaphysics of Indian-
hating," Charlie maintains that "in strict speech there can be no biography of
an Indian-hater *par excellence*" (150). Herein lies the account's "metaphysics": a
truly principled life lies outside the realm of biography. What makes a life uniform exists beyond remembrance or report. Consistency, the individual counterpart of the "grand points of human nature" that are "the same to-day they
were a thousand years ago" (71), is metaphysical, beyond the scope of simple
recollection even as reinterpreted by imagination.

What memory offers to the imagination is not consistency *par excellence* but
change. Only that which changes can be singled out as having a distinct, tem-
porally located identity, lodged in recollection, and turned into an imaginative
appeal. Don Benito in "Benito Cereno" asserts the humanness of recall, but in
fixing himself in the amber of his memories he consigns himself to the grave.

Memory is not metaphysical; its realm is the ever changing, ever inconsistent comedy of appearances.

The Confidence-Man, in its discussions of stories like that of Moredock, proposes the necessary interplay between simple recollection and its interpretation by the imagination. On a metafictional level, the end result of this interplay—of reading the book—is, in modern phenomenological terms, noesis rather than noema, knowledge of the patterns of mind rather than knowledge of externals.[9] To help one live successfully among the ever-changing phenomena which are our birthright, imaginative literature must preserve the space of the unspeakable— the metaphysical—and not, like Emerson, presume to represent it.

Chapter 33 establishes a bond of empathy between reader and author based on the author's memory of the imagined responses of the reader. The chapter goes a step further. It induces the reader's acquiescence ("and with this class we side") in seeking from literature "nature unfettered, exhilarated, in effect transformed.... It is with fiction as with religion: it should present another world, and yet one to which we feel the tie" (183). In equating fiction with religion, Melville now suggests that its calling is comparable to metaphysics. The combination of imaginative empathy, noetic memory, and shared witness which generates the novel's metafictional insights points to "another world," a counterpart of the space left unspeakable in Moredock's tale.

Chapter 44, Melville's third and final metafictional essay, asserts that what would be truly memorable would be an original character in fiction: "a grateful reader will, on meeting with one, keep the anniversary of that day" (238). Original characters are not metaphysical in an Emersonian sense, but, like the duck-billed beaver, they transcend the understood categories of remembered experience. Such a character would shine its light on existing memory-imagination relationships, giving the structure of the self a new look and creating "another world" out of our memories.

Whether or not the confidence man is meant to be taken as an original fictional character, Melville does not say. What he proposes as theoretically significant is the act of reading that emerges from the collusion of character, author, and reader. If character, narrator/author, and reader can, in their metafictional interplay, be rendered new, placed meaningfully among the "strangers" and "strangers still more strange" (8) that teem the decks of the *Fidèle*, the novel's originality, its substitute metaphysics, its memorability will have been witnessed.

In the novel's final comment on memory, the old man, ready for bed, asks, "'is there anything I have forgot,—forgot? Something I sort of dimly remember. . . . Oh, my poor old memory!'"(250). The cosmopolitan supplies the void in his memory by offering a chamber-pot as the life-preserver. The quest for "Providence," for "another world," leaves one embarrassingly dependent on life's fundamental functions. Metaphysics is brought back to earth.

The cosmopolitan, in discussing with the old man the "life-preserver" he has just proffered, admits that "I never use this sort of thing" (251). Apparently inhuman himself, he sells his victims their own basic humanness which, by undercutting memory, he can disguise as something greater. If *The Confidence-Man* is read allegorically, the confidence man represents author, fiction, and imagination in their parallel relationships with reader, experience, and memory. It is not by leaving memory for transcendental meanings that we reach a vision of enduring truth but rather by opening ourselves to the shared witness which selfhood enjoys as it carves its future out the interplay between remembered appearances, imaginative interpretations, and its inward looking awareness of its response patterns. For Melville, to remember in the profound and complex way that his novel seeks to remember is to participate in a genial "masquerade"—a dressing up for others similarly *en costume*—and at the same time to give oneself the crucial human guarantee that "Something further may follow."[10]

NOTES

1   *Piazza Tales* 116. Hereafter I use the following abbreviations for the Northwestern-Newberry editions of Melville's works: *Typee, T; Omoo, O; Redburn, R; Moby-Dick, MD; Pierre, P; Correspondence, C*.

2   Except where otherwise noted, all references to Melville's acquisition of particular books come from Sealts, *Melville's Reading*, revised and enlarged edition (hereafter abbreviated *S*).

3   Sealts, "Melville and Emerson's Rainbow" and "Melville and the Platonic Tradition," both in *Pursuing Melville*; Wenke, "Ontological Heroics," from Bryant's *Companion*; and *Melville's Muse*.

4   Interest in the possibility of correspondences between the material and spiritual underlies Melville's ongoing exploration of religion, as described by such scholars as Braswell, Goldman, Herbert, Sherrill, and Wright, and mythology as treated by Franklin and Sweeney.

5 Foster, in her introduction to the Hendricks House edition of *The Confidence-Man*, argues that the lamblike man is not a guise of the novel's hero: "at any rate, Melville clearly differentiates between him and the Confidence Man" (lii).

6 Montaigne argues that his poor memory encourages strength of judgment and a lively imagination. As a result, he claims, he is more truthful and reflective and better enjoys the rereading of good books (32-38). The Cotton translation cited here is the one Melville acquired (*S* 199). See Bryant (*Repose* 72-73) for a discussion of Melville's use of "Of Lies."

7 Bellis discusses at length the theme of continuity of the self, or identity (165-90).

8 Dryden (176-77) discusses the pottery/baking motif in the novel.

9 Noesis and noema for Husserl define the two parts of phenomenological description (660).

10 An extended version of this paper was published in *Arizona Quarterly* 55.1 (Spring 1999): [39]-65.

REFERENCES

Akenside, Mark. *The Pleasures of Imagination.* London: J. Dodsley, 1769.

Bellis, Peter J. *No Mysteries Out of Ourselves: Identity and Textual Form in the Novels of Herman Melville.* Philadelphia: U of Pennsylvania P, 1990.

Braswell, William. *Melville's Religious Thought: An Essay in Interpretation.* Durham, NC: Duke UP, 1943.

Bryant, John, ed. *A Companion to Melville Studies.* Westport, CT: Greenwood, 1986.

——. *Melville and Repose: The Rhetoric of Humor in the American Renaissance.* New York: Oxford UP, 1993.

Carlyle, Thomas. *Sartor Resartus: The Life and Opinions of Herr Teufelsdröckh.* Ed. Charles Frederick Harrold. New York: Odyssey, 1937.

Coleridge, Samuel Taylor. *Biographia Literaria.* New York: Macmillan, 1926.

De Quincey, Thomas. *Confessions of an English Opium-Eater, and Suspira de Profundis.* Boston: Ticknor and Fields, 1853.

Dryden, Edgar A. *Melville's Thematics of Form: The Great Art of Telling the Truth.* Baltimore: Johns Hopkins UP, 1968.

Emerson, Ralph Waldo. *The Collected Works of Ralph Waldo Emerson.* Vol. 7. *Representative Men: Seven Lectures.* Cambridge, MA: Harvard UP, 1987.

Foster, Elizabeth, ed. *The Confidence-Man: His Masquerade.* By Herman Melville. New York: Bobbs-Merrill, 1967.

Franklin, H. Bruce. *The Wake of the Gods: Melville's Mythology*. Stanford, CA: Stanford UP, 1963.

Goldman, Stan. *Melville's Protest Theism: The Hidden and Silent God in* Clarel. DeKalb: Northern Illinois UP, 1993.

Hartley, David. *Observations on Man, His Frame, His Duty, and His Expectations*. 1749 ed. New York: Garland, 1971.

Herbert, T. Walter, Jr. *Marquesan Encounters: Melville and the Meaning of Civilization*. Cambridge, MA: Harvard UP, 1980.

Hume, David. *The Philosophical Works*. Ed. Thomas Hill Green and Thomas Hodge Grose. Darmstadt: Scientia Verlag Aalen, 1964.

Husserl, Edmund. "Phenomenology." *Critical Theory Since 1965*. Ed. Hazard Adams and Leroy Searle. Tallahassee: U of Florida P, 1986. 658-63.

Locke, John. *An Essay Concerning Human Understanding*. 2nd ed. Amherst, NY: Prometheus, 1995.

Melville, Herman. *The Battle-Pieces of Herman Melville*. Ed. Hennig Cohen. New York: Thomas Yoseloff, 1963.

——. *The Confidence-Man: His Masquerade*. Ed. Harrison Hayford, Hershel Parker, and G. Thomas Tanselle. Vol. 10 of *The Writings of Herman Melville*. Evanston and Chicago: Northwestern UP and the Newberry Library, 1984.

——. *Correspondence*. Ed. Lynn Horth. Vol. 14 of *The Writings*. 1993.

——. *Journals*. Ed. Howard C. Horsford with Lynn Horth. Vol. 15 of *The Writings*. 1989.

——. *Mardi and a Voyage Thither*. Ed. Harrison Hayford, Hershel Parker, and G. Thomas Tanselle. Vol. 3 of *The Writings*. 1970.

——. *Moby-Dick; or, The Whale*. Ed. Harrison Hayford, Hershel Parker, and G. Thomas Tanselle. Vol. 6 of *The Writings*. 1988.

——. *Omoo: A Narrative of Adventures in the South Seas*. Ed. Harrison Hayford, Hershel Parker, and G. Thomas Tanselle. Vol. 2 of *The Writings*. 1968.

——. *The Piazza Tales and Other Prose Pieces, 1839-1860*. Ed. Harrison Hayford, Alma A. MacDougall, and G. Thomas Tanselle. Vol. 9 of *The Writings*. 1987.

——. *Pierre; or, The Ambiguities*. Ed. Harrison Hayford, Hershel Parker, and G. Thomas Tanselle. Vol. 7 of *The Writings*. 1971.

——. *Redburn: His First Voyage*. Ed. Harrison Hayford, Hershel Parker, and G. Thomas

Tanselle. Vol. 4 of *The Writings*. 1969.

——. *Typee: A Peep at Polynesian Life*. Ed. Harrison Hayford, Hershel Parker, and G. Thomas Tanselle. Vol. 1 of *The Writings*. 1968.

——. *White-Jacket; or, The World in a Man-of-War*. Ed. Harrison Hayford, Hershel Parker, and G. Thomas Tanselle. Vol. 5 of *The Writings*. 1970.

Montaigne, Michel de. *The Essays of Michel de Montaigne*. 3 vols. Vol. 1. Trans. Charles Cotton. London: G. Bell and Sons, 1913.

Rousseau, Jean-Jacques. *The Confessions*. Trans. J. M. Cohen. London: Penguin, 1953.

Sealts, Merton M, Jr. *Melville's Reading: Revised and Enlarged Edition*. Columbia: U of South Carolina P, 1988.

——. *Pursuing Melville 1940-1980*. Madison: U of Wisconsin P, 1982.

Sherrill, Rowland A. *The Prophetic Melville: Experience, Transcendence, and Tragedy*. Athens: U of Georgia P, 1979.

Short, Bryan C. *Cast by Means of Figures: Herman Melville's Rhetorical Development*. Amherst, MA: U of Massachusetts P, 1992.

Sweeney, Gerard M. *Melville's Use of Classical Mythology*. Amsterdam: Rodopi, 1975.

Wenke, John. *Melville's Muse: Literary Creation and the Forms of Philosophical Fiction*. Kent, OH: Kent State UP, 1995.

——. "'Ontological Heroics': Melville's Philosophical Art." *A Companion to Melville Studies*. Ed. John Bryant. New York: Greenwood, 1986. 567-601.

Wordsworth, William. *Poems*. Vol. 1. Ed. John O. Hayden. London: Penguin, 1977.

Wright, Nathalia. *Melville's Use of the Bible*. Durham, NC: Duke UP, 1949.

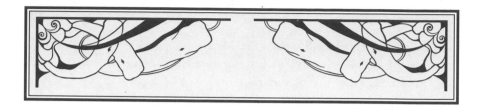

Andreas Kriefall

Esotericism, Sacrifice, Democracy
Alternative Politics of Tragedy in Nietzsche and Melville

I n his brilliant but little known book, *The Sacred Game*, Girardian critic Cesáreo Bandera makes a statement that succinctly defines a particularly modern form of tragic paradox: "One cannot fight or violently expel the sacred without perpetuating it."[1] By "the sacred" Bandera means a combination of killing and lies, a deep human drive to displace shared, social violence onto an arbitrarily chosen sacrificial victim, and to cover over this act of disavowing responsibility with distortive mythic justifications. Girard claims that this victimage mechanism forms the sacrificial kernel of religions world-wide, but even in modern attempts to overcome religion, the secularizing Western world has repeatedly taken the peculiar path of *scapegoating religion itself*, making it as if ideas of God and ritual, and not human beings themselves, were responsible for suffering and inhumanity. It is this self-undermining effort that leads to the problem Bandera points out: as it is the gesture of scapegoating, violent expulsion itself, that is the essence of the sacred, scapegoating religion cannot free humanity from its violent desires or from the tendency to evade its responsibility and cover up its guilt.[2]

The Girardian argument obviously presents us with a vast and complex theory of religion and culture, but this essay will draw from it a more specific thesis idea, using a variation on Bandera's formulation: sacrificial violence, and its attendant deception, is perpetuated through attempts to expel the sacred and create a modern myth of the state inimical to democracy. I will try to show how powerfully this religio-political dialectic illuminates similarities and differences in the tragic vision of Melville and Nietzsche. It provides, first of all, a fresh and illuminating way to interpret the tragic plot of Ahab's fight against the whale: a leader unifies and enslaves a democratic state threatened by violence by channeling its aggression toward a victim mythically portrayed as the incarnation of evil; the disastrous result of course is that an even greater violence completely engulfs both captain and crew. The specifically modern character of this sacrificial drama lies in the fact that Ahab undertakes the creation of a fatal myth on his own authority—autonomously, knowingly, deceptively—utterly without the communal sanction of shared experiences typical of premodern mythology, such as stories of ancestral origin, narrated dreams, and time-honored symbols.

Thus, what Ahab presents to his community as a clear and unifying direction is grounded not in socially acknowledged visionary insight, theophany, or traditional memory, but in the guilty laceration of his sovereign, solitary mind. The suffering of a myth-maker without faith in ancestors, god, or truth was experienced in strikingly similar ways by Friedrich Nietzsche. Though this philosopher is exoterically cast, and often celebrated, as the greatest (post)modern critic of religion, that is only because we have not yet grasped the esoteric logic through which fighting the sacred and killing gods actually perpetuates politically useful effects of the sacred. In this essay, I will try to elucidate this logic, to show how the threats to democracy anticipated in the tragic plot of Melville's novel are replayed in Nietzsche's attempt to undermine modern democracy—a potent philosophical *coup d'état* and *coup de théâtre* in which one can recognize precisely the forms of esoteric, sacrificial thinking exposed in *Moby-Dick*'s portrayal of Ahab. In other words, the moral and political catastrophe warned against in Melville's tragic, philosophical art is actively pursued in Nietzsche's artistic philosophy of tragedy. Getting to the heart of this surprising connection will require attention to the linked phenomena of esotericism and sacrifice in *The Birth of Tragedy* and *Moby-Dick*, topics that readers of Nietzsche and Melville have not yet explored.

SECTION ONE

Esotericism and Sacrifice as Practiced in Nietzsche's *Birth of Tragedy*

Nietzsche's famous slogan heralding "the death of God" is a euphemism for what he actually calls the *murder* of God, a sacrificial murder with momentous consequences: "How shall we comfort ourselves, the murderers of all murderers? What was holiest and mightiest of all that the world has yet owned has bled to death under our knives: who will wipe the blood off us? What water is there for us to clean ourselves? What festivals of atonement, what sacred games shall we have to invent?"[3]

This impassioned set of questions about killing God presents in a nutshell the central problems addressed by Nietzsche's philosophy of tragedy: sacrifice, guilt, the need for consolation, and the invention of sacred games. Unlike Marx and Freud, and unlike simplistic Enlightenment narratives of eliminating religion through the light of reason and the spread of science, Nietzsche implies that only a new religion can supplant the old, only a new myth of bloody sacrifice can break history in two and shape a new, post-Christian European politics. How is sacrifice related to politics? Section 859 of *The Will to Power* explains: "My ideas do not revolve around the degree of freedom that is granted to the one or to the other or to all, but around the degree of *power* that the one or the other should exercise over others or over all, and to what extent *a sacrifice of freedom*, even enslavement, provides for the emergence of a *higher type*. Put in the crudest form: *how could one sacrifice the development of mankind* to help a higher species than man come into existence?" (my emphasis in italics).[4]

Thus, these late texts suggest that the sacrificial killing of God has something to do with the sacrifice of freedom, the enslavement of the many for the benefit of the higher type. Already in *The Birth of Tragedy*, his first book, Nietzsche had begun exploring these interlinked religious and political dimensions of sacrifice, focusing on the tragic god, Dionysus. But Dionysus is not a figure whose meaning is easily grasped. What is a (post)modern thinker like Nietzsche actually recommending by ending *The Birth of Tragedy* with the invocation: "follow me to witness a tragedy, and sacrifice with me at the temple of [Apollo and Dionysus]"? This enigmatic, anachronistic reference to tragedy, gods, and sacrifice cannot possibly mean what it literally says—in this essay, I will present some evidence that we can best understand what Nietzsche is up to by assuming that the obscurity is intentional, that Nietzsche writes esoterically: "*The Greeks as Interpreters*—When we speak of the Greeks, we involuntarily speak of today and yesterday.... We take advantage of the freedom to speak about them in order to be silent about other things—so that these Greeks might themselves whisper something into the ear of the thoughtful reader. Thus for the modern man the Greeks facilitate the communication of many things which are difficult or hazardous to communicate."[5]

In speaking about speaking about the Greeks, Nietzsche draws us into a world of masks and hidden, perilous subjects, a labyrinth of language about language. This passage speaks of involuntary speech, deliberate silence, indefinite whispers, and dangerous communication—it is speech revealing only that it is concealing most of what it has to say. This is in fact just the sort of language we see at work in *The Birth of Tragedy*, which Nietzsche begins in this way: "We shall have gained much for the science of aesthetics once we have come not merely to logical insight, but to the immediate certainty of vision, that the continuous development of art is bound up with the duplicity of the Apollonian and of the Dionysian."[6]

Nothing means what it first appears to say in this text—within a short span Nietzsche will have inverted or refunctioned every one of the signifiers in his opening sentence: what purports to offer a gain for "science" will become an attack on it; "aesthetics" will be derided as the worst form of modern superficiality; "logical insight" will be flouted rather than supplemented; the "immediate certainty" of vision will be shown to be constituted by veils of dream and illusion ... and so on. Since it is clearly not "the science of aesthetics," what is Nietzsche really writing about? In speaking of art and duplicity, the text appears to do something similar to what Nietzsche's comment on the Greeks did: to speak about ways of communicating and generating secrecy without conveying a direct or specifiable content. Thus, the text functions in an artfully hermetic and self-referential way, *using its modern analysis of ancient musical and dramatic art to develop a disguised theoretical account of what the modern text itself tries to perform*. This is, in other words, esoteric writing about esoteric writing: Nietzsche's study of tragic art deploys a performative rhetoric masked as constative prose, producing at once a theory and a practice of deceptive discourse.

On this assumption, let us return to the obscure opening sentence of *The Birth of Tragedy* and substitute for art and aesthetics "Nietzsche's esoteric writing" as the real subject of the book. Such a substitution produces something like the following sentence: "we shall have gained much for understanding *Nietzsche's esoteric writing* if we come to see that it is bound up with the duplicity of the Apollonian and Dionysian." Not only is this sentence a good deal clearer than the one Nietzsche published, it is actually close to an unpublished draft of that sentence, which reads: "The Greeks, who express and simultaneously keep silent about the secret doctrine of their world view in their gods, erected as the double source of their art two godheads, Apollo and Dionysus."[7] We know enough by now to see that Nietzsche is talking about his own project here: it is in fact Nietzsche who conveys a secret world-view by inventing gods through a duplicitous art of double writing. Thus we are beginning to get a sense of what Nietzsche's "Dionysus" is: an invented god, an esoteric fiction designed to impart and disguise a secret doctrine.

What terrible "doctrine" requires such elaborate forms of encrypting and manipulation to be communicated? Perhaps the most effective way to penetrate the coded discourse of *The Birth of Tragedy* is to turn to a much shorter piece, "The Greek State," written at the same time (1871) but—because Nietzsche purposely withheld it from public scrutiny—written without the larger text's intentional obfuscations. From there we can move back to Nietzsche's book on tragedy with better understanding. "The Greek State" furnishes not only an essential guide to the secret doctrines of *The Birth of Tragedy*, but invaluable insight into the motives for esotericism in Nietzsche's writings generally. Here, then, one can see the "cruel" and "frightening" teaching that requires endless masking and esoteric communication:

The formation of culture, which is mainly a genuine need for art, rests on this frightening foundation: but this foundation lets itself be recognized in the vague feeling of shame. In order that there be a wide, deep, and fertile soil for the development of art, the vast majority must be in the service of the minority—beyond the measure of their individual necessity—slavishly subjected to the distress of life. Through their suffering, through their surplus labor, the advantaged class should be elevated above the struggle for existence, in order to produce a new world of need and desire. Correspondingly, we must agree to set forth this cruel-sounding truth: *that slavery belongs to the essence of a culture....* This truth is the vulture which gnaws on the liver of the Promethean patron of culture.[8]

In the private medium of unpublished writing, Nietzsche does not hesitate to add more cruel-sounding truths to this grim social vision of suffering, exploited slaves and artists who labor to free themselves from the shame of their own privilege. The slave class, for instance, emerges out of wars of conquest which build the power of the state, wars whose violence, like art, generates another of the dark enchantments that compel human beings to sacrifice themselves for something greater than their individual existence:

If indeed hearts instinctively swell at the magic of the becoming state, with the sense of an invisibly deep intention . . . if at that point the state is regarded, even with fervor, as the goal and summit of the sacrifices and duties of the individual, then out of all this the monstrous necessity of the state speaks, without which nature could not succeed in coming through society to its redemption in illusion, in the mirror of the genius. . . . Be it then pronounced that war is just as much a necessity for the state as the slave is for society, and who can avoid this verdict if he honestly asks himself about the causes of the never-equalled Greek art-perfection?[9]

With the help of these blunt pronouncements, we are now in a position to understand the horrific content of Nietzsche's obsessively masked doctrine of tragedy, the state secrets that require so many layers of art to be at once revealed and concealed. The violent state of nature expresses itself in warfare among human beings, but out of this chaos emerges a form of Apollonian order, what Nietzsche calls *the iron clamp* of the state. Through the power of the state the war of all against all is recast into a hierarchy of two distinct classes: slaves who labor to provide leisure for the ruling artist class, and artists who labor to provide an ideological justification for themselves and unifying delusions for the slaves. Attic tragedy, which grew out of a slave-supported society and a political history of constant warfare, represents for Nietzsche the most potent (though ephemeral) artform capable of simultaneously expressing unutterable pain and covering shame with consoling joy. He ends his essay with a fascoid vision of an esoterically governed state serving the genius: "every human being, with his

315

entire activity, only has dignity insofar as he, consciously or unconsciously, is the tool of the genius; from which one can readily draw the ethical consequence, that 'man in himself,' the absolute person, possesses neither dignity, nor rights, nor duties: only as a wholly determined being, serving unconscious purposes, can a human being justify his existence."[10]

Warfare, slavery, destruction of the individual, and control of society through "redemptive," collective illusion: to move from these overtly political fantasies in "The Greek State" to the aesthetic theory of *The Birth of Tragedy* is to sense the way Nietzsche uses tragic art as an esoteric metaphor for political ideology. If we keep in mind Nietzsche's comments about geniuses using men as tools, about creating gods and communicating deceptively, about guilt and consolation, passages like the following description of "the aesthetic phenomenon" take on a markedly sinister level of meaning:

At bottom, the aesthetic phenomenon is simple: let anyone have the ability to behold continually a vivid play and to live constantly surrounded by hosts of spirits, and he will be a poet; let anyone feel the urge to transform himself and to speak out of other bodies and souls, and he will be a dramatist. The Dionysian excitement is capable of communicating this artistic gift to a multitude, so they can see themselves surrounded by such a host of spirits while knowing themselves to be essentially one with them. And this phenomenon is encountered epidemically: a whole throng experiences the magic of this transformation.[11]

The processes characterized here as "vivid play," "artistic gift," "Dionysian excitement," and "magic transformation" correspond directly to the processes described in "The Greek State" as the need for illusion, the origin of the state, and the work of genius by which an enslaved mass comes to be "wholly determined," governed by "unconscious purposes." Here again, Nietzsche describes a hallucinatory effect of tragic art that he himself is trying to create with his fantastic, esoteric text: he conceals a theory and an act of rhetorical, political manipulation beneath aestheticized, mythic images of art and art deities. In both his political doctrine and the imagery he attaches to tragedy, he also happens to be providing descriptions which apply with remarkable cogency to Ahab's takeover of the *Pequod*. Before I cite a final passage from *The Birth of Tragedy*, allow me to insert an anticipation of my *Moby-Dick* thesis. I read Ahab as a Shakespearean version of the "poet" and "dramatist" that Nietzsche depicts above—surrounded by "spirits," driven to transform himself by transforming the whole throng of mates, harpooneers, and crew through the Dionysian magic of his violent, sacrificial fantasy. Throughout this performance, Ahab also remains keenly conscious of the way the very act of subjugating the crew involves sacrificing *himself* in some measure, giving himself over to a demanding, dangerous role he cannot fully control. Here again, I find the resonance between Ahab's tragic persona and Nietzsche's tragic philosophy striking: "In himself [Nietzsche writes of Aeschylus and his Prometheus myth] the Titanic artist found the defiant faith that he had the ability to create men and at least destroy Olympian gods, by means of a superior wisdom which, to be sure, he had to atone for with eternal suffering. . . . The best and highest possession mankind can acquire is obtained by sacrilege and must be paid for with consequences that involve the whole flood of sufferings and sorrows with which the offended divinities have to afflict the nobly aspiring race of men. . . . [This constitutes] the sublime view of *active sin* as the characteristically Promethean virtue. With that, the ethical basis for pessimistic tragedy has been found: the justification of human evil, meaning both human guilt and the human suffering it entails."[12]

Here we can clearly see the relevance of Bandera's formula: one cannot fight the sacred (destroy gods, commit sacrilege, sin actively) without perpetuating it (creating men, suffering from offended deities, seeking justifications). In Nietzsche's passage about murdering God, we saw a similar pattern—one cannot kill god(s) without inventing sacred games. Or, translated into the key terms from "The Greek State," one cannot inflict sacrifices and enslave humanity without suffering in turn from enduring shame, leading to a desire for consolation productive of mythic, esoteric art. As I read them, the comments on the "ethical basis for pessimistic tragedy" set the Dionysian agenda for Nietzsche's philosophy: to "justify" the human evils of violence, sacrifice, exploitation, deception, and order of rank by universalizing conditions of killing and lies. We began a reading of *The Birth of Tragedy* by asking what the author means by witnessing tragedy and sacrificing to art deities: this political program gives us some idea. It remains to be seen how far we can trace the analogy of this political philosophy of tragedy with Ahab's tragic Shakespearean performance on the quarter-deck.

SECTION TWO

Esotericism and Sacrifice as Exposed in *Moby-Dick*

One of *Moby-Dick*'s distinctive features as a novel is the way it shows how things are put together before they do anything. Unlike Ahab's fantasy of an undoubted deed, *Moby-Dick* obsessively sets words and deeds in the context of multiple presentiments, questions, doubts, and interpretive frames. Thus, we get in the book not just a whaling story, but reviews of how whaling stories have been told through millennia; not just a sermon, but a careful review of the chapel and the pulpit where it is performed; not just whale killing, but exhaustive analyses of implements and procedures; not just a genocidal catastrophe, but loomings of it. My thesis here is that perhaps *Moby-Dick*'s most stunning revelation is the insight it gives into the workings of esotericism and sacrificial violence. In other words, paradoxically, *where Nietzsche refunctions philosophy as the esoteric attempt to perform what it claims the artform of tragedy has accomplished, Melville refunctions the tragic artform to analyze the performative dynamics of violent esotericism.*

In the opening of Chapter 41, "Moby Dick," Ishmael provides us with a succinct overview of the effects of Ahab's quarter-deck speech: "I, Ishmael, was one of that crew; my shouts had gone up with the rest; my oath had been welded with theirs; and stronger I shouted, and more did I hammer and clinch my oath, because of the dread in my soul. A wild, mystical, sympathetical feeling was in me; Ahab's quenchless feud seemed mine. With greedy ears I learned the history of that murderous monster against whom I and all the others had taken our oaths of violence and revenge" (41:155).[13]

This single passage evinces nearly all the key markers of esotericism and sacrifice we uncovered in Nietzsche's texts. We find: a mythic, sacrificial fight— "Ahab's quenchless feud," "oaths of violence and revenge"; the vague feeling of guilt—"the dread in my soul"; the workings of subconscious, esoteric affect to unify leader and group—"a wild, mystical, sympathetical feeling was in me"; and, finally, the use of overdetermined, anachronistic symbols and myths to influence a contemporary political movement—"with greedy ears I learned the history of that murderous monster." Such a cluster of effects seems closely related to what *The Birth of Tragedy* calls the "aesthetic phenomenon," whereby a "dramatist" speaks out of other bodies and souls and a "whole throng" experiences Dionysian "transformation." Ishmael has lost his individuality, been possessed by Ahab and united with the crew: "Ahab's quenchless feud seemed mine," "my shouts had gone up with the rest; my oath had been welded with theirs."

Ishmael's description of this uncanny form of control is hardly an isolated example of the deep connection between Ahab's power and sacred violence. I can only provide a very condensed account here of the abundant evidence in the novel revealing esotericism and sacrifice at the heart of Ahab's character and project. Using the concepts derived from Nietzsche as an organizing principle, we will look for key references to sacrifice itself; for analyses of lying and esoteric control; for the complex appearance of "yesterday" in "today," that is, for anachronistic qualities in Ahab that parallel Nietzsche's use of the ancient Greeks to communicate dangerous truths in the modern world; and for the "aesthetic phenomenon," the quarter-deck stage as a site for enacting political manipulation.

Moby Dick is Ahab's sacrificial victim, and surrounding victimage (according to Girard) there grows a mythology. The whale's mythic resonance is not related to its identity as natural force or supernatural evil, it is engendered by the "Arkansas duellist" consciousness of the *Pequod*'s captain. Moby Dick is Ahab's mythic double:

The White Whale swam before him as the monomaniac incarnation of all those malicious agencies which some deep men feel eating in them, till they are left living on with half a heart and half a lung. That intangible malignity which has been from the beginning; to whose dominion even the modern Christians ascribe one-half of the worlds; which the ancient Ophites of the east reverenced in their statue devil;—Ahab did not fall down and worship it like them; but deliriously transferring its idea to the abhorred white whale, he pitted himself, all mutilated, against it. (41:160)

Melville's novel examines not only scapegoating but the mythopoesis connected with it, the cyclical process whereby humanity strives to achieve oneness by projecting inner divisions outside itself, only to create thereby new splits, ambiguities, and conflict. The identities and differences created in this unstable process lead to undifferentiation, symbolized in the spectacular shipwreck that ends Ahab's quest. The simulacrum of oneness in the *monomaniac incarnation* constitutes a *schizophrenic fantasy* generated by "malicious agencies" dividing the subject, such that a division expresses itself in a unity, and a psychic figment appears as flesh. Thus, the "fixed and fearless, forward dedication" of Ahab's gaze (28:111), his determined search for the real whale that "swims before" his ship is oriented by the imagined whale that "swims before" Ahab's mind, confounding the difference between reality and fantasy. Thus, the verb "swim" not only vacillates between a literal meaning (the whale's motion) and a figurative one (confusion), it designates the very vacillation or blur between metaphor and reality in the violent, mythic consciousness.

As Ahab himself later makes explicit in his famous "Candles" speech, the difference between worship and defiance collapses in the "delirious transference" of metaphor, too. The Ophites' worship consisted of making sacrifices to propitiate the devil, using violence to counteract the fear of violence. However fearlessly he may be doing so, in "transferring" the idea of the devil to the body of the whale and attacking it, Ahab merely repeats the sacrificial gesture of the Ophites at another level; he remains trapped in a relation of doubles where the only saving action imaginable is *elimination*. The text uses the image of the half—an entity created by splitting one into two and eliminating one—to symbolize this paradox of ongoing self-mutilation: evil consumes all but "half a heart and half a lung" in a person, and Christianity ascribes "one-half of the worlds" to the devil, thereby violating the unity of the subject and the goodness of God by drawing them into an antagonism with a counter-principle that can only be violent. The only pervasive, unifying element in Ahab's universe is the inherently disintegrative relation of conflict: "that intangible malignity which has been from the beginning." This underlying hostility undoes differences at every level—between reverence and resistance; between modern, monotheistic Christians and ancient, dualistic Ophites; between humanity and its evil gods; and between body and soul: "his torn body and gashed soul bled into one another; and so interfusing, made him mad" (41:160).

Ahab's soliloquy in Chapter 37, "Sunset," clearly shows the chain of repetitions into which this vortex of doubling and dedifferentiation drags him: "The prophecy was that I should be dismembered; and—Aye! I lost this leg. I now prophesy that I will dismember my dismemberer. Now, then, be the prophet and the fulfiller one. That's more than ye, ye great gods, ever were" (37:147).

Ahab proposes a fantastic attempt to reachieve a lost unity and indeed to transcend divinity through a compounded series of dismemberments. Again we find the economy of sacrifice perpetuating the process of elimination, the attempt to restore divided wholeness by cutting. In Nietzsche we observed a similar pattern: the sacrificial killing of God leads to the need for new sacred games, new forms of sacrifice and deception to provide consolation. His defiant Promethean artist destroys gods and creates men only to suffer from the vulture of shame, the answering wrath of offended deities within himself. *Moby-Dick* associates Ahab with Prometheus in terms that strongly resemble Nietzsche's: "God help thee, old man, thy thoughts have created a creature in thee; and he whose intense thinking thus makes him a Prometheus; a vulture feeds on that heart for ever; that vulture the very creature he creates" (44:175).

The doubling of esoteric communication, its divided language, thus has its root in a doubled condition within the communicator:

Captain Ahab was by no means unobservant of the paramount forms and usages of the sea. Nor, perhaps, will it fail to be eventually perceived, that behind those forms and usages, as it were, he sometimes masked himself; incidentally making use of them for other and more private ends than they were legitimately intended to subserve. The certain sultanism of his brain, which had otherwise in a good degree remained unmanifested; through these forms that same sultanism became incarnate in an irresistible dictatorship. For be a man's intellectual superiority what it will, it can never assume the practical, available supremacy over other men, without the aid of some sort of external arts and entrenchments, always, in themselves, more or less paltry and base. (33:129)

The paradoxes of Ahab's political performance are multiple. In order to strike through the mask that all visible objects present, Ahab needs to mask himself. In order to pursue his noble end, he must stoop to means that are base. In order to overcome the psychic disintegration within him, Ahab feels compelled to create external forms of hyperbolic bodily unity: his "monomaniac incarnation" of the scapegoat in Moby Dick; the embodiment of irresistible power in his person; and the dictatorship "incarnate" in the unified crew. Sacrifice, then, at once creates and fractures unity, in the self, in society, and in communication. As we saw in Nietzsche, too, this split condition forces Ahab to engage in a complex game of revealing and concealing: "the subtle insanity of Ahab respecting Moby Dick was noways more significantly manifested than in his superlative sense and shrewdness in foreseeing that, for the present, the hunt should be stripped of that strange, imaginative impiousness which naturally invested it" (46:183). Thus, esotericism gains power by masking it, enacts violence by covering it over, and endows sacrifice with meaning by marshalling and then diluting its inherent imaginative force.

The fullest, most astonishing image of divided being as the esoteric, sacrificial essence of power comes at the end of the "Moby Dick" chapter:

This is much; yet Ahab's larger, darker, deeper part remains unhinted. But vain to popularize profundities, and all truth is profound. Winding far down from within this spiked Hotel de Cluny where we here stand—however grand and wonderful, now quit it—and take your way, ye nobler, sadder souls, to those vast Roman halls of Thermes; where far beneath the fantastic towers of man's upper earth, his root of grandeur sits in bearded state; an antique buried beneath antiquities, and throned on torsoes! So with a broken throne, the great gods mock that captive king; so like a Caryatid, he patiently sits, upholding on his frozen brow the piled entablatures of ages. Wind ye down there, ye prouder, sadder souls! question that proud, sad king! A family likeness! Aye, he did beget ye, ye young exiled royalties; and from your grim sire only will the old State-secret come. (41:161)

From this rich passage, I will extract only three important points. First of all, we see here a graphic depiction of the effort I have claimed is essential in Melville's novel as a whole—that of "winding far down," unveiling and exposing the underpinnings of esotericism and anti-democratic political power. Unlike Nietzsche's text, whose esoteric depths only became apparent when decoded, *Moby-Dick* thematizes esotericism and its elitist presumptions as such. I take this to be the reason the text leaves Ahab behind after the first sentence to discuss secrets of power and history in general, and ends by turning to "young exiled royalties," whose "nobler, prouder, sadder" natures render them out of place among the "fantastic towers" of the liberal, democratic American state, "where we here stand." Second, as we observed in Nietzsche's cryptic suggestions about the Greeks as interpreters and in his use of Greek art deities in *The Birth of Tragedy*, one of the key features of esotericism is its relation to the ancient past. A crucial part of Ahab's domination, too, is the association he cultivates with kings, emperors, and non-Christian forms of religious and political authority: the prophet, the Titan, the sultan. The text's image of an imperial Roman underside to Christian civilization suggests that a superficial covering has been cast over a terrible, unchanging essence. Modern democracy will have to go deeper to face the disturbing persistence of the past if it is to vindicate its inherited Christian faith in the "just Spirit of Equality." In the tragic plot of the novel itself, of course, that reckoning fails to take place, and that is perhaps another reason the narrator turns to the reader explicitly at just this point: recognitions will have to come in the reading of the book.

Third, as I have been arguing, the "old State-secret," the terrible ancient essence that persists even below illusions of progress, is sacrifice, the violent basis of state power and civilization in warfare and killing. Clues for this reading are numerous. The dominant architectural metaphors of temple, tomb, and palace in this passage all relate to sacrifice and concealment: the temple as the site of killing and burning corpses; the tomb as the shrine where corpses are at once honored and hidden away;[14] and the palace as the locus of religiously sanctioned authority, a "bearded state" of patriarchal power throned on "torsoes," the broken bodies of the victims of war and sacrifice. The idea of the gods mocking the captive king evokes directly the ancient ritual connection explored by Girard between sacrificial victimage (traditionally involving crowning and mocking as echoed for example in Christ's passion narrative as well as carnival festivities) and the institution of kingship.[15] Our analysis of sacrificial myth as trapping the mythic, sovereign subject in crippling, distortive repetitions also illuminates the notion of the king as "an antique buried beneath antiquities," upholding "piled entablatures of ages," since these images combine a sense of death and burial with concealing, doubling, and ceaseless repetition through history, right down to the reader who sees in the king a family likeness, another double.

The surprising link between sacrifice and the origins of power is further confirmed by the central imagery in *Moby-Dick* as it relates to the names *Leviathan*, *Ahab*, and *Pequod*. In a verse of Isaiah immediately preceding a verse cited by Melville in the "Extracts" we read of an apocalypse, a revelation overturning earthly empires and uncovering concealed bloodshed and victims: "the earth also shall disclose her blood, and shall no more cover her slain." (Isaiah 26:21) The next verse links this uncovering to the *sacrifice of Leviathan*: "In that day, the Lord with his sore, and great, and strong sword, shall punish Leviathan the piercing serpent, even Leviathan that crooked serpent; and he shall slay the dragon that is in the sea" (Isaiah 27:1 as cited in "Extracts," 2). The name *Ahab* itself further extends this Biblical motif of sacrifice and sovereignty: it was during Ahab's reign as chronicled in 1 Kings 16-22 that this king is said to have made sacrifices to Baal, leading to Elijah's terrible competition with the prophets of Baal to establish which god ought to receive sacrifices. Ahab's name thus links him to the greatest sacrificial crisis in the Old Testament, one in which the very religious and political foundations of the state were at issue. Finally, *Pequod* was of course the name of the tribe with whom the Puritans had their earliest and bloodiest war; the Puritans narrated their massacre of that tribe as the providential seal of the legitimacy of their new covenant.

All three of these examples demonstrate important motifs that we have traced to sacrifice and esotericism. In each of them, a new order founds itself in an act of historical elimination vis-à-vis an older, darker world—Leviathan the dragon was a remnant of pre-Israelite myth, Baal was the supreme Canaanite deity before Israel's entrance into that land, and the Pequods were the indigenous peoples of the land the Puritans wanted to claim. In the way Ahab relates to these historical crises, he can be seen, like Nietzsche, to *resist* conforming to the providential and Christian sense of divine purpose (God's rule, Israel's prophet, Puritan covenant), and to draw strength from an identification with anti-Christian, pagan figures and their sacrificial rites (Leviathan, Baal, Indians). Ahab wants to assume God's role in the apocalyptic scenario, to sacrifice the Leviathan himself, for his own reasons, and he allies himself with Fedallah and with his pagan, heathenish crew—all of them remnants of that primordial, non-Christian order—in order to accomplish his object.

When Ahab first appears on the quarter-deck, Ishmael's description immediately associates him with the heretical victim of a fiery sacrifice: "he looked like a man cut away from the stake" (28:109). Ahab himself repeats this association of fire, sacrifice, and his identity in the opening words of his "Candles" speech, "Oh! thou clear spirit of clear fire, whom on these seas I as a Persian once did worship, till in the sacramental act so burned by thee that to this hour I bear the scar" (119:416). Ishmael's second image refers to a Greek example: "[Ahab's body was] . . . shaped in an unalterable mould, like Cellini's cast Perseus" (28:110). In the statue alluded to here, Perseus holds the head of the slain Titan monster, Medusa—another instance of new order emerging from the killing of a monstrous victim. The rest of the initial description of Ahab discusses the competing superstitions among the crew regarding his scar as either the trace of a lightning strike or a birthmark. Both of the competing stories suggest emphatically that Ahab is the subject of dark prophecy, a victim of divine violence and curse. In all of these elements in our first extended view of Ahab's character, the allusions point to a combination of sacred violence, sacrificial acts, sovereignty, and pre- or anti-Christian religion. This strain climaxes with crucifixion imagery, imagery implying that Ahab has usurped Christ's divine role as simultaneously suffering victim and all-powerful king: "moody stricken Ahab stood before them with a crucifixion in his face; in all the nameless regal overbearing dignity of some mighty woe" (28:111).

It is precisely the mesmerizing effect of this evocation of victimage and sacrifice that transforms the crew when Ahab presents his esoteric quarter-deck performance on the "true" purpose of the *Pequod*'s voyage: "And this is what ye have shipped for, men!" he declares with peremptory, illocutionary force, making it so by saying it (36:143). " More and more strangely and fiercely glad and approving, grew the countenance of the old man at every shout; while the mariners began to gaze curiously at each other, as if marvelling how it was that they themselves became so excited at such seemingly purposeless questions. But, they were all eagerness again, as Ahab, now half-revolving in his pivot-hole, with one hand reaching high up a shroud, and tightly, almost convulsively grasping it, addressed them" (36:141-42).

In this scene, Melville portrays the mythic, collective dynamic of sacrificial violence that runs through the most baffling, "irrational" episodes in modern history, not least of course in U.S. history, including lynchings, riots, mob violence, red scares, racism, revolutionary blood-baths, massacres, genocides, and mass warfare, all of which are modern forms of scapegoating that imperfectly and catastrophically try to recapture the unifying power of the sacred in a pluralized, secularized context. Although I will not have the space here to elaborate a reading of the essential "Quarter-deck" chapter, I will conclude with some brief suggestions about the relevance of my thesis to that complicated episode. The Girardian theory of sacrifice and the comparison with Nietzsche help us see the following in a new light: Ahab's ambivalent role as victim and heroic leader; his use of the hunt as scapegoating, and (in the speech to Starbuck) his attack on God as a particularly modern form of it; his use of Satanic and other non-Christian rituals and references; Ahab's alliance with the pagan harpooneers; the revelation of the "little lower layer" speech as another instance of exposing esoteric thought; the appropriation of Shakespearean tragedy, which itself had begun exploring the violent paradoxes of murder and state power in the modern world; the prominence of both stage theatrics and of grog as promoting intoxication; the scandalized discomfort of the American-born, more rational mates (esp. Starbuck) throughout the ceremonies.

As I have tacitly implied throughout my interpretation, I am critical of political readings of *Moby-Dick* that separate artificially (as nearly all of them have) its political from its religious themes: the novel's most radical political insights anticipate the esoteric critique of religion cum political philosophy that Nietzsche developed, and this prophetic character stems precisely from its exploration of the sacred roots of violent political elitism. The fact that neither this aspect of Melville's work, nor the esoteric politics of Nietzsche's writing have been well understood—in spite of the rich scholarly interpretations of both— suggests that we are just beginning to see the relevance of their alternative tragic visions for postmodern democracy.[16] In view of the tremendous prestige Nietzsche's esoteric philosophy currently enjoys, I would suggest that there are contemporary threats to the philosophical underpinnings of democratic society that we would do well to consider and call into question, and I believe *Moby-Dick* can help us in that vital effort. As Melville's novel implies and Girard makes explicit: "The whole of humanity is already confronted with an ineluctable dilemma: human beings must become reconciled without the aid of sacrificial intermediaries or resign themselves to the imminent extinction of humanity."[17]

NOTES

1   Cesáreo Bandera, *The Sacred Game: The Role of the Sacred in the Genesis of Modern Literary Fiction*, (University Park: Penn State UP, 1994), 39.

2   For the fullest versions of this thesis, see in addition to Bandera's book René Girard, *Things Hidden Since the Foundation of the World* (Stanford, CA: Stanford UP, 1987). [Henceforth noted as *Things Hidden.*]

3   Friedrich Nietzsche, *The Gay Science*, tr. Walter Kaufmann (New York: Random House, 1974), § 125, 181.

4   Friedrich Nietzsche, *The Will to Power*, tr. Walter Kaufmann (New York: Random House, 1967), § 859, 458.

5   Friedrich Nietzsche, *Human, All too Human*, Volume Two, Part One, "Assorted Opinions and Maxims," § 218, tr. R. J. Hollingdale (Cambridge: Cambridge UP, 1996).

6   Friedrich Nietzsche, *The Birth of Tragedy and The Case of Wagner*, tr. Walter Kaufmann (New York: Random House, 1967), § 1, 33. Translation modified. [Henceforth noted as *Birth* with section & page number.]

7   This piece is not available in English. The sentence is my translation of the opening line from the German "Dionysische Weltanschauung," published in Colli-Montinari, eds., *Friedrich Nietzsche. Sämtliche Werke. Kritische Studienausgabe* (Munich and Berlin: dtv and de Gruyter, 1988), Volume 1, 553. This edition of the complete works includes all of Nietzsche's writing, published and unpublished, in a carefully edited, definitive issue. The first volume will be cited henceforth as SW 1, with page number.

8   "Der Griechische Staat," SW 1, 767.

9   "Der Griechische Staat," SW 1, 770-71.

10   "Der Griechische Staat," SW 1, 776.

11   *Birth*, § 8, 64

12   *Birth*, § 9, 70-71.

13   Herman Melville, *Moby-Dick*, Norton Critical Edition, ed. Harrison Hayford and Hershel Parker (New York: Norton, 1967), 155. To facilitate reference to other editions, citations will be noted in parentheses with the chapter number followed by the page number.

14   Girard comments: "Tombs exist to honor the dead, but also to hide them in so far as they are dead, to conceal the corpse and ensure that death as such is no longer visible. This act of concealment is essential." *Things Hidden*, 163.

15   Girard, *Things Hidden*, 51-57.

16   My reading of Nietzsche is heavily indebted to the groundbreaking book by Geoff Waite, *Nietzsche's Corps/e* (Durham, NC: Duke UP, 1996), in which Waite explores the thesis that Nietzsche's esoteric writing has been the crucial determining factor in his 20th-century reception. Waite does not, however, link esotericism with Girardian theory of sacrifice as I have tried to do in this paper.

17   Girard, *Things Hidden*, 136.

REFERENCES

Bandera, Cesáreo. *The Sacred Game: The Role of the Sacred in the Genesis of Modern Literary Fiction*. University Park, PA: Penn State UP, 1994.

Girard, René. *Things Hidden Since the Foundation of the World*. Stanford, CA: Stanford UP, 1987.

Melville, Herman. *Moby-Dick*. Norton Critical Edition. Ed. Harrison Hayford and Herschel Parker. New York: Norton, 1967.

Nietzsche, Friedrich. *The Birth of Tragedy and The Case of Wagner*. Tr. Walter Kaufmann. New York: Random House, 1967.

——. *The Gay Science*. Tr. Walter Kaufmann. New York: Random House, 1974.

——. *Human, All too Human*. Tr. R. J. Hollingdale. Cambridge: Cambridge UP, 1996.

——. *Sämtliche Werke. Kritische Studienausgabe*. Ed. Giorgio Colli and Mazzino Montinari. Münich and Berlin: dtv and de Gruyter, 1988.

——. *The Will to Power*. Tr. Walter Kaufmann. New York: Random House, 1967.

Waite, Geoff. *Nietzsche's Corps/e*. Durham, NC: Duke UP, 1996.

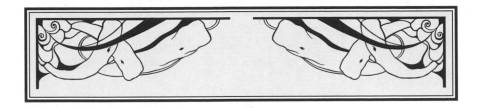

Anna Hellén

Melville and the Temple of Literature

Introduction

The body of critical works in recent years devoted to revaluating and reformulating the relationship between popular culture and the Romantic legacy or high culture, has also offered a revised account of Herman Melville's authorship. The prevalent view of Melville as the creative genius, misunderstood by his contemporary critics and readers and tragically tortured in the literary marketplace, has been challenged in favor of a more nuanced and historically more veracious appreciation of his writings in relation to the commercial forces which nevertheless controlled his achievements. Exploring the interrelations between Melville's development as a writer and the structural changes literature went through after the Romantic period, I will argue that Melville's way of understanding his position in relation to the literary marketplace reached a turning point with *Moby-Dick*. Previously known and cherished primarily for his popular travel narratives, he now set out to integrate his earlier mode of writing with a new literary orientation informed by Romantic theory. More explicitly, in *Moby-Dick* he sought to negotiate the incipient tension between highbrow and lowbrow culture by fashioning a literary space for his novel which enabled him to withdraw symbolically from the literary marketplace at the same time as it allowed him to fully acknowledge and respond to its demands. After *Moby-Dick*'s relative failure, however, Melville grew increasingly pessimistic about such a bivalent undertaking, and his later works are accordingly characterized by what may best be described as an unequivocal aversion to eclecticism and modern commercialism.

This paper falls into three parts. First, Melville and American antebellum culture will be related to what I will refer to as the Romantic temple, a metaphor which epitomizes the design to construct a revered cultural realm at one remove from what was seen as a disruptive and alienating commercialization of art and literature. Next, with an emphasis on the Etymology and Extracts scenes, I will argue that *Moby-Dick* can be read precisely as an attempt to establish a temple of literature set apart from the reductive Grub-Street aspects of literary production. However, instead of discarding the expressions of the literary market Melville sought to subsume them into the very groundwork of his temple through an act of literary sublimation. Samuel Johnson's extraordinary development from usher to sovereign of the world of literature (as it is depicted in Boswell's biography, which Melville read and most likely integrated into his image of the "pale usher") will be used in this context to further elucidate Melville's authorial aspirations. Last, I will suggest that Melville in his later career came to question and even distrust his sublimating capacities. In his lecture "Statues in Rome," the heterogeneous temple has consequently been replaced by a temple of Classical art, which is depicted as being exempt from commercialism and altogether uncontaminated by the social world of politics and technical and scientific progress.

1. Melville's "Botches": The Romantic Temple and American Antebellum Culture

In Romantic aesthetics the temple-building, devoid of specific sociopolitical connotations, is a common symbol for the ideal dwelling place for art. Hegel, for example, holds that the temple is where one can encounter Absolute Spirit *through* the work of art: "when architecture has prepared the temple, and the hand of sculpture has placed in it the statue of the god, then this sensuously present deity is confronted in the wide halls of his home" (qtd. in Ziolkowski 329).[1] In *Pierre*, Melville likewise compares literary creation with the construction of a temple, an undertaking which is presented as being intimately connected with theoretical awareness: "[T]here are immense quarries of fine marble but how to get it out; how to chisel it; how to construct any temple? Youth must . . . go and thoroughly study architecture. Now the quarry-discoverer is long before the stone-cutter; and the stone-cutter is long before the architect, and the architect is long before the temple; for the temple is the crown of the world" (*Pierre* 257). Before we go further into Melville's theoretical quarries, however, we must get a clearer idea of how the Romantic temple was first conceived.

The most concrete and successful realization of the Romantic project is most likely nineteenth-century museum culture. As Theodore Ziolkowski shows, taking the Altes Museum in Berlin of 1830 as his example, the art museum simultaneously embodies and corroborates the most significant conceptions of art that emerged during the Romantic period. The Altes Museum was the first museum to be designed exclusively for the display of art objects and was germinal to nineteenth-century museum architecture in the entire Western world. What made it epochal was first and foremost that its design was wholly bent on emphasizing the integrity, both of the individual art objects and of art as an integrated concept. For instance, the first floor was dedicated exclusively to statues, but these were not, as in the Louvre and other museums, randomly put against the walls but placed on special pedestals so that each statue could be contemplated in isolation. Above all, designed as a temple with a rotunda, the museum provided the art objects with a sacred and practically desocialized symbolical setting (Ziolkowski 309-21). Accordingly, side by side in an otherwise blank museum-space the objects mirrored, not primarily ancient cultures or systems of beliefs, but each other's status as art. Equally important, it was this radical decontextualization which made it possible to link together objects that originally served their purpose as parts of other institutions (as signs of political power or religious sanctity) under the new denomination *art*. According to André Malraux, "[a] Romanesque crucifix was not regarded by its contemporaries as a work of sculpture, nor Cimbue's *Madonna* as a picture. Even Pheidias' *Pallas Athene* was not, primarily, a statue. . . . [The museums] bulked so large in the nineteenth century and are so much part of our lives today that we forget that they have imposed on the spectator a wholly new attitude towards the work of art. For they have tended to estrange the works they bring together from their original functions and to transform even portraits into pictures" (13-14).[2]

In this temple-building, then, the Romantic idea of art was successfully realized. Analogously, the idea of an art of letters, which includes poetry, drama, and prose, is fundamentally Romantic and was unheard of until the very end of the eighteenth century. At this time, what had formerly been known by the more narrow terms "belles lettres" or "'poetry" gave way to a broader category which came to include all types of imaginative writing, regardless of genre or historical origin.[3] Hence in the potentially disintegrating process by which the written word fell off from the church and the crown and was left to fend for itself as a commodity in the marketplace, imaginative writing found a renewed authority and *raison d'être* in the generic constitution of literature.

Literature as a unified field thus came into being through a strategy of amalgamation, something which can be said to characterize the Romantic literary agenda at large: the early Romantics most typically conceived of imaginative writing as an open-ended and diversified field, capable of subsuming all genres and forms of knowledge. Accordingly, the temple of literature was not originally averse to eclecticism—in fact, its very foundation rested on eclectic ground. However, this eclectic constellation subsequently came to forge a new unity, which in due course would become set in a fixed mold. Seemingly paradoxically, as we have seen happening with the literary canon, what had come into being through a coalescence of a diversity of cultural expressions turned into a normative screen by which certain cultural expressions were incorporated and some excluded.

The museum as a manifestation of Romantic theory also has a more concrete literary counterpart. As Azade Seyhan has shown, the *Athenäum*, the journal which became the intellectual center of early Jena Romanticism, was also the center for an undertaking of impressive proportions whose aim it was to assemble fragments from different fields of knowledge, such as philosophy, rhetoric, criticism, science, and religion and weld them together in a great universal encyclopedia. Through this reconfiguration of knowledge—a kind of reversed interdisciplinary movement—the Romantics sought to reconstruct what was thought to have once been a unified body of texts but which had subsequently been dissociated and dispersed into different faculties. One can say that the encyclopedic enterprise, like the Romantic project as a whole, was governed by two different and to some extent also contradictory impulses. For on the one hand, it aimed at creating a total and completely coherent system; on the other hand the ideal form for this project was the fragment, which was to vouch for the open-ended and limitless constitution of the system. What was ultimately understood to keep the entire project together was the ascendant and unifying powers of literature (Seyhan 93). As Schlegel puts it, "the realization of the encyclopedia requires that all art and knowledge and criticism be resolved, in the final analysis, in poetry" (qtd. in Seyhan 96):[4] In fact, all discourses were believed to attain higher standing and truth-value *as* literature, which, however, is not the same as to say that the Romantics were naïve believers in the *representational* power of literature. On the contrary, when representation had become a problem for itself, especially in the aftermath of Kant's critical philosophy, literature seemed to offer a way out. Allegedly capable of transcending mere representation, aesthetic language was considered a suitable medium for the expression of higher truths, truths that no other discipline or discourse could lay claims on, let alone enunciate.[5] In Schlegel's view the ideal encyclopedic text is the Bible, which, re-examined in Romantic terms, becomes a "perfect literature" by virtue of its fundamentally *inclusive* nature. The Bible is, according to Schlegel, a "system of books," "eternally in a state of becoming" (qtd. in Seyhan 94). More interesting for my purposes, however, is that the novel—perceived by the Romantics as a blend of different forms of knowledge and genres—was also considered the model realization of the encyclopedia: for Schelling all writing, regardless of genre, that fulfills the encyclopedic project is *by definition* a novel. As we shall see, *Moby-Dick* agrees with the encyclopedic ideal delineated above, not only through its generic constitution, but also through its conscious design to employ "literariness" as a unifying device.

In mid-nineteenth-century America, Romantic ideas were only slowly starting to influence the cultural climate as a whole. In Lawrence Levine's analysis, this manifested itself as a "sacralization of culture," which he defines as the process by which the eclectic turns into the specific and the general into the exclusive, most notably accompanied by a rather vague religious terminology (Levine 146). However, most cultural manifestations were still characterized by a general eclecticism, an institutionalized heterogeneity, which also prevailed in the museums. Neil Harris has described the typical American museum in the first half of the nineteenth century: "paintings and sculpture stood alongside mummies, mastodon bones and stuffed animals. American museums were not, in the antebellum period, segregated temples of the fine arts, but repositories of information, collections of strange or doubtful data" (qtd. in Levine 146-47). It was not until the beginning of the twentieth century that Benjamin Ives Gilman, secretary of the Boston museum, declared that "a museum of art is in essence a temple" (qtd. in Levine 155).

Just as painting and sculpture occupied no sacred place set apart from other forms of expressive culture, there was no elevated novel genre during the period of Melville's career. Prose fiction, as Richard Brodhead argues, thrived as a kind of writing which "merged high and low into a 'universal' popular audience" (Brodhead 24). Melville's deprecation of his authorial achievements in a much quoted letter to Hawthorne has most typically been interpreted as a characterization of his own intermediary position between highbrow and lowbrow genres: "What I feel most moved to write, that is banned, it will not pay. Yet altogether write the *other* way I cannot. So the product is a final hash, and all my books are botches" (Leyda 412). However, as no such distinctive genres existed, "botches" is really a fitting description of antebellum American literary climate in general, at least as far as the novel is concerned. This is, of course, especially true of the mixed form narrative, a novel form which mixed fact and fiction, popular genres and metaphysical speculation.[6] A common and generally accepted genre in England as well as in America, it also served as the vehicle for Melville's temple construction in *Moby-Dick*.

With his third novel *Mardi*, Melville initially intended another travel narrative like *Omoo*, but, searching for an alternative novel space, he soon altered his course and started experimenting with the mixed form narrative. However, having obvious problems circumscribing this alternative fictional realm, he wrote to his publisher: "It is something new I assure you, & original if nothing more. But I can give you no adequate idea of it. . . . My instinct is better than acquired wisdom" (*Letters* 71). As Nina Baym points out, the reason for *Mardi*'s failure was probably not the mixed form per se, but that its overall purpose and aim were blatantly unclear, even to Melville himself (Baym 913). As one contemporary critic puts it with resignation, "we never saw a book so like a kaleidoscope. As for giving any idea of it, we have none ourselves" (Leyda 293). *Moby-Dick*, by contrast, makes use of the mixed form narrative with greater precision, and as we shall see, it also breathes new life into the genre through its Romantic and, more specifically, *encyclopedic* constitution.

2. *Moby-Dick*: Constructing the Temple

There are several indications that the trip to Europe that preceded the writing of *Moby-Dick* also had a bearing on the novel's general constitution and direction. In Melville's journal two recurrent activities stand out from beginning to end: museum visits and discussions about German Romantic theory with George J. Adler, professor of German at New York University. The following entry is characteristic: "We talked metaphysics continually, & Hegel, Schlegel, Kant &c were discussed under the influence of whiskey" (*Journal 1849-1850*, 4). When Melville subsequently returned to America, Adler wrote to their mutual acquaintance Evert Duyckinck that the "instinctive impulse of [Melville's] imagination to assimilate and perhaps to work up into some beautiful chimaeras . . . the materials he had already gathered in his travels, would not allow him to prolong his stay" (Leyda 343). Hence, filled with new experiences and with a heightened theoretical awareness he started writing *Moby-Dick* with a sense of a unifying design, which had been lacking in *Mardi*. As we have seen, however, in antebellum America there was no temple-space reserved for novels of "beautiful chimaeras," and the groundwork of Melville's temple would therefore differ from that of European high Romanticism: it would seek to conflate commercial and artistic aspirations.

Melville was not alone in this particular endeavor. In America the system of patronage had never taken root, and whereas the European Romantics generally saw the literary market as degrading and disruptive of a literary tradition, many American writers of the antebellum period acknowledged the interdependence between a commercialization of the literary text and writing as a specialized vocation released from genteel amateurism. Accordingly, several of the writers known today as the Transcendentalists, rather than turning their backs on the marketplace, sought to combine Romantic aestheticism with capitalist expansionism. A most overt example of this is Emerson's optimistic claim that "[t]he statue is so beautiful that it contracts no stain from the market, but makes the market a silent gallery for itself" (698). The statue, in other words, harbors

335

the power to turn the market into one vast temple of art. Analogously, what is fascinating is that Melville deployed the same strategy when seeking to stake out a new ground for his novel as the early Romantics did when first setting out to corroborate the idea of literature, but with one important exception: Melville's encyclopedic enterprise aspires to resolve all genres and perspectives in poetry (to repeat Schlegel's call above) *including* the expressions of the literary marketplace.

Many critics have commented on the self-reflexive strain of *Moby-Dick*; the constant reminders of its essential "literariness," a trait which was not lost on Melville's contemporary readers either: "Who would have looked for philosophy in whales, or for poetry in blubber?" a reviewer in *John Bull* asks enthusiastically (Leyda 431). More recently, Sheila Post-Lauria has explored how the novel offers "a new metaphysical—and metafictional—level," which she claims is an innovation in the mixed-form narrative in the sense that it blurs the distinction between physical reality and the "literary world of the narrative" (113). Paul Royster, finally, focuses on the novel's "conscious attention to the task of constructing itself as language," especially the intimate interplay between "industrial production and literary construction" (313). As we shall see, this intense preoccupation with its own status as a literary creation is manifest already in the novel's preliminary pages. Indeed, what makes the Extracts and Etymology sections so interesting is that they epitomize the quintessential scheme of the narrative as a whole. For though at once humorous and parody-like (an effect of the presumptuous yet naïve tone of the narrator), they nevertheless function as condensed mock-versions of the novel. Above all, as we shall see, what seems an arbitrary muddle of fragments in Extracts attains new purport in the literary rendering of the narrative.

Two encyclopedic stratagems emerge in the two introductory scenes. First, the fundamental openness of the novel is established: the narrator presents whale-knowledge from a great variety of disciplines and cultural realms, all supplied by a "poor sub-sub librarian" and a "consumptive usher to a grammar school." As this essential inclusiveness is characteristic of the novel as a whole it is symptomatic that Ishmael compares his work in the Cetology chapter, not to a temple, but to an unfinished cathedral of which he is the architect: "small erections may be finished by their first architects; grand ones, true ones, ever leave the copestone to posterity. God keep me from ever completing anything" (*Moby-Dick* 147). Seen in this light, Melville's novel does indeed appear to be an ideal encyclopedic text—"eternally in a state of becoming"—to repeat Schlegel's statement above. Equally important, however, the librarian has not only searched the libraries, or the "long Vaticans," for whale material but also the "street-stalls of the earth"—the place of purchase for more quotidian reading. The extracts he displays are accordingly not only taken from disciplines such as etymology, theology, and philosophy, but also include popular literary genres such as travel narratives and journalistic material such as newspaper articles. Correspondingly, as has been shown by a number of twentieth-century critics, the story of the white whale is by no means a unique creation of Melville's imagination, but has sources among a variety of popular writings.

Second, the ascendancy of literary power is affirmed, primarily through the exalted status of the writer who not only provides a "bird's eye view of what has been promiscuously said, thought, fancied, and sung of the Leviathan, by many nations and generations, including our own," but who also initiates a process of literary sublimation. In the two scenes described in the preliminary pages we are introduced to two pallid, powerless ghosts, whose voiceless isolation in their dungeons of books is at last penetrated by the narrator, who can relate to and sympathize with their predicament but who is also fully conscious of the fact that he does not belong there. His role is instead to be the spokesman for that which cannot transcend its paltry confinement: "So fare thee well, poor devil of a Sub-Sub, *whose commentator I am.* Thou belongest to that sallow tribe which no wine of this world will ever warm; and for whom even pale sherry would be too rosy-strong, but with whom one sometimes loves to sit, and feel poor-devilish too" (xxiii; emphasis mine).

Recovered from the dusty godforsaken shelves of the old disciplines and institutions *and* from the evanescence of the commercial realms, the extracts and etymological entries also presage a continuance in the sovereign realm of literature. In other words, their symbolic significance is poignant since the ensuing literary voyage is largely made up of a similar blend of material. Ishmael's having "swam through libraries" as he reminds us of in the in the Cetology chapter, is not intended to result in a superficial compilation of whale material—"no ordinary letter-sorter in the Post-Office is equal to it." On the contrary, Ishmael, although humble when facing his difficult task, hopes for nothing less than a glimpse of "the unspeakable foundations . . . of the world" (135). Accordingly, whereas other scientific books on whales are "full of leviathanism, but signifying nothing" (146), Ishmael sets out to search for that which cannot be adequately accounted for by "traditional" disciplines or modes of representation. Indeed, as "there is no *earthly* way of finding out precisely what the whale looks like" (274; emphasis mine), the sublimation of the whale material must involve taking it to a point beyond ordinary representation—even to the point where it becomes the "draught of a draught" (147). Conspicuously, Ishmael's systematization of the whale is accomplished by means of a bibliographical system—a genealogy of books—which he, equally conspicuously, leaves "standing . . . unfinished" since "any human thing supposed to be complete must . . . be faulty" (135).

What is emphasized in the preliminaries is also the distinction between two roles on the scene of literary production; that of the independent writer in control of his situation, material, and destiny, and that of the bondservant in the letter industry, the "mere painstaking burrower and grub-worm of a poor devil of a Sub-Sub." For like the librarian, the usher to the grammar school is caught in a literary nether world which gives a vague but deceitful intimation of transcendence: "The pale Usher—threadbare in coat, heart, body, and brain; I see him now. He was ever dusting his old grammars, with a queer handkerchief, mockingly embellished with all the gay flags of all the known countries of the world. He loved to dust his old grammars. It somehow mildly reminded him of his mortality." This character, however, remains elusive until we become aware of its derivation: a comparison between Melville's usher-figure and its eighteenth-century antecedent will further elucidate, not only the foundation of the Romantic temple in general, but also the impetus of Melville's specific sublimating strategies.

During his trip to England Melville bought Boswell's *Life of Johnson*. In Boswell's extensive biography a dismal period in Samuel Johnson's life, analogous to the usher's deplorable predicament in *Moby-Dick*, is depicted. Destitute and without a proper degree the young Johnson was compelled to accept a position as a grammar school usher, and, like Melville's usher, he is described as perishing in monotonous isolation: "In the forlorn state of his circumstances, he accepted an offer to be employed as usher, in the school of Market-Bosworth, in Leicestershire.... This employment was very irksome to him in every respect, and he complained grievously of it in his letters to his friend Mr. Hector.... The letters are lost; but Mr. Hector recollects his writing 'that the poet had described the dull sameness of his existence in these words, *'Vitam conitet una dies'* (one day contains the whole of my life); that it was unvaried as the note of the cuckoo; and that he did not know whether it was more disagreeable for him to teach, or the boys to learn, the grammar rules" (Boswell 84).[7]

The important difference between Johnson's and Melville's usher is of course that Johnson combined the roles of creative writer and wage slave, whereas it is the fundamental *difference* between the usher and the writer that is emphasized in Melville's version: Melville's narrator-writer is defined primarily through his distance from the usher, who is clearly that which the narrator is *not.* Indeed, the very absence of the writer in this scene emphasizes the contrast between the crude materiality of the usher's abode and the ethereal world of the narrator. Interestingly enough, Boswell's biography also makes it clear that the usher and the writer *should* not be the same person. When Johnson set up a private school he was nevertheless obliged to teach, something which Boswell regrets since his supreme intellectual capacity paradoxically made him ill-adapted for the task: "[H]e was not so well qualified for being a teacher of elements, and a conductor in learning by regular gradations, as men of inferior powers of mind. ... I am of opinion, that the greatest abilities are not only not required for this office, but render a man less fit for it" (Boswell 97-98).

In Boswell's interpretation, then, the writer-usher relation is practically a contradiction in terms. What eventually redeemed Johnson was above all his remarkable ability to adapt to, and subsequently also to master, the new conditions of the mechanical reproduction and commercialization of the literary text. The first important writer to make his way as a professional wage-earner, Johnson took great pride in his new role as a self-made man—free from the fetters of patronage and an incontestable sovereign of the world of literature. His remarkable career can therefore be described as a combination of willful dependence on the market and an alleged capacity to transcend a mere Grub-Street existence.[8] His boasting to Boswell that "[n]o man ... who ever lived by literature, has lived more independently than I have done" (Boswell 443) is no doubt an apt description of his status as a professional writer.

Struggling with his authorial identity in a commercialized literary environment, Melville must have been highly covetous of the self-assertive autonomy Johnson displays in Boswell's biography. However, two things of decisive importance had happened in between the careers of Johnson and Melville: namely the massive expansion of the literary market *and* the emergence of Romanticism as its ineluctable other. For it can be argued that Johnson not only participated in, but also to some extent controlled and mastered the forces of the literary market, and his authorial status can therefore be accounted for in terms of *real* power. What Romanticism provided Melville with, by contrast, was not a new authority or status in real terms, but a new way of *representing* literary activity and the role of the author. Above all, as the case of *Moby-Dick* reveals, it enabled him to construct a symbolic space in which authorial freedom and creativity are not at odds with commercial interests. Ishmael thus becomes Melville's ideal alter ego: without turning his back on the system of exchange like Thoreau, but sublimating it, he also fictionalizes a distance between the reductive and confining aspects of literary activity and the prophetic or Transcendental impetus. It is important to stress that Melville must have been only too aware that the distance indeed *was* fictional, which most likely also accounts for the ironic tone in the preliminary pages. This assertion is further supported by the fact that Melville too had, much to his dislike, been forced to work as a schoolteacher during a period of his life. The fact that he was subsequently able to live by his pen did not redeem him from an usher-like existence: only in a fictional temple-space such as *Moby-Dick* could he achieve such a thing.

3. Retreat into Museum Space

When he was condemned by the literary market, Melville in his turn condemned the market: two of his later novels, *Pierre* and *Israel Potter*, can both be read as mock-pleas for patronage. After several novelistic semi-failures (or worse) Melville more or less abandoned the novel form and entered the temple of "pure" art, or museum space—first as lecturer, then as poet. In the fall of

1856, in bad health and with borrowed money, he set out on a journey around Europe and the Levant, and as on his first journey to Europe a recurring event was visiting museums and various sites of historical interest. Home again, he turned to lecturing to support his family.[9] However, having lost his reputation as one of America's most entertaining and intriguing authors, he now also seems to have lost his belief in his sublimating power as writer. Interestingly enough, in his most famous lecture "Statues in Rome," he disregards his literary capacity altogether and reduces himself to a common museum visitor, or, perhaps more correctly, he leaves his role as the author with great creative powers and turns into a museum guide who can only marvel at the splendor of the art treasures and humbly convey these impressions to his audience: "Art strikes a chord in the lowest as well as in the highest. . . . With this explanation, I, who am neither critic nor connoisseur, thought fit to introduce some familiar remarks upon the sculptures in Rome, a subject which otherwise might be thought to lie peculiarly within the province of persons of a kind of cultivation to which I make no pretension" (Sealts 128-29).

Figuratively leading his audience through the city of Rome, Melville then deferentially contemplates the statues one by one in his attempt to "paint the appearance of Roman Statuary objectively" (129-30). Conspicuously, there is no hint of quotidian life or real persons behind the statues. To the contrary, it is "among the mute citizens that the stranger forms his most pleasing and cherished associations," and that constitute "the true undying population of Rome" (130). Hence, through Melville's eyes, the entire city of Rome turns into one vast museum: "On entering Rome itself, the visitor is greeted by thousands of statues. . . . Wherever you go in Rome, in streets, dwellings, churches, its gardens, its walks, its public squares, or its private grounds, on every hand statues abound" (130).

Melville concludes by comparing two ancient temples with two modern ones. First the Vatican, the temple of timeless art, is set up against the modern pseudo-culture of the Washington Patent Office, and the two are deemed totally incompatible: "The Vatican itself is the index of the ancient world, just as the Washington Patent Office is of the modern. But how is it possible to compare the one with the other, when things that are so totally unlike cannot be brought together? . . . [W]e boast much of our progress, of our energy, of our scientific achieve-

341

ments—though science is beneath art, just as the instinct is beneath the reason" (151-52). Next, the Colosseum is compared to the Crystal Palace, which in Melville's analysis is the prime temple of commerce and capitalism, representative of the decadence and transience of modern commercial society. Again the fundamental incompatibility of the modern commercialized world and the ancient world of great art is stressed—note also the utterly pessimistic attitude toward social change: "The ancients of the ideal description, instead of trying to turn their impracticable chimeras, as does the modern dreamer, into social and political prodigies, deposited them in great works of art, which still live while states and constitutions have perished, bequeathing to posterity not shameful defects but triumphant success. All the merchants in London have not enough in their coffers to re-produce the Apollo. If the Coliseum expresses the durability of Roman ideas, what does their Crystal Palace express? These buildings are exponents of the respective characters of the ancients and moderns. But will the glass of the one bide the hail storms of eighteen centuries as well as the travertine of the other?" (153-54).

After his short period as lecturer Melville turned to poetry, and just like "Statues in Rome," *Clarel* to a great extent reflects his Mediterranean tour of 1856-57. In this long poem Greek and Roman art constitute the organizing principle for his vision of the Holy Land, and what is emphasized is above all symmetry of form and completeness. If *Moby-Dick* is an unfinished cathedral—always in motion, never fixed—his last writings, with some exceptions, stand forth as temples of Classical art. *Moby-Dick* thus constitutes the critical moment in Melville's career when the coming together of different paradigms becomes the very momentum of literary creativity. This essentially optimistic attempt to achieve a synthesis of two potentially contradictory impulses is most likely also the reason why *Moby-Dick* is considered today, not only Melville's greatest achievement, but also one of the most intriguing expressions of American nineteenth-century literary culture.

NOTES

1   The German original in G.V.F. *Werke*, eds. Eva Moldenhauer and Karl Markus Michel, xiii (Frankfurt am Main: Suhrkamp, 1969-71).

2   Alvin Kernan has also drawn on Malraux's conception of the museum in *The Imaginary Library*, 18-21.

3   See for example Wellek, 20.

4   The German original in Friedrich Schlegel, *Kritische Augabe*, ed. Ernst Behler (Paderborn: Schöningh, 1958), IL 16: 419, no. 34 and 2: 265, no. 95.

5   Kant's critical philosophy gave rise to a deep uncertainty as to whether it is possible to represent the "thing-in-itself." Kant's successors, most notably Fichte and Schlegel, saw literature as the cure for this wound. The "thing-in-itself" could, it was argued, be truthfully represented within the realm of the aesthetic. On literature and the problem of representation, see further Lacoue-Labarthe and Nancy, 1-17.

6   For fuller information on the mixed form narrative, see Post-Lauria, 101-22.

7   In the last pages of his journal, under the heading "Memoranda of Things on the Voyage," Melville writes: "Dr. Johnson an usher—'intolerable'"; see *Journal of a Visit to London and the Continent*, 85.

8   For a more detailed analysis of Johnson and the literary marketplace, see Kernan, *Printing Technology, Letters and Samuel Johnson*, 16-23.

9   As Sealts points out, Melville had previously held lecturing in very low estimation. He had not only refused several invitations to lecture himself; in *Pierre*, he also ridicules a similar invitation. See further Sealts, 5.

REFERENCES

Baym, Nina. "Melville's Quarrel with Fiction." *PMLA* 94 (1979): 909-21.

Boswell, James. *Life of Johnson*. Ed. George Birkbeck Hill, rev. L. F. Powell. Vol. 1. Oxford: Clarendon Press, 1934-50.

Brodhead, Richard H. *The School of Hawthorne*. New York and Oxford: Oxford University Press, 1986.

Emerson, Ralph Waldo. *The Writings of Ralph Waldo Emerson*. New York: Random House, 1940.

Kernan, Alvin. *The Imaginary Library. An Essay on Literature and Society*. Princeton, NJ: Princeton University Press, 1982.

——. *Printing Technology, Letters and Samuel Johnson*. Princeton, NJ: Princeton University Press, 1987.

Lacoue-Labarthe, Philippe, and Jean-Luc Nancy. *The Literary Absolute.* Trans. Philip Barnard and Cheryl Lester. Albany: State University of New York Press, 1988.

Levine, Lawrence. *Highbrow/Lowbrow: The Emergence of Cultural Hierarchy in America.* Cambridge, MA, and London: Harvard University Press, 1988.

Leyda, Jay. *The Melville Log. A Documentary Life of Herman Melville 1819-1891.* 2 vols. New York: Harcourt, Brace and Company, 1951.

Malraux, André. *The Voices of Silence.* Princeton, NJ: Princeton University Press, 1978.

Melville, Herman. *Journal of a Visit to London and the Continent 1849-1850.* Ed. Eleanor Melville Metcalf. Cambridge, MA: Harvard University Press, 1948.

——. *Journal of a Visit to Europe and the Levant. October 11, 1856-May 6, 1857.* Ed. Howard C. Horsford. Princeton, NJ: Princeton University Press, 1955.

——. *Moby-Dick.* Oxford: World's Classics, 1988.

——. *The Letters of Herman Melville.* Ed. Merrell R. Davis and William H. Gilman. New Haven, CT: Yale University Press, 1960.

——. *Pierre; or, The Ambiguities.* Eds. Harrison Hayford, Hershel Parker, and G. Thomas Tanselle. Evanston and Chicago: Northwestern University Press and the Newberry Library, 1971.

Post-Lauria, Sheila. *Correspondent Colorings. Melville in the Marketplace.* Amherst: University of Massachusetts Press, 1996.

Royster, Paul. "Melville's Economy of Language." *Ideology and Classic American Literature.* Eds. Sacvan Bercovitch and Myra Jehlen. Cambridge, MA: Cambridge University Press, 1986. 313-36.

Sealts, Merton M., Jr. *Melville as Lecturer.* Cambridge, MA: Harvard University Press, 1957.

Seyhan, Azade. *Representation and Its Discontents: The Critical Legacy of German Romanticism.* Berkeley, Los Angeles, and Oxford: University of California Press, 1992.

Wellek, René. *What Is Literature?* Ed. Paul Hernadi. Bloomington: Indiana University Press, 1978. 16-23.

Ziolkowski, Theodore. *German Romanticism and Its Institutions.* Princeton, NJ: Princeton University Press, 1990.

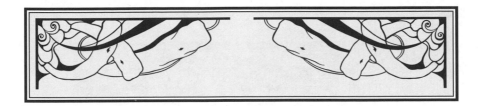

ZBIGNIEW BIALAS

PONDERING OVER THE CHART OF KOKOVOKO:

HERMAN MELVILLE AND THE CRITIQUE OF CARTOLOGICAL INSCRIPTION

Gentlemen, a strange fatality pervades the whole career of these events, as if verily mapped out before the world itself was charted (Moby-Dick, 281)

1.

et me try to establish first the link between the land-mass and the Whale-mass. It could perhaps be legitimately said that *Moby-Dick* is not a book about cartography. It could likewise be argued that cetology has nothing to do with cartology.[1] Yet, both these claims, commonsensical as they sound, would be superficial.

That whaling played an immense role (if not always positive) in the history of geographical discoveries is irrefutable.[2] Melville himself was aware of that: "for many years past the whale-ship has been the pioneer in ferreting out the remotest and least known parts of the earth. She has explored seas and archipelagoes which had no chart, where no Cook or Vancouver had ever sailed" (*MD* 120).[3]

That a post-medieval representative mode could link (if naively) whaling and cartographical inscription into a related image is also undeniable, and the woodcut of early whaling, *Walfang* (1555), elegantly testifies to it (Fig. 1).

345

Fig. 1: *Walfang. Holzschnitt, 1555* (after H. Pleticha & H. Schreiber, *Die Entdeckung der Welt*)

Abstracting from the representation of the earth leaning on the whale—a legacy of antiquity—here, noticeably, the mass of the whale functions as a junction between land and water. The boat on the represented sea is anchored to the body of the represented hulk, while people who chop the whale stand on the represented coast. The dimensions and the rules of perspective may be debatable, but that is of minor import, as the representation of the land-mass, the sea-mass and the whale-mass evidently constitutes a single image. The whale is a prolongation of the sea as a sea-creature but at the same time, as solid mass—a prolongation of solid land, *terra firma*. The word *terra* with reference to the sea does not create, hopefully, a sense of contradiction as far as Melville's textual practice is concerned.[4] After all, "[w]e know the sea to be an everlasting *terra incognita*," claims the narrator in Chapter 58 (*MD* 298). In the representation of *Walfang* our power of detailed denomination (e.g., horses, carts, castles, etc.) extends as far as the framed body of the represented beast. In *Moby-Dick* similarly, it might seem that casting off onto the sea, "Ishmael enters a marvelous indeterminacy of denomination" (Cowan 90); in the exiled waters Ishmael loses "the miserable warping memories of traditions and of towns" (*MD* 165). But the search for denomination never stops, even if it changes configurations. The sea's

346

infinity does not entail a lack of information, but rather its overload; hence the attempts at observing, delineating, and framing. The problem is, however, that something which comes under observation never remains the same.

Ishmael no doubt realizes that the question of dimensions is a question of pondering. "[O]ft repeated ponderings" and "earnest contemplation" change the delineation of the suspected "chaos bewitched" into ideas that are not altogether unwarranted. Ishmael articulates this awareness while entering the Spouter-Inn. Confronting the oil-painting of a Cape-Horner in a hurricane (*MD* 13) he notices how ponderous perception or perceptive and interpretative pondering changes the painting's meaning. Joseph Flibbert asserts that "[t]he painting requires interpretation, the ability to generalize, to extract from the black masses a representational concept, to see the symbolic in the particular. Ishmael's insight of the painting ... does just that. It is Ishmael's 'final theory,' not of what the painting is, but of what it 'represents'" (Flibbert 107). In the Spouter-Inn, where science is applied, even the footpad's goblets are surrounded by parallel meridians (*MD* 15), while intricate patterns of Queequeg's tattoo attain their mappable topography.[5] All that despite Ishmael's suspiciousness of structured or skeletalized imprints. In *Moby-Dick* immovable inscriptions cause despair—cf. e.g., the black-bordered sacrificial marbles in the Chapel (*MD* 41) where the blanks and voids left by beings placelessly perished discredit the non-referentiality of any framed representation.

2.

Although Melville's first novel of traveling adventures, *Typee* (1846), includes a map, no mention of one occurs in the text. Published three years later, *Redburn: His First Voyage* (1849), contains a famous episode on an outlandish old guidebooks (Chapters 30 and 31). Wellingborough Redburn, on landing in England, finds his father's map of Liverpool a complete delusion. As a result, Redburn's faith undergoes a "severe shock" (*Redburn* 218), but it is in *Moby-Dick* not in *Redburn* that cartography receives a fatal blow. Already in Chapter 12 the reader learns that "Queequeg was a native of Kokovoko, an island far away to the West and South. It is not down in any map; true places never are" (*MD* 61). On the one hand the narrator seems to be somehow fortified with Redburn-like harrowing experience, on the other hand the meaning of the latter part of the sentence, "true places never are" transcends Redburn's disillusionment, and it can be understood to have an underlying ontological dimension. For a philosopher the existence of maps is no proof of the existence of reality. The citation articulates an unremitting fear that true places *never are*. Only one of the possible meanings is that they never appear in maps. Two chapters later the narrator exclaims: "Nantucket! Take out your map and look at it. See what a real corner of the world it occupies" (*MD* 69). But a map is neither a pictorial simulacrum of the non-pictorial ground of reality nor a purely descriptive text. Which then is real: Nantucket (because it exists in the map) or Kokovoko (because it does not)?

Literary theorists more and more frequently revert to the concept of the map. For postcolonial criticism, deconstruction, feminism and (new)Left criticism, mapping or charting is liberally understood as almost any act of creating stereotypical representations. *To be mapped* means to be compulsively bounded and categorized; *a map* is used almost interchangeably with discourse or text; literature is also understood as *mapping*, and so is writing about literature. In the situation of increasing epistemological chaos it is useful, perhaps, to demonstrate that this awareness is not at all a postmodernist or a deconstructive achievement. Reducing the discourse of mapping *ad absurdum* Melville (alongside Lewis Carroll) should be seen in the context of the nineteenth-century budding Western critique of totalizing cartographical inscription and thus a precursor of the postcolonial attack on cartology.

Melville employs the figure of the map as a catalyst of the protagonist's perception. In *Redburn* the experience still remains in the sphere of puzzlement and epiphany. Reverentially unfolding the father's map, Redburn discovers and mentally follows the dotted lines traced with a pen, delineating the father's excursions and penetrations (*Redburn* 211). By palimpsestic selection the father symbolically instituted certain spaces. In the interest of orderliness, which paradoxically maximizes entropy (but of that Redburn is obviously ignorant), superfluous components are eliminated from a system, and those which are required are supplied (see: Arnheim 51)—hence the need for palliative activities. Puzzlement and epiphany aside, when Captain Ahab yields to his more pensive obsession of studying maps, he is (like Redburn's father but unlike Redburn) an expert practitioner of the reinscriptive cartographic palimpsest. Pondering over the charts, Ahab: "trace[d] . . . courses over spaces that before were blank. . . . Almost every night some pencil marks were effaced, and others were substituted" (*MD* 215).

Trying to negate the topographical tendency towards disorder by the building up of shapes, organizing divergent disorderly factors, by orderly delineation of some marks and erasure of what is thought to form irrelevancies, Ahab tends to believe in implied necessary existence. The systematic inscription of the supposedly uninscribed ocean is the exemplification of a structuralist wish to guarantee presence although stability cannot be guaranteed (Huggan 128): "For with the charts of all four oceans before him, Ahab was tracing a maze of currents and eddies, with a view to the more certain accomplishment of that monomaniac thought of his soul" (*MD* 215).

The methodically delirious Captain Ahab is a precursor of yet another narrative tradition—that of the love affair between the map maker and his map. Every desire can be transformed into discourse (Foucault 12), and maps could, indeed, be gazed at and interpreted erotically. The map does not have to result from the application of the actual cartographic, distant-prospect gaze. Instead, it may be a joint product of an obsession with visual perception and the map maker's libidinous drives.

When Redburn lovingly lingers over his father's volume (*Redburn* 208) and would rather sell his life than the green morocco guide-book, it may still be understood as filial affection. There is no such filial affection (which I admit is also suspect) when Captain Ahab takes the maps out of the locker. Almost every night, in secrecy, he spreads the charts on the screwed down table and studies them intently. In striking correspondence with the Lacanian psychoanalytic formulation of the equivalence between the act of visual perception and sexual impulses, Ahab's gaze directed upon the chart of the ocean evokes the eye-intense voyeuristic intercourse. In the act performed by the wrinkled Ahab on the wrinkled map even a pewter lamp participates, tracing lines and courses of shadows "upon the deeply marked chart of [Ahab's] forehead" (*MD* 215). While the application of the grid may symbolize the indispensible conceptual fishing-net spread all over the ocean—an ersatz denomination—the meaning of this scene consists not only in such an interpretation.[6] Neither does it consist solely in transferring Ahab from the public to the private and from "a nautical oratory" (*Typee* 21) to "writing" as an individualized form of forbidden pleasure. After the oratorical scene which reveals "a level of calculation masked by Ahab's public rhetorical power" (Cowan 103), studying the map simulates and enacts a mortal love affair between Ahab and the ocean (notoriously a female principle), between the calculator and the object of calculation.

No wonder one night Starbuck sees Ahab wet and with his eyes closed: "On the table beside him lay unrolled one of those charts of tides and currents which have previously been spoken of. His lantern swung from his tightly clenched hand. Though the body was erect, the head was thrown back so that the closed eyes were pointed towards the needle of the tell-tale that swung from a beam in the ceiling" (*MD* 256).

In the corporal aspect of representational correspondencies it is not only Ahab's forehead that simulates a map. Ahab figures up the latitudes on the little oval slate of smoothed ivory on the upper part of his artificial leg (*MD* 161, 515). This motif seems to echo an observation made already in *Typee*, concerning the remarkable peculiarity of the appearance of the timeworn savages' feet: their toes "like the radiating lines of the mariner's compass, pointed to every quarter of the horizon" (*Typee* 74). The Polynesian link could, in turn, lead us back to Queequeg. If we were to follow the hints from Chapter 110 and venture on providing constitutive elements of the mystical art of attaining the semblance of truth from the storehouse of Melville's own symbolism, we might extract the following: the hieroglyphic marks, undecipherable patterns, figures, drawings, lines and tattoos on Queequeg's body are grotesquely repeated on Queequeg's coffin—the instrument of survival, while wrinkled patterns and lines of Ahab's forehead are grotesquely repeated on Ahab's maps—eventually the agent of perdition. The apparent opposition of body and mind is matched by the parallel opposition of the life-saving coffin/buoy and life-threatening computations, profound magnetic meditations, the technology of "binnacle deviations," "azimuth compass observations," and "approximate errors" (*MD* 171).

3.

In view of the above sketch, what is the epistemological use of narrative cartography? In the times of the growth of the Empires only under the disguise of the absurd could one hint at the inadequacy and conceptual suspiciousness of the map in the discourse of traveling. In Lewis Carroll's *Hunting of the Snark*, the seminal poem of the absurd written by a mathematician in 1876, the Bellman leads an expedition in search of the mysterious and elusive Snark. Very adequately, the expedition is supposed to be facilitated by a map:

> He had bought a large map representing the sea,
> Without the least vestige of land:
> And the crew were much pleased when they found it to be
> A map they could all understand.
>
> "What's the good of Mercator's North Poles and Equators,
> Tropics, Zones, and Meridian Lines?"
> So the Bellman would cry: and the crew would reply
> "They are merely conventional signs!"
>
> "Other maps are such shapes, with their islands and capes!
> But we've got our brave Captain to thank"
> (So the crew would protest) "that he's bought *us* the best
> —A perfect and absolute blank!" (Carroll 683).

"The large map representing the sea / Without the least vestige of land" may remind us of *Moby-Dick*. The Bellman, haranguing and hypnotizing the crew, behaves like Captain Ahab; hunting for the Snark is like hunting for the White Whale. There exist marked differences, however. The chorus of the crew in the Bellman's expedition reveals an unusual insight into the conventions of both maritime and terrestrial geography in the times when Mercatorial maps shaped and totalized the collective imagination. The Bellman and the "mad" members of his crew know that the map is a lie which pacifies the mind through the use of codes, grids, and numerical calculations. They realize, above all, that maps do not have much to do with physical reality. The derogatory and distrustful tone of the crew towards Mercatorial convention, "such shapes" and their uncritical acceptance of

351

de-gridding, i.e., a global white spot as a solution, is precisely the opposite of the attitude of the non-absurd part of the traveling and colonial population busily engaged in the *ars apodemica* in the second half of the nineteenth century.

We find a comparably optimistic chorus about "our captain" in *Moby-Dick*. Led by the 1st Nantucket Sailor, the crew intone a popular shanty: "Our captain stood upon the deck, / A spy-glass in his hand, / A viewing of those gallant whales / That blew at every strand. / Oh, your tubs in your boats, my boys, / And by your braces stand, / And we'll have one of those fine whales, / Hand, boys, over hand!" (*MD* 187).

While the Bellman optimistically rejects a map, Ahab (in Chapter 118) bombastically curses the quadrant. He ponders over the numerous cabalistical contrivances of the vain toy, dashes it to the deck, and tramples on it with his live and dead feet: "Curse thee, thou quadrant!.... I trample on thee, thou paltry thing that feebly pointest on high; thus I split and destroy thee!" (*MD* 544).

But even if the Bellman's total rejection of a map may initially impress us as more radical (albeit doubtless less spectacular) than Ahab's trampling on the quadrant, Melville in fact goes further than Lewis Carroll. The Snark cannot be spotted; the White Whale can. That Moby Dick can be followed and found, unmistakably revealing his identity "in the limitless, uncharted seas" (*MD* 199), distressed a few generations of critics looking for *vraisemblance*. But we must realize that if someone is looking for something, he will find it. Because Columbus believed in Cyclopes, mermaids, etc., his belief permitted him to find them (Todorov 15), and then, in the Preface to the *Book of Prophecies* (1501), he admitted that "[f]or the execution of the enterprise . . . reason, mathematics and the map of the world were of no utility" to him (Todorov 22). The narrator of Thomas More's *Utopia* confirms this stance claiming that "nothing is more easy to be found, than be barking Scyllas, ravening Celaenos, and Laestrigonians devourers of people, and such like great and incredible monsters" (More 20). Hence, Ahab's monomaniac intercourse with maritime maps, no matter if they are "of utility or not," necessarily ends with a success. Moby Dick—the Ultimate White Spot on the unmappable "perfect and absolute blank" of the Ocean—is nevertheless located. What is more, it is located precisely where it is expected, and every time, during the three days of the final chase, it is rediscovered by Ahab—the creator of the

grid/net and its contents. Simply, the crew "has got the brave Captain to thank."
After all, in Ahab's maps Moby Dick probably is, as in the framed woodcut of
Walfang, "merely a conventional sign."

NOTES

1   *Cartology* will be understood as a preoccupation with both *carta* and *logos* (the latter symbolizing both verbalization and logistics)—thus a notion transcending that of cartography.

2   Cf. the entry on *Walfaenger* in Heinrich Pleticha and Hermann Schreiber, *Die Entdeckung der Welt: Ein Lexicon...*, p. 403.

3   All references to *Moby-Dick* (abbreviated throughout the text as *MD*) come from the edition of Harmondsworth: Penguin, 1992.

4   In the chain of the *floating* signifiers it is of course possible to relativize *terra firma* as well. In J. F. Cooper's *Deerslayer* the deck of Floating Tom's Ark is referred to as *terra firma* by comparison with the Hurons' rafts (332). The Ark is not *terra firma* per se; it can only be *terra firma* of civilization, on the strength of asserting a difference.

5   Cf. similar geometrico-geographical stylization in *Typee* where e.g., "all imaginable *lines and curves and figures were delineated* over ⌊Mehevi's⌋ whole body (60); Kory-Kory embellishes his face with "broad *longitudinal stripes* of tattooing" (65) while Marnoo's body is drawn all over with fanciful figures which "appeared to have been executed *in conformity with some general design* (110) [emphasis mine, Z.B.].

6   Cf. B. Cowan: Ahab coordinates "space and time in a projected line of motion, a conjunction inherent in the movement of his pencil. When magnified to oceanic proportions and considered for the degree of accuracy needed to attain his purpose, Ahab's charting takes on an aura of the numerical sublime, relying on sheer incalculability to impress the ordinary mortal with his insignificance before something vast" (95).

REFERENCES

Adam, Ian and Helen Tiffin, eds. *Past the Last Post: Theorizing Post-Colonialism and Post-Modernism.* New York: Harvester Wheatsheaf, 1993.

Arnheim, Rudolf. *Entropy and Art: An Essay on Disorder and Order.* Berkeley: U of California P, 1974.

Carroll, Lewis. *The Complete Illustrated Lewis Carroll.* Ware: Wordsworth Editions, 1991.

Cooper, James Fenimore. *The Deerslayer.* Harmondsworth: Penguin Books, 1987.

Cowan, Bainard. *Exiled Waters:* Moby-Dick *and the Crisis of Allegory.* Baton Rouge and London: Louisiana State UP, 1982.

Flibbert, Joseph. *Melville and the Art of Burlesque*. Amsterdam: Rodopi n.v., 1974.

Foucault, Michel. *The History of Sexuality*. Volume I: *An Introduction*. Trans. Robert Hurley. New York: Vintage Books, 1980.

Huggan, Graham. "Decolonizing the Map: Post-Colonialism, Post-Structuralism and the Cartographic Connection." Ian Adam and Helen Tiffin, eds., *Past the Last Post: Theorizing Post-Colonialism and Post-Modernism*. Calgary: U of Calgary P, 1990. 125-38.

Melville, Herman. *Moby-Dick; or, The Whale*. Harmondsworth: Penguin Books, 1992.

——. *Redburn: His First Voyage*. Harmondsworth: Penguin Books, 1986.

——. *Typee*. Ware: Wordsworth Classics, 1994.

More, Sir Thomas. *The Utopia of Sir Thomas More* [1515]. Trans. Ralph Robinson. London: Macmillan, 1958.

Pleticha, Heinrich, and Hermann Schreiber, eds. *Die Entdeckung der Welt: Ein Lexicon*. Wien: Ueberreuter, 1993.

Todorov, Tzvetan. *The Conquest of America: The Question of the Other*. Trans. Richard Howard. New York: Harper, 1992.

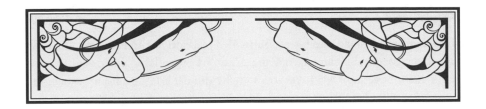

DAVID MITCHELL

THE LANGUAGE OF PROSTHESIS IN *MOBY-DICK*

Introduction: The Inflexibility of Prosthesis

nlike the important attention bequeathed to questions of race, class, and nationalist identifications in Melville's work (and in literary studies in general), little attention has been focused upon *Moby-Dick*'s vehement insistence upon the relationship between Ahab's "monomaniacal" personality and his dismemberment by Moby Dick.[1] My emphasis here is not upon the parallel drawn between monomania and dismemberment (there is a substantial critical tradition on this relationship alone), but rather upon the insistence in the narrative that these two facets of Ahab's identity are absolutely and inexorably linked. The fact that Ahab's "monomaniac mind" is said to be forged out of "the direct issue of a former woe"—namely the instant of his maiming or crippling—runs counter to the novel's overarching strategy of demonstrating the ultimate indeterminacy of meaning embedded in the relations of signifier and signified (385, 463-64).[2] This paper analyses the reasons why Ahab's crippling accident and subsequent prosthetic alteration bequeath to him a singular motivation and static identity that resist Ishmael's and the narrative's fluid and nuanced interpretational practices. Ahab's disability proves recalcitrant to the linguistic ambiguity that destabilizes the truth-telling systems of human knowledge addressed in the novel.

My contention in this paper is that there is a short-circuiting of narrative purpose that crystallizes around the physical *fact* of Ahab's prostheticized difference.

355

The repaired leg signifies a physical and metaphysical *lack* that cements the captain's identity as obsessive, overbearing, and overwrought. Yet, curiously, this static identity bequeathed to Ahab also provides the contrast against which the linguistically permeable universe of *Moby-Dick* unfolds. From the moment that Captain Peleg explains to Ishmael that the source of Ahab's "desperate moody, and savage" behavior commenced with the "sharp shooting pains in his bleeding stump," the riddle of Ahab's identity is largely solved (79, 77). Ishmael's access to the story of Ahab's dismemberment provides a physical myth of origins that the novel never sincerely interrogates or destabilizes. Thus, just as "the most poisonous reptile of the marsh perpetuates his kind," the "miserable event" of Ahab's dismasting "naturally beget[s its] like" (385, 464). Although the argument for the source of Ahab's compulsive behavior and violent vendetta is revisited on numerous occasions during the narrative, the monomaniacal result of his prostheticized body eventually becomes novelistic doctrine.

Ahab's Accessibility

The reasons behind the novel's singularizing explanation of Ahab's physical loss can be traced directly to nineteenth-century attitudes about perceived bodily differences and physical incapacities. Unlike previous historical moments which ascribed physical anomalies and bodily hardships to a sinful fate bequeathed from God or as the surface manifestation of satanic possession, the Victorian period witnessed the rise of an increasingly professionalizing medical ethos and ideology in relation to the body. The nineteenth-century study of pathology, as medical historian Georges Canguilhem has documented, developed out of a belief that bodily permutations could be empirically quantified as degrees of deviance from an idealized norm (Canguilhem, 154-55).

While Melville's captain alters himself and the maritime world around him to better accommodate his disability, he nonetheless fails to escape the fate of a medicalized determinism which pervades the novel. The captain's endeavors to provide himself with a "foothold"—both literally and metaphorically—in the traditionally able-bodied profession of whaling ironically solidifies the evidence of his single-minded arrogance and over-reaching nature. A lengthy catalogue is supplied by the novel with regard to Ahab's physical alteration of top-side ship life as if to fend off disbelief in Melville's readership that a one-legged captain could still manage to function in such a precarious environment: the "auger hole, bored about half an inch or so, into the plank" that steadied his "barbaric" bone leg (110, 124), the "iron banister" which he grips to "help his crippled way" (112, 127); the winch hook and specially designed saddle that carries him aloft into the ship's rigging; his unsuccessful request for a special allotment of "five extra men" from the ship's owners (Ahab fulfills this need secretively in the smuggling of Fedallah's crew on board); the "making [of] thole-pins with his own hands for what was thought to be one of the spare boats"; the addition of an "extra coat of sheathing in the bottom of the boat, as if to make it better withstand the point-ed pressure of his ivory limb"; and the "shaping of thigh board, or clumsy cleat, ... for bracing the knee" (198, 230). The final commentary on these numerous transformations of the ship by Ahab to accommodate his disability comes in an exhausted exclamation by Ishmael on the superfluous nature of Ahab's efforts at self-accommodation: "Hence the spare boats, spare spars, and spare lines and harpoons, and spare everythings, almost but a spare Captain and duplicated ship" (89, 96).[3]

Each of these innovations and inventions is paraded out not as evidence of Ahab's creativity or resourcefulness, but rather as evidence of the extent to which he will go to fulfill his "singular" quest: "But almost everybody supposed that this particular preparative heedfulness in Ahab must only be with a view to the ultimate chase of Moby Dick" (198, 230). The paradox for Ahab is that his need for physical alterations aboard the ship supply the tangible evidence of his "unnatural" and "unhealthy" perseverance. Unlike the slippery multiple mean-ings ascribed to the "monstrousest parmacetty that ever chipped a boat," the linkage of Ahab's subjectivity with his disability functions as a mystery without the force of revelation (69, 72). The significance of disability as a prescription for Ahab's mysterious behavior suggests that people with disabilities can be re-duced down to the physical evidence of their bodily differences. Disabilities rep-resent all consuming affairs that, as the anthropologist Robert Murphy argues, become the sum of one's entire personality canceling out all other attributes of one's multi-faceted humanity (Murphy 143). Ahab's dismemberment and "incom-plete" physicality—now simulated with an ivory substitute—supplies Melville's characterization with both a personal motive and an identifying physical mark. These two aspects function in the novel as a deterministic shorthand device for signifying the meaning of Ahab's *being*.

Although Ahab's single-minded identity is fixed by the presence of his artificial leg, there is a paradoxical purpose accorded to the captain's ivory supplement; prosthesis serves double-time as a metonym for the myriad "substitutions" which riddle the novel's plot (such as the ship-like pulpit from which Father Mapple sermonizes his congregation on land, or Queequeg's coffin that later serves as a life preserver for the sole-surviving Ishmael), and as a metaphor for the artificial operations of language that give "flesh" to that which is perceived as "natural" in the world.[4] Prosthesis functions in *Moby-Dick* as the mutable relation between natural and unnatural and as a deterministic principle buried within Ahab's identity. Such a paradox demonstrates that Melville simultaneously anticipated a primary postmodern conceit about the slippery function of language, and also condemned his disabled character to a limiting ideological myth of physical normativity.

The Language of Prosthesis

In his recent study entitled, *Prosthesis*, David Wills argues that the prosthetic relation between natural and artificial—the attempt to simulate a living appendage with a wooden or inorganic substitute—serves as the proper metaphor for the workings of language itself. Rather than assailing a living reality directly or absolutely, language disguises its inability to represent anything once and for all, and thus, the sign acts as an elaborate system of deception. The sign's ability to conceal that the relation of signifier and signified is a thoroughly artificial one seeks to perform a prosthesis upon the "Real." For Wills, the word is an artificial extension of the body seeking to capture an elusive essence: "Language inaugurates a structure of the prosthetic when the first word projects itself from the body into materiality, or vice versa; by being always already translation, constituting itself as otherness, articulation of the othernesses that constitute it, *language is a prosthesis*. Every utterance is as if spoken from a skateboard, written on crutches, relying on the prosthetic supplement" (Wills 300, my italics). In taking an "incomplete" or "maimed" physicality and turning it into an organizing metaphor for the operations of language itself, Wills displaces our notions that either language or the body exists in a natural relation to the worlds they inhabit and of which they endeavor to make sense.

Language, in Wills's analysis, cannot walk straight—its figures "limp or zig zag" (Wills 24). *Moby-Dick* also searches for an understanding of the question of linguistic relations and, in the end, anticipates Wills's own deconstruction of language as prosthesis. Melville's sea captain becomes stubbornly welded to a bone supplement which, by its very presence, demonstrates that the natural world exists only in a constructed—or *prostheticized*—relation to the artificial workings of language. Unlike the more fluid and flexible narrations on whaling and the whale offered up by Ishmael, Ahab is sentenced to the inflexibility of a prosthesis. This treatment of his character is distinct from the narrative's musings upon the meanings of the white whale whose multiple physical differences such as its albinism, "snow-white wrinkled forehead," "pyramidical humpedback," and "deformed lower jaw," fail to secure any absolute definition of its mammalian essence (159, 183). The mythic whale defies any human-made system's ability to discern a reliable natural patterning to its behavior or existence, and thus its "monstrous" physicality eludes capture as *knowledge*.

Yet, while the allegory of the whale may be explained as an exposé of the artificiality of language—a prostheticized bridge between the human verbalization of desire and "mute nature"—Ahab's own allegory is sedimented into a story of biological fact and personal (as well as physical) incapacity. In her book, *Empire for Liberty: Melville and the Poetics of Individualism*, Wai-Chee Dimock argues that the allegorical structure of *Moby-Dick* forwards characters who become agents of the textual exegesis rather than agents in their own right. This narrative strategy employed by Melville serves as a "personification" of character types that necessarily limits the "play" usually associated with developed characterizations: "In short, what makes the allegorical character powerless is precisely his fixedness, his materialization within a form that never changes. To be personified at all, from this perspective, is already to submit to the dictates of the timeless, the dictates of destiny. This point becomes especially clear when we consider the nature of 'agency' in allegory.... [If] allegory leaves no doubt about the character of its agency, that emblematic clarity is possible only because its 'agency' is always represented as 'image,' a bounded figure in space. Personification is really a kind of reification then: it reifies the category of 'agency,' investing it and confining it within a material form—in this case, a human form" (Dimock 25).

Interestingly, Dimock endeavors to prove her theory about the determinism of allegory through its numerous applications to the figure of Ahab: his character reveals a "blaming the victim" mentality in Melville's narrative because his agency is already delimited by the conventions of the novel's allegorized expression (Dimock 109). Yet, Dimock's theory overlooks Ahab's prosthesis as the organizational principle of the novel, while also ignoring the more political question in disability studies of why Ahab's figure proves so available for allegorization in the first place. While Dimock significantly points out that Ahab's agency is thoroughly compromised by Melville's larger thematic objectives, his singular status as a "bounded figure in space" demonstrates that what is at work here is a cultural penchant for allegorizing disability itself. Culturally, we imagine agency to be precluded by the fact of a disability—one is transformed into the principle of passivity where agency is only a lost or longed for ideal available to the normative inhabitant of an intact body.

In order to demonstrate that what is at stake in the novel's representation of Ahab's physical difference is more than a generalized question on the workings of agency in allegory, one could turn to Melville's reflections on the nineteenth-century sciences of physiognomy and phrenology in the chapters entitled, "The Prairie" and "The Nut." While Ishmael ends up dismissing these two "semi-sciences" as little more than a passing fad—and thus, gesturing toward Melville's critique of nineteenth-century empiricism in general—I want to go on to demonstrate that the novel continues to rely upon the very tenets of these disciplinary perspectives wherever Ahab's visage and physique are concerned. The means by which Ahab's "personification" occurs is more strictly connected to the material facts of his physiology than Dimock's argument recognizes; and thus, I want to argue that disability's "material form" plays host to the "confining" logic of identity which Dimock chalks up to the process of allegorization in general.

Ahab's missing leg debases his physical and psychological person by making him "too much of a cripple" (364, 437). The enigma of his figure translates into the static device that causes *Moby-Dick*'s philosophical pursuit of language's radical contingency to falter. In "The Sphynx," just nine chapters prior to the denunciation of physiognomy's pseudo-scientificity, Ahab offers up his own physiognomical correlative to the relationship between body and subjectivity: "O Nature, and O soul of man! how far beyond all utterance are your linked analogies! not the smallest atom stirs or lives in matter, but has its cunning duplicate in mind" (264, 312). Tellingly, this general principle of the mind following the course of the body (or matter) serves to pigeonhole Ahab most vehemently. Yet, this physiognomic philosophy fails at various other points in the novel when applied to the indeterminable meanings of the whale's external anomalies and to the other sailors' physical beings as well: "Only some thirty arid summers had [Starbuck] seen; those summers had dried up all his physical superfluousness. But this, his thinness, so to speak, seemed no more the token of wasting anxieties and cares, than it seemed the indication of any bodily blight" (102-3, 115). The narrative's refusal to assign any "bodily blight" to Starbuck's visible thinness demonstrates that neither "intact" human nor whale physiologies provide reliable surfaces for interpretation.

Ahab's self-condemning philosophy about the interrelated aspects of body and mind openly defies this pivotal aspect of the novel's moral lesson on the instability of language. In order to construct the narrative's insistence upon the mirroring relations of bodily surface and internal psychology, Ahab's confessions about his truncated humanity supply their own correspondent physical signs. The narrative's external vantage point on the character of Ahab could easily be refuted as mere projection upon his disabled figure, just as Doctor Bunger aboard the *Samuel Enderby* explains to Ahab that "what you take for the White Whale's malice is only his awkwardness" (368, 441). But there is a good deal of plot at stake in enforcing Ahab's unique and singular position with respect to the question of bodily signs taken for internal symptoms.

Ahab's "dented," "marked," "swelled," and "bent" forehead bears the signature of a violent internal upheaval that spills out upon the surface of his private physiognomy at nearly every point in his physical and psychological portrait. This pervasive emphasis upon correlations between external countenance and internal corruption effectively condemns Ahab as a product or victim of his own physiological make up. Since the primary use of physiognomic interpretations in the nineteenth century was to theorize a distinct visage of criminality and depraved humanity, the relationship emphasized by Melville is exclusively debilitating to the reader's interpretations of Ahab's behavior. The captain's body serves as the medium which reveals his disturbed personality, and his physical inadequacy symptomatically evidences his raging psychic life.

The Bodily Vulture of Narrative

As Rosemarie Garland Thomson has perceptively observed in her book, *Extraordinary Bodies: Figuring Physical Disability in American Culture and Literature*: "Ahab's outrage compensates for his vulnerability, rendering him both a sublime and a threatening version of the disabled figure" (45). Either the novel exhibits its own monomaniacal resort to this formative instance in Ahab's life, or Ahab's disabled exceptionality stubbornly thwarts authorial desire and the overarching thematic discourse upon the malleable nature of truth. If we apply Melville's own commentaries upon the creative process to the author's physiological method of characterizing Ahab's disabled body, one may reveal the irony of the narrative's parasitical principles: "God help thee, old man, thy thoughts have created a creature in thee; and he whose intense thinking thus makes him a Prometheus; a vulture feeds upon that heart for ever; that vulture the very creature he creates" (175, 202). The self-cannibalizing psychological principle that Melville identifies in this passage involves a question of authorship. Whose creature is Ahab exactly—his own, as is speculated in the above quoted comment, the murderous" Moby Dick's, or Melville's? From where does the vulture that feeds upon his heart hail from, and who has set it upon him?

Melville's Ahab belongs within the Romantic tradition of what I term a newly evolving literary aesthetic of *dire bodies*. The disabled body became an important means of artistic characterization in this period for it allowed authors to visually privilege something amiss or "tragically flawed" in the very biology of an embodied character. The literary disablement of fictional bodies represented a tactile device for quickly individuating a character within a complex social network of relations. "Ticks" of character abounded, and nineteenth-century writers—especially novelists—populated their fictional landscapes with "tragic" characters who embodied a range of physical and cognitive anomalies. The burgeoning of medicalized vocabularies and taxonomies of the body provided an impetus for the evolution of this *pathological aesthetic*, and nineteenth-century discourses of the body such as medicine and art mutually reinforced disabled bodies as sources of cultural fascination and leering contemplation.

Medicine and art bolstered this perception of singularity by exploring physical differences without acknowledging the social context that authored them as Other. Ahab's isolated experience as the sole physically disabled denizen of the *Pequod*—with the exception of the "shuffling and limping" negro cook, old Fleece, who is parodically described as having "something the matter with his knee-pans, which he did not keep well scoured like his other pans" (250, 294)—marks him as an unusual specimen among the multicultural human brood that occupies the *Pequod*. Disabilities are transformed into individually compelling idiosyncrasies bereft of their social stigma while paradoxically providing the means by which one becomes *interpretable* to an outside perspective. People with disabilities arrive with their limitations openly on display, and thus, their bodies are constructed as the most transparent of surfaces; consequently, their incapacities render them most incapable of eluding their textually bequeathed fates.

This textually bequeathed fate becomes increasingly evident during the sequence of events that make up the final chapters which narrate the deadly encounter with Moby Dick. Throughout these chapters, Ahab's bodily destiny surfaces as an ominous symptom that establishes the whale's superiority in what Ahab perceives to be their "mutual antagonism." When Ahab falls from his upturned whaling boat and Moby Dick tauntingly circles him so as to cut off the crew's access to him, Melville objectifies his character's disability by describing him as "half smothered in the foam of the whale's insolent tail, and too much of a cripple to swim" (450, 551). The scene focuses upon Ahab's physical displacement in the unctuous and unstable medium of the ocean where his prosthetic leg's immobility is further exacerbated. The quest to kill the white whale turns to farce and *Moby-Dick* becomes a black comedy "whose centre had now become the old man's head" (450, 551).

Later, when Ahab is finally rescued and laid out in the bottom of Stubb's less accessible whaling boat, the captain is forced to come to grips with his own biological failings: "Dragged into Stubb's boat with blood-shot, blinded eyes, the white brine caking his wrinkles; the long tension of Ahab's bodily strength did crack, and helplessly he yielded to his body's doom: for a time, lying all crushed in the bottom of Stubb's boat, like one trodden under foot of herds of elephants" (450-51, 551). In this manner the narrative reaches its final objective: to force Ahab to admit that his human frailty transcends any designs he may have on the conquest of nature and subsequent personal renown. To punctuate such a revelation Ahab finally declares: "Accursed fate! That the unconquerable captain in the soul should have such a craven mate [as his body]" (458, 560). Disability in *Moby-Dick* further concretizes this outrageous availability of human subjects to intangible processes for it represents a distressed and fallible body calling attention to itself. Its perceived deviations announce the material conditions by which it is apprehended by other outside perspectives and forces; its visible accessibility is imagined to disallow the subject any bodily subterfuge or physiognomic anonymity.

Within such a paradigm, Ahab is held singularly culpable for his actions in the narrative while paradoxically experiencing his life as already circumscribed by historical and mythological patterns: "Ahab is for ever Ahab, man. This whole act's immutably decreed. 'Twas rehearsed by thee and me a billion years before this ocean rolled. Fool! I am the Fates' lieutenant; I act under orders" (459, 561). Physical disability becomes synonymous in the text with the tragedy of a deterministic fate, for the body seems prematurely exposed to a future state of vulnerability and malfunction. The encounter with bodily deviations from an imaginary cultural standard or ideal of physicality challenges the expectation of a normative biological continuum or timeline.

Of course, literary timelines are in themselves altered and "disordered" affairs. Characters necessarily capitulate to the generic conventions which govern them and the untimeliness of their melodramatic structures. Some five hundred pages into the narrative, *Moby-Dick* barrels toward its inevitable and fixed conclusion in the matter of three chapters. Ahab is not so much doomed to a "natural" fate bequeathed by the gods, but rather an artificially contrived destiny that props up the captain's figure for a time and then "gives out" like a faulty prosthesis under the pressures of historically constructed assumptions about disability.

The day before Ahab succumbs to the whale's indomitable power, Ahab remarks that, "I feel strained, half stranded, as ropes that tow dismasted frigates in a gale" (459, 561). This sense of being simultaneously immobilized and towed by another vessel proffers a vision of the disabled body firmly yoked to the tragically specular logic of nineteenth-century discourses on physical difference. Disability conjures up a ubiquitous series of associations between corrupted exterior and contaminated interior. The pairing is no more *natural* or aesthetically arresting than a truncated leg buttressed by a whale-bone shaft, but the language of prosthesis would make it seem so.

NOTES

This essay is excerpted from a chapter in a new book that I am co-authoring with Sharon Snyder, entitled *Narrative Prosthesis: The Materiality of Metaphor in Western Narratives*. The work argues that literary narratives have historically depended upon disabled figures as a primary tool of characterization. In charting out this history of narrative reliance upon disability, we seek to analyze the ways in which disabled identities have been constructed in various genres and historical epochs.

1   For a further discussion of critical elisions of disability in literature see the introduction to my co-edited collection of essays entitled, *The Body and Physical Difference: Discourses of Disability*.

2   In this essay I will be providing page citations for both the Norton critical edition and the Northwestern/Newberry volume. In each case, the citations will appear parenthetically with the Norton pagination first followed by the corresponding pages in the Northwestern/Newberry version.

3   Many scholars in disability studies have pointed out the pervasive perception that disability accommodation changes the environment for too few people and thus appears as an adamantine request for "special accommodations." Ahab is faulted in a similar manner in *Moby-Dick*, for his attempts to make the ship conform to his own abilities and body are interpreted as willfully singular and superfluous to all but himself. This observation becomes the original onus for Ishmael's reading of Ahab as "monomaniacal" and "obsessive."

4   While instances of the novel's use of Ahab's disability as the explanatory source of his character abound, the following quote can act as a pointed example of this tendency in the novel: "It is not probable that this monomania in him took its instant rise at the precise time of his bodily dismemberment. Then, in darting at the monster, knife in hand, he had but given loose to a sudden, passionate, corporal animosity; and when he received the stroke that tore him, he probably but felt the agonizing bodily laceration, but nothing more. Yet, when by this collision forced to turn towards home, and for long months of days and weeks, Ahab and anguish lay stretched together in one hammock, rounding in mid winter that dreary, howling Patagonian Cape; then it was, that his torn body and gashed soul bled into one another; and so interfusing made him mad" (160, 184-85).

REFERENCES

Canguilhem, Georges. *The Normal and the Pathological*. New York: Zone Books, 1991.

Dimock, Wai-chee. *Empire for Liberty: Melville and the Poetics of Individualism*. Princeton: Princeton UP, 1989.

Melville, Herman. *Moby-Dick*. Ed. Harrison Hayford and Hershel Parker. New York: W. W. Norton and Company, 1967.

——. *Moby-Dick, or The Whale*. Ed. Harrison Hayford, Hershel Parker, and G. Thomas Tanselle. Vol. 6 of *The Writings of Herman Melville*. Evanston and Chicago: Northwestern UP and the Newberry Library, 1988.

Mitchell, David T. and Sharon L. Snyder. "Disability and the Double Bind of Representation." *The Body and Physical Difference: Discourses of Disability*. Ed. David T. Mitchell and Sharon L. Snyder. Ann Arbor: U of Michigan P, 1997.

Murphy, Robert. "Encounters: The Body Silent in America." *Disability and Culture*. Ed. Benedicte Ingstad and Susan Reynolds White. Berkeley: U of California P, 1995. 140-58.

Thomson, Rosemarie Garland. *Extraordinary Bodies: Figuring Physical Disability in American Culture and Literature*. New York: Columbia UP, 1997.

Wills, David. *Prosthesis*. Stanford, CA: Stanford UP, 1995.

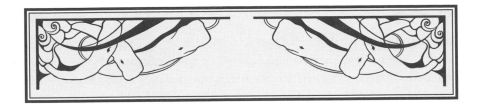

WILLIAM SPANOS

PIERRE'S SILENCE:

MELVILLE'S UNMAPPING OF AMERICAN SPACE

ince the essay I wrote for this conference is too long to give in its entirety, I will offer here only a part of it. But in order to provide a context, I want at the outset to summarize briefly what precedes. The general purpose of my reading of Melville's *Pierre* is to suggest that Americanist criticism, whether old or new, remains deeply inscribed by the myth of American exceptionalism. As a result this criticism is more or less oblivious to the degree to which Melville's fiction anticipates two fundamental—and indissolubly related—motifs of late postmodernist theory that have their origins in Europe. The first of these theoretical motifs, which, by this time, is more or less a familiar one, is the critique of hegemony by such thinkers as Antonio Gramsci, Louis Althusser, Michel Foucault, and Raymond Williams. By hegemony I mean the socially constructed discourse of the dominant social order that, by way above all of canon-formation, becomes the truth discourse of a culture: what, to underscore an underdetermined aspect of commentary on hegemony, is permitted to be said. In *Pierre*, this motif is articulated by the pervasive trope of monumentalization: the portraits of Pierre's grandfather, "grand old Pierre," and his father and its allotrope, the (canonical) narrative, which are the agencies of spatializing or reifying, of representing, charting or mapping, the irreducible ambiguities of being, not least in its historical manifestation. The second, more recently articulated, but still to be ad-

367

equately thought, motif is the effort to *think* (and say) the positive possibilities of the de-centering of the *logos*, the absence of presence disclosed by the destruction of metaphysics and the discourse of hegemony to which metaphysics gives rise. I am referring to the initiative, inaugurated by Martin Heidegger's urgent call for the rethinking of thinking itself, of theoreticians such as Jacques Derrida and, more radically, Gilles Deleuze and Felix Guatarri. In *Pierre*, Melville articulates the de-centering in terms of Pierre's "extraordinary e-mergency" and by the trope of *Silence*. By "silence" I mean that to which the discourse of hegemony/ monumentalization/mapping reduces the differential "Other." It is the latter which I will focus on in what follows.

I

What about this resonant silence? As I have suggested, the passages on the metaphysics of monuments and on narrative quoted above are written by Melville in the context of Pierre's "extraordinary emergency." They constitute *dis-closures* of the dark underside—the shadow—of the luminously white truth discourse of America. I mean this not simply in the sense of the negative effects of a totalized thinking/saying that claims to be positively ameliorative, but also in the sense of precipitating into *visibility* the "ambiguities" which, in its will to power over difference, it finally cannot accommodate to its discourse of Presence: the spectral non-being, as it were, that haunts the dominant discourse of Being. As Pierre puts this resonant, if unspeakable, revelation in lines immediately following the second passage on the metaphysics of monumentalization, lines, not incidentally, that conflate the metaphorics of memorialization and narrative: "As for the rest—now I know this, that in commonest memorials, the twilight fact of death first discloses in some secret way, all the ambiguities of that departed thing or person; obliquely it casts hints, and insinuates surmises base, and eternally incapable of being cleared. Decreed by God Omnipotent it is, that Death should be the last scene of the last act of man's play;—a play, which begin how it may, in farce or comedy, ever hath its tragic end; the curtain inevitably falls on a corpse. Therefore, never more will I play the vile pygmy, and by small memorials after death, attempt to reverse the decree of death, by essaying the poor perpetuating of the image of the original" (*P*, 197-98).

368

What Pierre is intuiting in thus discovering the irreducible and thus dreadful ambiguities subsuming his father's portrait—i.e., the hitherto totally charted world of Saddle Meadows—is precisely what Ishmael discovers in his narration of Ahab's pursuit of Moby Dick: the essential unnameabiity, the unpicturability, the unrepresentability, the unsayability of being itself.[1] In a way that uncannily anticipates the Derridean analysis of the non-concept *différance*, the act of naming/picturing/monumentalizing/mapping is simply the substitution or supplementation of a sign for that which would be brought to presence.[2] The process of representation, that is, whether it takes the form of a memorial portrait, a monument, a shrine, a narrative, a cultural model, or a structural "world," always already postpones or defers that which it would bring to presence, that which it would re-present. This motif of deferral, which is intrinsic to representation in general and to the American discourse of hegemony in particular, pervades Melville's novel. Indeed, it could be said provisionally that it constitutes the irreducible absence that haunts the *center* of Pierre's story. And its spectral force is underscored precisely because it is precipitated into "visibility" as a contradictory "Other" by the very fulfillment in violence of the imperial logic of the American discourse of hegemony.

A decisive example of this insistent motif of deferral occurs in Melville's commentary on Pierre's burning, but finally abortive, Titanic desire, in the face of the reigning "Olympian" gods, to write the "comprehensively compact" book that would "gospelize the world anew" (*P*, 273) after having "arrived" in the city and taken lodgings with Isabel in the "Church of the Apostles." Instigated by "the *unprecedented* situation in which [Pierre] now found himself" (*P*, 283; my emphasis), Pierre, thus "disburdened" of the last vestiges of the patriarchal tradition, *envisions* this book as The Book, *lex naturae:* a spatial miniature that would include "digestively . . . the whole range of all that can be known or dreamed" (*P*, 283).[3] In this form, this "comprehensively compact" book would thus "deliver what he thought to be new, or at least miserably neglected Truth to the world" (*P*, 283). Invoking the contradictorily inclusive visualism of this heroic Titanism, Melville underscores Pierre's paradoxical blindness to the things themselves of his vestigial universalist (i.e., metaphysical) narratological perspective: "He did not see [Melville foregrounds Pierre's visualism by repeating this locution three times in one paragraph] that all great books in the world are but the mutilated shadowings-forth of invisible and eternally unembodied images in the soul; so that they are but the mirrors, distortedly reflecting to us our own things; and never mind what the mirror may be, if we would see the object, we must look at the object itself, and not at its reflection" (*P*, 284). In its reliance on *mimesis*, that is, the "comprehensively compact" book Pierre would write reinscribes the dominant "Olympian" culture's essentially metaphysical/spatializing (Hegelian) notion of the work of art as a "microcosm" that *reflects* in miniaturized visible form the "macrocosm," which in its unmediated form is impossible to see and grasp.[4]

After thus disclosing the blindness of Pierre's over-sight, Melville then destructures what we can call his panoptic view. And he does this by invoking the sublime—that which Heidegger calls the "Nothing" and Lyotard, the "unpresentable"[5]—which it is the finally futile purpose of the "comprehensive" visualism of the dominant meta-physical perspective to re-present and domesticate (make docile): "But, as to the resolute traveler in Switzerland, the Alps do never in one wide and comprehensive sweep, instantaneously reveal their full awfulness of amplitude—their overawing extent of peak crowded on peak, and spur sloping on spur, and chain jammed behind chain, and all their wonderful battalionings of might; so hath heaven wisely ordained, that on first entering into the Switzerland of his soul, man shall not at once perceive its tremendous immensity; lest illy prepared for such an encounter, his spirit should sink and perish in the lowermost snows. Only by judicious degrees, appointed by God, does man come at last to gain his Mont Blanc and take an overtopping view of these Alps; and even then, the tithe is not shown; and far over the invisible Atlantic, the Rocky Mountains and the Andes are yet unbeheld. Appalling is the soul of man!" (*P*, 284).[6]

But Melville's destruction of Pierre's vestigial metaphysical vision does not culminate here. He goes on, in what might be called a Heideggerian repetition, to affiliate the vestigial subject-oriented panopticism of Pierre's "comprehensively compact" perspective with the tropes that he has insistently identified in the novel as the metaphors endemic to metaphysical/hegemonic perception and the agents of its imperial will to peace: the monument and inscription (i.e., writing as representation): "Ten million things were as yet uncovered to Pierre. The old mummy lies buried in cloth on cloth; it takes time to unwrap this Egyptian king. Yet now, forsooth, because Pierre began to see through the first superficiality of the world, he fondly weens he has come to the unlayered substance. But, far as any geologist has yet gone down into the world, it is found to consist of nothing but surface stratified on surface. To its axis, the world being nothing but superinduced superficies. By vast pains we mine into the pyramid; by horrible gropings we come to the central room; with joy we espy the sarcophagus; but we lift the lid—and no body is there!—appallingly vacant as vast is the soul of a man!" (*P*, 285)

The itinerary of the logical economy of naming, of representation, of mapping, whose end is to bring temporality and the differences that temporality always already disseminates to stand "ends" paradoxically in the deferral of the *end*, which is to say in the precipitation of the absence of presence. Representation claims as its narratological end a full totality, the perfection and beauty of the All, and is metaphorically represented as "arrival" and figured as the inclusive and plenary centered circle. But the fulfillment of its logical itinerary paradoxically discloses the evacuated circle, the zero: the nothing that precedes naming or, what is the same thing, the difference that is the condition for the possibility of Identity and that always already haunts the latter's authority.

In the novel, Melville calls this absent presence—the shadowy "Other" of metaphysical representation—"Silence." And, it should be noted, it resonates throughout *Pierre*, especially at points that refer to the epistemological perspectives that early Americanists have identified with the "American Renaissance." Thus, for example, in the passage, already quoted, where Melville mocks Plato, Spinoza, Goethe and, above all, the "preposterous rabble of Muggletonian Scots and Yankees, whose vile brogue still the more bestreaks the stripedness of their Greek or German Neoplatonical originals," Melville, we recall, writes: "The profound Silence, that only Voice of our God . . . ; from that divine thing without a name, those imposter philosophers pretend somehow to have got an answer; which is as absurd, as though they should say they had got water out of a stone; for how can a man get a Voice out of Silence?"

Melville's reiterated invocation of God should not deflect us away from the philosophical, narrative, and social margins to which his deviant text *as such* compels our attention, back, that is, into our inscribed adherence to the con-centering *logos*, and to the structure, the narrative, the monument, the map that are endemic to its imperial project. His reference to God in his text should be understood as being within quotation marks, an ironic comment on the still powerful Puritan Spirit in antebellum America. The Silence is, in fact, the Noth-ing that this secularized Puritan spirit would occlude. Or, more specifically, it is the ontological and sociopolitical condition vis-à-vis speech of having been bereft of the *logos* by emergency. It is for Melville, if not quite for young Pierre, the e-mergent unthinkable and unspeakable, the ex-orbited—peripheral—un-sayable, that returns as "visitant" to haunt the central, monumental, and imperi-al stony voice of the dominant metaphysical/hegemonic culture that would have nothing to do with "it."

Understood in the context of the thematics of the thinkable and unthinkable, the sayable and unsayable, Melville's evocation of Silence as the "end" of meta-physical/hegemonic thinking/saying constitutes another insight that is remark-ably proleptic of the postmodern occasion; namely, the recognition, first an-nounced by Heidegger, that the "end" of philosophy in post-Enlightenment modernity constitutes not simply the fulfillment of its logical economy, but its demise.[7] I mean the recognition that, in fulfilling its spatializing logic, in coming to closure, as it were, Western metaphysical thinking—thinking from after or above (*meta*) the temporal process—has transformed the be-ing—the always al-ready differential temporal dynamics—of being to a totalized "World Picture" (*Weltbild*)[8] and in so doing has exposed "to view" the temporality or, what is the same thing, the nothing that metaphysical thinking will have nothing to do with.[9] With the "triumph" of metaphysical thinking, which is to say, with its arrival at the limits of its logical economy, in other words, the Silence that metaphysical thinking cannot think shows itself as the shadowy contradiction—the irreducible excess—that delegitimizes its authority. Silence *e-merges*, as it were, as the spectral presence that haunts metaphysical thinking's "triumphant" hegemony.

The language of spectrality I have insinuated into my text to suggest the af-filiation of Melville's "extraordinary emergency" with the postmodern occasion is not gratuitous. In a late essay on the poetry of Georg Trakl, for example, Hei-degger refers to this occasion as *die Abgeschiedenheit*, "the place of apartness," and the poet who inhabits it, *der Abgeschiedene*, "the one who is apart." He is the "stranger" bereft of language—exiled from a discursive homeland—by the total mapping/colonization of saying by the "Spirit" of metaphysical thinking, but who finds, precisely in that diasporic condition of bereavement, a "spiritual" voice: the "ghostly" voice of silence: "The apartness [*die Abgeschiedenheit*] is 'ghostly.' This word—what does it mean?. . . 'Ghostly' means what is by way of the spirit, stems from it and follows its nature. 'Ghostly' means spiritual, but not in the narrow sense that ties the world to 'spirituality,' the priestly orders of their church. . . '[O]f the spirit' means the opposite of material. This opposition posits a differentiation of two separate realms and, in Platonic-Western terms, states the gulf between the supersensuous *noeton* and the sensuous *aistheton*. 'Of the spirit' so understood—it meanwhile has come to mean rational, intellectual, ideological—together with its opposites belongs to the world view of the decaying kind of man. But the 'dark journey' of the 'blue soul' [of the *Abgeschiedene*] parts company with this kind. . . Apartness is spiritual, determined by the spirit, and ghostly, but it is not 'of the spirit' in the sense of the language of metaphysics. . . . [¶] What, then, is the spirit?. . . . Trakl sees spirit not primarily as *pneuma*, something ethereal, but as a flame that inflames, startles, horrifies, and shatters us. . . . [¶] Trakl sees spirit in terms of that being which is indicated in the original meaning of the word 'ghost'—a being terrified, beside himself, *ek-static*."[10]

There are, admittedly, problems in Heidegger's definition of the "ghostliness" of *die Abgeschiedene*. It could be said with Derrida that it remains vestigially metaphysical.[11] But I want to identify the spectral "one who is apart" with the *Dasein* of *Being and Time*. I mean the being-in-the-world who, with a "break in the referential totality" (*Verweisungsganzheit*), e-merges from the world "as it is publicly interpreted"[12]—the de-differentiated or charted or colonized world, as it were, constructed by the privileged concentering *logos*. He/she is the stranger, the wanderer, the orphan, whose dis-location from the homeland compels him /her into the de-centered uncanny world of not-at-homeness, *die Unheimlichkeit*, where, all the points of reference as on a map having dissolved, he/she comes face to face in anxiety with the nothing.

It would be quixotically optimistic to identify this condition of lack in terms of the conventional understanding of the word "positive." And yet it is, precisely in its diasporic or dis-seminated character, a condition of positivity. This is because it dis-closes the lack of the *Abgeschiedene* not simply as lack but as the lack *of*—the lack that *belongs to*—the "plenary" totality of the imperial thinking that has driven him/her *out* of a homeland ("beside him/her self), because, that is, it reveals this lack as the silence that not only haunts what is permitted to be said by metaphysical thinking, but calls, precisely in its haunting, for the rethinking of (hegemonic) thinking itself. It is a positive condition, in other words, not only because it *opens up* the realm of temporality and possibility to a kind of "ec-static" thinking hitherto foreclosed by the achieved dominion of metaphysical thinking, but also because the condition of silence, in signaling an excess that is beyond the reach of metaphysical thought, *constitutes a directive to such a rethinking of thinking* that would render thinking adequate to the task of resisting the will to power informing what can now be called alternatively the spatial, monumental, cartographic, imperial imperatives of "the Truth."

Read in the context of this emergent, still to be adequately thought, postmodern initiative, Pierre Glendinning is the *Abgeschiedene*. With the dis-integration of the "world" of Saddle Meadows, Pierre undergoes an "extraordinary emergency" that renders him, in Heidegger's terms, an "ec-static in-sistence."[13] He becomes acutely *aware*, that is, of a "reality" that hitherto, in his mergent state, has been foreclosed to him. In his e-mergency he not only comes to realize that the truth of the "world" of Saddle Meadows is a lie, a construction imposed on it by the dominant imperial American culture. He also comes to the realization that his being-in-the-world is a condition of "thrownness," bereft of cartographic coordinates and thus of language. He becomes the one apart, the alienated stranger or nomad who has been exiled from the "homeland" of American discourse into the not-at-home (*die Unheimliche Welt*), where silence resonantly reigns.

The rhetoric Melville uses in *Pierre* to characterize the represented American homeland, as we have seen, circulates around the tropes of memorialization: the monument, the shrine, the relic (behind which lies the metaphor of the seed [*sporos*]), the portrait, the canon, the narrative. But if we read *Pierre* in the context of *Moby-Dick* (which, not incidentally, precedes *Pierre* by less than one year), as, that is, a domestic allotrope of the global scope of the earlier novel, in which the chart and the classificatory table predominate, it becomes clear that this metaphorical chain associated with memory and cultural formation also includes the trope of mapping, a trope which, of course, is endemic to and the *sine qua non* of, the colonialist project. In *Moby-Dick*, Melville overdetermines these geographical tropes in order to interrogate the geopolitical imperial project of the United States in the antebellum period.[14] In *Pierre*, as in *Israel Potter* (a novel, not incidentally, which also traces the genealogy of the American discourse of hegemony back through the American Revolution to its origins in the Puritan's providentially ordained "errand in the wilderness"), he overdetermines the metaphorics of memorialization in order to interrogate the American domestic hegemonic project. But these metaphorical systems circulating around memorialization and mapping and the American practices to which they refer, are, as I have been suggesting, not incommensurate, but indissolubly continuous: they spatialize history and the differences that history disseminates for the purpose of dominating it and them. "Culture" and "colonization" derive etymologically from the Latin *"colonus,"* the planter/settler who domesticates—at-homes—the *agr(i)os,* the wild and savage earth.[15]

For Melville, in other words, the "mapping" and "colonization" of America inaugurated by the Puritans' "founding" of the "unmapped" "New World" wilderness had been implicitly (theoretically) if not actually accomplished by the middle of the nineteenth century when he was writing *Moby Dick* and *Pierre*. I put these affiliated key terms—"founding," "mapping," "colonization"—in quotation marks not to indicate that they are simply metaphors drawn from the discourse of Western imperialism proper. Rather, in keeping with Melville's remarkably proleptic intention, I do it in order to suggest that they refer literally *both* to geographical space *and* to *thinking* itself, that is, to a Western thinking that, at least since the Romans and increasingly thereafter, is informed by a spatial metaphorics that represent the truth of being (knowledge) as a "territory" or "province" or "domain," or "field" or "region" to be won and dominated.[16] In other words, the being of American thought in *Pierre*, even more than the being of American space, has been reduced by an epistemological comportment towards "it" that *sees* its "darkly" differential, ambiguous, and ineffable dynamics from the end (all at once) to a classified space, to an (enlightened) comprehensively compact map, as it were. By putting every detail in time and space in its proper *place* within the larger identical whole, to put it alternatively, this epistemological comportment towards being—this spatializing thinking—facilitates imperial domination of the wild "Other." In short, the world of antebellum American thought in *Pierre* has been utterly colonized and domesticated (at-homed) under the aegis of the hegemonic discourse of Manifest Destiny. As Pierre's futile Titanic attempt against the "Olympian" gods to write a "comprehensively compact" book that would "gospelize the world anew" suggests, even the dissident who would resist the domination enabled by this totally mapped/colonized American thinking is compelled to do so in the imperial metaphysical language it privileges: the language of the "world" that must render Pierre's errancy "docile," the "benign" democratic American discourse, finally, that in effect murders Pierre.[17]

Pierre's silence—his failure to realize the indissoluble affiliation between the representation of being as such, of self, and of world, and thus to "say" what he has intuited about them—implies in one sense his utter defeat by "the world." But, as I have tried to suggest by way of invoking Heidegger's *Abgeschiedene*, Melville, as narrator of Pierre's "story," also suggests, paradoxically, something more positive, something that is only now, at the extreme limits of the late phase of the postmodern occasion, beginning to be thought: when, that is, the domestication and forgetting of the original emancipatory force of the postmodern initiative by its reduction to a periodizing reference that equates it to the logic of late capitalism has become in some degree manifest. Pierre's silence means that he has no language with which to resist the vengeful "world" that has closed in on him in his place of refuge. But for Melville, who, unlike Pierre, "completes" his novel *without* succumbing to the disabling metaphysical imperatives of "comprehensively compact" completeness, it also implies "e-mergence," an incipient understanding of the indissoluble continuum of being that is totally foreign to the representation of being that informs the "world's" discourse. As the one apart, as stranger, as exile, as outsider (within his homeland) Pierre in Melville's view is indeed the "barbarian" at the gates, not, however, in the negative sense given to this word by the imperial Romans, but in the positive sense, ultimately deriving from the ancient Greeks, given to it by the e-mergent discourse of contemporary postcolonialism: one who does not speak "Greek," that is, does not think in terms of—*refuses to be answerable to*—the accommodational imperatives of the truth discourse of the dominant order. As such, Pierre's death, which is to say, his silencing by the hegemonic American culture, precipitates his spectral return. Though he fails to think his occasion to its emergent end, Melville does not. For Melville, Pierre becomes the "ghost" that, according to Heidegger, haunts the reified and reifying thought of modernity which will have nothing to do with "ghosts," or, in Derrida's version (which, in politicizing the "trace," thematizes the imperial visualism that informs Western logocentric thinking), the *revenant*, the "dead" who returns to *visit* the (colonial) *visitor*.[18]

It is this resonant contradiction, this spectral silence, that e-merges with the fulfillment—the violent narrative end—of the circular logic of the "world" of antebellum America. The last spoken words of the novel, which Isabel pointedly addresses to the "world" that has murdered Pierre, are: "All's o'er now, and ye know him not" (*P*, 362). The dramatic narrative of Pierre's life has arrived at the denouement of its fifth act. But this end does not bring the peace—the *catharsis*—of canonical tragedy, which, in rendering the catastrophic ontologically intelligible, reconciles "Man" to Being. This "denouement," that is, does not enable us to *see* Pierre's tragic fate as an essential detail in a larger and meaningful structural or aesthetic whole. Instead, the "closure" of Pierre's story—his, Lucy's, and Isabel's deaths—releases this differential "detail" as an ominous and disconcerting irregular force. Isabel's last words, in other words, constitute a silent, irrepressibly phantasmic, accusation directed against the all-knowing American "world's" truth—and against the American reader/auditor who would sublimate social violence against the shadowy "Other" of the enlightened "world" in the name of the universal (tragedy, for example): the "Talismanic Secret." This "dark" Other that *returns* to haunt the "world" in the form of Isabel's ominous accusation is not restricted to the type of Pierre. According to the anti-logical logic of *Pierre*, it also includes women (the "dark" Isabel and the "deviant" Lucy Tartan), the working class (Dellie), and not least, if we are attuned to the historical (antebellum) context of the composition of *Pierre* and to the national framework in which Melville places his domestic "romance," the black slaves (including those in the North who have been "freed" since the days of "grand old Pierre"). In *thinking* the occasion of Pierre's extraordinary emergency, Melville makes thinking the spectral nothing and its worldly manifestations possible. We might say, in keeping with the metaphor of the monument (and that which is inscribed in Pierre's name), he has in some latent sense gotten "water out of a stone," which is to say, "a Voice out of Silence." This, not incidentally, is also the testimony of *Israel Potter*, of "Bartleby the Scrivener," of "Benito Cereno" of *Billy Budd*, and, if we understand Ishmael's errant garrulousness as the obverse face of silence, of *Moby-Dick*.[19] I am referring, of course, to those orphans of the Fatherland or, as Thomas Pynchon would say, those "preterites" that the hegemonic discourse of a divinely or historically "elected" America has passed over. Indeed, it might also be said that this is the resonant testimony of Melville's creative life itself after the publication of *Pierre*.

It is, I submit, this voice of silence—this "saying" of what the thinking of the dominant American culture renders unsayable—that constitutes Melville's most revolutionary legacy to the postmodern occasion. For in thus wrenching by violence a polyvalent positive content from Pierre's silence, Melville anticipates the postmodernist diagnosis of modernity as the "end" of philosophy. I mean, after Heidegger, its disclosure that the fulfillment of modernity's imperial spatializing logic in the "Age of the World Picture"—and, not incidentally, its ensuing pronouncement of the "end of history"—paradoxically precipitates into invisible visibility the nothing—the excess—that this reified and reifying, i.e., stony, logic necessarily cannot finally accommodate. Melville, as we have seen, insistently identifies this uncapturable nothing with the emerged errant orphan. I, in order to identify "it" with the underdetermined question of thinking itself, have followed Heidegger in identifying it with the *Abgeschiedene*, the one apart, the stranger, the wanderer. Whether "orphan" or "*Abgeschiedene*," or, for that matter, the "differend" (Lyotard)[20] or "catachrestic remainder" (Spivak)[21] or the "singular event" (Foucault)[22] or "specter" (Derrida)[23] or "nomad" (Deleuze and Guattari),[24] he/she is the spectral "non-being" who, at the extreme limit of the discursive empire, returns to haunt the Being of metaphysics and the hegemonic world that has constructed itself on its foundation: the "world" that, as it were, has buried him/her at its periphery in silence. And thus calls for thinking.[25]

But this is not all. If, as I think Melville intends, we read the domestic *mis en scène* of *Pierre* in the global geopolitical context of *Moby-Dick*, and if we attend to his insistent identification of his "defeated" preterites—social de-viants such as Pierre and Bartleby, "mariners, renegades, and castaways" such as the crew of the *Pequod*, women, blacks, native Americans, servants, and ethnic migrants—with the one who has been orphaned (exiled) from the Father(land) by the symbolic order, we are allowed—indeed, compelled—to project his proleptic thematization of the e-mergent specter into a wider social context. Specifically, such an intertextual perspective will enable us to see that Melville's infusion of a positive content into Pierre's silence is also, however inaugurally, proleptic of that polyvalent strategy of resistance to capitalist power that Gilles Deleuze and Felix Guattari, by way of positing a "smooth," "deterritorialized," "rhizomatic" thinking against the "striated" territorialized (mapped) thought of modern capitalist dispensation, have called "nomadology."[26] I am referring particularly to the late or post-postmodern theoretical initiative that, in infusing a positive emancipatory content into the minor—"errant"—term of the "triumphant" binary logic of Western metaphysical thought, has precipitated a certain inaugural polyvalent postcolonial discourse most suggestively, but far from adequately, exemplified by Edward Said's *Culture and Imperialism*, Gayatri Spivak's *The Postcolonial Subject*, Homi Bhabha's essays in *The Location of Culture*, and, in a more theoretical way, by Jacques Derrida's *Specters of Marx*. I mean the emancipatory postcolonial discourse that takes its point of departure precisely from the massive global demographic displacements that constitute the terrible legacy of modern Western imperialism, from, that is, the "extraordinary emergency" of a vast population of emigres, exiles, displaced persons, migrants—nomads, as it were—who have been unhomed, both as subjectivities and as citizens, by the depredations of modern, i.e., post-Enlightenment, colonialism: "[It] is no exaggeration to say that liberation as an intellectual mission, born in the resistance and opposition to the confinements and ravages of imperialism, has now shifted from the settled, established, and domesticated dynamics of culture to its unhoused, decentered, and exilic energies, energies whose incarnation today is the migrant, and whose consciousness is that of the intellectual and artist in exile, the political figure between domains, between forms, between homes, and between languages."[27]

It is, like Melville's in *Pierre*, a "deterritorialized" or "diasporic" or "hybrid" discourse that, in intuiting the impotency of the power of the binarist spatial logic of Western representational thinking, is learning not simply to refuse to be answerable to the *saying* of the imperial first world, but to turn that refusal—that silence—into an effective emancipatory practice. It is, in short, an e-emergent discourse, that, like Melville's at the site of domestic America, is learning to get a "Voice out of Silence."

The irony of Melville's e-mergent occasion should now be clear. It is not simply that his sustained effort since *Moby-Dick*—and especially in *Pierre*—to think his estrangement from the America homeland in the context of the history of Old World philosophy culminates in the explosion of the myth of American exceptionalism. In thinking his emergency—his being outside in the American cultural machine—he anticipates the de-centered and errant thought of the new Europeans and thus becomes a truly American exceptionalist.

NOTES

1   See Spanos, *The Errant Art of* Moby-Dick, (Durham, NC: Duke University Press, 1995), pp. 124-27; 127-31; 169-72; 197-201; 269-70.

2   Derrida, "Différance," in *Speech and Phenomena*, trans. David Allison (Evanston, IL: Northwestern University Press, 1973).

3   The image Pierre invokes to visualize the kind of book he would write is the atoll: "the primitive coral islets which, raising themselves in the depths of profoundest seas, rise funnel-like to the surface, and present there a hoop of white rock, which though on the outside everywhere lashed by the ocean, yet excludes all tempests from the quiet lagoon within" (*P*, 283). Pierre invokes this image because it ostensibly refers to the primordial nature at which he thinks he has arrived. But Pierre's description of this natural phenomenon is remarkably like the description of a man-made monument intended to resist the ravages of time. Indeed, it is, as Joseph Riddel, following the lead of Edgar Dryden, has brilliantly shown, remarkably like the pyramid that Melville invokes on the next page to deconstruct the Book Pierre, in his "unprecedented situation," envisions. See Riddel, "Decentering the Image," *boundary 2* (1979), pp. 165-66; and Dryden, "The Entangled Text," *boundary 2* (1979), pp. 162-63. The pyramid, it needs to be emphasized, is that fundamental spatial structure projected by civilized man not simply to transcend the ephemeral state of mortality but also, by way of its panoptic allotrope, to facilitate a dominant culture's domination of the "Other." Not too far behind the atoll/pyramid trope, as I am suggesting by way of invoking the metaphor of the microcosm, is the trope of the map.

4   As I have pointed out elsewhere, the word "comprehend," which is basic to the discourse of knowledge production in the West, derives from the Latin *com*, an archaic form of *cum* ("with")

used in compounds and meaning "together, in combination or union," "altogether, completely," and *prehendere* "to seize," "to take hold of," that is to say, from two complicitous *metaphorical* systems—seeing and grasping—that belie the originality of the truth of being. This etymology thus discloses the pursuit of knowledge in the West to be a process informed by the will to power over the be-ing of being. I mean the willful reduction of temporality to spatial form (a microcosm mirroring the macrocosm) or, what is the same thing, the reification of an essentially unreifiable being. Western epistemology, in other words, serves the function of annulling the anxiety of being-in-the-world and/or of transforming the difference that time disseminates to standing reserve (Heidegger) or "useful and docile body" (Foucault). "Comprehend," not incidentally, is one of the key philosophical words in the discourse of Hegel's metaphysical dialectics. See Spanos, *Heidegger and Criticism: Retrieving the Cultural Politics of Destruction* (Minneapolis: University of Minnesota Press, 1993), 141-44. See also the chapter entitled "Heidegger and Foucault: The Politics of the Commanding Gaze," pp. 132-80.

5   Martin Heidegger, "What Is Metaphysics?," in *Basic Writings*, revised and expanded edition, ed. David Farrell Krell (New York: Harper & Row, 1993), 100-101; Francois Lyotard, *The Postmodern Condition: A Report on Knowledge*, trans. Geoff Bennington and Brian Massumi (Minneapolis: University of Minnesota Press, 1984), 79-82.

6   As Dominique Arnaud-Marçais observed in an interesting paper entitled "Melville's French Connections" delivered at the conference on "Melville Among the Nations," in Volos, Greece, July 2-6, 1997, Melville seems to be consciously eliding the meaning of the French word, *blanc* ("white") with the English word "blank" ("the absence of presence") in the following passage from the chapter on "The Whiteness of the Whale" in *Moby-Dick*: "Is it that by its indefiniteness it shadows forth the heartless voids and immensities of the universe, and thus stabs us from behind with the thought of annihilation, when beholding the white depths of the milky way? Or is it, that as in essence whiteness is not so much a color as the visible absence of color, and at the same time the concrete of all colors; is it for these reasons that there is such a dumb blankness, full of meaning, in a wide landscape of snows—a colorless, all-color of atheism from which we shrink?" *Moby-Dick; or The Whale*, eds. Harrison Hayford, Hershel Parker, G. Thomas Tanselle (Evanston and Chicago: Northwestern University Press and the Newberry Library, 1988), 195. I would suggest that the reference to Mont Blanc in the crucial passage I am quoting from *Pierre* also plays with this double meaning and is thus fraught with the same ontological significance.

7   Martin Heidegger, "The End of Philosophy and the Task of Thinking," in *Time and Being*, trans. Joan Stambaugh (New York: Harper & Row, 1972), 55-73.

8   Martin Heidegger, "The Age of the World Picture," in *The Question Concerning Technology and Other Essays*, trans. William Lovitt (New York: Harper and Row, 1977), 115-54.

9   Hiedegger, "What Is Metaphysics?," 96.

10   Martin Heidegger, "Language in the Poem: A Discussion of Georg Trakl's Poetic Work," trans. Joan Stambaugh, in *On the Way to Language* (New York: Harper & Row, 1971), 177-79.

11   Derrida, *Of Spirit*, trans. Geoffrey Bennington (Chicago: University of Chicago Press, 1989).

12   Heidegger, *Being and Time*, 102-7; 164-66.

13   Martin Heidegger, "On the Essence of Truth," trans. John Sallis, in *Basic Writings*, 132-35.

14   See Spanos, *The Errant Art of* Moby-Dick, especially, pp. 191-203.

15   Wei-chee Dimock makes explicit the pervasiveness in *Pierre* of the metaphorics of empire and shows convincingly that the domestic topos which the novel overdetermines is utterly continuous with the geopolitical: "C. B. Macpherson, commenting on Hobbes's model of selfhood, makes just this point. A society of 'possessive individualism,' he argues, 'permits and requires the continual invasion of every man by every other.' The self that inhabits such a society must be an 'imperial' self then: in its defensive pose no less than in its appropriative venture, it must act like an imperial polity. From this perspective, there is nothing fortuitous about the presence of Manifest Destiny in *Pierre*, and nothing decorative about its allusions to empire. Those allusions describe, on the contrary, both the structure of its 'untrammelled' self and the structure of the environment that dictates to the self its particular shape. The imperial trappings of Love, especially, have everything to do with the 'internalization' of Manifest Destiny, with the constitution of the self as a 'dominion,' a terrain subject to sovereignty and expropriation both" (*Empire for Liberty*, Princeton, NJ: Princeton University Press, 1989, 148-49). But see my reservations about Dimock's use of this continuum in her reading of Melville's novel in *The Errant Art of* Moby-Dick, pp. 290-91, endnote 62.

16   "Region" (of knowledge), for example, derives from the Latin *regere*, "to command"; "province," from *vincere*, "to conquer"; "domain," from *dominus*, "master"; "territory," from *territorium*, "land of settlement as realm of command." See Michel Foucault, "Questions Concerning Geography," in *Power/Knowledge: Selected Interviews and Other Writings 1972-77*, ed. Colin Gordon (New York: Pantheon Books, 1980), 69.

17   In a provocative "New Americanist" reading of *Pierre*, Priscilla Wald interprets Pierre's declaration to "gospelize the world anew and show them deeper secrets than the Apocalypse!—I will write it, I will write it!" in the following way: "His use of 'gospelize' suggests that he *cannot* reject the basic tenets he thinks he has overthrown. Pierre *wants* to be the instrument through which an absolute eternal truth is filtered; he wants to transcribe rather than write." In this, Pierre is to Wald, following Donald Pease, "not only Ahab's heir . . . but Ishmael's as well." She thus reads Melville's attitude towards Pierre's declaration as one of mockery: "Pierre's text, which also features an author-hero, mirrors both Pierre and *Pierre*; the former is, again, not conscious of the full implications of reflection, whereas that latter exploits it. Melville ridicules Pierre, whose manuscript betrays not the darkness of his vision that horrified his publishers, but the ludicrousness that undermines his tragedy" (my emphasis; "Hearing Narrative Voices in Melville's *Pierre*," in "New Americanists: Revisionist Interventions into the Canon," boundary 2, 17.1 (Spr. 1990), p. 126). Wald, I think, is right in saying that Pierre "cannot reject the basic tenets he thinks he has overthrown." But I would take issue with her subtle restatement of this negative in positive terms: as *wanting* "to be the instrument through which an absolute eternal truth is filtered." Melville is not ridiculing Pierre's juvenile obtuseness. He is pointing, rather, to the depth to which Pierre is inscribed by the triumphant hegemonic dis-

course of America, that is, to the global scope and power of the discourse he would overthrow. He *cannot* reject it because no other language but that of the dominant imperial culture is available to him. For my critique of Pease's reading of Ishmael's narrative as an internalization of Ahab's mono-maniacal "acts of interpretation," which Wald appropriates for her reading of Pierre's abortive effort to "gospelize the world anew," see *The Errant Art of* Moby-Dick, pp. 224-25, 243-45, 274-75.

18 Derrida, *Specters of Marx: The State of the Debt, the Work of Mourning, and the New International*, trans. Peggy Kamuf (New York: Routledge, 1994), 99-102.

19 See *The Errant Art of* Moby-Dick, 271-74.

20 Jean Francois Lyotard, *Differend: Phrases in Dispute*, trans. Georges Van Den Abbele (Minneapolis: University of Minnesota Press, 1988).

21 Gayatri Chakravorty Spivak, "Marginality in the Teaching Machine," in *Outside in the Teaching Machine* (New York: Routledge, 1993), 53-76.

22 Michel Foucault, "Theatrum Philosophicum": in *Language, Counter-Memory, Practice: Selected Essays and Interviews*, ed. Donald Bouchard, trans. Bouchard and Sherry Simon (Ithaca, NY: Cornell University Press, 1977), 165-96. This essay is a review of Gilles Deleuze's *Difference et repetition* (1969) and *Logique du sens* (1969), which inaugurate Deleuze's sustained effort to think the "phantasmic" excess of the Western philosophical tradition that culminates in the rhizomatic thinking of the nomad in his and Guatarri's *A Thousand Plateaus*. See below.

23 Jacques Derrida, *Specters of Marx: The State of the Debt, the Work of Mourning, and the New International*, trans. Peggy Kamuf (New York: Routledge, 1994).

24 Gilles Deleuze and Felix Guatarri, *A Thousand Plateaus: Capitalism and Schizophrenia*, trans. Brian Massumi (New York: Routledge, 1987).

25 Priscilla Wald verges on thematizing this momentous post-metaphysical legacy: "Insofar as we come to see the narrator's perspective as an alternate narrative as, that is, *an* other, not *the* other narrative, then perhaps Silence can indeed speak to the attuned reader. The narrative unravelling that follows undermines narrative authority and alerts the reader to the possibility of an alternative discourse. Silence (and its counterpart, meaningless noise) emerges in resistance to narrative and meaningful language, not as an absence but as an alternative presence, the *embodiment*, perhaps of possibility" ("Hearing Narrative Voices in Melville's *Pierre*," 120). But because she is blinded by her vestigially American exceptionalist insight, she is compelled to refer to Pierre's predicament as a problem more or less of authorial identity and to contain Melville's *Pierre* within "the scene of writing." She thus fails to perceive the global scope of Melville's domestic "drama" and, above all, of the "possibility" vis-à-vis thinking inhering in his evocation of the Silence to which the American "world" reduces those who refuse their spontaneous consent to its truth.

26 Deleuze and Guatarri, *A Thousand Plateaus: Capitalism and Schizophrenia*, trans. Brian Massumi (Minneapolis: University of Minnesota Press, 1987).

27 Said, *Culture and Imperialism* (New York: Alfred Knopf, 1993), 332.

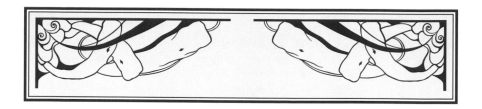

DILEK DİRENÇ

WHAT DO THESE WOMEN WANT?

PIERRE AND THE NEW WORLD OF GENDER

elville's *Pierre; or, The Ambiguities*, represents a shift in focus from the perilous seas of his previous narratives to the pastoral American scene. The novel concentrates especially on the social roles and individual needs of male and female characters. Although the hero in *Pierre* is only an "intellectual adventurer" and his quest does not take place in the middle of fierce gales or on faraway savage islands, it is still as dangerous and ultimately as destructive as Ahab's pursuit of the white whale. However, Pierre is not the only seeker in this novel, which interweaves the lives of Lucy Tartan, Pierre's fiancée at the opening of the novel, and Isabel Banford, Pierre's alleged illegitimate sister and later his make-believe wife. These young women are also on their quests while exhibiting the gender-based characteristics and constraints of American society in the mid-nineteenth century. The intent of this paper is to show that by playing with the conventional portrayal of the "dark" and "light" ladies of romance fiction as well as genteel concepts of "masculinity" and "femininity," Melville attempts to subvert the nineteenth-century clichés, stereotypes, and doublings and tries to counter them by presenting ambiguity, paradox, and irony in his portrayal of these women. An analysis of Melville's technique will show that in *Pierre* the molds of the dark temptress and the fair maiden are filled with more heterogeneous material than expected. Also, these seemingly passive and dependent women, at closer inspection, turn out to be on their own quest for power and

384

fulfillment, which, in itself, is a masculine privilege and tradition. Thus, gender stereotypes and the stereotypes of romance fiction become more complex, more contradictory, and more ambiguous in Melville's hands.

Pierre's mother, Mary Glendinning, is the only woman in *Pierre* who already has power and authority. As a widow, she is the head of the family; an attractive woman from an affluent family, she is very much aware of her advantages and privileges in life. Toward Pierre she exercises her power playfully and genially, but with demanding Oedipal overtones. Lucy and Isabel, however, are totally devoid of any kind of power at the beginning. Since she has neither money nor family, Isabel is an outsider with no means of acquiring power and achieving acceptance and recognition in society. Lucy, on the other hand, who comes from a respectable and wealthy family, is an insider; yet she is strictly limited by the conventions and expectations of society. The moment she dares to step beyond these, she becomes an outsider as well. These two young women search desperately for empowerment and fulfillment; Isabel, to be included in human kinship and to achieve love and intimacy, Lucy, to be free to decide for herself and to love and live accordingly.

As the novel opens, Pierre, his mother, and his promised bride occupy an ordered and peaceful world. There are no confusions or unsettling questions in their conformist lives. However, when Isabel gives Pierre the letter which reveals her identity, she threatens this ordered world. From the moment Isabel appears on the scene, she exerts a revolutionary influence on Pierre. However, as Phillip J. Egan points out, "Isabel revolutionizes Pierre's life not so much because she gets him to do unconventional things but because she gets him to think unconventionally, and this pulls him loose from the fixities of his early life" (100). Since her letter leads him to doubt, question, and search his past on the symbolic level, it becomes an invitation for Pierre to enter the world of the seekers, to leave the world of common men and earthly "horologicals" behind, and to embark on a quest in search of heavenly "chronometricals."

It is only after his confrontation with Isabel that Pierre gradually gains new insight into his own life; he awakens to the fact that the world he has occupied so far is a world of vanity, artifice, and hypocrisy, and that its superficial peace, order, and happiness are maintained at the expense of others. Through Isabel

385

Pierre also gains new insight into his mother's character and his father's early life. He sees that "[his] sacred father is no more a saint" and that his dear mother is "pride's priestess" (Melville 110). He realizes that she loves him "with pride's love," not with love "past all understanding"; she, in fact, loves "her own curled and haughty beauty" in her son (109-10). Part of this realization grows from his recognition of Falsgrave's cowardice and religious hypocrisy in the case of the wronged and abused Delly Ulver. Through Isabel, whose dark and bewildering presence is "the complete denial of everything in his mother's milky, blue, pink, and gold idyllic world" (Fiedler 420), Pierre gets a glimpse of the more enigmatic face of life.

Indirectly through Pierre, Isabel changes the lives of the other two women in Pierre's life. Mrs. Glendinning cannot accept the fact that her son can go against her will and that she is not in the center of his life anymore. Her once "docile" son's rebellion infuriates her. She reacts violently and disinherits Pierre. Following this act of revenge, as if she cannot continue living without seeing herself reflected in her son, she dies. Melville's portrayal of Pierre's mother does not present a traditional image of motherhood with its conventional attributes. Wilma Garcia sees her as a "parody as well as namesake of the mother of Jesus" (80). Whereas "the Biblical Mary was poor and humble," Mary Glendinning is a woman of wealth, social influence, and immense pride (80). Her pride and selfishness blind her not only to the needs of the helpless young woman, Delly Ulver, but also to those of her own son. Mary Glendinning wants power not to love and nurture, but to control and conquer. Instead of loving care and contact, she concentrates all her energy on acts of vengeance, control, and ego, ultimately destroying herself as well as her relationship with her son. Lucy, on the other hand, does not give up Pierre. Her long "swoon" that follows the news of Pierre's marriage to Isabel is an experience that ultimately liberates her from the social games and masks. Her inner journey causes a transformation, a renewal if not a rebirth, and, as a result of it, she emerges as a much stronger character. She offers Pierre what Mrs. Glendinning as a mother is unable to give, her unconditional and undemanding love.

Because Lucy, before Isabel's intrusion, nicely fits into Pierre's complacent life, she is usually identified with the quiet forces of the land, and Isabel with the restless forces of the sea. F. O. Matthiessen states that "Pierre's presentiment at first seeing [Isabel] is cast in the familiar Melvillian terms of the difference between the peaceful land in which Pierre has been living and the dangerous waters that lie ahead" (481). Joyce W. Warren emphasizes the same idea explaining that in Lucy and Isabel "Melville suggests the same polarity that in *Moby-Dick* he described as the lee shore and landlessness" (119). She maintains that in this novel "Lucy represents the safe, known, every-day 'inland' peace and 'blessed sereneness' of 'truth-blind' Saddle Meadows. When Pierre meets Isabel, however, he begins to probe and question and resolves to forsake Lucy and the 'green, gentle, and most docile earth' to embark with Isabel upon 'the appalling ocean' of the unknown" (119).

The description of Isabel throughout the novel makes it clear that she is not an ordinary woman; she does not seem to belong to the world she lives in. She is a wild being who belongs to the "wonder-world from which she had so slidingly emerged" (Melville 154). She has an alien quality which suggests that she has no connection to the land or the region. The first time she gets on a boat, she becomes ecstatic by recognizing the motion of the waves. She cries, "I feel it! I feel it! It is! It is!" (416) as if she has an inborn recognition of the sea. Lucy, on the other hand, is certainly a land woman. We are told that "though born among brick and mortar in a seaport, she still pined for unbaked earth and inland grass," and "every spring, this sweet linnet girl did migrate inland" (33). On the symbolic level, the two women might be seen as the representatives of the antithetical forces of the sheltered land and the open sea. Yet, Melville complicates this view, for Lucy later rejects the values of the sheltered land, and Isabel becomes a childlike figure lacking the depth of the open sea.

Lucy is the epitome of social propriety and conformity when she first appears on the scene. Described through the eyes of Pierre's mother, she is "His little wife, . . . beautiful, and reverential, and most docile" (Melville 27). Her fragility and ethereal qualities lead Pierre to think that Lucy will not be able to make a worldly wife; "one husbandly embrace would break her airy zone," he contemplates early in the story (72). However, she later shows a determination not expected from the traditional "little wife" and confounds Pierre with her newly acquired strength: "Such wonderful strength in such wonderful sweetness; such inflexibility in one so fragile," Pierre reflects (380). Isabel, however, is a more interesting and promising character at the beginning. She lives on the outskirts of society and is neither shaped nor limited by its values and expectations. She is independent because she is solitary. She is a doer and agent who finds Pierre and bewilders him with her ambiguous stories, and she decides when and what to tell him. Yet, as Egan points out, she "does not live up to the expectations she creates" and "never again quite achieves the quiet power she has when she first appears" (108). After she tells her obscure tales and plays her mysterious songs, her part seems to be completed, and she becomes totally dependent on Pierre. Although she first seems to be associated with the open sea, she soon proves not to have the depth to justify this association. She does not grow, mature, or change. Isabel tells Pierre that she "never knew a mortal mother," and that her lips "never touched a woman's breast" (Melville 137). Without ever being exposed to maternal love and care, Isabel has not matured emotionally. Her darkness is a manifestation of her inability to grow, to mature, and thus to complete her feminine nature. An incomplete character, Isabel is condemned to be "a child of everlasting youngness," denied maturity and fulfillment (167).

Similar to Mary Glendinning's, Isabel's quest for power is self-centered, although its purpose is to help her overcome isolation and gain human contact and inclusion in society. Isabel reaches Pierre and challenges him because, within the circumscribing conventions of nineteenth-century society, her influence on Pierre is her only route to power. Consequently, in Isabel's quest for power Pierre must be subordinate, but in Lucy's he must be the focus of unconditional love and support. Isabel manipulates Pierre no less than his mother did, but whereas Mrs. Glendinning limited his personal development, Isabel challenges him in ways that destroy them both. Lucy, on the other hand, adopts Pierre when he is deserted by everybody else, including his own mother. She becomes a surrogate mother to him because she comes "to serve" and "to guard" both Pierre and Isabel (Melville 361). With a very maternal concern, she even intends "to practice her crayon art professionally" so that she can contribute to the economic survival of the group (383). At this point of her quest, she seems to have achieved an alternative vision of self-identity outside the social and sexual convention. If, in his ethical rectitude, Pierre seems a putative Christ, Lucy seems even more the Virgin Mother determined not to desert Pierre and devote her life to him without expecting anything in return. Isabel, in contrast, easily accepts the sacrifices Pierre makes on her behalf. Although she does not directly ask for anything, she accepts whatever Pierre offers her without questioning their implications for him.

The physical descriptions of these beautiful women also symbolize their contrasting natures. Lucy is light and fair, her "cheeks were tinted with the most delicate white and red, the white predominating" (Melville 31); Isabel has a "dark-eyed, lustrous, imploring, mournful face" (46), and "her dark, olive cheek is without a blush" (58). Lucy is described by the narrator as washed in light: "The setting sun, streaming through the window, bathed her whole form in golden loveliness and light" (71). On the other hand, Isabel appears among "the thicker shadows" (133), "the death-like beauty of [her] face" spreading out "immortal sadness" (134). Pierre sees himself placed between "the fond, all-understood blue eyes of Lucy" and "the as tender, but mournful and inscrutable dark glance of Isabel" (153). When Isabel learns that Lucy is coming to join them in the city, she makes a comparison between herself and Lucy based on their physical characteristics. Claiming that Lucy's blue eyes and fair hair "make the livery of heaven" (365), Isabel compares herself and Lucy to the angels that "hover over every human soul"; Lucy is the good angel with her "heaven's own blue" eyes, and Isabel, "the other angel," because "a good angel with dark eyes" is anomalous (365). Isabel here uses the familiar association of dark with evil and light with good. Yet, the presence of these two women in Pierre's life and in the novel cannot be reduced to a conflict between good and evil. Isabel's dark presence in the novel is more mysterious than it is evil. Throughout the novel, "inscrutable," "unfathomable," and "inexplicable" are the adjectives repeatedly used in relation to her. She contributes to the "ambiguities" of the subtitle. Lucy is light, transparent, and as open to the eye as the clear "June skies" (365). At the beginning of the novel she represents simplicity, propriety, and seeming stability, but the foundation for these qualities is shallow in contrast to Isabel's mysterious depths. However, later in the story, when she is determined not to give up Pierre, Lucy becomes a more intriguing character compared to Isabel who becomes a shadow after the move to the city.

The descriptions of both women are drawn directly from the tradition of sentimental romances. Although Melville's mock-romantic attitude is obvious, even cloying as he parodies the themes of sentimental moralism and domesticity, he sets out with "conventional stereotypes, the angelic fair lady and the dark temptress" (Herzog 86). In *Pierre*, Isabel is seemingly related to the world of passions and psychological complexity, and Lucy to the world of ideals and pastoral simplicity. Noting that America as Eden had been the major theme of American literature in the previous century, Judith Fryer calls the female characters of the period "American Eves." (24-25). Fryer finds something of the dark and the fair faces of the "American Eves" also in *Pierre*. With her "saintly, virginal and ethereal qualities" (49), Lucy is the "pale maiden," "Eve before the Fall," whereas Isabel displays "all of the conventional trappings of the dark lady, of Eve the temptress" (54).

Fryer's description of the "pale maiden" and the "dark lady" as contrasting faces of Eve and her application of these female images to Lucy and Isabel exemplify the standard interpretation of these characters, though slight variations exist. Wilma Garcia, for example, agrees with Fryer that "Lucy is the epitome of the virgin saint" (84). However, she does not see Isabel as the dark woman; she believes that Isabel is only "another image of thwarted fertility" (86). Faye M. Lenargic, on the other hand, interpreting the novel as a portrayal of "the innocent hero's initiation into the mysteries of female sexuality," sees Isabel as a "Fatal Woman at her most destructive" who is responsible for the death of all three protagonists (143). Yet, is Lucy only "a virginal figure out of a fairy tale" who possesses "ideal purity," and Isabel "the dark woman, a temptation for Pierre toward sexuality"? (Haberstroh 69)

In sentimental fiction the contrasts are clear and unmistakable. In a novel subtitled "The Ambiguities," however, the characters cannot be expected to be as neat and tidy as stereotypes of fiction. Isabel is the dark lady and representative of the mysterious and dark forces of life. She is the temptress, not only in terms of sexuality but more importantly in the sense that she tempts Pierre to dive "deep down in the gulf of the soul" (Melville 319). Her temptation is an intellectual and psychological challenge; her influence turns Pierre from an ordinary swimmer into a "diver," the truth-seeker, so often admired by Melville. She forces him to confront the dark underside of idealized American pastoral, of family secrets, of religious faith, and cowardly conformity. If Isabel is a destructive force, what she destroys first is Pierre's romantic and complacent illusions about his life, but this might be interpreted as a beneficial influence leading him to maturity. Lucy, on the other hand, is the angelic fair maiden; but her virginal qualities do not prevent her from becoming a rebel, and her ethereal qualities do not blind her to the earthly concerns of survival. If Lucy's rejection of her family and its values might be interpreted as a feminine sacrifice, it is certainly not the self-effacing or the conventionally expected passive kind of sacrifice. Her decision is independently made and unquestionably non-conformist, a sign of her increasing self-confidence and maturity. Breaking the pattern of her yearly cycle, "this sweet linnet girl" does not this time migrate inland, and thus she breaks loose from the values of the land. In the world of the novel, as we see, Isabel and Lucy resist easy labeling.

In their discussion of "the tendency of romance fiction to split the hero's love into two figures, a 'dark' one and a 'light' one," Annis Pratt and colleagues go back to Northrop Frye's definition of "a polarization" in romances "between the lady of duty and the lady of pleasure" (81). She suggests that many novels written in the previous century were built upon the tension between these "dark" and "light" figures and, eventually, the tension "between a hero's passion for an unacceptable lover and [his] dutiful marriage" (81). Melville's portrayal of the dark lady and fair lady in Pierre's life is intentionally ambiguous. There is also a similar kind of ambiguity in Pierre's marriage to a dark temptress. Is this a marriage of duty where he attempts to fix his father's wrongdoing, or is it a marriage of passion which he desperately wants to see as a duty on his part? Does the possibility of Isabel's being his sister make her less than a temptress or more of a temptress? Who is "the lady of duty" and who is "the lady of pleasure" in this novel? Since he was betrothed to Lucy, Pierre also has a responsibility towards her; however, does he not sacrifice her too easily? Obviously, Melville here confutes the stereotypes of the dark and light ladies and their association with pleasure and duty, and thus he subverts the conventional assumptions of his culture and exposes their unreliability.

At the end of the novel, Lucy's life-giving powers are neutralized by Isabel's desperate femininity, so Lucy's whiteness solidifies into marble. In her restless search for a belated human bond and sympathy, Isabel comes closer to Ahab and Melville's other seekers. Her quest, like theirs, proves to be fruitless and destructive. She cannot have this human intimacy, which is symbolized in the mother's milk she has never tasted, either as a sister or as a wife. At the very end, the stone and marble imagery which pervades the novel culminates in Isabel's petrifying influence on Lucy and Pierre.

In this story of total destruction, as in *Moby-Dick* and later in *Billy Budd*, Melville asserts the idea that a world of polarized masculinity and femininity and a world of split womanhood is not a place of vitality and creativity, but a world of struggle, agony, defeat, death, and destruction. To Melville, the possibility of rebirth for the individual and society lies in the merging of all polarized forces of Western thought and culture. Laurie Robertson-Lorant explains that in *Moby-Dick* "Ishmael is saved from self-destruction" because he is able to "experience the 'melting' which the symbolic marriage with Queequeg allow[s] him to enjoy" (404). The significance of this "melting" lies in the fact that it "merges sexual and spiritual impulses into a union that annihilates Western polarities of body and soul, just as the orgasmic Nirvana of the late poem 'Buddha' dissolves dualities" (404). *Pierre*, on the other hand, offers no possibility of rebirth for either Pierre or his companions. Amid the currents of counterfeit femininity and religiosity, maternal hypocrisy and fraudulent art, human fulfillment is inevitably frustrated. However, Melville's attempt to expose and question the polarities of his time and culture may well communicate more successfully to readers today than to readers in his own time.

References

Egan, Philippe J. "Isabel's Story: The Voice of the Dark Woman in Melville's *Pierre*." *American Transcendental Quarterly* 1.2 (1987): 99-110.

Fiedler, Leslie. *Love and Death in the American Novel*. New York: Anchor Books, 1992.

Fryer, Judith. *The Faces of Eve: Women in the Nineteenth Century American Novel*. New York: Oxford UP, 1976.

Garcia, Wilma. *Mothers and Others: Myths of the Female in the Works of Melville, Twain, and Hemingway.* New York: Peter Lang Publishing, 1984.

Haberstroh, Charles J., Jr. *Melville and Male Identity.* Cranbury, NJ: Associated UP, 1980.

Herzog, Kristin. *Women, Ethnics, and Exotics: Images of Power in Mid-Nineteenth-Century American Fiction.* Knoxville: U of Tennessee P, 1983.

Lenargic, Faye M. "The Virgin Shapelifter: Melville's Quarrel with Maids." *Courage and Tools: The Florence Howe Award for Feminist Scholarship, 1974-1989.* Ed. Joanne Glasgow and Angela Ingram. New York: Modern Language Association of America, 1990. 136-54.

Matthiessen, F. O. *American Renaissance.* New York: Oxford UP, 1964.

Melville, Herman. *Herman Melville: Novels.* New York: Library of America, 1984.

Pratt, Annis, Barbara White, Andrea Loewenstein, and Mary Wyer. *Archetypal Patterns in Women's Fiction.* Bloomington: Indiana UP, 1981.

Robertson-Lorant, Laurie. "Melville's Embrace of the Invisible Woman." *Centennial Review* 34 (1990): 401-11.

Warren, Joyce W. *The American Narcissus: Individualism and Women in Nineteenth-Century American Fiction.* New Brunswick, NJ: Rutgers UP, 1984.

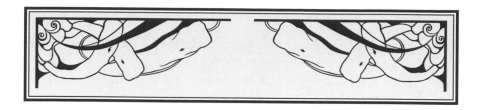

ATTILIO FAVORINI

THE EUTHANASIA OF NARRATIVE:

MULTIPLE ENDINGS IN *BILLY BUDD*

hat Herman Melville was at the time he was writing *Billy Budd, Sailor* preoccupied with endings may be understandable in view of the death of his son Stanwix in 1886, his own failing health, and the decay of his career. It is noteworthy enough that Melville wrote what became the ending of the novel before he began it—"Billy in the Darbies" predating the completed manuscript by three to five years.[1] But, in the end, the ballad proved to be only one of four endings Melville provided for his short novel, including the description of Billy's hanging, the concocted report supposedly published in "a naval chronicle of the time" (p. 130), and the comic dialogue of chapter 26.

Perhaps the oddest of these is the burlesque exchange between the Purser and the Surgeon, whose eschatological speculations take a scatological turn. The Purser offers the view that Billy's body did not jerk spasmodically at his hanging because Billy suppressed the climactic reflex by sheer power of will. The Surgeon superciliously dismisses the Purser's theory: "*Euthanasia*, Mr. Purser, is something like your will-power; I doubt its authenticity as a scientific term—begging your pardon again. It is at once imaginative and metaphysical; in short, Greek" (p. 125). Because the end of Billy Budd is also the ending of *Billy Budd*, I am convinced that the Surgeon's description also slyly characterizes Melville's novel, with its myriad references to chirons and "Delphic deliverances," to Apol-

394

lo, Achilles, Plato, Alexander, Agamemnon—and which itself comes to an end with a series of anti-climaxes.

Billy Budd's ambiguous endings, as well as its "Greek" qualities, have been frequently the focus of analysis.[2] What I intend to argue here is that the two features are essentially related: that the novel's multiple endings can be traced to multiple beginnings, that Greek tragedy was only one among several dramatic models Melville had in mind when he was writing *Billy Budd*, and that the key to the novel's construction is the discord of these dramatic models. My speculations therefore contribute less to a discussion of what *Billy Budd* means than to one of how it means.

To proceed as did Melville by beginning at the end, why, in a novella whose revisions mark a decided tendency towards exchanging the reported for the dramatic,[3] is there a final retreat from drama into pseudo-journalism and balladeering? The narrator's subtle answer—that "the symmetry of form attainable in pure fiction cannot so readily be achieved in a narration essentially having less to do with fable than with fact" (p. 128)—is more than ambiguous. It is manifestly a deception, for *Billy Budd* as an "imaginative" and "metaphysical" creation has more to do with fable. Yet it is true in a way the narrator does not intend, for Melville here—as throughout his career—invites consideration of how factual representation may be suffused with fictionality. And it is yet again false in the deepest sense, because what seems to engage Melville most is the fable-making itself. Indeed, the novel's "construed discordance"[4] derives also from the tension between the narrator's sly voice and the multivalent narrative Melville constructs for him.

Hayford and Sealts have demonstrated that Melville only increased such tensions in the course of composition, complicating the character of Vere, adding historical circumstance, deliberately leaving contradictions unresolved, and cultivating a noncommital alienation.[5] Though the debate over acceptance or irony, framed in the 1950s, still rages in some quarters, recent criticism tends to embrace the openness of the text, making it out to be a "retrospective allegory of Melville's rhetorical career," which Melville deferred completing as a way of resisting a final silence; or a story about the difficulty of writer or reader hitting the mark in matching understanding and composition; or by dubbing it a problem novel "to emphasize its parallels with and origins in the problem play"; or by seeing it as a fable of homosexual attraction and homophobia simultaneously.[6] While there can be nothing new about suggesting that Melville relished ambiguity or self-consciously scrutinized the narrative mode, I hope to show that the text of *Billy Budd* bears the traces of a handful of plays that treat the issues of the novel from divergent points of view.

Paradoxically enough, the enticement of dramatic irony that allowed Melville to "insinuate without endorsing"[7] various narrative positions has eluded the many dramatizers of the novel, whose adaptations, seven of which had appeared prior to the Hayford/Sealts edition, tend to resolve Melville's ambiguities one way or the other. Thus, Coxe and Chapman, the first dramatizers of *Billy Budd*, supply the scene of Vere communicating the death sentence to Billy which the novel's narrator only conjectures; they show Vere begging forgiveness and telling Billy the law is "all wrong, all wrong."[8] The libretto by E. M. Forster and Eric Crozier for the Benjamin Britten opera narrows the focus of the action by framing the story with a Prologue and Epilogue delivered by an aged Vere. In various adaptations, Claggart is over-determined as motivated by fear, pride, impotence, or homosexual attraction. A television adaptation in 1952 changed the setting to sailors on an American ship during the war of 1812 and featured a prologue justifying Vere as torn by personal feelings and duty to country but ultimately charged with maintaining discipline. This prologue was delivered on television by Admiral Halsey. By contrast, in a 1969 musical stage version Billy stands in for conscientious objectors, and his mates sing a song entitled "It Ain't Us Who Makes the Wars."[9] The Age of Aquarius, of course, had dawned in the meanwhile.

If subsequent dramatizations of *Billy Budd* tended to oversimplify the novel, its dramatic antecedents are another story—or, as I would have it, other stories. I have come to imagine the relationship of *Billy Budd* to the drama in an hourglass shape, as grains of drama (what Samuel Beckett called dramaticules) passing through the cinched waist of the novel which in turn yields a growing heap of dramatizations of itself. Among the dramatic antecedents only two—both of them nautical melodramas by Douglas Jerrold—were certainly and consciously used by Melville in the course of writing *Billy Budd*. The others I will adduce were certainly known to Melville—he possesed them in book form—and have left their marks on his text almost as clearly as did Jerrold. All together, the group constitutes an exhaustive array of dramatic models for dealing abstractly or allegorically ("metaphysically," the Surgeon would say) with the theme of justice and civil order by focusing on a cast of characters clustered around an ambiguous crime.

It is more than forty years since Jerrold's *Black Ey'd Susan* (1829) and *The Mutiny at the Nore* (1830) were identified as likely sources for the plot of *Billy Budd*, and I am here largely, though not entirely, recapitulating.[10] What is new in my perspective is the idea that these two and other dramatic models afforded Melville not just a fund of ideas and devices but together posed a compositional conundrum, evidence for which Melville chose to leave in the text. To travel the familiar ground first: between them, the two melodramas offered Melville a morally innocent sailor condemned to hang for striking a superior, a setting of a British man o' war during the post-French Revolutionary period, a condemned man bestowing a final benediction, and a moral dilemma for his judges. Uncommented on previously, however, are these minor echoes, which I take to be marks of Melville's experiencing one or the other melodrama in the theater: William in *Black Ey'd Susan* sings a reprise of a ballad just before he is to be hanged, a ballad which contains the image of a sailor "high upon the yard" and then descending by a cord to the deck; the court martial in Jerrold's play and Melville's novel takes place in the Captain's cabin laid out in careful symmetry; the subtitle of *The Mutiny at the Nore* is *British Sailors in 1797* and it was advertised as a "historico-nautical" melodrama.[11] Melville may have had more than a hundred opportunities to see *Black Ey'd Susan* in New York before he started writing *Billy Budd*, but that he sought out in May 1890 a library copy of the much less popular *Mutiny at the Nore*[12] is particularly interesting and may be reflected in his development of the court scene, absent from all but the latest stages of composition.[13]

Furthermore, Billy Budd is by no means purged of the vestiges of the Jolly Jack Tar stage character, whom Jerrold exploits and who predates the Jerrold melodramas by almost a hundred years. The prototype of the Jolly Jack Tar is generally taken to be Will Steady in James C. Cross's *The Purse; or, Benevolent Tar*

(1746). As the type developed, he emerged as sentimental, virtuous, loyal, patriotic, courageous, respectful, self-sacrificing, on the best of terms with his superiors, an accomplished singer, excellent company and as characteristically speaking in a comic nautical dialect.[14] William, the example in *Black Ey'd Susan* enters to a music cue with the following: "Huzza, huzza! my noble fellows, my heart jumps like a dolphin — my head turns round like a capstern; I feel as if I were driving before the gale of pleasure for the haven of joy" (p. 18). Melville both adopts and adapts the type for his Handsome Sailor, happily and perhaps deliberately suppressing the typical comic volubility in Billy's stutter. While a great deal has been written about the Handsome Sailor as noble savage archetype,[15] I suggest that Billy oscillates between archetype and theatrical stereotype: inside the narrative he is a comic figure to his mates.

In the melodramatic *Black Ey'd Susan* and *The Mutiny at the Nore*, then, Melville had models — the former resolved comically and the latter tragically, by the way — for rendering a theme of justice inflected with a moral and metaphysical dilemma. In Shakespeare's *Measure for Measure* he had an example of the same theme rendered in exquisite ambiguity and irony. Melville's debt to Shakespeare has been extensively documented, but if anyone has observed the parallels between *Measure for Measure* and *Billy Budd,* it has escaped my notice.[16] Yet, In Shakespeare's play we have the issue of justice vs. mercy and strict adherence to the law vs. anarchy presented, albeit ambiguously, as an allegory of Christian redemption. Indeed, as regards the shape and detail of the plot, as well as the theme, *Billy Budd* certainly owes more to *Measure for Measure* than to either *Othello* or *The Winter's Tale*, both of which have been adduced as analogues.[17]

Shakespeare's main characters are the disguised and "fantastical" Duke Vincentio (= "starry Vere"); his depraved surrogate ironically called Angelo (= Claggart); and the (almost) innocent siblings Claudio and the novice Isabella (male and female conflated by Melville into the androgynous Billy). Claudio has impregnated his fiancée, with whom he has announced the banns of marriage, and stands condemned to death on a strict interpretation of the law against fornication. He is visited in his cell by the Duke disguised as a monk who urges him to be resolute for death, recalling chapters 22 and 24 of the novel, in which Billy is visited first by Vere and then the chaplain. Vincentio wrestles aloud with moral issues in Vere-like exclamations, worrying that unless the law is enforced "strong statutes / Stand like the forfeits in a barber's shop" (V, i, 321-23) and soliloquizing "O, what man may within him hide, / Though angel on the outward side" (III, ii, 286-87)—both passages marked by Melville in his copy of *Measure for Measure*, which is the third most heavily marked play in his edition of Shakespeare.[18] Finally, in both Shakespeare's play and Melville's novel, the almost allegorical rendering of justice is refracted as through a dark prism: the difficulty of reading human situations from their appearances. Shakespeare's Isabella and Melville's Billy both demonstrate the congruence of appearance and reality, even as Angelo and Claggart demonstrate the opposite. So, what Barbara Johnson says of the novel is equally true of the play: "The story thus takes place between the postulate of continuity between signifier and signified ('handsome is as handsome does') and the postulate of their discontinuity ('a mantrap may be under the ruddy-tipped daisies')."[19]

Part of what renders both *Measure for Measure* and *Billy Budd* ambiguous as allegories of acceptance or redemption is the frailty of the human judges supposedly standing in for a metaphysical presence felt largely by its absence, an absence Melville alludes to in naming one of the ships in his story the *Athée*. The conventions of neither the Jacobean drama nor the nineteenth-century novel encouraged the direct and personified intervention of the deity. Greek dramatists, however, suffered from no such limitation. The gods manipulate the action in many Greek plays, but the circumstances most evocative of *Billy Budd* occur in Aeschylus' *Oresteian Trilogy*, which dramatizes the adjudication of an ambiguous offense committed by a victimized protagonist.[20]

As with his use of Shakespeare, the case that Melville was thinking of Aeschylus when he was writing *Billy Budd* must be made on internal textual grounds almost exclusively. Though we know Melville owned a copy of the Potter translation of the *Oresteia*, that copy has not resurfaced.[21] If there is anything like an extra-textual clue it is in the word "Agamemnon" circled and penciled with a question mark into Melville's manuscript on leaf 57 but not working its way into the text until leaf 109, when the Old Dansker is identified as an "*Agamemnon*-man" (p. 148). While it may be argued that the *Agamemnon* just happened to be the name of Nelson's ship, this argument can be turned on its head:

that Nelson allowed himself to be associated with the "leader of the naval hosts / The Royal Agamemnon" (*Furies*, ll. 496-97), as he is described in the Potter translation,[22] may have reverberated both with Melville's poetic sensibility and his historical bent.

In the first play of the trilogy, the eponymous Agamemnon with Cassandra as his mistress returns home in triumph from the Trojan War only to be murdered in his bath by his spouse, Clytemnestra, who is enraged that Agamemnon was willing to sacrifice their daughter Iphigeneia in order to win the war. In the second play, *The Choephorae* or *Libation-Bearers*, Orestes kills his mother and her lover Aegisthus. In the third play, significantly named in Potter's translation *The Furies* but now generally called *The Eumenides* or "kindly ones," Orestes is exonerated when Athena votes in his favor before the court of the Areopagus.

Counterparts to the main characters of the novel are as prominent as in *Measure for Measure*, but here extend even further throughout the cast of characters. Billy is Orestes who, acting in response to a crime, in effect "changed places" with the criminal, as Melville says of Billy and Claggart (p. 103). Not just the hard consonants of Claggart's name suggest Clytemnestra; both his actions and hers are motivated by an erotic sadism and ambiguous loathing of and attraction to male sexuality. The reverberations of "vir" and "veritas" in Vere's name not only intimate qualities ambiguously associated with Athena, but may also anagrammatically evoke Minerva, which is how Athena is called in the Potter translation. If Nelson is associated with Agamemnon it is logical that the Old Dansker, the *Agamemnon*-man given to "Delphic deliverances," is Cassandra. And there is more than likely a trace of the Furies in the sea-fowl that "flew screaming to the spot" (p. 127) where Billy's body disappeared beneath the waves. Finally, the coy narrator, both insider and outsider, is the Chorus who never leave the stage in Greek drama and who, at the beginning of the *Agamemnon*—to cite just one example of their slipperiness—switch from a lofty prediction of the action in anapests, to a less formal meter in which they characterize themselves as tired old men, then back to the omniscient narrator reporting on the sacrifice of Iphigeneia at Aulis—though they have just told us they spent the whole war at home.[23] Similar discrepancies about what the narrator knew and how he knew it characterize *Billy Budd*.

As well, structurally both novel and plays are aftermath stories—of the French Revolution and the Trojan War. And like Aeschylus, Melville was developing a trilogy of a sort, having composed the sections dealing with Billy, Claggart, and Vere in three distinct phases.[24] Although the satyr play which would have followed Aeschylus's three tragedies is lost, Melville's is to be found in the burlesque discussion of Surgeon and Purser I quoted at the outset.[25]

Whatever formal parallels there may be beween the situations of the Greek plays and the novel, there is also a profound modal one. Melville's narrator wears a mask he never removes, hiding behind a non-face that opens a gap between storyteller and story similar to that between Greek actor and character. But the mask is also a second face for the actor (narrator): it relates *to* him just as it relates *with* him. The hide-and-seek, revealing and concealing game played by the narrator of *Billy Budd* may be Melville's most dramatic device. While Ishmael often soliloquizes, the narrator of *Billy Budd* deploys the orality of a parlor recitation, sounding alternatively like a well-polished set piece, a personal narrative and a tall tale.

As in *Measure for Measure*, in which anarchy threatens simultaneously in the absence of enforcement of the law against fornication (resulting in libertinism) and its rigid over-application (resulting in tyranny), in *Billy Budd* and the *Oresteia* transgressive sexual desire is the sensational stimulus for raising issues of civil and cosmic order. In all three works this theme is signalled by the combination of violence and sexual imagery, in all three works sex points pornographically to death. Claudio is condemned to hang for fornication, and a morbid association of erections and hanging is imaged continually, e.g., when Pompey the imprisoned whorehouse-keeper is apprenticed to the hangman. Clytemnestra likens the blood of Agamemnon splattering her gown to the semen with which Heaven fecundates the Earth in the Spring (*Agamemnon*, ll. 1464-67). Billy's encounters with Claggart are charged with violent eroticism expressed in talk of loins, erectness, discharged cannon, ejaculate and spilled soup (pp. 72, 99), and I am convinced by Eve Kosovsky Sedgwick's argument that the hanged Billy, the "Pendant pearl from the yard-arm end," has, in effect, become Vere's [("vir's")] erection.[26] Aeschylus and Melville both exploit displayed bodies for their political, sexual, and religious significance. Sedgwick finds in the hanging of Billy the culmination of a theme of exhibitionism that links it to images of the "publication" of Nelson on the deck of his ship and the way in which Vere positions himself to be observed (pp. 58, 91).[27] (She ignores the religious "ecce homo" echo of the narrator's "behold Billy Budd" in Chapter 24 [p. 118], a resonance which maintains the [meta]physical dimension.) In associating the displayed body, either clothed or nude, with the horrid attraction of being gazed at,[28] Melville is also following Aeschylus, who has Clytemnestra bare her breasts to her son, has Agamemnon killed in his bath, and freely uses the Greek stage device of displaying dead bodies on the *ekkyklema*.

Noting this imagery and the fact that the homosexually intertwined Claggart, Billy, and Vere all end up dead, Sedgwick controversially concludes that Melville's novel reveals "a fantasy trajectory toward a life *after the homosexual.*"[29] Even here there is a troubling parallel to Aeschylus. In "The Dynamics of Misogyny: Myth and Myth-Making in the *Oresteia*," Froma Zeitlin finds the trilogy dealing with the archetypal myth of male triumphing over female, while on the way demonstrating female sexual voracity and hatred of the male, united in the image of Clytemnestra as both adulterous wife and hostile mother. "The *Oresteia*'s program," she contends, "is to trace the evolution of civilization by creating heirarchies of Olympian over chthonic, Greek over barbarian and male over female."[30] I suggest that the purging of "barbarian Billy," as he's called in chapter 24 (p. 120), effected by Vere's urging the court to "rule out" the "feminine in man,"[31] implies a similar program. The *Oresteia* is resolved once the threatening females are literally put in their place at the shrine of Athena, herself an "androgynous compromise"[32] between male and female (because no woman bore her, yet she is female). So, too, *Billy Budd* frames an action in which men's desire for other men is seen as a barely contained threat to the "masculinist heirarchies of Western culture,"[33] presided over by an ambiguously sexed Fairfax Vere.

Yet, to discover the misogyny in the *Oresteia* and the homophilia/homophobia in *Billy Budd* is not to exhaust their meanings. The allegorical vector of Melville's novel, like the needle of a compass drawn by several lodestones, responds waveringly to classical, Christian, Rousseauian, and homosexual attraction. Though this would appear to be more than enough for a short novel, the hermeneutic circle of *Billy Budd* encloses both allegory and—with its reference points to the *Somers* mutiny and maritime law—history. Here again, Melville had a model in Aeschylus. When Athena, exercising the patience Vere lacked, defers judgment and submits the matter of Orestes' guilt to the court of the Areopagus, Athenian audiences could not help but think of "the fierce constitutional struggle of the years ca. 463-458 BCE" which left the Areopagus reformed but intact.[34] Thus do allegory and actuality converge in *The Oresteia*, and these seemingly archaic plays take on a decidedly contemporary cast—just as the allegorical *Measure for Measure* makes specific reference to the problematic rule of James I, and Jerrold directed his dramatic efforts against the contemporary evils of impressment.

And in each case—in Aeschylus, Shakespeare, Jerrold, and Melville—it is, as Barbara Johnson argues *re Billy Budd*, "judging, not murdering"[35] we are ultimately asked to judge. Though Johnson does not notice the parallels I have adduced here, her assertion is supported by them. Indeed, we may grasp how deeply Melville felt about judging by recalling the source for the title of Shakespeare's play in the Sermon on the Mount: "Judge not, that ye be not judged. For with what judgment ye judge, ye shall be judged, and with what measure ye mete, it shall be measured to you again" (Matthew 7:1-2). The act of judgment had a personal resonance for Melville, whom the narrator, with his appeal to inside knowledge, his use of historical accounts, and references to an obscure writer (no doubt Melville himself),[36] ironically evokes. Dogged through his career by critics uncertain as to whether to judge his works as fiction or nonfiction, allegory or actuality, Melville hedged *Billy Budd* between fable and fact, sardonically, protectively, and finally positioning himself to judge his own judges.

We are brought back, then, to the fable, to the generic issue of what kind of story Melville wrote. None of his contemporary critics, I believe, fathomed what Melville intuited, what *Billy Budd* appears to demonstrate, and what the postmodern historian Hayden White has labored mightily to prove: that the same four modes of emplotment govern the "description of any field of events, whether imagined or real."[37] If, as I have suggested, Melville was evoking Aeschylus, Shakespeare, and Douglas Jerrold, then he may have deliberately decided to emplot his story all four ways at the same time—as tragedy, comedy, irony, and romance.

403

Thus, what the narrator in mock apology calls the "ragged edges" (128) of the story's fourfold endings are not so ragged. The hanging recapitulates the tragic motifs couched in self-conscious classical allusion; the burlesque discussion of Purser and Surgeon caps the comic motifs, developed in the description of the shipboard life of the crew and the attempt to socialize Billy; the distorted journalistic account ends the story ironically, the brute "facts" of history pulverizing attempts to render them meaningful; and the ballad ends the story romantically, restating the allegory of the noble savage. These four constitute the *euthanasia*, the good dying, of a novel that begins with the phrase "in the time before steamships" and ends with a ballad yet claims ironically to be "no romance" (p. 53), which insists on the tragic (Chapters 21 and 22, *passim*) nature of the events it recounts yet focuses the tragedy on a rustic who ascends to heaven in a divinely comic finale. For Melville at the end of his life, there was to be no Bartlebyan retreat from narrative, but an embrace of storytelling every which way.[38]

NOTES

1   Herman Melville, *Billy Budd, Sailor (An Inside Narrative)* ed. Harrison Hayford and Merton M. Sealts, Jr. (Chicago: University of Chicago Press, 1962), 1. All quotes are from this edition.

2   See, e.g., Richard Harter Fogle, "*Billy Budd*—Acceptance or Irony" and Edward H. Rosenberry, "The Problem of *Billy Budd*" in *Twentieth Century Interpretations of* Billy Budd, ed. by Howard P. Vincent (Englewood Cliffs, NJ: Prentice-Hall, Inc., 1971), 41-47, 48-55. Barbara Johnson, "Melville's Fist: The Execution of *Billy Budd*," *Studies in Romanticism*, 18, 4 (Winter 1979), 562-77, registers and brilliantly analyzes the multiple endings of *Billy Budd*—though she configures them differently than I. Her essay is reprinted in Harold Bloom, ed., *Herman Melville's* Billy Budd, "*Benito Cereno*," "*Bartleby the Scrivener*," *and Other Tales* (New York: Chelsea House, 1987), 47-80. My citations are from the reprint.

3   Hayford/Sealts, pp. 35-38.

4   Mark Troy, "'. . . its [*sic*] me, not the sentence they'll suspend'—Billy in the Darbies," *Orbis Litterarum*, 52 (1997): 241.

5   Hayford/Sealts, pp. 35-38. Stanton Garner, "Fraud as Fact," *San Jose Studies*, 4 (May 1978): 82-95, suggests that among Melville's obfuscating techniques is the trick of having his narrator deliberately get facts wrong in order to undermine his credibility.

6   Respectively, Bryan C. Short, *Cast By Means of Figures: Herman Melville's Rhetorical Development* (Amherst, MA: University of Massachusetts Press, 1992); Barbara Johnson (see note 2); Christo-

pher Sten, *The Weaver God, He Weaves: Melville and the Poetics of the Novel* (Kent, OH: Kent State University Press, 1996), 12-13; and Eve Kosovsky Sedgwick,*The Epistemology of the Closet* (Berkeley: University of California Press, 1990), 91-130. Mark Troy (see note 4) holds that the conflicting metanarratives embedded in the text nevertheless refocus the novella on the matter of individual ethics. It will be evident from my argument that I do not consider the novella unfinished, but almost the opposite: over-finished.

7   Hayford/Sealts, p. 38.

8   Louis O. Coxe and Robert Chapman, *Billy Budd* (New York: Hill and Wang, 1962), p. 81. The adaptation was first performed in 1949 under the title *Uniform of Flesh;* and subsequently revised.

9   On dramatic adaptations of *Billy Budd* see Kenneth D. Smith, "Dramatic Adaptations of Herman Melville's *Billy Budd"* (diss., Notre Dame University, 1970) and Mark Estrin, "Dramatizations of American Fiction: Hawthorne and Melville on Stage and Screen" (diss., New York University, 1969).

10   See B. R. McElderry, Jr., "Three Earlier Treatments of the *Billy Budd* Theme," *American Literature*, 27 (May 1955): 251-57; and Richard and Rita Gollin, "Justice in an Earlier Treatment of the *Billy Budd* Theme," *American Literature*, 28 (January 1957): 513-15.

11   The text of *Black Ey'd Susan* is handily available in *Nineteenth Century Plays*, ed. by George Rowell (London: Oxford University Press, 1953), 8-43. *The Mutiny at the Nore* was published in a Lacy's acting edition (n.d.). For the newspaper advertisement of *The Mutiny at the Nore,* see André Tsai, "The British Nautical Drama (1824-1843)" (diss., Ohio State University, 1964), 98.

12   On the availability of the two plays, on stage and page, to Melville, see McElderry, 252, n. 4 and the Gollins, 513, n. 2. For Melville's borrowing of a copy of *The Mutiny at the Nore*, see Merton M. Sealts, Jr. *Melville's Reading*, rev. ed. (n.p.: University of South Carolina Press, 1988), 189.

13   Hayford/Sealts, pp. 36-37.

14   Tsai, pp. 17-19.

15   See Thomas J. Scorza, *In the Time Before Steamships:* Billy Budd, *The Limits of Politics and Modernity* (DeKalb, IL: Northern Illinois University Press, 1979), chapter 1.

16   Julian Markels, *Melville and the Politics of Identity: From* King Lear *to* Moby Dick (Urbana, IL: University of Illinois Press, 1993), p. 151, n. 4, summarizes the scholarship on Melville and Shakespeare.

17   Robert Heilman, *Magic in the Web; Action and Language in* Othello (Lexington, KY: University of Kentucky Press, 1956), first noted the analogies to *Othello;* Richard Chase adduces *A Winter's Tale* in the introduction to *Selected Tales and Poems* by Herman Melville, reprinted in *The Merrill Studies in* Billy Budd, ed. by Haskell Springer (Columbus, OH: Charles E. Merrill Publishing Co., 1970), 32-35.

18   Markels, pp. 140 and 151.

19   Johnson, 55.

20   After writing this piece, I discovered that Roger Shattuck also sees parallels between the *Oresteia* and *Billy Budd*, though he merely mentions the fact without comment or analysis in *Forbidden Knowledge* (New York: St. Martin's Press, 1996), 157.

21 Sealts, 1988, pp. 46-47 and 189.

22 The Potter translation reprinted in the Harper Classical Library series was originally published in *Aeschylus*, tr. by the Reverend R. Potter (New York: Harper and Bros., 1839).

23 Peter Arnott, *Public and Performance in the Greek Theatre* (London: Routledge, 1989), 30-32.

24 Hayford/Sealts, pp. 2-3.

25 Though Melville could have no knowledge of Aeschylus's lost satyr play, John Harford's introduction to the Potter translation discusses the satyr play as a feature of Greek tragic performance.

26 Sedgwick, p. 126.

27 Ibid., pp. 105-9.

28 On such topics as shame, exhibitionism, and the gaze in Melville, see Joseph Adamson, *Melville, Shame, and the Evil Eye* (n.p.: State University of New York Press, 1997).

29 Sedgwick, p. 127.

30 "The Dynamics of Misogyny: Myth and Myth-Making in the *Oresteia*," in *Aeschylus's* The Oresteia, ed. and with an Introduction by Harold Bloom (New York: Chelsea House, 1988), 47.

31 Here the echo is of Posthumus threatening to dislodge "the woman's part in me": *Cymbeline*, II, iv, 171.

32 Zeitlin, p. 65.

33 Sedgwick, pp. 93-94.

34 John Herington, "No-Man's-Land of Dark and Light," in Bloom, p. 146.

35 Johnson, p. 72.

36 According to Hayford/Sealts, p. 38.

37 Hayden White, "Fictions of Factual Representation," in *Tropics of Discourse: Essays in Cultural Criticism* (Baltimore, MD: Johns Hopkins University Press, 1978), 129.

38 The author gratefully acknowledges the research assistance of David Pellegrini and the editorial advice of Joseph Flibbert and Haskell Springer.

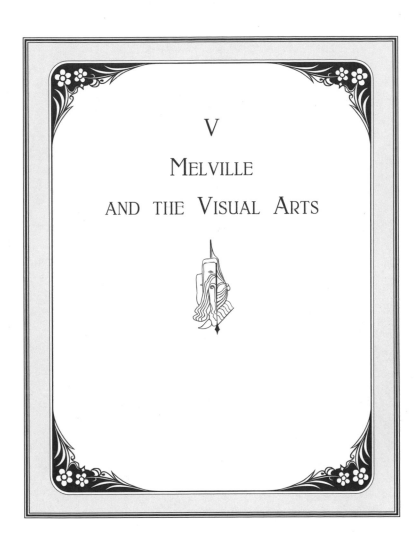

V

MELVILLE

AND THE VISUAL ARTS

ELIZABETH SCHULTZ

SEEING *MOBY-DICK* GLOBALLY

n *Melville's Foreign Reputation*, Leland Phelps acknowledges the significant contribution of Rockwell Kent's
illustrations for the 1930 Lakeside Press edition of
Moby-Dick to the international expansion of the reputation of Melville's novel.[1] Kent's images appeared
in the first illustrated edition of *Moby-Dick* published
outside the United States—a 1933 Czech translation,
followed soon after in 1935 by a Bulgarian translation, also featuring Kent's pictures. As a result of
his visits in 1949 and 1960 and of successful exhibitions of his paintings and
drawings in both Moscow and Kiev, Kent became well known in the Soviet
Union. Hence, it is not surprising that his illustrations, which accompanied the
first Soviet translation of *Moby-Dick* in 1961, prompted, according to Soviet literary critic Boris Gilenson, the popularity of the novel's Russian translation.[2]
Well into the 1970s, translations of *Moby-Dick* with Kent's powerful realistic
and symbolic illustrations continued to be published outside the United States—
in India, China, France, Israel, Lithuania, Norway, Pakistan, Poland, and Sweden, with eight different editions published in Japan alone.[3]

In 1976, Joachim Kruse, however, recognized that the aesthetic responses to
Moby-Dick throughout Europe and the United States extended well beyond Kent,
presenting an astonishing diversity of media, style, and interpretation. In that
year, at Germany's Schleswig-Holstein Museum, Kruse organized an exhibition
of *Moby-Dick*-inspired artworks in addition to editing an impressive catalog.[4]

Kruse's study, which calls attention primarily to the range of illustrations created by European artists for translations of the novel in the three decades following World War II, discusses them from diverse theoretical, historical, and cultural perspectives. Although he cites only one European edition of *Moby-Dick* published from the 1930s with an illustrator other than Kent—Alexander Noll of France, he notes three remarkable and distinctly different *Moby-Dick* illustrators of the 1940s—Otto Tschumi of Switzerland, René de Pauw of Belgium, and Will Sohl of Germany.

For the 1950s, Kruse's catalog lists twenty-one editions of *Moby-Dick* with illustrations by artists other than Kent and published outside the United States, twenty-nine for the 1960s, and seventeen for the 1970s. In these three decades, at least one edition of *Moby-Dick* with illustrations by artists other than Kent appeared in Australia, Austria, Belgium, Czechoslovakia, Denmark, England, Holland, Greece, Japan, the Soviet Union, Spain, and Sweden, with fourteen appearing in France, sixteen in Germany, and eighteen in Italy. As Phelps's study suggests, this international proliferation of *Moby-Dick* illustrated editions following World War II coincides with the restoration of commercial publishing in Europe and Japan, with an increase in new translations of Melville's works assisted by the American-based Franklin Book Program, and with a growth in worldwide Melville scholarship resulting from the United States-government-sponsored Fulbright Program.[5] It could also be argued that the increase in international editions of *Moby-Dick*—with illustrations by Kent as well as other artists—coincided with the increase in European and Japanese attention to American popular culture in light of American military and economic hegemony. In addition, during these post-war years it was common for literary scholars in the United States and abroad to praise *Moby-Dick* as belonging to world culture, comparing it to Homeric epics, Shakespearean drama, Goethe's *Faust*, Beethoven's symphonies. Given that many of these international illustrated editions were comic books or children's editions suggests that publishers worldwide also perceived the novel's appeal to an expanding audience, including children and young people as well as educated adults and scholarly readers. That the University of Kansas's collection of illustrated editions of *Moby-Dick* has added comic-book versions and illustrated children's editions printed in Brazil,

France, Italy, Japan, and Sweden during the 1980s and 1990s testifies that international popular and commercial interest in the novel has not diminished. On receiving a 1996 French children's illustrated edition, *Moby Dick: l'aventure et l'histoire*, for this collection, the director of the University of Kansas's Spencer Research Library recogized that the novel now makes an international environmental appeal, "I think this is the first edition with a lecture on endangered species and the chromosomes of whales, not to mention directions for making an endangered species mobile!"[6]

As the essays and reproductions in Kruse's catalog indicate, the visual responses to *Moby-Dick* by European illustrators between 1950 and 1980 are stunning in the diversity of their philosophical, political, psychological, and aesthetic interpretations. Whereas my 1995 study of *Moby-Dick* illustrations shows the focus of American illustrators to be primarily on the realistic, symbolic, or narrative aspects of the novel,[7] Swiss illustrator Otto Tschumi in 1942 and German illustrators Will Sohl in 1949 and Horst Janssen in 1957, however, deconstruct the images of men and whales in complex and entangled abstract terms. With his collages created from nineteenth-century illustrations, William Klien for a 1955 French translation of the novel literally emphasizes the text's and reality's multiple layers of meaning. If the realistic wood engravings of Sven Havsteen-Mikkelsen project the materiality of whales and men in a 1955 Danish version of *Moby-Dick*, the stark simplicity of their strong lines, which are often left open toward whiteness, also imply a mystical reading of the novel. Through comic figures, which appear as simple pen-and-ink doodlings, Günther Stiller succeeds ironically in baring the novel's tragic dimensions in a 1968 German translation.

Although American artists have been inspired since the 1930s to generate autonomous artworks in response to Melville's novel,[8] freestanding visual interpretations did not appear on the world scene until the 1960s. In focusing principally on *Moby-Dick*'s illustrations, Kruse identifies only a very few of these autonomous American and German artworks.[9] Primarily conceived as paintings and works on paper, these freestanding international *Moby-Dick* artworks fill multiple aesthetic categories, e.g., abstract expressionism, surrealism, constructionism, Pop Art. The international appearance of these freestanding pieces since the 1960s may reflect not only an increasing dependency on image in contemporary societies and an expanded art market, but also *Moby-Dick*'s increasing value as a commodity as well as its increasing acceptance as an international cultural icon.

As Kruse's catalog demonstrates the particular appeal of Melville's novel for German illustrators, its little lower philosophical and psychological layers seem to be equally fascinating for German artists.[10] Jan Koblasa cites the Czech translation of *Moby-Dick* with its Kent illustrations as a formative influence on his ponderous, 1963 wooden sculpture titled *Moby Dick*. After finishing this pitted and scarred, inner-directed sculpture, he wrote in his diary, "I have caught the white whale. So full of despair, this story of the search for one's own destruction appeals to me a great deal."[11]

Carl Barth's 1966 *Homage to Melville* (*Huldigung an Melville*, oil on linen, 100 x 130 cm) evokes the white whale's mysterious head. Barth seems literally to put that brow before his viewers, challenging them to read it if they can. Projecting both ferocity and dignity, the head appears entirely swathed, its overlapping bandages leaking blood, its secrets its own. According to art historian Karl Ruhrberg, *Homage to Melville* points to a significant continuity in Barth's career; it looks back to his first painting, *Prospect* (*Ausblick*), 1932, and ahead to *Still Life with White Head* (*Stilleben mit weissen Kopf*), done three years before his death in 1973.[12] Collectively, the three works, spanning four decades, reflect Barth's persistent interest in a mind's construction of space and vision, an interest shared with Melville, who pictured Ahab's head with "shifting gleams and shadows of lines upon his wrinkled brow, till it almost seemed that while he himself was marking out lines and courses on the wrinkled charts, some invisible pencil was also tracing lines and courses upon the deeply marked chart of his forehead."[13]

Henry Koerner, who fled Austria's Nazi regime in 1938, reaching the United States in 1939, creates a disturbing Edenic scene in his 1977-78 surrealistic painting, *Moby Dick* (oil on canvas, 102 x 88"). In fantastic contrast to the lush park of the upper half of the painting, where casually dressed acrobats fly free among the trees, is the black and white grid of the chess board in the painting's lower half, where legless, heavily garbed chess pieces are moved about by figures of Fate, helmeted with skull masks. Together these groups represent a diverse society, multi-ethnic, old and young. For Koerner, as for Ishmael, dualities are united. "There is no quality in this world that is not what it is merely by contrast. Nothing exists in itself," comments Ishmael (53); these figures form "one reality," comments Koerner.[14] Uniting the composition in his *Moby Dick* is a fantastic, fabricated right whale, its spout both waterfall and fountain. Not the white whale, but a replica of a whale Koerner remembered from his youth as being atop a restaurant in the pre-war Prater, it joins his personal past with his present, his knowledge of human evil with human innocence, his sense of tragedy with comedy.

In her 1991 assemblage, *Moby Dick* (43 ¾ x 27 ½ x 4 ½"), Rebecca Horn frames a copy of the novel, torn and open to "The Grand Armada" chapter, and puts it behind glass along with a pair of electric shoe warmers, and a merchandizing label, inscribed, "UNDER WATER, 100 ft. $20." Boxed together, these disparate elements are preserved as relics of the past, but as relics, they appear abandoned, disassociated from each other and from life, one no more meaningful nor valuable than the other. Horn's assemblage also comments on the process of *Moby-Dick*'s iconization; a work of art, its philosophical complexities, human tragedies, and aesthetic wonders are circumscribed, trivialized, and commodified. If the prickly blowfish, outside the frame, remains whole, it is irrelevant and ineffectual, a minor representative of Melville's masterless sea.

In a 1994 assemblage, also titled *Moby Dick*, Finnish artist Juhani Harri also preserves relics as if, according to Finnish critic Seppo Heiskanen, he were "in search of lost time" or even the eternal.[15] Painted in its entirety a ghostly white, his construction also seems to attempt to frame an apparition, to "grasp the ungraspable phantom of life" (5). Inside a rectangular frame, two model ships, their hulls stacked one upon the other, the mast, spars, and rigging of the upper ship a tangled mass, a hole bashed in its side, are set amidst a flurry of paint chips and what I take to be pharmaceutical pill packets. The remnants of disaster, these relics, like Ishmael, "survive the wreck" (573).

New Zealand artist, Colin McCahon, fuses multiple elements in his 1972 *Tui Carr Celebrates Muriwai Beach: Moby Dick Seen Off Muriwai Beach* (acrylic on canvas, 34 ⅛ x 69")—his appreciation of Melville's novel and of Pop Art's use of signs; his concern for New Zealand's natural beauty, its indigenous people, and his young grandson. Contending that McCahon has developed "an ingenuous primitive style of his own," New Zealand art historian and literary critic, Wystan Curnow notes further that in his work, "High art and low, past and present, turning both ends against the middle—this [is] part of a [conscious] cultural strategy."[16] A stylized depiction of the cliffs over Muriwai Beach on New Zealand's west coast, McCahon's painting is also his personal view from the masthead. Beyond the cliffs, represented by heavy, black vertical bars to the right, horizontally stretch the lavendar beach, the rippling breakers, the azure sea, and the soft apricot sky, with Oaia Island, a white hump resembling Moby Dick, balancing them to the left. Cliffs, sea, and whales require "NECESSARY PROTECTION," as McCahon testifies in capital letters at the top of the painting. A monumental and mysterious black "Y" in the center of McCahon's painting stabilizes it, suggesting that he keeps his grip on the masthead. Signifying the joy of the artist's part-Maori grandson, Matui Carr, at the moment of seeing the natural beauty of Muriwai Beach, this letter also evokes the boy's arms raised in ecstasy. In the lower left-hand corner, McCahon has written in Maori the words of a great nineteenth-century chieftain, "One chief falls, another rises and takes his place,"[17] a warning which, in conjunction with the natural setting and with *Moby-Dick*, whale and novel, assures his grandson and a future. McCahon's painting redeems Queequeg for his zeal in peddling New Zealand heads.

Moby-Dick has been a principal inspiration for Vali Myers, born in Australia and resident of Italy since 1970. Three works—*Moby Dick*, 1972-74 (pen, black ink, burnt sienna, watercolor, tempera on handmade paper, 11 x 16"); *The Whale*, 1980-83 (pen, ink, watercolor on handmade paper, 330 x 230 mm); and *The Whaler's Daughter*, 1990 (fine pen and diluted black ink on handmade paper, 9 x 13")—reveal the continuity of her interpretation of Melville's novel as both a condemnation of human violence against nature and a passionate endorsement of its wonders. As a feminist and an active environmentalist, Myers contends that Moby Dick is female and that every harpoon in the whale's body penetrates her own flesh. Working with a feather brush to create her intricate ink drawings, reminiscent of Persian miniatures or Celtic illuminations, Myers consistently represents the confrontational, climactic scene in *Moby-Dick* as a swirling nightmare. Dramatically juxtaposed with this scene of intentional slaughter, however, is the figure of a woman, who in *The Whale* fiercely protests the destruction with her raised hand and who in *Moby Dick* and *The Whaler's Daughter* suggests nurturing alternatives.[18]

Primarily an illustrator of children's books, Canadian Jules Prud'homme in 1992 sought to make *Moby-Dick* accessible to more readers by placing the novel's climactic scene in an ornate Italian operatic theater setting. By framing this scene with gaudy gold columns, heavy drapes, and footlights shaped like whales' tails, Prud'homme, on the one hand, honors the power of the novel's most tumultuous and terrifying moment, while on the other hand acknowledging that presenting it in realistic terms on stage is absurd. Given that he errs, however, in showing Ahab rather than Fedallah as strapped to Moby Dick, following in the wake of John Huston's film and subsequent other copy-cat misrepresentations, his *Moby-Dick* stage setting seems a charming mockery of the novel.

In a series of five paintings, created between 1989 and 1997, Athanasios C. Christodoulou, Melville scholar and translator of *Moby-Dick* into Greek, reflects on the implications of Ahab's intellectual and emotional response to his universe: *The Monomania of Ahab* (tempera, 30.5 x 12.7 cm), *The Thought of Ahab* (tempera, 30.5 x 12.7 cm), *The Catechism of Ahab* (tempera, 17.2 x 9.5 cm), *The Death of Ahab* (tempera, color crayons, Indian ink, 10.6 x 11.6 cm), and *The Triumph* (tempera, 18.5 x 17.5 cm). Created in the tradition of the Greek icon, Christodoulou's stylized paintings are small and intense, each centering a luminous symbolic form against an ominous, dark background. In the middle of *The Monomania of Ahab* is a portrait of Ahab's cadaverous face, framed by scarlet and gold bands and superimposed on blackness. The surrounding dark, the constricting frame, as well as his heavy top hat project the insanity of Ahab's "frantic morbidness" in identifying Moby Dick as the source "not only [of] all his bodily woes, but all his intellectual and spiritual exasperations" (184). Yet if within the portrait frame, the lower portion of Ahab's face is submerged in water, where a phantom white whale swims, its upper portion is blessed by a radiant light, from which emerge three golden lines, two of which lead to white doves, hovering and glowing above him, like twin images of the Holy Ghost. A naked corpse arches up from the base of *The Death of Ahab*. With neither head nor feet showing fully and tinted pale blue, the corpse also may be seen as a mighty muscular brain or as the earth's curving horizon. Unlike the background in Christodoulou's other four

Moby-Dick paintings, the background here is pale; inscribed with multiple carto-graphic hieroglyphs and with a pair of black sperm whales superimposed upon it so as to soar magically above the body/brain/globe, it resembles a medieval map similar to Queequeg's "mystical treatise on the art of attaining the truth" (480). In his most evocative painting, Christodoulou seems to imply that despite Ahab's attempt to solve them, the mysteries of cosmic and natural cartography, like the mysteries of *Moby-Dick*, remain after his death. For the final painting in his series, *The Triumph*, Christodoulou envisions a massive tidal wave; shimmering, very like that "grand hooded phantom, [very] like a snow hill in the air" (7), it rises up from the dark waters to dominate the painting and as if to overwhelm a small village pressed into the painting's right-hand side. However, its upward thrust is countered by the village, which sends multiple tentacles out and down-ward into the sea, anchoring it. Thus, Christodoulou creates a dynamic balance between the awesome presence of *Moby-Dick*'s legacy and the human communi-ty. In this brooding painting, a glimmer of a golden cloud mountain appears in the upper left-hand corner as if to consecrate this balance and to signify that "the triumph" of Melville's novel is in keeping "the great flood-gates of the wonder-world" swung open (7).

Paul Metcalf, the American writer and Melville's great-grandson, proposes an affinity between *Moby-Dick* and the recent work by English painter, Lucian Freud. Although Freud, whose ancestry is no less distinguished than Metcalf's, nowhere alludes to *Moby-Dick* in his paintings of the 1990s, a shared aesthetic between them and Melville's novel makes a comparison irresistible. Describing a general affinity between modern art and *Moby-Dick*, Metcalf writes, "It can be argued that Melville's career as a writer was destined to fail, he simply could not be understood—until [the Abstract Expressionists] had opened the door for him. When painting passed from representational to abstract, a recognizable face was erased. The canvas became faceless—with a new language of hiero-glyphics."[19]

Applying this "new language of hieroglyphics," which insists on the inter-section of the representational and the abstract, Melville constructs the mysteri-ous and magisterial body of the white whale in words while Freud constructs the monumental white bodies of his models, Leigh Browery and Sue Tilley, in paint. Melville's and Freud's methods of creativity are also comparable. Whereas Melville implies in *Moby-Dick* that his method of writing is synonymous with organic growth—"Out of the trunk, the branches grow; out of them, the twigs. So, in productive subjects grow the chapters" (289)—Freud maintains that manipulating paint in his portraits is synonymous with manipulating flesh: "I want paint to *work as flesh*. . . As far as I am concerned the paint is the person. I want it to work for me just as flesh does."[20] The young Ishmael dreads whiteness for being "a dumb blankness, full of meaning" (195) and joins Ahab's fiery quest, thinking to destroy the formless, ambiguous, mutable, paradoxical abstraction he fears, but an older Ishmael discovers meaning in the very process of acknowledging and expressing such abstraction. Freud discovers that in painting these massive human beings in their full nakedness from several perspectives—seated, sprawled, standing—he can, like Ishmael in his descriptions of Moby Dick, represent whiteness as colorless and paradoxically as containing all color; in addition, he can give a flat surface the spatial depth and heft of boulders and from this surface evoke the illusion of tactility and, as Metcalf indicates, an overpowering sense of smell.[21]

When the crew of the *Pequod* finally see Moby Dick in the flesh in the novel's final chapters, Melville's adjectives of the white whale are multiple and contradictory—"lovely," "leering," "bewitching," "serene," "dazzling," "steady," "glistening," "broad," "glorified," "divine," "mild," "calm," "shrouded," "rainbowed," "appalling," "furious," "mighty," "tremendous," "blank." Similarly, a series of contradictory adjectives can be applied to Freud's representation of the immense nude figures of Browery and Tilley. Their flesh seems tough, rough, soft, smooth, scaly, resilient, rubbery, tender, damp, melting, rotting. Browery is simultaneously smug, audacious, cavalier, cocksure, and yet suffering from AIDS. Tilley is simultaneously self-assured, imposing, uncompromising, pudgy, mountainous, and yet characterized by the daintiest of feet. If Ishmael describes the sight of a dying whale as "most pitiable" (354) and its death as "most piteous" (358), Freud imbues these massive mounds of human flesh with profound vulnerability.

The ubiquity of *Moby-Dick*—and perhaps its consequent immortality, for, as Ishmael says, "immortality is but ubiquity in time" (183)—extends beyond the world's libraries and art museums, however. The image of Melville's whale thrives around the world in marketplaces and in popular imaginations. It is, for example, reincarnated as a toothy ferry boat in Berlin and as Japanese origami; it emerges in a Paris bar, an Istanbul restaurant, a Zagreb coffee shop; it is associated with a travelling maritime exhibition in Germany and loans its name to a Greek yacht supplier and to sailing vessels in ports throughout the seven seas. The ubiquity as well as the commercial and inspirational power of Moby Dick as an icon is apparent in the 1996 Australian film, *Shine*, for which Geoffrey Rush won the Golden Globe as best dramatic actor. Playing the role of a psychologically disturbed pianist, he is restored to miraculous health at a piano bar called Moby's, where the readily recognizable talisman of good karma—a white whale—is everywhere in evidence—in neon posted over the door and stitched over the pockets of all the servers.

The persistence and the proliferation of these visual responses to *Moby-Dick* suggest that Melville's novel has escaped the all-grasping world of American scholars, artists, and entrepreneurs. Like the Declaration of Independence, like jazz, like McDonald's, Coca-Cola, and Mickey Mouse, *Moby-Dick*, since the 1960s, has been up for grabs. The diversity of these worldwide visual interpretations of *Moby-Dick* proves that Melville's novel now belongs to the world at large, and that the world has joined the United States in attempting to see both the novel and the whale more fully and more clearly.

NOTES

1   Leland Phelps, *Herman Melville's Foreign Reputation* (Boston: G. K. Hall, 1983), xviii-xix.

2   Boris Gilenson, "*Moby-Dick* in Russian," *Soviet Life* (Nov. 1969): 18.

3   Phelps, xix.

4   *Illustrationen zu Melvilles "Moby-Dick,"* ed. Joachim Kruse (Schleswig: Schleswiger Druck und Verlagshaus, 1976).

5   Phelps, xv, xvi, xviii.

6   Alexandra Mason, letter to Haskell Springer, 7 September 1996.

7   Elizabeth Schultz, "Illustrating *Moby-Dick*," "*Unpainted to the Last*": Moby-Dick *and Twentieth-Century American Art* (Lawrence: U P of Kansas, 1995), 13-122.

8   Schultz, 123-28.

9   The autonomous artworks which Kruse identifies are by Americans Jackson Pollock,

Thessaloniki; Remains of a Roman Stoa with Carytids, or the "Idols" ("encantadas"); Copperplate, drawn by F. L. S. Fauvel, engraved by F. Sorrieu, from Esprit Marie Cousinéry, *Voyage dans la Macédoine: Contenant des recherches sur l'histoire, la géographie, et les antiquites de ce pays.* 2 vols. Paris: Imprimiere Royale, 1831. [Georgodaki, "Herman Melville in Thessaloniki," 85–107]

Thessaloniki; The Arc of Galerius; Copperplate, drawn by F. L. S. Fauvel, engraved by F. Sorrieu, from Cousinéry, *Voyage dans la Macédoine.* [Georgodaki, "Herman Melville in Thessaloniki," 85–107]

(*Above*) *Medusa Rondanini*. Courtesy of Foto
Marburg/Art Resource, New York. [Berthold,
"Melville's Medusas," 287–96, figure 1]

(*Left*) Benvenuto Cellini, *Perseus with the Head of
Medusa,* Alinari/Art Resource, New York. [Berthold,
"Melville's Medusas," 287–96, figure 2]

M. S. *Moby Dick* ship, postcard, Berlin. [Schultz, "Seeing *Moby-Dick* Globally," 409–19]

Moby Dick, Ltd., Yachts Service truck, Athens. [Schultz, "Seeing *Moby-Dick* Globally," 409–19]

William Kienbusch, *Dirigo Island.* Courtesy of The Art Museum, Princeton University. Gift of James H. Beal, Class of 1920, and Mrs. Beal. [Kelley, "Kienbusch, Melville, and the Islands," 420–28, figure 2]

Guido Reni (?), *Beatrice Cenci.* Courtesy of Scala/Art Resource, New York. [Watts, "Energy and Gentleness Doublehooded," 440–54]

Elihu Vedder, *Vain Questioning (Illustration for Rubaiyat of Omar Khayyam).* Courtesy of the Smithsonian American Art Museum. Museum purchase and gift from Elizabeth W. Henderson. In memory of her husband Francis Tracy Henderson. [Kleitz, "Questions of the Sphinx," 455–62, black-and-white figure 1]

THE SCHOOL OF HOMER.
(Scio)

Edward Finden after J. M. W. Turner, *The School of Homer (Scio).* Courtesy of the Indianapolis Museum of Art. [Wallace, "'Aloof' and 'Aloft,'" 463–71, figure 1]

Edward Finden after J. M. W. Turner, *Temple of Minerva, Cape Colonna.* Courtesy of the Indianapolis Museum of Art. [Wallace, "'Aloof' and 'Aloft,'" 463–71, figure 2]

J. T. Willmore after J. M. W. Turner, *Temple of Minerva Sunias, Cape Colonna.* Courtesy of The Metropolitan Museum of Art, The Elisha Whittelsey Collection, The Elisha Whittelsey Fund, 1949 (49.50.150). [Wallace, "'Aloof' and 'Aloft,'" 463–71, figure 3]

W. Miller after J. M. W. Turner, *The Death of Lycidas—"Vision of the Guarded Mount."* © Copyright The British Museum. [Wallace, "'Aloof' and 'Aloft,'" 463–71, figure 4]

The temple at Cape Colonna on the morning of July 2, 1997. Photograph by Robert Wallace. [Wallace, "'Aloof' and 'Aloft,'" 463–71, figure 5]

[Moorish Arch], from "The Manchester and Liverpool Rail-Road." *Monthly Supplement of the Penny Magazine of the Society for the Diffusion of Useful Knowledge* 69 (March 31–April 30, 1833): 164. [Marr, "Mastheads and Minarets," 472–84, figure A]

Thomas Cole, *The Voyage of Life: Youth*. 1840, Oil on canvas, 52⅞ x 76¼ inches.
Munson-Williams-Proctor Art Institute, Museum of Art, Utica, New York.
[Marr, "Mastheads and Minarets," 472–84, figure B]

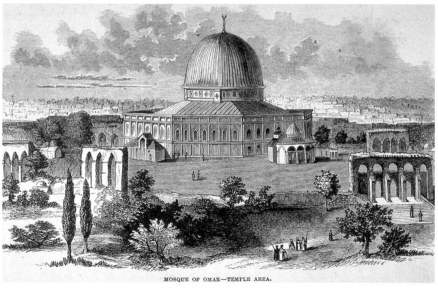

MOSQUE OF OMAR—TEMPLE AREA.

"Mosque of Omar—Temple Area," from William Thomson, *The Land and the Book* (New York:
Harper's, 1871). [Marr, "Mastheads and Minarets," 472–84, figure C]

Robert Indiana, Robert Del Tredici, and Gilbert Wilson, and Germans Willi Baumeister, Ekkehard Thieme, and Jan Koblasa. I have been unable to see either Baumeister's four colored serigraphs printed between 1949 and 1951 or Thieme's twelve engravings printed between 1959 and 1969. See Kruse for a listing of these works, 163-65, 229-31.

10 For a discussion of the German interest in *Moby-Dick* see Leland Phelps, "*Moby-Dick* in Germany," *Comparative Literature* 10.4 (Fall, 1958): 349-55.

11 Kruse, 200.

12 Karl Ruhrberg, "Einheit in der Vielfalt: Das Nachkriegswerk von Carl Barth," *Carl Barth* (Düsseldorf: Galerie Remmert und Barth, 1986), 108-9.

13 Herman Melville, *Moby-Dick* (Evanston and Chicago: Northwestern University Press and the Newberry Library, 1988), 198. Subsequent references to this work will appear parenthetically in the text.

14 Gail Stavitsky, *From Vienna to Pittsburgh: The Art of Henry Koerner* (Pittsburgh: U of Pittsburgh P, 1983), 70.

15 Seppo Heiskanen, "Juhani Harri—The Enchantment of the Old," *Harri* (Helsinki: Amos Anderson Art Museum Publications, 1996), n.p.

16 Wystan Curnow, Introduction, *I Will Need Words* (Wellington, NZ: National Art Gallery, 1984), n.p.

17 For this translation, I am again indebted to Wystan Curnow, "The Shining Cuckoo," *Interpreting Contemporary Art* (New York: HarperCollins, 1991), 43.

18 For an extended discussion of Myers's paintings, see Schultz, 281-83.

19 Paul Metcalf, "Melville and Freud (Lucien [sic], that is)," *Sulfur* 35 (Fall 1994): 243.

20 Quoted by Metcalf, 245.

21 Metcalf, 245.

W𝐘𝐍 K𝐄𝐋𝐋𝐄𝐘

KIENBUSCH, MELVILLE, AND THE ISLANDS

illiam Kienbusch's 1966 painting *Ahab* (figure 1) is probably familiar among Melville scholars only to those who have seen it reproduced in Elizabeth Schultz's *Unpainted to the Last*. This Abstract Expressionist painter (1914-1980) was also an avid reader, admirer, and collector of books by Melville, although he had many other literary passions besides *Moby-Dick*.[1] Building on the work of Stanley Clifford, Donelson Hoopes, Carl Little, and Elizabeth Schultz, all of whom have discussed the painting in recent years, and drawing on Kienbusch's markings of his copies of *Moby-Dick,* I would like to help explain how he responded to Melville's book. Ultimately it would be difficult to show exactly what this painting "means"; Kienbusch's reading of the text surely destabilizes, almost dissolves, interpretive certainty. I would like instead to focus on what I have found most remarkable in his visual reading of the text, namely his handling of a forward movement into receding space. This problem, the representation of movement into space, appears most visibly in Kienbusch's paintings of islands, islands in Maine and, notably, islands in Greece. Kienbusch's treatment of the island in this painting responds to a philosophical problem in Melville's text, that of the artist's literal and metaphysical approach to his elusive subject.

Let me first suggest, though, the seductions and difficulties of explaining what this painting "means," starting with the title. Although Kienbusch insisted that "*Ahab* is completely nonobjective" (letter to Stanley Clifford, July 27, 1966), he usually gave his paintings representative titles. With early pictures like *Two Ducks —Stonington, Maine* (1941), or *New England Stove* (1948), the title is not as necessary for meaning as it would be in his more abstract landscapes. Although Kienbusch could be playful in his use of titles, he was generally and straightforwardly descriptive and offered his titles as guides to the painting. With some works, his choice of prepositions indicates how he expects a viewer to read the images and their relationships: as, for example, *Island in the Spruce* (1975) or *Island Balancing on Rose Hip Bushes* (1972). As Kienbusch frequently explained in his interviews, he tried to paint the synchronous relationship between objects: "At a certain point, instead of looking at a rock, a pine, and an ocean, I looked at a . . . rock/pine/ ocean . . . these forms started to merge, coalesce, come together" [quoted in Hoopes 47]. Kienbusch's titles tend to make those meanings and those mergings clear.

I take him at his word, then, in viewing this painting's subject as Ahab. There are several problems with this reading, however. For one thing, that white mass at the center looks a lot more like a whale than a one-legged captain. And since Kienbusch rarely painted human subjects, it is hard to see anything *but* Moby Dick in the picture. Then is the painting allegorical? Does it show Ahab's mind perceiving Moby Dick? Possibly. But what, then, are we to make of the colors and their arrangement? The brushwork, with its energetic, sinuous lines, certainly suggests the intensity of Ahab's character. The way the blue encloses the white seems to refer to Ahab's feeling of imprisonment, especially in the chapter Kienbusch often quoted, "The Quarter-Deck," where Ahab ringingly declares, "If man will strike, strike through the mask!" Yet at the same time, the classical, geometric order of the rectangles, the cerulean blues and luminous whites, the profound depth suggest the meditative Ahab of "Sunset" and "The Symphony," or more properly, the meditative Ishmael.

Critics have certainly reached varying interpretations of this problem. Elizabeth Schultz sees the whiteness as "emblematic of either the solitary Ahab or the white wall against which he feels himself to be shoved. . . . Kienbusch's title and ambiguous central image raise the possibility that Ahab, isolated in his yearnings, is himself as inscrutable as the white whale" (143). Carl Little, referring to the "strike through the mask!" passage, comments on "the artist's mission to go beyond surface concerns, to seek the essence of the subject—the object, the figure, the landscape—a goal Bill strived for in his own work" (23). Donelson Hoopes feels that this "elusive subject demanded a format appropriate to the rhapsodic metaphorical prose of Melville's narrative" (38) and that the painting registers the artist's struggles with ambiguity by "shifting the viewer's perception back and forth between the delicate reality of the painted surface and the obscure symbolic content hovering within" (38). All these readings point to the symbolic power and mystery of the painting, which seems to these writers, even as they differ, a passionate and profoundly conceived tribute to Melville's work.

Stanley Clifford, however, sees the painting more in terms of its place in the artistic canon. He does connect it closely to the text: "The reason it is Ahab and not Moby Dick can be found in Ahab's own characterization of himself at the end of the book in 'The Chase—The Third Day.'...[2] Ahab, addressing Starbuck, says, 'and I feel now like a billow that's all one crested comb.' A 'comb' is short for 'comber,' a breaking wave. His life, like the life of a wave ending in a burst of white water, is ending. 'I am old.' This image of the white, breaking wave, is the central image of the picture." Clifford goes on to argue, "That centered wave is almost an icon of American painting," found in works by Winslow Homer, John Marin, and Marsden Hartley, all well known to Kienbusch. Clifford sees the painting as about Ahab's quest, but by extension about Kienbusch's quest for mastery of a specific artistic theme, the breaking wave: "He [Kienbusch] pursued Ahab as relentlessly as Ahab pursued Moby Dick, and like Ahab, cornered his quarry in a burst of blue and white" (letter to Wyn Kelley, August 30, 1996).

If the painting alone presents problems of interpretation, then the literary context complicates the matter even further. Of the thirty or more books by or about Melville in his library, Kienbusch owned nine different editions of *Moby-Dick*. Five of his *Moby-Dicks* were illustrated: two by Rockwell Kent (one inscribed "Sgt. W. Kienbusch"), one by Alfred Staten Conyers, one by Mead Shaeffer, and, the only one you won't find in Schultz's book, a Danish edition illustrated by Sven Havsteen-Mikkelson. He also had *Moby-Dick* in Greek, and he had the Classics Illustrated comic book version of 1969. In 1963 he bought the Washington Square Press paperback, abridged edition, edited by Maxwell Geismar, and wrote on the cover, "Kienbusch, Peggy's Cove, 1963." Ironically this cheap, incomplete edition is the one he marked up significantly, giving us a chance to follow his reading of the book. And in 1965, on his round-the-world trip, he bought an Oxford edition and wrote on the inside front cover, "William Kienbusch, Hongkong—Feb 24 '65," and underneath, "Bangkok, Calcutta, Katmandu, New Delhi," the cities he visited while rereading the volume. Kienbusch did buy editions of Melville's other works (including "Benito Cereno" in Greek), but *Moby-Dick* is the only one of which he bought multiple copies.

Although he was reading the Oxford edition just a year before commencing the painting, he did not mark it, so we must turn to his 1963 text to get any sense, however partial, of his response to the novel. Here we quickly see that certain passages and chapters mattered far more to him than others. He doesn't mark anything before Ahab's "pasteboard mask" speech (136);[3] but that page is dogeared (the only one) and the whole long speech scored with a marginal line. The book contains about eighty other markings, including his writing the date, "Oct 17,'63," on which he finished reading it. Of these, twenty-seven mark speeches *by* Ahab, many of them long, including his most defiant: his "I am madness maddened" ("Sunset"), the "Ego non baptizo te in nomine patris" ("The Forge"), his "queenly personality" speech ("The Candles"), the "what nameless, inscrut-able, unearthly thing is it; what cozening, hidden lord and master" from "The Symphony," and most of his speeches from "The Chase" chapters. He also marks long passages *about* Ahab, especially Ishmael's description of how he lost his leg ("Ahab's Leg"), movingly illustrated, as Schultz points out, in the Rockwell Kent edition.[4] No other *character* receives as much attention, although Kienbusch marks Ahab's conversations with the Carpenter, Starbuck, Pip, and Stubb. Especially if I were doing a biographical analysis here, I would be struck by Kienbusch's response to Ahab's fiery rhetoric; the issues of insanity, paternity, and identity which bedevil Ahab; and Ahab's violence.

These markings and references to Ahab, however, don't fully explain the painting to me, since visually it seems beautiful, mysterious, powerful, yet serene in a way that Ahab seldom is. The many descriptive passages Kienbusch marked, usually Ishmael's philosophical meditations on nature, seem here equally relevant. For example, in "The Whiteness of the Whale," he underlines a single phrase, "shoals of combed white bears were swimming round him" (160), which, besides using the word "comb" that Stanley Clifford points out, also conveys the wondrous, perhaps sinister quietness of the picture. I would expect this chapter, with its endless ruminations on color and its strong visual imagery, to appeal to a painter, and indeed Kienbusch made nine markings. Underlining "Antarctic seas" (161), he wrote "A Gordon Pym Poe" in the margin. Double left marginal lines mark "Though in many of its aspects this visible world seems formed in love, the invisible spheres were formed in fright," as well as the line, "Is it that by its indefiniteness it shadows forth the heartless voids and immensities of the universe" (162). And he underlines "the butterfly cheeks of young girls . . . whose allurements cover nothing but the charnel-house within" (162-63) in Ishmael's discussion of the way Nature assumes the seductive colors that conceal her essential whiteness and colorlessness. It seems very clear that Kienbusch read this chapter with an avid eye.

He circled the title of the chapter "The Pacific" and marked the passage that describes the way "that serene ocean rolled eastwards from me a thousand leagues of blue" (262). This chapter seems not only to have stimulated his inner eye but also to have given him a sense of the motion he later reproduces in the painting: "There is, one knows not what sweet mystery about this sea, whose gently awful stirrings seem to speak of some hidden soul beneath; . . . And meet it is, that over these sea-pastures, . . . the waves should rise and fall, and ebb and flow unceasingly; for here, millions of mixed shades and shadows, drowned dreams, somnambulisms, reveries; all that we call lives and souls, lie dreaming, dreaming still; tossing like slumberers in their beds; the ever-rolling waves made so by their restlessness" (296). "The Gilder" is another chapter whose title he circled and where he marks Ishmael's description of the unceasing motions of life: "Would to God these blessed calms would last. But the mingled, mingling threads of life are woven by warp and woof: calms crossed by storms, a storm for every calm. There is no steady unretracing progress in this life" (305). This "warp and woof" reappears visually in the painting and in its tension between movement and rest. Kienbusch also marked, among several critical passages in "The Symphony," the opening sentence: "Hither, and thither, on high, glided the snow-white wings of small, unspeckled birds; these were the gentle thoughts of the feminine air; but to and fro in the deeps, far down in the bottomless blue, rushed mighty leviathans, sword-fish, and sharks; and these were the strong, troubled, murderous thinkings of the masculine sea" (359). All these passages taken together suggest that the colors and structures of the painting refer as much to nature and to Ishmael's meditations on the sea as to Ahab himself.

The "Chase" chapters contain about twenty more markings and represent, besides the chapters already discussed, the most densely marked section of the book. Here Kienbusch seems to have been equally excited by Ahab's eloquent speeches ["I am the Fates' lieutenant; I act under orders" (383); "Some men die at ebb tide; some at low water; some at the full of the flood" (388); "from hell's heart I stab at thee"(396)]; but equally so by Ishmael's gorgeous descriptions: "Before it [Moby Dick], far out on the soft Turkish-rugged waters, went the glistening white shadow from his broad milky forehead, a musical rippling playfully accompanying the shade; and behind, the blue waters interchangeably flowed over into the moving valley of his steady wake" (366); "But suddenly as he [Ahab] peered down and down into its depths, he profoundly saw a white living spot no bigger than a white weasel, with wonderful celerity uprising, and magnifying as it rose" (368); "So suddenly seen in the blue plain of the sea, and relieved against the still bluer margin of the sky, the spray that he raised, for the moment, intolerably glittered and glared like a glacier" (378). If I were doing a straight literary-artistic comparison, these passages would be convincing evidence that the painting is both "about" Ahab and "about" the whale or the philosophical implications of the conflict between them.

The book and the painting also seem to mesh, though, in another, more structural way. Ahab is always moving toward something he both longs and dreads to meet. Kienbusch employs a similar movement in many of his island pictures, and in this sense the *Ahab* seems a significant rethinking of a favorite motif. For in this painting, the desired object seems both to recede from the pursuing viewer and at the same time to come forth, to loom out of the picture. It is that paradoxical tension, that trompe l'oeil, that rests at the heart of Kienbusch's work and links him most strikingly to Melville.

For me, Kienbusch's 1951 *Dirigo Island* (figure 2) is his quintessential early island picture, and it shows him imagining the *approach* to the island, with the intermediary stages represented geographically in lines or blocks, as just as critical as the island itself. Other early island pictures position the island in the distance as

425

a simple, black shape, distinct yet mysterious, both near and far. Although Kienbusch did many different island views, he liked this concept of the distant island that seems both to come forward and move away as the viewer approaches.

Kienbusch alternated this hard-edged abstract style with a more lyrical, romantic one that used more vivid colors. His journey to Greece in 1959, Donelson Hoopes remarks, "probably accelerated this direction his work had already been taking" (37). As the paintings from Crete make clear, Kienbusch was fascinated by the blues and oranges, juxtaposed with black and white, that he found there. He also began to experiment with more dynamic zigzagging lines within his rectangular forms, as in *Knossos, The Sea* (figure 3). Here we see him begin to enclose his central form with the sea in a way that anticipates the *Ahab*. The islanded forms move to the center of the picture, within the surrounding ocean.

In his letter to Stanley Clifford in the summer of 1966, Kienbusch explains that "the *Ahab* one comes out of 2 winter (last) pictures based on the Blue Door theme" (July 27, 1966). Kienbusch did a number of paintings, then and later, that placed a significant object in the center of the ocean, especially *Oceandoor* (1971), *Red Bandanna, Red Ocean* (1970), and *Blue Bandanna, Blue Ocean* (1970) (figure 4). Like *Ahab*, these paintings make the island seem to move out of the picture plane, toward the viewer. During the same period, Kienbusch began to paint the approach-to-islands again as a theme. Here, however, the approach impinges aggressively on the distant shore; approach (often in a boat) and island become merged. *Rowboat to Island # 1* (1972) (figure 5), for example, makes an island of the boat itself, suggesting an ambiguous relationship between the moving boat and its object; and *Entrance to the Island* (1971) (figure 6) seems to break up and merge both the approaching vessel and the distant shore. Kienbusch, who himself usually rowed his small boat, the *Epo-Bid*, back and forth between the islands, here thematizes and problematizes the artist's approach to his subject.

Kienbusch marked with a double left marginal line Ahab's last words in *Moby-Dick*: "Towards thee I roll, thou all-destroying but unconquering whale; to the last I grapple with thee; from hell's heart I stab at thee; for hate's sake I spit my last breath at thee. Sink all coffins and all hearses to one common pool! and since neither can be mine, let me then tow to pieces, while still chasing thee though tied to thee, thou damned whale!" (396-97). *Ahab* shows the snaking whale lines, the many other lines, that tie the viewer to the quarry he seems to be pursuing. The painting positions the viewer as an Ahab who stabs in vain at the whale who comes forth to meet the gaze yet eludes the understanding.

Kienbusch's title, then, in part reminds the viewer of his or her own Ahabness, that longing to possess. But Ahab hates the whale that frustrates him, whereas Kienbusch's painting makes that mysterious island an image of the loved and desired self: "But even so, amid the tornadoed Atlantic of my being, do I myself still for ever centrally disport in mute calm; and while ponderous planets of unwaning woe revolve round me, deep down and deep inland there I still bathe me in eternal mildness of joy" (253), a passage in "The Armada" that Kienbusch marked. That "eternal mildness of joy" seems as hard to find, as much to be cherished, as the other remote islands of Kienbusch's work. Rosanna Warren's elegy of Kienbusch speaks movingly of his devotion to those charmed oases of, or beyond, the self: "On our / island, alders shimmied in sunlight, deer / browsed through cranberry bogs. / But there are / other islands, and already, while we sat / here with you chatting of ours with its goldenrod, / what you heard / was the other islands."[5]

Not long after my last visit to Cranberry in 1979, a visit in which Kienbusch and I discussed our ideas on Melville, a painting arrived in the mail. Called *Islands in the Wake*, it shows a rowboat *leaving* an island. The title has a distinctly funereal double meaning, and the islands appear portentous and foreboding. Kienbusch died after a hip operation about six months later.

NOTES

I would like to thank Stanley Clifford, Katherine Kaplan of the Kraushaar Galleries, and Carl Little for their help with this essay. I would also like to thank the Kraushaar Galleries and the Princeton Art Museum for permission to reproduce images from their collections.

1   Kienbusch was also my uncle, and I draw here from many discussions between us. His Melville books are in my possession.

2   Kienbusch did indeed mark this passage. Stanley Clifford is an artist, a longtime friend and neighbor of Kienbusch, and his executor.

3   I use the page references from the Washington Square Press edition, with apologies to readers with more authoritative texts.

4   Since Kienbusch encountered the Rockwell Kent editions early in his career, I'm reasonably sure that he was affected by the illustrations and may have had Kent's graphic picture of the

prostrate, wounded Ahab in mind as he marked this passage. I'm indebted to Elizabeth Schultz's cogent reading of the picture for this speculation.

5   From "'Sea-Gate and Goldenrod' (Cranberry Island Elegy)," 82-83.

REFERENCES

Hoopes, Donelson. "William Kienbusch (1914-1980)," in *William Kienbusch: A Retrospective Exhibition, 1946-1979*. Ed. Pamela J. Belanger. Rockland, ME: The Farnsworth Art Museum, 1966. 28-48.

Little, Carl. "Strike Through the Mask!: An Appreciation of William Kienbusch," in *William Kienbusch: A Retrospective Exhibition, 1946-1979*. Ed. Pamela J. Belanger. Rockland, ME: Farnsworth Art Museum, 1996. 16-27.

Melville, Herman. *Moby Dick, or, the White Whale*. An Abridged Edition. Ed. Maxwell Geismar. New York: Washington Square Press, 1962.

——. *Moby Dick, or, The Whale*. Introduction by Viola Meynell. London: Oxford University Press, 1963.

Schultz, Elizabeth A. *Unpainted to the Last: Moby-Dick and Twentieth-Century American Art*. Lawrence: University Press of Kansas, 1995.

Warren, Rosanna. *Each Leaf Shines Separate*. New York: W. W. Norton & Company, 1984.

ROBERT K. WALLACE

CIRCUMNAVIGATING THE GLOBE WITH FRANK STELLA'S *MOBY-DICK* SERIES

rank Stella began his *Moby-Dick* series in 1985. He has completed it in 1997. He has created one or more art works for every chapter title of the novel. He has created 138 separate designs from which he has made 264 unique artistic works (and more than 2,700 individual objects if you count all editioned prints, reliefs, and shawls). These works are scattered literally all over the world.

Thirty of Melville's chapter titles have materialized as prints on paper. *Ahab* (color plate 1) is one of thirteen *Wave* prints (1985-89). In it, Stella has collaged a lot of shapes together. The whale-and-wave-like shape that is printed in pink and black on gray paper will be an important shape throughout the series. The brick-like pattern within the circular lattice shape will also appear elsewhere in the series. Specific to this print is the saw-tooth shape in the lower extremities. Like William Kienbusch in Wyn Kelley's presentation, Stella is presenting a psychological portrait of Ahab in abstract form.

Ninety-six of Melville's chapter titles have materialized as various kinds of metallic reliefs. One of these is *The Whiteness of the Whale* (color plate 5), one of sixteen titles in Stella's IRS-reliefs (1987-88). Like most of the metallic reliefs in the series, this one has been made in two versions, one twice the size of the other. The large version, pictured here, is twelve feet tall by ten feet wide by four feet deep. Two abstract wave shapes combine to suggest the shape of a white whale. Within the shape of the white whale-head you can see other shapes as well: a small white bird protruding from the forehead, the head of a seagull cut in the negative space at the back. Stella has built his metallic frame, and painted its abstract shapes, in such a way as to suggest a white whale in a green sea. You have to see the work from the side to see the lattice shapes that are part of the design. These derive from Chinese lattices similar to the one in the *Ahab* print.

Seven of the titles in the *Moby-Dick* series have been created as freestanding sculptures. One of these is *The Town-Ho's Story* (color plate 6), made mostly of scrap that Stella found in a Connecticut junk yard. It rises twenty-three feet high in the Metcalfe Federal Building in Chicago. This 1993 sculpture incorporates two other *Moby-Dick* titles. *Postscript* is mounted within the upended table in the lower left center of color plate 6. This unpainted relief in cast stainless steel does not appear in any official photograph. You have to go to Chicago to know it is there. Its metallic body articulates the same whale-and-wave-like shape that was printed on paper in the *Ahab* print. Like Ishmael, Stella gives us whales in paint, in sheet-iron, and in a variety of abstract spaces.

I first learned about Frank Stella, and his *Moby-Dick* series, in November 1989. I walked into a gallery in Cincinnati, Ohio, across the river from my home in Kentucky, and saw a print that turned out to be *The Whale as a Dish*. This was one of seven brand-new *Wave* prints in the show. Another was *Moby Dick*, the source of the whale-and-wave shape that is embedded in the *Ahab* print. In *Ahab's Leg*, the profile of that same whale-like shape is absent at the very center of the design. Through the presence or absence of such shapes, Stella creates an abstract narrative throughout the series as a whole. Physical disembodiment is as central to the series as it is to the novel.

I was hooked as soon as I saw the *Wave* prints. I wanted to learn whatever I could about the series as a whole. I quickly learned that to do so I would have to travel widely. You have to see Stella's three-dimensional works in person to feel their scale—and even to see some of their shapes. You can no more know them from photographs or slides than Ishmael could know the whale from the "monstrous pictures" he had seen in books. As with the whale in the open sea, you have to see them in their own places and spaces.

I soon learned that very few of the works in the series were on public display in the United States. In 1991 I decided that if I were serious about the series I would have to go to Japan. Ten *Moby-Dick* reliefs were scheduled to arrive at the Kitakyushu Municipal Museum of Art in October. The first two I saw were *Merry Christmas* and *The Spirit-Spout* from 1987. *The Pipe* (1988) is dominated by a smooth metallic version of the whale-and-wave shape I had seen on paper in *Ahab* and *Moby Dick*. In the 1988 relief entitled *The Shark Massacre* (color plate 7) I saw a new wave shape for the first time, a double-headed wave in an uncomfortable position. That same wave shape was featured in *Cistern and Buckets*, a 1990 work in which Stella was beginning to incorporate unpainted honeycomb aluminum along with the aluminum he was painting. In *The Mast-Head* (1990) Stella used no paint at all. He was on the way to being a sculptor but he had not yet left the wall.

I met Stella in Kitakyushu. I got a photo of him, appropriately, next to *The Sphynx* (1988). The next morning we had the first of many interviews about the series (see my essay "Sounding Out Stella"). Our next interview was in New York, in Stella's studio on East 13th Street, around the corner from the Fourth Avenue address at which Melville had begun *Moby-Dick* in 1850. I visited the studio for the first time in April 1992. On that same visit I also got out to Tyler Graphics in Mount Kisco, New York, where the newest series of *Moby-Dick* prints, the *Moby-Dick Domes*, were in production. In the print shop these were called the pregnant prints because they are printed on dome-shaped paper that swells out from the wall. *Jonah Historically Regarded* is one of five brightly colored *Domes*, each of whose designs had appeared a year earlier as one of the *Moby-Dick Engravings*, flat and mostly black-and-white.

Another print in production that day was *The Fountain*. This became a twenty-three-foot woodblock and intaglio print printed on three sheets of Kozo paper custom-made in Japan. Like the sperm whale at the end of "The Fountain" in *Moby-Dick*, this print is crowned, at one end, with a rainbow. Its wide expanse includes ten different wave shapes that have appeared elsewhere in the series. Some of them are from *The Symphony*, an Embassy print that Tyler Graphics made in 1990. It was printed in an edition of 175 so it could hang in every U.S. Embassy around the world. It has quite literally gone to "all the isles of the sea" and to "all the ends of the earth" (in Ishmael's phrasing from "Knights and Squires").

On my next visit to Tyler Graphics in June 1993, Stella was creating another series of prints, the *Moby-Dick Deckle Edges*. These were to have their inaugural exhibition in Ulm, Germany, in November. The Ulmer Museum asked to me write an essay about the prints for their catalog and I became interested in some Japanese characters that I noticed toward the bottom of *The Affidavit* (color plate 2). It turned out these were from *Miyamoto Musashi and the Whale* (c. 1848-52), a woodblock triptych print that Kuniyoshi had created in Japan while Melville was writing *Moby-Dick* in New York. The Japanese characters that Stella has appropriated from Kuniyoshi's print tell the heroic story of Musashi killing the whale, but Stella undercuts the samurai swordsman in *The Affidavit* by juxtaposing those Japanese characters against liquid bubbles also taken from Kuniyoshi's print (and by blotting out Kuniyoshi's depiction of Musashi with the bright blue anchor-like shape).

Stella's brightly colored *Deckle Edges* prints made a striking impression against the white walls of Richard Meier's *Stadthaus* in Ulm. His *Moby-Dick* prints were the inaugural exhibition in Meier's 1993 building. In addition to seeing the print exhibition in Ulm, I was also able to see works from the *Moby-Dick* series in Zurich, Basel, Dresden, Luxembourg, and Brussels. But my most intense overseas itinerary came the following summer, during an eight-day visit to Japan in August 1994.

In January of that year I had seen a large collage in the *Deckle Edges* style in the New York studio. Its imagery was then being transferred to huge canvas panels for an upcoming installation at the Kawamura Memorial Museum in Sakura in April. The installation was part of an exhibition of Stella's sculptural and architectural projects that seemingly had nothing to do with either Melville or the *Moby-Dick* series. When I received the Sakura catalog in May, however, I learned that the large installation on canvas was called *Hooloomooloo*. This is the name of the "Isle of the Cripples" in Melville's *Mardi*, so of course I wanted to see it. I was becoming more and more like Ahab—or Ishmael—sometimes I was not sure which. I decided to make the trip when I discovered that there were several new *Moby-Dick* sites in Japan that I could visit on my way to Sakura.

The first one was the paper mill near Tokushima that had made the paper for *The Fountain*. Near the mountain on which the kozo grows, I visited the Fuji Paper Mill Cooperative, a modern factory in which all the paper is still made by hand. From Tokushima I then took a train to Takamatsu and a ferry to Naoshima, where two of Stella's *Moby-Dick* reliefs had recently been installed at Benesse House, the island's Museum of Contemporary Art. There, at the bottom of a long ramp, was my old friend *The Shark Massacre*. Next to it was *The Grand Armada* (color plate 8). Standing beneath the latter work, I was able to sense the delicacy of the small wave shape that rises umbilically at the top of the structure. This is the whale-like shape from the *Ahab* and *Moby Dick* prints. Here it is stamped with the lattice from *Ahab's Leg*. Even so, it seems to float free from the surrounding commotion—much like the baby whale that rises to Ishmael's sight in the "Grand Armada" chapter. As I was taking notes on these side-by-side metallic reliefs, smoke from a forest fire began to rise in the picture window that looked out on the Inland Sea. It was still expanding, above and behind the liquid bubbles from the ferry, on the way back to Takamatsu.

The next day I took a train from Tokushima across the island of Shikoku to Kochi. I knew that Kochi's new 1993 museum had acquired one of the three versions Stella had made of *The Pequod Meets the Rosebud*, but I did not know that this version had been installed right inside the door (color plate 3). Stella's *Rosebud* painting is the centerpiece of Kochi's "Ark of Art." Like the painting Ishmael encounters right inside the door of the Spouter-Inn, this one can make you think of "chaos bewitched." But in this one, too, you can make out, if you try hard enough, the "shape of the great leviathan himself." Underneath all of the overpainting to the lower left is the metallic body of the whale shape from the *Ahab* and *Moby Dick* prints.

From Kochi I flew that same evening to Kitakyushu, where I gave a lecture the next day on *The Town-Ho's Story*. People in Kitakyushu were interested in *The Town-Ho's Story* because Stella had installed a similar sculpture in their own city in November 1993. *Yawata Works* shared considerable imagery with the towering sculpture that had been installed in Chicago two months earlier. Stella had found much of the scrap for this sculpture in Japanese scrap yards. He created its manufactured shapes at the Nippon Steel plant in Yawata, where he poured molten stainless steel over the entire sculpture after constructing it. This is really working "Among the Nations."

From Kitakyushu I flew to Tokyo. Four *Epilogue* reliefs that I had hoped to see were in storage, but I did see a small version of *The Spirit-Spout*. I also had

433

the pleasure of meeting Arimichi Makino, editor of *Sky-Hawk*, the Japanese jour-nal of Melville studies. I then went on to the Kawamura Museum in Sakura. Two of my old friends, *The Sphynx* and *The Mast-Head*, were side by side as part of the permanent collection there. And *Hooloomooloo* (color plate 4) was part of the temporary exhibition. The Kawamura Museum had intended to purchase this site-specific work, but it turned out they were not able to do so. After the exhibition, *Hooloomooloo* had to be broken up into separate parts. These have since been exhibited and sold separately. I am exceedingly glad to have seen the entire work in its original state. Its irregular shapes were as uninhibited as those on the fictional island in *Mardi*.

Hooloomooloo turned out to be the first of several titles that Stella took from non-*Moby-Dick* books by Melville. Another is *Loohooloo*, the name from *Omoo* that Stella gave to an installation at the Knoedler Gallery in New York in October 1994. A year later the same installation was dedicated as a conference room in the School of Architecture and Planning at Wyn Kelley's school, M.I.T. A few months after that, *Heads or Tails*, a *Moby-Dick* relief from 1988, was dedicated in the lobby of the Tang Business School at M.I.T.

Although individual works from the series continued to appear from time to time in the United States, the larger congregations of them continued to be found overseas. In September 1995 a number of *Moby-Dick* works I had never seen were included in a retrospective of Stella's career at the Reina Sofía Muse-um in Madrid. I was not able to attend that exhibition because I was in Kansas for Beth Schultz's symposium on *Moby-Dick* and American Art in connection with her exhibition *Unpainted to the Last*. There I saw Kienbusch's *Ahab* for the first time, a work one of my students became obsessed with when we went to see *Unpainted to the Last* at Northwestern University in February 1996.

In March 1996 I caught up with the Madrid retrospective in Munich, where it now included more than seventy works reaching back to Stella's pre-Black paint-ings of 1958. There I got to see *Enter Ahab; to Him Stubb* (1988), and watch one of my favorite wave shapes move from the bent fencing in the lower part of that work across into the boisterous action of *Forecastle—Midnight* (1990), where its metallic body is even more disguised by vivid paint than in *The Pequod Meets the Rosebud*. In *The Dart* (1990) that same wave shape is crucified at the very center of the design, hanging by its head from a longhorn curve like a sheet on a line. In *Ahab and the Carpenter* (1990), however, the wavelike shapes are again active and buoyant. The Munich retrospective also included *Hooloomooloo 4*, a part of the installation I had seen in Sakura. This work is remarkably self-contained. If you had never seen the whole, you would not imagine that four of its five parts were missing. In the June 1997 issue of *ARTnews*, I discovered that a circular extract from this large rectangular fragment was soon to materialize as a floor medallion by Stella in the new addition to the Washington National Airport.

Early in 1997 Stella completed the *Moby-Dick* series with *The Prairie* (color plate 9). In March he exhibited this sculpture, twenty-seven feet long, at the Gagosian Gallery on Wooster Street in New York. In April I went there to see it, eager also to find *The Ship*, a smaller work he had incorporated in the larger one, but which did not appear in the official photo sent by the Gallery. *The Prairie* is created from three large, found objects: a crushed industrial tank, a circular industrial tumbler, and pieces from a nuclear submarine. *The Ship*, only nineteen inches long, was made of much smaller objects. I am glad I saw it when I did because it has since disappeared, lost or stolen after the close of the exhibition.

A day before seeing *The Prairie* at the Gagosian Gallery, I had seen *Juam* at Tyler Graphics. Juam is the first name from *Mardi* that Stella has given to one of his prints. *Juam* is the last of twenty-five Imaginary Places prints, but it also incorporates imagery from the *Moby-Dick Deckle Edges*. Many of its actual printing elements derive from screens, rings, and spirals in aluminum and steel that Stella had used in his *Moby-Dick* reliefs and sculptures. Stella crosses boundaries in his art as much as Melville does in his, in media as well as in imagination. They have both created challenging art that speaks to people "Among the Nations," among whom it is widely distributed.

One of our challenges at this international conference is to try to discover just what it is in Melville's art that allows him to appeal so deeply to people of many cultures and languages, in pictorial languages as well as verbal ones. I am grateful to Beth Schultz for asking me to be part of this panel on Melville and the visual arts, and I hope that the relatively small slice of Stella's *Moby-Dick* series that I have been able to share with you will be a useful strand in the overall weave of the loom.

One generalization I would like to leave you with is this: Melville's art is universal because it addresses the generic dimension of living experience. He is interested not just in Ahab but in Ishmael and Queequeg and the carpenter and Pip. He is interested not just in Moby Dick but in the whale that is killed in chapter 61, and in the old bull whale in chapter 81, and in the baby whale in chapter 87. He attends to the globe and its living creatures in a way we all need to do more attentively as a new century approaches. He does so, as Stella does, not by telling us what to do but by inviting us to see, to see and to feel what it can all add up to, at either its best or its worst. Each but puts that brow before us and trusts us to read it if we can.

Stella's art is universal in part because it is abstract. You do not have to know anything about Captain Ahab or even Moby Dick to experience his *Moby-Dick* series because he is not illustrating those individual, culture-specific images. He is creating generic whale and wave shapes that are activated in a larger psychological and material landscape whose ultimate dimensions and implications are to be determined by the active imagination of the viewer(s). Stella's abstract imagery is open to anyone, with or without prior knowledge of the novel. To someone who does know the novel, of course, the series can become as symbolically rich and structurally multi-stratified as Melville's text.

Stella's series, like Ishmael's whales, must be sought out around the world. You have to work hard just to see the works in the series (unless you just happen upon some of them, as I first did in Cincinnati). After you do see them, you have to do your own thinking about what they mean and what they are for, and why others respond to them in the way they do. In this way Stella's art works are like Melville's chapters, individual creations that invite, and even require, a communal interpretation from the peoples of the world.

REFERENCES

In English

Rubin, William. *Frank Stella, 1970-1987.* Catalog of traveling exhibition originating at the Museum of Modern Art, New York (October 10, 1987-January 5, 1988).

Leider, Philip. "Shakespearean Fish: Frank Stella Meets Moby Dick." *Art in America* 78 (October 1990): 172-91.

Wallace, Robert K. "Sightings of the White Whale." *Contemporanea* 24 (January 1991): 60-67.

Wallace, Robert K. "Frank Stella's Embassy Print, *The Symphony*." *The Print Collector's Newsletter* 23 (July-August 1992): 88-90.

Schultz, Elizabeth. *"Unpainted to the Last"*: Moby-Dick *and Twentieth-Century American Art*. Lawrence: University of Kansas Press, 1995.

Wallace, Robert K. "Sounding Out Stella." *Melville Society Extracts* 107 (December 1996): 1-19.

Wallace, Robert K. *Frank Stella: "Juam" and "Juam, State I."* Mount Kisco, NY: Tyler Graphics, 1997.

Wallace, Robert K. *Frank Stella's* Moby-Dick: *Words and Shapes*. Ann Arbor: University of Michigan Press, 2000.

In Japanese

Amagasaki, Kikuko. *Frank Stella Exhibition*. Catalog of exhibition at the Akira Ikeda Gallery, Taura (November 5, 1988-April 30, 1989).

Kuroiwa, Kyosuke, et al. *Frank Stella: 1958-1990*. Catalog of exhibition at the Kawamura Memorial Museum of Art, Sakura (April 27-June 16, 1991), and the Kitakyushu Municipal Museum of Art (October 19-December 1, 1991).

The Museum of Art, Kochi. *The Inaugural Exhibition 1993*. Catalog.

Hiromoto, Nobuyuki, et al. *Frank Stella: A Vision for Public Art*. Catalog of exhibition at the Kawamura Memorial Museum of Art, Sakura (April 29-August 28, 1994).

Richard Meier/Frank Stella: Architecture and Art. Catalog of traveling exhibition opening at the Aichi Prefectural Museum of Art, Nagoya (February 2-April 7, 1996).

In German

Strelow, Hans. "Frank Stellas Malerei Vom Schwarzen Bild zum Drama im Raum." In *Positionen heutiger Kunst*. Catalog of group exhibition at the Nationalgalerie, Berlin (June 23-September 28, 1988). Pp. 78-101.

Wallace, Robert K. "Stella and Melville: Seeing and Thinking at the Same Time" (tr. Christian Timm; also in English). In *Frank Stella, Moby-Dick Series; Engravings, Domes, and Deckle Edges*. Catalog for exhibition by the Ulmer Museum in the Ulm Stadthaus, Richard Meier architect (November 12, 1993-January 16, 1994). Pp. 19-37. Reprinted by Cantz (Stuttgart, 1994).

Gassner, Hubertus. "Frank Stella: Der Raum bewohnbarer Illusionen" (also in English). In *Frank Stella*. Catalog of exhibition at Haus der Kunst, Munich (February 9-April 21, 1996). Pp. 63-151 and 273-306.

In French

Rubin, William, et al. *Frank Stella, 1970-1987* (tr. Claude Grimal, with original essay in French by Christian Derouet). Catalog of exhibition at the Musée Nationale d'Art Moderne, Centre Georges Pompidou, Paris (May 18-August 28, 1988).

Lévy, Bernard-Henri. *Frank Stella: Les Années 80*. Catalog for exhibition at the Galerie Beaubourg, Paris (February 3-March 10, 1990).

Wallace, Robert K. "Frank Stella sous le signe de Melville, encore" (tr. Frank Straschitz; also in English). *Art Press* 200 (March 1995): 18-25.

In Italian

Tolomeo, Maria Grazia, et al. *Richard Meier/Frank Stella: Art e Architettura*. Catalog of exhibition at Palazzo delle Esposizioni, Rome (July 8-October 3, 1993).

In Spanish

Goldman, Judith, et al. *Frank Stella*. Catalog of exhibition at Museo Nacional Centro de Arte Reina Sofía, Madrid (September 25, 1995-January 9, 1996).

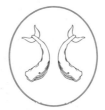

CHARLES WATTS

ENERGY AND GENTLENESS DOUBLE-HOODED:

THE FIGURE OF BEATRICE CENCI IN SHELLEY, HAWTHORNE, AND MELVILLE

This paper examines a figure of innocence and its appearance in an evil world—or, rather, in a world so shot through with ambiguity and dualism that appearances and representations of good and evil at times seem to be or to become their opposites.

The figure is that of Beatrice Cenci, the victim, heroine, and villain of a family tragedy of late sixteenth-century Rome. Her story and fate are those of a young woman of noble family, no more than a girl, who, raped and degraded by a cruel father, plotted his murder with other members of her family and, shortly thereafter, was tried and condemned to death with her stepmother and her brother by a Papal court for the crime of parricide. This *cause célèbre*, widely reported at the time of the trial and executions, became a popular legend down the centuries. The legend emphasized Beatrice's innocence; her father's, Count Cenci's, crimes; and the Papal government's duplicity in having ignored Count Cenci's outrages, including murder, in favor of his wealth, but condemned Beatrice, her step-mother, and brother while professing to protect the weak and innocent.

A painting, long and erroneously attributed to Guido Reni and said to be the portrait of Beatrice Cenci on the eve of her execution, became the image of outraged innocence which united with the Cenci story in the popular imagination of Europe. By the time Percy Bysshe Shelley saw the painting in 1819, Beatrice was, according to Stuart Curran, "one of the most famous attractions of Rome; reproduced ubiquitously, the portrait was hardly less compelling to visitors than the Bernini fountains or the Sistine frescoes."[1] But what Shelley saw in the portrait would make Beatrice a figure in the Romantic imagination, famous in the English-speaking and reading world, and would compel first Herman Melville and then Nathaniel Hawthorne to make a pilgrimage to the sites of the painting and the tragedy.

Beatrice's image and her story moved Shelley to write a verse-tragedy in the Shakespearean manner, in five acts, *The Cenci* (1819). In the preface to the play he describes the image which the artist had rendered and which so attracted him:

There is a fixed and pale composure upon the features: she seems sad and stricken down in spirit, yet the despair thus expressed is lightened by the patience of gentleness. Her head is bound with folds of white drapery from which the yellow strings of her golden hair escape, and fall about her neck. The moulding of her face is exquisitely delicate; the eyebrows are distinct and arched: the lips have that permanent meaning of imagination and sensibility which suffering has not repressed and which it seems as if death scarcely could extinguish. Her forehead is large and clear; her eyes, which we are told were remarkable for their vivacity, are swollen with weeping and lustreless, but beautifully tender and serene. In the whole mien there is a simplicity and dignity which, united with her exquisite loveliness and deep sorrow, are inexpressibly pathetic. Beatrice Cenci appears to have been one of those rare persons in whom energy and gentleness dwell together without destroying one another: her nature was simple and profound. The crimes and miseries in which she was an actor and a sufferer are as the mask and the mantle in which circumstances clothed her for her impersonation on the scene of the world.[2]

Thirty-eight years later Herman Melville, traveling in Rome, would take some trouble to visit Shelley's grave and "Thence to Cenci Palace. . .Tragic looking place enough"; then he would confront the famous portrait and remark in his journal, in the terse style meant primarily for his private rumination: "Expression of suffering about the mouth (appealing look of innocence) not caught in any copy or engraving."[3] Melville had been thinking of Shelley's Beatrice at least since the summer of 1849, when he wrote in *White-Jacket*, alluding to the occurrence of homosexual rape on American naval vessels, "There are evils in men-of-war, which, like the suppressed domestic drama of Horace Walpole, will neither bear representing, nor reading, and will hardly bear thinking of. The landsman who has neither read Walpole's *Mysterious Mother*, nor Sophocles's *Oedipus Tyrannus*, nor the Roman story of *Count Cenci*, dramatized by Shelley, let that landsman guardedly remain in his ignorance of even worse horrors than these, and forever abstain from seeking to draw aside this veil."[4]

Two years after Melville, and forty years after Shelley, Nathaniel Hawthorne would stand before the painting and then meditate in his journal:

It is the very saddest picture that ever was painted, or conceived; there is an unfathomable depth and sorrow in the eyes; the sense of it comes to you by a sort of intuition. It is a sorrow that removes her out of the sphere of humanity; and yet she looks so innocent, that you feel as if it were only this sorrow, with its weight and darkness, that keeps her down upon the earth and brings her within our reach at all. She is like a fallen angel, fallen, without sin. It is infinitely pitiful to meet her eyes, and feel that nothing can be done to help or comfort her; not that she appeals to you for help and comfort, but is more conscious than we can be that there is none in reserve for her. It is the most profoundly wrought picture in the world; no artist did it, or could do it, again. Guido may have held the brush, but he painted better than he knew. I wish, however, it were possible for some spectator, of deep sensibility, to see the picture without knowing anything of the subject or history; for no doubt we bring all our knowledge of the Cenci tragedy to the interpretation of the picture.[5]

The figure of Beatrice Cenci imposed itself on the imaginative writing of both Melville and Hawthorne, as it had on Shelley's work. A copy of the portrait makes an enigmatic appearance in a critical scene just before the climax of Melville's *Pierre; or, The Ambiguities* (1852). Another copy is an important presence in Hawthorne's *The Marble Faun* (1860). And a partial image, a metonymic ghost of an image of Beatrice, appears to Clarel's gaze in a sudden and fleeting expression on the mouth of Vine, in Melville's verse novel, *Clarel: A Poem and Pilgrimage in the Holy Land* (1876).[6]

In this paper I will consider the figure of Beatrice as it appears in *The Marble Faun* and in *Pierre*, with some reference to Shelley's *The Cenci*. My intent is to show how both Melville and Hawthorne brought forward characters whose special and particular innocence and purity seem to draw them to the portrait, as though both authors felt compelled to confront this image of innocence amid evil with a complementary image of unassailable innocence, an image which they describe as angelic, but which both authors, Melville more demonstrably, view with ambivalence.

For Hawthorne's part, the desire to formulate a character whose purity allows her a clearer, more telling view of Beatrice is announced in the journal entry quoted above: "I wish, however, it were possible for some spectator, of deep sensibility, to see the picture without knowing anything of the subject or history; for no doubt we bring all our knowledge of the Cenci tragedy to the interpretation of the picture." When Hawthorne wished for such a spectator, it was Shelley's depiction he wanted, if only for a moment, to wish away. Stuart Curran reports that "The fame of the portrait in the English-speaking world of the nineteenth century rested on [Shelley]"; as Henry A. Murray has remarked, "Shelley's *Cenci* (1819) was largely responsible for the compelling fascination exerted by Guido's head upon the intellectuals and *spirituelles* of the succeeding generation."[7] Hawthorne was moved to re-imagine the Cenci story in modern Rome and to fabricate himself a spectator whose ability to empathize with the image of Beatrice's innocence in the painting would permit her for a time to forget, to be completely innocent of the Cenci history and its tragedy. In "Beatrice," Chapter VII of *The Marble Faun*, Hilda, a young American painter living in Rome who has devoted herself to copying the works of the great Italian masters, shows her recently completed copy of the portrait of *la Cenci* to her friend and fellow painter, Miriam. Miriam remarks on the copy's extraordinary likeness to the original, and asks Hilda, "can you interpret what the feeling is, that gives this picture such a mysterious force? For my part, though deeply sensible of its influence, I cannot seize it." Hilda replies:

Nor can I, in words. . . . But, while I was painting her, I felt all the time as if she were trying to escape from my gaze. She knows that her sorrow is so strange, and so immense, that she ought to be solitary forever, both for the world's sake and for her own; and this is the reason we feel such a distance between Beatrice and ourselves, even when our eyes meet hers. It is infinitely heart-breaking to meet her glance, and to feel that nothing can be done to help or comfort her; neither does she ask help or comfort, knowing the hopelessness of her case better than we do. She is a fallen angel, fallen, and yet sinless; and it is only this depth of sorrow, with its weight and darkness, that keeps her down upon earth, and brings her within our view even while it sets her beyond our reach.[8]

Here we see Hilda echoing Hawthorne's words as he set them down in his journal. She is his conception of an almost angelically innocent witness in the novel. When Miriam asks in reply to Hilda, "You deem her sinless?" and reminds her of Beatrice's history, remarking on her perception that "Beatrice's own conscience does not acquit her of something evil, and never to be forgiven," Hilda responds, "shuddering," "I really had quite forgotten Beatrice's history, and was thinking of her only as the picture seems to reveal her character. Yes, yes; it was terrible guilt, an inexpiable crime, and she feels it to be so. Therefore it is that the forlorn creature so longs to elude our eyes, and forever vanish away into nothingness! Her doom is just" (906).

Miriam exclaims, "Oh, Hilda, your innocence is like a sharp steel sword," calling the reader's attention to the inflexible judgmental edge of Hilda's saintliness. She goes on to wish passionately that she were able to empathize with the ancient victim: "if I could only get within her consciousness! If I could but clasp Beatrice's ghost, and draw it into myself! I would give my life to know whether she thought herself innocent, or the one great criminal since time began!" Here Miriam's expression suddenly appears to Hilda to be exactly like that of the image in the painting—a sign in Hawthorne's semiology that Miriam shares or will share somehow in Beatrice's ruined innocence.

Later in the novel, Hilda beholds a doubling of her own image with the face in the portrait. Afflicted with the knowledge of sin which she has gained by witnessing Miriam and her lover, Donatello, at the moment when he hurls Miriam's tormentor, Antonio, to his death from the Tarpeian Rock, Hilda recognizes in a mirror near the painting in her studio her own likeness to Beatrice's expression of despair: "She fancied nor was it without horrour that Beatrice's expression, seen aside and vanishing in a moment, had been depicted in her own face, likewise, and flitted from it as timourously. 'Am I, too, stained with guilt?' thought the poor girl, hiding her face in her hands." The narrator hastens to deny this possibility ("Not so, thank Heaven!"), explaining that perhaps Beatrice's forlorn expression is due to "the intimate consciousness of her father's sin," just as "It was the knowledge of Miriam's guilt that lent the same expression to Hilda's face" (1022).

444

Here is Hawthorne's imagination of an innocence of vision which has "quite forgotten" the painful history manifesting itself in Beatrice's gaze, until it is made forcibly aware of such history by direct witness; here also is an experienced vision which so empathizes with Beatrice and her history that it momentarily assumes Beatrice's look—looks out with her eyes. Both the "innocent" and the "experienced" vision are doubles or copies of the portrait's aspect—moreover, they are doubles of each other, interpenetrating one another—as they take on consciousness of evil. This confrontation, doubling and interpenetrating an innocence with an experience of vision, forms one basis for the action of Hawthorne's novel.

Another and a prior innocent, like Hawthorne's Hilda an amateur artist and a kind of angel—in some ways she is a model for Hilda—Lucy Tartan is Herman Melville's unworldly spectator before the portrait of Beatrice. Lucy, the girl to whom Pierre Glendinning is engaged at the opening of *Pierre; or, The Ambiguities*, seems there so ethereal as hardly to be made of flesh, she "hath floated as stilly through this life, as thistle-down floats over meadows."[9] This ethereal Lucy, who shares with Pierre what seems an ideal love, is abandoned by Pierre without explanation when he pretends to elope with Isabel Banford, the woman he has secretly come to believe is his unacknowledged half-sister, his father's undeclared and apparently illegitimate daughter. Lucy suffers the agony of this abandonment, lapsing into a "swoon" which verges nearly on death. (Isabel had herself suffered the abandonment of mother—through her early death—and father—by his unwillingness to forthrightly declare his paternity and then by his death.)

Yet Lucy recovers, transformed by her ordeal, and sends to Pierre a letter reinvoking her undying love for him, confessing her intuition of the "superhuman, angelical" heroism of his action in appearing to marry Isabel, which she regards as both a gesture of self-sacrifice for Pierre and one of many "cruelest disguises" to which Isabel has been forced. In this letter Lucy announces that she is coming to Pierre to "guard and serve" him and Isabel as a "nun-like cousin," to fulfill a "superhuman office" as angelic sister and servant in the expectation that her true wedding to him is in heaven (309-11). And she does come to them, in defiance of her mother, brother, suitor and the world, to dwell with them in uneasy communion in their rooms at the abandoned and converted Church of the Apostles. Lucy, whose name means *light*, whom Isabel calls Pierre's "good angel" (314), is the extraordinary woman who stands witness, in Book XXVI, to what the narrator calls "a very tolerable copy" of the portrait of Beatrice—"that sweetest, most touching, but most awful of all feminine heads—the Cenci of Guido."

The wonderfulness of which head consists chiefly, perhaps, in a striking, suggested contrast, half-identical with, and half-analogous to, that almost supernatural one—sometimes visible in the maidens of tropical nations—namely, soft and light blue eyes, with an extremely fair complexion, vailed by funereally jetty hair. But with blue eyes and fair complexion, the Cenci's hair is golden physically, therefore, all is in strict, natural keeping, which, nevertheless, still the more intensifies the suggested fanciful anomaly of so sweetly and seraphically *blonde* a being, being double-hooded, as it were, by the black crape of the two most horrible crimes (of one of which she is the object, and of the other the agent) possible to civilized humanity—incest and parricide. (351)

This metaphorical double blackness, invisible in the painting itself, imbues it with horror, tragedy, and pathos by virtue of the history and legend of Beatrice, a matter of narrative. Lucy, so far as we know, is unaware of this history. It is the narrator, the one who is telling the history of Pierre and Isabel and Lucy, who puts us in mind of this double veil. But why should it appear in the narrative of *Pierre* at just this moment?

A double hood of (narrative) blackness invests the struggle of Pierre and Isabel to live free of the trammels of the past, just as it invests this image of Beatrice Cenci. One hood is an emblem of the crime of incest. Pierre and Isabel, brother and sister to each other, are living outwardly as husband and wife, and Pierre's unspoken desire for Isabel, which she ambiguously reciprocates and passively resists, brings them both under the sign of incest (192, 272-74). The other hood emblematizes the crime of patricide. Pierre has metaphorically murdered his father's sacred memory by burning his youthful portrait and by renouncing him ("now all is done, and all is ashes! Henceforth, cast-out Pierre hath no paternity, and no past" [198-99]); the consequence of his proclaiming his marriage to Isabel is his banishment from his mother's house and his expected inheritance; a worse consequence is his mother's early, bitter death (285-86). And when, soon after Lucy confronts Beatrice Cenci's portrait, Pierre madly, desperately kills his cousin and former childhood companion, Glen Stanly; he "extinguishe[s] his house in slaughtering the only unoutlawed human being by the name of Glendinning" (360).

This last disaster holds the bitterest irony for Lucy. For by her decision to join Pierre and Isabel, hoping to serve them as a "good angel," she draws her vengeance-seeking brother and cousin down on them; Lucy's presence visits this penultimate blackness on them, as exterminating angel—a final irony. It is thus to the "seraphically blonde" Lucy that the image of Beatrice Cenci appears.

We have noted that Isabel calls Lucy a "good angel." She does so not from admiration, but in a high pitch of anguish, jealousy, and terror at the prospect of Pierre favoring Lucy over herself. She tells Pierre that she has seen Lucy's image in a dream, "her blue eyes turned beseechingly on me; she seemed as if persuading me from thee;—methought she was then more than thy cousin;—methought she was that good angel, which some say, hovers over every human soul; and methought...that I was thy other, thy other angel, Pierre. Look: see these eyes, —this hair—nay, this cheek;—all dark, dark, dark,—and she—the blue-eyed—the fair-haired—oh, once the red-cheeked!" Isabel thinks Lucy a "good angel" by contrast with herself, "the other angel"—a dark angel, conventionally signifying evil and death. Referring to her "ebon tresses" and her "ebon eyes," she asks, "Say, Pierre; doth not a funerealness invest me? Was ever hearse so plumed?—Oh, God! that I had been born with blue eyes, and fair hair! Those make the livery of heaven! Heard ye ever yet of a good angel with dark eyes, Pierre?—no, no, no—all blue, blue, blue. . . . But the good angel shall come to thee, Pierre. Then both will be close by thee, my brother; and thou mayest perhaps elect,—elect!" (314).

Thus Pierre is flanked by the "good angel," blonde, blue-eyed Lucy with skin the pallor of white marble (328), and the "other angel," ebon-haired, olive-skinned Isabel, when the three enter the gallery where two portraits will capture their respective attentions: the "dark, comely, youthful man's head" known as "A Stranger's Head by an Unknown Hand," and the "seraphically blonde" head of Beatrice Cenci.

Melville further elaborates the confrontation and doubling of light and dark in explicating the "suggested fanciful anomaly" of the Cenci portrait. Several critics have pointed out the peculiar blending and reversal of the traditional light-dark/good-evil dualism in this passage. Not only does the narrator imply a racial mixing in talking of an "almost supernatural" blending of blue eyes, fair skin, and black hair in "the maidens of tropical nations," but as Leon Chai suggests, the image also blends the contrary characteristics of the two "sisters": "as a 'dark' yet 'seraphically *blonde*' heroine, [Beatrice Cenci] simultaneously suggests both Isabel and Lucy."[10] Louise K. Barnett remarks: "This verdict on the portrait of Beatrice Cenci implicates Melville's two heroines, styled at times the 'good angel' and the 'bad angel.' By the end of the novel, the fair, nun-like Lucy and the dark and passionate Isabel have merged like the two opposed qualities of Beatrice. Unable to resolve the ambiguities of the situation, Pierre renounces both women and his own life."[11] Thus the narrator metonymically superimposes the "almost supernatural" image of "the maidens of tropical nations" on the image of Beatrice, doubling the light with the dark, Lucy with Isabel. But while light and dark appear merged, they are also, like Blake's contraries, at war: vertiginously blended yet distinct. By the final scene, for desperate Pierre, in prison and under imminent sentence of death for the impetuous murder of Glen Stanly, they have become like the phantoms which had haunted him on first meeting Isabel: "Ye two pale ghosts, were this the other world, ye were not welcome. Away!—Good Angel and Bad Angel both!—For Pierre is neuter now!" (360).

This communion of light and dark is present even in the placement of the two portraits in the gallery: "Now, this Cenci and 'the Stranger' were hung at a good elevation in one of the upper tiers; and, from the opposite walls, exactly faced each other; so that in secret they seemed pantomimically talking over and across the heads of the living spectators below" (351). And while he tells us nothing of what Lucy thinks or feels in gazing at the Cenci portrait,[12] the narrator describes those very different yet fatally bound-together responses of Pierre and Isabel to the Stranger's Head by an Unknown Hand: Pierre, shocked at the portrait's uncanny likeness to the "chair portrait" of his father as a young man, the portrait which had so reminded Pierre of his father's secret and seemingly dishonorable life that he had burned it; Isabel, struck by the portrait's resemblance to the man who had so rarely visited her as a child and whom she had come to regard as her father. And yet Pierre knows that this Renaissance painting can portray neither him nor her father, even as Isabel vividly affirms that it somehow magically *is* her father's image. So it is the image of the father, an image inflected by mystery and sexual transgression, and yet with an "unequivocal aspect of foreignness, of Europeanism," and of impossible ambiguity about it, which seems to hold secret parley with the portrait of Beatrice.

The narrator adds only, regarding this painting: "With the aspect of the Cenci everyone is familiar" (351). With this remark, Melville anticipates Hawthorne's lament over the universal awareness of the Cenci story by seven years. But what may this apparently perfunctory sentence mean? For instance, what is "the aspect" of the Cenci? Perhaps it is the "look" or the "appearance" of Beatrice's face that is meant. But in addition to "look," "countenance," "appearance," *aspect* may also mean the "act of looking at"; the "gaze."[13] Beatrice does in fact gaze from within the space of the portrait out to the viewer. We meet her gaze, even if, with Hawthorne's Hilda, we feel that she is trying to escape our own. And then, how is it that "everyone" is "familiar" with this "aspect"? On the surface of it, it is simply the image with which everyone is familiar, as the Cenci was one of the most reproduced paintings of the nineteenth century. But cunningly (or casually) concealed in this innocent sentence is the notion that everyone is familiar with the *gaze* of the Cenci: that is, that everyone has a *family* relation to that gaze. The narrator is very quietly, nonchalantly, saying that Beatrice's aspect is archetypal; that she is a universal sister and daughter; and that the infinitely painful and tragic meaning of her gaze is universally recognized and recognizable—recognizable, that is, for all those who will look. This aspect is a matter of family relations gone terribly, tragically wrong. And that, of course, is the text—not the subtext or the pretext, but the very texture, the weave—of *Pierre; or, The Ambiguities.*

In the gallery scene, public "familiarity" with the painting's "aspect" is contrasted with the uncanny foreign-familiarity of the "Stranger's Head." But the superficial public celebrity of the Cenci portrait does not fully explain its attraction for Lucy, who, passing unconcerned, "without the least special pause" by the portrait which so haunts and undoes Pierre and Isabel, turns to stand "motionless" before this "very tolerable copy." And yet what has been said in explication of Pierre's and Isabel's sudden interest in the "Stranger's Head" can as much be ascribed to Lucy's sudden arrest before Beatrice: "No one who has passed through the great galleries of Europe . . .—no calm, penetrative person can have victoriously run that painted gauntlet of the gods, without certain very special emotions, called forth by some one or more individual paintings, to which, however, both the catalogues and the criticisms of the greatest connoisseurs deny any all-transcending merit, at all answering to the effect thus casually produced. . . . [I]t is not the abstract excellence always, but often the accidental congeniality, which occasions this wonderful emotion" (350).

What arrests Lucy, then, who stands motionless as the marble woman (or angel) Pierre perceives she has become—"Her head sat on her shoulders as a chiseled statue's head; and the soft, firm light in her eye seemed as much a prodigy, as though a chiseled statue should give token of vision and intelligence" (328)—is what she perceives, hovering on the expectant edge of the final swift, tragic action which binds up the lives of Pierre, Isabel, and herself, of "the accidental congeniality" of her own image with that of Isabel in this "very tolerable copy":

Beatrice Cenci appears to have been one of those rare persons in whom energy and gentleness dwell together without destroying one another: her nature was simple and profound. (*Cenci* 278)

To Pierre's dilated senses Isabel seemed to swim in an electric fluid; the vivid buckler of her brow seemed as a magnetic plate. . . . The occasional sweet simplicity, and innocence, and humbleness of her story; her often serene and open aspect; her deep-seated, but mostly quiet, unobtrusive sadness, and that touchingness of her less unwonted tone and air; these only the more signalized and contrastingly emphasized the profounder, subtler, and more mystic part of her . . . it seemed well-nigh impossible that this unassuming maid should be the same dark, regal being who had but just now bade Pierre be silent in so imperious a tone, and around whose temples the strange electric glory had been playing. (*Pierre* 152)

Such wonderful strength in such wonderful sweetness; such inflexibility in one so fragile, would have been matter for marvel to any observer. . . . As if sterling heavenliness were incompatible with heroicness. These two are never found apart. Nor, though Pierre knew more of Lucy than anyone else, did this most singular behavior fail to amaze him. Seldom even had the mystery of Isabel fascinated him more, with a fascination partaking of the terrible. (*Pierre* 327)

Isabel also was most strangely moved by this sweet unearthliness in the aspect of Lucy.

Edward Lear, *Thessaloniki and the Thermaic Gulf*. Courtesy of the Ashmoleon Museum, Oxford, England. [Georgoudaki, "Herman Melville in Thessaloniki," 85–107]

Flemish School, *Medusa*. Courtesy of Alinari/Art Resource, New York. [Berthold, "Melville's Medusas, 287–96]

Carl Barth, *Homage to Melville (Huldigung an Melville).* Courtesy of Peter Barth.
[Schultz, "Seeing "Moby-Dick Globally," 409–19]

Vali Myers, *The Whale.* Courtesy of Vali Myers. [Schultz, "Seeing "Moby-Dick Globally," 409–19]

Athanasios C. Christodoulou, *The Monomania of Ahab*.
[Schultz, "Seeing "Moby-Dick Globally," 409–19]

William Kienbusch, *Ahab.* Courtesy of the Estate of William Kienbusch. [Kelley, "Kienbusch, Melville, and the Islands," 420–28, figure 1]

William Kienbusch, *Knossos, The Sea.* Courtesy of the Estate of William Kienbusch. [Kelley, "Kienbusch, Melville, and the Islands," 420–28, figure 3]

William Kienbusch,
*Blue Bandana, Blue
Ocean.* Courtesy of
the Estate of William
Kienbusch. [Kelley,
"Kienbusch, Melville,
and the Islands," 420–
28, figure 4]

William Kienbusch,
Rowboat to Island #1.
Courtesy of the
Estate of William
Kienbusch. [Kelley,
"Kienbusch, Melville,
and the Islands," 420–
28, figure 5]

William Kienbusch, *Entrance to the Island.* Courtesy of the Estate of William Kienbusch.
[Kelley, "Kienbusch, Melville, and the Islands," 420–28, figure 6]

Frank Stella, *Ahab*. © 1999 Frank Stella / Artists Rights Society
(ARS), New York. [Wallace, "Circumnavigating the
Globe," 429–38, color plate 1]

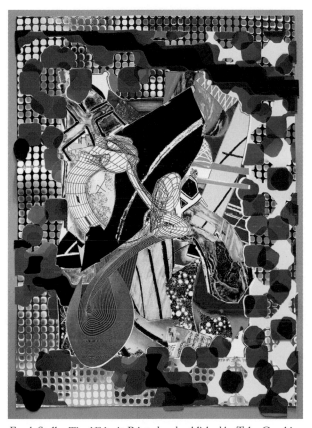

Frank Stella, *The Affidavit*. Printed and published by Tyler Graphics, Ltd., 1993; © 1999 Frank Stella/Tyler Graphics Ltd./Artists Rights Society (ARS), New York. Photo: Steve Sloman, NYC. [Wallace, "Circumnavigating the Globe," 429–38, color plate 2]

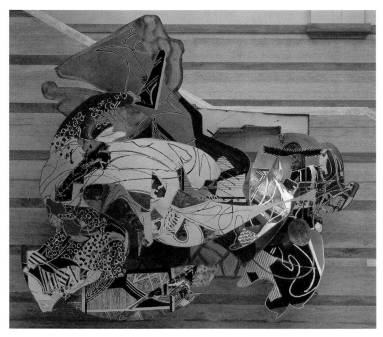

Frank Stella, *The Pequod Meets the Rosebud*. © 1999 Frank Stella / Artists Rights Society (ARS), New York. [Wallace, "Circumnavigating the Globe," 429–38, color plate 3]

Frank Stella, *Hooloomooloo.*
© 1999 Frank Stella /
Artists Rights Society
(ARS), New York.
[Wallace, "Circumnavigat-
ing the Globe," 429–38,
color plate 4]

Frank Stella, *The Whiteness
of the Whale.* © 1999 Frank
Stella / Artists Rights
Society (ARS), New York.
[Wallace, "Circumnavigat-
ing the Globe," 429–38,
color plate 5]

Frank Stella, *The Town Ho's Story.* © 1999 Frank Stella / Artists Rights
Society (ARS), New York. [Wallace, "Circumnavigating
the Globe," 429–38, color plate 6]

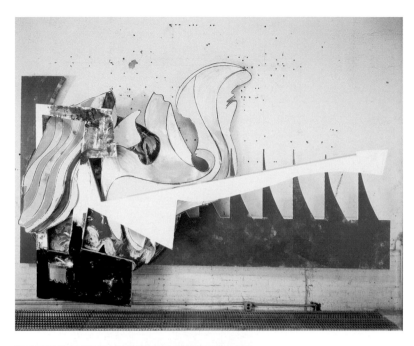

Frank Stella, *The Shark Massacre*. © 1999 Frank Stella / Artists Rights Society (ARS), New York. [Wallace, "Circumnavigating the Globe," 429–38, color plate 7]

Frank Stella, *The Grand Armada*. © 1999 Frank Stella / Artists Rights Society (ARS), New York. [Wallace, "Circumnavigating the Globe," 429–38, color plate 8]

Frank Stella, *The Prairie*. © 1999 Frank Stella /Artists Rights Society (ARS), New York.
[Wallace, "Circumnavigating the Globe," 429–38, color plate 9]

Elihu Vedder, *The Lair of the Sea Serpent.* Courtesy of the Museum of Fine Arts, Boston.
Reproduced with permission. © 2000 Museum of Fine Arts, Boston. All Rights Reserved. [Kleitz,
"Questioners of the Sphinx," 455–62, color plate A]

Elihu Vedder, *The Questioner of the Sphinx.* Courtesy of the Museum of Fine Arts, Boston.
Reproduced with permission. © 2000 Museum of Fine Arts, Boston.
All Rights Reserved. [Kleitz, "Questioners of the Sphinx," 455–62, color plate B]

Elihu Vedder, *The Cumaean Sibyl,* 1876. Founders Society Purchase, Merrill Fund.
Photograph © 1991 The Detroit Institute of Arts.
[Kleitz, "Questioners of the Sphinx," 455–62, color plate C]

But it did not so much persuade her by any common appeals to her heart, as irrespectively commend her by the very signet of heaven. (*Pierre* 328)[14]

The crimes and miseries in which she was an actor and a sufferer are as the mask and the mantle in which circumstances clothed her for her impersonation on the scene of the world. (*Cenci* 278)

This mixture of energy and gentleness, strength and sweetness, the terrible in the sublime, is a birthright and a circumstance common to Lucy, Isabel, and Beatrice. This figure of the angelic under the censure of the earthly moved Melville's "Expression of suffering about the mouth—(appealing look of innocence) not caught in any copy or engraving." It is what drew Hawthorne, following Melville's lead both in art and in life, to reconsider this portrait of Beatrice: "It is a sorrow that removes her out of the sphere of humanity; and yet she looks so innocent, that you feel as if it were only this sorrow, with its weight and darkness, that keeps her down upon the earth and within our reach at all." And it is what moved Melville, long before he saw the actual painting, to pair his American double image of womanly victimhood and passion—the "rural bowl of milk" he had promised Sophia Hawthorne turned now to living white marble, shaded by "ebon vines"—with the famous Renaissance image of saintly pathos and tragic horror, a sainthood deprived of its canonicity by the very action which gave it tragic dignity—Lucy with Isabel with Beatrice.

NOTES

1   Stuart Curran, *Shelley's* Cenci: *Scorpions Ringed with Fire* (Princeton, NJ: Princeton University Press, 1970), xi. Twentieth century critics have concluded that the portrait is not by Guido Reni, nor is it probably that of Beatrice Cenci, but rather an idealized depiction of a sibyl. See, for example, Arthur McComb, *The Baroque Painters of Italy: an Introductory Historical Survey* (1934: rpt. New York: Russell & Russell, 1968), 26, 31. Interestingly, however, the brass identifying plate on the painting, which remains in the Palazzo Barberini, now the Galleria Nazionale d'Arte Antica, still names the painter as Guido Reni, the subject as Beatrice.

2   Percy Bysshe Shelley, "Preface" to *The Cenci*, in *Shelley: Poetical Works*, ed. Thomas Hutchinson, new edition corrected by G. M. Matthews (Oxford & New York: Oxford University Press, 1970), 278.

3   Herman Melville, *Journals*, ed. Howard C. Horsford and Lynn Horth. *The Writings of Herman*

Melville, Vol. 15 (Evanston and Chicago: Northwestern University Press and the Newberry Library, 1989): 108.

4   Herman Melville, *White-Jacket; or, The World in a Man-of-War*, ed. Harrison Hayford, Hershel Parker, and G. Thomas Tanselle. *The Writings of Herman Melville*, Vol. 5 (Evanston and Chicago: Northwestern University Press and the Newberry Library, 1970), 376.

5   Nathaniel Hawthorne, *The French and Italian Notebooks*, ed. Thomas Woodson. *The Centenary Edition of the Works of Nathaniel Hawthorne*, Vol. XIV (Columbus: Ohio State University Press, 1980), 92-93.

6   See *Clarel: A Poem and Pilgrimage in the Holy Land*, ed. Harrison Hayford, Alma A. MacDougall, Hershel Parker, and G. Thomas Tanselle. *The Writings of Herman Melville*, Vol. 12 (Evanston and Chicago: Northwestern University Press and the Newberry Library, 1991), 287 (3.7.16-24).

7   Curran, xi; Murray, in Herman Melville, *Pierre or, The Ambiguities* (New York: Hendricks House, 1949), 503.

8   *The Marble Faun*, in *Nathaniel Hawthorne: Novels* (New York: The Library of America, 1983), 906. Further references to this work will be cited parenthetically in the text.

9   Herman Melville, *Pierre; or, The Ambiguities*, ed. Harrison Hayford, Hershel Parker and G. Thomas Tanselle. *The Writings of Herman Melville*, Vol. 7. (Evanston and Chicago: Northwestern University Press and the Newberry Library, 1971), 25. Further references to this work will be cited parenthetically in the text.

10   *The Romantic Foundations of the American Renaissance* (Ithaca and London: Cornell University Press, 1987), 419.

11   "American Novelists and the 'Portrait of Beatrice Cenci,'" in *New England Quarterly* 53.2 (June 1980): 176-77.

12   Discussing the subjective nature of Pierre's response to another painting, the youthful "chair portrait" of his father, Leon Chai observes, "The transformations of the face as Pierre continues to hold his imagined colloquy with it attest to the subjective nature of even the actual lineaments of the representation. For this reason Melville abstains from describing Beatrice Cenci: her importance lies not in her appearance but in what she symbolizes for Pierre and the subjective consciousness which pervades Melville's novel" (421).

13   *Webster's Collegiate Dictionary*, Fifth Edition (Springfield, MA: G. & C. Merriam, 1948).

14   This involuntary persuasion, "commended" (commanded) by heaven, is confirmed for Isabel when she recognizes Lucy's communion with the divine by a sign that she, too, like Isabel, can evoke the voice of the sublime, the departed mother in heaven, through the voice of the guitar: "And when it so chanced, that—owing perhaps to some momentary jarring of the distant and lonely guitar—as Lucy was so mildly speaking in the presence of her mother, a sudden, just audible, submissively answering musical, stringed tone, came through the open door from the adjoining chamber; then Isabel, as if seized by some spiritual awe, fell on her knees before Lucy, and made a rapid gesture of homage; yet still, somehow, as it were, without evidence of voluntary will" (328). That "distant and lonely guitar" (whose "secret name" is Isabel)—for Isabel the metonymic

sign of the deceased and translated mother, the source for her (and through her, for Pierre) of power and mystery (148-50)—is, it seems to me, one remarkable instance of this book's extraordinary imaginative richness—as the withheld and "vailed" "aspect" of Beatrice is another.

REFERENCES

Barnett, Louise K. "American Novelists and the 'Portrait of Beatrice Cenci.'" *New England Quarterly* 53.2 (June 1980): 168-83.

Chai, Leon. *The Romantic Foundations of the American Renaissance*. Ithaca, NY, and London: Cornell University Press, 1987.

Curran, Stuart. *Shelley's* Cenci: *Scorpions Ringed with Fire*. Princeton, NJ: Princeton University Press, 1970.

Hawthorne, Nathaniel. *The French and Italian Notebooks*. Ed. Thomas Woodson. *The Centenary Edition of the Works of Nathaniel Hawthorne*, Vol. XIV. Columbus: Ohio State University Press, 1980.

——. *The Marble Faun*, in *Nathaniel Hawthorne: Novels*. The Library of America. Texts Selected and Annotated by Millicent Bell. New York: Literary Classics of the United States, 1983.

McComb, Arthur. *The Baroque Painters of Italy: An Introductory Historical Survey*. 1934. Rpt. New York: Russell & Russell, 1968.

Melville, Herman. *Clarel: A Poem and Pilgrimage in the Holy Land*. Ed. Harrison Hayford, Alma A. MacDougall, Hershel Parker, and G. Thomas Tanselle. *The Writings of Herman Melville*, Vol. 12. Evanston and Chicago: Northwestern University Press and the Newberry Library, 1991.

——. *Journals*. Ed. Howard C. Horsford and Lynn Horth. *The Writings of Herman Melville*, Vol. 15. Evanston and Chicago: Northwestern University Press and the Newberry Library, 1989.

——. *Pierre; or, The Ambiguities*. Ed. Harrison Hayford, Hershel Parker and G. Thomas Tanselle. *The Writings of Herman Melville*, Vol. 7. Evanston and Chicago: Northwestern University Press and the Newberry Library, 1971.

——. *White-Jacket; or, The World in a Man-of War*. Ed. Harrison Hayford, Hershel Parker, and G. Thomas Tanselle. *The Writings of Herman Melville*, Vol. 5. Evanston and Chicago: Northwestern University Press and the Newberry Library, 1970.

Murray, Henry A., ed. Introduction to *Pierre; or, The Ambiguities*, by Herman Melville. New York: Hendricks House, 1949.

Shelley, Percy Bysshe. *The Cenci.* In *Shelley: Poetical Works.* Ed. Thomas Hutchinson. New edition corrected by G. M. Matthews. Oxford & New York: Oxford University Press, 1970.

Webster's Collegiate Dictionary. Fifth Edition. Springfield, MA: G. & C. Merriam, 1948.

DORSEY KLEITZ

QUESTIONERS OF THE SPHINX:

MELVILLE, VEDDER, AND ORIENTALISM

rientalist elements in Herman Melville's writings have been extensively cataloged in Dorothee Finkelstein's *Melville's Orienda* (1961). Since Finkelstein's book, however, and in spite of the discussion sparked by Edward Said's influential but now outdated *Orientalism* (1976) and his more recent *Culture and Imperialism* (1993), little follow-up work has been done. This essay clarifies Herman Melville's brand of Orientalism by examining his interest in the work of the visionary artist Elihu Vedder.

The nature of the relationship between Melville and Vedder is an intriguing footnote in Melville scholarship. Though there is no hard evidence they ever met, the links between these two men are strong. Elihu Vedder was one of Melville's favorite American artists. Part of the reason Melville was drawn to Vedder probably lies in the artist's imaginative intensity. Like Melville, Vedder was fascinated by the mysteries of the universe and formulated original symbolic ways of articulating them.

A good example of Vedder's visionary style is in *The Lair of the Sea Serpent* (1864) (color plate 1), a painting Melville could have seen when it was exhibited at the National Academy in New York in the spring of 1864. Due to a discrepancy in scale, the painting turns a faithful representation of a snake lying in seaside dunes into an unresolvable threatening puzzle. Neither the setting nor the serpent seems fantastic, yet the lack of a point of reference makes their juxtaposi-

455

tion unsettling. Like the tortoises of Melville's "Enchanted Isles," "mystic creatures . . . of unutterable solitudes," the "Sea Serpent" expresses a feeling of "dateless, indefinite endurance." In a letter to Vedder, one viewer praised the artist for having "lifted the low life of earth into a monarch, and endowed the repulsive with grandeur. . . . The whole picture is asleep. . . . It is greater . . . for what it suggests—in the dim marvelous with which it fills the mind—than in what it exhibits."[1] One is reminded of Ishmael's comment in "The Doubloon" chapter of *Moby-Dick* that "some certain significance lurks in all things, else all things are little worth and the round world itself but an empty cipher."[2]

A scene in *Moby-Dick* which provides a direct connection between Melville, Vedder, and the Orient is in Chapter 70, entitled "The Sphynx" (355-57). This chapter comes at the end of several chapters describing the process by which blubber is taken off a whale. At one point, Melville discusses the unusual scars etched into the skin of the whale, which were caused by battling other whales. "To the quick, observant eye," he says, "these marks are hieroglyphical; that is if you call those mysterious cyphers on the wall of the pyramids hieroglyphics." Finally, the body and head are separated, the head is hoisted against the ship's side, and the crew goes below for noon dinner. Silence descends on the deserted deck. "An intense copper calm, like a universal yellow lotus, [unfolds] its noiseless, measureless leaves upon the sea." The whale head is described as hanging "to the Pequod's waist like the giant Holofernes's [head] from the girdle of Judith." It is "black and hooded," and "hanging there in the midst of so intense a calm, it [seems] the Sphynx's in the desert." Ahab appears on deck and addresses the head: "Speak thou vast and venerable head . . . which, though ungarnished with a beard, yet here and there lookest hoary with mosses; speak, mighty head, and tell us the secret thing that is in thee. Of all divers thou hast dived the deepest. That head upon which the upper sun now gleams, has moved amid this world's foundations. . . O head! thou hast seen enough to split the planets and make an infidel of Abraham, and not one syllable is thine!"

Ahab's soliloquy suggests that knowledge of the universe leads to a state of non-believing, or a state where one religion may be as good or as useless as another. The mixing of biblical references with allusions to the mysteries of ancient Egypt suggests that Melville sees all these spiritual paths as ways to the same end.

Ahab's soliloquy is Melville's version of Hamlet's musings in the graveyard when he addresses Yorick's skull. In the Orientalist world, the Sphinx serves the same purpose the skull serves in the West. It is a mute point of reference, if not exactly a memento mori, then certainly a symbol of the mysteries of life. In "The Sphynx" chapter, the Christian tradition of meditating on a skull is fused with the story of Oedipus confronting the inscrutable sphinx.

In 1863, twelve years after the publication of *Moby-Dick*, Elihu Vedder painted *The Questioner of the Sphinx* (color plate 2), a visual paraphrase of Melville's sphinx chapter. Vedder's work shows an Arab crouching at the mouth of the Sphinx in the moonlight. The scene is desolate and enigmatic. The body of the Sphinx is totally covered by sand, so only the head is visible. The desert in the background is littered with broken columns stretching away in the darkness. The Arab is a worn figure who has dropped his staff and rests on his knees listening. At the bottom right is a human skull half-buried in the sand.

Although there are key differences between the two works, there are also provocative similarities. The silence and "copper calm" of Melville's scene find a parallel in the mysterious atmosphere and lighting in Vedder's painting. Melville's scene takes place at noon and Vedder's takes place at night, but in each of them the eerie light conveys a sense of timelessness, of eternity. Both Ahab and the Arab seek knowledge that transcends thought and time. In each piece, questions involving the nature of the universe have been or are asked and are answered only with silence. Both figures are alone in different kinds of wastelands—one watery, the other desert. One is reminded of Melville's comment during his visit to Egypt that the desert was as fearful to look at as the ocean. In the topography of Melville's imagination the desert and the ocean are equally empty, desolate, and terrifying, yet they are also places conducive to spiritual rumination, places where, stripped of the distractions of civilization, one has at least the possibility of questioning God.

Both pieces have a powerful, dramatic quality. The two figures are probably about the same age, and while one has an ivory leg and holds himself steady with a crutch-like spade the other kneels beside his staff. In both scenes, too, death is present: in *Moby-Dick* it is present in the huge severed head of the whale; in Vedder's painting it is suggested by the toppled columns, the blank eyes and massive chipped visage of the Sphinx, and ultimately by the skull in the sand.

One other aspect important here is the point of view in each piece. The viewer and reader are about the same distance from the action in each work. Though the works share a theatrical melodramatic veneer, there is a sense that on a deeper level the author and the artist are personally involved and that Ahab and the Arab are, in part, personas. Through Ahab, Melville questions the whale's head, and through the Arab, Vedder questions the Sphinx. Both sphinxes suggest promise of inner meaning; neither immediately fulfills that promise.

This is not to claim a direct link between "The Sphynx" chapter in *Moby-Dick* and *The Questioner of the Sphinx*, but to point out a similar interest in and use of Oriental materials. Both the text and the painting appeal to contemporary views of the Orient as a land of mystery, but both also go beyond the Orient as mere stage scenery to suggest more profound implications. It is the intangible aspects of the Orient rather than its colorful or exotic customs which intrigue Melville and Vedder.

An example of a possible artistic dialogue carried on between Melville and Vedder can be seen in the following three works centering on prophecy. Melville's poem, "'Formerly a Slave'," which was included in his Civil War collection, *Battle-Pieces and Aspects of War* (1866), was inspired by a portrait by Vedder entitled *Jane Jackson—Formerly a Slave*, which Melville saw when it was exhibited at the the National Academy in New York in the spring of 1865. The poem appears near the end of *Battle-Pieces* and focuses not on the war itself, but on the social injustice which started it and on the dimly seen future:

> The sufferance of her race is shown,
> And retrospect of life,
> Which now too late deliverance dawns upon;
> Yet is she not at strife.
>
> Her children's children they shall know
> The good withheld from her;
> And so her reverie takes prophetic cheer—
> In spirit she sees the stir
>
> Far down the depth of thousand years,

And marks the revel shine;
Her dusky face is lit with sober light,
Sibylline, yet benign.[3]

Here the freed slave, the mother with "dusky face" "sibylline, yet benign," has "prophetic" power allowing her to see "far down the depth of thousand years." The tone is one of guarded hope.

Eleven years later, Vedder, perhaps following the hint given by Melville, used the same brooding face of Jane Jackson for a large canvas entitled *The Cumaean Sibyl* (color plate 3), in which the former slave is transformed into an aging sibyl, clutching her scrolls, striding with determination across a wild windswept landscape. Like the sphinx, the sibyl possesses profound knowledge of the universe. She can see the future and reveals it in riddling prophecies. Here the link between author and artist mixes the wisdom of the ages with the contemporary social and political issues of slavery and race.

Philosophically, Melville and Vedder were kindred spirits. In 1886 Melville acquired a deluxe edition of Edward Fitzgerald's *Rubaiyat of Omar Khayyam* illustrated by Vedder. Vedder's *Rubaiyat* with its fifty-four drawings was the masterpiece of his late years and brought him international acclaim. Just as Fitzgerald had taken liberties to make the Oriental text his own, Vedder rearranged the verses to fit his personal interpretation. He carefully designed each element of the book including the eccentric lettering used for the quatrains. For Vedder the *Rubaiyat* does not center on the transience of all earthly things which is usually considered to be the main theme, but on fate, immortality, and the origin and destiny of human life—exactly the kinds of themes that would have appealed to Melville. Vedder's interest is in the dilemma of life rather than in the acceptance of its evanescence. The illustration *Vain Questioning* (black and white plate 1), whose title resonates with Ahab's soliloquy in "The Sphynx" chapter and with *The Questioner of the Sphinx*, accompanies verses 37 through 39:

37

Up from Earth's Centre through the Seventh Gate
I rose, and on the Throne of Saturn sate,
　　And many a Knot unravell'd by the Road;
But not the Master-knot of Human Fate.

459

38

There was the Door to which I found no Key;
There was the Veil through which I could not see:
    Some little talk awhile of Me and Thee
There was—and then no more of Thee and Me.

39

Earth could not answer; nor the Seas that mourn
In flowing Purple, of their Lord forlorn;
    Nor rolling Heaven, with all his Signs reveal'd
And hidden by the sleeve of Night and Morn.[4]

In reading Vedder's *Rubaiyat*, Melville must have experienced what can only be described as a shock of recognition. The restless fatalism in the verses quoted is reminiscent of Melville's own reasoning on "Providence and futurity" when he visited Hawthorne in Liverpool on his way to the Levant in 1856.[5] More specifically relating to *Moby-Dick*, the veil in verse 38 is a lyrical echo of the pasteboard mask and the wall in "The Quarter-Deck" chapter, and the unanswering earth, seas, and heaven in the last stanza remind one of the mute whale's head in "The Sphynx" chapter. In the illustration Omar, the Persian poet-astronomer, leans back and turns his head to gaze up at the star-pricked heavens. His hands rest on his manuscripts. Alongside and pushed away from the front of the desk lie a compass, try square, and ball of twine suggestive of tools used for astronomical calculation. There is little of the popular Oriental exoticism of the earlier *Questioner of the Sphinx*; the focus here is all on the theme, on the inability of science to convincingly explain the phenomonology of life. The figure of Omar setting aside the astronomical tools can be seen as a different version of Ahab destroying the quadrant toward the end of *Moby-Dick*. Ahab's curse that the quadrant "canst not tell where one drop of water or one grain of sand will be to-morrow noon," parallels Omar's understanding that all his calculation cannot predict the future. Finally, of course, the bearded Omar in *Vain Questioning*, is an image of Melville himself confronting the silent stars. The view from the window is at once foreign and familiar: it is the timeless Oriental landscape of the *Rubaiyat*, and it is Mount Greylock seen from Melville's Arrowhead study where *Moby-Dick* was finished.

When, in 1891, Melville dedicated his last book of poems, *Timoleon*, "To My Countryman, Elihu Vedder," he was not simply acknowledging that he and Vedder were both Americans. The real country they shared, according to Melville's understanding, was the artistic and spiritual landscape of the Orient. In a note accompanying a copy of *Timoleon* sent to Vedder after Melville's death, Elizabeth Melville made clear that the dedication was in response to the imaginative genius that produced the *Rubaiyat*. "I take pleasure in now sending you the little volume," she wrote, "believing that it will give you pleasure to know that a spirit so appreciative as my husband's estimated your artistic rendering of the profound and mysterious 'quatrains' of the poet (of which he never tired) in the manner which appealed so powerfully to his own imagination and enlisted his sympathy with the artist."[6] Vedder's own collection of verse, published in 1922, thirty years after Melville's death, was called *Between Faith and Doubt*, a title which could almost serve to describe Melville's life.

In recent discussions of Western attitudes toward the Orient, there is a common tendency to view Orientalism as essentially a Western way of creating and managing the Orient. Knowledge claims authority over its object. By rendering an object comprehensible within a conceptual system, we define, limit, and authorize a certain view of that object, and it is within this field of knowledge that we act. It seems to me, however, that while the history of colonial power in the Middle East and the creation of "an" Orient go hand-in-hand, it is wrong to view Orientalism as a closed system. On a purely economic and political level it may be, but on a creative level, the anxieties of engaging an Oriental Other cannot so easily be defined. They are much more various and dynamic than the popular thesis allows. An examination of Herman Melville's brand of Orientalism reveals this narrow position. Captain Ahab may be an allegorical representation of the American world quest, "obsessed, compelling, unstoppable, completely wrapped up in his own rhetorical justification and his sense of cosmic symbolism,"[7] but it must be remembered that, at least on these terms, Melville is critical of Ahab, and through Ahab he is critical of his own culture. He does not want to control the Orient or authorize a particular view of it. On the contrary, as seen in Melville's interest in Vedder, Melville looks to the Orient not so much as a site where answers are found, but as a site where questions are asked.

NOTES

1   Joshua C. Taylor, "Perceptions and Digressions," in *Perceptions and Evocations: The Art of Elihu Vedder* (Washington, DC: Smithsonian Institution Press, 1979), 66.

2   Herman Melville, *Moby-Dick* (New York: Vintage Books, 1991), 438. All subsequent quotations from *Moby-Dick* come from this edition.

3   Herman Melville, *Battle-Pieces and Aspects of the War* (New York: Da Capo Press, 1995), 154.

4   *Rubaiyat of Omar Khayyam. The Astronomer-Poet of Persia, Rendered into English Verse by Edward Fitzgerald with Accompaniment of Drawing by Elihu Vedder* (Boston: Houghton, Mifflin, 1884), unpaginated.

5   Herman Melville, *Journals*, eds. Howard Horsford and Lynn Horth (Evanston and Chicago: Northwestern University Press and the Newberry Library, 1989), 628-29.

6   David Jaffee, "Sympathy with the Artist: Elizabeth Shaw Melville and Elihu Vedder," *Melville Society Extracts* 81 (May 1990), 10.

7   Quoted in Edward Said, *Culture and Imperialism* (London: Vintage, 1994), 349.

ROBERT K. WALLACE

"ALOOF" AND "ALOFT":

CAPE COLONNA IN MELVILLE'S POEM AND TURNER'S ENGRAVINGS

"Off Cape Colonna" is one of the poems that Melville published as "Fruit of Travel Long Ago" in *Timoleon* in 1891. *Timoleon* is one of the volumes of poetry that Melville published after his career as a novelist ended in 1857. The visual art of J. M. W. Turner was as important to Melville's work as a poet as it was to his work as a novelist.[1] Turner's influence on Melville's poetry is most explicit in "The Temeraire," the poem he published in *Battle-Pieces* in 1866, nine years after seeing Turner's *The Fighting Temeraire* in London on the way home from his 1856-57 Mediterranean voyage.[2] Turner's influence is pervasive, if less explicit, in *Clarel*, published in 1876, and in *Timoleon* in 1891. So is the influence of Melville's personal print collection.

By the time Melville died in 1891, he had collected more than 400 prints and engravings that I have been identifying and cataloging since in 1986. Twenty-six of these were engravings after paintings by Turner. These included *The Fighting Temeraire*, *Snow Storm—Steam-Boat*, *Peace—Burial at Sea*, and other powerful late seascapes.[3] Melville also owned engravings after Turner in many of the illustrated books that he collected. Among these were twenty-one engravings in Cosmo Monkhouse's illustrated biography of Turner (Sealts, no. 365), and another seventeen in the sixteen volumes of *The Life and Works of Lord Byron*, an American reprint of the celebrated 1832-33 John Murray edition (Sealts, nos. 112, 369). These engravings of Turner's visual art were a rich repository of imagery and association as

463

Melville published his poetry later in life. So were engravings after painters as diverse as Claude Lorrain, Piranesi, Raphael, Van de Velde, Richard Wilson, and Herman van Swanevelt, to mention only several of the many artists whose recently discovered prints from Melville's collection offer powerful interpretive avenues for understanding the imaginative range and imagistic precision of Melville's poetry.

In several recent and forthcoming essays, I have shown how a variety of poems in *Timoleon* can be illuminated by various prints from Melville's collection. The prints include Claude Lorrain's *Embarkation of the Queen of Sheba* and Turner's *Regulus Leaving Carthage* for the poem "Art," Piranesi's *Arch of the Emperor Marcus Aurelius* for the poem "The Age of the Antonines," and Vedder's illustrations of the *Rubaiyat* for the poem "Magian Wine." They also include Richard Wilson's *Evening* and Turner's *The Golden Bough* for the poem "Pausilippo," and Turner's "Venice" vignette for Melville's poem "Venice."[4] The latter two poems bring us back to the "Fruit of Travel Long Ago," and to "Off Cape Colonna," the focus of this paper.

"Off Cape Colonna" is one of eighteen poems published as "Fruit of Travel Long Ago." All of these 1891 poems derive, in one way or another, from Melville's Mediterranean tour of thirty-five years earlier. The first six poems are set in Italy, the next ten in Greece, and the last two in Egypt (reversing the direction of Melville's actual itinerary). In writing the poems, some of which may have been drafted as early as 1860, Melville was drawing upon the journal he had kept during his travels—as many commentators have pointed out.[5] He was also drawing upon the expanding repertoire of visual art that was filling his mind during the Mediterranean journey—and that would continue to grow as he acquired the vast collection of engravings and book illustrations by which he was surrounded in his New York home when he published his "Fruit of Travel Long Ago" in 1891.

Turner's illustrations for *The Life and Works of Lord Byron* were one obvious visual touchstone for Melville's Mediterranean journey, for they encapsulate Turner's and Byron's own responses to many of the places that Melville had himself visited, to some degree with both of these predecessors in mind. Among Turner's images of Italy in Melville's edition of Byron were *Genoa*, *Venice—the Bridge of*

Sighs, and *Santa Maria della Spina, Pisa*. Among the images of the Near East were *The Plains of Troy* and *Santa Sophia, Constantinople*. Among the images of Greece were *The Gate of Theseus, Scio*, and *The School of Homer (Scio)* (figure 1).[6] I emphasize these Byronic illustrations in part because Byron is an obvious literary reference for Melville's "Off Cape Colonna."

Byron mentions the Cape, also known as Cape Suniam, in *Childe Harold* and again in *Don Juan*. Byron's visits to the ruins of the temple on the promontory of the Cape in 1810 had been an important touchstone for his entire Greek experience—as indicated not only in the poetry but in the notes of Melville's edition of Byron. In those notes, Melville would also have read of Byron's interest in Cape Colonna as "the actual spot of Falconer's shipwreck." William Falconer survived a shipwreck off Cape Colonna in 1750. His poem *The Shipwreck* was "reprinted no less than 83 times between 1762 and 1887" (Shanes, p. 110). Melville had already alluded to Falconer's *Shipwreck* in both *White-Jacket* and *Moby-Dick* (Cohen, pp. 247-48). In "Off Cape Colonna," the actual shipwreck becomes central to the action, and mood, of the poem.

Melville's journal for February 8, 1857, the day he sailed from Syra to Pireus en route to Athens, does not record any vision of Cape Colonna or the columns of its celebrated temple. Instead, he records a "cold, comfortless" day in his berth as the ship battled "Head wind, head sea." Approaching Pireus "toward sunset," he noted only the "bare & bald aspect of the shores & isles" (*Journals*, p. 98). Whenever he composed his poem "Off Cape Colonna," he probably envisioned its setting in a kind of projected retrospect, perhaps somewhat in the spirit of the engraving he owned of *Byron Contemplating the Coliseum* (now at the Berkshire Athenaeum). In writing this and other Greek poems in "Fruit of Travel Long Ago," Melville found his own way of combining "books, pictures, and the face of nature" (to borrow one of his favorite phrases from William Hazlitt).[7]

The poem itself is in two unequal stanzas. The first stanza is the longer of the two:

> Aloof they crown the foreland lone,
> From aloft they loftier rise—
> Fair columns, in the aureola rolled
> From sunned Greek seas and skies.

465

They wax, sublimed to fancy's view,
A god-like group against the blue.

This stanza corresponds to the best-known of Turner's two depictions of the site, engraved in 1832 as *Temple of Minerva, Cape Colonna* (figure 2).[8] The engraving was made by Edward Finden for *Finden's Landscape Illustrations to the Life and Works of Lord Byron*, published as a supplement to the multi-volume John Murray edition later acquired by Melville.

Finden's engraving from a Turner watercolor anticipates Melville's poem in both imagery and mood. You can envision the "aloof" and "aloft," the "fair columns," and the "foreland lone." You can see the "aureola rolled," and the "sunned Greek seas and skies." You have the "God-like group against the blue," except that the blue of Turner's watercolor is necessarily absent from Finden's engraving.[9]

Much of Melville's poetic imagery in the first stanza would also apply to a second, but much lesser-known image that Turner created of the columns above the Cape. *Temple of Minerva Sunias, Cape Colonna* (figure 3) was engraved by J. T. Willmore in 1854. The topography is the same, but the mood is entirely different, in part because of the small spot in the sea off the Cape to the left. In its nautical action, as well as its mood, this engraving after Turner is a perfect complement to the second stanza of Melville's poem: "Over much like gods! Serene they saw / The wolf-waves board the deck, / And headlong hull of Falconer, / And many a deadlier wreck" (*Collected Poems*, p. 248).

The wreck, in both cases, is Falconer's. Turner, like Byron, knew of this piece of nautical history; Falconer's *Shipwreck* volume was in his library. Eric Shanes was the first scholar to closely examine this comparatively rare engraving after Turner; in 1990 he drew attention to the two "wolves" in the foreground. One of them is howling as the ship goes down (Shanes, p. 110). These are fit companions to the "wolf-waves" in Melville's poem.

Turner himself had never seen Cape Colonna; he made several trips to Italy but never got to Greece. The small watercolor that he had drawn for Finden in 1832 had been based on a sketch by Thomas Allason. Turner evidently used the same sketch as the topographical basis for his shipwreck scene. For this he drew a much larger watercolor (see Brown, plate 28). He is thought to have completed this work in 1834, but he never saw it engraved. J. T. Willmore was not able to engrave it until 1854, three years after Turner's death and two years before Melville's Mediterranean voyage. Willmore engraved it "exclusively for members of the Association for the Promotion of the Fine Arts in Scotland" (Shanes, p. 110). That is one reason it was not widely known. Another is that Turner's original watercolor had rarely, if ever, been exhibited. In addition, Willmore's engraving was published as a single image and did not benefit from being associated with a large literary publishing project, like Finden's or Murray's editions of Byron. In Melville's lifetime, only someone with his kind of interest as a viewer and collector of Turner's prints is likely to have seen it. Melville's copy of Turner's *The Golden Bough* had been engraved by Willmore in 1856, two years after Willmore had engraved the Suniam shipwreck scene in the same large format.

Willmore's 1854 engraving of the ship sinking off Cape Colonna is not among the 26 engravings after Turner currently known to have been in Melville's collection. The engraving was rare enough that Melville may never have had a chance to see it, much less buy it. If he did see it after writing "Off Cape Colonna," he would have recognized a remarkable counterpart to his own poem. If he saw it before writing his poem, he may have been directly inspired by Turner's vision (either in responding to the Willmore engraving alone or in contrast with the 1832 Finden engraving, a very widely circulated image that he surely would have known). Melville's poem reads as a conflation of Turner's two engravings, the first stanza stressing the sublime grandeur of the columns that rise aloof and aloft, the second stressing the irony of a deity that would tantalize men about to drown with the false promise of deliverance. The shipwreck watercolor by Turner is another expression of the Fallacies of Hope that dominated so many of his ambitious history, landscape, and seascape paintings of the 1830s and 1840s, including a number that Melville acquired in engraved form: *The Fighting Temeraire, Snow Storm—Steam-Boat, Peace—Burial at Sea, Regulus Leaving Carthage, The Golden Bough.*

Let us now look at another of the literary illustrations that Turner had created in the 1830s (figure 4). Turner's original watercolor for *The Death of Lycidas— "Vision of the Guarded Mount"* dates from 1834.[10] W. Miller published the engraving in an 1835 edition of Milton's *Poetical Works.* In the uppermost regions of *The Death of Lycidas* is the glorious, sunstruck cathedral on the promontory—the English equivalent of the Greek temple at Cape Colonna. Beneath it is the storm, with lightning, that has destroyed a ship whose sinking crow's nest is all that remains visible. Beneath everything else, at the bottom of the image, is the raised, rigid arm of Lycidas, about to drown, in a situation as ironic as that of the sinking ship in the wolf waves off Cape Colonna. Melville is likely to have known the engraving from the late 1840s, when he had access to it in the library of his friend Evert Duyckinck, who owned nearly all of the books containing Turner's literary engravings (*Melville and Turner*, p. 138). Melville continued to use Duyckinck's library again in the 1850s, before and after his trip to the Mediterranean.

In his 1856-57 Mediterranean journal, Melville makes many striking comparisons between scenes he was seeing in Greece or the Near East and those he had seen in England and Scotland at the beginning of his journey. Turner's mind was working in the same way in 1834, when his tiny *Lycidas* watercolor and his large *Colonna* watercolor had brought together two of the most famous shipwrecks in English literary history, one off St. Michael's Mount in Cornwall, the other off Cape Colonna in Greece, each occurring in the face of a temple to the gods both aloof and aloft. Melville, in writing "Off Cape Colonna," brought together Greece and England as well as Turner, Falconer, and Byron. He drew upon his past travels as well as his personal collection of books and pictures. He blended all of these components into one of his own most characteristic (and Turneresque) blendings of books, pictures, and the face of nature (while at the same time enriching his own earlier allusion to Cape Suniam in *Clarel*).[11]

As a coda, I would like to mention a curious fact I came across when researching Turner's watercolor of the shipwreck off Cape Colonna. David Blayney Brown speculates that Turner drew the shipwreck scene as a companion to *Lord Byron's Dream*, an 1827 painting by Charles Lock Eastlake, for in 1834 Willmore engraved Eastlake's painting in the same format he was later to use for the Cape Colonna watercolor that Turner was creating in that same year. Brown indicates that Eastlake painted this work "for his friend the Earl of Leven and Melville" (Brown, p. 84). This friend of Eastlake had been the lost link to the Melvill clan of Scotland. In 1818 Herman's father Allan Melvill had managed to visit the Earl—but without being able to establish any hereditary rights. In 1856

Herman had followed his "father's footsteps" into this ancestral region of Scotland on his way to the Mediterranean. He was not, however, able to visit the Earl or his art collection, in part, it appears, owing to "an ugly injury to his face" (*Journals*, p. 386). He did, however, visit Edinburgh for five days, and he was "much pleased there." In the print shops of that city Melville might easily have seen Turner's Suniam shipwreck scene as Willmore had engraved it two years earlier for the Association for the Promotion of the Fine Arts in Scotland. Unfortunately, his journal is an absolute blank for those five days.[12]

We may never know exactly when Melville may first have had access to Willmore's engraving. But we do have access to the poem that Melville wrote, to the image that Turner and Willmore created, and to the cosmic energy that flows between them. Hoping to tap some of that energy, I visited Cape Colonna on the morning of July 2, 1997 (figure 5). The bright sun and a driving wind provided an auspicious beginning to a day that ended, after a long bus ride and some time after the sun had gone down, with the convivial gathering that opened our conference in Volos.

NOTES

1   For Turner's influence on Melville's work as a novelist, see Wallace, *Melville and Turner*, especially chapters 3, 6-9.

2   Melville explicitly acknowledged the influence of Turner's painting in his note to the poem (*Collected Poems*, p. 449); he recorded his visit to the painting in his 1857 London journal (*Journals*, p. 128).

3   Nineteen of the Turners are among the 287 engravings in my 1986 catalog of "Melville's Prints and Engravings at the Berkshire Athenaeum," pp. 79, 81-82, 86. Among the Turner engravings that have surfaced more recently are two early seascapes, *Dutch Boats in a Gale* and *Calais Pier* (figures 16 and 17 in my essay "Melville's Prints: The Ambrose Group").

4   These interpretive connections are made in the essay on "The Ambrose Group," in "Melville's 'Venice,' Turner's Vignette, Ruskin's *Stones*, and Darwin's Voyage," and in "David Metcalf's Prints and Tile" (forthcoming from the *Harvard Library Bulletin*).

5   The editors of the Northwestern-Newberry edition of the *Journals* make many such connections in their notes to individual entries. So does Hennig Cohen in his notes to *The Selected Poems*. So does Ekaterini Georgoudaki in "Melville's Artistic Use of His Journeys to Europe and the Near East."

6   The engraving after Turner's *The School of Homer (Scio)* is easy to miss in Melville's sixteen-volume set of Byron's *Life and Works*, now in the Houghton Library at Harvard. Rather than ap-

pearing as a frontispiece or title vignette (as do most of the other engravings), this engraving appears deep in volume X of the *Works*, facing p. 263.

7 Melville twice underlined the phrase "books, pictures, and the face of nature" in the copy of Hazlitt's *Criticisms on Art* that he acquired in 1870 (Sealts, no. 263a). Hazlitt considered those "three pleasures in life" to be the only ones that are "pure and lasting" (*Melville and Turner*, p. 11).

8 For Turner, Melville, and their contemporaries, the ruins at Cape Colonna were thought to be from the Temple of Minerva. The archaeological evidence identifying them as from the Temple of Poseidon was not discovered until 1898.

9 David Blayney Brown reproduces the 1832 engraving of the *Temple of Minerva, Cape Colonna* alongside the watercolor from which it was made in *Turner and Byron* (nos. 51 and 52, pp. 102-3). His book was extremely helpful in my research for this paper.

10 Turner's *Lycidas* watercolor is at the Taft Museum in Cincinnati, Ohio. For an excellent analysis of the work (and clarification of its name), see Eric Shanes, *J. M. W. Turner: The Foundations of Genius* (Cincinnati: The Taft Museum, 1986), no. 47.

11 In *Clarel* Melville had invoked the ruins of the temple at Cape Colonna to characterize Rolfe: "He rose, removed his hat to greet, / Disclosing so in shapely sphere / A marble brow over face embrowned: / So Suniam by her fane is crowned" (1.31.9-12). Fane, an archaic word for temple, had been memorably used by Tennyson in stanza 56 of *In Memoriam*, a book that Melville had acquired in 1871 in the form of a present to his wife (Sealts, no. 505). At the peak of the poem's "song of woe" at the death of Tennyson's friend Arthur Hallam is the image of "fanes of fruitless prayer" to a God who repays faith with senseless death. For Melville's marginal notations to stanza 53 in his copy of the poem (which juxtapose water, burial, and marble) see Cowen, 2: 684. For a recent discussion of the allusion to Suniam in *Clarel*, see Robillard, pp. 137-38. Robillard notes that an engraving of the temple at Suniam appears in Melville's copy of the 1844 edition of Christopher Wordsworth's *Greece: Pictorial, Descriptive, and Historical* (acquired in 1871, Sealts, no. 563). The book engraving resembles Finden's 1832 engraving of the temple as much as it differs from Willmore's 1854 engraving.

12 Our only direct account of Melville's non-visit to the Earl of Leven (and of the unspecified "pleasures" of his five days in Edinburgh) comes from a letter he sent from Liverpool to his brother Allan in New York in November 1856 (*Correspondence*, pp. 300-305).

REFERENCES

Brown, David Blayney. *Turner and Byron*. London: Tate Gallery, 1992.

Cohen, Hennig. *The Selected Poems of Herman Melville*. New York: Fordham University Press, 1991.

Cowen, Walker. *Melville's Marginalia*. 2 vol. New York: Garland, 1987.

Georgoudaki, Ekaterini. "Melville's Artistic Use of His Journeys to Europe and the Near East." Ph.D. dissertation, Arizona State University, 1980.

Melville, Herman. *Clarel*. Evanston and Chicago: Northwestern University Press and the Newberry Library, 1991.

——. *Collected Poems*, ed. Howard P. Vincent. Chicago: Hendricks House, 1946.

——. *Correspondence*. Evanston and Chicago: Northwestern University Press and the Newberry Library, 1993.

——. *Journals*. Evanston and Chicago: Northwestern University Press and the Newberry Library, 1989.

Robillard, Douglas. *Melville and the Visual Arts: Ionian Form, Venetian Tint*. Kent, OH: Kent State University Press, 1997.

Sealts, Merton M. *Melville's Reading: Revised and Enlarged Edition*. Columbia: University of South Carolina Press, 1988.

Shanes, Eric. *Turner's Human Landscape*. London: Heinemann, 1990.

Wallace, Robert K. *Melville and Turner: Spheres of Love and Fright*. Athens: University of Georgia Press, 1992.

——. "Melville's Prints and Engravings at the Berkshire Athenaeum." *Essays in Arts and Sciences* 15 (June 1986): 59-90.

——. "Melville's Prints: The Ambrose Group." *Harvard Library Bulletin* n.s. 6 (Spring 1995): 13-50.

——. "Melville's 'Venice,' Turner's Vignette, Ruskin's *Stones*, and Darwin's Voyage." In *Mediterranean Perspectives* 2 (1997): 21-35.

Timothy W. Marr

Mastheads and Minarets:

Islamic Architecture in Melville's Writings

*For the Immeasurable's altitude is not heightened by the arches of Mahomet's heavens; and were all
space a vacuum, yet it would be a fullness; for to Himself His own Universe is He.*
Herman Melville, Mardi and a Voyage Thither [1]

Scholars have not adequately appreciated Melville's
rich engagement with the Islamic orient since Dorothee Metlitsky first surveyed *Melville's Orienda* in 1961.[2]
Euroamerican images of the Islamic world at the time
that Melville wrote were paradoxical, partly reflecting the changing political fortunes of the Ottoman
empire in the mid-nineteenth century. On the one
hand, Islam had been a religious enemy of the Christian lands since the Crusades, and orientalist descrip-
tion had long figured the Turk as a cruel and fanatic despot, a notion revived in
the United States by its engagement in the Barbary "wars" and the Greek War of
Independence. On the other hand, a more romantic heritage of literary orientalism had arisen from biblical notions of eastern wealth which mixed with the fantastic and entertaining tales of the Arabian Nights: *The Book of the Thousand Nights
and One Night*. These images were expanded through increasingly available travelers' vignettes of indolent patriarchs with captivating harems to render the Islamic world one of the more desirably exotic areas of the globe. This romantic tradition, refined—by such authors as William Beckford, Robert Southey, Thomas
More, Thomas Hope, and Lord Byron—fostered a dual image of Islamic orien-

talism with two contrasting valences: a dark, diabolical gothicism and a sublime, opulent romanticism.[3] Melville had imbibed these literary conventions of orientalism through his wide reading and frequently emphasized both resonances in his writings.

One example of Melville's deployment of orientalist rhetoric is in his literary characterizations. His tyrannical ship captains (such as Riga, Claret, and Ahab), were often described as imposing a Turkish despotism upon their sailors. Fedallah in *Moby-Dick*, the Moor in *Clarel*'s Timoneer's tale, and the Persian alchemists in the poems "The Rose Farmer" and "The New Zealot to the Sun" all represented standard stereotypes of the dark and cunning Asian. Nevertheless, Melville also gained a Byronic release for his narrators by investing some with the trappings of orientalist liberation: from Omoo's nickname "The Basha with Two Tails"; to Taji seeking Yillah throughout Mardi in his Emir's robe; and ultimately with Melville's annunciation of Ishmael, a biblical character most widely known in the nineteenth century as the Abrahamic ancestor of the Arabs.

This paper addresses another major location of orientalist modalities in Melville's writings: his changing representations of Islamic architecture and his metaphorical orientalization of imaginary space. In his longer works of fiction, Melville frequently hung his rhetorical hammock in an imagined Islamic orient. "Give me plenty of room to swing it in," he had White-Jacket rhapsodize; "let me swing it in between two date-trees on an Arabian plain; or extend it diagonally from Moorish pillar to pillar, in the open marble court of the Lions in Granada's Alhambra."[4] Melville's versatility in expressing the romantic resonances of oriental space ranged from such an Irvingesque projection to employing the "Hall of Eblis," popularized in such works as William Beckford's *Vathek* (1786), as a representation of a diabolical hell. Although such patterns influenced his initial perceptions during his 1856-57 journey to the Near East, it was there that Melville began to reappraise the romance of the Orient as it clashed with the experience and perspective he gained from his travels, producing a decidedly altered view of the resonances of Islamic architecture by the time of the publication of *Clarel: A Poem and Pilgrimage in the Holy Land* in 1876.[5] As Bryan C. Short has noted, "Melville's responses to architecture reveal an imagination at war with itself, a visionary sensibility in conflict with the evidence of vision."[6]

Melville's disenchantment while in the actual Orient helped to confirm his rejection of the sufficiency of both romantic and theological verbal doctrine, an underlying theme in *Clarel*.

In *Redburn* (1849), Melville depicted the contradictory valences of Islamic architecture through the contrasting melodramas of two innocent characters who serve as foils to Redburn: Harry Bolton, the English aristocratic lad; and Carlo, the Italian organ-boy. Part of the low esteem with which Melville held "beggarly" Redburn must partly reside in his over-reliance on literary convention for effect, and the presence of these two characters was especially censured by Melville's contemporary critics as implausible intrusions into an otherwise realistic text. (It has been suggested that Melville created these characters of Bolton and Carlo late in the ten-week process of composing his book to enlarge the manuscript up to proper publication length.)[7] Nevertheless, the cases of Bolton and Carlo demonstrate how Melville had digested the conventions of romantic orientalism, as each clearly represent the polar brands of Melville's exotic use of Islamic architecture.

Reviewers of *Redburn* criticized most roundly the mysterious night that Redburn spends with Harry Bolton at "Aladdin's Palace" in London, calling it "absurdly improbable" (*Albion*); a "palpable invention" (*Holden's Dollar Magazine*); and "the very stalest of minor-theatre melodrama" (*Blackwood's*).[8] Melville portrays the palace of Aladdin with a mystifying density of allusion, an important facet of which figures it as an orientalized space where standard moral strictures are relaxed. Described as "some semi-public place of opulent entertainment," the main room of Aladdin's palace is a "hall of pillars" featuring "numerous Moorish looking tables, supported by Caryatides [*sic*] of turbaned slaves." The private chamber of "long lounges" and "oriental ottomans," to which Harry and Wellingborough ascend, entraps them in a scene of mystery. "[M]ethought I was sinking in some reluctant, sedgy sea," claims Redburn, "so thick and elastic the Persian carpeting." But Redburn's visions of "metropolitan magnificence" are soon transformed into a realm controlled by "the serpent of vice," and Redburn falls victim to the cultural paranoia about the "infernal" poison of the East. "The whole place seemed infected; and a strange thought came over me, that in the very damasks around, some eastern plague had been imported. This must be some house whose foundations take hold on the pit. But these fearful reveries only enchanted me fast to my chair; so that, though I then wished to rush forth from the house, my limbs seems manacled." The scene evokes a dual charge of enchantment and horror that exemplifies Melville's use of Islamic orientalism even in his least contemplative moments.[9]

The handsome Italian boy, Carlo, another "poor and friendless son of earth" in *Redburn*, fares better than Bolton because he possesses an authentic artistic gift. Melville orientalizes the rhapsody of Carlo's music in order to intimate the "subtle power" and "divine ravishments" of musical expression.[10] Carlo is described by Redburn as the "architect of domes of sound, and bowers of song," which are heard by Redburn as "the gush of the Fountain of Lions . . . a mixed and liquid sea of sound, that dashes its spray in my face." But the limits of narration prevent Melville's expression of music's own melodic structures, and he turns instead to a description of the material organ itself. Redburn begins by portraying the carved organ as a Gothic cathedral but then reconsiders its "sculptured arches, leading into mysterious intricacies" and pauses: "But stop! 'tis a Moorish iniquity; for here, as I live, is a Saracenic arch; which, for aught I know, may lead into some interior Alhambra. Ay, it does."

Redburn's rhapsodical mood "magnifies [the organ] into grandeur," which reveals its interior as "the inner palace of the Grand Mogul," replete with "gilded columns . . . [and] fountains; canopies and lounges," featuring a courtly pageant of "martial men . . . in crimson turbans, . . . with jingling scimeters" and "jet black Nubian slaves" who perform acrobatic tumbling for an array of European nobles hosted by a Muslim sultan. In this depiction of what one critic called the "rigmarole" of Carlo's organ, Melville expanded Carlo's musical world into a sublime opera, a masquerade of oriental nobility.[11]

Melville's application of the dual valences of romantic orientalism in 1849 is also shown in his treatment of another arch, the Moorish one that Redburn sees in Liverpool and calls "handsome." (See Figure A.) Redburn actually sees three images of this arch: first in a copy of the *Penny Magazine* years before his journey; then, while he is in Liverpool where he feels he has seen it before; and again in the *Magazine* several months after he returned to America. This complex nexus of recall demonstrates the purchase that the novelty of what Melville calls "saracenic scenery" had on his awareness.[12] However, in *White-Jacket*, the book he wrote the same summer he finished *Redburn*, Melville invests the same arch with evil connotations. The *Neversink's* master-at-arms—a man named Bland who is a clear forebear of Claggart in *Billy Budd*—is portrayed as a polished gentlemen with "snaky black eye" and a "small, Moorish-arched, and wickedly delicate mouth."[13]

Melville's most sublime staging of orientalism, however, is enacted during his masthead visions during which he literally evokes castles in the air. The region of the Pacific into which Melville launches his narrator into the worlds of *Mardi* is introduced by a fabulous panorama which transforms Taji's desire to leave the *Arcturion* into a frenzy: "In the distance what visions were spread! The entire western horizon high piled with gold and crimson clouds; airy arches, domes, and minarets; as if the yellow, Moorish sun were setting behind some vast Alhambra. Vistas seemed leading to worlds beyond."[14]

Likewise, Melville celebrates *Mardi's* most exalted intimations of paradise in images of oriental opulence. Babbalanja's invocation of the "furthest worlds" portrays these heavens with "[r]uby columns: minarets of amethyst: diamond domes!" Even Serenia's apostle can evangelize the glory of Alma only through a transcendence of this oriental sublime: "He is all we pray for, and beyond; all, that in the wildest hour of ecstasy, rapt fancy paints in bright Auroras upon the soul's wide boundless Orient!"[15] It is not surprising that contemporary reviewers of *Mardi* found the book "full of all oriental delights," and felt that Polynesia was "becoming to romance what the 'fabled east' has been for more than thirty centuries."[16]

White-Jacket also glimpses these sublime visions during his journey from the Pacific back to the Atlantic. During the treacherous turn around Cape Horn, he describes the icy islands as "towering in their own turbaned snows, . . . like the diamond watchtowers along heaven's furthest frontier."[17] Later, while traveling north from Rio to the Equator, White-Jacket experiences a "glorious" masthead spectacle on a moonlit night where "[t]he three shrouded masts looked like the apparitions of three gigantic Turkish Emirs striding over the ocean."[18] Such imagery replicated *Redburn's* description of a great fleet of merchant ships under weigh off Liverpool as their "white sails glistened in the clear morning air like a great eastern encampment of sultans."[19] Ishmael similarly rhapsodizes in *Moby-Dick* about mounting the astronomical Cetus and "leap[ing] the topmost skies" to discover whether "the fabled heavens with all their countless tents really lie encamped beyond my mortal sight!"[20]

Atop his rhetorical masthead, unrestrained by verisimilitude, Melville employs the minaret and the caravanserai to ground his mystic visions and to intimate the sublimity of natural beauty. By describing the exaltation of his vision through orientalist diction, Melville subtly attests to the incapacity of traditional Western symbolism to strike a deep enough chord in expressing the fuller resonances of human experience, highlighting the attraction of orientalism as a romantic resource. In these examples, Melville summons the energies of the oriental exotic to dramatize the moment where language transcends the knowable world to exude instead the romance of the mirage. An analogue to this process can be seen by Thomas Cole's placement of an oriental dome in the distance of his painting *Youth* in his series *The Voyage of Life* (1840, 1842). (See Figure B.)

Melville brought his enchantment with the romance of islamicized architecture along with him to the actual orient in 1856 where his expectations of eastern splendor were sustained well into his journey. Melville's first descriptions of Muslim lands in his *Journal* are seen through the perspective of romantic literature, much like the narrator's projections in "The Piazza," the last short story that Melville wrote and annexed to the volume of tales he published the year he left for Europe and the eastern Mediterranean. To Melville, the coast of Algiers has a "[p]iratical corsair look" that reminds him "of one of [the] passages in Don Quixotte [sic], 'Story of the Morisco.'"[21] Perhaps recalling the high spirit of enthusiasm with which he had first planned a "glorious Eastern jaunt" during his trip to Europe seven years earlier, Melville expects that his first view of Constantinople will conform with the magnificence of Thomas Hope's description in *Anastasius*, a book he had twice purchased on that earlier trip.[22] About sailing up the Dardanelles, Melville writes that the Sultan had "a sublime approach ... to his capital. Antichambers [*sic*] of seas & lakes, & corridors of glorious straits." He does not allow a heavy fog to dispel this orientalist fantasy when first viewing the city on December 12, 1856, after a day-and-a-half delay. The fog

477

has lifted from the "skirts" of the city, leaving the "crown of it hidden wrapped in vapor." Melville extends this metaphor into an allegory in which he likens the city to the "magic effect" of the "coy disclosure" of a "Sultana . . . veiled in her ashmack."[23]

This sublime perspectivism is operative during much of Melville's stay in the Turkish capital. The next day Melville writes about the minarets of the mosques, which, as he later remembered, "gleam like lighthouses" and comprise "the most conspicuous objects" that caught his attention. In his journal, Melville describes minarets as "wonderfully venerable" and wonders whether they were derived from the shape of the cypress trees that soar up from the cemeteries. In an insight he would later expand into his poem "The Continents," Melville muses about the cypresses and minarets, the two objects which tower above the eastern landscape: "[t]he intermingling of the dark tree with the bright spire expressive of the intermingling of life and death." Melville describes the mosque of Sultan Ahmad as "six towered . . . soaring up with its snowy spires into the pure blue sky, Nothing finer." While in the mosque of Sultan Suleiman, Melville imagines that he was inside a tent of which the minarets are the stakes. At the end of his entry for the next day, describing the cityscape from the distance of a bridge, Melville envisions "a spreading, still further, of the tent" where the mosques, built on the domed hills, themselves become the stakes of a tent that contain the whole city.[24]

This transformative vision is active again when Melville imagines the fezzes of the dense crowd in the bazaar as paving his way with tiles. Melville is deeply impressed by the fortress of Rumeli Hisar, whose foundations were shaped into an Arabic initial in honor of a Sultan Mahmud II, and he appreciates the honor of a man who would "solidly build [his name] up in walls upon the enduring rocks." Melville's sensitivity to the fabulous is likewise apparent when describing the kiosks and fountains on a visit to the Bosphorus. "One is amazed to see such a filigree, such delicate and fairy-like structures out of doors," he claims, "[o]ne would think the elements would visit them too rudely; that they would melt away like castles of confectionery."[25]

Despite these many examples, Melville's romantic approach to the eastern Mediterranean was progressively eroded by the "rude elements" he encountered

during his journey: his fear of alleged pickpockets and assassins, his claustropho-
bia amidst the dirty streets and busy crowds, and "[t]he rotten & wicked looking
houses" which he calls "[s]o gloomy & grimy seems as if a suicide hung from
every rafter within."[26] As this imagery suggests, Melville had also brought his
Gothic prejudices of the orient with him, and the exultation he experienced in
Constantinople is largely replaced by the despair he feels in Egypt and Palestine.
For Melville, the Holy Land proves to be a barren wasteland rather than a land
of milk and honey. After witnessing the stony terrain of Judea, Melville writes,
"as the sight of haunted Haddon Hall suggested to Mrs. Radcliffe her curdling
romances, so I have little doubt, the diabolical landscapes [of a] great part of
Judea must have suggested to the Jewish prophets, their terrific theology."[27]

Although Melville returned to some of the romantic valences of Islamic orientalism in his late poetry (especially in the figure of the earthly rose), both the
sublimity and the gothicism of Melville's descriptions of Muslim architecture
were chastened during the nineteen-year hiatus between his trip to the Near East
and the publication of *Clarel* (1876). In the Jerusalem described in his poetic pilgrimage, minarets loom over the devastation of the Jewish and Christian holy
places, potent symbols of Islam's ascendancy and Turkey's political supremacy,
both of which deepen Clarel's doubt about the capacity of the Christian faith
to sustain the modern world. As Melville had attested in *White-Jacket*, "some sub-
stances, without undergoing any mutations themselves, utterly change their col-
or, according to the light thrown upon them."[28] For Melville, this change in val-
uation represented a disenchanting fall from the masthead of romance into the
dust and rock of the Holy Land, like the pieces of early Christian mosaic that
Melville picked up off the floor of a church in Thessaloniki that had been transformed into a mosque.[29]

Islam's triumph over the rest of Jerusalem is most clearly communicated to
Melville by the central position of Mount Moriah in his account of the urban
landscape. (See Figure C.) This hill features the mosque of Omar, the Dome of
the Rock, the second holiest Islamic shrine and the place from where Muslims
believe Muhammad underwent his night ascent to heaven. Melville views the
Dome of the Rock, constructed from the stones of Solomon's Temple and looming over the Wailing Wall, as a symbol of both the inaccessibility of Islam and of

the triumph of the Turk over the Jewish dispensation. But if the western gate of Moriah symbolizes the subordination of the Jews to Melville, its eastern gate typifies the subjection of Christianity. The Wonderful or Golden Gate, through which Christ entered the city on Palm Sunday, was walled up by the Muslims and a lawn of graves planted on the slope outside. Melville sees this in his *Journal* as "expressive of the finality of Christianity." Permission from Westerners to visit the Dome of the Rock during Melville's time was "almost impossible to obtain." In *Clarel*, Melville describes Moriah's green courts, guarded by fierce "Mauritanian guards," as another symbolic "islet" of paradise from which he was debarred. He closes his description of Moriah in *Clarel* with a forlorn rhetorical question: "But of the reign / Of Christ did no memento live / Save soil and ruin?"[30]

The Christian holy places in *Clarel*'s Jerusalem are dominated by the towering Muslim minarets and the frequent echoes of their calls to prayer. Rolfe speaks his first words in the poem from a hill above Gethsemane as the pilgrims look down at a "Saracen shaft and Norman tower" rising above the dome of the Church of the Holy Sepulchre. "Look, by Christ's belfry set / Appears the Moslem minaret!.../ The tower looks lopped; it shows forlorn— / A stunted oak whose crown is shorn; / But see, palm-like the minaret stands / Superior, and the tower commands."[31]

This proud, "palm-like" minaret refuses to humble itself before the "blank towers" of Christ's dispensation, forming a graphic portrait of Christian emasculation in the face of Muslim superiority. When Clarel hears the morning prayers of the Muslim muezzin from atop the minarets of the city (in a Canto titled "Under the Minaret"), he is assailed by dooming thoughts of the indifference of God towards the apparent blasphemy of heathens in the Holy of Holies.[32] Although the blindness of the muezzin is to prevent him from peeping in on the open privacies of the families beneath, for Christian doubters like Clarel it functions as a symbol of the distance of God. "While over all those fields of loss / Where now the Crescent rides the Cross, / Sole at the marble mast-head stands / The Islam herald, his two hands / Upon the rail, and sightless eyes / Turned upward reverent toward the skies."[33]

While here the minaret is figured as a "marble mast-head," in Melville's sea fiction the metaphor is transposed and the masthead described as a minaret from which sailors, described as muezzins, issue their calls: such as Tashtego's "vivacious cries" for the whale and the old tar of Liverpool's "floating chapel" who calls the strolling sailors to devotions in *Redburn*.[34] While White-Jacket describes the "monitory sound" of the Muslim call to prayer as "magical," in Jerusalem it rings out a sinister irony for Melville: the knell of Christian doom.[35] In his journal, Melville describes himself retracing the path of Christ carrying the cross while before him and behind him sound reminders of Islam's presence. "Wearily climbing the Via Dolorosa one noon I heard the muezzin calling to prayer from the minaret of Omer [sic]. He does the same from that of Mt Olivet."[36] For Melville, the blind and remote muezzin atop his minaret becomes the voice of the wilderness, haunting in its annulment of Christ's passion. In *Clarel*, Islamic architecture loses its romance. Installed in the spiritual heartland of the Bible, aloof from east and west, Muslim architecture symbolizes not the celebration of spiritual mystery, but rather the eclipse of Christianity's "deeper faith" and the impenetrability of God's will. In his trip to the Near East, Melville learned the same unsettling lessons as had Clarel: the "ill-content" arising from the realization that "Terra Firma can Deceive."[37]

NOTES

1   Herman Melville, *Mardi and a Voyage Thither* (Evanston and Chicago: Northwestern University Press and the Newberry Library, 1970), 230.

2   Dorothee Metlitsky Finkelstein, *Melville's Orienda* (New Haven and London, CT: Yale University Press, 1961).

3   On this tradition see Martha Pike Conant, *The Oriental Tale in England in the Eighteenth Century* (New York: the Columbia University Press, 1908); Marie E. de Meester, *Oriental Influences in the English Literature of the Nineteenth Century* (Heidelberg: C. Winter, 1915); and Byron Porter Smith, *Islam in English Literature*. S. B. Bushrui and Anahid Melikian, eds. 2nd ed. (1939; Delmar, NY: Caravan Books, 1977).

4   *White-Jacket; or, the World in a Man-of-War* (Evanston and Chicago, IL: Northwestern University Press and the Newberry Library, 1970), 79.

5   Melville wrote about the effect of his journey to the eastern Mediterranean in the lecture on "Travelling" that he took onto the circuit in 1857: "The Spanish matador, who devoutly believes in the proverb, 'Cruel as a Turk,' goes to Turkey, sees that people are kind to all animals; sees docile horses, never balky, gentle obedient, exceedingly intelligent, yet *never beaten*; and comes home to his bull-fights with a very different impression of his own humanity. The stock-broker

goes to Thessalonica and finds infidels more honest than Christians.... In the Levant where all nations congregate, unpretending people speak half a dozen languages, and a person who thought himself well educated at home is often abashed at his ignorance there." *The Piazza Tales and Other Prose Pieces, 1839-1860* (Evanston and Chicago: Northwestern University Press and the Newberry Library, 1987), 422-23.

6   For essays on Melville and architecture that do not discuss Islamic representations, see Timothy Dow Adams, "Architectural Imagery in Melville's Short Fiction," *American Transcendental Quarterly* 44 (Fall 1979): 265-77; Vicki H. Litman, "The Cottage and the Temple: Melville's Symbolic Use of Architecture," *American Quarterly* 21 (1969): 630-38; Gordon V. Boudreau, "Of Pale Ushers and Gothic Piles: Melville's Architectural Symbology," *ESQ* 67 (1972): 67-82; and two essays in *Savage Eye: Melville and the Visual Arts*, ed. Christopher Sten (Kent, OH: Kent State University Press, 1991): Sanford E. Marovitz, "Melville's Temples," 77-103, and Bryan C. Short "'Like Bed of Asparagus': Melville and Architecture," 104-16. The quotation is from Short, 105.

7   "A few of the longer reviews mentioned Carlo, generally in condemning the importation of so romantic a character into so minutely realistic a book. But most reviewers singled out Harry Bolton as the only implausible character and what the *Spectator* called the 'episodical trip to London' as the only instance of Melville's aiming 'at effect by melodramatic exaggeration'." Hershel Parker, "Historical Note," *Redburn* (Evanston and Chicago, IL: Northwestern University Press and the Newberry Library, 1969), 339, 332.

8   William Young, *Albion* (24 November 1849): 561; Charles F. Briggs, *Holden's Dollar Magazine* 5 (January 1850): 55-56; Frederick Hardman, *Blackwood's Edinburgh Magazine* 56 (November 1849): 567-80. These reviews were originally unsigned and can be found in Watson G. Branch, ed. *Melville, the Critical Heritage* (London and Boston: Routledge & K. Paul, 1974), 206, 213, 197.

9   *Redburn*, 228-36. The metaphorical language reflects the account of the bottomless pit in the Bible's Book of Revelation (9:1-12), routinely seen in Protestant eschatology as a site for explaining the source of Islam's rise. This conflicted mood resembles that found in Melville's first published writing: the "Fragments from a Writing Desk" that he had composed immediately prior to his own trip to England in 1839. While visiting a concealed villa in the Second Fragment, the narrator is hoisted up to an apartment that is described as "a spectacle as beautiful and enchanting as any described in the Arabian Nights," one "filled up in a style of Eastern splendour," in which Inamorata, with "Turkish sleeve" and "Andalusian eyes," reclines upon her "ottoman," deaf and dumb to any earnest entreaty. *The Piazza Tales and Other Prose Pieces*, 200-204.

10   Melville would later include a similar evocation of the rhapsody of music in the "mysterious melodiousness" of Isabel's guitar in *Pierre; or, The Ambiguities* (Evanston and Chicago, IL: Northwestern University Press and the Newberry Library, 1971), 125-27.

11   *Redburn*, 249-51. *Holden's Dollar Magazine* criticized the hand organ rhapsody as distracting "rigmarole," "Historical Note," 335.

12   *Redburn*, 206. The term "saracenic scenery" appears in "The Paradise of Bachelors and the Tartarus of Maids," *The Piazza Tales and Other Prose Pieces*, 321.

13 *White-Jacket*, 187.

14 *Mardi*, 7-8.

15 *Mardi*, 616, 630.

16 See reviews of *Mardi* from *The Home Journal* and *Sartain's Magazine* in Jay Leyda, *The Melville Log*. 2 vols. (1951; New York, Gordian Press, 1969), 1: 299, 311.

17 *White-Jacket*, 116.

18 *White-Jacket*, 311.

19 *Redburn*, 240.

20 *Moby-Dick; or, The Whale* (Evanston and Chicago: Northwestern University Press and the Newberry Library, 1988), 271.

21 *Journals* (Evanston and Chicago, IL: Northwestern University Press and the Newberry Library, 1989), 52. Melville is here referring to Chapters 39-41 of *Don Quixote* in which Captain Ruy Pérez de Viedma recounts his escape with the Moorish maiden Zoraida. Chapter 41 includes images of sailing along the North African coast.

22 The "grandness" of a possible trip to the east resonated through Melville's mind during his 1849 crossing on the *Southampton* (*Journals*, 7-9). Melville's first copy of *Anastasius* was seized by British customs (39). *Anastasius* describes his mood upon encountering Constantinople: "with eyes riveted on the expanding splendours . . . entranced by such a magnificent spectacle, I felt as if all the faculties of my soul were insufficient fully to embrace its glories: I hardly retained power to breathe; and almost apprehended that in doing so I might dispel the gorgeous vision, and find its whole vast fabric only a delusive dream!" Thomas Hope, *Anastasius; or, Memoirs of a Greek*. 2 vols. (London: Richard Bentley, 1855), 1: 51-52.

23 *Journals*, 57-58. This perhaps reflects Melville's own examination of the "very pretty" Turkish ladies in yashmaks aboard the ship that brought him to Constantinople, some of whom had to come below to remove their yashmaks and sit before the fire because of the rainy weather (57).

24 *Journals*, 55, 74, 65, 59, 60, 63. Elements of this enchantment are still in his mind in his description of camping in Jericho, a rare moment of contentment while in the Holy Land: "—tent—fine dinner—jolly time—sitting at the door of the tent looking at the mountains of Moab—tent the charmed circle keeping off the curse" (83). See "The Continents," *Collected Poems of Herman Melville*, ed. Howard P. Vincent (Chicago: Hendricks House, 1947), 409.

25 *Journals*, 63, 67, 65.

26 *Journals*, 61. Melville responds to being trailed by "an infernal Greek, & confederates" by bringing to mind Schiller's "Ghost-seer" (64).

27 *Journals*, 89. The collision of the romantic with the gothic is clearly communicated in Melville's account of the Arab guides who showed him the pyramids in Egypt. In his *Journal*, Melville oscillates between viewing them as angels and demons. He begins by viewing his Arab guides "in flowing white robes" as "tender . . . angels" conducting him to heaven; but, soon after, this mood is replaced by terror and panic: "Dread of the Arabs. Offering to lead me into a side-hole" (75).

28 *White-Jacket*, 186.

29 *Journals*, 55, 392n.

30 *Journals*, 86, 434n. *Clarel: A Poem and Pilgrimage in the Holy Land* (Evanston and Chicago: North-western University Press and the Newberry Library, 1991), 31 (I, x, 24-26). Melville's treatment of Moriah differs in tone from the sources he consulted which celebrate the romantic beauty of the Dome of the Rock. See Arthur Penhryn Stanley, *Sinai and Palestine* (London: J. Murray, 1856), 167-68; and *A Handbook for Travellers in Syria and Palestine.* 2 vols. (London: John Murray, 1858), which calls it the most beautiful and interesting building in the Holy City: "we feel we are indeed in that gorgeous East which fancy pictured when we used to revel in the *Arabian Nights*" (1:132).

31 *Clarel*, 97 (I, xxxi, 73, 67-68, 76-79).

32 "Side by side in impartial equality appear the shadows of church & mosque, and on Olivet every morning the sun indifferently ascends over the Chapel of the Ascension." *Journals*, 85.

33 *Clarel*, 48 (I, xv, 36-41).

34 *Moby-Dick*, 341; *Redburn*, 175.

35 *White-Jacket*, 287. After visiting a family of American missionaries who had migrated to Palestine, Melville wrote, "[m]ight as well attempt to convert bricks into bride-cake as the Orientals into Christians. It is against the will of God that the East should be Christianized." *Journals*, 81.

36 *Journals*, 89.

37 *Journals*, 85; *Clarel*, 53 (I, xvi, 136-37).

VI

PROJECTION AND REFLECTION

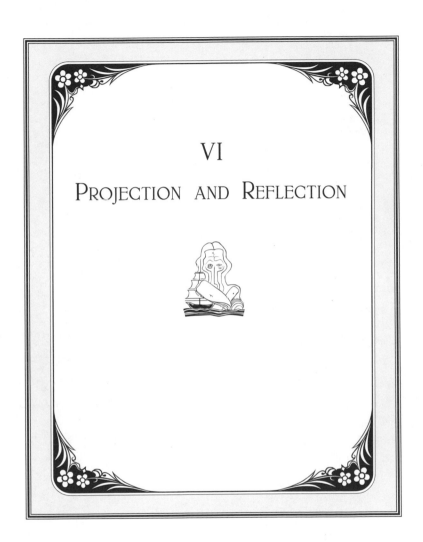

JINCAI YANG

TEACHING HERMAN MELVILLE IN CHINA

O fficially, Herman Melville was introduced to Chinese students through literature courses in the late 1920s. At that time, Tsinghua University personnel were very active in introducing American literature, for example, Professor Ye Gongchao who taught and wrote on the subject. Literary scholars like Wu Guangjian also played a very important role. Along with the introduction of American literature, Melville's name began to appear in some periodicals such as *The Fiction Monthly*.[1] Articles written then were not really critical in nature but were often summaries of the novels. No Chinese version of Melville's works appeared until the 1930s when Wu Guangjian translated *Typee* into Chinese, unfortunately not in a complete edition but an abridged one.[2]

Since then Melville has been taught in various Chinese universities though few significant changes have taken place regarding the teaching of his works. Chinese teachers seem to have stressed the significance of American literature by quoting from D. H. Lawrence's "Foreword" to his *Studies in Classic American Literature*, in which Lawrence maintains that in modern literature the American literature of the "old people" like Hawthorne, Poe, Melville, and Whitman is on the verge of change (viii). Professor Zhou Jueliang (from Beijing Institute of Foreign Languages) said with regard to Melville's literary work that he was a rare writer of his time who expressed a great deal of variety of the elements of his age. It is emphasized, therefore, that Melville should be studied not only as an individual writer, but also as an important representative in the history of American literature.[3] It is a pity that Professor Zhou did not do any further exploration.

During the chaotic Cultural Revolution, there arose in China an "ultra-Left" trend of thought in the world of literature and art. Nearly all Western thought except Marxism was refuted and ruthlessly attacked as anti-socialism. Western modernism suffered the most. It was severely condemned and mercilessly abused. For most Chinese literary critics, Western modernists were counter-revolutionary and therefore should be critiqued; for example, T. S. Eliot was strictly banned from the classroom.[4] In contrast, some American writers were treated somewhat better. Walt Whitman, for instance, was respectfully regarded as a liberator and revolutionary model. One of his contemporaries who also fared well was Herman Melville. Although he was much less known than Whitman, Melville was fortunate enough to survive the age of turmoil. Not a single word could be found about him in Chinese periodicals. However, the name of *Moby-Dick* was maintained in some Chinese English textbooks.[5] According to the compilers, this novel is very critical of U.S. capitalism. Perhaps it is just because of the narrow-minded political assumption that Melville is critical of American capitalism that he was allowed to enter the classroom in that particular era.

It is quite true that traditional scholars in China tend to focus their attention on the "gloominess of Melville." A case in point is Li Wanjun who largely considered Melville as a pessimistic writer.[6] Dong Hengxun and his fellow compilers made similar remarks.[7] The darkness of Melville, they believe, is neither the gloom of nihilism nor the coldness of misanthropy. It is the darkness that evolves when the indomitable human soul, trying to solve the question of good and evil by delving deep into the heart of reality, reaches the very limit of the human mind. In other words, it is a stoic view of the human fate. From darkness like Melville's we can observe the ultimate phase of man's destiny. No wonder Melville is often associated with the pessimists in our country.

Early in the 1980s, we ran headlong into an academic turmoil about the teaching of American literature that was to have a profound effect on the way in which it was to be taught at most universities and colleges from that time forward. Central in this turmoil was the revolt against the "survey course." This kind of course, long traditional in the Chinese way of dealing with foreign literature, had usually taken the form of a genial canter through literary history, with biographies of authors, summaries of the plots of major works, bits of social history, and of the history of ideas and bits of genre-history all mixed up together. This was in fact very much like church sermons with the professor lecturing all the time. There was no communication and of course it was very boring to attend such a course. But imagine, if you had a professor who combined depth and range of knowledge with liveliness of mind. Attending the course could be quite an experience. But taught by a run-of-the-mill teacher, such a course can be a confused and dreary business, involving the doling out of information about literature rather than the direct confrontation of literary texts.

It was not until the late 1980s that this aspect of the survey course came under serious attack. A group of scholars from Nanjing University such as Professor Liu Haiping and Professor Wang Shouren, who were then leading figures, discarded the original way of teaching American literature through history and started to turn to literary texts. They bravely worked out a new syllabus for the course. As far as the teaching of Melville is concerned, they added, in addition to "Bartleby, the Scrivener," all the other chapters of *Moby-Dick* to the reading list. As one of their graduates, I benefited from their lectures. Instead of dwelling too much on historical facts, they encouraged us to read the short story first. Our curiosity was thus aroused about Melville's humor and rhetorical style. The parodic and satirical features of "Bartleby" led us to browse over *Moby-Dick*.

Today, no one would want to teach a course of literature without emphasizing a specific text. Considered as a work of literary art, a novel is no longer simply a document in the history of ideas or in the biography of the author. Knowing that historical and biographical information is not entirely irrelevant to critical appreciation, nearly all literature teachers will focus on a particular text while still keeping an eye on bits of history and biography, Melville not excepted.

As has been indicated, in China Melville is taught along with the course of American literature, which is offered at nearly all universities and colleges for students of the arts. As it is intended for different audiences, there is much diversity of requirements for the course. Generally speaking, we have two specific kinds of students: majors and non-majors. The former refers to those who specialize in either English or Chinese while the latter major in other areas of the arts, and those interested in American literature in particular. In line with this, Chinese scholars have worked out various textbooks concerning the teaching of American literature. Among them the most representative are perhaps *A Short History of American Literature*, *History of American Literature and Its Selected Readings*, *A Brief History of American Literature*, and *Selected Readings of American Literature*.[8] None of these is a book-length study of Melville, but each of them devotes a long chapter to the writer. It is perhaps odd to note that all of them deal with *Moby-Dick* only. Needless to say, all the discussions are more or less similar and therefore lack innovation. In other words, Chinese teaching of Melville is strictly limited to a few general interpretations of some episodes of *Moby-Dick*.

What follows is a survey of how we teach Melville. For undergraduates of English, a few lectures are given followed by a short discussion of *Moby-Dick*. As we ask our students to read only one or two chapters of the novel,[9] the discussion is more often than not focussed on the linguistic problems, for the purpose of teaching American literature, as stated in the syllabus of the course, is to expose our students to a limited scale of original texts so as to enhance their reading ability and help them foster a habit of appreciating literature. Obviously, we are not teaching literature at all. What we are required to do in this course is to help our students read some chapters of original texts. I can still remember my undergraduate teacher Professor Zhu Li (at Suzhou University) explaining word by word the first three chapters of the novel. We had no idea whether he was teaching us intensive reading or literature. The only difference I could tell then in his course was the repeated phrase "symbolic meaning" which we rarely heard for a reading course. This is the typical way of teaching Melville that most Chinese English teachers have adopted. It was only recently that many foreign experts have joined us in our way of teaching. For instance, Fulbright Professor Fair C. Meeks has taught Melville both at Nanjing and Tianjin. Her combination of history and text has been highly acclaimed among students of English in these two regions.

The students majoring in Chinese can also come across Herman Melville in their course of American literature. Usually, a lecture is given to the survey students who passively listen throughout. As most of them have difficulty in reading the original text due to their limited knowledge of English, they often read the Chinese version of *Moby-Dick*.[10] Although they have not read anything that is original, these students seem to be very active in their discussion. I cannot tell how much they are possibly misled by the Chinese translation, but I do feel they are much more involved in their reading response. Only they are responding to the Chinese version of the novel, not the original text.

Similar lectures are also offered to students of other majors. As they are non-majors, we have no specific requirement for them. All the lectures are no more than surveys of Melville's personal history and summaries of his books, and they are given at night. Course participants are not asked to write critical essays but have to pass a certain test on lectures.

Although some universities in China are teaching Melville in the new ways, many still insist on a heavy dose of literary history. A careful reading of Chinese textbooks will confirm that this is the case. It seems to me that Chinese compilers have paid too much attention to historical facts. None of their Melville chapters are critical, and their selections of *Moby-Dick* are certainly random. How can a reading of one or two chapters of one major work illustrate a great artist? It is far from adequate.

In all, our reading of Melville has suffered from the comparative absence among us of a seriously critical habit of mind and of those methods of sound criticism that go with it. Whether in the academic world or in the more or less uncultivated reading public (here referring to the students), we too often find, in the place of criticism, one or the other of two flagrantly uncritical habits of thought: either exaggerating the author's pessimistic frame of mind or over-generalizing on him as a social critic of capitalist society. Such simple generalization is almost commonplace among Chinese readers. Therefore, we have a long way to go in order to get a more complete picture of Melville, for his ultimate appeal, as Professor John Bryant has observed, lies in his art: his mighty lines, his concrete and surprising images, his palpable ideas, his penetration into mind and being, his exposure of that human longing for the eternal, and his evisceration of American myth (xix). I know it will take years, or perhaps decades, to get close to the treasure of Melville, but we are confident we can if we really dedicate our lives to him.

Take me as an example. I came across Herman Melville in 1983 when I was pursuing my undergraduate studies in Suzhou University. I was then attending Professor Zhu's class in which he was lecturing on *Moby-Dick*. I did not follow him, but I did have a sense that the novel was extraordinary. Ever since then Herman Melville has been a hard nut to crack. However, from the onset, his frequently innovative style as well as his intricate mind of thought has held a strange and lasting fascination for me, and this fascination has grown with closer acquaintance. My endeavors to both read and teach Melville have caused me endless headaches and many sleepless nights, but they have also provided me with many an exciting moment when a happy solution to a tricky problem was finally found.

Even though it is quite true that Herman Melville has been little studied in China except for a few sporadic remarks by some noted Chinese literary critics,[11] one can hardly ignore the fact that this American writer has enjoyed an audience among Chinese college students, and students of literature in particular. Today, Melville is widely acknowledged as part of the greatest of American literature and his name can be witnessed in almost all foreign literature textbooks compiled in China. In view of the long-standing teaching of Melville we can safely predict a prolonged life for Melville in China.

Finally, I wish to leave you with these thoughts. (1) The teaching of Melville in our country has a long tradition but still has a long way to go compared with our partner nations. The Japanese scholars, for instance, have set a very good example in this regard. (2) The teaching of Melville should be much broadened and improved. We should not limit our eyes to only one or two works of Melville as we have all along been doing. Instead, we must broaden our vision. We should not only import the existing Melville scholarship and introduce it to our students but also keep in touch with world scholars. Meanwhile we should train more scholars of our own so that they can take up the subject sooner or later. (3) Much has to be done concerning the translation in order to attract more attention. Up to now, we have only one sound or presentable Chinese version of Melville's *Moby-Dick* and an incomplete abridged version of his *Typee* while so many other works remain entirely untouched in China. With more translation of Melville's other texts, I am sure a nationwide interest in Melville will soon emerge in China. Personally, I will do my best. I am currently working on Herman Melville's Polynesian Trilogy, which I hope will arouse no small interest among Chinese literary critics.

Recently, my home advisor, Professor Liu Haiping, has written to indicate that we are going to offer a "Melville Seminar" at Nanjing University. Although I cannot tell at this moment how much we can influence the Chinese academic world, I do feel optimistic about our plans. As this is the first seminar on Melville in China, we will certainly take the lead in this respect. It, I am sue, will cause no small repercussion, for the more students we train, the more theses and papers will be written on Melville. Our seminar is an attempt to devise the plainest possible elementary lectures on Melville's fiction. This is a deliberately broad way of approaching his works, and it is basically a teaching device. In it, we will try to be concise and lucid, and to make students understand that it is possible to respond to his works in spite of reading difficulties. We will gradually examine Melville's works individually, from his earliest practice to his last accomplishment. As most of his writings have been totally neglected, we would like to reveal them to our students in the hope of rendering a more panoramic view of Melville. Of course, it is no easy matter to achieve all this. It is a painstaking business, but we find it worthwhile to do so nevertheless.

NOTES

1   The *Fiction Monthly* was one of the influential periodicals in Shanghai in the 1920s and 1930s. It played a very important role in introducing Western literature to China.

2   This abridged Chinese version of *Typee* was published by the Commercial Press in 1934.

3   In his book review of Cao Yong's translation of *Moby-Dick*, Zhou Jueliang made a survey of Melville's art, asserting that Melville deserves more attention. For further reference, see his "The White Whale: *Moby-Dick*," *Western Language and Literature*, 2, no. 1 (1958): 120-24.

4   For instance, Yuan Kejia (from the Chinese Academy of Social Sciences) once rebuked T. S. Eliot. For him, Eliot's literary theory was an adverse current against the socialist culture; see *Review of Literature* 6 (1960): 58. In 1962 *Selected Essays* by T. S. Eliot was translated and published in Shanghai in order to criticize Eliot's literary ideology, calling for a rejection of the poet.

5   See, for example, Yu Dayin, *English*, Vol. 6 (Beijing: Commercial Press, 1961), 124.

6   Li Wanjun, "A Tentative Study of *Moby-Dick*," *Foreign Literature*, no. 3 (1988): 3.

7   Dong Hengxun et al. ed., *A Short History of American Literature* (Beijing: People's Literature Press, 1978), 95.

8   Dong Hengxun et al., ed., *A Short History of American Literature* (Beijing: People's Literature Press, 1978); Wu Weiren, *History of American Literature and Its Selected Readings* (Beijing: The Foreign

Language Teaching and Research Press, 1990; Chang Yaoxin, *A Brief History of American Literature* (Tianjin: Nankai University Press); and Chang Yaoxin et al. ed., *Selected Readings of American Literature* (Tianjin: Nankai University Press, 1991).

9   Usually, Chapter 84 of *Moby-Dick* is chosen for classroom discussion. The choice is based on Professor Carl Bode's Manuscript *Highlights of American Literature*, Book II (1971). Sometimes Chapter 1 of the book is also selected.

10   *Moby-Dick*, trans. Cao Yong, 1957; rpt., Shanghai Translation Press, 1982.

11   See Lou Guangqing, "On Melville's *Moby-Dick*," *Outside Learning*, no. 4 (1985); Qian Mansu, "Melville and His *Moby-Dick*," *Chun Feng Translation Series*, no. 3 (1986); Wu Jia, "On Melville's 'Bartleby,'" *Foreign Literature*, no. 7 (1986); Zhou Jueliang, "Billy Budd: An Inside Story," *World Literature*, no. 6 (1987); Yang Xianghu, "On Melville's Short Story 'Bartleby, The Scrivener,'" *Journal of Fuyang Teachers College*, no. 2 (1988); and Li Wanjun, "A Tentative Study of *Moby-Dick*," *Foreign Literature*, no. 3 (1988).

REFERENCES

Bryant, John. "Introduction" to *A Companion to Melville Studies*. Ed. John Bryant. Westport, CT: Greenwood Press, 1986. xvii-xxviii.

Dong, Hengxun et al., ed. "Herman Melville" in *A Short History of American Literature*. Beijing: People's Literature Press, 1978. 93-99.

Lawrence, D. H. "Foreword" to *Studies in Classic American Literature*. D. H. Lawrence, 1923; rpt., New York: Viking Press, 1961. vii-viii.

Li, Wanjun. "A Tentative Study of *Moby-Dick*." *Foreign Literature* 3 (1988): 1-6.

Yu, Dayin. *English*. Volume 6. Beijing: Commercial Press, 1961.

Yuan, Kejia. "T. S. Eliot: A Hack Writer of British and American Imperialism." *Review of Literature* 6 (1960): 50-58.

Zhou, Jueliang. "The White Whale: *Moby-Dick*." *Western Language and Literature*, 2, no. 1 (1958): 120-24.

RALPH MAUD

CHARLES OLSON AND THE MELVILLE SOCIETY

obert Bertholf's article, "Charles Olson and the Melville Society" (*Extracts* 10 [January 1972], 3-4), needs some emendation, as the author recently acknowledged to me in conversation. It was largely on the basis of guesses by Luther S. Mansfield that Bertholf identified the three persons satirized in Olson's notorious "Letter for Melville 1951" as Howard Vincent, F. O. Matthiessen, and Perry Miller. Howard Vincent as the "Congregational minister's son" is obviously correct. However, the "very bright man" at the end of the poem is not Perry Miller but Newton Arvin. Arvin was listed as one of the main speakers on the preliminary program that Olson received, but was not on the final program. This may have caused the confusion, though it should not have; if Olson's referring to him as a "neuter" was not enough, Newton Arvin's book *Herman Melville* in the American Men of Letters series is quoted several times. The other "main speaker" who "will talk about democracy" is Perry Miller. F. O. Matthiessen is not mentioned at all in the poem. The poet is therefore released from Bertholf's accusation that "Olson attacked people who had been so kind to him." Matthiessen had been Olson's close mentor at Harvard, but there is no evidence that Perry Miller was. Arvin was not someone Olson knew personally at all. Even Vincent met Olson only twice and was, at best, an acquaintance. So Olson's offense in "Letter for Melville 1951" is not treachery toward former friends.

There is no doubt, however, that the poem involves personal defamation and general vilification that may still offend. It is not my intention to intrude such matters into a meeting of the Melville Society forty-six years later. If Melville scholarship has had its gods, their squabbles will sometimes seem like a bad day on Mt. Olympus. Let me bound over the *Dunciad*-like parts of "Letter for Melville 1951" and reach the very interesting conclusion to the poem, which is a noble reaffirmation of Melville's unique value: "it is not the point / either of the hook or the plume which lies / out on this brave man's grave /—on all of us—/ but that where they cross is motion, / where they constantly moving cross anew, cut / this new instant open—as he is."

If the "hook" (or anchor) is the sea life, and the "plume" (a quill pen actually appears on Melville's gravestone) is the writer's life, the intersection of the sea and the writer in this case produced the masterpiece of motion, *Moby-Dick*. Moreover, it is proposed that, with all of us, our lives move forward (if they do) by the constant cutting open of the instant to release its possibilities. As Olson had already written in June 1951 in the "Human Universe" essay: "If there is any absolute, it is never more than this one, you, this instant, in action" (*SelWr*, 55). But since the essay was not printed until after "Letter for Melville 1951," the poem stands as Olson's first published announcement of his postmodernist position.

From February to July 1951 Olson had been outside the United States for the first time in his adult life, looking at America, its history, its problems, and its future, from the objective distance of the Yucatan. He was troubled. On the basis of two ingredients of his experience there—the physicality of the people and their self-reliant poverty—Olson intuited the need "to get on to some alternative to the whole Greek system," which we have inherited: "Plato may be a honey-head, as Melville called him, but he is precisely that—treacherous to all ants, and where, increasingly, my contemporaries die, or drown the best of themselves" (*SelWr*, 55). As Olson put his new thoughts into shape in the "Human Universe" essay, he realized that the Greek "logic and classification" have "so fastened themselves on habits of thought that action is interfered with, absolutely interfered with." "The harmony of the universe," he asserts, "is the order of any created thing," involving "direct perception" and "contraries." It is "particularity" that has to be "fought for anew" in opposition to the "generalizing" in our time, "at least since 450 B.C." (*SelWr*, 53).

Olson did not use the word "postmodern" in the "Human Universe" essay, but he did soon afterward in a letter to Robert Creeley in August 1951. In fact, what may not be widely known, Olson was the first critic to use the term "postmodern." Subsequently, many meanings have been claimed for the word. I cannot follow most of them. I am just glad I am old enough to have gained tenure before it became compulsory to read Paul de Man. What I gather is that postmodernism is an intensification of modernism, the alienation escalating to a hyper-self-consciousness where objectivity is obliterated. One does not experience a work or a thing, but one talks interminably about the limits to the possibility of experiencing anything. Olson's original use of the word was in total contradiction to these developments. Postmodernism is the act of the instant, not thinking about the instant.

Melville was very important to Olson in reaching this definition of the postmodern. It was Melville, along with Dostoyevsky, Rimbaud, and D. H. Lawrence, who "broke the spell and put us forward into the going live present": "they engaged themselves with modern reality in such fierceness and pity as to be of real use to any of us who want to take on the postmodern" (*HumUniv*, 112). This is from a 1952 review of a new edition of *Moby-Dick*, and in opening the book Olson "felt the wonder all over again of Melville's knowingness of object and motion, those factors of a thing which declare what we call its physicality" (*HumUniv*, 113). Melville was a master at apprehending the "visible truth," which is "the absolute condition of present things." Olson was fond of quoting these words from Melville's well-known letter to Hawthorne (for instance, in *SelWr*, 47, silently correcting the spelling) and of citing the chapter "The Tail" as showing Melville's "ability to go *inside* a thing, and from its motion and his to show and to know, not its essence alone . . . but its *dimension* . . . how it comes in on us as a force peculiar to itself and to ourself in any of those instants which do hit us and of which our lives are made up" (*HumUniv*, 113).

For Olson, the instant is always an intersection between the active person and the external world: "where they cross in motion, / where they constantly moving cross anew, cut / this new instant open."

Or as the "Human Universe" essay has it: "The meeting edge of man and the world is also his cutting edge. If man is active, it is exactly here where experience comes in that it is delivered back. . . . And his door is where he is responsible to more than himself" (*SelWr*, 62). Or as he later put it with great assurance in the poem "Maximus to Gloucester, Letter 27 [withheld]": "I have this sense, / that I am one / with my skin / Plus this—plus this: / that forever the geography / which leans in / on me I compell / backwards I compell Gloucester / to yield, to / change / Polis / is this" (*Maximus Poems* II.15).

This passage from a poem of December 1954 shows that Olson had learnt particularity from Melville; he had learnt physicality, and space; and he had learnt the weight on each individual of each one's share in upholding the moral structure at every instant.

In the development of this postmodern position of Olson's the Melville Society itself played a small but strategic part. In the Yucatan Olson had not been thinking about Melville very much. The mail he picked up on his return contained the invitation to the Melville Society's weekend celebration of the centenary of *Moby-Dick*. It goaded him into writing a flamboyant satire on the "Melvilleans," but it also caused him to pay his own tribute to Melville, acknowledging him as one of the precursors of the postmodern, one of the chief writers who "projected what we are" (*AddPr*, 40). Olson ended his "Letter for Melville 1951" with the image of the "new instant" being cut open as Melville himself was cut open, an image of a self-sacrifice that helped to give us our future. This is what we can take away from the poem as of use—even those who may have no use for the rest of it.

BIBLIOGRAPHICAL NOTE

"Letter for Melville 1951" was first published as a broadside, printed at Black Mountain College on 30 August 1951. A copy was delivered to Eleanor Melville Metcalf at the Melville Society meeting at Williams College on 3 September 1951. It was included in *The Distances* (New York: Grove Press, 1960) and in *The Collected Poems of Charles Olson* (Berkeley: University of California Press, 1987). This passage and others quoted in this paper from the writings of Charles Olson have been used with the permission of the Charles Olson Papers, Archives & Special Collections, Thomas J. Dodd Research Center, University of Connecticut Libraries.

Other writings of Olson cited are the "Human Universe" essay, first published in *Origin* 4 (Winter 1951-52), and collected in *Selected Writings of Charles Olson* (New York: New Directions, 1966), pp. 53-66; "Equal That Is, to the Real Itself," in *Selected Writings of Charles Olson*, pp. 46-52; review of the Mansfield-Vincent edition of *Moby-Dick*, "The Materials and Weights of Herman Melville," first printed in the *New Republic* (8 and 15 September 1952), and collected in Donald Allen, ed., *Human Universe and Other Essays* (New York: Grove Press, 1967), pp. 109-116; and "The Present Is Prologue," in George F. Butterick, ed., *Additional Poems* (Bolinas, CA: Four Seasons Foundation, 1974), pp. 39-40.

A preliminary survey of Olson's use of the term "postmodern" may be found in George F. Butterick, "Charles Olson and the Postmodern Advance," *Iowa Review*, 11 (Fall 1980); 4-27, and in Ralph Maud, *Charles Olson's Reading: A Biography* (Carbondale: Southern Illinois University Press, 1996), the chapter "Yucatan, Archaeology of the Postmodern," pp. 87-95.

DOMINIQUE MARÇAIS

THE PRESENCE AND SIGNIFICANCE OF FRANCE

AND THE FRENCH LANGUAGE IN *MOBY-DICK; OR, THE WHALE*

The references to specific places, to significant events and episodes in past or contemporary French history, the allusions to many famous French figures— kings, politicians, scientists, artists, and writers—as well as the presence of some French words in *Moby-Dick; or, The Whale* point to the importance of France in the novel. In this essay I do not propose to explore the impact of France on Melville from a historical or biographical point of view. I wish, in fact, following Melville's injunction in "The Whiteness of the Whale," to use both "imagination" and "subtlety" to dive into the "hidden" depths of Melville's text: "can we thus hope to light upon some chance clue to conduct us to the hidden cause we seek? [¶] Let us try. But in a matter like this, subtlety appeals to subtlety, and without imagination no man can follow another into these halls" (ch. 42, 192).

From such a perspective I will try to show how France and French, "subtly" related to monarchy and the spirit of revolution on the one hand and to naming and writing on the other hand, function as "chance clues" which operate in turn as catalysts or as masks.

I

Monarchy and Democracy: Sovereignty and the Spirit of Revolution

Versailles (267), "the palace of the Tuileries" (xvii, 456), "the rue Dauphine in Paris" (456), the "Hotel de Cluny" (185) and the "Bastile" (494), such are the

500

places related to France which are mentioned in *Moby-Dick; or, The Whale*. These names suggest either monarchy and nobility or the revolution. In the same way, the French historical figures referred to are either kings and emperors like Charlemagne (246), Louis le Gros (417), Louis XVI (109), Louis Philippe, the citizen king (155), the royal house of Bourbons (443), Napoleon, Louis the Devil (alias Napoleon III) (155), or revolutionaries like Anacharsis Clootz (121), Louis Blanc (155), and the anonymous street fighters of the 1848 revolution to whom Steelkilt and the mutineers of the *Town-Ho* are compared—being described as "sea-Parisians entrenched ... behind the barricade" (250). The leader of the mutiny (Steelkilt) and his followers finally manage to escape legal retribution by being picked up in Tahiti by two "French ships sailing for France" (258), perhaps hinting at a relation between France and survival. Paradoxically, in all these instances, monarchy is inseparable from democracy and the spirit of revolution. Thus the description of the *Pequod* and the thirty members of her crew, clearly a metaphor of America with its thirty states in Melville's time, combines these paradoxical themes. "Her old hull's complexion was darkened like a French grenadier's, who has alike fought in Egypt and Siberia. ... Her masts stood stiffly up like the spines of the three old kings of Cologne (ch. 16, 69). ... She was apparelled like any barbaric Ethiopian emperor" (70). This "noble craft" (70), however, "federates along one keel" a motley crew likened to "an Anacharsis Clootz deputation" (121), that is, to a band of revolutionaries.

The captain of the *Pequod* is compared to a sultan, a czar, an emperor, and a king and endowed with "all the outward majestical trappings and housings of a king" (148). He dons "a royal mantle" (117) and assumes "the Iron Crown of Lombardy" (167) which was said to contain relics of Christ (Beaver 770). He is a "god-like" king, a monarch by divine right. But Ishmael also speaks of Ahab "as a poor whale hunter" (148). Moreover, in the early description of the crew, Ishmael compares them to "An Anacharsis Clootz deputation from all isles of the sea and all the ends of the earth, accompanying Old Ahab in the Pequod to lay the world's grievances before that bar from which not very many of them ever come back" (ch. 27, 121).

Although called elsewhere "supreme lord and dictator" (121) and "lord and master" (149), Ahab is clearly identified here with the enthusiastic supporter of the French revolution. Similarly, Steelkilt, the leader of the *Town-Ho* mutiny, is invested with regal insignia and associated with the imperial theme: "Steelkilt was a tall and noble animal with a head like a Roman, and a flowing golden beard like the tasseled housings of your last vice roy's snorting charger; and a brain, and a heart, and a soul in him, gentlemen, which had made Steelkilt Charlemagne, had he been born son to Charlemagne's father" (ch. 54, 246). Real nobility replaces merely inherited nobility.

Ishmael's comments on the whaling industry point to the same contradictions since whaling is presented both as a noble, royal and even imperial activity and a democratic and even revolutionary one. Ishmael extols the whaling industry as the herald of democracy and praises commerce "which eventuated the liberation of Peru, Chili and Bolivia from the yoke of Old Spain" (ch. 24, 110). Significantly he traces back the origin of the whaling industry to 1775 (443), that is, just a year before the American Declaration of Independence. But according to him, the British trading company—the famous whaling house of Enderby and Sons which initiated this long-standing tradition of freedom comes "not far behind the united royal houses of the Tudors and Bourbons (ch. 101, 443). Ishmael also points out that "Louis XVI fitted out whaling ships from Dunkirk at own personal expense" (ch. 24, 109) as if the revolutionary whaling industry had eventually cost his royal life. The whale hunt—which is that of a "royal fish"—actually turns into "a revolutionary celebration as the beheading of the whale marks the beginning of the ritual of extracting and refining spermaceti. Blubber is boiled down to oil and the remaining scraps are jettisoned overboard as if the crew sought to obliterate any trace of the former feudal order" (Derail 24): "You would have almost thought they were pulling down the cursed Bastile, such wild cries they raised, as the now useless brick and mortar were being hurled into the sea" (ch. 115, 494).

The production of sperm oil "in its unmanufactured, unpolluted state" (114) indispensable for the coronation of kings and queens clearly depends on the whalemen's work and sweat. Because they "supply this coronation stuff" (114), these revolutionaries contribute to maintaining monarchy. This implies that paradoxically monarchy holds its sovereignty from the people. The nostalgia for monarchy goes hand in hand with its questioning as evidenced by the parody and derision present in the following passage: "Certain I am, however, that a king's head is solemnly oiled at his coronation, even as a head of salad. Can it be, though, that they anoint it with a view of making its interior run well as they anoint machinery" (ch. 25, 113).

The references to France and especially to French history show the contradictions inherent in monarchy and democracy and underline their basic contiguity. Focusing on the dynamic tension between monarchy and democracy, such allusions call for new definitions of hierarchy, authority, order, and disorder. Thus, France, imaginary rather than ideal or idealized, operates as a catalyst, susceptible to help the new American democracy to define its own identity between two seemingly opposite poles.

II

France and the French Language as Masks

But France and the French language also function as masks hiding the true nature of the quest and above all the nature of Moby Dick as a metaphor for Melville's writing. Errors, spelling mistakes, inversions, misdirections and puns of all kinds—all related to France—hint at the deceitful, ambiguous, and even equivocal character of the artistic, scientific, literary, and linguistic representations of the whale.

In chapter 55, "Of the Monstrous Pictures of Whales," 56, "Of the Less Erroneous Pictures of Whales, and the True Pictures of Whaling Scenes" and 57, "Of Whales in Paint; in Teeth; in Wood; in Sheet-Iron; in Stone; in Mountains; in Stars," Ishmael examines "those curious imaginary portraits of the whale" because he feels "it is time to set the world right in this matter by proving such pictures of the whale all wrong" (260).

Among the numerous authors of such "pictorial delusions" are two French scientists whom Ishmael labels as aristocrats, "Bernard Germain, Count de Lacépède" and "the scientific Frederick Cuvier, brother to the famous Baron" (262) and the plebeian commentator of Lacépède's *Histoire Naturelle*, Desmarest. Several accusations are leveled against them. In Lacépède's "scientific systemized whale book," not only are "most of the pictures of the different species of the Leviathan incorrect, but the picture of the Mysticetus or Greenland whale

(that is to say, the Right Whale)" simply does not "have its counterpart in nature" (267). "Cuvier's Sperm Whale is not a Sperm Whale, but a squash" (262)
and Desmarest "got one of his authentic abortions from a Chinese drawing"
(263). The cause of "this blundering business" is to be ascribed to the lack of
experience of these scientists who have never seen "the living Leviathan" but
take their drawings from "the stranded fish" (263). Significantly in chapter 32,
"Cetology," which questions the very principle of classification, Lacépède, the
two Cuviers, and Desmarest are also mentioned. Melville gives the French ap-
pellation of the Right Whale or True Whale as "Baliene ordinaire" instead of
"Baleine." This curious inversion associating French and error hints at the unreliability of scientific classifications.

After denouncing the inaccuracy of scientific drawings, Ishmael gives examples of "less erroneous pictures of whales." Among them are "two large French
engravings taken from paintings by one Garnery" ([*sic*] 266). The English spelling
of the name Garneray is all the more curious as later the narrator insists on his being French: "The French are the lads for painting action" and speaks of "the natural aptitude of the French of seizing the picturesqueness of things" (266-67). Ishmael also mentions "two other French engravings worthy of note, by some one
who subscribes himself 'H. Durand'" (267). Garneray's battle pieces which convey "the real spirit of the whale-hunt" are worthy of being exhibited "in that triumphant hall at Versailles; where the beholder fights his way, pell-mell, through
the consecutive great battles of France; where every sword seems a flash of the
Northern Lights, and the successive armed kings and Emperors dash by, like a
charge of crowned centaurs" (267).

The narrator is obviously both critical of and fascinated by the spirit of conquest. Could the pseudonym H. Durand, common among French engravers and
woodcarvers (Beaver, 815) hide the name of Albert Dürer, referred to as "that
fine old Dutch savage" in the following chapter? Engraving, because it involves
cutting into wood or stone, is thus a mimetic representation of the whale hunt,
inseparable from violence, savagery, and the barbaric history of conquest.

The French word for whale—*baleine*—is one of the 13 names listed in "Etymology" pointing to the multiplicity of linguistic and cultural representations.
The central position of French, between English and Spanish, two languages as-

sociated with world powers, links France, once again, to the imperial theme of conquest. The presence of French is significant too in the tentative definition or classification established in chapter 32, "Cetology," between the Sperm Whale and the Right Whale—the Sperm Whale being "the present Cachalot of the French" and the Right Whale designated as "the Baliene Ordinaire" with the mistake already alluded to. The Sperm Whale is presented at length in a vague and joking way: "This whale among the English of old vaguely known as the Trumpa whale and the Physeter whale, is the present Cachalot of the French and the Pottsfich of the Germans, and the Macrocephalus of the Long Words" (137-38).

These names call the reader's attention to the importance of different languages and to the question of errors. Trumpa whale, a name invented by Melville, suggests the French *tromper*—to cheat (Sachs 42). Melville gives the reader an indication of his deceitful writing. He diddles the readers just as Stubb, through a mock translation, diddles the French captain of the *Bouton de Rose* in chapter 91, "The Pequod Meets the Rose-bud." In this chapter the word cachalot is used for the second time in the narration when the American and French ships exchange news on the White Whale. Melville plays on the French and English names of the ship and creates a word, "Bouton-de-Rose-bud" that contains both the French name of the ship, *Bouton de Rose* and the English one, Rose-bud, an indication which points to the existence of a similar pattern in the word cachalot. Cachalot can be interpreted as *cache* (hide) a lot, the Sperm Whale cheats and hides a lot (Vatanpour 50). Stubb addresses the Guernsey-man: "'Well, then, my Bouton-de-Rose-bud, have you seen the White Whale?' [¶] '*What* whale?' [¶] 'The *White* Whale—a Sperm Whale—Moby Dick, have ye seen him?' [¶] 'Never heard of such a whale. Cachalot Blanche? White Whale—no'" (404).

The error in gender in the French name "Cachalot Blanche" reminiscent of the inversion in the French name of the Right Whale, questions the sexual identity of the Sperm Whale for *cachalot*, being masculine, should be qualified as *blanc*.

The use of French and fake translation eventually allow Stubb to "diddle" the French captain into releasing the blasted whale that smells so terribly. Digging into his body, Stubb extracts the ambergris, that precious and incorruptible substance "worth a gold guinea an ounce" (407). Ambergris is associated with France, inversion, and the royal metaphor. The word ambergris is, according to the text, "the French compound for grey amber" (408). Referred to as "a curious substance" and "an essence" used by "fine ladies and gentlemen to regale themselves" (408), it combines contradictory if not paradoxical elements. It is considered by some "to be the cause, and by others the effect, of the dyspepsia in the whale" (408). Although found in "the heart of decay" (409), it is "most fragrant" and is associated with corruption and incorruption, dishonor, and glory. The description of ambergris evokes that of plum pudding, a "term bestowed upon certain fragmentary parts of the whale's flesh" (416) and related to the French King Louis le Gros. Ambergris is described as "something that looked like Windsor soap or rich mottled cheese; very unctuous and savory withal . . . worth a gold guinea an ounce" (ch. 91, 407), and plum-pudding, which tastes like a "royal cutlet from the thigh of Louis le Gros" is similarly "unctuous," of "an exceedingly rich mottled tint, with a bestreaked snowy and golden ground" (417).

Another instance shows how French functions as a mask. In chapter 42, "The Whiteness of the Whale," the French word *requin*, whose etymology "*Requiem in eternam*" suggests the "ghostliness of repose and the stillness of death" (190), hides its English counterpart "shark" which in *Moby-Dick* symbolizes cannibalism and self-destruction.

A similar use of the French language as mask occurs in the same chapter. The translinguistic pun on the words blank and blankness which mean "white" in French and "empty" in English helps the narrator to find the significance of whiteness. If whiteness is but a "phenomenon" (193), something "laid on from without" (195), it becomes meaningful and represents the essence of the universe only when related to blankness: "Or it is, that in essence whiteness is not so much a color as the visible absence of color, and at the same time the concrete of all colors; is it for these reasons that there is such a dumb blankness, full of meaning, in a wide landscape of snows—a colorless, all-color of atheism from which we shrink?" (195).

Thus whiteness which envelops or covers up both the world and the whale like a *blank*-et hides the underlying blackness of the universe. The reference to Louis Blanc (155), the famous French revolutionary, can also be interpreted as further illustration of the use of the French language as mask.

Some of the references to France and French clearly show the tensions and paradoxes which are at the core of *Moby-Dick; or, The Whale*, thus contributing to the dynamics of the text. But others which involve errors, inversions, spelling mistakes, and translinguistic puns are more insidious. They may be "the chance clues" alluded to in chapter 42, but they mislead the reader rather than "conduct [him] to the hidden cause [he] seek[s]" (192). By masking the nature of things and beings, they suggest that truth is undistinguishable from error, that in fact truth is in error just as error is in truth.

REFERENCES

Beaver, Harold, ed. *Moby-Dick; or, The Whale*. By Herman Melville. London: Penguin, 1986.

Derail, Agnès. "Melville's Leviathan: *Moby-Dick; or, The Whale* and the Body Politic." *L'Imaginaire-Melville: A French Point of View*. Saint Denis: P U de Vincennes, 1992. 23-31.

Melville, Herman. *Moby-Dick; or, The Whale*. Ed. Harrison Hayford, Hershel Parker and G. Thomas Tanselle. Vol. 6 of *The Writings of Herman Melville*. Evanston and Chicago: Northwestern U P and the Newberry Library, 1988.

Sachs, Viola. "American Identity and the Counterfeit Whale." *L'Imaginaire-Melville: A French Point of View*. Saint Denis: P U de Vincennes, 1992. 33-45.

Vatanpour, Sina. "Of Money, Cash and Writing in *Moby-Dick; or The Whale*." *L' Imaginaire-Melville; A French Point of View*. Saint Denis: P U de Vincennes, 1992. 47-52.

507

LAURIE ROBERTSON-LORANT

MELVILLE'S FRENCH CONNECTIONS

hen Sanford E. Marovitz asked over a year ago if I would like to submit a paper for this conference, I had just arrived in France to teach at an American school in Rennes, the provincial capital of Brittany. Eager to explore the influence of France on Melville and Melville's influence on French writers, I decided to do a paper on "Melville's French Connections." As I saw it, this paper would have two parts: "Melville and the French" would focus on the Biographical and Textual References, and "The French and Melville" would focus on the Critical and Literary Reception of his work. As a corollary, I hoped to be able to figure out how well Melville knew the language.

Thanks to Merton M. Sealts, Jr., Jay Leyda, Leon Howard, Mary K. Bercaw Edwards, and others, we know that Melville mined Pierre Bayle's *Dictionary* for information, and we know that his work echoes Rabelais, Montaigne, Rousseau, and Pascal. Hugh Hetherington, Harrison Hayford, Hershel Parker and others have documented the reception of Melville's books by French critics E. D. Forgués, Emile Montégut and Philarète Chasles, and Sanford E. Marovitz has presented an overview of Melville's international reputation in his essay "Herman Melville: A Writer for the World." Thanks to the recent work of Sheila Post-Lauria and Wyn Kelley, we have become better aware of Melville's debt to Balzac, Le Sage, Eugene Sue, and the French sensationalists.[1]

Early critics followed the lead of Philarète Chasles, who published a rambling article entitled "Voyages réels et fantastiques d'Herman Melville" in the *Revue des deux mondes* in 1849. Although he praised *Typee* and *Omoo* for their astonishing *"fraicheur"* and *"profondeur des impressions,"* Chasles pronounced Melville devoid of originality and greatness of soul, and he dismissed *Mardi* as an *"oeuvre inouie, digne d'un Rabelais américain sans gaieté, un Cervantes sans grace, un Voltaire sans goût."* Soon after, the same *Revue* published E. D. Forgues's laudatory notice of *Moby-Dick* and Émile Montégut's translation and discussion of passages from *Israel Potter*, which he claimed illustrated the "Americanness" of which Chasles had written earlier.[2]

Melville was eclipsed throughout the remainder of the nineteenth century in Europe and America, as these early reviewers established the tone of French criticism until the Melville Revival reached France in the mid-1920s. Then, as Sanford E. Marovitz observes, Régis Michaud and Réné Galland rediscovered *Moby-Dick* through Raymond Weaver's biography. No longer condescending to Melville's Americanness, they portrayed Melville not as a merely picturesque storyteller, but as a mythmaker *extraordinaire*, one of the giants of world literature. Inspired by Michaud and Galland, the French began taking Melville more seriously, and Melville began to influence French writers.[3]

In 1930, novelist André Gide wrote in his journal, *"Je viens d'achever l'admirable* Moby-Dick." For Gide, as for many French readers, *Moby-Dick* was *"le plus glorieux"* of all the great books of the sea. It had *"un grand vent"* blowing through it, and an *"air chargé de parfums étranges, d'orages et de détresses et d'embruns."* Drawn to civilizations freer from guilt and inhibition and more sensual and harmonious than ours, Gide extolled the Greeks as the great exemplars of *"la harmonie de l'individu, et des moeurs, et de la cité."* Melville extolled the noble savages of the Marquesas for similar virtues, as have painter Paul Gauguin, Breton poet-novelist Victor Segalen, and all others who have dreamed *"la rêve Polynésian."*[4]

After Jean Simon published his dissertation entitled "Herman Melville, marin, métaphysicien et poète," a team of translators headed by novelist Jean Giono started translating *Moby-Dick*. For decades, Melville has been known to French readers primarily through Giono's *La Baleine blanche*, a kind of *traduction imaginaire*, and his wildly inaccurate *Pour saluer Melville*, a book audaciously advertised as a "biography." This bizarre tribute to Melville starts out with an eloquent appreciation of *Moby-Dick*, which Giono aptly calls *"une partie de notre rêve commun,"* a recognition of our inner oceans and our personal demons. *"On a ses propres oceans et ses monstres personnels,"* writes Giono, *"des terribles mutilations interïereures qui irriteront eter-nellement les hommes contre les dieux."*[5] Giono's descriptions of Melville's style are equally wonderful: *"La phrase de Melville est à la fois un torrent, une montagne, une mer,"* he writes. *"Comme la montagne, le torrent ou la mer, cette phrase roule, s'élève et retombe avec tout son mystère. Elle importe; elle noie."*

Unfortunately, after this promising opening, *Pour Saluer Melvill*e degenerates into a grotesquely fictionalized, completely fanciful and self-indulgent narrative that focuses almost exclusively on Melville's 1849 visit to London, for which Giono shamelessly invents characters and scenes. Oddly enough, he says noth-ing about Melville's 1849 visit to Paris, a subject to which I will return later.[6]

In 1958 Jean-Jacques Mayoux's richly illustrated *Melville par lui-même* appeared. This little book, which was translated into English by John Ashbery, skillfully weaves pictorial and literary material with biographical and geographical infor-mation. Providing an overview of Melville's life and writings, with a focus on images of cannibalism, Mayoux provides a much needed corrective to Giono's self-indulgent fantasy, while retaining a sense of the mystery and strangeness of Melville's world.[7]

By affirming Melville as a grand mythmaker and *Moby-Dick* as one of the great masterpieces of world literature, Simon, Giono, and Mayoux kept Melville stud-ies alive in France. Then in 1979 Charles Pérotin included Melville in his study of *"Les Ecrivains anti-esclavagistes aux Etats-Unis de 1808-61."* Identifying Melville's search for Truth as a quest for justice, he wrote, *"Le voyage de marin lui apparut de plus en plus comme l'archetype de la quête de l'homme à la recherche de sa propre verité."*[8]

Melville's ocean voyage struck both Jean-Paul Sartre and Albert Camus as an epic metaphor for existential striving. We haunt—we are obsessed by—the Ab-solute, wrote Sartre, *"mais personne, a ma connaissance, personne sauf Melville ne tente cette extraordinaire entreprise: retenir en soi le goût indefinissable d'une qualité pure—de la qualité le plus pur: la blancheur—et chercher dans ce goût même le sens absolu qui le dépasse."* For Sartre, *"la chasse"* in *Moby-Dick* forges a link between man and animal, *"un rapport de vertige et de mort."* It is this rapport between dizziness and death that makes Melville *"le plus 'moderne' des écrivains"* in the eyes of Albert Camus.

Camus praised Melville's ability to construct symbols *"sur le concrêt, non dans le matériau de rêves."* For Camus, Melville was the Homer of the Pacific, a creator of myths whose symbols are grounded in reality, not fantasy. Contrasting Melville with Franz Kafka, Camus wrote that Melville's symbols are not chimeras of imagination, but flashes of perception, profound insight into the deep structures of things, moments of sheer genius. Camus found Kafka's rendering of *"l'expérience spirituelle"* monotonous when compared with Melville's exuberance and humor. Camus found in *Moby-Dick* *"La santé, la force, un humeur jaillissant, le rire de l'homme, y éclatant,"* finally paying homage to Melville in *La Peste* by adapting the "doubloon" technique of multiple points of view in order to render *"l'équivalence profonde des points de vue individuels en face du même absurde."*[9]

French philosophers Gaston Bachelard and Gilles Deleuze, both prolific writers of scientific and literary critiques, were as fascinated by Melville as their existentialist predecessors Sartre and Camus. Their attempts to synthesize philosophical, psychological, and literary studies paved the way for recent analyses of the hidden text that, in the words of Viola Sachs, functions *"comme un voile, un masque qui cachait un monde holistique, sacré, un Tout originel dont l'expression était non-verbale."* Sachs and other French scholars connected with the *Laboratoire de Recherche sur l'Imaginaire Américain* of the University of Paris VIII see linguistic and meta-linguistic signs, esoteric lore, and textual errors as keys to Melville's creation of a "hidden text." By decoding the astrological, numerological, cabalistic, and hermetic signs as well as textual errors they consider intentional, they seek to show how Melville's writings interrogate and ultimately refute conventional formulations of American national identity.[10]

According to Sachs, *Moby-Dick*'s hidden text is a *"contre-Bible,"* an inverted version of the scriptures. Both Sachs and her colleague Sina Vatanpour discuss Melville's manipulation of linguistic signs, citing plays on the English and French words "cash," *"cacher"* and *"cachalot"* as evidence of his attempt to "write the other way." Pointing to Ishmael's inclusion of the fictitious "Trumpa whale" in his Cetology, Sachs points out that the French verb *"tromper"* means "to trick or cheat," another indication that Melville was attempting to subvert the national mythology by deconstructing the myth of American exceptionalism.[11]

Melville has many fans in France. While I was in Rennes last year, Gallimard published *Typee*, *Omoo*, and *Mardi* in its prestigious *Bibliothèque de la Pléiade*, thereby canonizing Melville and admitting him to the pantheon of great writers. Among the French scholars who are at work editing and translating Melville for the *Pléiade* edition of his writings, Dominique Marçais, Phillippe Jaworski, and Michel Imbert have all published books and articles on Melville. On January 9, 1997, *Le Figaro Littéraire* featured three articles on Melville. *"MELVILLE: L'AME AVENTUREUSE"* read the headline over the 1860 photo of Melville superimposed on an idyllic South Seas scene. *"Ses romans paraissent dans la Pléiade. Avec eux allait établir le malentendu qui a longtemps réduit le père de* Moby-Dick *au rang de simple auteur de récits d'aventures,"* read the caption beside editor Jean-Marie Rouart's introduction of Melville as *"l'un de ceux qui ont forgé le mythe de l' Océanie heureuse. Un précursor de Gauguin, en quelque sort."* Reviewer Christian Charrière wrote: *"Tout le talent et tous les themes chers à Melville apparaissent dans ce premier livre, qui, de loin, est l'oeuvre la plus réussie du volume de la Pléiade. On sait que l'auteur de Moby Dick était hanté par une idée toute simple: l'erreur de l'Occident."* Citing *Typee*, Charrière identified this as a religious error based on a Christian civilization whose intentions Melville deemed corrupt because it justified conquest by preaching the false idea that material progress would bring about spiritual benefits when, in fact, colonialism destroyed the native cultures.[12]

Enthusiasm for Melville runs high in Brittany, a sea-girt region of France with Celtic orgins which Melville would undoubtedly love as much as I do. Breton writer Hervé Hamon takes as the epigraph for his recent book, *Besoin de Mer*, several lines from *Moby-Dick* *"Mais ça ne leur suffit pas. Rien ne peut plus les contenter sinon la plus extreme limite de la terre."* Calling Melville a writer who voyages through spiritual as well as temporal seas, Hamon explains that Melville creates ambiguity in his writing in order to force us to deeper awareness and a sense of how to live life with passion, gusto, and courage. This lust for life is similar to what Philarète Chasles meant when he wrote of Melville's *"soif d'émotions"* in *Typee*, a thirst for a life lived alternately in the teeth of the gale, in the eye of the hurricane, in the bosom of a blissful bower whose fragrances intoxicate the senses and ravish the soul.[13]

How well did Melville speak French? Could he carry on a conversation? Could he read books in French? We know that Melville's father knew French well enough to write letters and converse with business associates in Paris and Lyon. Although Herman evidently never studied French in school, as a boy he liked to listen to the "liquid syllables" of the language as his father talked with a serving-man who claimed to have been born in Paris, or with his Uncle Thomas,

who had lived in the French capital in the wake of the American and French Revolutions. Thomas Melvill, Jr., worked in a bank and served as acting American
consul in Paris. His acquaintances included the Marquis de Lafayette, Joel Barlow, and James Monroe, and he married Françoise Lamé Fleury, the niece of
Madame Récamier, and brought her back to the family's Pittsfield farm in 1811.

Thomas Melvill made a lasting impression on Herman, who later described
him as "mild and kindly, with a faded brocade of old French breeding." Clad in
his Sunday clothes, "partly leaning on his slanted rake, [he] gracefully helped himself to a pinch of snuff" from a "smooth-worn box of satin-wood," presenting
"the shadowy aspect of a courtier of Louis XVI, reduced as a refugee, to humble
employment, in a region far from the gilded Versailles." Remembering how his
uncle would sit by "a late October fire on the great hearth of the capacious kitchen
of the old-farm-mansion . . . gazing into the embers," Melville imagined that in his
reveries he was "carried far away over the ocean to the gay Boulevards" of Paris.[14]

Melville's father, an importer of *de luxe* dry goods designed to satisfy the taste
of social-climbing Americans for Parisian fashions, made several business trips
to France shortly before Herman was born. An 1818 letter to his wife suggests
that Allan Melvill was both attracted and repelled by Paris: "France is still a delightful place to visit, & many of the Inhabitants preserve their virtues inviolate,
[but] Paris is a dangerous place for any Man, for there the gorgon's head of vice
is concealed between the mask of beauty, & the artificial flowers of love bestrew
the path of infamy, the force of bad example is ever in operation, & the temptation to evil bewilders the senses, folly usurps the place of reason, fashion toler-
ates infidelity, reflection is abashed by the arrogance of art, & the past & the future, time & eternity, are all lost in the present moment, & the gay and thoughtless multitudes who throng the avenues of Paris, pursue the phantom pleasure,
with avidity." Maria Melville may have saved her husband's letters to show to
her children, as many widowed mothers did in those days, but Melville did not
have to see his father's letter to have grown up associating Paris with the kind
of "foreign intrigue" that pervades *Pierre*, as Eugene Sue's *The Mysteries of Paris*
and other French sensational romances were quite popular in America.[15]

Neither a prig like his father nor a Puritan like his mother, Melville had no fear
of the "gay boulevards" of Paris, but when he spent a fortnight there in 1849, he

did not find them particularly gay, and on the whole, his journal gives a rather disappointing account of that great capital. His first impression of Paris when he arrived at the end of November 1849 was of "a garrison town," as there were some 60,000 troops stationed on the streets of the French capital. Louis Napoleon had put down an armed rebellion the previous summer, and he had not dared to withdraw his troops.

The first night, Melville stayed at the Hotel Meurice on the Rue de Rivoli, a hotel William Thackeray wryly credited with saving Englishmen the trouble of realizing they had left London for a foreign land. There he enjoyed "splendid" but unidentifiable French dishes and chatted with two Englishmen before strolling over to Galignani's reading room to check the American newspapers for notices of his books, perhaps because he found it difficult, even impossible, to read newspapers and magazines in French. After one night at the Meurice, Melville checked out of the hotel and crossed the river to find the rooming house recommended by fellow New Yorker Augustus Kinsley Gardner. It seems that he left the Meurice because he could not afford it, not because he wanted to immerse himself in French culture, as he took many of his meals at the "Rosboeuf," a restaurant that catered to English tourists.

In his journal, Melville notes that he "sat and jabbered as well I could" with his landlady, Mme. Capelle, while waiting for his friend George Adler. Although this could be seen as evidence that Melville spoke French, it illustrates the kind of problem of interpretation of such statements that distresses biographers. What exactly did Melville mean by "jabbering"? Does this self-deprecating phrase suggest halting, ungrammatical, incoherent French, or fluent small talk?[16]

Melville may have understood some French because he paid 25 sous to see three "comical comedies" with "plenty of babies & wet napkins &c." at the Palais Royal. A few days later, he and Adler made two attempts to see *Phèdre*, but both performances were sold out. Did Melville feel confident he would understand the play, or did he just want to see "the celebrated Rachel" whether or not he could understand the text? It is impossible to say.

His only comment on a performance of the *"Opéra Comique"* was "splendid orchestra," and with the sole exception of "Pont," used as a name, no French words appear in his journal. Nowhere in it does he slip into French or write a

French word because it is more expressive or evocative than an English one. From this it appears that Melville did not feel at home in the French language.[17]

As far as I can tell, Melville read little or no French in 1849. Although he bought "a copy of Telemachus for self near the Louvre" for two francs, the editors of the Northwestern-Newberry *Journals* identify the volume as Bishop François Fenelon's *Les Aventures de Télémaque*, a satire of Louis XIV, "presumably in English." Merton Sealts's assertion that Melville purchased French books in translation seems borne out by Melville's noting that he bought an English translation of Rousseau's *Confessions* for eleven shillings when he got to London.[18]

So just how much French did Melville know? Sifting through the evidence we have so far, I would have to conclude that Melville probably spoke little more than the nineteenth-century equivalent of "high school French," and read much less well than I did when I arrived in Rennes last August. He did not study the language in school, as far as we know, and if he learned words and phrases on his own, there is little evidence of it in his published or unpublished writings. Given Melville's love of language and his ability to teach himself everything he wanted to know, I find it surprising that the only French writers included among the "Extracts" in *Moby-Dick* are Rabelais and Montaigne, both translated into English. Moreover, if my estimate is correct, there are more French words in Walt Whitman's "Song of Myself" than in all of Melville's writing.

In the end, Melville's knowledge or lack of knowledge of French remains a mystery. His writings reveal an ambivalence toward France that may account for his not learning to speak or read the language well. In *Typee* he describes "black-hulled" French frigates patrolling Polynesia, taking pot shots at islanders for recreation, demolishing grass huts with their eight-pounders; in *Omoo* he satirizes the affected and barbarous "wees-wees" who colonized and destroyed the indigenous culture of Tahiti, and in *Mardi*, *Redburn*, *White-Jacket*, and *Moby-Dick* he frequently alludes to the French revolutions of 1789 and 1848. Philarète Chasles, thanking Melville for warning France about the danger of revolution, exclaimed *"Salut, mon Amérique libre, terre du printemps!"* French bellicosity plays no role in Redburn's fascination with his father's French books and engravings or the glass model of *La Reine Blanche* with its tiny sailors and delicate sails. Redburn's recollections seem to express Melville's boyhood fascination with France as a symbol of aestheticism and high culture, while later references associate France with pleasure and temptation.[19]

As Dominique Marçais's paper will show, *Moby-Dick* is full of allusions to France and the French, but other than *"cachalot blanc"* and *"bouton de rose,"* Melville uses few French words in that text. Although he chose a French name for the eponymous hero of *Pierre*, a novel that owes an enormous debt to the French sensational romance, France plays almost no role at all in Pierre's story except as a kind of "foreign feminineness" associated with Isabel, who describes her almostforgotten maternal language as "a bonny tongue . . . pure children's language . . . so twittering—such a chirp." In this melodramatic novel, Pierre Glendinning's life undergoes a dramatic *bouleversement* when a mysterious woman named Isabel shows up claiming to be his sister, the illegitimate daughter of his revered late father and an unnamed mistress in France. Weaving together Pierre's personal and national identity, Melville creates a sense that layers of history, like family entanglements, are coeval with the deep and complex strata of the mind.[20]

References to France and the French are few and far between in Melville's short fiction. Israel Potter meets Benjamin Franklin and John Paul Jones in Paris, and the narrator of "I and My Chimney" praises "Louis le Grand of France" for building a one-story cottage-style palace at Versailles, saying, "Any man can buy a square foot of land and plant a liberty-pole on it; but it takes a king to set apart whole acres for a grand Trianon." While most references to France in the short fiction are brief and largely ornamental, many commentators have pointed out that Jimmy Rose seems partially modeled on Thomas Melvill, Jr. The story's setting evokes France: The "heavy-moulded wooden cornices, paneled wainscots, and carved and inaccessible mantles of green horticultural and zoological devices" evoke the Hotel de Cluny in Paris. "Dim with longevity, the very covering of the walls still preserved the patterns of the time of Louis XVI"—paper hangings of "the most gaudy style" that "could only have come from Paris—genuine Versailles paper— the sort of paper that might have hung in Marie Antoinette's boudoir, with great diamond lozenges, festoons of roses, and an 'over-arbored bird cage.'"[21]

Subsequent references to France are less rococo, and often less significant. In *The Confidence-Man*, the Indian-hater is portrayed as "one evidently not so preposessed as Rousseau in favor of savages." In *Clarel*, however, the French Revo-

516

lutions of 1789 and 1848 figure prominently in the conversations of admirable characters such as Rolfe and Ungar—conversations that resemble those of the roving philosophers of *Mardi*. And finally, in *Billy Budd*, the French Revolution casts such a long shadow over a British vessel that its captain orders the execution of an innocent young sailor because of a deep-seated fear of shipboard rebellion,[22] an order seen as fundamentally unjust.

In *Melville's City* Wyn Kelley notes that Melville first saw Paris as a symbol of America's only ally in the revolution against British tyranny, then as a "place of freedom and delight, shabby but not Sodom-like or perverse." It is a indication of Israel Potter's naiveté that as soon as his foot touches French soil, he "freely declares himself to be an American," only to have his freedom taken away by the sly Dr. Benjamin Franklin, a fellow known to have enjoyed himself on the "gay boulevards" of Paris. At times, as Kelley points out, Melville resembles Baudelaire's *flâneur*, the cosmopolitian observer whose promenades through the city reveal the "little lower layer" of savagery lurking beneath the surface of civilized life.[23]

It is not surprising that the writings of the the grandson of two heroes of the American Revolution would incorporate references to France and the French in his writings. For Melville, as for so many of his countrymen, France was seductive, mysterious, and a little worse for wear. Thomas Gold Appleton quipped, "Good Americans, when they die, they go to Paris," but despite his many "French connections," Melville evidently did not consider Paris heaven, nor did he hope to spend Eternity in France, as some of us poor sinners do.

NOTES

1   Merton M. Sealts, Jr., *Melville's Reading*. Columbia: University of South Carolina Press, 1988; Jay Leyda, ed., *The Melville Log: A Documentary Life of Herman Melville, 1819-1891*, 2 vols. New York: Harcourt Brace and Company, 1951; reprinted with additional material, Fairfield, CT: Gordian Press, 1969; Leon Howard, *Herman Melville: A Biography*. Berkeley: University of California Press, 1967; Mary K. Bercaw, *Melville's Sources*. Evanston and Chicago: Northwestern University Press and the Newberry Library, 1987; Sheila Post-Lauria, *Correspondent Colorings: Melville in the Marketplace*, Amherst: University of Massachusetts Press, 1996; Wyn Kelley, *Melville's City: Literary and Urban Form in Nineteenth-Century New York*. New York: Cambridge University Press, 1996; Hugh Hetherington, *Melville's Reviewers, British and American, 1846-1891*. Chapel Hill: University of North Carolina Press,

1961; Hershel Parker and Harrison Hayford, eds., *Moby-Dick as Doubloon: Essays and Extracts* (1851-1870), New York: W. W. Norton & Company, 1970. I am indebted to Sanford E. Marovitz, "Herman Melville: A Writer for the World," *A Companion to Melville Studies*, edited by John Bryant. Westport, CT: Greenwood Press, 1986. Of the doctoral dissertations on Melville written in the past few decades, at least three deal specifically with questions of influence and reputation: Edward Alderson, "L' Influence française dans l'oeuvre de Herman Melville" (Ph.D. diss., University of Toulouse, 1951), Henry Yeager, "La Fortune littéraire d' Herman Melville en France" (Ph.D. diss., University of Paris, 1961), and Yael Amzalak, "Herman Melville en France" (Ph.D. diss., University of Paris, 1970).

2   Philarète Chasles, "Voyages réels et fantastiques d' *Herman Melville. Typee.—Omoo.—Mardi*," *Revue des deux mondes* 19 (15 May 1849), 541-70; E. D. Forgues, "Moby Dick, la chasse à la baleine, scenes de mer," *Revue des deux mondes* 23 (January-March 1853), 491-515; Emile Montégut, "Israel Potter, Legende démocratique américaine (Etude de quelques traits démocratiques d'après le roman *Israel Potter*)," *Revue des deux mondes* 25 (July-September, 1855), 5-56.

3   Régis Michaud, "*Herman Melville*, coureur des mers," *Nouvelles Litteraires* (December 25, 1926), and René Galland, "Herman Melville and *Moby-Dick*," *Revue Anglo-Américaine* 5 (October 1927), 1-9.

4   André Gide, entry for July 21, 1930, *Journal 1889-1939*. Paris: Nouvelle Revue Française, 1939.

5   Jean Simon, *Herman Melville, marin, métaphysicien et poète*. Paris: Boivin, 1939; and Jean Giono, *Pour Saluer Melville*. Paris: Gallimard, 1941/1974, 8-9.

6   Giono, 12.

7   Jean-Jacques Mayoux, *Melville par lui-même*. Paris: Aux Editions de Seuil, 1958; translated into English by John Ashbery as *Melville*. New York: Grove Press, 1960.

8   Charles Pérotin, "Les Ecrivains anti-esclavagistes aux Etats-Unis de 1808-61," *Recherches* 35. Paris: Sorbonne, 1979, 299-327

9   Albert Camus, *Carnets 1937-39*, Paris: Gallimard, 1949; and *Les Ecrivains célèbres, Editions Mazenod*, vol. 3, 1952.

10   Phillippe Jaworski, *Melville: Le Désert et L' Empire*. Paris: Presses de l'Ecole normale supérieure, 1986; Dominique Marçais, "Order and Disorder: Transmutation of Identity in Melville's *White-Jacket, or The World in a Man-of-War*," *Littérature d'America* 27 (1988), 51-67; "Les Jeux sur le blanc et le noir chez Melville," Figures 6 & 7 (1991), 173-86. "Revolution and Identity in Melville's *White-Jacket* and *Israel Potter*," *L' Imaginaire-Melville: A French Point of View*. Paris: Presses Universitaires de Vincennes, 1992, 53-64, and Michel Imbert, "Cash, Cant and Confidence: Of Paper Money and Scriptures in *The Confidence-Man*," in *L' Imaginaire-Melville*, 77-93.

11   Viola Sachs, *The Game of Creation: The Primeval Unlettered Language of* Moby Dick, or The Whale, Paris: *Editions de la Maison des Sciences de l'Homme*, 1981, originally, *La Contre-bible de Melville*: Moby Dick *dechiffré*. Paris and The Hague: Moulton, 1975; and "American Identity and the Counterfeit Whale," *L' Imaginaire-Melville: A French Point of View*, 33-46; and Sina Vatanpour, "Of Money, Cash and Writing in *Moby-Dick, or, The Whale*," *L' Imaginaire-Melville*, 47-52.

12   Marovitz cites Henry Yeager, "La Fortune littéraire d' Herman Melville en France" (Ph.D. diss., University of Paris, 1961) and Yael Amzalak, "Herman Melville en France" (Ph.D. diss., Uni-

versity of Paris, 1970), but not Edward Alderson, "L' Influence française dans l'oeuvre de Herman Melville" (Ph.D. diss., University of Toulouse, 1951). I was unable to locate a copy of this thesis, however. *Le Figaro Littéraire*, Jan. 9, 1997, also featured Claude Michel Cluny's "Les Tribulations d'un incompris," and *Le Monde*, March 21, 1997, ran a review by Hector Bianciotti entitled "Lorsque Melville se découvre écrivain."

13 Hervé Hamon, *Besoin de Mer*. Paris: Seuil, 1997.

14 Herman Melville, "Sketch of Major Thomas Melvill, Jr., By a Nephew," published in part by J. E. A. Smith in his *History of Pittsfield* (1876) and reprinted by Merton M. Sealts, Jr., *Pursuing Melville, 1940-1980*. Madison: University of Wisconsin Press, 1982, see 67-77.

15 Allan Melvill to Maria Gansevoort Melvill, July 29, 1818, Gansevoort-Lansing Collection, New York Public Library.

16 *Journals*, 31.

17 *Journals*, 32.

18 *Journals*, 33. Merton M. Sealts, Jr., *Melville's Reading: A Checklist of Books Owned and Borrowed*. Cambridge: Harvard University Press, 1948; 1952; 1966.

19 Mark Niemeyer, an American teaching in France, writes on *"Moby-Dick* and the Spirit of Rebellion," in *The Critical Responses to Herman Melville's Moby-Dick*, ed. Kevin J. Hayes. Westport, CT: Greenwood Press, 1994.

20 *Pierre, or The Ambiguities*. Vol. 7 of *The Writings of Herman Melville*. Evanston and Chicago: Northwestern University Press and the Newberry Library, 1971, 117.

21 *The Piazza Tales and Other Prose Pieces, 1839-1860*. Vol. 9 of *The Writings*. 1987, 354 and 337.

22 *The Confidence-Man: His Masquerade*. Vol. 10 of *The Writings*. 1984.

23 Wyn Kelley, *Melville's City: Literary and Urban Form in Nineteenth-Century New York*. New York. Cambridge University Press, 1996, 227.

ARIMICHI MAKINO

MELVILLE AMONG JAPANESE MELVILLEANS

elville mentions Japan at least ten times in *Moby-Dick*, and we can sense in these references a keen desire to enter a country that had been deliberately closed to Western countries. "If that double-bolted land, Japan, is ever to become hospitable, it is the whale-ship alone to whom the credit will be due; for already she is on the threshold" (*MD*, chap. 24). The fact that it was white Christian civilization being shut out must have instigated Melville's imagination, as is explicit in *Typee*. In *Typee*, through the viewpoint of a simple sailor named Tommo, Melville criticizes the missionary rhetoric and imperialistic forces intruding into the Pacific Ocean, while drawing a favorable portrait of life among non-Western Typees.

Of course, in many ways the Japanese were different from the Typees. But, as Tommo observes, if "the penalty of the Fall presses very lightly upon the valley of Typees" (*Typee*, chap. 26), it is not unreasonable to presume that Melville was eager to learn about a non-Christian culture. If possible, he would even hope to "intrude" into Japan peacefully and "by chance," as he did into the Typee valley. But Melville regrettably failed in his attempt to enter Japan. In spite of his last efforts to be a member of Commodore Perry's "conquest of Japan," his hopes were left ultimately unrealized "on the threshold."

Reciprocating Melville's interest in Japan, enthusiastic Japanese Melvilleans have ever pursued his works, through which they seek to understand the cultural background of Western civilization. As the bibliography below shows, more than twenty book-length studies of Melville's works have been published.

Since most of them are written in Japanese, the status of Melville studies in Japan has not been sufficiently introduced to foreign scholars. To rectify this situation, the following list identifies the major studies by Japanese scholars.

Japanese Scholarship on Melville's Writings—Books

[J] : in Japanese. [E] : in English.

1. Abe, Tomoji. *Melville*. Tokyo: Kenkyu-sha, 1934. [J]
2. Hayashi, Nobuyuki. *A Study of Melville*. Tokyo: Nanun-do, 1958. [J]
3. Terada, Takehiko. *Silence of God—The Essence of Herman Melville and His Works*. Tokyo: Chikuma-shobo, 1968. [J]
4. Kanbara, Tatsuo. *A Lonely Pilgrim—A Study of Herman Melville*. Tokyo: Kobian-shobo, 1975. [J]
5. Maeno, Shigeru. *A Melville Dictionary*. Tokyo: Kaibun-sha, 1976. [E]
6. Tanimoto, Taizo. *Herman Melville's Tragic Ambiguity and Beyond*. Tokyo: Kobian-shobo, 1977. [E]
7. Kitagawa, Teiji. *A Moby-Dick Dictionary*. Tokyo: Hokusei-do, 1981. [E]
8. Maeno, Shigeru. *The Sources of Melville's Quotations*. Tokyo: Kaibun-sha, 1981. [E]
9. Sugiura, Ginsaku. *Melville—Voyager to Spiritual Wreck*. Tokyo: Toju-sha, 1981. [J]
10. Ohashi, Kenzaburo, ed. *Whale and Text—Melville's World*. Tokyo: Kokusho-kanko-kai, 1983. [J]
11. Maeno, Shigeru & Inazumi, Kaneaki, eds. *A Melville Lexicon*. Tokyo: Kaibun-sha, 1984. [E]
12. Sakamoto, Masayuki. *The Sea of Desert—A Reading of Melville's Works*. Tokyo: Kenkyu-sha, 1985. [J]
13. Yagi, Toshio. *Anatomy of the White Whale*. Tokyo: Kenkyu-sha, 1986. [J]
14. Sakashita, Noboru. *Melville's Keywords—A Genesis of American Language*. Tokyo: Kokushokanko-kai, 1989. [E]
15. Sengoku, Hideyo. *Toward the Inside of the White Whale—Melville's World*. Tokyo: Nanun-do, 1990. [J]
16. Hoshino, Katsutoshi. *Herman Melville—The Abysm and the Star*. Tokyo: Liber Press, 1991. [J]
17. Nakamura, Koichi. *Narrators of Melville's Works*. Kyoto: Rinsen-shobo, 1991. [J]
18. Ohashi, Kenzaburo, ed. *Melville and Melville Studies in Japan*. Westport, CT: Greenwood Press, 1993. [E]

19. **Maeda, Reiko.** *The White Whale—Hellenism and Christianity.* Osaka: Osakakyoiku-tosho, 1994. [J]

20. **Fukuoka, Kazuko.** *Transforming Text—Melville's Novels.* Tokyo: Eiho-sha, 1995. [J]

21. **Makino, Arimichi.** *White Phantom over the World—Melville and American Ideology.* Tokyo: Nanun-do, 1996. [J]

There must be many reasons why Japanese readers remain fascinated by Melville's works. One would have to hold a high interest in narratives about the sea. On opposite sides of the Pacific Ocean, America and Japan are but neighbors who share an interest in sea adventures, trade, and whaling. The sea, nature to be symbolized in various ways, has been a fascinating subject for the Japanese imagination, too.

For all the Japanese writers' interest in the sea, however, no one has produced a monumental literary work on the subject like *Moby-Dick*. Considering the wonderful symbolism in *Moby-Dick*, I suggest that the second important reason is probably its mysticism. Discussions of Melville's mysticism, as related either with Gnosticism or the Western tradition of idealistic philosophies, constitute a large part of Japanese scholarship on Melville. Of particular interest is the cultural background of Christianity reflected in Melville's works. Yet other critics are attuned to Melville's bitter criticism of the Christian "civilized" world. Some detect a subversive message not only in *Moby-Dick* but also in Melville's other works. Their readings share some of the perspectives of new historicist and postcolonial criticism. In general, however, most Japanese readers appreciate Melville's artistic talent. They are amazed at his liberal imagination and the intricate development of his narratives.

In addition, the explication of Melville's unique terminology has long attracted scholarly efforts in Japan. Dictionaries and lexicons on his works have been published here although mostly in English.

As for articles on Melville published in Japan, I will only record the number brought out for each of his works, as too many exist to refer to them all by titles. In 1983, I edited "A Bibliography of Melville Studies in Japan" for *Whale and Text* (No. 10 of the list above), and since then I have edited "Appendix to A Bibliography of Melville Studies in Japan" in *Sky-Hawk*, the academic magazine issued by the Melville Study Center of Japan. Most of articles cited in these bibliographies have been published in academic magazines and university periodicals throughout Japan. The following chart indicates the number of articles on Melville published in Japan since 1920.

Subject	Biblio. in *Whale and Text* (1920-1983)	Appendix in *Sky-Hawk* (1983-1997)	Total
General	212	167	379
on *Typee*	16	16	32
on *Omoo*	3	2	5
on *Mardi*	25	4	29
on *Redburn*	9	6	15
on *White-Jacket*	2	5	7
on *Moby-Dick*	163	96	259
on *Pierre*	59	27	86
on *Israel Potter*	2	3	5
on *The Confidence-Man*	25	28	53
on "Bartleby"	30	21	51
on "Benito Cereno"	28	18	46
on "The Encantadas"	4	2	6
on "The Bell-Tower"	1	7	8
on "The Lightning-Rod Man"	0	1	1
on "I and My Chimney"	0	3	3
on "Cock-A-Doodle-Doo!"	4	2	6
on "The Fiddler"	2	2	4
on "The Paradise of Bachelors and the Tartarus of Maids"	2	0	2
on "The Two Temples"	1	0	1
on "The Gees"	0	1	1
on Poems	9	4	13
on *Clarel*	5	7	12
on *Billy Budd*	40	24	64

Needless to say, many Japanese scholars have done their best to translate Melville's works into Japanese. Though translation has always been a hard job, Japanese scholars have endeavored to conquer Melville's difficult rhetoric. The following is a historical list of translations (the year indicates the publication of the first complete version):

Typee: Hashimoto, Fukuo (1943); Honda, Kikuo (1950); Toki, Koji (1976); Sakashita, Noboru (1981).

Omoo: Meguro, Masumi (1943); Sakashita, Noboru (1982).

Mardi: Sakashita, Noboru (1981).

Redburn: Sakashita, Noboru (1982).

White-Jacket: Sakashita, Noboru (1982).

Moby-Dick: Hirai, Toyokazu (1939); Tanaka, Nishijiro (1950); Hanamura, Susumu (1954); Abe, Tomoji (1955); Tomita, Akira (1956); Miyanishi, Toyoitsu (1959); Nozaki, Takashi (1972); Takamura, Katsuji(1973); Sakashita, Noboru (1973); Ikuno, Hiroshi (1980); Hara, Hikaru (1994).

Pierre: Sakashita, Noboru (1981).

Israel Potter: Sakashita, Noboru (1982).

The Confidence-Man: Sakashita, Noboru (1983), Yamamoto, Tadashi (1983); Hara, Hikaru (1995).

The Piazza Tales & Other Short Stories: Sugiura, Ginsaku (1983); Hara, Hikaru (1991).

"The Piazza": Katsurada, Shigetoshi (1957).

"Bartleby": Hayashi, Tetsuya (1948); Terada, Takehiko (1957); Abe, Tomoji (1960); Kitagawa, Teiji (1960); Tanaka, Nishijiro (1966); Sakashita, Noboru (1979). Toki, Koji (1979); Sakamoto, Masayuki (1988)

"Benito Cereno": Hayashi, Tetsuya (1948); Kasegawa, Koh (1964); Hayashi, Nobuyuki (1972); Sakashita, Noboru (1979); Toki, Koji, and Sengoku, Hideyo (1979).

"The Encantadas": Hayashi, Nobuyuki (1972).

"Bridegroom Dick": Makino, Arimichi; Okamura, Jinichi, and Hamada, Kurashi (1994).

Clarel: Suyama, Shizuo (1994).

Billy Budd: Harada, Keiichi (1960); Sakashita, Noboru (1976); Hara, Hikaru (1997).

Contemporary Melville studies are strongly supported in Japan, especially by the activities of the Melville Study Center in Tokyo. Every year since 1985, it has published *Sky-Hawk*, whose contents include works by American critics although the emphasis is on bibliography and criticism written by Japanese scholars. The contents of a few selected issues are as follows:

No. 1 (1985):

Arimichi Makino, A Foreword [J]; Merlin Bowen, "The Melville Revival—A Personal Report," trans. the Melville Study Center [J]; Curriculum Vitae of Prof. Merlin Bowen [E]; Sanford E. Marovitz, Abstract of "'Some Beautiful Chimeras' from Europe and the Writing of *Moby-Dick*" [E].

No. 2 (1986):

Arimichi Makino, "By way of Cairo and into 'Fever & Ague'—Melville's *The Confidence-Man*" [E]; Jinichi Okamura, "A Bird's Eye View of *Moby-Dick*" [J]; Haruo Yamanishi, "From Head to Head—on 'The 'Gees'" [J]; Appendix to "A Bibliography of Melville Studies in Japan," ed. the Melville Study Center [J & E].

No. 3 (1987):

Kenzaburo Ohashi, "Modern 'Doubts' in *Clarel* in Relation to Nature" [J]; Shizuo Suyama, "On *Clarel*—If There Be No God" [J]; Arimichi Makino, "*Clarel* Studies in Japan" [E]; Appendix to "A Bibliography of Melville Studies in Japan," ed. the Melville Study Center [J & E].

No. 7 (1992):

Arimichi Makino, "Introducing Prof. H. Bruce Franklin" [J]; (Announcement) Three "Melville plays" with an Introduction on interpretation by dramatization by Joyce Sparer Adler [E]; H. Bruce Franklin, "Home and Homelessness in Melville," trans. & comment, Teruo Kameyama [J]; Hisao Fukushi, "*Billy Budd*, or the Inside Narrative as a Poetical Criticism" [J]; Kazuyoshi Takano, "Young Melville and the Intellectual Declaration of Independence of Young America" [J]; Appendix to "A Bibliography of Melville Studies in Japan," ed. the Melville Study Center [J & E].

No. 10 (1995):

John Bryant, "Killing Indians" (from *Melville and Repose*), trans. Arimichi Makino, Masafumi Yoneyama, Tamayo Tomita, Masaaki Uno, and Akinobu Hayasaka [J]; (Review) Kazuko Fukuoka, "New Melville" (*American Literature* 66.1 [March 1994]) [J]; Seiji Aihara, "A Wistful Narrator—On 'Cock-A-Doodle-Doo!'" [J]; Appendix to "A Bibliography of Melville Studies in Japan," ed. the Melville Study Center [J & E].

No. 11 (1996):

(Call for Papers Announcement) "Melville 'Among The Nations'" [E]; Jane Faulders, "Melville's Home: An American Literary Monument" [E]; (Announcement) "A Summer Celebration in the Beautiful Berkshires" [E]; Robert K. Wallace, "Turner's Influence on Melville" (from *Extracts*), trans. Arimichi Makino, Jinichi Okamura, Seiji Aihara, Akinobu Hayasaka, Hiroyoshi Iizuka, and Yumiko Nara [J]; Masahiro Tateno, "Passion for Incompleteness: Melville, Turner, Ruskin, and Leviathan" [J]; Yoshitaka Aoyama, "Heavenly Sanity and Earthly Madness: An Introduction to Melville" [J]; Appendix to "A Bibliography of Melville Studies in Japan," ed. the Melville Study Center [J & E].

The Melville Study Center of Japan seeks essays for *Sky-Hawk* not only from Japanese scholars but also from the international community. The Center cooperates with "Ishmail," the Internet service managed by Professor John Bryant of Hofstra University, who is also the editor of *Extracts*, the journal of the Melville Society. The Melville Study Center of Japan is not a large organization like the Melville Society in America, and *Sky-Hawk* is but a young bird compared with *Extracts*. Further we know that in the last chapter of *Moby-Dick*, "the sky-hawk" sinks far out in the waters near Japan with the *Pequod*: "and so the bird of heaven, with archangelic shrieks, and his imperial beak thrust upwards, and his whole captive form folded in the flag of Ahab, went down with his ship" (*Moby-Dick*, chap. 135). Yet, insofar as we preserve a high admiration for Melville's great works, the Japanese *Sky-Hawk* rises from the darkest sea and, like a Catskill eagle, flies over the Pacific ocean and beyond.

GORDON POOLE

"BOMBA" AND THE ITALIAN HENDECASYLLABLE

T here is a certain ambiguity in my position before you today. Although I have published several articles on Melville, as well as an edition of "The House of the Tragic Poet" and an edition of "At the Hostelry" and "Naples in the Time of Bomba," it is not as a scholar but as a translator that I want to address you. Nor as a teacher of literary translation, which I have also been at my Institute.

The distinctions are important to me because the long labor of turning "Naples in the Time of Bomba" and "Pausilippo" into Italian has split my intellectual personality in a, to me, surprising fashion. To put it simply, in order to do the job I had set out to do, I must put aside my "curial robes" (as Machiavelli called his scholarly garb) and become or try to become a poet, which is, I have discovered, quite a different creature from the scholar, as if other brain lobes were being activated than those one uses for literary criticism. When the last period in my text became a truly full stop and I had realized my intent, I was reminded of the remarks of the late John Ciardi in his notes on translating Dante into English. After showing the several metamorphoses of one exemplary tercet from a literal paraphrase into its final poetic form, Ciardi's ultimate self-justification was, "It sounds right to me."

I hope, therefore, that you will be interested in what my guidelines were in translating Melville, who for sheer thorniness, if for nothing else, can be compared to Dante. Schematically, these consist in the feeling I had for Melville's text, the feeling I have for Italian as a literary language, and my sense of who I was writing for.

Let me say, then, that there were some language traits in "Bomba" I found rebarbative and, hence, was not interested in translating. Remember, I am not speaking as a scholar, but on a—so to speak—gut-level, as a translator. Melville leaves out too many articles and pronouns and is sometimes too syntactically involute for my taste. He says things like "In season when the vineyards mellow" (v. 6) instead of "In *the* season" and "To feet I spring" (v. 44) for "To *my* feet" and "From balcony roguish girls laugh out" (v. 51) instead of "From *their balconies*." As a scholar, I might offer an explanation for the resulting sense of constipation; as a poet translator I censor with confidence and determination because my feeling is that in these cases Melville is having trouble with his meter and has opted for an easy way out. I realize that also a certain wry jocularity can result when these artifices are being successfully controlled, but I can communicate that in other ways, without skipping articles, etc.

This is virtually the only aspect of Melville's poetics that grates on my ear, and sometimes I even find it very effective, well worth rendering. As in lines 20-26:

> *"Signor," exclaims my charioteer,*
> *Turning, and reining up, the while*
> *Trying to touch his jaunty hat;*
> *But here, essaying to condense*
> *Such opposite movements into one*
> *Failing, and letting fall his whip,*
> *"His Excellency stops the way!"*

Clearly the tangled verses are formally correlative to the tangle the coachman has gotten himself into trying to do too many things at once. In Italian I hit on the following:

> "Signore!" grida forte il mio cocchiere,
> mentre, girando, frena e al tempo stesso
> vuol sfiorare il cappello, disinvolto,
> senza poter così diversi impulsi
> in un sol movimento combinare,

sì che di man gli cade infin la frusta:
"Vostra eccellenza ha bloccato il passaggio."

Another feeling I have about the poetry is that the moments of poetic entanglement are often followed by the relief of narrative and sometimes lyrical freedom where the poet finds his most felicitous dimension. An example of narrative ease (vv. 620-36):

> *Anon*
> *The files wheeled into open view.*
> *A second troop a thousand strong*
> *With band and banners, flourished blades,*
> *Launched from a second cannoned den*
> *And now in countermarch thereon;*
> *The great drum-major towering up*
> *In aigulets and tinsel tags—*
> *Pagoda glittering in Cathay!*
> *Arch whiskerando and gigantic*
> *A grandiose magnific antic*
> *Tossing his truncheon in the van.*
> *A hifalutin exaggeration,*
> *Barbaric in his bearskin shako,*
> *Of bullying Bomba's puffed elation*
> *And blood-and-thunder proclamation,*
> *A braggadocio Bourbon-Draco!*

This was a lot of fun to translate into Italian, along with the alliteration:

> Infin le fila in marcia ecco apparire,
> mille soldati, ancora più di prima,
> con banda e bandierine, e i brandi in pugno,
> da qualche tana corazzata usciti
> ed ora in contromarcia per tornarvi.
> Il capobanda era alto più di tutti,
> d'orpelli, piastre e aghetti agghindolato,
> brillava come un tempio di Catai!

Arci-baffuto, buffo e gigantesco,
stracolmo di grandiosa bizzaria,
pomposo egli lanciava il suo bastone
in alto, il più in alto che poteva.
Barbaro dal chepì di pelle d'orso—
di Bomba tracotante gonfio bullo,
retore degli editti truculenti
del vanesio borbonico Dracone!

Here is a more lyrical example of Melville as a charmer (vv. 284-301):

Ah, funeral urns of time antique
Inwrought with flowers in gala way,
Where faun and bacchanal dance in freak,
Even as of pagan time ye speak
Type ye what Naples is alway?
Yes, round these curved volcanic shores,
Vined urn of ashes, bed on bed,
Abandonment as thoughtless pours
As when the revelling pagan led.

I tried:

Or vedo antiche urne funerarie,
con sovra impressi fiori gai, e fauni
che trescano sfrenati con baccanti:
scene pagane, eppure prefigurano
la Napoli di sempre; un' urna è il golfo,
urna frondosa di cinerei strati,
spiagge vulcaniche disposte attorno,
e ci si sfrena adesso come alle orge
facevano i pagani spensierati.

Now let me come to my second consideration, the sense of Italian as a liter-ary language. A couple of technical points need to be made, if only to show that I do have an awareness of them. Unlike English, which is a syllabo-accentuative language, Italian is syllabic. This is to say that the isochronism of Italian is not measured in terms of ictuses or beats, as in English, but by mere syllable count. To clarify, in English the spondaic line "One year floods rose" and the line "Whose woods these are I think I know" are both tetrameters and hence of the same length (duration), although the second has twice as many syllables as the first.[1] This sort of accentual measurement is foreign to the Italian tradition of poetic diction, in which an eight-syllable line lasts twice as long as a four-syllable one and stresses are used for emphasis, not for measurement.

What does this have to do with translating Melville? Well, the accentual sameness of his tetrameters, already a source of misgiving to some readers of "Bomba," "Hostelry," *Clarel*, and some other works, is partly alleviated in English by the fact that the beats are, in a sense, discounted because, as I have said, they are the stuff of verse measurement, not of emphasis, which is expressed in other ways (notably, playing off rhythm against meter). If I had turned his tetrameters into what is formally the closest Italian equivalent, the octosyllable, I would have found myself dealing with the most irritatingly stressed verse form in the language, 750 sledgehammer lines that would have tired my readers to no end.

On a more general level, choosing the longer Italian line allows compensation for the fact that English is rich in monosyllables, while Italian has few. You either have to lengthen the line or increase the number of lines. The latter option would have been a rather severe departure from the poet's choice. In fact, Melville makes little use of enjambement; his lines are syntactic elements that segment his poetic discourse markedly, giving rise to units that are individually significant. So I went for the longer line and kept the line count. Yet, even with the greater length of the hendecasyllable compared to the tetrameter, it was wonderfully challenging to accommodate Melville's highly condensed poetic language without losing something.

Ultimate justification: it just felt right to me to recast the poem into the noble hendecasyllable, which has a long tradition in Italian culture of use for narrative poetry (Boccaccio, Ariosto, Tasso, etc.) as well as lyrical poetry (*dolce stil novo*, Petrarch). For a fleeting instant, as a scholar, I had qualms, but it worked for me as a poet translator, so I just went ahead and never had any second thoughts about the matter.

Coming quickly to my final point, my sense of an addressee. I have always taught my students that poetry ought to be read aloud or listened to. But only when my job was done did I realize, upon reflection, that I had been translating for a listener rather than a silent reader. I was unwittingly attuned to Melville's sonority. If I had to let an occasional case of alliteration or onomatopoeia go by without expressing it in Italian, I more than made up for it by taking Melville's hint and alliterating and onomatopoeicizing even when he did not. Such devices, after all, are not always at hand, so when the felicitous chance turns up, the wise poet seizes upon it. Forgive me a few more comparative quotations where alliteration is the issue:

The battlements black-beetling hang (v. 82)
Neri e sporgenti s'ergono gli spalti

She charms us glum barbarians still,
Fleeing from frost, bad bread, or duns,
Despotic Biz, *and devils blue...* (vv. 172-74)
Così ci incanta ancor, noi tristi barbari,
fuggendo geli, cambiali e cattivo
pane, dei soldi il despotismo, e i demoni
della malinconia.

What Mohawk of a mountain lours! (v. 272)[2]
Che monte è qui? minaccia come un Mohawk.

The darling of the mob; nine days
Their great Apollo; then, in pomp
Of Pandemonium's red parade,
His curled head Gorgoned on the pike... (vv. 460-63)
Idolo della folla, nove giorni
il loro grande Apollo; poi in gran pompa,
del Pandemonio la parata rossa,
e il capo riccioluto era impalato...

So much for alliteration. Let me close with an example of onomatopoeia, which, considering theme and speaker, I translated into the Neapolitan dialect rather than into standard literary Italian, which struck me as possibly stilted in the street context of these particular verses:

"Hark, the stir
The ear invading:

"Crowds on crowds
All promenading;

"Clatter and clink
Of cavalcading;

"Yo-heave-ho!
From ships unlading;

"Funeral dole,
Thro' arches fading;

"All hands round!
In masquerading;

"Litany low—
High rodomontading;

"Grapes, ripe grapes!
In cheer evading;

"Lararus' plaint
All vines upbraiding;

"Crack-crick-crack
Of fusillading!

"Hurly-burly late and early,
Gossips prating, quacks orating,
        "Daft debating:
Furious wild reiteration
And incensed expostulation!

533

"Din condensed
All hubbub summing:
Larking, laughing,
Chattering, chaffing,
Thrumming, strumming,
Singing, jingling,
All commingling—
Till the Drum,

"Rub-a-dub sounded, doubly pounded." (vv. 569-601)

And here it is in Neapolitan:

Sentite 'o fru-fru,
ca tras' int' 'e recchie,

'na folla de gente
'nu struscio pe' 'e vie,

'nu zuoccolo-zuo',
surdate a cavallo,

òi issa, guagliù'!
so' 'e navi into' 'o puorto,

tin-tin, fatte 'a croce,
ca passa 'o viateca,

che aspiette 'a balla'?
'a festa cu' e' maschere,

diasille e ammenne,
o smargiassarie!

Bell'uva, chi 'a vo'?
allegra 'sta voce!

Ma Lazzaro piccia:
e a me chi me penza?

534

Crak—crik—crak!
e so' fucilate.

Che manicomio 'e gente a tutte l'ore!
che chiacchiere 'e capère e sparapalle!

Parole a schiovere!
Diceno ridiceno e straridiceno,
si 'nciarmano si 'nquartano e s'acciùppulano!

'N'ammuina 'e pazzi,
'na sbafunarìa!
Pazzeano e ridono,
alluccano e sfottono,
cantano e sonano,
sescano e jocano.
Ma â 'ntrasatta:
oilanne, *'o tammurro!*

Ra-ta-bum risuona, ta-bum ingombra.[3]

To conclude, this sonority, that I was concerned to project through the Italian version of "Bomba," and my sense of writing to be read aloud were appreciated by two Italian actors, the rising Neapolitan actor Riccardo Zinna, a versatile comic, and the well-known Achille Millo, also a Neapolitan. Both Zinna in Naples and, more recently Millo at the Teatro dell'Orologio in Rome have recited "Bomba," with the accompaniment of original musical scores, to very receptive audiences. Furthermore, plans are afoot to make a radio show out of this text. As you can imagine, all of this has been very gratifying for the translator.[4]

NOTES

1   See Geoffrey Leech, *A Linguistic Guide to English Poetry* (London and New York: Longman, 1969, 1991) on this.

2   Only an American could compare Vesuvius to a Mohawk Indian.

3   I thank my daughter Susanna, an accomplished actress, for reciting these lines at Volos.

4   Quotes are from Herman Melville, *Napoli al tempo di Re Bomba*, G. Poole (ed.), with facing

text (Naples: Filema, 1996). This edition is based on my examination of the manuscript at the Houghton Library, Harvard Univ., with reference to the Constable Edition (1924); Hedricks House Edition, ed. Howard P. Vincent (1947); and *Melville's Poetry: To the Enlarged Heart*, ed. Aaron Kramer (1972).

The Motif of the Book

In the Works of Herman Melville and Bruno Schulz

erman Melville and Bruno Schulz. Where could there be a common cruising-ground for a possible gam of the strikingly different narrative vessels of one Ishmael whose fate was to sail wild, distant, and forbidden seas round the world, and of one Joseph, whose wanderings seldom led beyond the last, suburban, weed-flooded backyards of his hometown in the Polish Galicia, the extreme limit of his native land but a backwater place truly which, according to Schulz's description in "The Republic of Dreams," followed its own, private, uncharted way and attempted single-handedly "to constitute a world"? Could we *imagine* one key to those isolated fictional halls: the room in Drohobycz where Joseph covers handfuls of old newspapers, folios, and ledgers with his ingenious drawings, inspired "zigzags that knot themselves suddenly into anagrams of visions, enigmas of bright revelation"; the cabin on the whaling ship where Ahab, a pencil in his hand, piles of old log-books beside him, traces new courses over the blank spaces of the charts; the chamber in New York City where Pierre, "a pile of folios on his back," struggles to remain loyal to "whatever transcendental object" some usurper mood in him "so tyrannically suggests"?

In asking these questions we already mean to imitate that universally recognizable, narcissistic gesture of analogy, the seductive force of which both Melville and Schulz repeatedly felt compelled to acknowledge. By confessing Hawthorne, Melville tells the readers, "you thereby confess others; you brace

537

the whole brotherhood." He writes to Hawthorne: "I feel that the Godhead is broken up like the bread at the Supper and that we are the pieces. Hence this infinite fraternity of feeling." "We are all of us dreamers by nature, after all, brothers under the sign of the trowel," Schulz tells his readers, and in a letter written to another Polish author on account of his having understood *Cinnamon Shops*, a collection of Schulz's stories first published in 1934, he comments on the need "to feel that [his] world borders on other worlds, that at these borders the worlds cross and interpenetrate, exchanging currents and ripples. . . . I feel as if we were on close neighborly terms somewhere, as if we knocked against the same wall from opposite sides. . . . In the realm of intellect, distance loses its authority."[1] In Melville's words: "Genius, all over the world, stands hand in hand, and one shock of recognition runs the whole circle round."

It is the nostalgic evocation of the "ineffable socialities" as a common narrative thread in the writings of Melville and Schulz that encourages us to disregard geographical and cultural latitudes and meditate on confluences of the "rounded eternities" of "Dreams" in *Mardi*, the somnambulistic "fabled undulations" of the Pacific in *Moby-Dick*, and the wide-rolling plains of "The Republic of Dreams" with "the ready contours of myth suspended over [them]." To follow the dream, Schulz writes in a passage which may remind us of the stoneless grave of Bulkington and the mast-head reveries, is "to surrender our lives to this torrent of the fabulating element," let ourselves "be carried away by its surging waves without a will of our own." For those in his story who, like Noah, heard an inner voice: "The spirit of nature was by its very essence a great storyteller. Out of its core the discourse of fables and novels, romances and epics, flowed in an irresistible stream." A way of driving off the Galician spleen and finding an antidote against Emperor Franz Joseph's "gospel of prose," his likeness on each coin confirming the stability and immutability of the world, was to quietly proclaim the Republic of the Young, "part fortress, part theater, part laboratory of visions": "As in Shakespeare, this unleashed theater spilled over into nature, expanding into reality, soaking up impulses and inspirations from all elements, undulating with the great tidal ebb and flow of natural currents."[2]

If, ignoring literary and existential dangers, one persists in the enjoyment of "the *all* feeling," names themselves may lose their authority and become diffused

in the vision of "the Authentic" (Schulz) or "the very axis of reality" (Melville).
Schulz draws an imaginary map of the province—with the names of Homer,
Shakespeare, Dante, Goethe, Poe, Mann, Kafka, and Kubin but a handful of those
more distinctly marked in its maze of references and allusions—to let the garden
plots look across the fences and over the tollgates into the infinity of some
anonymous, nameless, self-sufficient land. No wonder the adventurous gaze cannot be separated from a sense of belatedness and "sadness" presiding over the
no-man's, every-man's place. In a story from under the sign of the hourglass, the
suburban Indian-summer day is compared to "that old crafty librarian groping
his way up ladders in a faded dressing gown and trying spoonfuls of sweet preserves from all the centuries and cultures"[3]—a modernist image which in this
room and at this hour makes us think again of the late consumptive Usher and
his "queer handkerchief." The authority of the names of all the fine authors
brought together by "a poor devil of a sub-sub-librarian" creates an imaginative,
perhaps vulturous fancy of their being "fictitious ones . . . simply standing as they
do, for the mystical, ever-eluding Spirit of all Beauty, which ubiquitously possesses men of genius" ["Hawthorne and His Mosses"]. If you kindly excuse this enchanted mood of piling up quotations, I would like to add a few more. One that
was surely among Schulz's favorites comes from another great student of the
risky business of confusing natural and fictitious currents, Hans Castorp. On the
verge of his being lost forever in the whiteness of the snow, he had a vision that
took him to a beautiful bay on a Mediterranean island (it could be Italy or Greece,
he tells us) where the temple precincts become the site of a cruel, sacrificial rite.
"Now I know," he concludes when his identity comes back in horror, "that not
out of our single souls we dream. We dream anonymously (and communally) if
each after his own fashion. . . The great soul of which we are a part may dream
through us, in our manner of dreaming, its own secret dreams."[4]

It may also be appropriate to remember here the confession Mallarmé made
in a letter to Verlaine about his decision to "collect... the countless little bits" of
his poetry in an *Album*, which, like the book Pierre Glendinning writes in the
Church of the Apostles, would be distinct from that most exclusively private and
hence all-embracingly anonymous work where "the Text would speak for itself
without its author's voice." Mallarmé calls for a spiritual brother to share his

chimerical belief that "all books contain the amalgamation of a certain number of age-old truths; that actually there is only one book on earth . . . the earth's true Bible," which can be "suggested" by the miscellaneous fragments, the small parts a writer can do.[5] Pierre's lesson is to learn that all the great books in the world must be "federated in the fancy and so regarded as a miscellaneous and Pantheistic whole" and even then be recognized as "but the mutilated shadowings-forth of the invisible and eternally unembodied images of the soul."[6] Despite his father's words: "As a matter of fact, there are many books" and the warnings of Bianca, the girl he wants to rescue from the prosaic fate of a wife: "You are ridiculous with your sense of mission," Joseph declares his readiness to "collect these allusions, these earthly approximations . . . like the fragments of a broken mirror" and to risk a regressive journey into "one and indivisible," the Age of Genius. Joseph—A Galician Ahab and his own oarsman—is, like Ishmael, willing to "try all things," and his narrative is a belated gaze across the patchwork of literary plots into what he calls at some place "the regions of great heresy."[7]

Bruno Schulz and Herman Melville, as we know, were ready to make the sacrifice and like Mallarmé's alchemists, "burn their furniture and the beams of their house to feed the furnace of the Great Work."[8] Remembering Schulz in Argentina, Witold Gombrowicz wrote: "Even though he demonstrated a profound moral sense in all his dealings, he was not at all disposed to morality conceived as doctrine. . . . So only art remained. And indeed I saw him completely devoted to it, consumed by it with a zeal and concentration I had never seen in anyone else—he, a fanatic of art and a slave . . . a false ascetic, sensuous saint . . . nihilistic fulfiller, a monk without God."[9] There are moments we seem to hear Ahab and Pierre say the same of Herman Melville, for they all become "Fast-Fish" to the idea of the mythical Book—an empty space of a missing text, originating from a loss, winning its grandeur by always becoming lost in the sea-matrix of metaphor, cross-references, allusiveness, ever-changing and ever-recurrent perspectives of approximation. For Ahab, the albino whale appears ultimately to signify that desperate and self-consuming thirst for the unattainable which the reader, through the agency of Ishmael, is repeatedly prompted to identify with the whiteness of the page, challenging the limits of the writer's imagination.

The Book is at the center of Joseph's earliest memories in *Sanatorium Under the Sign of the Hourglass*. Joseph and his father, Jacob, spend their days alone ("Mother had not appeared yet") in the room "as large as the world." The Book lying on father's desk and occasionally approached by the son is seen in a process of dazzling transformations of light, color, and shape. Mother's appearance breaks the self-sufficiency of the relation: "Seduced by my mother's caresses I forgot my father." The miraculous world is forgotten until the night the boy awakens to "rave confusedly . . . about the old lost Book." Furious and despairing, he searches through Father's bookshelves and tries to describe to a stunned audience an indescribable thing. Father offers him the Bible; on its pages flocks of birds fill the sky, processions of animals head for distant lands. Yet, the child rejects the Scriptures calling it "a corrupt apocrypha . . . a thousandth copy . . . a clumsy falsification." When Jacob explains: "The Book is a myth in which we believe when we are young," the child refuses to accept Father's logic and scornful, full of bitter, dogged pride, declares the Book to be a "postulate," a "goal." Some time later he aproaches a servant-girl, Adela, in order "to enjoy the scent of her body" and becomes attracted by a cheap mail-order catalog or calendar she is reading. Among many anecdotes, advertisements, and announcements there is a story of Anna Csillag, "similar in construction to the story of Job," telling of a cure for baldness, illustrated with a photograph of the apostle of hairiness, who, having received the signs and portents, concocted the miraculous mixture for her own benefit, the benefit of her family, of her native village, and of the whole world. Hiding the script under a pile of other books, Joseph now knows that he found the "holy Original," however degraded and humiliated its last, unofficial pages may look. Whenever the calendar is re-opened, the pictures are not the same and the stories are always new, changing in the process of being read. This, according to the narrator, testifies to its being the "authentic" Text. "How dull all my other books now seemed!"

Joseph announces that his story approaches the "age of genius."[10] It begins with a perception of a square of sunlight on the carpet. He greets it with "alien curses," feeds the "column of fire" with stacks of printed materials and, in an ecstatic rage, draws thousands of pictures across them. The room becomes then the frontier and the tollgate for colorful processions of "humped and horned creatures, encased in the varied costumes and armors of zoology." They expect Joseph to "solve their riddle." In the opinion of the local swindler, Shloma, "the world has passed through [Joseph's] hands in order to renew itself" at the time "when everything is shut tight, when all meaningful things are walled up, and when you constantly knock against bricks, as against the walls of a prison." Joseph shows Shloma the remnants of the "great Original," placed in the drawer together with the dress and high-heeled shoes of Adela.[11]

In the longest story of the volume, "Spring," he discovers a parallel version of the divine text in a postage stamp collection of his friend, Rudolph. There he finds "strange abbreviations and formulae, recipes for civilizations, handy amulets that allowed [him] to hold between his thumb and finger the essence of climates and provinces."[12] Intoxicated by the magic of the countries' exotic names (*Republica del Ecuador* appearing on one of them) Joseph recognizes in the album "the book of truth and splendor . . . a compendium of knowledge about everything human" and a final release from the prosaic boredom of Franz Joseph's unchanging profile. All the imaginative threads—a flux of categories, concepts, suggestions, allusions—converge towards Bianca in her white dress, the girl who can do nothing unnecessary, who can simply be herself without any strain or artifice, inaccessible in her serious, saddened knowledge of everything there is to know. "What can I say about Bianca, how can I describe her?" Joseph despairs, yet describe her he must. The sensuous lover of the ineffable, the passionate collector of the scattered fragments of the whole, is now ready to examine the miracle of the spring dusk. This is when dissolved words return to their true etymology, re-enter their distant obscure roots in the mythical Underworld. We are back in the dark sub-sub-terranean passages of the Book: "There is a lot of movement and traffic, pulp and rot, tribes and generations, a brood of bibles and iliads, multiplied a thousand times! Wanderings and tumult. . . Here are the great breeding grounds of history, factories of plots, hazy smoking rooms of fables and tales."[13]

Schulz's references to the Book direct us to the bookshelves (or computer files) with biblical, cabbalistic, alchemical, psychoanalytical studies, and the names of the great theorists of Its inheritance. My intention here is only to point to those patterns in the transformations of Schulz's Book which I believe run parallel to the recurrence of some motifs in Melville's work.

Lombardo's "I have created the creative" is echoed in Schulz's description of *Cinnamon Shops*, which, according to the author, "offers a certain recipe for reality, posits a certain special kind of substance."[14] The theme of the rediscovery of the Book or the rediscovery of the theme of the Book invites, despite the self-ironic mood in a reader of many books, ejaculatory, annunciative, and sacrificial imagery of a space from which God seems to have withdrawn, which needs to be filled in through the agency of the artist's work. There is an expansion of creative force envisaged by the opening of the flood-gates to a multitude of forms: "endless pilgrimages of beasts and animals" in Joseph's story and "endless processions of the whale" in Ishmael's. "It is then that the revelation took place: the vision of the fiery beauty of the world suddenly appeared, the secret message of good tidings, the special announcement of the limitless possibilities of being. Bright, fierce, and breathtaking horizons opened wide, the world trembled and shook its joints, leaning dangerously, threatening to break out from its rules and habits"—this is the voice of Joseph opening the stamp album and thinking of saving the grief-stricken Bianca from the world circumscribed by Franz Joseph I.[15] We may easily take it, however, for the voice of Pierre at the time he opens the letter brought by the secret hooded messenger and the ever-flowing thoughts of Isabel, "flashing revelations of grief's wonderful fire," displace the world of solid objects around him.

In the sexual-mystical imagery of Joseph's, Pierre's, Ishmael's creative experience (where the recollection of the gesture of the "hand" becomes a significant literary image), the "adventure" of the Book or the "adventure" of the critique of the Book is associated with the sad satisfaction of discovering a realm of plasticity, potentiality, pulsation, excess. Theirs would be a theologically grounded troubled pleasure, known so well to the modernist and post-modernist writers and critics, of recognizing the paradox of the "ungodly, God-like" activity—resurrecting the idea of some authoritative text in need of continual revision and completion. The substance of the reality of his book, Schulz writes, "exists in a state of constant fermentation, germination, hidden life. It contains no dead, hard limited objects. Everything diffuses beyond its borders, remains in a given shape only momentarily, leaving this shape at the first opportunity," and thus "a principle of sorts appears in the habits, the modes of existence of this reality:

universal masquerade. . . A certain extreme monism of the life substance is assumed here, for which specific objects are nothing but masks."[16]

Presiding over this visionary theater of migrating forms or masks is the figure of the Schulzian father, the present and absent owner of a textile store, possessing the authority of failure and bequeathing this authority to his symbolic son as he leaves to him the Book and the illustrated map of Drohobycz. As the gates of the wonder-world swing open to the readers of *Cinnamon Shops, Sanatorium Under the Sign of the Hourglass, Pierre,* and *Moby-Dick,* they may wonder at the striking correspondences in the authors' use of paternal metaphor and the way it spreads to narrative discourse. Schulz's description of literary strategies in *Cinnamon Shops* would fit into a Lacanian reading of *Moby-Dick,* emphasizing the book's concern with "generation and accretion, with how things come to life, are produced by a play of forces" where, "without a clearly identifiable source, no line can remain straight, everything bifurcates and forks out in increasingly complex patterns."[17]

The Ishmael-Ahab pattern of continual change within the rigid discipline of continual change becomes a characteristic feature of Schulz's work. The principle of the migration of forms in the evocation of the myth of the Book is mirrored by the repetition of images of renewal and freshness. In "Sanatorium Under the Sign of the Hourglass," a story of the father's death, repetition itself is linked to *re*-volution and *re*-staurant, playful fluidity of language which like the Polish word for the bookbinder, "introligator," appearing in the same story and suggestive of interrelatedness ("liga") and perhaps Torah ("tor"), remains inseparable from the notion of unity and totality. In "Dead Season," Joseph wonders at the significance of the memory of his father who, loaded with books, goes downstairs to open the shop on the street level of the building. For a moment father becomes flat, grown into the facade: "How many other fathers have grown forever into the facades of houses at five o'clock in the morning, while on the last step of the staircase? How many fathers have thus become the concierges of their own gateways, flatly sculpted into the embrasure with a hand on the door handle and a face dissolved into parallel and blissful furrows, over which the fingers of their sons would wander later, reminiscing about their parent, now incorporated forever into the universal smile of the house front?"[18]

In the "vegetative ignorance" of "the great and sad machinery of spring," old trees with roots steeped in old chronicles wake up with twigs; the humus of disembodied, timeless stories wants to be absorbed again "in your young life, in your bloodstream." "The greenness will once more make them new and fresh as in the beginning, and stories will become rejuvenated and start their plots once again, as if they had never been."[19]

In Melville's work, Pierre's unending thought of Isabel, his father's open hand, and his unfinished, ever-to-be-attempted book, are compared to those "wonderful rivers which once bathed the feet of the primeval generations, and still remain to flow fast by the graves of all succeeding men, and by the beds of all now living."[20] The old man is shot out of the whaling boat on the third day of "all pervading azure" when the air smells as it does for the mowers sleeping amid greenness of the new-mown hay and the sea rolls "as it rolled five thousand years ago." When on the new-mown clover Melville indulges in his melancholy musings over the "perennial green" of Hawthorne's *Mosses*, "men not very much inferior to Shakespeare are . . . born on the banks of the Ohio," "the world is as young as it was created and this Vermont morning dew is as wet to [his] feet as Eden's dew to Adam's." "Countries are after all only a pretext," and next time Joseph meets Bianca it will perhaps be in the state of Louisiana, he says. Joseph ends his imaginative journey to the mythical underworld of the Book with the vision of Its nameless forerunners, novels without a title, shapeless bardic tales, formless plots, giants without a face, and behind these—unwritten books, eternal pretenders and lost books. Schulz's builders of the Republic of the Young would recognize with satisfaction a sign of brotherhood in Melville's statement that "In Shakespeare's tomb lies infinitely more than Shakespeare ever wrote."

It is a sign of all the wrestlers with the angel of Art whose experience it was, quoting from Rilke's poem, "to be deeply defeated by ever greater things."[21] Attracted by the absence of the Book, silence, and the whiteness of the page, both Melville's and Schulz's works gesture towards an elusive and paradoxical territory, explored by Derrida, Jabes, Blanchot, which, at the time art comes under suspicion without ever ceasing to be an absolute, belongs as much to mystics as to masqueraders. If the visionary glance is inseparable from the ironic awareness of the makeup—paradigms, encapsulations, iconic images, "like"-"unlike" repetitions—and if the artist as character tends to evolve into a clown, a Pierrot, a prestidigitator, a confidence-man, it is not because those writers believed art is weak but because the power of art reaches beyond any individual manifestation. To be at the threshold of the Book, to have the desire and entertain the nostalgia of creating and reading a book, is, as we know, to recognize the most powerful attribute of the Book—a totalizing construct suspended alchemically in the realm of dislocation and fragmentation. Like the famous passage from Book I to Book II in Don Quixote's story, the Book assumes the shape of some trashy scrap of paper to be picked up among the trading world of everyday transactions—in the market-place, the store, the whaler—by those few elect, true, imaginative readers in whom the Book trusts. Schulz's Authentic is the "unofficial supplement, the tradesman's entrance full of refuse and trash"; Pierre's resolution is followed by his discovery of the crumpled, miserable, sleazy rag of Plinlimmon's pamphlet, which looked like "some shred of a long-exploded advertisment" and whose "conclusion was gone": "It must have been accidentally left there by some previous traveller, who perhaps in drawing out his handkerchief, had ignorantly extracted his waste paper."

Melville's and Schulz's evocation of the imagery of the mythical Book stems from their fascination with absolutes and their desire to perceive the creative activity in terms of mystical mediation. They both chose to speak of what transcends language. In the self-referential reality of their works, they felt compelled to include imaginative illustrations of the necessary failure to grasp the final significance of the creative act. In the world of language, where everything must be mediated, the Book becomes a gate to the mystery of incompletion. Magically illuminated, atemporal, and universally accessible, it marks that liberating, catastrophic end to distinctions, boundaries, and distances, which also points to the destruction of the image itself.

Around the year 1935, Bruno Schulz was commissioned by his friend, Stanislaw Weingarten, a Lodz businessman, to make a catalog of his library collection. Schulz, who was also a recognized graphic artist, illustrated each of the letters of the alphabet in the catalog with pencil drawings referring to motifs from his own books as well as from those in Weingarten's collection. The catalog is canvas-bound and has all the characteristics of Schulz's Book of all Books: it is trashy, faded, stained, its torn spine is coming off. *Moby-Dick* could not have been one of about two thousand books listed there. The complete version of Melville's masterpiece was not published in Poland until twenty years later. The cover of the catalog, however, has on it an ink drawing, "a boggy, soggy, squitchy picture truly, enough to drive a nervous man distracted," one that we might continually be tempted to approach and converse with others about. It seems to present a man amid the stormy waves of the sea. Disguised in a costume of a magician, a hat on his head, he is struggling to keep balance on what bears resemblance to a foundering barrel. Behind him, there is a tower, the Tower of Babel perhaps, leaning in a gale. In a theatrical gesture that makes you think of some mythical reality where beginnings and endings merge, he is holding an open book in his hands and looking directly at you.

NOTES

1   Jerzy Ficowski, ed., *Letters and Drawings of Bruno Schulz with Selected Prose* (New York: Harper & Row Publishers, 1988), 36-37.

2   *Letters and Drawings of Bruno Schulz*, "The Republic of Dreams," 217-22.

3   *The Fictions of Bruno Schulz: The Street of Crocodiles & Sanatorium Under the Sign of the Hourglass*, translated by Celina Wieniewska (London: Picador, Pan Books Ltd., 1988), 221.

4   Thomas Mann, *The Magic Mountain*, translated by H. T. Lowe-Porter (New York: Random House, 1947), 495.

5   Stephane Mallarmé, *Selected Prose Poems, Essays & Letters*, translated by Bradford Cook (Baltimore: John Hopkins University Press, 1956), 15-16.

6   Herman Melville, *Pierre or, The Ambiguities*, in The Library of America Edition (New York: Literary Classics of the United States, Inc., 1984), 331.

7   *The Fictions of Bruno Schulz*, 138.

8   Mallarme, *Selected Prose Poems*, 15.

9   Witold Gombrowicz, "On Bruno Schulz," *New York Review of Books* (April 13, 1989), 24.

10   *The Fictions of Bruno Schulz*, "The Book," 127-39.

11   *The Fictions of Bruno Schulz*, "The Age of Genius," 140-49.

12   *The Fictions of Bruno Schulz*, "Spring," 157.

13   *The Fictions of Bruno Schulz*, "Spring," 169.

14   *Letters and Drawings of Bruno Schulz*, 113.

15   *The Fictions of Bruno Schulz*, 158.

16   *Letters and Drawings of Bruno Schulz*, 113.

17 Regis Durand, "'The Captive King': The Absent Father in Melville's Text," in *The Fictional Father. Lacanian Readings of the Text*, edited by Robert Con Davis (Amherst: University of Massachussets Press, 1981), 163.

18 *The Fictions of Bruno Schulz*, 223.

19 *The Fictions of Bruno Schulz*, 170.

20 *Pierre*, 168.

21 Rainer Maria Rilke, *The Book of Images*, translated by Edward Snow (San Francisco: North Point Press, 1991), 213.

JILL B. GIDMARK

CLAREL AND *OMEROS*, "ODES" WITH A GRECIAN TURN:

AN INTERCULTURAL READING

ome eight years ago, addressing the Melville Society, Richard Blevins paired both *Clarel* and *The Confidence-Man* with Edward Dorn's *Gunslinger* in a recasting that teased out commonalities among three frustrated searches for faith and meaning: *Clarel*, a journey across the Holy Land by an ardent and naive theological student and other pilgrims; *The Confidence-Man*, a shadowy masquerade of "original characters" duped aboard a riverboat in the heart of America; and *Gunslinger*, a New World "trip" to Las Vegas taken by a hip stranger-poet and his friends, including a talking, stoned horse. While I'm not convinced that the hotwired, postmodern *Gunslinger* resonates to *Clarel*'s content or form in a timeless or significant way, I do believe that examining asynchronous, compatible works side by side can be a way of finding new relevance in old truths. And I believe that there's something about both the timelessness of John Keats's "Ode on a Grecian Urn" (1820) and its sense of reversals that is intrinsically shared by the two landmark poetic works that are the subject of this paper, both written and published after Keats's ode.

Herman Melville's philosophical 18,000-line epic *Clarel* has, I propose, deep kinship with the searching, evocative 8,000-line modern epic *Omeros*, by poet and playwright Derek Walcott. While *Omeros* projects more discovery and celebration than pilgrimage, it does chart the course of several figurative and literal journeys: by Middle Passage slaves aboard ship, by an angst-ridden poet with writer's block, by Native American Ghost dancers, by a symbolic sea-swift, and by a string of ants which an African voodoo-woman noses after on the ground searching for a special, healing herb. The deeply layered storytelling, the shape-shifting personas, the confluence of epochs and seas, religions and cultures make *Omeros* a compelling document for our time and, I'll suggest, a mythical extension of what *Clarel* might have become in a more intentionally intercultural milieu.

"Ah, what reverses time can own!" (4.19), proclaims Derwent, *Clarel*'s Broad-Church clergyman. As he speaks, the pilgrims are near the end of their journey, but they seem still isolated and confounded; what's the "Old World" and what's the "New World," and which of them are "offspring" (4.19) of which? But it's the "reverses" that are important. Though wracked with religious questioning, each pilgrim nevertheless is, in Walter Bezanson's words, "outside the Church, and for all of them the Cross is a symbol of pain, not hope" (565). A negotiation of opposites, Keats's "Ode on a Grecian Urn" presents like *Clarel* a balance and reversal of potential thwarted; it presents, like *Omeros*, warm transitory sensuality and promise frozen in the eternity of an artifact. Keats's urn continually reverses time in its preservation of a fleeting moment. One can turn the urn around and around again, and the same scene repeats itself unchanged. *Clarel* and *Omeros*, too, reverse chronology by repeating journeys backwards in time and in mind; this retrospective, this regression, produces a new vision that brings their characters forward in a powerful way.

Separated by more than a century, *Clarel* (1876) and *Omeros* (1990) are spawned from the same classic roots, from like-minded tortured genius and intellect, and, when juxtaposed, reflect each other's sensibilities in stunning reverse. Denuded, desolate Palestine is the setting for one epic; lush, fragrant Caribbean the other. One is a detached dialectic of ideas; the other is vigorous human drama. Melville's work—while granting its sea imagery, sea tales, and sea analogues—remains an epic of the wilderness. Walcott's work—for all its seductive tropical geography—is an epic of the sea. *Clarel* and *Omeros* could be said to form twin pictures in a locket, two halves of the same globe.

Melville's four-line poem "Greek Architecture" cites "reverence for the archetype" (248) as a desideratum of art, and his slightly longer poem "Art" spells an anguished poet wrestling with creative opposition to achieve that archetype:

A flame to melt—a wind to freeze;
Sad patience—joyous energies;
Humility—yet pride and scorn;
Instinct and study; love and hate;
Audacity—reverence. These must mate,
And fuse with Jacob's mystic heart,
To wrestle with the angel—Art (231).

Walcott's artistic reverence involves anguish, too, and his aesthetic gets complicated by the matter of his ethnicity. Walcott is a Caribbean of mixed-race heritage, whose depiction of his native St. Lucians becomes an emblem of all minority peoples, dispossessed, all but obliterated by traditional accounts and majority intentions. We see in a few fairly early lines in *Omeros* Walcott's aggressive yet humble agenda: he likens his writing to the toil of sweating, proudly turbaned native women carrying coal to a ship, the real heroines of and inspiration for his writing:

Kneel to your load, then balance your staggering feet
and walk up that coal ladder as they do in time,
one bare foot after the next in ancestral rhyme.
Because Rhyme remains the parentheses of palms
shielding a candle's tongue, it is the language's
desire to enclose the loved world in its arms;
or heft a coal basket; only by its stages
like those groaning women will you achieve that height
whose wooden planks in couplets lift your pages
higher than those hills of internal anthracite. . .
. . . They walk, you write; . . . give those feet a voice (75-76).

The sweating women groan and toil, "staggering" yet rising, their present ascending also a descent backwards "in time," forming the very ancestral rhyme that is Walcott's anguish and that is Melville's, too.

Both Melville and Walcott merge classical Grecian and contemporary American themes in a number of short poems. Both studied art: Melville lectured on Roman statues and collected prints and engravings; Walcott produces seascapes in watercolor. Both are myth-makers whose writing is plagued by demons of

Western civilization and of their own mid-life crises: Walcott dogged with failed marriages and allegations of sexual misconduct, splitting his time between Boston or New York and St. Lucia; Melville with the romance of marriage gone, a financial failure as writer and farmer, suffering from sciatica and weak eyes, plumbing the causes of his melancholy with a seven-month trip abroad. Remarkably, both men published at mid-life an elusive and powerful extended narrative along similar Grecian/American lines, which are convoluted searches for truth and identity through society and science, religion and philosophy, self and other. Walcott's epic, assessed with his drama and other poetry, fast won him international acclaim, including the world's most esteemed literary tribute, the 1992 Nobel Prize; Melville's epic was brusquely dismissed even at home (if it was read at all), and even in resurgent interest in the 1970s it was deemed ambiguously metaphysical, though a major psychological document of Melville's later years.

Seamus Heaney, friend of Walcott and himself the Nobel Prize winner in literature in 1995, has written a play called *The Cure at Troy*, a version of Sophocles' *Philoctetes*. Published in 1990, the same year as *Omeros*, Heaney's play offers an intriguing gloss to a major piece of Walcott's epic and even to Melville's— in its focus on an outcast hero, in the understanding it presents between public and private morality, and in its presentation of victims of injustice becoming devoted to, even obsessed with, the contemplation of their wounds.

Heaney's Philoctetes is *Omeros'* Philoctete. Walcott is overt in declaring that he has "stitched ... wound[s]" into all of his characters because "affliction is one theme / of this work" (28), but the wound that most obviously and constantly grieves is the festering, puckered, starfish-shaped sore on Philoctete's shin, incurred from a rusty anchor. For a dollar he'll display it to tourists for snapshots; he moans about it the whole poem long, drinking himself into daily oblivion at the No Pain Cafe, in desperate anguish tearing out tender white yams from his own garden by the roots, then finally, blessedly, healed by a voodoo woman who bathes his leg with tincture of a special herb.

The wound exceeds personal injury; it is a shameful feature of Philoctete's black ancestry, a "tribal sorrow" marked by "the chained ankles / of his grandfathers" (*O*, 19). In *Clarel*, the four "monomaniacs" (Walter Bezanson's term for this dark quartet [573]) are all sorely wounded: Celio—humpbacked with the twisted body, Mortmain—malevolent and misanthropic, Agath—beaten by robbers and shipwrecked, forearm tattooed with a crucifix, and Ungar—sabre-scar on his neck, blue powder-burn on his temple. It is, of course, the wild Swede Mortmain with his obsessive sense of evil, with his emblematic black skullcap—drinking the bitter waters of the Dead Sea, gnawing away at his own hand in a dream "as a wolf-hound a bone" (3.25, 20)—who is the most darkly despairing, the most deeply wounded figure. His deprivation by loveless unmarried parents, his apostrophe to Sodom and the star called Wormwood, the theft of his cap by a gier-eagle—to say nothing of behavioral tics like fierce outbursts, burning eyes, hissing, hating—all signify a wound for which there can be no cure. If in death Mortmain casts rheumy, hopeful eyes up toward those symbolic palm branches, and if an enigmatic eagle feather settles on his dead lips, then nature could be said to salve or soothe or save him, but his destruction is self-willed and non-reversible.

The opening chorus of Heaney's *The Cure at Troy* echoes this wounding:

> Heroes. Victims. Gods and human beings.
> All throwing shapes, every one of them
> Convinced he's in the right, all of them glad
> To repeat themselves and their every last mistake,
> No matter what.
> People so deep into
> Their own self-pity, self-pity buoys them up.
> People so staunch and true, they're fixated,
> Shining with self-regard like polished stones.
> And their whole life spent admiring themselves
> For their own long-suffering.
> Licking their wounds
> And flashing them around like decorations (2).

Unaware that he was doing so, Heaney has with these lines provided an insightful depiction of Melville's and Walcott's walking wounded, particularly Mortmain in *Clarel* and Philoctete in *Omeros*, who both lick their wounds and flash them around like badges, emanating a heroism that is a mask for their perceived victimization.

Though Melville and Walcott adamantly disparage "mere book-knowledge" (*Pierre* 283), it is a commonplace that these authors are omnivorously well-read. Sealts's *Melville's Reading*, Bercaw's *Melville's Sources*, Coffler's *Melville's Classical Allusions* reveal many volumes of print sources in addition to the whale-ships that Melville acknowledged to be his Yale and Harvard. And though the "odours of the sea" are in Walcott's armpits and "each phrase [of what he writes] go be soaked in salt" (as he says in "The Schooner *Flight*," [*CP* 347]), Walcott, raised in a Caribbean fishing village, enjoyed a privileged British education that steeped him early and thoroughly in the classics. Geert Lernout has hailed *Omeros* as not only a modern version of the *Odyssey* and the *Iliad*, but as "the centre of an intertextual web that contains strands from all major works of Western literature, from Virgil and the Bible to James Joyce" (96-97). From Dante's *Divine Comedy*, in itself a confluence of biblical and classical references, Walcott takes the terza rima that he uses in *Omeros*, the descent into hell, and the poet's sulfurous purgation in scalding lava pits. The pilgrims in *Clarel* make a descent, too, in the "Inferno" that is Part Two, down "through arid ravines and ugly turns of ground" (*C* 558). They seek purgation from sin and doubt, but the water they camp beside is the acrid Dead Sea, which does not offer baptism but a threat of intolerable introspection, even annihilation. The slimy Siddim Plain that they cross is a Dante-world of the soul's eternal torment, and the Jerusalem at the end of their dusty trail is not a blessed city of God offering refuge, but a cursed, fallen city of lepers, of plundered tombs and death.

The closer one looks, the more convincing the reverse parallel between *Clarel* and *Omeros* becomes. Melville, of course, is a "mariner and mystic" of thoroughly Yankee stock who peoples his epic with a Greek timoneer, a handsome if hump-backed Italian youth, an Anglican priest, a Mexican war veteran, a Jewish geologist, several midwestern American expatriates, and a host of other characters who are either one-dimensional, many-sided, or impenetrable. Walcott is the grandson of two white men and two black women, a "divided child" he proudly calls himself, whose duality fuels his black/white, minority/majority aesthetic. The cast of *Omeros* is, importantly, simple Caribbean fisher-folk with derivative Greek names—Hector, Achille, Helen, Philoctete—who swill white rum, swear in French patois, bounce to Marley reggae, and lust in the hot sun.

There are also a pair of long-married, pretty decent British colonialists who have moved to St. Lucia to retire, and a protean narrator who suffers and spellbinds. This chameleon figure is, by turns of page, Homer, a carved white marble bust, a blind old man named Seven Seas who keeps a khaki dog, Omeros the salt-sea life-force and inspiration, and the poet Walcott himself, who visits his mother in a nursing home, gets jilted by a promiscuous Greek lover whom he fruitlessly pursues throughout Boston, and who experiences a profoundly liberating sea-change that is his call and blessing to henceforth celebrate his native people in their own voice. *Clarel* has been said to have little, if any, plot—or, perhaps, as Basem Ra'ad has argued, an elaborate design of plots of death (14). *Omeros* has plots and subplots to spare, and they essentially affirm life. *Clarel* follows a scripted, liturgical chronology from Epiphany vigil to Whitsuntide in a single narrative line. *Omeros* may begin at dawn and conclude at dusk the same day, but spans as much as three hundred years in its many time-warp flashbacks.

Now, what if Clarel, the orphaned, naive wanderer, who, in my reading, re-enters Jerusalem after the pilgrimage every bit as confused as he left it, matured and found himself, realized his quest and mustered the nerve to assuage his angst? Might we have Walcott's narrator, the multi-faceted, multi-cultural persona who discovers his salvation within himself and his people, his land, and sea? Mortmain and the monomaniacs obviously prefigure Philoctete in their woundings and bitter pain. We can also venture that Rolfe and Vine—those middle-aged Americans, mature and sensitive men of genius whom Melville intimately identified with—in an intercultural reversal are models for Hector and Achille—those brawny, sensual Caribbean fishers of the sea with which Walcott's identity is so bound up. Hector and Achille both brawl over a magnificent black Helen and love her by turns, though Helen, uncertain which of them has conceived her unborn child, is fiercely independent: she will be owned by no man. The chaste, constant, and meek vision which is Clarel's Ruth is reversely mirrored in two Walcott women: the false Greek lover Antigone and the proud "panther" (322) Helen.

Walcott imposes yet another significant layer upon the character of Helen in the poem: she is his island St. Lucia. In a complicated linguistic argument also involving the island's native iguana and the Aruac Indians, the poem makes a convincing case for an etymological connection between the names "Helen" and "St. Lucia." Moreover, Helen is promiscuous, "possessed" by many and owned, finally, by none; as Walcott reflects on Caribbean history, possession of St. Lucia changed fourteen times between the French and the English before it gained independence in 1979. Walcott overtly uses mammary imagery to enforce the identity between woman and island. The notable geographical feature of St. Lucia is its two lush and magnificent Grand Pitons, certainly a sexy image. Melville gives us "twin peaks" in *Clarel*, too, the twin towers of the great stone hive Mar Saba, the fifth-century Greek monastery, but they are chaste by comparison, pious in intent if not in fact. The gate of Mar Saba was unbarred to male travelers only. Here the *Clarel* pilgrims (minus Clarel) revel with song, story, and flasks of St. Saba wine. As in *Omeros*, an "island" functions meaningfully in *Clarel*, too, though Melville's allusion is to something barren or virginal, not sexual: "The Island" is the title of the third canto of Part Four, where an old Greek pilot "schooled by the inhuman sea" (4.13) describes a lonely, haunted, parched place, inhabited only by a tortoise with a hollow, white carapace. This island is devoid of sensual allure.

In the last analysis, Melville's hero eschews the senses. He doesn't participate in the Mar Saba revel; he doesn't become sexual with Ruth or Vine; he looks backward and inward and seems fixated there, or backward and inward and upward and sees nothing helpful. He can't pray; the tongues of Pentecostal flame offer him no light. Walcott's hero embraces, even hallows, sense experience over theory and artifact; he looks backward and inward and then forward, ingesting the salty exultation of the sea with its smell, singing the deep hymn of his "wide country, the Caribbean Sea" (320).

At the close of the epilogue, the narrator urges Clarel to emerge "from the last whelming sea" (4.35.33). Achille leaves the beach in the concluding line of *Omeros*, and "the sea was still going on" (325). For Melville, the sea "went on" after *Clarel*, with *John Marr and Other Sailors* and with *Billy Budd*. The sea is still "going on" for Walcott, too, as attests his latest collection of poems, *The Bounty* (1997). Three years after *Omeros* Walcott published a stage version of *The Odyssey*. Commissioned by Britain's Royal Shakespeare Company, it is another inspired counterpointing of Homeric and Caribbean themes. Odysseus's protracted wanderings are interspersed with pungent commentary by blind singer Billy Blue—

a name which calls to mind Billy Budd—who is given the last speech. How appropriate if we take this final word to be not only homecoming for Odysseus, but also epitaph for Melville and epigraph for Walcott—and, above all, homage to Homer, wellspring of inspiration for them both:

> I sang of that man against whom the sea still rages,
> Who escaped its terrors, that despair could not destroy. . ..
>
> And a house, happy for good, from a swallow's omen,
> Let the trees clap their hands, and the surf whisper amen.
> For that peace which, in their mercy, the gods allow men (160).

REFERENCES

Blevins, Richard L. "Recasting Melville: *The Confidence-Man* and *Clarel* in Ed Dorn's *Gunslinger*." *Melville Society Extracts* 77 (May 1989): 15-16.

Dorn, Edward. *Gunslinger 1 & 2*. London: Fulcrum Press, 1969.

——. *Slinger*. Berkeley, CA: Wingbow Press, 1975.

Heaney, Seamus. *The Cure at Troy: A Version of Sophocles' Philoctetes*. New York: Noonday Press, 1991.

Lernout, Geert. "Derek Walcott's *Omeros*: The Isle is Full of Voices." *Kunapipi* 14.2 (1992): 90-104.

Melville, Herman. *Clarel: A Poem and Pilgrimage in the Holy Land*. Ed. Harrison Hayford, Alma A. MacDougall, Hershel Parker, G. Thomas Tanselle. Historical and Critical Note by Walter E. Bezanson. Vol. 12 of *The Writings of Herman Melville*. Evanston and Chicago: Northwestern University Press and the Newberry Library, 1991.

——. *Collected Poems of Herman Melville*. Ed. Howard P. Vincent. Chicago: Hendricks House, Packard & Co., 1947.

——. *Pierre, or the Ambiguities*. The Kraken Edition. Ed. Hershel Parker. Harper-Collins Publishers, 1995.

Ra'ad, Basem L. "The Death Plot in Melville's *Clarel*." *ESQ* 27 (1st Quarter 1981): 14-27.

Walcott, Derek. *Collected Poems 1948-1984*. New York: Noonday Press, 1986.

——. *The Odyssey*. New York: Noonday Press, 1993.

——. *Omeros*. New York: Noonday Press, 1991.

INDEX

Characters from Melville's works have been entered by first name.

559

565

CONTRIBUTORS

BERCAW EDWARDS, MARY K.: Dr. Bercaw Edwards teaches Literature of the Sea for the Williams College-Mystic Seaport Program. Her interest in Melville began when she sailed around the world with her family at the age of 16. She leads the demonstration squad on the world's only surviving wooden whaleship, the *Charles W. Morgan*, at Mystic Seaport. Dr. Bercaw Edwards earned her Ph.D. under Harrison Hayford's guidance at Northwestern Univ., where her book, *Melville's Sources*, was published in 1987. She is co-editing Wilson Heflin's 1952 dissertation, "Melville's Whaling Years," with Thomas Farel Heffernan (forthcoming from the Univ. of Texas Press), and she is on the editorial board of the first encyclopedia of sea literature, ed. Jill Gidmark. In 1999 she co-directed a conference on "Melville and the Sea" at Mystic, CT.

BERTHOLD, DENNIS: Professor of English, Texas A&M University. Prof. Berthold earned his Ph.D. in 1972 at the Univ. of Wisconsin. His research focuses on the relationships between nineteenth-century literature and landscape aesthetics, painting, and iconography, with a special emphasis on politics and ideology. He has published on Charles Brockden Brown, Hawthorne, Lowell, Twain, and Joshua Slocum as well as Melville, and has co-edited two books, *Dear Brother Walt: The Correspondence of Thomas Jefferson Whitman* and *Hawthorne's American Travel Sketches*. He has contributed essays to *America and the Sea* and *Savage Eye: Melville and the Visual Arts*, and is completing a book on Melville in Italy.

BIALAS, ZBIGNIEW: Assistant Professor of English Lit., Univ. of Silesia, Sosnowiec, Poland, where Prof. Bialas has taught since 1982. He earned his Ph.D. in 1992 at Nicholas Copernicus Univ. at Torun, Poland, and completed his Habilitation at the Univ. of Essen, Germany, in 1997. He has published widely and presented numerous papers on symbolic aspects of literature, especially relating to matters of identity and colonialism, and he holds a major interest in the literature of South Africa.

BRYANT, JOHN: Professor of English, Hofstra Univ., NY. Having earned his Ph.D. at the Univ. of Chicago, Prof. Bryant taught at Penn State Univ., Shenango Valley, before accepting the post at Hofstra. With help from the Melville Society, he compiled *Melville Dissertations, 1924-1980: An Annotated Bibliography and Subject Index* (1983); since then, he has edited *A Companion to Melville Studies* (1986) and the Penguin edition of *Typee*, co-edited *Melville's Ever-Moving Dawn: Centennial Essays* (1997), and authored *Melville and Repose* (1993) as well as many essays in critical books and journals. In addition to editing *Melville Society Extracts* and *Leviathan*, he is now collaborating on the Melville Electronic Library, working on a study of the *Typee* manuscript, and writing a book to be entitled *The Fluid Text*.

CHRISTODOULOU, Athanasios C.: Co-director of "Melville Among the Nations," Mr. Christodoulou is a lawyer, writer, artist, translator, and Melville scholar. A resident of Volos, Greece, he has written *The Strophe of Seferis* (1981-84), a three-volume study of the poetry of George Seferis; two novels, *The Lady Noemi* (1986) and *The Thorn, or Pantelis Vlastos* (1992); four poetical syntheses, *Laws* (1982), *The Brother* (1984), *Diptych* (1990), and *The Tree* (1993); a drama, *The Angel* (1998); and essays on Melville (1981-83), Laurence Stern (1992), and Hawthorne (1994). Having translated *Moby-Dick* into Greek, he has prepared a bilingual edition of that novel in five volumes, the first of which was published in 1997. Mr. Christodoulou is the director of a continuing series of books for the Gutenberg Press in Athens under the title *Gutenberg Orbis Literae*. His pictorial chronological biography of Melville and his art work on *Mardi* and *Moby-Dick* have been recently exhibited in the United States.

COFFLER, GAIL H.: Professor of English, Suffolk Univ., Boston, MA. After completing her dissertation on Melville under the direction of Merton M. Sealts, Jr., at the Univ. of Wisconsin, Prof. Coffler received her Ph.D. there in 1981. She held a Fulbright Lectureship at Stuttgart Univ. after which she taught for three years at the Univ. of Kansas. Since 1985 she has been at Suffolk. In addition to numerous articles and chapters, she has published *Melville's Classical Allusions: A Comprehensive Index*, and forthcoming is *Melville's Allusions to Religion: A Comprehensive Index*.

COHEN, HENNIG: Late John Welsh Professor Emeritus of History and English Literature, Univ. of Pennsylvania. After Prof. Cohen earned his B.A. and M.A. from the Univ. of South Carolina, he went to Tulane Univ. and received his Ph.D. there in 1951. He returned to South Carolina, and after working briefly as a news editor, he directed public relations there. In 1960 he became a Guggenheim Fellow; in the same year and again in 1970 he received ACLS grants. He held Fulbright posts in London and Budapest, and lectured in several other countries as well. From 1962-65, he taught first at Bryn Mawr College, then at Swarthmore. During those years and more, he was exec. secretary of the Amer. Studies Assoc., editor of *American Quarterly*, and secretary and president of the Melville Society. In 1965 he began teaching at the Univ. of Pennsylvania, where he taught English and American Studies until his retirement. Prof. Cohen was a prolific scholar. He edited *White-Jacket*, *Israel Potter*, and *The Confidence-Man*, novels which had been receiving relatively little critical attention at the time, and his edition of *Selected Poems* testifies to his early recognition of the merits of Melville's poetry. In addition to his work on Melville, Prof. Cohen brought out a text edition of old Southwestern humor that has not yet been superseded. Cancer took his life on Dec. 12, 1996.

DALSGAARD, INGER HUNNERUP: Ms. Dalsgaard received her B.A. and M.A. from the Univ. of Aarhus, Denmark, in 1994; she has received her Ph.D. in American Studies at King's College, Univ. of London. In 1995-96 she held a visiting scholarship at MIT. Her research and publications focus on the writings of Mary Shelley and Thomas Pnycheon in addition to Melville. In their work she is investigating their critiques of the changing location of science, technology, and industrialization in the social imagination over the past two centuries. Ms. Dalsgaard has presented papers on these subjects in Denmark, Great Britain, and the United States; she is teaching American literature at the Univ. of Aarhus.

DIRENÇ, DILEK: Dr. Direnç teaches English and American literature at Ege Univ., Turkey, where she earned her B.A. and M.A. degrees. In 1992, she traveled to the United States on a Fulbright scholarship; two years later she received an International Fellowship from the Amer. Assoc. of Univ. Women Ed. Found., which enabled her to complete her doctoral studies at Arizona State Univ.; there she received her Ph.D. in 1996, having written her dissertation on the fiction of Eudora Welty.

EVANS, LYON, JR.: Professor and Chair of English, Viterbo College, WI. After earning a B.A. in History at Swarthmore, and an M.A. in History at the Univ. of Michigan, Prof. Evans turned to the State Univ. of NY at Buffalo, where he received his M.A. and Ph.D. in English. He has published on Melville in the *New England Quarterly* and *Extracts*.

FAVORINI, ATTILIO: Professor and Chair of Theatre Arts, Univ. of Pittsburgh. Prof. Favorini received his Ph.D. from Yale. He is the author of the documentary drama *Steel/City* and the editor of *Voicings: Ten Plays from the Documentary Theater*. The Founding Chair of his Department, he was also founder and, for 13 years, the producing director of the Three Rivers Shakespeare Festival. He is on the editorial board of the *Encyclopedia of American Literature of the Sea and the Great Lakes*.

FISHER, MARVIN: Professor Emeritus of English, Arizona State Univ. A past president of the Melville Society and recipient of four Fulbright lectureships, Prof. Fisher has been teaching American literature "among the nations" since 1961. He held two of these lectureships at Aristotle University in Thessaloniki, where six of his former students currently teach—a circumstance that makes him *koumbaros* to the American Literature Section. Among his Melville publications are *Going Under: Melville's Short Fiction and the American 1850's* and the York Press monograph on Melville's life, work, and criticism.

GARNER, STANTON: Visiting Professor, Southwest Texas State Univ. After graduating with a B.S. from the U.S. Naval Academy and serving as a regular naval officer for a decade, Prof. Garner received his Ph.D. from Brown Univ., subsequently joining the English faculty there. He later taught in the Univ. of Texas system, from which he retired in 1987. He has been a visiting professor at the Naval Academy and held three Fulbright lectureships in Brazil and Portugal. Having been general editor of The Harold Frederic Edition, he has published extensively on Frederic as well as Melville and other authors. Among his publications are his edition of *The Captain's Best Mate: The Journal of Mary Chipman Lawrence on the Whaler Addison* (1966), "Fraud as Fact in Herman Melville's *Billy Budd*" (1978), and *The Civil War World of Herman Melville* (1993). He has served as both secretary and president of the Melville Society.

GEORGOUDAKI, EKATERINI: Formerly Professor of American Literature and Director of the American Lit. and Culture Dept., Aristotle Univ., Thessaloniki, Dr. Georgoudaki retired in

1998. After earning her B.A. and M.A. degrees at Aristotle Univ., she received her Ph.D. from Arizona State Univ., having written her dissertation on Melville's travels, under the guidance of Marvin Fisher. She represents the Hellenic Assoc. in the European Assoc. for American Studies, and she works with Women's International Studies Europe. In spring 1997 she chaired the committee that organized the 3rd annual conference of the HAAS. In addition to her articles on Melville, she has published internationally on American authors, particularly on modern poetry and African-American writing. These two interests are combined in her book of 1991, *Race, Gender, and Class Perspectives in the Works of Maya Angelou, Gwendolyn Brooks, Rita Dove, Nikki Giovanni, and Audre Lorde*.

GIDMARK, JILL B.: Morse-Alumni Distinguished Professor of Literature and Writing at the Univ. of Minnesota, Minneapolis. Prof. Gidmark has published articles and reviews on multicultural literature, midwestern drama and memoirs, and contemporary fiction. Her *Melville Sea Dictionary: A Glossed Concordance and Analysis of the Sea Language in Melville's Nautical Novels* will be followed by her forthcoming volume for Greenwood Press, *An Encyclopedia of American Literature of the Sea and the Great Lakes*, of which she is editor-in-chief. In 1999 Prof. Gidmark co-directed a conference on "Melville and the Sea" at Mystic, CT. She is also an active freelance flutist.

HARDACK, RICHARD: After receiving his Ph.D. in American literature from the Univ. of California at Berkeley, in 1994, Dr. Hardack taught at Haverford College and Bryn Mawr. His scholarship focuses on connections between American transcendentalism, postmodernism, and African-American literature. His most recent articles have appeared in *Callaloo, Studies in the American Renaissance, Arizona Q.*, and *ESQ*, among several other journals. Dr. Hardack is finishing a book on pantheism, gender, and transcendental identity for the Cambridge University Press. He has recently returned to Berkeley, where he is now studying law.

HARMON, MARYHELEN C.: Associate Professor of English, Univ. of South Florida. Since earning her Ph.D. at Florida State Univ., Prof. Harmon has been active as an officer in regional professional associations, and she has published on Melville and Hawthorne. She has held a Fulbright Lectureship at the University of Paris, served with the Florida State Univ. Florence Program, and received three undergraduate teaching awards.

HELLÉN, ANNA: Doctoral candidate, Univ. of Göteborg, Sweden. After receiving her M.A. in Education, Ms. Hellén is writing her dissertation, which will include readings of Melville, Dickens, and Emily Bronte. In 1992 she published an article on work by Peter Kihlgård and Marianne Hörnström in *Res Publica*, and in 1998-99 she held a research fellowship at Harvard to study American Romanticism.

KELLEY, WYN: Lecturer, Dept. of Literature, Massachusetts Institute of Technology. After graduating from Yale and Stanford Universities, Dr. Kelley has been publishing extensively on Melville. Her book *Melville's City: Literary and Urban Form in Nineteenth-Century New York* was published by the Cambridge Univ. Press in 1996. She has essays in *Savage Eye: Melville and the Visual Arts, Evermoving Dawn: Essays in Celebration of the Melville Centennial,* and *The Cambridge Companion to Melville.* Her articles and reviews have appeared in *American Literature, Partisan Review, Melville Society Extracts,* and *Resources for American Literary Study.* She is Assistant Editor of *Extracts.*

KLEITZ, DORSEY: Associate Professor of English, Tokyo Women's Christian Univ., Japan. Since earning his Ph.D. from the Univ. of New Hampshire, Prof. Kleitz has held Fulbright Lectureships in Mauritania and Hungary. He has published articles on nineteenth-century American literature, including an essay on Benjamin Britten's opera *Billy Budd,* and he has several more forthcoming. He is completing a study of Orientalism and American Romanticism.

KRIEFALL, ANDREAS: Visiting Assistant Professor of English, Union College, NY. Prof. Kriefall received his Ph.D. in Comparative Literature from Cornell Univ. in 1992. Before accepting a visiting post at Union College, he taught from 1993-96 at Deep Springs College, a small experimental school in the mountains of eastern California. He is finishing a book-length manuscript entitled "In the Horizon of the Infinite: Nietzsche, *Moby-Dick,* and the Question of Multicultural Ethics."

MAKINO, ARIMICHI: Professor of English, Meiji Univ., Tokyo. After receiving B.A. and M.A. degrees at Tokyo Univ., Prof. Makino earned another M.A. from the Univ. of Iowa in 1975. On returning to Japan he taught for six years at Gakugei Univ. before joining the English faculty at Meiji, where he has been since 1981. Prof. Makino has long been central to Melville Studies in Japan; he is the founding editor of *Sky-Hawk,* published by the Melville Studies Center at Meiji, and he has published widely on Melville over the years. Among his important recent books are *White Phantom Over the World* (1996) in Japanese and *Melville and Melville Studies in Japan,* which he edited; it was published by Greenwood in 1993.

MARÇAIS, DOMINIQUE: Professor of English, Univ. de Orléans, France. Upon completing a dissertation on Melville, Professor Marçais received her Doctorate from the Univ. of Paris in 1988. She has published extensively on Melville's fiction for over two decades and is an associate editor of the new edition of Melville's prose being brought out by Gallimard.

MAROVITZ, SANFORD E.: Co-director of "Melville Among the Nations." Professor Emeritus of English, Kent State Univ., OH. He received his B.A. from Lake Forest College (1960), his M.A. and Ph.D. from Duke Univ. (1961, 1968), where he was a Woodrow Wilson Fellow in 1960-61. He taught from 1963-65 at Temple Univ.; from 1965-67 under the Fulbright Program at the Univ. of Athens, Greece; and at Kent State from 1967-96. In 1976-77 he was a visiting prof. at Shimane Univ., Japan. Prof. Marovitz co-edited *Artful Thunder: Versions of the Romantic Tradition in American Literature in Honor of Howard P. Vincent* (1975), and co-authored with Clarence Gohdes *Bibliographical Guide to the Study of the Literature of the U.S.A.,* 5th ed. (1984). His most recent book is *Abraham Cahan* (1996). Published widely in critical collections and journals, he has also served as secretary and president of the Melville Society.

MARR, TIMOTHY W.: Assistant Professor of English at Western Connecticut State University. Having earned degrees from Williams College and Stanford Univ., Prof. Marr received his Ph.D. in American Studies at Yale Univ. with a dissertation on Islamic Orientalism in nineteenth-century America. His interest in the subject originated when he was teaching *Moby-Dick* in Pakistan in the 1980s. For 1999-2000, he was awarded a Faculty Fellowship from the Pew Program in American History and a Mellon Post-Dissertation Fellowship from the American Antiquarian Society to complete his first book, tentatively entitled "Imagining Ishmael: Studies of Islamic Orientalism in America."

MASZEWSKI, ZBIGNIEW: Adjunct Faculty, Dept. of American Literature and Culture, Univ. of Lodz, Poland. After receiving his M.A. from the Univ. of Lodz in 1977, Dr. Maszewski taught ESL in Poland and spent two years as a teaching assistant at the Univ. of Missouri and Texas State Univ. In 1991 he completed his doctoral work at Lodz with a dissertation on Melville, Hawthorne, and Poe. In 1994 he studied at Harvard as an ACLS Fellow. He has published mostly on American Romantic literature, though his most recent article is a comparative study of Faulkner and modernist Polish authors.

MAUD, RALPH: Professor Emeritus of English, and Associate of the Institute for Humanities, Simon Fraser Univ., Canada. After early schooling in Yorkshire, England, Prof. Maud earned his M.A. and Ph.D. at Harvard. He spent his first working years in Buffalo, where he published extensively on the writing of Dylan Thomas; in addition to editions of Thomas's poetry and notebooks, he brought out a critical reading of the poems and a full-scale bibliography. In 1965 Prof. Maud moved to Simon Fraser Univ., where he developed an interest in local native traditions and published his editions of Salish writings. For two years, he and Charles Olson were simultaneously at the State Univ. of NY at Buffalo; since then, he has been collecting a replica of Olson's library and planning to restore Olson's home as a research center. In 1996 Southern Illinois Univ. published his *Charles Olson's Reading: A Biography*; he is now editing selected letters of Olson for publication.

MITCHELL, DAVID: Assistant Professor of English, Northern Michigan Univ. Upon receiving his B.A. and M.A. in American literature from the Univ. of New Hampshire, Prof. Mitchell earned an additional M.A. and his Ph.D. in American Cultural Studies from the Univ. of Michigan. He has published essays on narrative strategies in the writings of contemporary women of color such as Louise Erdrich, Julia Alvarez, and Cristina Garcia. Recently, he directed an award-winning documentary, "VITAL SIGNS: Crip Culture Talks Back," which uses activist footage, performances, dramatic readings, and interviews by academics and artists with disabilities to discuss the evolution of a culture of disability. The Univ. of Michigan Press recently published his co-edited collection, *Discourses of Disability: The Body and Physical Difference in the Humanities*.

NEUBURGER, HENDRIKA KLIJN: Independent Scholar, Montreal. Born in the Netherlands, Ms. Neuburger moved to Canada in 1955. She earned her B.A. and M.A. at Concordia Univ.

in Montreal; her thesis, which discusses *Redburn*, *Moby-Dick*, and *Pierre* as a triptych, is entitled "Stepson of Heaven." A collection of her essays, stories, and poems—*Pot-Pourri of E-S-P*—was published in 1996. She is a docent at the Montreal Museum of Fine Arts.

OSHIMA, YUKIKO: Associate Professor of English, Fukuoka Univ., Japan. After receiving her B.A. from the Fukuoka Women's School in 1980, Prof. Oshima earned her M.A. at the Univ. of Iowa two years later. Since then she has been on the faculty at Fukuoka Univ. Her major publications in English include: "A Study of *Moby-Dick*: The Orphanhood of Ishmael" (1985), "A Theme of Perseverance in *Israel Potter*: Value in Homespun" (1987), "An Aesthetic Approach to 'Rip Van Winkle's Lilac': The Picturesque against the American Sublime" (1989), and "Pilgrimage in *Clarel*: Clarel's Rebellion against God" (1994).

PERMENTER, RACHELA: Associate Professor of English, Slippery Rock Univ., PA. Prof. Permenter received her Ph.D. from Northern Illinois Univ. with a dissertation on Melville, D. H. Lawrence, and postmodernism. Since then her publications have been in film studies, including "The Blakean Dialectics of *Blade Runner*" and "*The Piano* on (Dis)location."

POOLE, GORDON: Tenured *Ricercatore*, Istituto Universitario Orientale, Naples. Dr. Poole received his B.A. from Boston Univ. in 1961 and his Ph.D. in medieval Italian literature from the Univ. of California at Berkeley in 1975. In the same year, he entered the Istituto Univ. Orientale as an English language teacher, and he was tenured there in 1981. He has edited and written numerous books and articles on Italian, Neapolitan, and American literature, including many on Melville's writing. In 1989 he published his estimable bilingual scholarly edition of Melville's "At the Hostelry" and "Naples in the Time of Bomba."

RA'AD, BASEM L.: Associate Professor of English Literature and Language, Al-Quds Univ., Jerusalem. After receiving his Ph.D. from the Univ. of Toronto, Prof. Ra'ad also has taught at Birzeit Univ. and others in North America and the Middle East. His critical studies have appeared in *ESQ*, *Literature East and West*, *American Speech*, *Modern Fiction Studies*, *American Literature*, PMLA, and elsewhere. His essay on Melville's journals is included in *Savage Eye*. Professor Ra'ad is particularly interested in developing curricula for teaching Western literature in non-Western contexts and is currently studying color theory and landscape aesthetics. He held a visiting appointment at the Univ. of Toronto in 1999-2000.

REIGELMAN, MILTON: Cowan Professor of English, Centre College, KY. Prof. Reigelman earned his B.A. in philosophy at William and Mary College, his M.A. at the Univ. of Pennsylvania, and his Ph.D. from the Univ. of Iowa. He held Fulbright Lectureships at both the Univ. of Warsaw and later at the Univ. of Kiev, and he now directs the Centre-in-Europe Program located in Strasbourg, France. An ex-journalist, he is the author of *The Midland: A Venture in Literary Regionalism* and various articles on American literature and culture. He also serves as Dean of the Kentucky Governor's Scholars Program.

ROBERTSON-LORANT, LAURIE: English Teacher, St. Mark's School, Southborough, MA. After graduating from Radcliff College, Harvard Univ., Dr. Robertson-Lorant received her Ph.D. from New York Univ., having written a dissertation on Melville and race, which has been called "a pioneering work." In 1992-93 she was an ACLS Fellow. Her major work thus far, *Melville: A Biography*, has received much favorable commentary since its publication in 1996. In addition, Dr. Robertson-Lorant has written articles on a variety of subjects, and her poems have appeared in the *Radcliffe Quarterly*, *American Voice*, *Birmingham Review*, and elsewhere.

RYAN, JAMES EMMETT: Assistant Professor of English, Auburn Univ., AL. Prof. Ryan received his doctorate at the University of North Carolina, having recently defended his dissertation entitled "Inventing Catholicism: A Contest for American Spirituality." A chapter from this study appeared in an issue of *Religion and American Culture*.

SCHULTZ, ELIZABETH: Chancellor's Club Teaching Professor of English, Univ. of Kansas. Prof. Schultz has written on American autobiography, nineteenth-century American fiction, African-American literature, American women's fiction, and Japanese culture. President of the Melville Society in 1997, she has focused her work in Melville studies on the relationship between his fiction and its representation in the visual arts, notably in her book, *"Unpainted to the Last": Moby-Dick and American Art*, which was the basis for an outstanding series of symposia and conferences at the Univ. of Kansas in 1995 and a traveling exhibition afterward.

SHORT, BRYAN C.: Professor of English, Northern Arizona Univ. Prof. Short earned his B.A. from Yale, his M.A. and Ph.D. from Claremont Graduate School. He has taught at Northern Arizona since 1967. He is the author of *Cast by Means of Figures: Herman Melville's Rhetorical Development* (1992) and various articles and book chapters, including "Form as Vision in Herman Melville's *Clarel*," which won the 1979 Norman Foerster Prize. He is currently working on a study of Emily Dickinson's rhetoric.

SPANOS, WILLIAM: Professor of English and Comparative Literature, State Univ. of NY at Binghamton. Prof. Spanos is the founding editor of *Boundary 2* as well as the author of many essays and several books on postmodern literature and theory. Among the latter are *Repetitions: The Postmodern Occasion in Literature and Culture* (1987), *The End of Education: Towards Posthumanism* (1993), *Heidegger and Criticism: Retrieving the Cultural Politics of Destruction* (1993), *The Errant Art of Moby-Dick: The Canon, the Cold War, and the Struggle for American Literary Studies* (1995). In 1999 the Univ. of Minnesota Press published his most recent book, entitled *America's Shadow: An Anatomy of Imperialism*. He held a Fulbright Lectureship in 1969-70, and he was awarded an honorary degree by the Univ. of Athens in 1987.

STEN, CHRISTOPHER: Professor of English, George Washington University, Washington, DC. After Prof. Sten received his B.A. from Carleton College, he earned his M.A. and Ph.D. at Indiana Univ. He has been at George Washington Univ. since 1970. In 1975-76 he held a Fulbright Lectureship at Würzburg Univ. in Germany. While publishing on many authors over the years—

Twain, Cather, W. C. Williams, Ellison, and others—he has maintained a strong interest in Melville. His articles have appeared in *American Literature*, *Texas Studies*, *Modern Language Quarterly*, *Studies in the Novel*, and elsewhere. In the past few years, he has edited *Savage Eye: Melville and the Visual Arts* (1992) and published two critical books *The Weaver-God, He Weaves: Melville and the Poetics of the Novel* (1996) and *Sounding the Whale:* Moby-Dick *as Epic Novel* (1996), all with the Kent State Univ. Press. He is currently working on a study of American writers and the federal city, to be entitled *Washington: The Politics of American Writing*.

WALLACE, ROBERT K.: Regents Professor of Literature and Language, Northern Kentucky Univ. Prof. Wallace received his B.A. from Whitman College and his Ph.D. from Columbia Univ. He has been teaching at Northern Kentucky since 1972. He has published books on Josef and Rosina Lhevinne, on Jane Austen and Mozart, on Emily Bronte and Beethoven, and on Melville and Turner. His book on Frank Stella's *Moby-Dick* series was published by the University of Michigan Press in 2000. In addition to the books, he has published essays on Stella's *Moby-Dick* series and on Melville's print collection in various distinguished art magazines and professional journals. Prof. Wallace has also curated an exhibition of Melville's prints for the New Bedford Whaling Museum.

WATTS, CHARLES: Mr. Watts was a doctoral candidate in English at Simon Fraser Univ., Canada. He had earned his B.A. from the Univ. of California at Davis and his M.A. at Simon Fraser with a thesis on Ezra Pound. Since 1980 he was assistant curator of Special Collections and Rare Books in the library at Simon Fraser, and he was the publisher of Tantrum Press Books. He served on the editorial boards of three contemporary literary reviews and published a number of poems, including a collection, *Bread and Wine* (1987). Mr. Watts succumbed to cancer in August 1998.

YANG, JINCAI: Associate Professor at Nanjing University. Prof. Yang received his B.A. in 1985 from Suzhou Univ. and his M.A. from Nanjing Univ. in 1991, after teaching from 1985-89 at Zhenjiang Teachers College. He continued teaching at Zhenjiang TC and at Nanjing, where in 1997 he received his Ph.D. with a dissertation on Melville. He was a Visiting Fellow at the Harvard-Yenching Institute, 1997-98. Mr. Yang has brought out many articles on American authors, including Melville, but chiefly on 20th-century writers, including Wharton, Dreiser, Eliot, Faulkner, Williams, and Rita Dove, among others; he is revising his dissertation to be published as a book.